MW01485756

INFANTA

INFANTA

The Short, Remarkable Life of Catalina Micaela

MAGDALENA S. SÁNCHEZ

YALE UNIVERSITY PRESS
NEW HAVEN AND LONDON

For information about this and other Yale University Press publications, please contact:
U.S. Office: sales.press@yale.edu yalebooks.com
Europe Office: sales@yaleup.co.uk yalebooks.co.uk

Set in Adobe Garamond Pro by IDSUK (DataConnection) Ltd

Printed and bound in the UK using 100% renewable electricity at CPI Group (UK) Ltd

Library of Congress Control Number: 2025942012
A catalogue record for this book is available from the British Library.
Authorized Representative in the EU: Easy Access System Europe, Mustamäe tee 50, 10621 Tallinn, Estonia, gpsr.requests@easproject.com

ISBN 978-0-300-28283-2

10 9 8 7 6 5 4 3 2 1

Supported by the Spanish Ministry of Education, Culture, and Sports

CONTENTS

PLATES

1. Sofonisba Anguissola, *Philip II*, 1573. Oil on canvas, 88 × 72 cm. Prado Museum, Madrid. Heritage Image Partnership Ltd / Alamy.
2. Juan Pantoja de la Cruz (after an original by Sofonisba Anguissola), *Elisabeth of Valois*, 1605. Oil on canvas, 120.1 × 84 cm. Prado Museum, Madrid. Carlo Bollo / Alamy.
3. Workshop of Alonso Sánchez Coello, *Infanta Isabel Clara Eugenia and Infanta Catalina Micaela*, c. 1571. Oil on canvas, 134 × 145.8 cm. Royal Collection Trust / © His Majesty King Charles III 2025.
4. Attributed to Sofonisba Anguissola, *Infanta Catalina with a Marmoset*, 1572–1573. Oil on canvas, 56.2 × 47 cm. Private collection.
5. Alonso Sánchez Coello, *Infanta Isabel Clara Eugenia with Magdalena Ruiz*, 1585–1588. Oil on canvas, 207 × 129 cm. Prado Museum, Madrid. classicpaintings / Alamy.
6. Jan Kraeck, *Carlo Emanuele I, c.* 1590. Oil on canvas, 194 × 108 cm. Courtesy of Museo Civico Casa Cavassa, Saluzzo, Italy.
7. Jan Kraeck, *Catalina Micaela of Savoy, c.* 1590. Oil on canvas, 194 × 108 cm. Courtesy of Museo Civico Casa Cavassa, Saluzzo, Italy.
8. Jan Kraeck, *The Dukes of Savoy, Carlo Emanuele I and the Infanta Catalina Micaela, with their Children: Filippo Emanuele, Vittorio Amedeo, Emanuele Filiberto, and Margarita, c.* 1589. Oil on canvas, 64.2 × 51 cm. Abelló Collection, Madrid.
9. Jan Kraeck, *Princes Vittorio Amedeo, Emanuele Filiberto, and Filippo Emanuele of Savoy, c.* 1592–1593. Oil on canvas, 177.1 × 142.2 cm.

NOTE ON NAMES AND SOURCES

I HAVE MAINTAINED THE form of a person's name customary in his or her country of origin. So, for example, I refer to Catalina's mother as Elisabeth of Valois, and not as Isabel de Valois, as she was known in Spain. The only exceptions are when the person's name is well recognized in English. Accordingly, I have used Philip II, Charles V, and Archduke Albert, not Felipe II, Carlos V, or Archduke Albrecht.

The book's title, *Infanta*, is taken from the designation of a Spanish king's legitimate daughter, not the heir apparent. Catalina retained the higher-ranking and her preferred title of *infanta* even after her marriage also made her duchess of Savoy.

All quotations from the correspondence between Catalina and Carlo are quoted directly from the manuscripts held in the Archivio di Stato (Corte) in Turin, Italy, in the Lettere di Duchi e Sovrani section of the archive. When citing these letters, I have abbreviated the references with AST followed by the *mazzo* number. When quoting, I have retained the sixteenth-century spelling, without post-sixteenth-century accents, except in cases where it would be confusing to the reader.

Most of Catalina's letters have been printed in an unedited collection: *Catalina Micaela d'Austria: Lettere inedite a Carlo Emanuele I* (1588–1597), 3 volumes, edited by Giovanna Altadonna (Messina: Il Grano, 2012). Because Altadonna's volumes may be more accessible to readers, I have cited them alongside the citations to the manuscript letters. Altadonna has done a meticulous job of organizing and transcribing Catalina's letters, and

I am deeply indebted to her edition. However, her volumes fail to incorporate a few of Catalina's dated letters and include none of her undated letters, her secretarial letters, or her autograph postscripts on secretarial letters; for those I give only the manuscript references. When citing Altadonna's *Lettere inedite*, I give her name followed by the volume and page number.

ACKNOWLEDGMENTS

In August 2008, I went to the Archivio di Stato in Turin to search for the letters exchanged between Philip II's two daughters, Isabel Clara Eugenia and Catalina Micaela. With four sisters of my own, I was intrigued by letters between sisters and thought the correspondence of the two *infantas* might also shed light on Isabel's last decade and a half at the Spanish court. Unable to find their letters, though, I discovered instead the correspondence between Catalina and Carlo. Fascinated by this unusually rich correspondence between wife and husband, I decided to shift my focus from the two sisters (especially Isabel) to the married couple (especially Catalina). It was the best decision of my scholarly life.

Over the years, Richard Kagan, my dissertation adviser at Johns Hopkins, has been a model of scholarly research and committed mentorship. He fosters friendships and builds connections, and many besides myself have benefited from his encouragement and good cheer. I first presented on Catalina at "Kagan's Kaleidoscope," a mini-conference to celebrate Richard's sixty-fifth birthday, and the encouraging comments I received there convinced me of the promise of this research. It was through Richard that I met Geoffrey Parker, whose support and assistance have been invaluable. He reached out on my behalf to Heather McCallum, Managing Director at Yale University Press London, and without that connection I doubt that Heather would have considered reading a manuscript on a Spanish *infanta* relatively unknown in the

English-speaking world. I'm very thankful to Heather for allowing me to pitch my book to her and for then publishing it.

Many friends and colleagues have assisted me. I am particularly grateful to María José del Río Barredo, who has helped me every step of the way. Our friendship grew closer with my research on Catalina and she has shared research notes, thought through archival questions, co-authored an essay with me, and read and commented on the entire manuscript. She is a great resource and a dear friend, and her husband, Marcello Bruzzo, has quietly, behind the scenes, fielded many questions on Italian terms and translations, and I thank him as well.

Fernando Bouza originally told me about the correspondence of Catalina and Carlo, and his edition of Philip's letters to his daughters has aided me enormously. Likewise, Bernardo García has included me in research projects and conferences, helped me secure funding from Hispanex, and remains a close colleague and warm friend. My trips to Madrid would have been much less pleasant without the company of Bernardo and his wife Rosa.

In Turin, I benefited greatly from talking with Blythe Alice Raviola, Paolo Cozzo, and Pierpaolo Merlin. Both Alice and Paolo read and commented on individual chapters of the manuscript, and Pierpaolo graciously gave me a copy of his book *Tra guerre e tornei* and answered last-minute research questions. I also greatly appreciated getting away from the archives to enjoy the kind hospitality of Paolo Manzoni and Cristina Milillo, who invited me to their home every time I visited Turin.

Anne J. Cruz prompted my work on the *infantas* when a comment in her review of my first book, *The Empress, the Queen, and the Nun*, led me to research Isabel Clara Eugenia; and when I switched to Catalina, Anne proved equally interested and continued to encourage me. She graciously read and commented on a draft of the manuscript, saved me from some errors, and helped me especially with translations of several tricky passages. Through Anne I met Silvia Mitchell, who has been warmly supportive, and whose own work on Mariana of Austria has served as a model of scholarly research.

Vanessa de Cruz Medina has always generously shared her publications with me, and I am particularly grateful to her for giving me a copy of her unpublished manuscript on the letters of Ana of Dietrichstein.

Elisa García Prieto and Rocío Martínez López have both discussed different aspects of Catalina's life with me, offering helpful bibliographic references and archival assistance. Bill Bowman took a break from his own research in Vienna to photograph documents for me at the Haus-, Hof-, und Staatsarchiv.

Invitations from Jim Amelang and Joan-Lluís Palos gave me forums in which to test my ideas early on in the research, and María Cruz de Carlos Varona shared her research with me, presented with me at an RSA conference, and strongly encouraged my work.

A Hispanex grant from the Spanish Ministry of Culture and another from the Renaissance Studies of America came at crucial moments when I was in particular need of external validation of my research. The Faculty Development Committee and Provost's Office at Gettysburg College have generously supported my research over the years and I am grateful to them. I am also grateful to my colleagues in the history department at Gettysburg College, some of whom have read and commented on parts of this book. In teaching senior seminars on letter-writing, I have profited and learned from discussing epistolary culture with my students.

I am indebted to the archives and libraries in which I worked in Turin, Milan, Venice, Florence, Madrid, Simancas, London, Geneva, and Vienna. I have enjoyed working with and greatly benefited from the friendly, efficient, and professional staff at Yale London—Production Editor Meg Pettit and Production Director Stuart Weir, cartographer Martin Brown, who designed the map, and copy-editor Rachel Bridgewater, who read the manuscript with a keen eye for mistakes and infelicities. In particular I would like to thank Associate Editor Katie Urquhart, who patiently helped me obtain the images, and Managing Editor and Design Manager Rachael Lonsdale, who went through the final manuscript meticulously. I am also grateful to Cecile Berbesi Rault for her careful review of the final proofs of my book.

Part of Chapter 3 was published earlier in my essay, " 'She Grows Careless': The *Infanta* Catalina and Spanish Etiquette at the Court of Savoy," in *Early Modern Dynastic Marriages and Cultural Transfer*, ed. Joan-Lluís Palos and Magdalena S. Sánchez (Burlington, VT: Ashgate, 2016), 21–44. Chapter 7 is a revised and expanded version of " 'I would not feel the pain if I were with you': Catalina Micaela and the Cycle of Pregnancy at the Court of Turin, 1585–1597," *Social History of Medicine* 28, no. 3 (2017): 445–64. Chapter 9 is a revised, expanded, and translated version of my essay, "Vísperas, Misas Cantadas y Sermones: Prácticas Devocionales de la Duquesa de Saboya Catalina Micaela," in *De puño y letra: Cartas personales en las redes dinásticas de la Casa de Austria*, ed. Bernardo J. García García, Katrin Keller, and Andrea Sommer-Mathis (Madrid: Iberoamericana, 2019), 51–78. I thank the three presses for permission to use this material.

This book has been long in the making. Begun when my elder son was starting high school, my second son in elementary school, and my daughter in pre-school, they are now full grown and I am grandmother to twin boys. I thank my son Lucas and daughter-in-law Jenna for bringing the two boys into my life. I would like to thank my husband, Bill Bowman, and my children, Lucas, Matías, and Angela, for long living with this project. Angela and Matías in particular remember coming downstairs in the morning to find me working on my "*cartas*" at the kitchen table. They are no longer home every day and I have moved from the kitchen table to my home office, but this book has been a constant in the life of my family for close to seventeen years and has occasionally tried everyone's patience. Regular long-distance conversations with my sister Rosa dragged me out of the sixteenth century and re-anchored me in the present. Last but not least, I should mention Zelda, my daughter Angela's dog, but since she—Angela, not the dog!—has gone off to college, Zelda has been my daily companion. Making sure that I got up early every morning and ensuring that I not sit at my computer for too many hours in a row, she taught me to appreciate Catalina's loving devotion to her many pets.

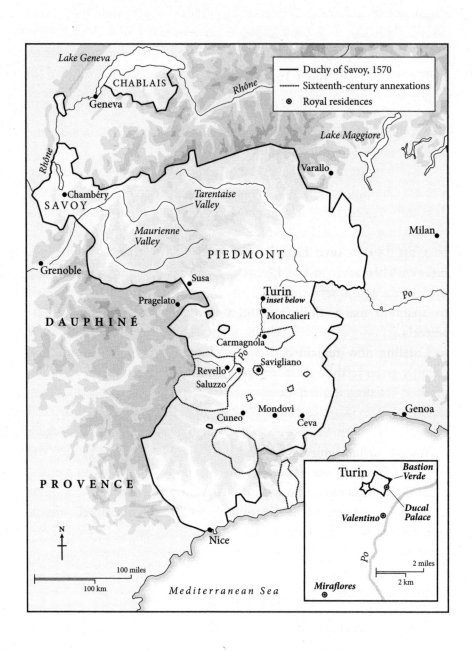

Lake Geneva

CHABLAIS

Geneva

Rhône

Rhône

Lake Maggiore

Varallo

SAVOY

Chambéry

Tarentaise
Valley

Milan

Maurienne
Valley

PIEDMONT

Grenoble

Po

Susa

Turin
inset below

DAUPHINÉ

Pragelato

Moncalieri

Carmagnòla

Po

Revello

Savigliano

Saluzzo

Mondovì

Genoa

PROVENCE

Cuneo

Ceva

N

Nice

100 miles

100 km

Mediterranean Sea

| Duchy of Savoy, 1570 |
| Sixteenth-century annexations |
| Royal residences |

Turin

Bastion
Verde

Valentino

Ducal
Palace

Po

2 miles

2 km

Miraflores

INTRODUCTION
An Overlooked *Infanta*

IN APRIL 1591, CARLO Emanuele, duke of Savoy, traveled to Spain to meet with his father-in-law, Philip II. He stopped first in Barcelona and then in Zaragoza, retracing his trip of 1585, when he had journeyed to Spain to marry Philip's younger daughter, the *infanta* Catalina Micaela.

Catalina now remained in Carlo's capital, Turin, where she had recently given birth to their fifth child. From Zaragoza, where they had married six years earlier, Carlo wrote to her, recalling their wedding night:

> You can well imagine how much I enjoyed seeing that city, although I did not see my eyes [Catalina] there, even though I went looking in all the walls of that house and shed not a few tears remembering the good time that I had there with my life [Catalina] and that bedroom with the golden key—you understand [my meaning] well.[1]

Catalina responded:

> If you have shed tears at not finding me there and in the room of the golden key, I promise you that I have not shed fewer at reading [your letter] and at every time that I remember that I am so far away from you and that I remember when we have been together.[2]

1

The room with the golden key, to which both Carlo and Catalina referred, was the bedroom where they had consummated their marriage on the night of 11 March 1585, an act that an anonymous chronicler noted "had pleased all."[3]

While wedding guests, courtiers, chroniclers, and even Catalina's father, Philip II, were pleased that the marriage had been consummated, what might Catalina—just seventeen and a half at the time—have been feeling as her wedding approached, and what might have been her reaction to this arranged marriage to someone once described as "small and ugly"?[4] Six years and five children later, Catalina could recall the wedding-night bedroom nostalgically, but in 1585 when she entered it, she must have felt understandable misgivings about sexual intimacy with a man she had known for less than forty-eight hours and with whom she had yet to spend a minute of complete privacy.

This later exchange of letters between Carlo and Catalina displays their mutual affection and demonstrates that, now very comfortable with each other, they had developed both a strong partnership and a loving marriage. In 1585, however, Catalina might for multiple reasons have had strong reservations about marrying Carlo. She was unhappy to leave her family and the places and people in Spain familiar and dear to her. She might even have felt as if she were being sacrificed to her father's political and military designs. Above all, perhaps, she could hardly have known she would grow to love her husband. Marriage between aristocrats—especially those of the highest rank—was hardly predicated on affection, and she had no reason to feel confident that she and her husband would bond emotionally. Yet Carlo would win her over, and, adapting well to life in Turin, she would soon switch her loyalties from Philip and her older sister Isabel Clara Eugenia to Carlo and their children.

Her journey in 1585 from Madrid to Zaragoza and then Turin began at the Spanish court, where she grew up with her sister Isabel under the watchful eyes of Philip II. "I am from Madrid," she told Carlo in 1591, stating not a simple biographical fact but an assertion to him that her character, tastes, and interests had been shaped by her years at Philip's court.[5]

STUDYING CATALINA

Catalina has not fared well in the historical record. Observers in her own day and historians afterward have been much more interested in her famous father and the major political events of the day than in a young girl who married the duke of Savoy and left Spain at seventeen. For the most part, modern scholars (particularly of the Anglo-American world) have ignored Philip II's daughters because neither ruled as a queen or governed one of the principal monarchies of the early modern period. When they have studied them, moreover, most historians have overlooked Catalina and given more attention to her older sister, Isabel Clara Eugenia. The editor of a recent book on Habsburg women justifies the inclusion of an essay on Isabel rather than one on Catalina by claiming, without citing evidence, that of Philip's two daughters, "Isabel Clara Eugenia's personality stands out particularly."[6]

Even in the sixteenth century, contemporaries tended to focus on Isabel because she was the older of the two and, in the absence of a male heir, stood to inherit the Spanish throne. Some observers claimed that Philip favored Isabel even over his male heirs. Matteo Zane, Venetian ambassador to the Spanish court from 1580 to 1584, reported in 1584 that "her father loves her much more tenderly than any of his other children," while also claiming that "she is endowed with such virtue and prudence as would make her very worthy of ruling."[7] Commenting on a theatrical performance the year before, in which both *infantas* participated, a court valet told Mateo Vázquez, Philip II's private secretary, that Isabel was the better performer.[8] The duchess of Alba, the *infantas'* governess from 1568 to 1570, remarked to Catherine de' Medici, their grandmother, that she was amazed at how much the girls knew, "especially the *señora infanta* Isabel. I think anyone who sees her thinks her much older than she is."[9]

As early as 1569, when Isabel was only three, Philip's secretary of state described her as "the cutest creature born in Spain and she already has greater authority than her father in everything she does, and she is as inclined toward writing as he is, so much so that for the duchess [of Alba] to quiet her down and make her do as she [the duchess] wants, there is no better means than with paper and ink, and with that she is happier than with any other thing they could give her."[10] While these observations might well have been accurate (though the comment about Isabel having greater authority than her father is obviously absurd), it is clear that to sixteenth-century observers Isabel was the more important and gifted daughter precisely because she was the elder of the two girls and the potential heir to the Spanish crown. It is not surprising that in his dispatches to Emperor Rudolf II, imperial ambassador Hans Khevenhüller dismissed Catalina as the "other *infanta*," giving pre-eminence to Isabel, whom Khevenhüller thought destined to marry Rudolf.[11]

Preference for Isabel has continued into the modern period. In the early twentieth century, three well-researched biographies of Isabel were written in English, French, and Spanish, respectively, primarily for a popular audience, all leaning heavily on Antonio Rodríguez Villa's 1906 publication of the correspondence between Isabel and the duke of Lerma, Philip III's royal favorite.[12] The published letters themselves indicate the attention given to Isabel, though mostly because she was corresponding with a principal (male) political actor. More recently (in 2004), a biography of Isabel, based on printed rather than archival sources, was published in Spanish, and a book of scholarly essays about her appeared several years later.[13]

By comparison, the twentieth and twenty-first centuries have seen on the subject of Catalina only a twenty-five-page publication of a lecture discussing her early years at the court in Turin and a 2002 romanticized biography of her in French, with limited circulation and many errors.[14] Catalina was also the subject of a 2009 scholarly conference (mostly in Italian), the proceedings of which were published (also mostly in Italian) a few years later.[15] These essays, well researched and insightful, were the first step toward a serious study of Catalina, and taken together they begin a much-needed examination of aspects of the *infanta*'s life, though none makes comprehensive use of her correspondence or pays more than passing attention to her marriage with Carlo. No full biography of Catalina has ever been published in English or Spanish. How can we know that Isabel had a stronger, more vivacious personality than Catalina's when hardly anyone has studied the younger *infanta*? The almost universal neglect of Catalina among early modern historians is all the more unfortunate, moreover, because her extant correspondence with Carlo, comprising more than 3,000 letters in less than a decade, constitutes the fullest and richest exchange of letters between a married couple in the early modern era and reveals Catalina's high intelligence, strong feeling, and forceful personality.

A few examples from Lucy Klingenstein's 1910 biography of Isabel show the historical bias toward Philip's elder daughter. Citing the sixteenth-century court chronicler, Luis Cabrera de Córdoba, Klingenstein remarked that as a young girl, Isabel helped Philip II with his paperwork: "As quite a child she was admitted into his study, to bring him the sheets to be folded up and put into packets to be addressed to his secretaries." In fact, Cabrera de Córdoba had noted that both Isabel and Catalina helped Philip in this way; Klingenstein simply chose to overlook Catalina. She also suggested that Philip favored Isabel: "Philip had already begun to make a companion of Isabel, the one being whom he loved to the end of his life." Klingenstein further argued that Isabel "was held to be peerless, and writers of prose and verse vied with each other in extolling not only her person, but her intellect. Skilled in all sports, she played and danced well, and was a great lover of music and poetry; she was her father's pupil in history and the science of politics. Her sister, Catherine, a year younger than herself, though neither as handsome nor as gifted, lent by her light-hearted, merry disposition an air of gaiety to the Court."[16] Klingenstein's source for this assessment of Catalina seems to have been Zane, who claimed that Catalina was neither "as beautiful nor as graceful as her sister, but is more cheerful and more jovial."[17] To Klingenstein (and to Zane), Catalina was less talented and less attractive than Isabel and noteworthy primarily for her lively nature rather than her intellect, a perception that has persisted to this day. Several years ago, seated at dinner next to a pre-eminent historian of early modern Spain, I mentioned that I was researching Catalina Micaela. He pondered a moment, and then asked, "But was she intelligent like her sister?"

The countess of Villermont, author of a biography of Isabel published in 1912, held opinions similar to Klingenstein's, arguing that from a young age Isabel was known for her "vivacity and intelligence" and

ranked as Philip II's favorite daughter.[18] Villermont drew this information from the letters of the duchess of Alba to Catherine de' Medici. Yet
the duchess had remarked on Isabel's intelligence when the girl was no
more than four years old, and the duchess's assessment of Isabel was
anything but objective, as she was writing to please and impress the
infantas' grandmother.[19] For her own biography, Villermont relied
heavily on a never completed and unpublished biography of Isabel that
Philippe Chifflet, a priest in the archducal chapel in Brussels, wrote
soon after her death.[20] But while Chifflet had known and spoken exten-
sively with Isabel when she governed the Netherlands, he had not
known her as a child, nor had he ever met Catalina. This, however, did
not stop him from claiming that at twenty, Isabel was "thought to be
the prettiest, the wisest, and the most accomplished of all princesses"
and that "everyone who saw her judged her to be completely perfect."[21]
Yet Chifflet had never met Isabel when she was twenty and had to rely
on what she herself had later told him about her youth in Spain. These
exaggerated assessments of Isabel, from both the seventeenth and twentieth centuries, inaccurately diminish Catalina, consistently making her
out to be less favored and less gifted than her older sister.

The scholarly neglect of Catalina and greater scholarly attention
given to Isabel can be explained in several ways. As the oldest surviving
child of Philip II, Isabel stood to inherit the throne if Philip's male heirs
died, as in fact all but one did. Even the one survivor, Prince Philip,
who eventually ruled as Philip III, was sickly, and perhaps for this
reason Philip II kept Isabel by his side until his own death in 1598. At
that point, Isabel finally married and left Spain at thirty-two to govern
the Netherlands for thirty-five years, until her death in 1633 at sixty-
seven. Isabel's many years in Spain close to Philip II—himself the
subject of numerous biographies—and her longevity have made her
more important to historians.

By contrast, Catalina left Spain for Savoy in 1585 and died in Turin
twelve years later, at only thirty. While the Netherlands figure prominently in the political history of early modern Europe, the duchy of
Savoy was a principality whose history has mistakenly been considered
peripheral to the principal events of the period.[22] Historical attention
given to the two sisters has thus been shaped by historians' greater

interest in the geographical and political realms in which the two women lived their adult lives, by which measure Catalina has fared the worse.

Prizing a royal woman's political influence, scholars have tried to document Isabel's informal introduction to statecraft at the Spanish court, arguing that Philip carefully trained her in political matters, whereas Catalina received no political education because she married early and left Spain at seventeen. To be sure, there is evidence of Isabel's involvement in political matters in the last decade of her father's life. In the 1590s, she had access to state papers, gained knowledge of governance, and shared her views with Philip II, who valued them.[23]

Nevertheless, Isabel's political role prior to 1598 pales in comparison with that of Catalina, whose influence was not limited to advising her husband informally. Rather, without any direct experience in ruling until 1588, Catalina governed Carlo's territories during her husband's long absences from then until her death in 1597. While other aspects of her life are at least as interesting as her role in statecraft, it is still surprising that politically focused scholars, who ordinarily welcome examples of women who have exercised political power, have yet to discover this young duchess who ruled. For the most part, and particularly in the English-speaking world, Catalina remains a little-known figure in early modern European history, and this book, a product of many years of archival research, is my effort to introduce her to a broader audience.

CHAPTER I

AN *INFANTA* AT THE ROYAL COURT IN SPAIN

I am from Madrid.

Catalina to Carlo, 20 May 1591

AT HER WEDDING CELEBRATION in Zaragoza in 1585, observers noted Catalina's rich attire, her poise, and her grace. Music and dancing figured prominently in the festivities, and the first evening concluded with two couples—Catalina with Carlo and the *infanta* Isabel with Prince Philip—dancing an *alemana* most gracefully. The second evening's festivities ended with just Catalina and Isabel dancing together. On subsequent days, the royal party, accompanied by many attendants, visited churches and monasteries and observed tournaments and bullfights.[1] The magnificence and splendor of the Spanish court was on display in Zaragoza, and a principal element of that splendor was Catalina. Philip II could rest assured that his daughter would look and act regally because, by the time she reached Zaragoza at the age of seventeen, she had been well trained to perform all the ceremonial functions expected of a royal woman at an early modern court. Though she would have much to learn in Turin, in 1585 she was very much a product of the upbringing she had received at the Spanish court.

BIRTH AND UPBRINGING

Born in October 1567, second daughter of Elisabeth of Valois and Philip II (see plates 1 and 2), Catalina should have been a boy. The year before, Elisabeth had given birth to a daughter, Isabel Clara Eugenia, and while Philip rejoiced at having a strong, healthy daughter, he still desired another male heir, especially because Don Carlos, his son by his first wife, María Manuela of Portugal, was physically and mentally weak. Indeed, Elisabeth and Philip had expected a son; at the birth of Catalina Micaela, Philip expressed his disappointment by absenting himself from the court immediately afterward, missing even her baptism. The birth of a second female heir was so inconsequential that some foreign ambassadors did not even dispatch a message reporting it.[2] In the months right after her birth, her governess, the duchess of Alba, writing to Catalina's grandmother, Catherine de' Medici, felt compelled to defend her. Catalina "is worth two sons," the duchess told Catherine, and "we would not exchange her even for two sons because she is very pretty."[3] No doubt the governess knew that Catherine and others shared Philip's disappointment at the birth of a daughter. Catalina's mother, Elisabeth of Valois, insisted in a letter to her brother, Charles IX, that she was pleased to have had a girl:

> I cannot help being pleased with Caterine, and for this reason, I am not sorry not to have had a son, except insofar as in such times as these, he would have been of service to you, although I hope that you remain so feared and obeyed that you will not long have need of it [his service]. I thank you very humbly for what you said about your impressions of the painting of your niece because I am fully aware that you said it because she is my daughter. If she is fortunate enough to live to the age of twelve, or even beyond, I will consider myself the most blessed woman in the world.[4]

Ironically, Elisabeth's strong defense of her infant daughter shows the pressure to produce a male heir, and suggests that she, too, was a little disappointed. Had she borne a son, there would have been no discussion of regrets at not having had a daughter. Everyone recognized the importance of male heirs. Years later, when Anna of Austria, Philip II's fourth wife and niece, miscarried a girl, one of her court attendants reported everyone's grief but noted that it would have been much worse if the child had been a boy.[5]

Catalina never knew her mother, who died in 1568 in premature labor with her third child, another girl. Nevertheless, Elisabeth of Valois, apart from bequeathing her possessions to her two daughters, exerted a posthumous influence over Catalina's upbringing. Known for spending extravagantly and for managing her household carelessly, Elisabeth enjoyed a relatively frivolous life, playing cards, going on excursions with her ladies-in-waiting, attending and participating in court perfor-mances, and delighting in court gossip.[6] Philip loved her deeply, confided in her about political matters, and turned a blind eye to her spending and debts, but when he married Anna of Austria, Philip decided that the queen's household needed to be reformed. He told the marquis of Ladrada, the new queen's *mayordomo mayor* (lord high steward), that "It is not suitable to continue the arrangement [of the household] of the late queen."[7] He ordered a set of rules (*etiquetas*) to be drawn up, and these rules, compiled over the course of four years, from 1571 to 1575, in most respects codified what had been informal practice before Elisabeth of Valois's arrival at the Spanish court.[8] However, the *etiquetas* made clear that Philip II wanted any future queen of his, along with his daughters (whose household was subsumed under that of the queen), to live in a closely supervised household with strictly limited and controlled access to the outside world. All their contact with male courtiers would be carefully regulated, as would all their outings.[9] These modifications to the queen's household, prompted by Elisabeth's lax court supervision, directly affected Catalina's daily life.

The queen's household was under the control of a male *mayordomo mayor*, but the *camarera mayor* (first lady of the bedchamber), in charge of the queen's apartments, also exercised great authority. She accompa-nied the queen at all hours and ensured that the women in the house-hold behaved appropriately. She helped monitor the queen's rooms, sleeping (with several additional ladies) in the queen's bedroom when the king was absent. The *infantas* had their own *aya* (governess), and in the absence of a queen, the *aya* exercised maximum authority, but when there was a queen, as was the case from 1570 to 1580, the *infantas* and their *aya* formed part of the queen's household and were technically under the authority of her *camarera mayor*. The new *etiquetas* stipulated that *dueñas de honor* (ladies-in-waiting) would attend the *infantas* at all times when the *camarera mayor* could not. Contact with men, even the male servants in the *infantas'* household, was closely regulated. For example, at the *infantas'* meals, male servants could bring food to the door, but there they had to hand the plates to the ladies-in-waiting, who alone were allowed to approach the table to serve the young girls. To ensure that these rules were followed, a *dueña de honor* was to stand guard by the doorway to the *infantas'* apartments.[10]

Philip believed that restricting access to the new queen, his daughters, and their female attendants would enhance his and their dignity. Moreover, if the principal nobles were to send their daughters to live at the Spanish court, they needed to be reassured that their virtue would be well protected. Not without a struggle were these changes implemented; in 1571, several of the ladies-in-waiting, including the painter Sofonisba Anguissola, protested strongly when grates were placed over the windows of their apartments to prevent them from being seen from without and also to prevent their conversing through the windows with men. When, using wooden rods, the court ladies pried off the grates, only through Queen Anna of Austria's intervention did they escape serious punishment.[11] In 1571, Catalina and Isabel were too young to realize that their movements would be more restricted than before, nor would they in any event have had any power to oppose the changes.

In practice, the *etiquetas* could be either relaxed or strictly enforced. So, for example, the women's apartments were occasionally left unlocked, or a lady-in-waiting could ask permission from the queen to leave the palace or to talk with a man.[12] However, when in 1580 Philip, Queen Anna, and the two *infantas* left for Badajoz, that Philip might there wait near Portugal, hoping with the success of his armies to cross the border to take up the Portuguese throne, they left behind female attendants at the court in Madrid to look after the two youngest royal children. During Philip and Anna's absence from the court, the rules governing access to the ladies-in-waiting were more rigidly enforced. Ana of

Dietrichstein, one of the women left behind, reported that they were confined (*enparedadas*—literally between walls, or cloistered) to their palace apartments and had strict instructions not to talk to "brother, father, nor to our fathers' servants, nor to friars." Ana chafed at these restrictions, complaining that, as she and the other women had been left with no one who could even enter their apartments to make the beds, she was forced to make her own. No gentlemen (*galanes*) could enter the palace or the chapel, greatly frustrating Ana, who felt as if she were an enclosed nun.[13]

Anna of Austria's death from influenza while in Badajoz changed Philip's plans, and the *infantas* returned to Madrid in December 1580, where they too were enclosed. Ana of Dietrichstein reported that hardly anyone could see them, though in fact the royal sisters quickly began to take on more public roles. Ana also related that at this time the *infantas* often played with her own younger sister and pressured Ana to play with them as well, suggesting that even if Isabel and Catalina were confined to the palace apartments (or the Descalzas, a royal convent in Madrid where they lived for part of the time Philip was in Portugal), they found ways to stay busy and could command their attendants to entertain them.[14] Moreover, Ana of Dietrichstein's strong complaints indicate that such strict observance of the rules was not the norm and had been imposed because neither king nor queen was in Madrid to supervise the women and children.

Five years later, Catalina took the new rules of etiquette to Turin with her, and Philip expected her to implement them there to lend a royal air to the ducal court.[15] In Turin as in Madrid, though, the rules could and would be bent.

A FAMILY CIRCLE AT THE SPANISH COURT

Catalina grew up surrounded by her father, siblings, aunts, and cousins, with whom she cultivated close, affectionate relationships and from whom she learned what was expected of her as a Spanish *infanta*. Her personality would be formed during these early years in Spain. After their mother's death, Catalina and Isabel, still very young girls, were supervised by their governess, the duchess of Alba, until 1570, and by their aunt, Juana of Austria, until her death in 1573.[16] If we can extrapolate from Philip's relationship with his other children, he was probably a largely absent father during these early years. When informed in 1575 that a visit to his sick three-year-old son might lift the boy's spirits, Philip had refused to comply, saying that "he is not old enough to derive any benefit from a visit by me," directing instead that his son be given specific foods for his health. When pressed again to see him, the monarch noted that the boy's governess was more likely than he to convince the boy to eat the prescribed food. Similarly, Philip undoubtedly left the *infantas*' governess to look after his daughters, even if he gave detailed instructions for their care. His hands-off fathering did not imply any lack of affection. As he told Catherine de' Medici after the death of Elisabeth of Valois, "I love the *infantas* so much that as Your Majesty says, there is little need for you to entrust them to me, because they are the only comfort left me after Our Lord deprived me of the company of their mother."[17]

In 1570, when Philip II married his niece, Anna of Austria, the girls passed into her household. Anna was the only one of Philip's four wives to speak Castilian, so the couple could converse easily, and in their marriage Philip found "a tranquility that he had never experienced."[18] By all accounts, Anna and Philip enjoyed a loving marriage; the Venetian ambassador reported in 1578 that Philip visited his wife three times a day, and they slept in "two low beds, about two palms [of the hand] apart, but a low curtain encloses them making them look like one [bed]. The king loves his wife most tenderly . . . seldom leaving her side."[19] When apart, they exchanged letters once or twice a week.[20] Between 1571 and 1580, the queen gave birth to five children, four sons and a daughter, who grew up with Catalina and Isabel.[21] The *infantas* must have enjoyed the close-knit family this marriage fostered, and, as one scholar has noted, "they formed a perfect household."[22]

Anna became Catalina and Isabel's surrogate mother (she was the second of Catalina's "two mothers," as Philip referred to her and Elisabeth of Valois), and they accompanied her everywhere, traveling with her whenever she left Madrid and remaining with her when their father left the capital.[23] Together with Anna, they also spent time with their father, even when he was busy with state matters. For example, in

November 1578 Ana of Dietrichstein noted that the queen and the *infantas* spent two hours in the afternoons and two in the evenings with Philip II.[24] While these times together were occasioned by their sorrow at the death of Anna's and his son, Fernando, heir to the Spanish throne, and were not necessarily the norm, they do illustrate that the queen and the *infantas* had access to the monarch and that Philip found comfort in their presence.

Fernando, the eldest of Anna's four sons, had been born in 1571, and his birth altered Isabel and Catalina's status at court because he supplanted them as direct heir to the throne. Three more sons, Carlos, Diego, and Philip, were born in 1573, 1575, and 1578, respectively, although Carlos would die when almost two, Fernando at six, and Diego at seven, so that by 1582 four-year-old Philip was the only male heir. How did Isabel and Catalina react to the births of these four half-brothers, relegating them to a secondary position in the succession? They would have witnessed the greater attention and importance given to these boys and might even have seen their father's particular joy at having male heirs. At Fernando's birth, for example, Philip refrained from official business for several days, took part in the elaborate public procession for his son's baptism, and pardoned several criminals in thanksgiving for the birth of a son.[25] On that occasion, the young *infantas*, only five and four, remained with the queen, watching the festivities from a palace window and greeting people afterward, but in 1584, at the public swearing in (*juramento*) of Prince Philip as heir to the throne, the *infantas*—now eighteen and seventeen—participated fully.[26] They entered the church on either side of the prince, sat on pillows placed below the prince's chair, and listened while their official fidelity to the prince was proclaimed for all to hear. Afterward, they knelt before the prince, their half-brother, kissed his hand, and pledged to remain loyal to him.[27] The ceremony was designed to emphasize the subordination of the female to the male line, as evidenced by Empress María, Philip II's sister, preceding the *infantas* and performing the same ritual. We have no record of the *infantas'* reaction to this ceremony or to the birth of male heirs who would displace them in the line of succession, but they grew up in a world in which sons took precedence over daughters and must have accepted it as the natural order of things.

In all probability, the two girls had been trained to expect that their future was marriage to a foreign prince and not rule of the Spanish kingdoms. Even as early as 1570, when Isabel was only four, there was discussion about a possible match between her and Mary Stuart's son (the future James I, king of Scotland and England), and in the 1570s, several French princes were proposed as potential candidates.[28] But the match pursued most seriously was that with Archduke Rudolf. In 1570, Empress María was already writing to Philip II about a possible marriage between her son and Isabel, a match which a Spanish courtier had mentioned two years earlier to the French ambassador.[29] The idea persisted; in 1576, Ana of Dietrichstein referred to the hoped-for marriage between Isabel and Rudolf, and four years later, she reported that Isabel had promised to take care of her and her sisters when she went to Central Europe to marry Rudolf, who by then was emperor. Ana's letters indicate that when Isabel was not even ten years old, her marriage to the future Holy Roman Emperor was openly discussed in the queen's household in Spain, and by 1580 fourteen-year-old Isabel thought she might become Holy Roman Empress. Though she clearly knew of the proposed marriage, the death of all but one of her half-brothers by 1582 and the remaining prince's weak health left open the possibility of her succession to the Spanish throne. When informing her mother of the death of Prince Diego in 1582, Ana of Dietrichstein noted that now there was talk that Isabel would not marry anyone, except perhaps Archduke Ernst, and that instead Catalina might be "given to the emperor [Rudolf II]."[30]

In a similar fashion, Catalina, too, would have seen an arranged marriage in her future, and by 1580 gossip already circulated at the Spanish court that she would marry the duke of Savoy.[31] For these reasons, it seems unlikely that there was any ill will between the two *infantas* and their younger half-siblings over the succession to the throne, because Isabel and Catalina knew that the chance of their succession was slim at best. Evidence suggests that the girls loved their half-siblings, and, after Anna's death, the *infantas* would tutor their three younger half-siblings, teaching them to read, write, and pray.[32]

But the *infantas'* family circle was not limited to the king and queen and their children. When Anna traveled from Central Europe to Madrid in 1570 to marry Philip II, she was accompanied by two of her brothers, eleven-year-old Archduke Albert (1559–1621) and nine-year-old Wenceslaus (1561–1578). The brothers were following in the footsteps of their older brothers, Rudolf and Ernst, who had returned to Vienna when Albert and Wenceslaus arrived in Spain.[33] Because their father, Maximilian II, had Protestant leanings, these four boys were sent by their devout Catholic mother, Empress María, and their grandfather, Ferdinand I, to the Spanish court for a more orthodox Catholic upbringing, as well as to strengthen the Spanish monarchy's bonds with the Austrian Habsburgs by familiarizing the boys with Philip II and the Spanish kingdoms.[34] Should Philip II die without an heir, one of these Austrian archdukes might eventually inherit his Spanish kingdoms, and he grew to care for these nephews as if they were his own sons.[35]

When Albert and Wenceslaus arrived at the Spanish court, Isabel was only four and Catalina three, so the girls grew up with their two older cousins close by. The two archdukes not only followed a strict schoolboy schedule, but they also accompanied the royal family on their outings, allowing the girls to get to know them well.[36] During summer evenings at the Escorial, the royal family would stroll through the gardens together to enjoy the cooler air.[37] Their close association was cut short first in 1578 when Wenceslaus died and then when Albert left for Portugal in 1580, to remain there as governor until 1595.

Philip's sister, Juana of Austria, was yet another central member of the family circle, until her death in 1573. Although Juana had married the prince of Portugal in 1552, he died shortly before their son, Sebastian, was born. She was recalled to Spain to serve as regent during Philip's marriage to Mary Tudor (1554–1559). Juana had been close friends with the *infantas'* mother, Elisabeth of Valois, and had joined and encouraged her in all her many court entertainments. In the Alcázar palace in Madrid, Juana had her own household, separate from that of the king and queen, and her own apartments, connected by a passageway to those of the queen. After Elisabeth of Valois's death, Juana cared for Catalina and Isabel, vowing to love them as if they were her own daughters, and the *infantas* lived in her apartments until Philip remarried.[38]

Taken by the spirituality of the Jesuits, Juana secretly joined their order—the only woman ever to do so—and decided to found a royal convent in Madrid, where she planned to retire. This convent—the Descalzas Reales—was still unfinished on her death in 1573, and Juana maintained her rooms in the Alcázar to the end.[39] In her rooms, she organized festivities to which she invited the *infantas*, the queen, and the two archdukes.[40] In Juana, Catalina and Isabel had the example of a woman who had exercised political authority, was a cultural patron and a lover of theater, music, and art, and had a strong commitment to the religious life. However, at her death, Isabel was only seven and Catalina six, so their memories of this aunt could not have been particularly vivid, though they would maintain a close relationship to the Descalzas Reales.

Perhaps a stronger influence and model might have been Juana and Philip's sister, Empress María, who, after having lived in Central Europe for thirty years and serving as Holy Roman Empress for the last twelve, returned a widow to Madrid in March 1582, where she resided in the Descalzas Reales. By all accounts a formidable woman, Empress María bore her husband, Emperor Maximilian, sixteen children, among them Queen Anna, archdukes Albert and Wenceslaus, and two other sons—Rudolf and Matthias—who would rule as emperors. Shortly after arriving in Madrid, the empress went to Lisbon to see Philip II, who asked her to serve as vicereine of Portugal. She declined, preferring to live in the Descalzas Reales. Because she never took religious vows, however, she was free to leave the convent at will and spent a great deal of time with Philip II and his children. Catalina and Isabel grew to know her well, and during Catalina's last two years in Spain she saw her aunt regularly.

For most of the 1570s, therefore, Catalina and Isabel were part of a close-knit family, but the unity of this family was shattered every few years by the deaths of some of its beloved members: Juana of Austria in 1573; Prince Carlos in 1575; Prince Fernando in 1578; Archduke Wenceslaus in 1578; Queen Anna of Austria in 1580; Prince Diego in 1582; and Anna's youngest child, the *infanta* María, in 1583. With each death, chroniclers noted the king's sorrow; at Fernando's, Philip II "wept, refused to eat, and secluded himself in a convent to mourn." At Wenceslaus's death, the monarch himself commented that "it is certainly a tragedy, but God (who is responsible) must know better." When

Diego died in 1582, Philip wrote to a minister that "it is a terrible blow," and when María died nine months later, the "grief prevented him from doing anything else."[41] Hans Khevenhüller, imperial ambassador to the Spanish court, reported that María's death saddened the monarch so greatly that he "stopped attending to other matters."[42]

The historical record is silent on how the *infantas* felt at the deaths of these relatives, except to note their wearing of mourning clothes and their questions about modifying their mourning attire at the wedding of one of their attendants.[43] However, Catalina and Isabel must have keenly felt the deaths of those around them, especially that of Queen Anna, because the girls had for ten years lived with her and her attendants. After her death, Philip was absent from Madrid for two years in order to claim the Portuguese throne, and during this time Catalina and Isabel remained by themselves in Madrid and would have had to mourn Anna's death without their father by their side.

They must also have mourned their two half-siblings, Diego and María. With Philip in Portugal, the two girls took responsibility for their half-siblings, Diego, Philip, and María, acting as mothers to them and tending to them when they were ill. In November 1582, Catalina, Diego, and María, along with many of their attendants, contracted *viruelas* (smallpox), and though Catalina and María recovered, Diego did not. In his letter to the *infantas* when Diego contracted the disease, Philip told them that he could not relax until he received an update on his illness, but he was sure that "with the care that you give him, he will be well."[44] Diego died thirteen days later.

To make matters worse, during the smallpox outbreak, Catalina and Isabel were kept apart to shield Isabel from the disease, so the two girls could not even console each other at Diego's death. Writing to Catalina in early January 1583, Philip commented that he was glad that Isabel had finally been able to visit her, because "you must have been very alone without her these days and also she without you." Two weeks later he again expressed his joy that the two sisters could now be together.[45] Though Philip made no mention of Diego's death in these letters to his daughters, the loss of his seven-year-old heir must have weighed heavily on his mind, and also on the minds of the two girls, who would likely have grieved for their half-brother.

In addition to family members dying, the girls also experienced the deaths of three governesses. The first, María Chacón, served as *aya* from 1570 until her death in 1576, important years for Isabel and Catalina as under Chacón's tutelage they grew from four and three years old respectively to ten and nine. Chacón was replaced on her death by María Magdalena Manrique, who died two years later. Inés Manrique, countess of Paredes de Nava, served next, until her death in 1583. These three women served the *infantas* at all hours and accompanied them everywhere. Thus, the girls might have mourned their deaths but would have grown used to a certain amount of turnover in their household, perhaps even expecting that they would have a new governess every few years.

DAILY LIFE AT THE SPANISH COURT

Despite the deaths of several close relatives, the decade of the 1570s was for the most part a happy, stable time for Catalina and Isabel. During these years, they joined Queen Anna's household and enjoyed the many activities of the queen and her ladies. As young girls, they played with dolls and enjoyed dressing up, and Luisa de Carvajal, the Catholic reformer who as a young girl lived for four years in the Descalzas Reales, later recalled playing with them at the Descalzas, running around the cloisters and disturbing the nuns with their ruckus.[46] They were educated both formally by tutors (usually the royal almoner) and informally by their female attendants, and they were taught to be cultured young women who could preside graciously over an early modern court. They were also instructed in Catholic devotional practices to inculcate the faith and prepare them to promote and defend Catholicism. Their manners, education, and demeanor were designed to reflect the majesty of Philip II and his court.[47]

Catalina and Isabel received an education befitting a Habsburg princess in the second half of the sixteenth century. No written instructions for their education have survived, whereas we have Charles V's written instructions for Philip II's education, for example, so we must rely on brief archival references to piece together how the *infantas* were taught and what they learned.[48] From earliest youth, they were educated by their governess and a few chosen court women, who would have taught them basic prayers and also begun to teach them to read and write. Around 1570, when Queen Anna arrived at the court, Juan de Zúñiga y Ercilla, a royal chaplain, was appointed to educate the royal children, but he did not begin to teach the girls until 1574, when they were eight and seven respectively. In teaching the two girls, Zúñiga initially followed the educational model used for Philip II's sisters, which prioritized religious instruction and sought to prepare the *infantas* for the various social and cultural roles that would fall to them at the court. However, educational reform in the 1570s also influenced Zúñiga's methods, and he might well have introduced the *infantas* to the reading of a range of texts that would have moved them beyond devotional subjects.[49]

They might have followed a daily schedule similar to that which Philip II instituted for their cousins, archdukes Albert and Wenceslaus. The two archdukes attended an early mass before beginning their lessons, which consisted of history, statecraft, and rhetoric in Latin and lasted from eight until ten in the morning. After a midday break for lunch and an hour of music between noon and one, they then had three more hours of lessons in Latin before breaking at four for physical exercise with other nobles and again before dinner at six.[50]

Like the archdukes, the *infantas* rose early, a practice that began when very young. In 1572, the king told the marquis of Ladrada, the queen's *mayordomo*, that if the girls "go to bed late, it is clear that they cannot get up early because they need to sleep well. But if they go to bed early, they could get up early and it would be good that they adopt this practice starting now."[51] Philip's comment suggests that up until 1572 the girls' schedule was not very strict but that by six and five years of age they were expected to conform to more stringent rules, possibly because they were beginning their more formal education. Catalina and Isabel also attended daily mass, either at the court chapel or in the queen's private oratory. (Catalina's own children would begin to attend complines before retiring when they were about two and a half, and mass when they were three.) Occasionally, the queen would leave the palace in late morning to attend a second mass or another religious service in one of the nearby churches, and the *infantas* sometimes accompanied her.[52]

After mass and breakfast, the *infantas* had morning and afternoon lessons, with time set aside for outdoor activities. The girls received lessons in Latin, "mathematics, natural philosophy, history, and literature."[53] Catalina and Isabel read devotional and secular literature, and, left to themselves, as when Philip was in Portugal, they preferred the popular romances of chivalry (*libros de caballería*), a taste they had no doubt acquired in Queen Anna's household, where the ladies-in-waiting took turns reading while the others did needlework or sewed.[54] When Philip was off in Portugal, their tutor complained to him that the girls were reading too many of these books and should instead read more devotional works, if only to serve as good role models for their ladies. He also noted that the *infantas* should know that Philip was informed if they used their time unwisely, suggesting that the girls sometimes tried to take advantage of their father's absence. The king ordered the situation remedied. Although the tutor mentioned their "innocence," the girls could no doubt be mischievous, and two months after their tutor's concerned appeal, Philip instructed his daughters to obey their governess in all matters, suggesting that the *infantas*, now teenagers, might have grown at least mildly rebellious.[55]

Some scholars have claimed that the girls attended a literary academy or school at court comprising the smartest and most gifted female attendants from the principal aristocratic families, in which they wrote and recited poetry and read literary works.[56] The documentary evidence for such a school is slim and the claims exaggerated, though it is fully plausible that aristocratic girls residing at the court would have been educated alongside Philip's two daughters.[57]

The *infantas* were tutored in Latin, but because neither Catalina nor Isabel was being trained to rule, it is doubtful that they read the same texts as their male cousins, whose Latin lessons were designed to teach them history and statecraft. Albert's and Wenceslaus's afternoon lessons focused on oratory, a skill not considered necessary for a princess.[58] Nevertheless, whereas Philip II's sisters had learned Latin only for devotional purposes, Isabel and Catalina received more formal training in the language. Initially, they were probably taught by one of Anna's ladies, Magdalena de Bobadilla, who knew Latin well, but afterward they were given a male tutor.[59] The Spanish humanist, Pedro de

Guevara, even designed a game for them to learn and practice Latin grammar. That they received the game no earlier than December 1582 tells us that the girls were studying Latin well into their teens, but they may have received the game only because they were having trouble with their Latin lessons.[60]

As women in the Renaissance usually stopped their education at marriage, Catalina's training in Latin ended at seventeen when she married the duke of Savoy.[61] Although she must by then have been able to read Latin, she did not fully comprehend spoken Latin. On their way to Zaragoza to celebrate Catalina's marriage, Philip stopped with his children at the University of Alcalá de Henares to listen to a lecture and gave instructions that the lecture be delivered in Castilian. Perhaps this was for the benefit of his seven-year-old son, whose Latin would still have been very rudimentary, but one observer specifically noted that the lecture was given in Castilian so that the prince and the *infantas* could understand it.[62] Other evidence suggests that Catalina's command of spoken Latin was not strong. In 1589, she wrote that she planned to see a play performed by the students of the Jesuits in honor of St. Mauricio, but as it would be in Latin, just thinking about it left her exhausted, knowing she would understand nothing.[63] Again, in 1592, when the students of the Jesuits in Turin put on a religious play in Latin, she commented that she had not understood anything.[64] It could be that by 1589 Catalina had forgotten whatever spoken Latin she had learned, but more likely, she had been taught only written Latin. In her day-to-day life in Turin, she had little need of Latin beyond following the mass and saying prayers. As Isabel, by contrast, continued to read Latin texts at Philip's court, her command of the language likely exceeded Catalina's.

The girls also learned French and Portuguese, probably from female attendants who were native speakers of the languages and not through formal instruction. French, their mother's language, could have been taught by French women who had served in their mother's household and joined that of Anna of Austria.[65] Catalina and Isabel wrote to their grandmother, Catherine de' Medici, in French, and both would continue to use French for diplomatic purposes as adults. Carlo would occasionally use French words in his letters to Catalina, suggesting that he knew she would understand their meaning.

The girls also knew Portuguese well enough that when Philip was in Portugal, he asked them to teach their brother the language, "because you understand it so well." He also commented that they must understand Portuguese well because they had been able to read an account he had sent them when even he could not understand several of the words.[66] Flattering the girls, Philip was no doubt encouraging them to master the language. As with French, Portuguese might be a useful tool for communicating with ambassadors or a future spouse; should one of the girls inherit the Spanish throne, she would be able to communicate with her Portuguese subjects. Though neither had much occasion to use Portuguese after she left the Spanish kingdoms, both had plainly learned it as young girls.

Their female attendants, who themselves had learned and practiced handwriting, taught Catalina and Isabel in their early youth how to shape their script.[67] A letter of 1573 from Isabel to the marquis of Ladrada, her *mayordomo mayor*, asking for clothing made of green and red fabric that she had seen in the queen's room, indicates that by seven, Isabel was capable of writing a letter of request, and while still very young, both girls would pen letters to their maternal grandmother, Catherine de' Medici.[68] Zúñiga, the *infantas'* tutor, made certain that both girls received formal training in handwriting, which would have included learning cursive script and epistolary conventions of salutations, spacing, and letter-folding.

Writing was not merely learning how to shape attractive, legible script and follow epistolary conventions. Nor was it simply a leisure activity to help the girls pass idle time. Letter-writing was conversing at a distance, and the *infantas* needed to learn how to express themselves clearly and pungently. Letters served to connect one with both family and political and religious leaders and were also a means to conduct business. Aristocratic women were active letter writers, and the women of the Habsburgs spearheaded an extensive correspondence network. By learning to write letters, Isabel and Catalina were introduced to what would be an expected and important familial responsibility. Both would eventually master the art of letter-writing, as evidenced in Isabel's letters to the duke of Lerma and in Catalina's to her husband.[69]

As part of their education in the social and cultural life of an early modern court, the *infantas* were also instructed in music and dance.

Both took lessons in harp, violin, and other string instruments. Violins were new to the Spanish court, having been introduced from France by the *infantas'* French mother, Elisabeth of Valois.[70] A group of violinists accompanied her to Spain and were given court offices in order to have regular access to the queen's apartments and give lessons to the *infantas* and to their ladies. These violinists would also have provided music for the *saraos* (evening parties with music and dance) and theatrical presentations, regular features of the court. In addition to the harp and violin, Isabel learned to play the guitar—or at least owned one—while Catalina might have learned to play the clavichord, as she inherited one from her mother, which she had in her rooms in Turin.[71]

Music accompanied another central court activity: dancing. As it was a necessary skill for all courtiers, the *infantas* began to receive dancing lessons when young. Like the violinists, dancing instructors were given offices in the queen's household, specifically to change bed linens, so that they would have access to the queen's private apartments, where they could teach the queen and the *infantas* to dance.

Changes in etiquette in the early 1570s also affected dancing. The marquis of Ladrada, in charge of drafting the new etiquette, suggested that some modification be made to dancing in the queen's apartments. "When her Majesty [Elisabeth of Valois] danced in her room and the ladies [danced] with the princes, everyone who ordinarily had access to these rooms was allowed in." Ladrada suggested that access should now be restricted to only a few attendants and servants whenever the queen and the *infantas* were dancing. Dancing, too, needed to be modest, and dancing lessons should be private.[72] At *saraos* or court masques, however, where all the aristocrats of the court gathered, the royal family would join their guests and dance in public. The queen and royal children needed to learn how to dance competently and elegantly, as the *infantas* would have been required to dance in public when very young. By the time Catalina and Isabel danced at Catalina's wedding celebration, they had been carefully trained.

Music and dancing came together in yet another essential feature of court life: theater. Court theater was a principal pastime at Philip II's court, but productions were organized and financed by the queens. Accounts from the households of Elisabeth of Valois and Anna of Austria show that theatrical presentations were extravagant and expensive endeavors, with elaborate costumes and musical accompaniment.[73] The girls were early exposed to court theater because their aunt, Juana of Austria, regularly sponsored performances and invited the queen (both Elisabeth of Valois and afterward Anna of Austria) and the girls to attend. On one occasion, when they saw a play (*comedia*) in Juana of Austria's apartments with Queen Anna and the archdukes, the queen's *mayordomo* reported to Philip that the girls, four and three at the time, had enjoyed the presentation as if they were twenty years old.[74] The Augustinian friar Juan de San Gerónimo reported that in 1578 at the Escorial, the royal family watched tragedies performed by the best actors in Spain.[75] The *infantas* themselves sometimes performed in plays, for example, by dressing as Turks in a *farsa* (farce) in 1579.[76]

After Queen Anna's death, the *infantas* and their ladies organized the plays themselves, practicing their parts, memorizing lines, and staging performances. We have little information about what plays were staged, but we do know that both girls acted in Luis Gálvez de Montalvo's pastoral work, *El pastor de Fílida,* which the author wrote to be performed at the court of Philip II. Gálvez de Montalvo included a detailed, laudatory description of both *infantas* and the aristocratic girls in their entourage. These plays, often with classical themes, were performed in Anna's or Juana's apartments at the Alcázar in Madrid; in the royal apartments at the Escorial and Aranjuez; in Empress María's rooms at the Descalzas; and even in the residence of Mateo Vázquez, Philip II's secretary, suggesting that they might have been staged in other noble residences as well.[77] These performances also occasionally took place outdoors in the gardens of royal or aristocratic residences. Catalina and Isabel took great pleasure in these theatricals, and Catalina and her ladies would carry the practice with them to Turin.

The women of the queen's household taught Catalina and Isabel domestic skills such as sewing and embroidery. While they might have helped to sew costumes for the theatrical performances, they also made altar cloths for churches and shrines. Catalina would become adept at a type of netting needlework known as *red,* on which she would later spend long hours while the duke was away from Turin. She would also sew many personal items for her husband and coverings for religious images and altars for churches in the duchy of Savoy.

The *infantas* were taught other arts as well. The ladies in the queen's household perfumed gloves, a skill the *infantas* also probably learned.[78] Sofonisba Anguissola, who had given drawing and painting lessons to their mother and who served the *infantas* after their mother's death, probably taught them to draw and paint.[79] They also learned to cook and bake. For example, Ana of Dietrichstein reported that for entertainment she and the *infantas* sometimes made stews (*guisar potages*), inviting the queen to eat with them.[80] They also made dishes with game they had hunted. Llanos y Torriglia, a Spanish historian who authored an early-twentieth-century biography of Isabel, claimed that the girls once cooked an entire pig they had hunted and served it to their father in a variety of dishes.[81] In Turin, Catalina would continue to cook special dishes to send to her husband on his campaigns.

Far from forcing his daughters to remain inside the palace dedicated solely to domestic work or study, Philip urged them to get physical exercise. As one of his ministers told the marquis of Ladrada, "It seems to His Majesty that the *infantas* should go outside sometimes, so that they can get fresh air, because there is no plant that can grow without it."[82] We have reports of the girls playing with their young female attendants, court buffoons, and dwarfs in the gardens of the Escorial, but, from an early age, Catalina and Isabel also learned to hunt with crossbows (*ballestas*) and harquebuses, one of Philip II's favorite pastimes.[83] They accompanied their father to the woods of Segovia, to the Fresneda, to Aceca, and to other royal lodges used for hunting and fishing. The girls hunted deer, boar, game birds, rabbits, and hares. Jerónimo de Sepúlveda reported that whenever the royal family went to the Escorial, they made excursions to hunt, and the girls would shoot much game. Competing with each other, "they placed their bets and did not forgive the other anything."[84] Sepúlveda also noted that the girls were adept at shooting. Philip delighted in his girls' hunting; when he was in Portugal and the girls wrote to him about their hunting, he responded that he was pleased they had killed so many rabbits and hares and complimented them at handling the crossbow well.[85]

With these early hunting experiences, the girls were introduced to an important aspect of aristocratic culture. Carlo shared Catalina's love of hunting, so it is not surprising that in October 1584, the duke's ambassador in Madrid detailed the *infanta*'s prowess to her soon-to-be husband, reporting that Catalina had brought down a large deer with a crossbow. She was a veritable Diana, the ambassador noted. Both Catalina and Isabel would continue to hunt into adulthood, and Catalina would hunt even when pregnant.[86]

The *infantas* also played and bet at cards, and they might also have played board games such as the popular game of the goose (*juego de la oca*).[87] We have records of them being given small amounts of money with which to play; while not specifically stating that they were playing cards, the account entry certainly indicates that they were betting. Card-playing and betting were regular activities in the queen's household. Elisabeth of Valois was known to bet at cards, even having sometimes to borrow money from her attendants to be able to keep playing, and her daughters did the same.[88] We should not assume, however, that card-playing was strictly a female activity or confined to the women's household. In fact, Philip II played cards with his daughters.[89]

Sepúlveda's comment about the girls challenging each other in shooting matches and the evidence that they bet at cards suggest that there might have been some competition between Isabel and Catalina, who were only fourteen months apart. The French ambassador at the Spanish court reported that when Anna of Austria met the *infantas* for the first time, she sat Catalina to her left and Isabel to her right, giving the latter the higher-ranking position.[90] This and other distinctions, while so routine that they are rarely recorded, would have made Catalina conscious on a daily basis of her sister's higher status. There is no evidence, however, that she felt resentful. Years later in Turin, comparing herself to Isabel, Catalina wrote to her husband, who was in Spain and reporting to her on her family there, that Isabel was a better person than she, more patient and forgiving.[91] Although adding that she knew Isabel loved her—"as she should" (*zierto me lo debe*)—she told the duke that she was happy to hear it from him.

The girls also had a menagerie of animals, including different kinds of birds, dogs, and monkeys, with which to amuse themselves. When they visited the Escorial with Empress María and her daughter Margarita, the monks gave them a docile squirrel with a collar and chain as a pet.[92] The *infantas* treated these animals like dolls, dressing them up in fancy clothes and having carts built for them. Portraits of the girls when very young, such as that of both girls by Alonso Sánchez Coello in *c.* 1571, now in Buckingham Palace (plate 3), or the portrait by Sofonisba Anguissola of a young Catalina with a marmoset (plate 4), show them holding songbirds, dogs, or monkeys. Court inventories indicate that, far from being mere props or symbols, the animals depicted were owned and domesticated by the *infantas*. Cages were constructed to transport the parrots, songbirds, squirrels, and monkeys from one royal residence to another. In 1585, cages were built so that Isabel could take animals with her on the wedding trip to Zaragoza; did other cages allow Catalina to take some of her animals with her to Turin?[93]

Their father, who delighted in exotic animals, had a pit constructed at the Real Alcázar in Madrid to house four lions sent to him by Suleiman II. At all his palaces, but particularly at Aranjuez, he kept animals such as goats, camels, ostriches, elephants, and a rhinoceros. He was elated when his viceroy in Goa sent an elephant to his young son, Prince Philip.[94] In 1583, he even allowed an elephant and a rhinoceros, whom Khevenhüller described as a "very fierce beast," to wander through the courtyard and hallways of the Escorial, no doubt relishing the monks' dismay.[95] For the youthful Catalina and Isabel, however, these animals were simply part of their daily lives, amusing and entertaining them at their different residences.

RELIGIOUS LIFE

As evident, palace life was anything but tedious for the *infantas*, yet, although they were busy with a range of worldly activities, religious devotion was also an essential part of their days.[96] As noted above, they attended at least one daily mass and began to attend daily devotions such as complines or vespers when they were about three years old. We have no record of when they received their first holy communion, but in the late sixteenth century children were often confirmed before they received communion, or received both sacraments at the same time. We know that Catalina and Isabel were confirmed at the Escorial in May 1575, when Catalina was seven, the age stipulated by the Council of

Trent.[97] Around the age of six, they would have learned how to pray the rosary. Other devotional practices included participation in religious processions during Holy Week and on Corpus Christi and many Marian and other feast days, so the girls needed to be taught how to participate. For example, the marquis of Ladrada, Anna of Austria's *mayordomo mayor*, noted that "Tomorrow it is customary to have a solemn procession in the hallways (*corredores*) and Your Majesty [Philip II] should see if the queen our lady should attend mass in the *sala* and if the *señoras infantas* should go upstairs to process (*andar la procesion*) with Her Majesty [Anna of Austria]."[98] Participating in such rituals was an important part of the girls' education.

Accompanying the queen or their father, Catalina and Isabel also visited monasteries and religious sites. In Madrid they went regularly to the convent of the Descalzas Reales and even stayed there from July to November 1581 when their father was in Portugal.[99] They also visited the Jeronimite monastery of San Jerónimo, which had royal apartments and where Prince Philip was sworn in as heir to the Spanish throne. They spent many summer months at the Escorial, including the summers of 1575, 1576, and 1578, though they had to cut short their stay in 1578. In 1580, on their way to Badajoz, the royal family stopped to visit the Jeronimite monastery at Guadalupe.[100] Journeying to Zaragoza for Catalina's wedding and subsequently to Barcelona for her embarkation, they visited first the Cistercian monastery of Santa Fe as they approached Zaragoza, then the Jeronimite monastery of Santa Engracia in Zaragoza, the Cistercian monastery of Santa María de Poblet, and the Benedictine monastery of Santa María de Monserrat, along with many churches, such as Nuestra Señora del Pilar in Zaragoza. In these ways, devotion to religious orders, monasteries, convents, and pilgrimage sites were inculcated in both girls. In later years, Isabel in the Netherlands would visit convents and develop close friendships with nuns, while Catalina in Savoy would visit and help promote pilgrimage sites and patronize several religious orders.

However, these visits to churches and monasteries were not strictly devotional. At the Escorial, for example, still under construction when the royal family began to visit the monastery, the king and his family had their own apartments. Accompanied by their many attendants, they went to the Escorial to escape the heat of Madrid—Philip to escape his audiences and meetings with ambassadors, as well, and the girls to spend time playing in the gardens.[101] They had greater access to and more frequent contact with their father at the Escorial, because he tended to be more relaxed, taking breaks in his crowded schedule. On these visits, Philip would have the monks show him and his family around. When they went in May 1575 for Catalina and Isabel's confirmation, they first visited the library, where they saw "paintings, tapestries, and silver objects, along with books of great value." On other visits, they saw the monastery's collection of relics, and when they went with Empress María in February 1582, they were shown the "books, paintings, images, along with the things from China."[102] In visiting the Escorial, Catalina and Isabel were being trained not only to follow the devotional life of the Habsburgs, but also to appreciate and imitate the Habsburg practice of collecting valuable and exotic items.

From the Escorial, the royal family often went to other royal residences, such as La Fresneda, Aranjuez, and Aceca, as well as to the woods of Segovia. Aranjuez was known for its beautiful gardens with rare flowers and fruit trees. La Fresneda was Philip's favorite residence for fishing, and the royal family usually accompanied him on these outings. Aceca and the woods of Segovia were excellent for hunting, the *infantas* practicing their shooting and archery there. Catalina recalled these places fondly; when her husband Carlo went to Spain in 1591 and reported on the sites he had visited, Catalina commented that she was very pleased that he had gone to Aranjuez and hoped he would be able to see Aceca at least in passing.

On their visits to royal residences, the *infantas* were accompanied by family as well as their attendants, and these excursions were therefore lively outings designed to entertain. When the royal family visited the Escorial in June 1576, Fray Juan de San Gerónimo, a monk there, reported, "a throng of gentlemen [came] with the royal family and all the many ladies who were in Madrid with them, important ladies, ladies-in-waiting, and servants, who all made up a large number." In June 1579, the same monk noted that Queen Anna of Austria toured the entire monastery with "many ladies-in-waiting," visiting first the relics but then the "library, dining room, wardrobe, infirmary, and pharmacy," before retiring to their rooms.[103] In the 1570s, Anna's two brothers, Albert and Wenceslaus, accompanied the royal family on hunting excursions and visits to royal residences. Visiting the Escorial for Corpus Christi in 1575, the family participated in the processions and also saw a theatrical performance in Latin and Spanish put on by the seminarians, along with two performances about the history of the Eucharist by the boys of the seminary. These Corpus Christi performances seem to have been annual rituals. In 1576, they attended them again, and in 1584, the boys of the seminary put on a dance about the history of the Eucharist, as well as a play.[104] Though these performances were religious in nature, they were festive and theatrical. When at the Escorial in September 1576, the *infantas* saw a bullfight in the village, requested by Philip II's half-brother, Juan de Austria.[105] For Catalina, these visits to the Escorial and other royal residences outside Madrid were formative experiences. She would later try to duplicate Aranjuez in her residences at Miraflores and Valentino, outside Turin.

THE *INFANTAS* AND THEIR FATHER

Catalina's and Isabel's lives changed dramatically after the death of their stepmother, Queen Anna of Austria, in 1580 and their return to Madrid from Badajoz. They did not see their father for two years and three months, obliging them, as the eldest members of the royal family in Madrid, to assume some of the family's official duties and meet occasionally with ambassadors and papal nuncios, as in December 1581 when their *aya* reported that the two girls were busy with "councils, ambassadors, and bishops."[106] Philip II charged them with greeting and welcoming his sister, Empress María, who in March 1582 arrived in Madrid from Central Europe with her daughter. He also asked the girls to write news of their arrival and reception: "Write me very good news of her [Empress María] . . . and [tell me] if she is fat or thin and if we still look somewhat alike as we used to and I well believe that she has not aged as much as I have. Also write me about your cousin [Margarita] and if you understand her well, as don Antonio de Castro told me he had not understood her because she speaks little Castilian. In short, write me lots of news about everything."[107]

We know of this period largely through the letters Philip wrote to them from Portugal. The *infantas* wrote to their father regularly, but after reading their letters, Philip burned them. He instructed his daughters to burn his as well, but the girls disobeyed, and Catalina took her father's letters with her to Turin, where they survive to this day. From these letters, we can often deduce or guess what the girls had written in theirs, since he often commented on their letters and responded to the topics they had addressed. Philip's letters to his daughters provide us with insight not only into the girls' daily lives but also into their relationship with him.[108]

Even from afar, Philip remained well informed about his daughters' activities; famously obsessive and micromanaging, he tried his best to control what they did. Yet he was also an affectionate and caring father who missed them and was interested in what they were doing. He encouraged them to write often, asking questions that he expected them to answer and thanking them for responding to everything that he had written.[109] For the girls, writing was a means to reach out to their father, whom they in turn missed.

In his letters, Philip described his activities in Portugal, indicating not only his own preferences but also what he thought the *infantas* would enjoy hearing about. He told them about his visits to monasteries, often with Archduke Albert, and the religious services that they attended there: a sermon, sung mass, vespers. He would often comment on the monastic buildings, the views from the monasteries, and especially the gardens. On one occasion, he stated that he intended to copy the plans for a garden he had seen, apparently to imitate it in Spain. In turn, the *infantas* told him about religious services at the Descalzas, where they were living, and about their trips to Aranjuez, Aceca, El Pardo, and the Escorial. Catalina wrote to him that there were citrons (*cidras*) in Aranjuez, and Philip responded that he was happy to hear it. He asked for news on the progress of the construction of the palace in Aranjuez, wondering if the fountain was operational, if the chapel was finished and the altarpiece in place, and if the clock was running. Several times, Philip commented that he envied their ability to visit these places, mentioning that what he missed most about Aranjuez was the song of the nightingales.[110] He described in detail a trip he had taken by boat, noting that he had done so to make them envious. These exchanges reveal that the king and his daughters connected over their mutual love of gardens and the outdoors, as well as their religious devotion.

Philip's letters also regularly mention the *gente de placer* (buffoons, dwarfs, jesters) who accompanied him and for whom he seems to have felt genuine affection. In particular, he mentioned the widowed dwarf Magdalena Ruiz, originally in the household of Philip's sister Juana and now in Philip's retinue in Lisbon, whom he likely saw every day.[111] (See plate 5 for a portrait of the *infanta* Isabel with Magdalena.) He joked about Magdalena's antics, reporting that she was annoyed with him and had been arguing with Luis Tristán, another court figure, possibly a dwarf, who had accompanied Philip to Lisbon.[112] Magdalena had left the court in a fury, threatening to kill Tristán, Philip told his daughters, but "I think by tomorrow she will have already forgotten." To the girls' report about eating strawberries in Aranjuez, Philip responded that Magdalena was jealous. Catalina and Isabel would have appreciated their father's jokes about these figures, since the two girls knew them well—several had been their playmates—and, from Portugal, Magdalena and Tristán wrote often to them.[113]

In another letter, Philip thanked his daughters for congratulating him on the momentous occasion of his official swearing in as king of Portugal. Still in mourning for the death of Anna of Austria, he knew they would understand his complaint that "they wanted to dress me in brocade much against my will."[114] He told them that he wished they had been able to observe the event from a window, but that he was sending them a detailed account (*relación*) of the *juramento* for them to look over and keep for him, so that when he returned he would look it over with them. His comments not only suggest that the *infantas* knew their father would be uncomfortable in brocade but also that he wanted them to know the importance of his swearing in and would later take time to review the details of the ceremony with them.

Edible gifts, especially with a particular connection to the giver, fostered affection at a distance. On at least one occasion, the *infantas* sent Philip apricots, which unfortunately did not survive the trip: he described them as having arrived unrecognizable. He noted that he was especially sorry because the apricots had come from one of the garden trees close to the *infantas'* window, which made the gift even dearer to him. In turn, Philip sent his daughters a box of horticultural items: sweet limes (*limas dulces*), Spanish limes (*limoncillos*), roses, and blossoms from a lemon or orange tree. He told them to try the limes and write to tell him whether in fact they were sweet, because he had never seen any so big and thought they were probably lemons. He also explained that he sent the roses and the blossoms to show them what grew in Lisbon, adding that he had seen violets but no jonquils, which apparently were grown in Spain. He also sent them beads from the Indies, Agnus Dei, rosaries, and pardon beads (*perdones*) given to him by the papal legate.[115]

Philip's letters also reveal other kinds of information, both personal and political, that he discussed with his daughters. We learn, for example, that he gave them New World shipping news: "The fleets from the Indies have already arrived, as you have heard, except for one that was thought lost but afterward we have learned that it arrived in the island of Madeira, and so I think that nothing will be lost." A year later he again reported the fate of the Indies fleet, saying that one ship had returned but that they awaited news of the others. Several days later, responding to Isabel's report that she had heard that the galleys (*galeras*) from the Indies had arrived, he corrected her by explaining that they were large *naos*, not galleys, and proceeded to give more details of their arrival.[116] Isabel and Catalina were well aware how important the arrival of the fleet was, and the status of the fleet was undoubtedly a regular topic at the Spanish court. Their father shared whatever information he had, but he also used the occasion to teach his daughters about proper nautical terminology.

Personal matters also figure prominently in Philip's letters, which tell us that the king knew his daughters well and did not shy away from sensitive subjects. For example, in October 1581, he told Catalina to be careful with her cheek, because he knew how often it swelled. To Isabel's report of a nosebleed, Philip replied that she would probably continue to have nosebleeds until she began to menstruate. Two months later, congratulating Isabel on her fifteenth birthday, he added that she had not yet become a woman, which would suggest that his daughter had still not had her first period.[117]

When his daughters withheld news, Philip sometimes learned of it from others, as when he wrote that "you have kept quiet about the fall that you, the younger one [Catalina], had in Aranjuez and I think [you have hidden] other things as well."[118] Philip did not disclose his source, though he told them they were wrong to suspect one of his officials, Tofiño, an *aposentador* (official responsible for palace lodgings). He also mentioned that he knew who might give him further details, making plain to the girls that he had back channels to learn of their activities.

His letters also reveal their shared fund of knowledge. When Philip mentioned Badajoz, the city where Queen Anna had died, he commented that he would rather not remember "such a bad place." He had no need to say more, because the girls would have understood his reference. All of these allusions suggest the intimacy between father and daughters, and the ease with which they communicated. Philip reassured them that he missed them and their siblings; he asked the girls to tell their half-brother that he was sending him an elephant and would give him books of paintings upon his return to Spain. As he told his daughters, "I would like to see all of you in more than just portraits."[119]

Once their father returned to Madrid, they resumed the monarch's festive court life, interacting regularly with the empress and many aristocrats.[120] In Catalina's last few years in Madrid, she and Isabel gradually assumed roles usually given to the queen and took over many activities that Anna of Austria had once organized. They often joined their father in his excursions outside Madrid, as they did in November 1583 when they spent many days in the royal hunting lodge of El Pardo, enjoying frequent walks with him.[121] In May 1584, the French representative at the Spanish court, Pierre de Ségusson, lord of Longlée, reported that the *infantas* and the prince were in Aranjuez with their father, where they spent mornings walking in the gardens and afternoons making boat excursions and hunting. "From morning to evening, their highnesses never lose His Majesty from view," Longlée related, "and it is a company that he [Philip] loves greatly." In the years between Philip's return from Portugal and Catalina's departure for Savoy, the girls spent many hours with him—Khevenhüller reported in July 1584 that the *infantas* were always with the king—once again enjoying the life they had shared with him in the 1570s.[122]

To Catalina, Madrid was her father's court, centered in the palace of the Real Alcázar but extending to the churches and monasteries close by, and peopled with the relatives, courtiers, and attendants she knew so well. That Madrid of the royal court was her home, and she identified herself with it. When Carlo wrote to her from the Real Alcázar in 1591 describing his visit there, telling her about the ladies, the palace rooms, and the furniture, his detailed account prompted Catalina to respond that she was happy to hear that he liked it all because "I am from Madrid, and I wish I could have been with you there."[123]

By the time of her marriage to the duke of Savoy, Catalina had received the education and training of a Habsburg princess. Graceful and poised, confident when conversing, fond of hunting, and at home in the cultural capital of Europe, she was the paragon of a cultured princess.

CHAPTER 2

A RELUCTANT BRIDE

She went holding a handkerchief in front of her eyes so that it would not seem as if she were crying.

> Henry Cock, *Relación del viaje hecho por Felipe II en 1585, á Zaragoza, Barcelona, y Valencia*

As the daughter of the most powerful monarch in Europe, with a large retinue of attendants to serve her, Catalina had enjoyed a privileged and even pampered youth. Her father might have controlled what she learned, where she went, with whom she interacted, and even what she wore (she needed his permission to wear the platform shoes—*chapines*—that court ladies wore), but she was certainly doted on and accustomed to people around her meeting her every need. She was fully conscious of her standing as the daughter of Spanish and French royalty—a rank above any of the ducal families in the Italian territories—and might well have believed that she lived in the most refined of European courts. She had never traveled outside the Iberian Peninsula, one of the territories ruled by her father, and everything in her youth had worked to make her think that the world revolved around her family circle. Even the resources of the vast Spanish Empire were there to meet all her material needs and comforts.

Like most other early modern royal women, Catalina played no role in negotiating her marriage, and sources suggest that she was unhappy to marry Carlo and reluctant to accede to her father's decision that she do so. Although she had known since September 1584 that she would marry the duke of Savoy, she probably looked at the upcoming wedding with trepidation. It would remove her from everyone and everything familiar to her, and she could only guess at what lay in store for her in Turin. She also knew that by marrying a duke, she was marrying beneath her royal status. Did she believe her father had sacrificed her to his political designs, and, if so, was she resentful? Did she think love was possible in an arranged, aristocratic marriage? After all, her father had enjoyed a loving marriage with her mother, Elisabeth of Valois, and her "second mother," Anna of Austria.

Little did Catalina suspect that she would grow to love her husband intensely, form a strong partnership with him, and wholly identify with his goals and interests. As she set off from Madrid in late January 1585 to celebrate her wedding in Zaragoza, her strong and affectionate marriage with Carlo was scarcely foreseeable.

NEGOTIATING THE MARRIAGE

From the early 1570s, when his daughters were still young, Philip II proposed to Emanuele Filiberto, duke of Savoy, that he consider a marriage alliance to unite their two families. Philip recognized the strategic importance of Savoy, a duchy through which the Spanish Road to Flanders passed, and he was aware that France was courting the duke as well. Emanuele Filiberto himself was married to a French princess, Marguerite of Valois, daughter of the French king Francis I, and several of Emanuele's advisers were Francophiles.[1] If Savoy were to ally with France, Spain's passage to Flanders would be seriously jeopardized, and, with outbreaks of rebellion in the Dutch provinces since 1560, Philip needed to safeguard the vital Spanish Road. Eager to strengthen his alliance with Savoy, he offered to have one of his daughters marry Emanuele Filiberto's heir, Carlo Emanuele, and the duke of Alba, former Spanish governor of the Netherlands, recommended that Isabel be the one to marry Carlo because, with a better chance of inheriting the Spanish throne, she might add the strategic Savoyard territories to the Spanish monarchy.[2]

Emanuele Filiberto, for his part, considered different potential spouses for his son, weighing the advantages of a marital alliance with

Spain against one with France or another European power. In 1579 Philip specifically proposed Catalina Micaela for Carlo, but at Emanuele Filiberto's death in 1580, no marriage had been settled. Carlo, his heir, considered his options, which included Princess Christina of Lorraine; the daughter of an Italian prince, such as the duke of Mantua or the Grand Duke of Tuscany; an Austrian Habsburg or German princess; or perhaps an English bride. Even the future saint, Carlo Borromeo, Archbishop of Milan, well known in his day as a leading reformer, expressed an opinion, recommending to Carlo the eldest daughter of the Grand Duke of Tuscany, as did the Venetian ambassador.[3] In the end, though, Carlo recognized the advantages of marrying the daughter of Europe's most powerful sovereign.

The marriage between Catalina and Carlo was arranged strictly for political reasons. Philip needed to secure his supply lines to Flanders, and Carlo sought to profit from the vulnerability of Spanish lines of communication. Carlo wanted territorial gains by marrying Catalina and initially tried to make the marriage contingent upon acquisition of the duchy of Monferrato, an imperial fief that Carlo thought Philip could secure for him. If Catalina did not bring any territory to the marriage, Carlo expected Philip at least to commit to placing a battalion permanently at his disposal. Paolo Sfondrato, Philip's ambassador to Savoy, negotiated with Carlo, with whom he got along well, and attempted to convince the duke to accept Philip's terms, which included no territorial cession.[4] He also tried to dissuade Carlo from other marriage proposals, noting, for example, that if he married a daughter of the Grand Duke of Tuscany, he would, after the first day, regret marrying "a woman of lower status." He consistently advised Carlo to be content with the privilege of allying himself by marriage to "the greatest king of the world," and eventually Carlo agreed. As a royal bride who was a potential heir to the French as well the Spanish throne, Catalina boosted Carlo's status vis-à-vis other Italian princes.[5] Carlo must also have calculated that Philip II would be much more likely to lend military and financial support to him if he became his son-in-law. This was powerful motivation for a young, ambitious duke who believed it his destiny to regain the Savoyard land seized by France years before.[6]

However, Carlo, twenty years old in 1582, weighed more personal concerns when choosing a bride. Early in the negotiations, he had instructed his ambassador in Spain, Carlo Pallavicino, to ascertain the *infanta's* measurements, which Pallavicino was finally able to obtain secretly in December 1581 from one of his Madrid agents, who was friendly with the *infantas'* tailor.[7] When he sent Catalina's measurements to Carlo, Pallavicino noted that she was still not wearing *chapines* but rather small boots with double soles (*botitas de dos suelas*), so that Carlo could better calculate Catalina's height. No doubt he wondered whether his prospective wife was attractive, but, more importantly, whether she could bear children. The expanse of her hips, for example, might have given some indication of whether she could readily give birth.

In turn, Philip had secretly instructed Sfondrato's predecessor as ambassador to Savoy, Guillén de San Clemente, to send a detailed report on Carlo, specifically whether he seemed able to sire children.[8] In 1580 one observer had noted that at eighteen, Carlo looked to be only fourteen, with no beard and very thin.[9] Requesting the physical characteristics and measurements of potential spouses was common in the early modern period, so we should not be surprised that Carlo and Philip both found surreptitious ways to assess the other half of the potential match.

Carlo also wondered about Catalina's features and wanted an informal portrait of his bride-to-be. A formal court portrait would idealize and enhance her features, and, having heard that Catalina had contracted smallpox in late 1582, he no doubt wished to know if the illness had disfigured her face. As in many royal marriages, the exchange of portraits featured prominently in the marriage negotiations between Spain and Savoy; Carlo was not unique in attempting to obtain an accurate likeness. From the early 1570s the court in Savoy had portraits of the young *infantas*, which Carlo reportedly compared to those of the princess Marie Elisabeth of France, born in 1572, asking courtiers whom they thought the most attractive. Likewise, Philip II obtained a portrait of the duke in 1581 that hung by his desk, where he could see it regularly.[10] Carlo Pallavicino told the duke that Philip never tired of looking at it.

Procuring a candid portrait of Catalina proved difficult. Because a portraitist had to receive permission to paint the *infantas*, his depiction might not be as informal and accurate as Carlo wanted. While Philip II was in Portugal from 1580 until 1583, moreover, the *infantas* in Madrid were forbidden to go out in public or receive many visitors. Ambassador Pallavicino negotiated privately with a few of Philip's closest ministers, including the duke of Idiáquez and Philip's secretary Mateo Vázquez, for permission to have an informal portrait painted, but in 1582 he still had not received the authorization. Pallavicino joked with Idiáquez that since the duke of Savoy would be getting the original—that is, Catalina—he should also be able to get the copy. Nonetheless, Philip II delayed authorizing a portrait until Catalina had fully recovered from the smallpox that had left her with facial pockmarks (though Khevenhüller, imperial ambassador to the Spanish court, noted that because she was the daughter of such an important king, the marks would make no difference in her marriage prospects).[11] Pallavicino had to wait until 1584 to acquire a small but realistic likeness of Catalina when she and her sister visited their aunt in the Descalzas convent.[12] The portrait must have been approved by Philip, as Carlo subsequently thanked the king for the painting, stating that the *infanta*'s pockmarks seemed like pearls to him. Reporting on the duke's reaction, Sfondrato commented that "there is no doubt that painters, like poets, are prone to exaggeration (*son grandes amigos de amplificar*), as was the painter of the portrait of the duke that I am sending."[13] Neither the portrait of the duke nor that of Catalina was fully accurate, Sfondrato suggested, but he noted that Pallavicino, after seeing Catalina at the Descalzas, told the duke that she was very beautiful (*hermosisima*). In September 1584, Pallavicino sent Carlo a carefully executed portrait of Catalina done by the Spanish court painter, Alonso Sánchez de Coello, perhaps the one that now hangs in the Prado Museum.[14]

As these negotiations show, however, even if physical appearance mattered, Carlo and Catalina's marriage was a political arrangement, calculated to bring concrete strategic advantages and heirs to both the duke of Savoy and the king of Spain, so there was little reason to expect any deep affection between Catalina and Carlo. Catalina evidently played no role in assessing Carlo as a potential spouse and at most would have heard gossip about the negotiations from the court ladies. One wonders if Philip shared with her any report about the duke sent by his earlier ambassador to Savoy, Guillén de San Clemente.

Even as the marriage between Carlo and Catalina was negotiated, it was done furtively, leaving much room for speculation. Philip knew that Empress María and Emperor Rudolf II, her son, did not favor the match, and he did not want to harm the chances of a marriage between the emperor and the *infanta* Isabel Clara Eugenia. Khevenhüller reported certain disturbing signs that suggested that a marriage was being discussed but found it hard to believe that Philip would negotiate the marriage of his younger daughter before that of his elder.[15] Monsieur de Longlée, the French representative at Philip's court, also wrote as late as February 1584 that informed observers argued that Philip would not allow Catalina to marry until her sister had wed Emperor Rudolf II and, even then, not until it was clear that Isabel could have children. The diplomat speculated that Philip was reluctant to have his nephew, Archduke Albert, ordained as a priest because he planned to have him marry one of his daughters, presumably Catalina. "I believe that in the end, the duke of Savoy will be disappointed in his hope [to marry Catalina]," Longlée remarked. As late as June 1584, the same diplomat reported that Carlo, frustrated by the delays, was once again considering marriage to the daughter of the duke of Florence. Rumor still had it that Catalina might marry one of her Austrian Habsburg cousins instead of Carlo.[16]

Longlée, who never actually held the title of ambassador at the Spanish court, did not have direct access to Philip II, so his information was second hand at best, but his reports still suggest that Philip II was playing his cards close to his chest.[17] In fact, by early March 1584 Philip had agreed to the marriage but refused to announce it publicly, frustrating the Savoyard ambassador, and no doubt Carlo too.[18] Philip might also have calculated that if the marriage were not announced, he could still back out.

Although Catalina grew up aware that the duke of Savoy was considered her most likely potential spouse—she was about eleven when the negotiations began in earnest—she still had reason in mid-summer 1584 to think that her marriage to Carlo was far from certain. Had she heard the rumor, reported by Khevenhüller in August 1584, that orders had been given to court bakers to design confections that incorporated Catalina's and Carlo's coats of arms? Even then, Empress María refused to believe the rumors, and Khevenhüller also had his doubts, so perhaps Catalina held out hope that the marriage agreement had not been finalized.[19]

THE MARRIAGE CONTRACT

In August 1584, unknown to all but a few select courtiers, Philip and Carlo settled on the terms of the proposed marriage, also petitioning the pope for a dispensation because Catalina was Carlo's first cousin once removed. Philip made no territorial cession to his daughter, but he agreed to give her a sizeable dowry of 500,000 ducats, which, the marriage agreement stated, should satisfy Catalina and Carlo, and she should consider herself well compensated since it was "much more than she was rightly entitled to" either through the paternal or the maternal line.[20] In addition to this sum, the contract stipulated that Philip grant her 40,000 ducats annually. Though she received the dowry in exchange for surrendering any claims she might have to lands or property either through Philip or Elisabeth of Valois, this did not preclude her from succeeding to the Spanish kingdoms should all of Philip's other heirs die. In that case, "her right will remain protected, without the renunciation prejudicing or harming them [Catalina and her heirs] in any way." If Catalina and Carlo were by the death of other heirs to succeed as monarchs of the Spanish kingdom, the agreement stipulated that they must follow and keep "the laws and customs, manner and style of proceeding which these kingdoms follow."[21]

The marriage agreement also specified that if for any reason the marriage were dissolved with no children, the duke or his heirs would be obligated to repay the dowry. If she were to die while married but childless, Catalina would be free to bequeath the property acquired through her dowry (*bienes dotales*) as she wished, but no other part of her inheritance. This clause probably anticipated the possibility of her death after having inherited the Spanish kingdoms. In this case, she would not be free to bestow the crown on whomever she wished, but rather succession would follow a predetermined order. The duke agreed that within two months of Catalina's arrival in his territories, he would give her 166,000 ducats as a bridal gift (*arras*), along with jewels and "adornments to her person and house." Carlo, who like all husbands would control his wife's dowry, also promised to provide a total of 60,000 ducats, part of which would come from the dowry's interest, in order to maintain Catalina's household.[22] The marriage agreement stipulated that, should the duke die first, Catalina and her household would be free to return to the Spanish kingdoms. The substantial dowry, generous especially for marriage to a duke, would become the standard for subsequent marriage contracts for Spanish *infantas*.[23] Moreover, Carlo was very likely pleased that Catalina and their heirs would maintain the right to inherit the Spanish kingdoms, even if their chances of doing so were slim.

What might Catalina have made of this contract? Did she read it before signing it? Did she care to maintain her rights and those of her heirs to the Spanish throne? She probably had no say in the contract and would have been virtually forced to accept anything which her father and her soon-to-be husband together stipulated. Philip might later have summarized the agreement to his seventeen-year-old daughter, perhaps reassuring her that in the event of all his other heirs dying, she and her heirs would inherit. He might also have pointed out that he was giving her a large dowry, sufficient to continue to live in the style of a king's daughter, and that she should therefore not be upset that he was not ceding any territory to her and Carlo. Probably doubting that she would in fact inherit the throne, Catalina might still have been pleased that she retained her rights of succession, as they made her a desirable bride and gave her greater cachet with a husband whose temperament and habits she had yet to discover. The large dowry was consolation for marrying a duke, but her retention in the line of succession emphasized that she was still a king's daughter, as did her continued use of the title "*infanta*" (used by a legitimate daughter of a Spanish king who was not immediate heir to the throne), rather than "duchess."[24]

On 23 August 1584, Carlo signed the contract, and Paolo Sfondráto, Philip's ambassador to the Savoyard court, signed for the king, who agreed to sign it himself within two months. Catalina was obligated to confirm it three days after her marriage was consummated, though in the event she did so only after three months, as she prepared to board ship in Barcelona for the voyage to Italy.[25] The bride's *post facto* confirmation of the contract was in most respects typical of marriage agreements of the time. All marriage contracts had to be ratified after the marriage was consummated, after which the marriage customarily could not be annulled. Because some delay in ratification was often to be expected, Catalina's delay in ratifying the contract until leaving Spain does not necessarily suggest that the marriage had not been consummated earlier.

Three weeks after Carlo and Sfondrato signed the marriage contract in Chambéry (the Savoyard capital until the move to Turin in 1563), Catalina was officially notified that, her father and Carlo having come to an agreement, she would marry the duke. The notice apparently caused her some pain or displeasure, as is suggested by an anonymous account that circulated at the Austrian Habsburg court detailing how she had learned of Carlo's agreement to marry her.[26] On 16 September 1584, the account relates, having requested permission to carry a letter from Carlo to Philip II, the Savoyard ambassador to the Spanish court, Pallavicino, traveled to the Escorial. In this letter, the duke thanked Philip for the great honor of allowing him to serve him as a son, thus making the marriage agreement public.[27]

After delivering the letter to Philip, the account goes on, Pallavicino, knowing that Philip would share the news with Catalina, waited with the gentlemen of the court to observe the two *infantas* as they made their way to their father's apartments. The king, while talking with Isabel, handed Carlo's letter to Catalina and told her to read it. When she saw the signature, "she was so indignant that she turned red as hot coals, and they even say she had tears in her eyes." She returned the letter to her father without having read it, despite his urging her twice to do so. Philip II then spent a long time alone with the two *infantas*. As Philip and the *infantas* left the king's apartments, Catalina's half-brother, Prince Philip, the count of Barajas, *mayordomo* of the *infantas*, and all the ladies-in-waiting came to congratulate Catalina, and that evening the ladies of the court celebrated the announcement with dances and other "very tasteful" merriments. Philip II announced that from that day forward, the *infantas* and their ladies could wear *chapines*, an indication that the *infantas* had come of age.[28]

Although the account's author could not have witnessed Philip and his daughters' private meeting, his detailed description suggests that he received his information from someone who had been present, perhaps one of the *infantas'* ladies-in-waiting. Written for an Austrian Habsburg court that did not look favorably on Catalina's match with Carlo, the account might well have been trying to flatter the court's disapproval of Philip, yet it is the only source we have of Catalina's reaction to the news of her marriage. If the account is accurate, Philip's behavior on the occasion is particularly intriguing. Why, for example, did he casually hand Catalina the letter while chatting with Isabel? Did he want to give Catalina time to read the letter carefully and with greater privacy, distracting Isabel from observing her sister? Perhaps fearing Catalina's displeasure, the king wanted to observe her reaction.

In refusing to read the duke's letter, however, Catalina did not respond the way he probably anticipated. Carlo's signature alone told her that he had agreed to marry her, so she now knew the rumored marriage had been contracted. Nevertheless, if her reaction was as emotional and forceful as the account suggests, she was unhappy and even angry to learn the news, which seems to have taken her by surprise. Perhaps the evening festivities and the concession to wear *chapines* were Philip's ways of appeasing Catalina and encouraging her to reconcile herself to the marriage. Even if she did not wish to wear the *chapines* worn by married court women, she now had no choice. It is hardly surprising that when discussing Carlo's letter to Philip, Pallavicino and the king spoke only of the great pleasure and benefit the marriage would bring to Carlo and Philip himself, with no mention of what the marriage would mean to Catalina.[29]

Because his wife had recently died, Pallavicino when delivering Carlo's letter to Philip was dressed in mourning, and at the end of his audience with the king he was reprimanded for wearing mourning clothes when communicating such joyous news. As a token of Philip's displeasure, Pallavicino was not allowed to congratulate the *infanta* in person nor celebrate the news with the rest of the court. Instead, he was instructed to meet privately with a few Spanish councilors before returning that evening to Madrid.[30] One wonders if Philip seized on the ambassador's innocent faux pas to prevent him from witnessing what

Philip might have feared would be a vivid demonstration of Catalina's chagrin.

Catalina's apparent unhappiness at learning she was contracted to marry Carlo was shared by her aunt, Empress María, who had urged Philip II to marry both his daughters to her sons, the archdukes of Austria. She herself had married her Austrian Habsburg cousin, Maximilian II, while Philip had taken as his fourth wife the empress's daughter—his niece. Empress María would have wished that Philip's daughters follow her own example in marrying her cousin, thereby strengthening the ties between the Spanish and the Austrian Habsburgs. Moreover, if her two archduke sons married Isabel and Catalina, their chances of inheriting the Spanish kingdoms would improve. By marrying Catalina to the duke of Savoy, Philip slighted Empress María's sons, and he was aware of the empress's disapproval.[31] The imperial ambassador to Spain, Hans Khevenhüller, also objected, admitting that he was "never of the opinion that the marriage with the [duke] of Savoy was suitable"[32] because it would harm the Austrian Habsburgs:

[On] the fourth [of September 1584] the marriage of the king's second daughter, the *infanta* doña Catalina, to the duke of Savoy was made public. And given that I had always been opposed to it because [it would be] prejudicial to the House of Austria, they hid [the marriage negotiations] from me as much as possible. And while I had previously heard about [the negotiations] indirectly, I [now] expressed in writing my strongest complaint to the king for this development.[33]

Khevenhüller added that Philip pursued the negotiations "even though the marriage seemed a bad idea to many."[34]

Catalina probably knew that the empress and the ambassador did not favor a union with Savoy, as they had made their sentiments well known at the Spanish court.[35] Moreover, as Catalina saw her aunt and the imperial ambassador regularly in Madrid, they would have had many opportunities to express their opinions to her directly. Not surprisingly, when the royal family left Madrid to travel to Zaragoza for Catalina's wedding, the headstrong empress forbade Khevenhüller from accompanying the court. Catalina apparently shared the empress's and Khevenhüller's misgivings, though perhaps not for the same reasons. While they were concerned about the archdukes' ambitions for the Spanish throne, she was more concerned about marrying only a duke. Reporting from Zaragoza in March 1585, the Florentine ambassador to the Spanish court remarked that Catalina showed every sign of being displeased and that at every opportunity she reminded Philip II that he was forcing her to marry beneath her status (*che l'habbia maritata bassamente*). Khevenhüller, too, reported that Catalina was unhappy with the impending marriage.[36]

The last formality was for Philip II to sign the marriage contract, which he had thus far done only by proxy. In October 1584, when the duke of Savoy's half-brother, Amedeo, arrived in Madrid with the contract signed by Carlo, Philip showered him with favors. He allowed him to visit the Escorial, asking the monks to show him the building, the sanctuary, and the relics. With Philip's permission, moreover, Amedeo visited the royal residences and gardens at Aranjuez and Aceca and continued to Toledo to see "notable things of the holy church of Toledo and the Alcázar."[37] Principal courtiers invited him to their homes for elaborate festivities, including a *comedia*, a bullfight, and hunting excursions. Even Khevenhüller, despite his opposition to the marriage, hosted a dinner for Amedeo. In his private diary, Khevenhüller described Amedeo as the duke's "bastard brother," objecting that he was addressed as "Your Excellency" and allowed to keep his head covered in the king's presence.[38] The Florentine ambassador reported that everyone was surprised that Amedeo was addressed, presumably with the king's permission, as "Excellency," a title ordinarily reserved for dukes, viceroys, and generals.

The Florentine ambassador recorded that Philip had invited Amedeo twice to El Pardo to visit the royal family and to hunt, and treated him with a familiarity (*domestichezza*) that seemed extraordinary.[39] An anonymous report from the first of these visits noted that Amedeo had asked to kiss Philip's hand and had knelt before him but that the king had told him to rise, welcoming Amedeo warmly with open arms.[40] Philip then gave Amedeo permission to visit his children, who were awaiting him in the gallery. Dressed in rich fabrics reserved for formal occasions, the *infantas* wore velvet taffeta dresses with parti-colored sleeves encrusted with pearls and were accompanied by all their attendants, "marvelously adorned and richly dressed." Isabel and Catalina remained standing, with the young prince Philip between them. As Amedeo approached, all the ladies bowed, though when he went to Prince Philip and knelt before him, wanting to kiss his hand, the prince did not allow him to do so.[41] Amedeo then related a message to him in Italian from the duke of Savoy, while the Savoyard ambassador to the Spanish court translated. As Prince Philip was only six and a half, the eighteen-year-old *infanta* Isabel told him what to respond.

The same anonymous observer claimed that Amedeo's initial approach to the prospective bride herself did not go smoothly, either. Despite the Savoyard ambassador's entreaties, Catalina spurned Amedeo's attempt to take her hand, yet he nonetheless remained talking with her.[42] Another observer, the Florentine ambassador, noted, perhaps critically, that Amedeo greeted her almost too warmly, placing his arms on Catalina's shoulders in a familiar fashion.[43] Afterward, Amedeo and his Savoyard attendants greeted the *infantas'* attending ladies, all of whom were impressed by his carefree attitude (*desenfado*) and great courtesy.

As a further sign of royal favor, on a third visit to El Pardo, Amedeo accompanied Philip, the *infantas*, and Prince Philip on an outing to hunt rabbits and hares.[44] Pallavicino reported that Philip had killed sixty, the prince two, the *infanta* Isabel fifty, Catalina forty-three, and Amedeo only thirty-seven, though he had had the least opportunity to shoot. In total, they had killed 300 rabbits.[45] In honor of Catalina's engagement, the court ladies staged a play for Philip II, Isabel, Catalina, Prince Philip, a few select courtiers, and Empress María, who had traveled to El Pardo to join the royal family.[46] Lasting from 7 to 10 in the evening in the rooms of the *infantas*, the play was well received; one report noted that when Philip returned to his rooms at the end he was very pleased.[47] Pallavicino remarked that "all is joy and happiness" at the court. Praising Catalina's upbringing, modesty, and manners, Pallavicino wrote to Carlo that he could rejoice in the beauty of her body and of her soul. In short, he gushed, her qualities were "more angelic than human."[48] Catalina's reaction to all this festivity and happy talk is unrecorded.

On his last day in Madrid, Amedeo attended the swearing in of Prince Philip as heir to Castile and witnessed Catalina and Isabel making obeisance and acknowledging his precedence in the line of succession. Philip had perhaps timed the ceremony to ensure that Amedeo might witness the important event. Before taking leave of the royal family, Amedeo asked Catalina if she had any message for her future husband. Catalina responded politely, "I am pleased to have learned from my father that the lord duke will soon be in these lands [the Spanish kingdoms]. You may kiss his hands and tell him to come soon because he is expected."[49] In so doing, Catalina fulfilled the courtesy expected of her, though nothing in her message suggests enthusiasm or excitement.

PREPARATIONS

To prepare for Catalina's departure from the Spanish court, Philip arranged for a division of the jewels, precious stones, and other valuables that she and Isabel had inherited from their mother, Elisabeth of Valois. A secretary compiled an inventory with a brief description and estimated value of each item, and each signed the document settling the partition and bound herself to live by its terms, though whether either *infanta* had a say in choosing specific objects is unknown.[50] Catalina took with her to Turin her share of the inheritance, with full liberty to dispose of it as she wished. It is unclear where the objects had been kept before they were divided up or whether they were in regular use by the *infantas*, but many of them, especially the jewels, were probably already in their possession. If so, they would have served in later years to remind Catalina in Turin of her years at the Spanish court.

The division at least partially reflected the two *infantas'* respective circumstances: Catalina was starting married life at a smaller court still in the process of formation, whereas Isabel remained unmarried at a wealthy and established Spanish court. Catalina, for example, was given five armchairs, while Isabel received only one; Catalina also inherited more rugs and cushions than her older sister. A marten decorated with precious jewels went to Catalina, no doubt because the marten, a talisman for fertility, was thought more appropriate for the *infanta* getting married.[51] Among other items Catalina received were her mother's clavichord, a book of hours, and a golden rose the pope had bestowed on Elisabeth of Valois.[52]

Other possessions she inherited were several objects bearing the coat of arms of her mother, as well as a small book with portraits of the kings and queens of France. She also received a cameo with Philip II's portrait. An image of the Virgin Mary painted by Master Jorge de Toledo, which Elisabeth of Valois kept by her bed, was also apportioned to Catalina, along with numerous objects for her oratory.[53] All this property together constituted Catalina's movable inheritance. In Turin, Catalina probably displayed and used some of these items allotted to her; we know, for example, that certain jewels she took from Spain she had reset in Turin into newer, more fashionable settings. Gems were generally a sound investment because they retained their value better than gold.[54] Shortly before embarking for Savoy after their wedding, Carlo was, not surprisingly, shown the document recording this partition.[55] These inherited items and valuables formed a large part of the wealth that Catalina brought into the marriage; they were quite literally the baggage that she carried to Turin.

A retinue of around one hundred attendants would accompany Catalina to Turin, and Philip II's ministers would have to work hard to persuade them to agree to leave the Spanish kingdoms. Transfer to Turin meant leaving behind family and familiar territory for an unknown land and unknown conditions, where many would be expected initially to foot their own expenses with only a dubious promise of future repayment. As Juan de Zúñiga, *mayordomo* to the royal children, explained, "no one wants to go to Savoy unless given a substantial promotion." One lady-in-waiting, Beatriz de Mendoza, initially refused to go but ultimately went, "against the will of her mother and her uncles." Another, Luisa Mexía, made it clear that she would go only if given substantial inducement (*mucha merced*). The list of those to accompany Catalina was not made public until 20 March 1585, after the wedding. She would go to Turin with a female entourage of a *camarera mayor*, eight ladies-in-waiting and six maids-in-waiting, along with at least five male attendants: a keeper of the jewels (*guardajoyas*), a *repostero de cama* (official who guarded the door to the bedroom and had charge of the bedding), an almoner, a confessor, and a *mayordomo*.[56] Paolo Sfondrato would serve as Catalina's *mayordomo mayor*—the head of Catalina's household.

For an *infanta* accustomed to living in a household with several hundred attendants, Catalina's entourage represented a reduction in status and service. She must have been well aware that most of the women who served her in Spain had no wish to follow her to Turin; like them, she must have wondered how her own living conditions would change. No doubt her attendants' reluctance to relocate to Turin mirrored her own hesitation to leave Spain and begin life in a foreign land as a duke's wife instead of a king's daughter.

THE JOURNEY TO ZARAGOZA

Although, by 1585, Philip did not travel long distances easily, he was compelled to make this journey for two distinct purposes: first, to marry Catalina to Carlo in Zaragoza and accompany them to Barcelona to board the ship bound for Savoy, and second, to attend the meeting of the Aragonese *Cortes* (representative assembly) in Monzón to receive the kingdom's formal acknowledgement of his young son as his heir. Even in this respect, Catalina may very well have thought that her wedding was secondary to the king's larger goal of the prince's investiture.

Observers described the royal progress from Madrid to Zaragoza as a leisurely, pleasant trip. Philip and his children left Madrid on 19 January, stopping first at the Descalzas to bid farewell to the empress and her daughter, and continuing to Barajas, a town on the outskirts of Madrid, to attend the wedding of the daughter of the count of Barajas. The royal party next stopped in Alcalá to visit and hear a lecture at the university and venerate the remains of Fray Diego de Alcalá (d. 1463), a Franciscan lay brother to whom Philip II was greatly devoted.[57]

From there they went on to Guadalajara, where they stayed at the house of the duke of Infantado and visited the Jeronimite monastery of San Bartolomé de Lupiana. As they passed through the smaller towns, all of them belonging to the duke of Infantado, residents came out to greet the royal party and show their pleasure by dancing and playing castanets. In the town of Brijuela, dancers organized into two groups—savages (*salvajes*) and laborers—and led Philip and his entourage to their lodging. Rain and snow slowed down the royal party, but on 12 February they reached the border of Castile and Aragon, where they remained for a few days to allow the customs authorities to inspect all the items being taken across the border, including those that Catalina had inherited from her mother. As the royal party crossed the border, Castilian judicial officials, following ancient custom, put down their rods of power.[58] Aragonese officials then guided the party to various towns, where crowds flooded the streets to see the king, perhaps for the first and only time in their lives, with the focus on the monarch himself and not on the soon-to-be-wed *infanta*.

In the town of Daroca, to show their pleasure at the royal visit, the people ran cows through the streets toward the palace where the royal party lodged—apparently a traditional festivity—and later acted out the scene of St. George killing the dragon, spectacles the prince and the court ladies observed from a window. In Cariñena, a large crowd greeted Philip and his children "with great joy."[59] On 24 February, the royal party finally entered Zaragoza, where silks and tapestries decorated the windows of houses and crowds gathered to greet the king and his children. The royal party lodged first at the viceroy's palace before moving to the episcopal palace, where they prepared for and awaited the duke's arrival.

Calling the pace of this progress "glacial," a modern historian has emphasized the difficulties Philip faced, particularly in the Crown of Aragon, where officials and aristocrats were determined to show the limits of royal power.[60] Undoubtedly, this must have been an exhausting trip for the king, who preferred the privacy of his royal residences and shunned the company of most. Traveling through territories frigid in February, and occasionally compelled to observe outdoor public performances at night, Philip must have had to feign interest and admiration, especially because the cold would have exacerbated his persistent gout.[61] And all of this—or at least much of it—to hand over his beloved daughter to a man he had never met.

Catalina may have enjoyed these days with her family, since sharing a coach with her sister, half-brother, and father for most of the trip she would have had time to talk at length with them. The detailed account of the progress written by Henry Cock, an archer in Philip's service, does not mention the young *infanta's* reactions, most likely because for Cock, Philip was the main attraction, perhaps rightly so. Nevertheless, Catalina may have grown anxious as the royal party neared Zaragoza and as her female attendants perhaps chaffed and counseled her about the approaching wedding night. She would also have had abundant time to brood on her own misgivings about the marriage.

THE WEDDING

Catalina's attitude toward her marriage may be further explored by considering briefly the nuptial bedroom—the room with the golden key—where the drama of the wedding night played out. Located in the archbishop's palace in Zaragoza, the room was richly decorated with tapestries of gold-embroidered silk designed with large *mascarones* (grotesque architectural masks popular in the Renaissance and thought to ward off evil spirits).[62] The bedroom, with only a bed, a chair, pillows, and velvet rugs, was clearly furnished strictly as a space in which to sleep or to engage in sexual intercourse. In an adjoining dressing room was a silver table (*bufete de plata*) for Carlo to place his clothes on. Philip II had personally seen to the decoration and outfitting of the room, as well as of those where the celebrations would take place, making sure to bring along the rich tapestries of Charles V's victory at Tunis, always displayed at major royal celebrations.[63] Hung in the hall for the betrothal ceremony, these tapestries emphasized the power and majesty of the Spanish monarchs, possibly serving to remind the duke of the favor Philip was granting him: his daughter's hand. Philip had also given detailed instructions on how the evening after the ceremony was to proceed. Until the moment the duke entered the marriage bedroom, Carlo and Catalina followed a carefully choreographed plan.

Carlo had arrived in Barcelona in mid-February, waiting there until early March, when Philip II officially summoned him to Zaragoza. In the meantime, he enjoyed himself by engaging in local Carnival festivities such as riding through the city on horseback, donning a mask, and tossing oranges at the young girls who watched from open windows.

Carlo had originally planned to travel to Spain with two hundred courtiers, but, with no way of lodging so many people, Philip restricted him to eighty.[64] In a letter to Sfondrato, Philip stipulated that if the duke would not reduce the size of his entourage, at the very least he should not add to the number.[65] In the end, the duke arrived with one hundred courtiers, although their servants and attendants must have made his party much larger.[66]

On Sunday, 10 March, when Carlo's arrival was expected in Zaragoza, Philip, accompanied by all his courtiers and guards, set out to greet the duke outside the city walls and escort him to the archbishop's palace, where the royal family was residing. Carlo was delayed, however, which displeased Philip until he learned that the delay had been caused by the collapse of a bridge over the Gállego river that had threatened the lives of several of the duke's men.[67] When Carlo finally arrived, both he and Philip dismounted and embraced. Carlo conspicuously demonstrated his subservience to the Spanish king, initially refusing to ride on his right and afterward insisting on riding a few paces behind Philip. By contrast, Philip kept slowing down his horse to shorten the distance between himself and the duke. Henry Cock, who described this elaborate game of etiquette, was in a good position to observe it all because the archers flanked the king and the duke.[68] As they approached the palace, Philip pointed out his daughters, who were observing their approach from a window; Cock noted that Carlo looked several times at the window but did not immediately recognize his bride-to-be. The Venetian ambassador, on the other hand, reported that the *infantas* observed the duke's entrance into Zaragoza from afar but were themselves unseen.[69] Carlo was shown to his apartments, to prepare for the secular part of the marriage ceremony: the *desposorio* or betrothal.

Catalina and Carlo lived during a period when the ceremony of marriage was in a state of flux. For many years the *desposorio* had been considered the legal wedding, with couples cohabiting after the ceremony, but the Church increasingly insisted that marriage was a sacrament to be celebrated in a church.[70] The Church referred to the *desposorio* as merely a betrothal, and consummation of the marriage was licit only after the church blessing.[71] Catalina and Carlo celebrated the *desposorio* on a Sunday evening, retired to separate bedrooms that night, and attended a nuptial mass at the cathedral the following morning, sharing a bed only that evening. Recalling these events years later, Catalina wrote to Carlo on 11 March 1592 that exactly seven years had passed "since we were betrothed," but in fact she was slightly mistaken. They had been betrothed in the *desposorio* on Sunday, 10 March and married the day after, so 11 March was the anniversary of their church wedding and not their betrothal.[72] This small error would suggest that Catalina did not necessarily distinguish between the betrothal and the wedding, using the term *desposorio* to refer to them collectively but still observing the date of the church wedding as the official anniversary.

The actual *desposorio*, enacted in an elaborately decorated hall of the episcopal palace on the evening of the duke's arrival in Zaragoza, was presided over by Cardinal Antoine Perrenot de Granvelle. Three other prelates were present: Cardinal Rodrigo Castro de Osorio, Archbishop of Seville; Andrés Santos de Sampedro, Archbishop of Zaragoza; and Bishop Ludovico Taverna, papal nuncio in Spain. The Venetian ambassador, Vincenzo Gradenigo, processed in with the prelates, all of them entering the hall directly in front of the king.[73] Four brocaded chairs were placed under a costly crimson velvet canopy for the bride and groom, Philip II, and the *infanta* Isabel Clara Eugenia, in addition to a smaller chair for the seven-year-old Prince Philip.

At the *desposorio*, the bride, dressed in white, and groom gave their promise to each other, and Henry Cock noted that the duke placed an expensive ring on Catalina's hand. Another chronicler recorded that before Catalina gave her consent, she knelt before her father to ask for his blessing; at the conclusion of the ceremony, both Catalina and Carlo bowed to Philip and kissed his hand. Once Philip gave his permission to the marriage, the *desposorio* was concluded, allowing for the grandees, courtiers, and ladies to approach the canopy amidst the "noise of hornpipes" to offer their congratulations not only to Catalina and Carlo but also to Philip II, Isabel, and Prince Philip.[74]

Afterward, the court celebrated with a *sarao*. Philip II and his family participated in it only at the end, when they formed two couples— Catalina and Carlo; Isabel Clara Eugenia and Prince Philip—for the last dance. The evening—and the civil or secular part of the marriage— concluded with the *infantas* returning to their apartments and Philip II and the duke to theirs. One chronicler remarked that at the end of the day Catalina seemed happy.[75] Carlo, too, was apparently pleased. As he subsequently wrote to the marquis d'Este, whom he had left in charge of his lands, he was impressed by "the great favor that His Majesty has deigned to show me," but even more so because Catalina had "all kinds of excellent qualities that exceed all that I had been told and all my own expectations."[76]

The church ceremony took place the following morning at 11 at the cathedral in Zaragoza, thereby confirming what had been anticipated by the *desposorio*.[77] The wedding followed Tridentine practices, which stipulated that, to be valid, a marriage must be performed in a church, formally witnessed by two observers, and officiated by a priest.[78] Catalina went dressed in crimson silk embroidered with large pearls and with buttons, collar, and cuffs decorated with diamonds. On her head she wore an extraordinarily beautiful cap encrusted with jewels and large pearls, delighting onlookers, who marveled at her appearance.[79] Philip II and Isabel Clara Eugenia served as Catalina's sponsors (*padrinos*), functioning as the witnesses required by the Council of Trent, and Catalina and Carlo exchanged vows at the royal chapel within the cathedral, before attending a sung mass at the high altar.[80] At the conclusion of the mass, Catalina knelt before her father, asking for his hand, but instead the king embraced her and afterward the duke, and all were moved by the affection and tenderness of the gestures. The royal party then returned to the palace amidst fanfare and blaring of trumpets, where they and the duke took the midday meal in the company of courtiers before returning to their separate apartments. All went smoothly except for the *infanta* Isabel suffering a nosebleed as they were to sit down for the midday meal.[81] One observer noted that the king seemed very happy throughout the meal but that Catalina seemed somber, as was to be expected in a new bride.[82] The evening brought another elaborate *sarao* that, according to the Venetian ambassador, lasted four hours.[83] Afterward, they all retired to take the evening meal in private, as Catalina and her sister withdrew to the women's apartments. To mark the occasion, the duke sent Catalina costly gifts; that evening he was given the famous golden key to the nuptial bedroom, where the couple consummated their marriage.

How did Catalina react to sexual intercourse with a man she had known for scarcely twenty-four hours? Carlo had already fathered a child, but Catalina had no sexual experience and might well have been terrified.[84] Most observers did not look at it from the young *infanta's* point of view, however, instead choosing to see it from Carlo's perspective. Angelo Corazzino, a captain in the duke's guard, described the marriage night in martial language. In the Italian version of his account, he reported that after receiving the bedroom key, the duke, dressed in a fine robe and slippers, entered the room to find Catalina in bed, whereupon he lay down with her. The following day neither was seen in public, but word got around the court and the city that the duke had jousted valorously. The Spanish version of Corazzino's account, however, which he sent to the duchess of Osuna, left out these details, narrating only that the duke and Catalina had slept together and that the following day it was known that they were happy and content.[85] Perhaps because Corazzino translated his account for a Spanish lady, he felt it appropriate to be more discreet in his description of the wedding night, eliminating the particulars of the duke joining Catalina in bed and the jousting metaphor.

Henry Cock also used martial language to describe the wedding night, writing that the duke, when "preparing for the tournament, dressed at midnight, and without offensive arms went out into the battlefield; opening the door to the much desired room of his wife, [he] found her lying in bed. How he kissed her is no concern of ours."[86] Both Corazzino and Cock had served in military guards, so it is therefore not surprising that they employed the fairly conventional language of tournaments to describe the wedding night. While colorful, neither of the accounts suggests that the authors received their information from someone at court, as their descriptions are commonplace.

The Venetian ambassador to Spain, who was in Zaragoza but could not have witnessed the rituals of the wedding night, nevertheless reported that the duke, dressed in night clothes (*veste di notte*) and accompanied by three of his closest courtiers, received the key to the bedroom from Philip II, who briefly whispered in the duke's ear. Upon entering the bedroom and seeing no one, the duke lay down, only to discover his bride behind a curtain.[87] The Venetian ambassador to Savoy reported from Turin that sources informed him of the marriage's consummation, and that he had received word from Zaragoza that the king was very happy, and Catalina the happiest of all.[88]

But another account, sent to Adam of Dietrichstein, who had served as imperial ambassador at the Spanish court from 1563 until 1571 but who by 1585 had long resided at the court in Prague, provides a much more detailed and complicated picture of the wedding night. The anonymous author of the Dietrichstein wedding account relied on female court informants, lending greater credibility to the events described. Precisely because his descriptions are so intimate, he was careful to validate his report by citing the sources of his information. He explains that he had heard about the wedding night from Leonor de Ayala when she was in Madrid at the house of the countess of Riela. Since Ayala based her own knowledge on a letter received from the palace in Zaragoza, she must have had one of the *infantas'* female attendants, who most certainly were the closest observers of the wedding night, relay the information to her.[89]

According to the account, at the conclusion of the evening meal Philip II walked to the *infantas'* apartments to meet Catalina and escort her to his own apartments. Two ladies-in-waiting—Sancha de Guzmán, Catalina's *camarera mayor*, and Francisca de Rojas, countess of Paredes (*infanta* Isabel's *camarera mayor*)—accompanied Catalina. Philip talked privately with Catalina for an hour, perhaps advising her about her marital duties, before instructing the two ladies to accompany Catalina to her marriage bedroom and prepare her for bed. Once the women had left, Philip called the duke to his apartment, walking about with him for half an hour before sending him back to his room, accompanied by Juan de Zúñiga, *mayordomo* to the royal children. Zúñiga handed Carlo the golden key to the marriage bedroom, explaining that the countess of Paredes would knock on the door connecting his room to Catalina's after she prepared the *infanta* for bed. The duke hurried to change into a dressing gown (*ropa de levantar*); when the knock came, he unlocked the door with the golden key and opened it to find the *infanta* in bed.

The account narrated what happened next: the duke parted the bed curtains, knelt before the *infanta*, and asked her what she desired. "She begged him very much that because the day had been so burdensome, he should go to his own bed because he would [later] have her whenever he wanted (*siempre que quisiese le tendria*)." Taken aback by this disconcerting response, the duke asked the ladies-in-waiting what to do, to which they responded, "Your Highness, do what you must do," adding that they were there only to blow out the candles. The duke shed his dressing gown and climbed into bed, while the *camareras* blew out the candles and left the bedroom. The next morning Philip sent the count of Chinchón to visit the duke and ask how the night had gone. The duke tactfully responded that all had gone very well and that he was now truly Philip's son.[90]

Clearly this was a carefully scripted evening, for Philip, micromanager that he was, thought he had taken care of everything, even counselling the newly married couple immediately before they were to consummate their marriage. The duke certainly showed himself willing to follow the script, though apparently he was momentarily confused when Catalina rebuffed his initial approach. She followed the plans until the last moment when, if the Dietrichstein account is to be believed, she tried to postpone their first sexual encounter despite the instructions of her father, who surely expected the marriage to be consummated that night. Catalina seems to have been happy enough with the wedding festivities but apparently balked at sharing her bed with a man she hardly knew.

In fact, we cannot know for certain whether the marriage was consummated on the wedding night, though given the act's political importance, it very probably was. Nor do we know whether Catalina and the duke slept together the rest of their time in Spain. She did not become pregnant for another four months, even though, as she was to have ten children in the next twelve years, she was certainly fertile. Had she persuaded the duke in Zaragoza to wait four months before sharing her bed regularly?

The Venetian ambassador noted that Catalina was not seen the following day, though the duke did leave the bedroom and was heartily congratulated by everyone. He spent two hours with Philip II, and, in their presence, Diego de Córdoba, Philip II's master of the stables, entertained them with many jokes.[91] Did Córdoba joke about the wedding night? Another account recorded that the morning after the marriage was consummated, Carlo gave his bride three necklaces, three ribbons, three garlands, and three bracelets of pearls, rubies, and diamonds.[92] On the second evening following the wedding day, Catalina and the duke appeared together at a window of their apartments, where they would have been seen by the court and the public, to watch a tournament (*gioco di caroselle*). The third day following, the newlyweds accompanied Philip II, Isabel, and Prince Philip to hear mass at the church dedicated to Santa Engracia, the patroness of Zaragoza. This public outing marked their first formal appearance as a married couple.[93] Scarcely two weeks after the wedding, the Venetian ambassador in Turin reported, rather optimistically, that he had heard that Catalina and Carlo were already in love and that Philip II was very pleased with the duke's qualities and his serious but graceful manner.[94]

THE FINAL STAGE

Three months elapsed between the wedding and Catalina and Carlo's embarkation for Savoy—months filled with not only excursions to monasteries, convents, and churches, sumptuous festivities in noble palaces, and public celebrations of the marriage, but also ceremonies to mark the visit of the country's sovereign. Before arriving in Barcelona, the royal party spent a week at the monastery of Montserrat, and Carlo would later fondly recall the stay, though he remembered that when they visited the cliffside hermitages, it rained.[95] On one of their last evenings in Barcelona, one of the duke's engineers orchestrated a display of flaming wheels and flares, one of which hit Catalina in the neck, almost igniting her ruff collar.[96] Reports of the festivities and Carlo's extravagant spending alarmed aristocrats back in the Piedmont, who also worried that if the *infanta* became pregnant, the ducal couple would remain even longer in the Spanish kingdoms.[97]

Until June 1585, when she finally boarded the ship that would take her away forever from the Spanish kingdoms, Catalina was under her father's authority. During that time, she was still living with her sister and sharing Isabel's household. Angelo Corazzino explained that on 31 March in Zaragoza, Philip II inducted the duke of Savoy into the

Order of the Golden Fleece, and afterward "the *infantas* came out of their apartment" to greet Philip and Carlo. That same day Carlo "sent many and diverse jewels for her to distribute to her ladies."[98] Corazzino's use of the verb "send" suggests that Catalina and Carlo were not living together, which would not be at all surprising, since, like kings and queens, dukes and duchesses kept separate apartments. Another chronicler noted that on 13 June, the day of Catalina's departure from Spain, the *infantas* spent the afternoon with their father but then went to have a light meal (*merendar*) in their apartment, again suggesting that Catalina and Isabel were residing together, though perhaps Catalina would leave her apartment at night to sleep with the duke.[99] Sharing her days with her sister, surrounded by the attendants who had served them all their lives, Catalina's life for the three months after her marriage (expect perhaps at night) had apparently not changed very much.

Moreover, while on Spanish soil Catalina was still not fully incorporated into the House of Savoy. This was evident on the feast of the Annunciation, 25 March, an important day for the House of Savoy, which had a military order called the Annunziata.[100] Carlo celebrated on the eve of the feast in Zaragoza by leading a procession to the cathedral, followed by all his courtiers. Afterward, he met with the members of Annunziata to propose seven new members. Philip II and his daughters observed the procession from the palace windows. On the morning of 25 March, when the duke and his courtiers went to mass with members of the military order, Catalina once again did not participate, but only observed the mass with her father and sister from an oratory window overlooking the chapel.[101] Because it was a military order, it is perhaps not surprising that the duke did not include Catalina in any of the festivities, but it also indicates that although she had married the duke of Savoy, she still had not assumed any public role as his duchess and a recognized member of the House of Savoy.

Occupying this liminal space—as Philip's daughter but also Carlo's wife, on Spanish soil but heading to Savoyard territories—Catalina must have had time to reflect on how much her life was about to change. She must have realized that, upon boarding the ship, she was unlikely ever to set foot on Spanish soil again, or ever to see her father and sister again. When the day arrived for her to board, observers noted that both

Catalina and Isabel were inconsolable. The sisters hugged each other dearly (*con un entrañable amor*). Apart from later letters and gifts she received from Isabel, Sofonisba Anguissola's portrait of a seven-year-old Isabel, today in the Galleria Sabauda in Turin, may have been all of her beloved sister to which Catalina could cling for the rest of her life.[102]

Philip II, known for his stoic public demeanor, had a difficult time controlling his emotions when Catalina knelt before him, kissing his hand while crying profusely. Catalina's sadness brought tears to Philip's own eyes, compelling him to turn away from her without a last word for fear that they would both break down in public.[103] The author of the Dietrichstein chronicle recorded that Philip's "sadness was very great, and he had never been seen to express his feelings and affection so openly; with a handkerchief to his face, he spilled forth a flood of tears."[104]

To hide her tears and a face swollen from crying, Catalina placed a handkerchief over her face as she walked to the ship. The ladies accompanying Catalina to Turin also cried profusely at taking leave of their homeland and of those staying behind. One observer commented that the women's lamentations made it seem like judgment day.[105] Henry Cock noted, dramatically:

> The most noble Catalina de Austria, embracing her beloved father, said goodbye with tears in her eyes. Who will tell of the sighs of the two sisters at their leave-taking? Who will tell of the sadness of the ladies who left and those who stayed? Who is not surprised at His Majesty's constancy? This sad farewell lasted until seven o'clock when the duke, taking his beloved wife by the hand, took her to the royal ship. She went holding a handkerchief in front of her eyes so that it would not seem as if she were crying.[106]

Expecting the parting to be emotional, chroniclers such as Cock were pleased to see such a public demonstration of filial love and paternal affection, commenting that Catalina's sorrow demonstrated her great love for her father.[107] While the reports' accuracy cannot be ascertained, they are plausible, as the farewells must have been extremely difficult for Catalina, as well as for her father and sister. A year apart in age,

Isabel and Catalina had been inseparable. They had also been Philip II's constant companions since his return from Portugal three years earlier. For Catalina, marriage to the duke of Savoy and a relocation to Turin meant a lifelong separation from those dearest to her, and she plainly felt the rupture deeply.

Catalina had other misgivings that she did not hesitate to express. The Florentine ambassador reported several times that Catalina was unhappy with the marriage, constantly rebuking her father for having arranged a marriage to someone beneath her in status, and in response Philip had arranged elaborate festivities befitting her royal rank to entertain and appease her.[108] Fray Jerónimo de Sepúlveda, a monk in the Escorial monastery who wrote a chronicle of the years 1584 to 1603, reported that a few days before Catalina left Barcelona, her father gave her a bowl of pearls—the biggest and prettiest ever seen—but that Catalina took only two or three. When Philip insisted they were all for her, she tearfully replied that three were sufficient for a duchess.[109] None of the other chroniclers mentions this incident, and Sepúlveda, known to have made mistakes in his account, was not an eyewitness.[110] Nevertheless, he knew Philip personally, so he may well have heard the story from Philip himself. Even if apocryphal, the account suggests that after the wedding, rumors persisted that Catalina was not entirely happy with a marriage to a "mere" duke.

Nonetheless, while she may have felt a lingering resentment about her marriage, Catalina could be thankful for several promising circumstances. Most royal weddings took place by proxy, which in the majority of cases obligated princesses to travel to a new country where their new husband awaited them. Philip II, for example, married four times, each time by proxy, and only in the case of his marriage to Mary Tudor did he travel to meet his wife—because she was a queen and he was then only a prince. And as in that case, royal couples usually did not speak the same language. It was up to the bride to learn the language of her new court. Moreover, a princess might travel with a large retinue of women who had cared for her from youth, but in most cases her new husband sent those ladies and servants home, at times gradually, but sometimes quickly—instead installing his own trusted servants in the bride's service. Thus isolated from family and friends, princesses were forced to conform quickly to a new culture and were restricted from seeking to exert political influence.[111]

Catalina's case differed significantly. Carlo, not she, made the long trip to marry, while most of the Spanish ladies and servants who accompanied her to Turin remained with her until her death. Carlo never attempted to replace them with Savoyards, although over the years Catalina's household grew to include many Italians, and several principal office-holders in her household—her first *mayordomo mayor*, her *caballerizo* (master of the stables), and at least one *mayordomo*—were the duke's close advisers. As soon as his marriage to Catalina was confirmed, Carlo, still in Turin, began to dress in the Spanish style (*a la española*), requiring his attendants to do likewise. (From Zaragoza the Venetian ambassador to Spain reported that Carlo had made it known that he was no longer Piemontese but rather Spanish, and had begun to imitate "the customs of the king [Philip II].")[112] Rather than oblige Catalina to conform to Savoyard practices, he himself adopted Spanish ways, and Catalina's household in Turin continued to follow Spanish rules of etiquette. Carlo was also devoutly Catholic—an important factor in a Europe increasingly torn by religious struggles. Most importantly, Carlo spoke and wrote Spanish fluently, so that from the beginning of their marriage he was able to converse with Catalina in her own language. He composed poetry in Spanish and was cultivated enough not only to write verse but also to interest himself in art patronage and architecture. He was also only five years older than she. All these facts might have made her politically arranged marriage more palatable to the seventeen-year-old *infanta*, as they introduced the possibility of more intimate communication and closer affinity than one might have expected from such a marriage.

Lacking the perspective to compare her marital situation with that of other princesses, Catalina may not have given much thought to these auspicious features of her marriage. Nevertheless, they proved important, ultimately helping her forge an emotional bond with her husband that she could never have expected to enjoy.

CHAPTER 3

FROM SPANISH *INFANTA* TO DUCHESS OF SAVOY
Early Years in Turin

Every day they go out hunting and . . . racing in carriages . . . one day
they eat early and the other late . . . I confess that it is a comfortable life
for the young or for strong people who can stand it.
Cristóbal de Briceño to Mateo Vázquez, 20 October 1586

THE NEXT FEW YEARS would be both a honeymoon and an apprentice-ship for Catalina, during which she and Carlo cemented their marriage and partnership. Reluctant and overwhelmed with sadness on leaving her father and sister, Catalina seems nonetheless to have adapted quickly to her new home and husband. She made the most of her independence from her vigilant father and a rigid court etiquette, relishing her new position as duchess of Savoy and mistress of her own court. From her arrival in the duke's lands in late June 1585 until the duke's departure from Turin on military campaign in September 1588, Catalina enjoyed herself greatly, dividing her time between indoor and outdoor pursuits, and combining religious and secular activities. Carlo would woo her effectively, and they would discover that they enjoyed each other's company. (See plates 6 and 7 for joint portraits done in the early 1590s.)

Cultural and personal tensions added drama to this lively court as Catalina's Spanish attendants argued with Savoyards over precedence and etiquette and as several members of Catalina's household tried to exploit the new environment to their own advantage. Catalina and Carlo would make mutual cultural adjustments, and he, assessing her

66

ability to govern, would be ready by 1588 to risk leaving her in charge of the duchy in his absence. Never again, after these honeymoon years, would Catalina have the luxury to enjoy such an extended time with her husband.

ARRIVAL

After boarding their ship in Barcelona on the evening of 13 June 1585, Catalina and Carlo sailed to Nice. By then, they had spent the better part of two months together, but always accompanied by her sister and father. This voyage was the first time they were not under Philip II's direct supervision. The crossing proved difficult for Carlo, who had been sick even before boarding and felt seasick before dinner on the first evening at sea.[1] Catalina, on the other hand, had better sea legs, and Paolo Sfondrato, who accompanied the couple from Zaragoza to Turin, reported that she was very strong (*bravissima*) and had acted half-sick only in sympathy with her husband. Sfondrato also observed that Catalina had "great goodness and valor," and, in her presence, the duke had told him that "this is one admirable woman who will govern me completely," to which Sfrondato responded that, if so, the duke would not be poorly governed.[2]

Writing to one of Philip II's closest ministers, Sfondrato undoubtedly wanted to praise the young *infanta* and indicate not only that she was performing her duties well but also that the duke appreciated her. Others also remarked on Catalina's strength; Andrea Provana di Leynì, Carlo's admiral, military commander, and councilor who traveled with the ducal couple, wrote that Catalina had shown herself fearless and able to tolerate turbulent seas.[3] From the moment she and Carlo embarked on the ship taking them away from the Spanish kingdoms, observers would comment on Catalina's strong character and suggest that she was adapting well to life as duchess of Savoy. They noted that she and the duke seemed happy together.

The duke had made sure that when they arrived in Nice, which at that time was Savoyard territory, there would be a magnificent reception awaiting his bride. Twelve small galleys, towing three sea monsters carrying people dressed as "Neptune, Thetis, tritons, nymphs, and sirens," met their ship and escorted it to shore. The nymphs presented the keys of the city to the duke and duchess and recited verses in Italian to Catalina. From Nice the duke took Catalina and her entourage for a seven-and-a-half-week tour of his duchy, attempting to impress her with the beauty and the extent of his territories. Everywhere they went, Catalina was greeted, fêted, and showered with many gifts, and no doubt Carlo wanted to show off his royal bride, since his marriage to the daughter of the king of Spain was a significant honor. Catalina, just a few months shy of her eighteenth birthday, dressed in royal finery and accompanied by her eight well-dressed ladies as well as many attendants, must have presented a striking sight, and observers speculated as to whether she was already pregnant.[4]

Looking ahead even before he left for Spain to the *infanta*'s entrance into Turin, Carlo had asked the municipal authorities in Turin to construct a new door at Porta Susina, as well as a baldachin (with six staffs instead of the usual four, to emphasize Catalina's royal status) and three triumphal arches. He gave detailed instructions to the marquis d'Este, whom he had left as his lieutenant, about how the Savoyard cities should prepare for the ducal entrance and welcome his new wife.[5] D'Este negotiated with the towns to ensure that the ducal couple should be greeted in a fitting fashion, instructing them to construct elaborate temporary structures celebrating the duke's marriage, and governors responded with their plans, such as creating archways made of greenery adorned with first the *infanta*'s coat of arms, and then the joint arms of Catalina and Carlo.[6] The governor of Ceva noted that the city was constructing a baldachin made of dark red damask with a gold fringe and black silk. The governor of Savigliano worried that too many poor would be visible on the street through which the duke and duchess were scheduled to enter the town and proposed a different point of entrance, though he doubted that all would be ready in the eight to ten days d'Este had given them. The governor of Cuneo, on the other hand, seemed less worried and indicated that in approximately an hour the town could put the coat of arms of the duke and duchess on top of the gate through which they would enter. The governors of other towns scrambled to prepare and asked d'Este for the precise dates when they should expect (and be prepared for) the ducal visit.[7] The towns were also required to present a donation (*donativo*) to Catalina, which must have further strained local resources and perhaps soured their attitude to the new duchess. She in turn gave money to churches and convents in the towns visited in these first two months.[8]

Toward the end of their slow progress toward Turin—as they left the city of Moncalieri—the duke arranged for the entire party to travel by boat along the river Po to Valentino, a palace located a mile outside the walls of Turin. Along the way they stopped at a small island on which the duke had orchestrated an elaborate reception: where a youth dressed as a god greeted them and recited verses in Catalina's honor and others dressed as mythological figures emerged from caves to welcome and serenade the young *infanta*. The duke also had ordered refreshments and led Catalina and her ladies to a table decorated with silk flowers and colored feathers and had them served sugared confections and wine while Venus and Cupid recited a dialogue in Italian and the nymph Echo responded in Spanish.[9] This elaborate reception with mythological themes was plainly designed not only to entertain Catalina but also to impress her with her new husband, his territories, and the cultural richness of his court.

Carlo and Catalina remained in Valentino until 10 August, the feast of St. Lorenzo, the day Carlo had chosen for the formal ducal entrance into Turin. The feast of St. Lorenzo had significance for both the Spanish monarch and the House of Savoy. In the battle of San Quentin, Philip II's troops had defeated the French on the feast of St. Lorenzo twenty-eight years earlier; as governor of the Netherlands, Carlo's father had led Philip's troops in this victory, which in turn had restored most of the Piedmont to the dukes of Savoy. Now, in the days preceding Carlo and Catalina's entry, four to five thousand people entered Turin daily, according to one account. On 10 August, courtiers lined the road between Turin and the palace at Valentino to escort them into the city. Cristóbal de Briceño, one of Catalina's *mayordomos* who had accompanied her from Spain, reported that more than two thousand infantry and twelve companies of light cavalry and harquebusiers processed from the city to salute and then usher them into Turin.[10] Another account, anonymous, noted that the city had constructed eight triumphal arches and claimed that they had marshaled four thousand cavalry and four thousand infantry to salute the ducal couple.[11]

The grand ducal entrance into Turin was a spectacle, with Catalina and Carlo entering through Porta Susina, the western gate of the city, which had been closed since 1536, when the French invaded and seized Turin, but had now been renovated according to Carlo's instructions and reopened for the occasion. Ephemeral statues had been erected and houses along the streets leading from Porta Susina to the cathedral had been restored, repainted, and embellished with tapestries. Representatives from the council of state, city magistrates, university doctors, and others greeted the ducal couple, and crowds lined the streets to observe them, others watched from windows, and still others perched perilously on rooftops.[12]

Catalina and the duke spent the day observing the festivities and at dusk went to the Cathedral of San Giovanni, where they were greeted at the entrance by the archbishop and the priests of the city and welcomed with "excellent music played on the organ and with all sorts of instruments," and with many orations and blessings. From there, under cover of night, they went to the palace by the temporary covered walkway (*pasadizo*) that had been constructed for that day. The Spaniard Briceño reported that "the city is very orderly and the palace houses are well adorned with a large interior garden. Her Highness should be comfortable here."[13]

The next day, a Sunday, the duke and duchess, accompanied again by the entire court, left the palace to attend mass at the cathedral, and afterward the duke and his attendants threw coins to the people watching—a total of 500 escudos. The festivities continued for two days, with the duke participating in a tournament that Catalina and her ladies observed from a castle window. An anonymous source reported that Catalina was indeed pregnant, that she had been vomiting and showed "other well-known signs" of pregnancy, and that perhaps for this reason the duke was the happiest prince in the world and did his best to "treat his wife regally and please her. They eat and dine most times together and only those servants who are absolutely essential enter to serve them."[14]

The two months the ducal couple spent processing from Nice to Turin were similar to the royal progress to Zaragoza that Catalina had made with her father for her wedding and afterward that to Barcelona for her departure, except that now, as she was introduced to the territories which would be her home, she was the center of attention.

IMPLEMENTING SPANISH COURT ETIQUETTE

Once arrived in Turin, though, Catalina and her entourage faced certain practical issues because the duke's palace complex there was still under construction. Turin had become the ducal capital only after the Treaty of Cateau-Cambrésis (1559), when Carlo's father had regained the Piedmont from the French. In February 1563 Emanuele Filiberto entered Turin and established it as his capital. The city had served the French primarily as a military outpost, and its most notable buildings were a castle (*c.* 1260), the cathedral, and the episcopal residence. The castle had included living quarters for the military commander, but when Emanuele Filiberto arrived in Turin, he chose to live in the episcopal residence because the castle was too small to accommodate his and his wife's households. In 1578, the family's most prized possession, the Holy Shroud, was transferred from Chambéry to Turin.[15]

Carlo continued his father's efforts to construct a worthy ducal capital, and beginning in 1583, when Carlo acquired the episcopal palace from the Vatican, the architect Ascanio Vitozzi set to work designing a new residence to be situated between the episcopal residence and the castle and connected to both. Construction on the new palace had already begun when Catalina arrived in 1585, and it would remain under construction throughout her years in Turin. Meeting her in Zaragoza, Carlo had learned of her love of gardens, and he sent word to the marquis d'Este, his lieutenant in Turin, to incorporate such features in the spaces where she would live.[16] "Because my wife derives great pleasure from gardens and fountains, you will . . . immediately see to the large fountain that is in the middle of the garden and because there is not enough time to have it done in marble, you will have it done in painted and gilded timber and place in the center the large statue of Venus."[17]

Knowing that the palace would take years to finish, Carlo in the meantime bought or seized several houses adjacent to the episcopal residence and had them remodeled; one of them was the house of the count of Racconigi, who as a supporter of a French alliance had left the court even before Catalina's arrival and did not return until after her death.[18] Carlo instructed d'Este to prepare this house for Catalina, and other adjoining houses were outfitted for Catalina's ladies and their servants.[19] Structural changes were made to link the houses. For example, a doorway was cut and a covered passageway constructed to connect the Racconigi residence to the houses of Catalina's ladies. Another covered passageway connected Catalina's apartments to the episcopal residence. After Catalina's arrival, her *mayordomo*, Cristóbal de Briceño, described the previously free-standing Racconigi house as "placed in the palace." He referred to all these quarters as the "palace houses," indicating that though the ladies' rooms were detached from those of the *infanta*, these neighboring dwellings were an extension of the ducal residence.[20] Sometime after Catalina began to bear children, they and their attendants would live in the castle (connected by a long gallery to the rest of the palace). Taken together, these houses along with the former episcopal residence, the castle, the gallery, and the "new palace" designed by Vitozzi would form the palace complex (see plate 14).[21]

The physical layout of the court immediately created difficulties, because, following the practice of the Spanish court, access to Catalina and her ladies was to be closely regulated. When she had left Spain, Philip had sent with her a copy of the rules that had been elaborated in the 1570s for the household of Queen Anna and modified slightly for Catalina.[22] They mandated very strict enclosure for Catalina and her female household, sharply limiting access to her apartments and restricting interaction between the *infanta's* ladies and outsiders. The rules included detailed instructions on how Catalina and her ladies were to behave both within the palace and outside it, that the *infanta's* household might be a model of decorous behavior.

Philip II directed that the *infanta's* apartments and those of her ladies be "well secluded," in "respectable places," with doors and windows well guarded.[23] All should be ordered with the "safety, decency, and authority" appropriate for the daughter of the Spanish king. These were not the rules currently governing Carlo's household, nor those of his mother's time.[24] The windows of the palace and adjoining houses were not covered with bars, as were those of the *infantas'* quarters in

Madrid, and to implement Spanish etiquette, changes would have to be made and someone appointed to oversee the process.

Catalina would have been familiar with the complicated rules governing her household; they were essentially the same that she and her sister had observed at the court in Madrid. Nevertheless, she was not charged with personally ensuring that her household in Turin conform to the rules; her *mayordomo mayor*, rather, was expected to see to their implementation. Catalina's *mayordomo mayor*, Baron Paolo Sfondrato, a Lombard, had served as Emanuele Filiberto's ambassador in Milan and then as Spanish ambassador to the court in Turin.[25] In 1585 he was appointed Catalina's *mayordomo mayor* even as he continued as Philip II's ambassador in Turin. Sfondrato, who had never served at the court in Madrid nor ever held the position of *mayordomo mayor*, was unfamiliar with Spanish court etiquette and did not understand or necessarily appreciate its finer points.

When appointed *mayordomo mayor*, Sfondrato asked for clarification of numerous issues of etiquette, no doubt recognizing his shaky grasp on Spanish court practices. He had been shown the rules governing the Spanish queen's household but requested a copy which addressed the special case of the court in Turin, where "the manners and customs" greatly differed from those in Spain.[26] Sfondrato, who had accompanied Carlo to the wedding with Catalina in Zaragoza, received a copy of the rules specifically designed for the *infanta*'s household before he left Spain in June 1585 but did not issue them to members of Catalina's household until December 1585—six months after he had received them and four months after Catalina and the duke's ceremonious entrance into Turin.[27] In consequence, Catalina's attendants did not necessarily know what rules they were to follow, even if most of them had previously served at the Spanish court. Moreover, the duke, his courtiers and attendants, and Catalina's attendants who were Italian had no experience of Spanish court etiquette and were wholly unacquainted with how it might govern access to the new duchess and her ladies.

Shortly after Catalina's arrival in Turin, an anonymous source claimed that Spanish court etiquette had been implemented in the *infanta*'s apartments, following "the enclosure and withdrawal used there [in Spain] as the *infanta* has demanded and wants."[28] Yet, according to at least one critical observer, Sfrondrato had failed to apply the Spanish rules, leading to disorder within Catalina's household. Her Spanish *mayordomo* (she had a Spanish and an Italian steward as well as a lord high steward), Cristóbal de Briceño, was appalled by Sfondrato's delay as well as by his ignorance of Spanish court etiquette. When Sfondrato finally issued the orders, Briceño was pleased because "with the law in hand, one can better tighten [the reins] so that Her Highness will be served with the authority that is just."[29] Subsequently, Briceño took it upon himself to implement Spanish etiquette in Turin, and from 1585 to 1586 he wrote regularly to Juan de Zúñiga, a close adviser to Philip II, reporting the problems he was encountering. His letters detailing his frustration shed light on Catalina's arrival at the Savoyard court and suggest that what he saw as disorder might actually have been Catalina and her ladies willingly bending the rules for their own benefit. The *infanta* was greatly enjoying herself and not much inclined to follow all of her father's instructions, at least was in no hurry to do so. Her ladies were also enjoying the festive atmosphere of the court in Turin. In recording his difficulties, Briceño unwittingly painted a captivating portrait of Catalina's court in Turin during its first year, told from the perspective of a man three times her age, and one whose life had been completely enmeshed in the protocol of the Spanish court.

Briceño detailed a long list of complaints about Catalina's court, almost all having to do with Spanish etiquette. The problems had begun almost immediately after arriving at Nice en route to Turin. Catalina's household was multi-tiered. At the top were her ladies (*damas* or *dueñas de honor*, widows for the most part), headed by her *camarera mayor*, Doña Sancha de Guzmán. The second tier were the ladies of the chamber (*cámara*, who were unmarried), headed by Luisa Mexía.[30] When the women of the *cámara* (referred to as *camaristas* by Briceño) were allotted fewer carriages than necessary and wanted to travel in carriages reserved for the *infanta*'s ladies, Briceño tried to stop them, upon which the *camaristas* complained and the *infanta* took their side, allowing them to ride in the *damas'* carriages.[31] Later, however, on the last leg of the journey to Turin, the *infanta* and her *damas* traveled on boats on the Po, but, thanks to Briceño's intervention, the *camaristas* were not allowed to do so. When the *infanta* and her household arrived in Turin, settled into the palace, and began to hold court entertainments, other breaks with Spanish etiquette occurred. The women of the *cámara* were allowed to enter the *sala* (a large room) to watch musical performances, whereas in Spain they would have watched from the doorway. Moreover, the *camaristas* were given rugs to sit on at these performances, a privilege reserved in Spain for the *infanta's damas*.[32]

Briceño blamed the head of Catalina's *cámara*, Luisa Mexía, for these breaches of etiquette, because she wanted for herself and several of her nieces also in the *cámara* privileges similar to those given the *damas*. In fact, Briceño claimed, when the ladies of the *cámara* had not been allowed to ride in boats on the Po, Mexía had complained to the *infanta*, telling her that the *camaristas* came from the principal families of Spain; that the *infanta's* mother (Elisabeth of Valois) had never been served by women from such important families; and that the *infanta* would never learn to be a woman if she allowed the *camaristas* to be treated in this fashion. Apparently, Mexía was arguing that in order to assume her role as duchess, the *infanta* needed to assert herself vis-à-vis people like Briceño—or at least not follow the rules of etiquette rigidly. The *infanta's* strong-willed attendant, taking advantage of the distance from Spain to revise or disregard court etiquette, enjoyed great favor with the *infanta* and, in the eyes of Briceño and other observers, exploited Catalina's partiality.[33] At least initially, Catalina saw no need to rein in Mexía or follow the Spanish rules of etiquette to the letter. From her experience at the Spanish court, Catalina knew that the rules could at times be relaxed or even bent.

Most frustrating to Briceño were breaches in Spanish etiquette that allowed men to have much freer and unsupervised contact with Catalina's ladies than was allowed at the Spanish court. He reported, for example, that the Spanish medical doctor Juan Madera sat around in the *infanta's* apartment telling stories, chatting, and playing cards (*naipes*) with the ladies and would enter the rooms of sick palace women unattended, thereby setting a poor example for the doctor who occasionally relieved him. When Mariana de Arce, one of Catalina's attendants, gave birth, she did so in the servants' house adjoining the Racconigi wing of the palace, in order that other palace ladies could easily visit her.[34] This house could be entered from both palace and street, and, by way of the street, men and women from outside palace circles stopped to visit Mariana, allowing Catalina's ladies to interact with visitors not necessarily approved or sanctioned by the court. Such laxness was completely unheard of at the Spanish court, where ladies-in-waiting were closely supervised for fear their honor or reputation might be tarnished, and Briceño insisted that these unseemly practices in Turin had to be remedied. Likewise, he complained that one of Doña Sancha's principal male servants, Acacio de Loaisa, a *guarda dama* (guard of the ladies), entered from the servants' house to the women's apartments in the palace because he had a key and sometimes stayed for two or three hours in the evening, chatting with the ladies after the doors had been locked. Briceño noted that as a *guarda dama*, Loaisa was thought to be trustworthy and allowed to have keys, but he did not have license to come and go at will and was supposed to enter the palace only through the usual entrance (and not through the doors between the adjacent servants' house and the ladies' palace apartments). Briceño worried about the possibility of illicit interaction with Catalina's female attendants because Loaisa was young (*no peina canas*—he does not comb white hair).

As *mayordomo mayor*, Sfondrato was supposed to prevent such breaches of etiquette, but Briceño suggested that Sfondrato was so preoccupied with juggling two offices (Catalina's *mayordomo mayor* and Spanish ambassador) and so engaged with questions of precedence between himself and the duke's *mayordomo mayor* as to be insufficiently concerned with the minutiae of Spanish etiquette in the *infanta's* household. Sfondrato's ambassadorial responsibilities kept him from attending the *infanta's* meals—a feature of court life governed in Spain by strict rules, stipulating that ladies alone should serve the meals. Briceño observed that when Carlo dined with Catalina, his male servants put the meat on the table. Appalled by this irregularity, he insisted that male servants give the food to young pages (*meninos*), who in turn would hand it to the *infanta's* ladies, ensuring that adult men did not enter the room while Catalina was dining. The presence of male servers was inappropriate, Briceño told the duke, who gave orders to conform in mealtime customs to the instructions which had accompanied

Catalina from Spain. Briceño also protested that at what was supposed to be a private meal given by the *infanta* to her ladies on Epiphany, "even the male servants" of courtiers had crowded the room, forcing Briceño to eject them two or three times because a careless guard kept allowing them to return. Instead of praising him for his efforts, the guard and Luisa Mexía criticized him, and neither Sfondrato nor Carlo defended him.[35]

He was particularly scandalized because in Turin courtiers were accustomed to freer access to court women and to less formal rules regulating their gallantry than in Madrid. As Briceño noted, "manners [in Turin] are more liberal and with greater license." He reported, for example, that one of the duke's courtiers, the lord of Scalenghe, spent too much time with the *infanta*'s women. Such extended contact was inappropriate, and, Briceño complaining about it, the duke curbed Scalenghe's access to Catalina's apartments. Worse yet, Briceño lamented, the duke's half-brother, Amedeo, and other courtiers wanted in Catalina's absence to spend time with the ladies. Though this free mixing of the sexes had been the practice at the court of Carlo's mother, Briceño remarked, it now needed to be stopped. Most shocking to him was the duke's men, in helping the *infanta*'s ladies as they descended from carriages, "putting their hands on their arms and [committing] other vulgarities" (*groserias*).[36] Spanish court etiquette allowed only the *mayordomo* to assist court ladies from their carriage.

Briceño also reported that on one wintry occasion, the duke and Amedeo wanted the ladies to accompany them on a sleigh ride and asked for them to come outside to join them. Etiquette demanded that they be accompanied from their rooms by a *mayordomo* or the *caballerizo mayor*, but none was present. Briceño had not been at the palace at the time, but when as a *mayordomo* he had been summoned, he admitted, he had purposely delayed so that the ladies would not be able to go. (He had had enough of ladies and courtiers racing around Turin on sleighs.) Taking matters into his own hands, however, the duke escorted two of Catalina's female attendants, who rode with him and Amedeo in separate sleighs. Briceño found it unseemly for the ladies to go racing in sleighs with men through the streets, unchaperoned. When he expressed his concerns to Sfondrato, the latter became annoyed but agreed to communicate Briceño's concerns to the duke. Carlo did not take his complaint well, Briceño inferred—how else could he explain that when a masque was held in Catalina's room several nights later, he was informed that he was not welcome, and that he was also excluded from the two following performances at court?[37] While he ascribed this reprisal to Carlo, it could well be that Catalina and her ladies had also had enough of Briceño.

On another occasion, Sfondrato invited the ladies to the midday meal at his house when his wife was away, provoking Briceño's protest. He was horrified by the prospect of scandal, especially because Sfondrato as *mayordomo mayor* should have known better. In order that his grievance reach Catalina's ears, Briceño groused to several members of the *infanta*'s household. His protest was again successful—informed of it by the *camarera mayor*, Sancha de Guzmán, the *infanta* changed the plans. Instead, the duke and *infanta* held a midday meal at Valentino, their estate on the outskirts of town, and invited the court, including Sfondrato. At the end of the evening, when the ladies were embarking on boats to return to Turin, the duke jokingly questioned Sfondrato—in easy earshot of Briceño—whether he thought Spanish etiquette also had rules for river travel (or for how court ladies entered and rode on *barcas*).[38] To the duke, such attention to minute questions of etiquette seemed almost ludicrous, and Briceño may well have been the butt of many jokes, because, for the most part, Catalina and her ladies seemed eager to ignore the finer points of Spanish etiquette as they went on excursions and enjoyed the company of the duke and his male attendants.

Briceño's grievances extended even to Catalina herself. One day she and Carlo went in a carriage, accompanied by Doña Sancha de Guzmán but with no other ladies and no *mayordomo*, to spend the afternoon and evening in Miraflores, their retreat 5 miles outside Turin. Briceño found this unseemly because in public Catalina should always be accompanied by her ladies, and he reprimanded her when she returned. She responded that to go on an excursion and enjoy themselves, she and the duke needed no one else, and that she had seen Barcelona without her ladies. Briceño, on the other hand, noted that although Turin was a small city, many foreigners (mentioning the French specifically) passed through and that it was unseemly for the *infanta* to be seen in public without a retinue befitting a Spanish princess, because without it she seemed to have so little authority (*tan poca autoridad*).[39]

Briceño also was greatly disturbed that a former mistress of Carlo (and mother of a child of his) was allowed to enter Catalina's private apartments, and that, rather than dismissing her, Catalina stood and watched as his ex-mistress sang and played the clavichord. Everyone in Turin knew of Carlo's former affair with this woman, Briceño reported, and "the Marquis d'Este and Amedeo and all the young men of the chamber, who know well this story and probably laugh at this," had watched as the woman performed in Catalina's bedroom. Such behavior betrayed Catalina's lack of authority at court, as well as a lack of respect shown her by the duke and his men—or so Briceño alleged.[40]

One of Catalina's female attendants, Juana Manrique, celebrated for her beauty, attracted the attention of one of the duke's male attendants, referred to in the documents only as El Forno. Briceño detailed how Carlo encouraged El Forno's interest in Juana, allowing him to bestow gifts on all the ladies after a tournament, but saving the best—a golden crown—for Juana. Suspecting that Carlo somehow stood to gain from a marriage between El Forno and Juana, Briceño believed Carlo was giving Juana the mistaken impression that El Forno had a sizeable income. Juana came from a prominent, wealthy family, however, whereas El Forno was "a very ordinary gentleman and poor."[41] Much to Briceño's dismay, Catalina seemed to favor the match, and Juana apparently welcomed El Forno's attentions. Taking it upon himself to talk with Juana, who, seeing the logic of his arguments, henceforth stayed away from her would-be suitor, Briceño incurred Catalina's wrath. A now-married Catalina could serve as a matchmaker for her ladies and apparently did not welcome his interference. (Juana Manrique would eventually return to Spain and marry a much older man, and Catalina would have occasion to reflect on that marriage.) While the incident demonstrates the *mayordomo*'s willingness to take matters into his own hands, it also reveals a youthful, even reckless *infanta* enjoying the privileges which marriage afforded her.

When Catalina did try to exercise authority, according to Briceño, she blundered publicly in a way unbecoming a Spanish princess. After returning from one of her unaccompanied outings with the duke, the *infanta* was annoyed that her ladies did not come down to the garden to greet her as warmly as she would have liked, suggesting that while she occasionally made light of Spanish court etiquette, she still demanded that her attendants conform to it when it suited her. On the occasion of her attendants' lackadaisical greeting, Catalina was so infuriated with them that she decided to play a trick on them, and a few days later she announced that they were going on an outing with her and should meet her in the courtyard. When they gathered there, with the marquis d'Este and other male courtiers present, the *infanta* laughed, stepped into a carriage, and ordered that, with the exception of Sancha de Guzmán and two female attendants (*meninas*), the ladies should return to their rooms because she had decided not to take them. Briceño complained that it was unseemly for an *infanta* to humiliate her ladies in public, especially as they had done their best to conform to Spanish etiquette and had not abused the extra freedoms given to women at the Turin court. As Briceño explained, the "ladies have not wanted to take advantage of the license that is found in this land concerning the treatment of ladies. Rather, they have maintained their dignity and decorum as if they were in the palace in Madrid."[42] Unlike the punctilious ladies, and much to Briceño's dismay, Catalina failed to follow standards of conduct appropriate for a Spanish *infanta*, exposing her ladies-in-waiting to ridicule in front of the duke's Italian courtiers. The less rigorous court ethos in Turin allowed and even encouraged the *infanta* to disregard her proper Spanish courtly education, he felt. If Briceño is to be credited, Spanish etiquette at the *infanta's* court was being disregarded and flouted on all fronts, even by the *infanta* herself.

In almost all these cases, Briceño succeeded in enforcing Spanish etiquette at the court in Turin, prevailing on Philip II's closest ministers to bring the matter to the attention of the king, who in turn wrote to the *infanta*. Catalina evidently defended Sfondrato from Briceño's criticism, because Philip acknowledged that Catalina had every reason to be happy with Sfondrato, but he also noted that Briceño had grounds for dissatisfaction with the conduct at Catalina's court. Philip urged her to follow the instructions which he had sent with Sfondrato, to discuss them with the duke, and ultimately to do what best suited her and the duke.[43] Even if his comments suggest that Philip was turning over the matter to Catalina and Carlo, in fact he was plainly trying to control matters from afar.

While Briceño was primarily concerned about implementing Spanish etiquette at the court in Turin, thereby protecting the reputation of Catalina and her ladies, his letters also suggest that Catalina herself was much less concerned than he about court etiquette. She had already formed an emotional bond with her husband and was plainly enjoying herself. She and Carlo felt free to go off on their own with a minimum of attendants and shared private jokes at the expense of others, including Briceño. For the first time in her life, Catalina had independence to do as she liked, unchaperoned by her father and sister, and she made the most of the opportunities, recreations, and pleasures that the duke and his court offered. Newly married, only eighteen years old, she had energy and a taste for excitement, and she was strong-willed enough to resist Briceño's attempts to rein her in.

RECREATIONS AND COUNTRY RETREATS

As Briceño's letters indicate, Catalina, Carlo, and their ladies and courtiers enjoyed themselves greatly in Catalina's first few years at court. The duke organized outings and activities to entertain his new bride and her ladies. "Every day they go out hunting and return at night," Briceño reported. "They go racing in carriages, their Highnesses one way and the ladies the other, going up the hills. One day they eat early and the other late, in sum, there is restlessness (*emquietud*) in everything. I confess that it is a comfortable life for the young or for strong people who can stand it" (but not for Briceño, fifty-five and often out of favor at the court).[44] As he was writing about Catalina's hunting, racing, and restlessness, she was at least three months pregnant, but that does not seem to have deterred her from feverish activity. Her behavior suggests a young impetuous woman, attracted to her young husband, delighting in her newly acquired independence from her father and his ministers.

As he had done during their journey from Nice to Turin, Carlo did his best to court his wife and win the favor of her ladies. Fancying himself a courtier poet, he composed verses extolling her female attendants and had his court artist, Jan Kraeck, known as "the Flemish one," *El Flamenco*, make charcoal drawings of the ladies (see plate 13).[45] Carlo's surviving verses, probably composed in late 1585 or early 1586, praise the beauty and virtue of Catalina's ladies. He wrote throughout his life, including sacred and profane poetry and historical works, so it is not surprising that as a young newly married gallant he composed poems in honor of Catalina's ladies and of Catalina herself. Written in Spanish, they demonstrate not only his gallantry but also his desire to flatter the ladies, whose good opinion he sought, as they were his wife's constant companions. To one, Doña Constanza, he wrote that her beauty was such that a knight (*caballero*) would give his life for her, while his verses to another, Doña Antonia Manrique, praised her eyes. To Doña Matilda (his half-sister), he wrote that, as a loving father, he wished to make her happy, calling her a "handsome and pretty rose" who would be most fortunate.[46] While he entertained himself by composing light-hearted verses of courtly love, his deeper motives were likely to create a refined, cultured environment appealing to the daughter of a king.

In keeping with a tradition established by monarchs such as Philip II and followed by Carlo's father, Emanuele Filiberto, Carlo and Catalina purchased residences outside Turin's city walls. These retreats provided rulers with the ability to escape the city, relax in greater privacy, and enjoy pursuits such as hunting and fishing. They were also means by which rulers extended their presence and power in the surrounding countryside, controlled the major roads leading into the city, and gained lands that could be cultivated to meet the appetite of a growing court.[47]

In 1585, Carlo acquired the palace of Miraflores from his cousin, the son of the duke of Nemours, and it quickly became his favorite retreat. Miraflores, as its Spanish name ("gaze at flowers") implies, featured beautiful gardens, and Carlo outfitted the residence to please the *infanta*, adding to the gardens many fountains, which Carlo had learned that Catalina loved.[48] Located in the countryside south of Turin, Miraflores was ideal for escaping from the city, while nonetheless close enough that the ducal couple could go and return the same day. Beginning in spring 1586, Carlo and Catalina often visited Miraflores, sometimes for the day but at some times for several weeks at a stretch. Writing from Miraflores in June 1586, for example, Briceño reported that the entire court had stayed there for two weeks, probably to escape the city during the warm summer months. However, the Venetian ambassador, who had not been invited to Miraflores, griped that Catalina and Carlo and their entourage had gone to "this place of pleasure" primarily to please Catalina, and that she and the duke were spending lavishly to have the residence renovated even though their finances were already stretched to the limit. Catalina and Carlo worked to mold the residence to suit their needs and tastes, planning second-story rooms for Catalina's ladies, and in 1587 they began to cultivate Miraflores' lands and to stock its ponds with fish from the Sangone river.[49]

In January 1586, Philip II wrote to Catalina that he had heard that the duke had given Miraflores to her, that they were renovating it, and that Catalina was the one responsible for the architectural plans, which he hoped she would share with him. Three months later, however, Philip remarked that the duke still had not given the house to Catalina.[50] Perhaps Carlo had changed his mind or perhaps Philip had been misinformed, because Carlo had not in fact given Miraflores to Catalina, but gave her instead another palace, Valentino, which he had acquired from the marquis d'Este in July 1586.[51] Located even closer to Turin than Miraflores, Valentino was designed as a leisure retreat, and Catalina could easily travel there for a few hours and return to the city the same day.

When Catalina and Carlo had been waiting to enter Turin in August 1585, the marquis d'Este had regaled them at Valentino, and the *infanta* had been taken with its beauty and location.[52] The palace lay on the banks of the Po, with its principal entrance facing the river. Recalling her father's multiple residences and hunting lodges, Catalina set out to have Valentino and its grounds renovated and enhanced so that she, the duke, and their children could relax, hunt, and enjoy the outdoors there. She decreed that no one other than the ducal family could hunt on Valentino's acres, and she had the gardens replanted. Her accounts indicate numerous payments for work on these gardens and also for restoring the walls around the estate grounds.[53] She had fountains constructed and soon had the land around the house put into cultivation. Valentino's grounds included woods, an orchard, and a vineyard, and the gardens eventually produced a rich variety of flowers and vegetables. Catalina strolled the gardens regularly, often with her children, for exercise. When Carlo was absent, she wrote to him detailing the condition of the estate, and by 1590 she was able to send him asparagus grown at Valentino.[54] By 1595, she turned to renovations of the palace itself, employing architects to add a more elaborate entrance (*la gran porta*) and restoring the chapel, among other improvements.[55]

DAILY LIFE

Catalina might occasionally go off alone with just the duke or travel with her court to Miraflores or spend the afternoon in Valentino, but for the most part she remained in Turin and followed a daily routine very similar to that which she would have followed in Spain. Religious observations were a central part of her day. She would attend a morning mass, usually in her oratory, either by herself or with her ladies. Perhaps because of palace renovations, Catalina also heard mass, at least occasionally, in the room of her *camarera mayor*, Doña Sancha; the accounts list the purchase of a green silk cloth to put in front of the wall "where Her Highness hears mass in Doña Sancha's room."[56]

On feast days or other special days, Catalina and Carlo would leave the palace together to attend mass publicly at one of the churches in the city. In these first years in Turin, Catalina also participated in the hourly devotions—matins, vespers, and complines. Briceño reported, for example, that she and Carlo had attended vespers on the eve of Corpus Christi in 1586, and her letters from later years indicate that she regularly took part in these daily religious rituals, as she had done at the court in Madrid.[57]

Catalina's accounts document a bustle of activities as she established herself at a new court in these early years in Turin. She ordered items of personal clothing; the accounts provide a long list of items of feminine fashion at that time, including the doublet (*jubón*), the Spanish farthingale (*verdugado*), the overskirt (*basquiña*), and oversleeves (*manguillas*). She also ordered fabric to make clothing and purchased blankets, sheets, and mattresses for herself and her many attendants. She sent away to Genoa for leather to have platform shoes (*chapines*) made for herself and her ladies, as well as simpler shoes for both the ladies and Carlo. She purchased a silver bell for her bedroom, presumably to summon a servant, and spent money on decorating the palace. Her accounts record that she purchased bedding for the bed in which she slept regularly with the duke (*en la que duermen de ordinario*).[58]

As a wedding gift, Catalina received a rich cloth from the city-state of Lucca and used it to have items made for herself, the duke, and her ladies, as well as for religious purposes. Among them was a cover for a desk; a bodice (*corpiño*) for Luisa Mexía; a cloak (*manto*) for the marquis d'Este's daughter; and a covering for a small crib that Catalina gave the newborn child of one of her *damas*, Mariana de Arce.[59] As she awaited the arrival of her own first child, Catalina ordered items not only for the infant but also for the women who would serve the newborn. For the midwife she ordered a bed, and after the birth she ordered a black velvet dress for the midwife's daughter, no doubt in gratitude for a successful delivery. Some purchases indicate that Catalina was traveling. In fall 1586 she ordered a wooden box covered in leather and lined in taffeta to transport hats. She also began to reset jewels which she had brought from Spain or which Carlo had given her when newly married. Finally, she ordered clothing and bedding for her attendant ladies about to be married. Clearly, Catalina was busy making herself at home in Turin, spending freely and sometimes even frivolously. She ordered fur-lined damask outfits for two of her dogs.[60]

In the late mornings and early afternoons, she and her ladies would sew or embroider. Her accounts are filled with entries for sewing materials—needles, golden thread, fabrics of all types—purchased for her ladies' needlework in her rooms. She ordered "a piece of very fine cloth" be given to her ladies to make shirts for Carlo and still other materials to make pleated collars and fans for her own use. In this way, Catalina's household was very similar to that of her mother, Elisabeth of Valois, at the Spanish court, or that of her second mother, Anna de Austria, both of whom supervised their ladies' sewing.[61] This needlework was not only designed to keep Catalina and her ladies busy, but it also served a practical purpose, as the women made objects for devotional and personal use. For example, Luisa Mexía, who was in charge of receiving and dispensing all the materials for Catalina's household, received a piece of fabric to make liturgical vestments (albs and amices) for priests celebrating mass in the oratory.[62] Mexía also received 8 pounds of colored silk to sew objects related to Catalina's service, and silver fabric and red taffeta to make small birthday gifts (*regalillos*) for Catalina.[63] Catalina herself also sewed, as well as embroidering altar cloths and veils for sanctuaries and Marian statues in her new lands.[64]

But the ladies also engaged in other, less sanctioned activities. Catalina's accounts indicate that she spent money to play (*jugar*), suggesting that she was gambling at cards or dice.[65] Moralists might criticize card-playing and gambling, but by the 1580s such activities were central to court life, and Catalina seems to have enjoyed them thoroughly. In October 1588, when she heard that the duke had been gambling, she made him a small bag for his winnings (the size of the bag might have been a joke, suggesting that his winnings would be few), and wrote to him that she would have liked to have participated in the game because "you know how *taura* I am, though not with dice."[66] (In describing herself as *taura*, Catalina seems to have playfully feminized the masculine noun *tahur*—gambler.) Briceño also noted that Catalina's ladies played cards, and when doing so they were probably gambling.

During Catalina's first winter in Turin, the duke, his half-brother Amedeo, and other male courtiers would outfit seven or eight sleighs to take her and her ladies for rides around the city—the sleigh rides that vicariously exhausted Briceño.[67] This was a completely new experience that she relished fully and described in a letter to her father, prompting him to reply that "I think you enjoyed the sleigh [rides]," while lamenting not being able to see them in Spain. In addition, she described other festivities (*fiestas*), including masques (*máscaras*) and hunting excursions. She reported that Carlo had killed a serval wolf (*lobo cerval*), but Philip gently corrected her, commenting that in Spain he thought the animal was called a serval cat (*gato cerval*).[68] From youth, Catalina had excelled in hunting, and she continued to enjoy the sport in Turin, both with and without the duke and even when pregnant. In February 1588, over seven months pregnant (she would give birth on 17 April), Catalina often went hunting with Carlo, choosing "comfortable places" close to Turin, and Pallavicino recounted that they would go off "to watch the falcons fly, sometimes to see herons and other times owls, which is a great pastime, and on their way back they always chase hares, of which there are very many."[69]

The theatrical productions that members of the court organized regularly were a principal source of entertainment for Catalina. Briceño reported that in early 1586, Catalina staged a masque in her bedroom, attended by the duke and eight of his men, along with all the *infanta*'s attendants, both male and female. Music was a central part of masques and other court performances, and Catalina's accounts show payments to violinists and other musicians, some of whom came from Milan, suggesting that she was not fully satisfied with the musicians available in Turin and could attract musicians from further afield to her court.[70] To celebrate her birthday in 1585, her ladies staged a pastoral drama, apparently with comic elements, because Catalina's accounts list the purchase of items for the character of a simpleton (*bobo*). Pastorals were considered more refined and appropriate for women, and in the regulated, closed space of Catalina's apartments, her ladies could perform freely in private (throughout most of Europe, with the exception of Spain, women were not allowed to perform in public).[71] For the occasion, Catalina bought her ladies colorful taffeta dresses and breeches (*greguescos*), hoods, white boots, and "anything else needed for the play and the dance."[72] (The wide breeches would suggest, not surprisingly, that the ladies performed male roles.)

For the duke's birthday on 22 January 1586, the ladies once again staged a play (*comedia*), for which Catalina purchased three pastoral dresses, made of red and yellow satin and decorated in colorful taffeta. Catalina's ladies also put on a masque for her and Carlo during Carnival season, and her accounts document the purchase of ribbons and feathers for the ladies' costumes.[73] She must have praised the Carnival celebrations in Turin to her father, because he responded that they had to have been better than what he had witnessed in Valencia and were probably better than those in Barcelona.[74] Entertainments like these were typical of the Spanish court, and Catalina and her Spanish attendants would have been very familiar with them. It was also typical of the Spanish court to celebrate birthdays with plays and to stage masques during Carnival.

Epiphany in early January brought other occasions for celebration, which included still other theatrical performances, but of a slightly different nature. On one evening in January 1586, the duke and his male attendants put on two plays in the duke's private apartments, inviting Catalina and all her ladies. The duke treated them to a performance of the very popular commedia dell'arte form, with the duke playing the character of the Venetian—a stupid, avaricious merchant— and also that of Graciano (or Doctor Graciano), whose role varied considerably but who was often in love with a young woman. For these comedies, the duke also employed a professional actor, whom Briceño described simply as Arlecchino, "one who lives by bringing *comedias*."[75] Was this Tristano Martinelli, who popularized (and might even have created) the character of Arlecchino, subsequently a stock character in the commedia dell'arte?[76]

Catalina might earlier have seen commedia dell'arte at the Spanish court. One of the leading commedia dell'arte actors, Ganassa, performed first in Toledo in 1579 (with Philip II's permission) and then in Madrid for several months. In 1580, Ganassa was in Valladolid, and he continued to perform in Spain for the next several years, acting in Madrid in late December 1583 and early 1584 when Catalina was still there and old enough to attend one of his performances.[77] Regardless of where she first encountered commedia dell'arte and whether she liked it, in Turin theatrical performances were under the sponsorship of the duchess, much as Spanish queens and Philip II's sisters financed court theater in Madrid. Although in 1586 Arlecchino performed with Carlo, Catalina paid for his performances, and in March that year she made a payment of 1,000 ducats—a relatively large sum—as a donation or favor (*merced*) to a group of actors (*comediantes*).[78]

Whereas Catalina's ladies performed masques and plays with pastoral themes, both considered appropriate for women, the duke chose the more earthy commedia dell'arte, which he and others performed in front of mixed audiences. The commedia dell'arte performances would probably have been in Italian or the Piedmontese dialect (or, in the cases of Doctor Graciano or Pantalone, another stock character, in a Venetian dialect). Catalina and her Spanish attendants, though relative newcomers to Turin and still not completely familiar with the language, would nonetheless have understood and enjoyed the slapstick comedy central to such performances.[79] The duke may have chosen this form of comic theater knowing that Catalina and her ladies would appreciate the humor even if they did not understand the dialogue. By 1591, she was familiar enough with the commedia dell'arte that, recounting the visit of a very angry Venetian ambassador in April, she told Carlo that she wished he had heard the ambassador's talk, "more sermon than anything else and with facial expressions like Pantalone."[80] As Pantalone was an avaricious Venetian merchant in the commedia dell'arte, Catalina's reference to him in describing the Venetian ambassador was less than complimentary.

She seems to have embraced the commedia dell'arte and other theater that she was exposed to in Turin, and her tastes might well have changed after she left the Spanish kingdoms. When the duke visited Madrid in 1591, she wrote to him that she imagined he had grown very tired of a performance (*farsa*) that had been put on for him because it must have seemed unsophisticated (*fria*) to someone accustomed to Italian theater.[81]

Other festivities, often corresponding to seasonal celebrations, punctuated Catalina's life during her first three years at the Turinese court. For the feast of St. Nicholas in early December, they celebrated the "Feast of the Shoe" with musical and theatrical performances. On the eve of Epiphany, commemorating the visit of the Magi to the Christ child, they celebrated "The Night of the Kings" with a masquerade, a practice that Catalina had brought with her from Spain.[82] The masquerade must have involved choosing a queen among the court ladies, because in January 1586 Catalina's beautiful lady-in-waiting Juana Manrique was chosen as queen, and Catalina honored her by sharing a light meal (*merienda*) with her and her other ladies. Between Christmas and Ash Wednesday, *comedias* were performed regularly at the court.[83] On 23 June, the eve of the feast of St. John, which coincided with midsummer festivities, Turin held a contest to see which archer could hit a popinjay placed high on a spire and also celebrated with bonfires; the ducal family participated by lighting one of them.[84] Processions during Easter season, religious plays put on by students at Jesuit schools, and other festivities added variety to the daily routine.

Carlo, Catalina, and their attendants occasionally made pilgrimages to nearby shrines, as they did in September 1586, traveling to the Marian sanctuary of Sacro Monte di Varallo. Catalina's accounts show that before setting out she had boxes made for her hats, for carrying rugs and tapestries, and for transporting her own and her ladies' dresses for the trip.[85] Traveling by boat and litter (the pregnant *infanta* in a chair), braving rain and overflowing rivers, Carlo, Catalina, and their entourage visited hermitages, hunted hares, pheasants, and boars, including one weighing 750 pounds, and stopped to visit a castle where the count of Masino entertained them regally.[86] Although ostensibly for devotional reasons and to give thanks for Catalina's recovery from a serious illness, the trip included many secular diversions, and Carlo reported that they greatly enjoyed themselves. (Briceño enjoyed it rather less, complaining that they were away for twenty-five days and that he was soaked the entire time and waist-deep in mud transporting the women in litters.) Carlo was so sure Philip II would like the Marian sanctuary in Varallo that he promised to have a painting of it made and sent to him.[87]

The birth of her first son, Filippo Emanuele, in April 1586 was the occasion for great thanksgiving. The Venetian ambassador reported that, immediately after the birth, an overjoyed Carlo showed off the infant to all his courtiers, ordering prayers to be said at the Cathedral of San Giovanni along with a procession of the Holy Sacrament. The next day a mass of thanksgiving was sung at the cathedral, even though it was Good Friday (the one day of the year on which mass is ordinarily not celebrated), and on subsequent days the birth was celebrated with intermezzos, bonfires, and jousting (literally, "running of the lances"). The archbishop of Turin privately baptized the baby shortly after his birth but reserved the baptismal anointing for the public celebration of the baptism a year later.[88] Carlo felt such joy at the birth of Filippo Emanuele, according to the Venetian ambassador, that he wanted everyone to come to see the baby so that they could share in his happiness. Carlo had promised to visit at the first possible moment the holy house of Loreto to give thanks to God for the birth of a male heir.[89]

Principal among the court festivities was the carefully choreographed public celebration of the baptism of Filippo Emanuele, held a year after his birth (and after the birth of their second son, Vittorio). The elaborate festivities, in planning for a year, included a carriage pulled by two lions, the construction of a passageway from the palace to the highest level of the cathedral, a procession into the cathedral, the pouring of water from gold goblets on the hands of the godparents, a rich meal afterward, and to conclude the day's events, fireworks. Catalina received gifts from her family and others. From Spain her sister Isabel sent a necklace with diamonds and rubies, and her brother, Prince Philip, a diamond ring. The Signoria of Venice gave a table of ebony decorated with precious stones. Still recovering from childbirth, Catalina did not participate, but her ladies attended along with foreign ambassadors and representatives of the city, guilds, university, and senate. Even the Shroud was displayed for public veneration. A day after the public ceremonies, the bishop of Turin and the ambassador of Malta celebrated mass in Catalina's private rooms; afterward they presented her with a relic, the finger of St. Catherine, in a crystal case decorated with jewels.[90]

Special events like the baptism were spread out through the year, lending zest to the lives of Catalina and her attendants. Such festivities and rituals, typical of early modern aristocratic culture, served as well to integrate members of her household into court life and highlighted the splendor of the ducal court. In February 1588, for example, Carlo Pallavicino, who at Sfondrato's death had been appointed Catalina's *mayordomo mayor*, reported that masques had begun again. Twice a week, Carlo and his men engaged in jousting exercises and games, and Pallavicino commented that these knightly exercises lent a festive atmosphere to the court, and that when the duke of Pastrana soon visited, there would be *juego de cañas* (jousting on horseback with reeds), *cuadrillas la mitad a la gineta* (troops, half with short stirrups), and a beautiful pastoral performed by the ladies.[91]

Contemporary accounts of these first three festive years refer casually to Catalina's pregnancies. In fact, she was pregnant twenty-eight of her first thirty-eight months in Turin; pregnancy was the backdrop to her court activities from August 1585 to September 1588. Even as she participated with gusto, Catalina was performing her dynastic duty by giving Carlo male heirs.

END OF AN APPRENTICESHIP

Amidst the dancing, music, theatrical performances, hunting, sleigh rides, and escapes to Miraflores and Valentino, Carlo must also have talked with Catalina about the political and military issues that concerned him, preparing her to govern the duchy in his absence. There is little documentary evidence that she busied herself formally with political negotiations in these first three years in Turin, but she did meet occasionally with ambassadors and certainly met with the Spanish governor of Milan, the duke of Terranova, when he passed through Turin in December 1585.[92] Carlo might well have used the occasions when they were alone to tell her about his designs on territories such as Saluzzo, because based on the reports of Venetian ambassadors, the subject was frequently discussed at the court in Turin.[93] The efficiency and ease with which she assumed political control when, in late September 1588, Carlo left Turin to besiege Saluzzo suggests that she was familiar with his plans, understood well what he expected of her, and already knew how to work with his ministers and negotiate with ambassadors and governors.

During these three early years, she also corresponded with far-flung family, especially with her father and sister in Spain, often requesting assistance for Carlo and in this way unofficially apprenticing in a political role. To solicit aid for Carlo, she had to have known his plans.[94] Further to help him advance his agenda, she also wrote to Spanish officials in Italy, such as Terranova, and she may have been present at informal negotiations Carlo conducted with ambassadors in Turin. According to Francesco Vendramin, the Venetian ambassador to the Duchy of Savoy, Carlo often preferred to discuss important matters with Catalina alone rather than with his advisers.[95] Though Vendramin was writing in 1589, by which time Catalina had governed the duchy for a year, he was commenting on what he had observed since 1586, suggesting that even before departing for Saluzzo, Carlo had regularly consulted with Catalina on matters of state.

Did Carlo also postpone any territorial aggression until he felt he could afford an extended absence from Turin? By September 1588, he had succeeded in fathering three healthy sons with Catalina. When he left toward the month's end on his first military campaign, she was almost two months pregnant with her fourth child. He had an heir, two spares, and a wife he trusted.

By September 1588, Catalina's apprenticeship and the couple's extended honeymoon were over. Vendramin reported that, now alone in Turin after Carlo's departure, Catalina had retired to two rooms in the palace and no longer visited the gardens or devoted herself to court entertainment because she was busy governing the duchy and also wanted to demonstrate to the duke how much she missed him. The duke's absence while campaigning in Saluzzo also marks the beginning of their correspondence, and Vendramin noted that they now "visited each other" through a daily exchange of letters carried by couriers.[96] Until Catalina's death in 1597, they would write to each other constantly.

CHAPTER 4

WRITING LETTERS TO "ENDURE THE SOLITUDE"

My soul, you do not need to apologize for your bad script because to me,
everything yours is good and I would like to be the paper [you write on]
so as to be with you, regaling you.

Catalina to Carlo, 9 September 1590

LETTER-WRITING WAS A NECESSARY skill for an aristocratic woman in
the late sixteenth century, and by 1588 Catalina had mastered it. It was
understood that women would play a prominent role in letter-writing
at early modern courts, using letters to maintain diplomatic and familial
connections and develop patronage networks. For Catalina as for other
aristocratic women, letter-writing could also have direct political appli-
cation because, left to govern a duchy while her husband was away, she
relied on letters as her principal way to give updates to and receive
instructions from her absent husband. But Catalina's and Carlo's letters
served much more than political and administrative purposes; they also
served to maintain their close, intimate relationship, and the letters
document their affection, habits, and personal concerns.

LEARNING TO WRITE AT THE SPANISH COURT

Expecting that his daughters would assume important political roles,
Philip II made sure they were trained in letter-writing, and both would
become excellent correspondents. In the earliest surviving letter (dated

3 April 1581) from Philip to his daughters when he was in Portugal and they were in Madrid, he implored them to write to his sister, Empress María, in Central Europe.[1] He also sent them a sealing wax stamp (*sello*) and urged them to use it to seal the letters to Empress María, to their grandmother, Catherine de' Medici, and to himself.[2]

With the seal, he indirectly taught his young daughters that letters could be political tools, drawing their attention to the revamped design of the seal, now incorporating the coat of arms of Portugal. In Portugal to claim and defend his right to the Portuguese throne (he would be officially acclaimed king by the Portuguese *Cortes* at Tomar on 16 April 1581), Philip would also proclaim his accession to the Portuguese throne in letters his daughters would send to their grandmother in France and aunt in Central Europe.[3] The seal was meant not only to close letters but also, in a metaphoric sense, to impress or stamp his rights visibly.

As a young girl, Catalina seems to have had more difficulty than Isabel in learning to compose a letter correctly. In 1576, when Catalina was almost nine, one of the *infantas'* maidens-in-waiting, Ana of Dietrichstein, wrote to her mother excusing herself for varying her handwriting so often in one letter. She explained that she had often been interrupted in writing in order to "serve as a secretary" for Catalina "because they make me write first what she writes to her grandmother [Catherine de' Medici]," so that Catalina would learn how to shape her script. Ana added that she did not have to do the same for Isabel, who "already writes very well."[4] By 1581, Catalina's handwriting had improved, as her script was distinctive enough that her father could (he claimed) detect her state of health just by looking at her letter.[5] Catalina and Isabel were trained to write in humanistic cursive script, a style known as "Spanish *bastarda*."[6] The attention paid to women learning this cursive style was a relatively new development at early modern courts, and Philip's fourth wife, Anna of Austria, who wrote well in this style, probably encouraged Philip to ensure that his daughters also learned it.[7] Catalina and Isabel would come to write far more legible script than did their father, their half-brother Carlos (d. 1568), or their aunt, Empress María.[8] Catalina's adult script was also clearer and better formed than that of her husband, Carlo.

In one letter to his daughters when he was in Portugal, Philip II mildly chastised Isabel for wrongly putting an "o" instead of an "a" and omitting a word, causing him to conclude that she had written too quickly.[9] In a culture where time spent writing indicated a writer's esteem and affection for the recipient, Isabel's sloppiness was a blunder. His daughters could expect that their father Philip would comment on not only the content of their writing but also the composition. From an early age—Isabel was fourteen and Catalina was thirteen when Philip went to Portugal—the two *infantas* were trained and encouraged to write letters that would distract, entertain, and inform, mimicking conversation at an early modern court.

While in Lisbon, Philip also assumed that his daughters would teach their younger siblings to read and write, and he instructed them on how to help their brother Diego learn to write the alphabet, urging them to ensure that he work slowly so as not to tire. To encourage Diego to write, Philip offered to send him a desk from the Indies. Had he rewarded his daughters in a similar fashion when they were younger and just learning to write?[10]

When responding to his daughters, Philip usually had their letters close at hand so he could refer to them and address any questions or matters they had raised. (After leaving Spain, Catalina and Isabel would follow a practice similar to their father's when responding to letters.[11]) On one occasion, he told them he was unable to respond directly to their letters because he had put them away in a desk and lacked leisure to rummage through all the paperwork to find them. Philip occasionally admitted that, pressed for time, he could not respond to all their questions. In one letter he wrote that so long had passed since he had read their letters that he was uncertain he had answered all their queries; in another, that having accumulated too much paper, he intended to burn all their letters and so they should tell him if he still needed to respond to something concrete.[12] Though expecting his daughters to write to him regularly, he had no time to re-read their letters and evidently attached little sentimental value to them. Unlike Philip, Catalina held dear her letters from Spain, and when in Turin would carefully retain all those she received from both her father and her sister.[13]

LETTER-WRITING AT THE COURT IN TURIN

After Philip returned from Portugal to Madrid in March 1583, his correspondence with his daughters ended for the time being, although on a few occasions when he traveled to his other palaces without them, they exchanged letters. Catalina and Isabel continued to practice their letter-writing skills by writing occasionally to their father and to their grandmother, Catherine de' Medici, and probably others as well. Certainly, by the time she married Carlo in 1585, Catalina was an experienced letter writer, and she wasted no time in writing to her family once she embarked in Barcelona, sitting down to write the following morning. She boarded the ship on 13 June 1585 and within five days her father had written to her that he, Isabel, and Prince Philip had received her letters and that she had done well to write them. He was pleased with her news of the sea crossing, especially that she had not felt too seasick.[14] For the rest of her life, she would continue to write to Philip and Isabel often, but her correspondence with her husband eclipsed them all.

Catalina and Carlo's correspondence began in late September 1588, when Carlo left Turin on a campaign to seize the marquisate of Saluzzo. After successfully taking Saluzzo, he moved on to other military campaigns in the following years, though sometimes returning to Turin for days, weeks, or even months. There are breaks in the correspondence when Carlo was in Turin or when he and Catalina were together in Nice from April to August 1592. When apart, however, they wrote to each other frequently, and their letters continue until Catalina's death in November 1597. In the days immediately after Carlo departed for Saluzzo, Catalina, now alone in Turin and missing him, wrote Carlo as many as four letters a day, but by early October she had settled into a pattern of writing once or twice a day. Until the end of her life, she wrote to the duke almost every day they were apart, apologizing if she missed a day.

Catalina and Carlo's correspondence is the fullest, most intimate, and most revealing marital correspondence surviving from early modern Europe, and their letters provide the strongest testament to their partnership and affection. In the course of these nine years, Catalina and

Carlo would exchange at least 3,217 letters. Of Catalina's letters to Carlo, 1,804 survive, 981 of which were autograph—meaning that she herself wrote and signed them—and 823 written by a secretary.[15] From Carlo to Catalina, 1,413 letters survive, 488 autograph and 925 secretarial. In addition, Catalina and Carlo often added autograph postscripts to the secretarial letters, in a few cases longer than the letters themselves.

If letters give the deepest insight into the character and marriage of early modern husbands and wives, we may know more about Catalina and Carlo than about any other couple in early modern European history. This correspondence is particularly impressive when compared to other women's and married couples' letters surviving from this period. The closest comparison is an exchange of approximately three thousand letters between Isabella d'Este (1474–1539) and her husband, Francesco Gonzaga (1466–1519), spanning twenty-nine years.[16] Like Catalina and Carlo's correspondence, that of Isabella d'Este and Francesco has been well preserved, in part because scribes made copies of all their letters before they were sent and gathered them together in bound volumes. Like Catalina, Isabella governed in her husband's absence, in her case from Mantua, and regularly communicated with him via letters to inform him of political matters, commenting on family and personal topics as well.

Unlike Catalina, however, Isabella relied on a scribe to write most of her letters, and her relationship with her husband, while affectionate, became strained over the course of their marriage. Scholars have argued that Isabella trusted her scribe, expressing herself openly and without restraint, but did look over secretarial letters before sending them. They have also argued that Isabella knew the value of an autograph letter, occasionally writing her own letters for maximum effect.[17] Nevertheless, the difference between Isabella's and Catalina's letter-writing is striking because Catalina wrote in her own hand far more often than by a secretary's, and the letters she and Carlo exchanged were concentrated in a span of only nine years, whereas roughly the same number between Isabella and Francesco were diffused over about three decades. As we shall see, Catalina and Carlo engaged in a more intensely personal correspondence and enjoyed a more affectionately intimate relationship than did Isabella and Francesco.[18]

It is particularly unusual to find such an extensive collection of letters written by a woman. In addition to Isabella d'Este, another apt comparison to Catalina is Anna of Saxony (1532–1585), who wrote roughly 12,500 letters to many different correspondents, including her husband. In most cases, though, Anna relied on a scribe, and her letters were more thinly stretched over a much longer period than Catalina's.[19] Finally, in the English world, Bess of Hardwick (1527–1608) is known for her letter-writing skills. James Daybell has called her "the best documented of any sixteenth-century English woman with the possible exception of Elizabeth I." Approximately 250 of Bess's letters, written to over 60 people, survive.[20] Nevertheless, her extant correspondence is miniscule compared to that of Catalina, and few of her letters are to her several successive husbands. While Catalina and the duke also wrote to others, in this chapter and for most of this book I will concentrate on their letters to each other, especially Catalina's to Carlo.

CONVENTIONS AND MECHANICS OF LETTER-WRITING

In writing to the duke, Catalina followed conventions learned in her youth at the Spanish court. Whenever possible, she wrote in her own hand. In the court culture of early modern Europe, a recipient appraised a letter by its length and by whether the sender had written the letter himself or herself. Time spent writing to a person was a sign of affection and respect, especially if the writer had other responsibilities. Philip II's letters to his daughters, when he was busy with the annexation of Portugal and with governing the Spanish kingdoms from Lisbon, are a good example. The language of letters was supposed to imitate conversation, and the writer sought to entertain the recipient, mimicking the spontaneity and conventions of oral exchange. In her letters to Carlo, Catalina passed freely from one subject to another without clear paragraph breaks or even periods. Occasionally, she used a tilde (~) to indicate that she had finished a particular subject and was passing to another. When writing to Carlo, she felt she was conversing with him, as she remarked in July 1597: "Forgive such a long letter, so poorly written that I fear you will not understand it, but I do not know how to stop because it seems to me that I speak with you, my eyes, and I am all yours."[21] Although she apologized for the length of her letter, presumably because Carlo would have to spend so much time reading it, its length demonstrated that she had spent much time thinking of him and writing to him.

Letter-writing was central to the culture of early modern courts, and not surprisingly, Catalina's and Carlo's letters show their familiarity with its protocols. A letter reflected a writer's character and training, demonstrating that he or she had been fully integrated into noble culture and was adept at courtly arts. Even when writing to each other, Catalina and Carlo carefully followed epistolary conventions, dating their letters (almost always giving the day of the month, the month, and the year), noting the city or location where the letter was written, and always placing the salutation in the same place, and the closing likewise. Their salutation, for example, was typically centered at the top of the page. When writing to a person of equal rank, a writer would center his or her salutation. (To a superior, the salutation would be on the right-hand side, and to inferiors, on the left.) Spacing was also important and indicated the relationship between the sender and the recipient. To a social superior, a writer would leave "significant space" between the salutation and the body of the letter, signifying respect. When writing social superiors, the signature was supposed to be at the bottom right-hand side of the page. Use of paper also indicated the sender's social rank. Because paper was expensive, to leave a large area of a letter blank immediately told the reader that the writer could afford a liberal use of paper.[22]

For the most part, Catalina and Carlo conformed to these conventional formalities when writing to each other. Catalina centered the salutation, leaving a gap (usually of about 2 inches) between the salutation and the body of the letter, and also, when possible, leaving a gap between the end of the letter and the signature, always at the lower right-hand corner of the page. She did not start a new page just to leave space between the body of the letter and her signature, however, but often crammed her signature into the bottom right-hand corner. Even in the way they utilized paper, Catalina and Carlo demonstrated their courtly education and attention to epistolary conventions.

Carlo also centered his salutation and left a space before the body of the letter, but on the whole he seems to have been more conservative in his use of paper than Catalina. He typically wrote to the bottom of the page and then turned the paper 90 degrees counter-clockwise to conclude his letter. In a few cases, he turned the paper another 90 degrees to add an additional note. His signature was always on the bottom right-hand side corner (though if he had turned the page, it was on the lower right-hand side corner of the turned page) (see plate 20). A postscript might also be squeezed onto the left margin of the page. Often writing from a military encampment, Carlo would have been dependent on Catalina to keep him supplied with paper and so probably had less to waste. Catalina also occasionally included postscripts or concluded a letter on the left side of the page, presumably to conserve paper.[23]

She ordinarily wrote on a sheet of cream-colored paper, approximately 12.2 × 16.4 inches (31 × 41 centimeters), folded vertically to form two leaves (creating four writing pages, each about 12.2 × 8.2 inches or 31 × 20.5 centimeters), with the fold on the left-hand side.[24] She left a narrow margin on the left side of each page but none on the right or the bottom. Visualize a four-page booklet. She began the letter on the front page of the booklet, then wrote on the back of that page, then filled the third page and continued on to the back of that third page—the last page of the booklet (see plates 17–19). If she needed additional space, she followed the same pattern over two new leaves (or another four-page booklet). When on one occasion she made a mistake and began to write with the fold on the right-hand side instead of the left, beginning therefore on page four of the booklet, she apologized twice to the duke for writing "backwards," even giving him brief directions for how to read the letter correctly (inserting a note in the top margin of the final page of her letter saying "inside is the beginning.") Her apology indicates that Catalina took care to follow epistolary convention, though she also explained that she would not rewrite the letter so as not to hold up the mail.[25]

In today's world of text messages, Twitter (X), and emails, we have little understanding of the time and effort writers such as Catalina spent composing letters. She wrote in ink, using a quill pen. The color of ink varied from year to year and occasionally from month to month, from very dark brown (almost black) to a much lighter brown, though the color might have faded with age. (Sometimes the ink color helps to date a given letter.) She would have dipped her pen in the inkwell regularly, used a flat, even surface for writing, and blotted the ink with sand so that she could turn a page over and write almost immediately on the back side. She employed both portable and stationary desks, some of them no doubt works of art which she valued enough to have covers made for them. Carlo, often writing in the field, faced greater difficulties. In December 1589, he told Catalina that his hand was so cold he could hardly hold the plume.[26] In a letter in which every inch of the single sheet of paper was covered with his writing and multiple blots of ink, the duke grumbled about the quality of the paper and his quill; Catalina responded that regardless of the bad paper and poor quill, she greatly appreciated his letter.[27] A month later—October 1592—the duke complained that "this plume is so bad that I have barely been able to write these few lines."[28] Quills, pen-cutting knives, ink, ink wells, paper, sand, blotting paper, and desks were all standard items in an aristocratic household (although a servant would probably have trimmed the edges of the quill for her), and Catalina would have kept Carlo well supplied with these items when he was away from Turin. Writing was a costly and time-consuming process requiring concentration and skill.

With few exceptions, Catalina wrote long, detailed letters to the duke. Most fill at least two or more leaves, front and back—that is, four pages of script; one of her letters, filling five leaves, front and back, she characterized as "long," but many others were much longer.[29] Each leaf contained about 125 words on each side. Given the mechanics of letter-writing in the sixteenth century, a letter must have taken hours to complete. Yet Catalina's letters are remarkably free of errors or corrections, and there is little evidence that she wrote rough drafts and then corrected them in a clean draft; her letters' length alone suggests that she would scarcely have had time to write both a first draft and a final version (although her comment that she would not rewrite the letter she had written backwards may imply that she occasionally rewrote letters).

Her penmanship is smooth and easy-flowing, with carefully shaped letters, clear script, and little blotting. Though she occasionally apologized for poor penmanship, ascribing it to lack of time or to distraction, and though a few letters have some blotting out and corrections, her letters on the whole show little sign that she was rushing, and her script remained strikingly neat and uniform through the years.[30] Before committing words to paper, she must have pondered what she wanted to tell the duke, and she expressed her ideas fluidly and cogently. For a woman with other responsibilities and other correspondents, it must have been difficult to devote hours to her letters to the duke, but she often assured Carlo that she had no greater pleasure. Amidst her daily activities, she gave priority to writing to him, as he would have expected, and letter-writing must have taken up a large part of her day.

AUTOGRAPH AND SECRETARIAL LETTERS

Perhaps because autograph letters were so time-consuming, Catalina and Carlo also employed secretaries to write some of their letters. Differences between their autograph and secretarial letters indicate that Catalina and Carlo thought of their autograph letters as private correspondence, in which they could freely express their thoughts, while secretarial letters were largely confined to business matters. Recognizing that Carlo was busy and overworked, she exhorted him not to wear himself out trying to respond to all her letters and reassured him that "I will be content for you to respond by a secretary's hand to all business matters."[31] Even as she saw the value of secretarial letters, she waited for Carlo's autograph letters to give her a detailed account of his actions, opinions, and feelings, and she made the same distinction between her own autograph and secretarial letters.

Though it was not Carlo's first language, the autograph letters of both are entirely in Spanish, suggesting that he and Catalina also conversed in Spanish. He was plainly comfortable in Spanish, expressing himself easily and clearly, with occasional differences in spelling from Catalina's: for example, he spelled "*señora*" as "*segnora*." (Spanish orthography was not standardized at the end of the sixteenth century, so these differences cannot necessarily be ascribed to Carlo's lack of familiarity with the language.) He sometimes inserted Italian words and, curiously, Catalina did as well. So, for example, for "wet nurse" Catalina used the Italian word "*balia*" rather than the Spanish "*ama de leche*" or "*nodriza*."[32] She also used the Italian phrase "*le belle parole*."[33]

The secretarial letters of both, on the other hand, are wholly in Italian, which in Catalina's case raises interesting questions about her familiarity with Italian, as well as the process she employed for dictation. She saw these secretarial letters very much as her own, writing to Carlo on numerous occasions that she had "written by the hand of a secretary," or describing a secretarial letter as "my letter by secretary's hand."[34] Likewise, she referred to Carlo's letters, written by a secretary, as "your letters by secretarial hand." On one of her secretarial letters written in Italian she added in her own script a sentence in Italian before dating the letter and inserting a short paragraph in Spanish.[35] This would suggest that she was fairly comfortable in Italian, which she must have been able to understand in order to communicate with Carlo's Savoyard advisers and attendants (or with his doctor, Argenter, who also treated her, though he and the duke's advisers may also have spoken Spanish). At least once she noted that she was responding to Carlo's secretarial letters, and, on another occasion, he added a postscript in Italian to a secretarial letter he sent Catalina.[36] These examples imply that Catalina understood Italian, unless someone translated them for her, for which there is no evidence. When employing a secretary for her own letters, did she dictate in Spanish while the scribe extemporaneously translated what she said into Italian? Did she tell the secretary in general terms (and probably in Spanish) what she wanted to write, leaving him to compose the letter on his own?

Catalina's letter to Carlo of 25 October 1589 suggests that the latter might have been the case. She explained that Agostino Ripa, her secretary, "has written my other [letter], whose substance was given to him by the marquis [d'Este]."[37] In this case, Catalina sent the marquis d'Este to Ripa with instructions about what Ripa should write, but these instructions were apparently conveyed in oral, not written, fashion. An intermediary was not the norm, however, but an ad hoc expedient because Ripa's knee pain (brought on by gout) confined him to his rooms. Ripa normally met with Catalina, and his secretarial letters are written in the first person, suggesting that in most cases he took dictation and presumably translated Catalina's Spanish into Italian. Her and Carlo's autograph postscripts to secretarial letters (Catalina's in Spanish and Carlo's in both Spanish and Italian) also indicate that they looked at—and possibly edited—what secretaries had written before the letters were dispatched.

Trusted with confidential political information, secretaries were important officials at a court, and they needed to be familiar with epistolary etiquette. In May 1585, as Catalina was about to leave Spain for Savoy, her *mayordomo mayor*, Paolo Sfrondrato, suggested that Philip appoint a secretary for her.[38] Sfrondrato was uncertain about how Catalina should address foreign rulers, either in person or in writing, and he asked for clarification, adding that because of these issues of protocol, a secretary would be beneficial.[39] Philip replied that when communicating with other rulers, Catalina should write in her own hand using the appropriate titles and formalities as clarified in a list that he sent to Sfrondrato.[40] After writing once to a ruler, Catalina could then rely on a secretary for subsequent letters. If she needed to address someone outside the list of people provided to Sfrondrato, Philip continued, Catalina should rely on the duke to inform her of the appropriate title. But rather than taking a Spanish secretary to Turin with her, Catalina should employ a secretary from the duke's household, Philip directed. Moreover, he told Sfrondrato that "it is well understood" that letters to Spain had to be in her own hand, so she would need a secretary only for other languages, not Spanish, which left little reason for her to take a secretary from Spain.[41] Catalina knew that when she left Spain she would be expected to write all letters to her family in Spain in her own hand and that she would employ a secretary only for limited purposes. Carlo would appoint his own secretary, Agostino Ripa, to serve as Catalina's as well, and in addition to penning letters for Catalina, Ripa often traveled back and forth between Turin and Carlo's camp, carrying Catalina's and Carlo's autograph and secretarial letters.

Catalina might have needed a Savoyard secretary to help her adopt the correct forms of address for foreign rulers, but at the Spanish court she would have learned the forms of address to use in personal letters. The autograph letters between Catalina and Carlo all begin with ardent salutations that seem almost saccharine to a modern reader. Yet similar salutations can be found in early modern Spanish love letters, probably influenced by literary models, and thus providing conventional language for aristocrats to articulate affection, whether feigned or real.[42] Catalina employed four terms to address Carlo: "my soul," "my heart," "my life," and "my eyes," often combining those terms for variation. So, for example, she wrote, "Lord of my soul," "Lord of my heart," "Lord of my soul and my life," "Lord of my life and my eyes," or "Lord of my life and my heart," interchanging such salutations randomly. To draw attention to her salutations, she could also embellish them, as when, addressing Carlo in one undated letter as "My lord of my heart" (*Señor mio de mi corazon*), she drew a heart shape over the "*s*" in *señor*.[43] Only twice in all her extant correspondence with him did she employ a simpler salutation.[44]

Carlo also used variations of the same four terms (soul, heart, life, eyes), usually preferring to combine two, such as "Lady of my eyes and my soul." In one letter he even dispensed with "lady" and wrote only "Life of my soul" (*vida de mi alma*), and in another, expressing his joy in her safe delivery of their second daughter, he addressed her as "Lady of my eyes and soul and mother of two daughters."[45] Poetically inclined, he seems to have preferred more flowery terms than did Catalina, adding words, as in "Lady of my heart and all mine." By 1591, however, Carlo was addressing her almost exclusively as "Lady of my soul and my life," not varying his salutations in any way, perhaps because he was so engrossed in military business. The evolution of Carlo's salutations suggests that earlier he crafted his salutations carefully, but afterward hardly thought about these salutations and used the same formula by rote.

When writing by a secretary, Catalina and Carlo refrained from salutations associated with intimacy and affection. The secretarial letters often begin simply "Most Serene Lady" or "Most Serene Lord" (*Serenissima Signora/Serenissimo Signore*), the standard formal salutation prescribed in letter manuals for proper address to princes.[46] The address denoted respect and social distance, and Catalina never used it in her autograph letters to Carlo. Even in autograph letters to Philip II, she addressed him only as "*señor*," a much less formal title befitting social equals.[47] Secretaries writing Catalina's and Carlo's letters would have used the salutations prescribed in letter-writing manuals, and perhaps Catalina and Carlo did not even dictate the salutation.

The closings in the secretarial letters also differ from those in autograph letters. Catalina's secretarial letters to Carlo ended simply with "I kiss your hand," followed by "the *infanta* doña Catalina," a conventional closing and standard mark of respect to someone of higher status. Her autograph letters afforded latitude for greater expressiveness. When she first wrote to Carlo in September 1588, Catalina ended her autograph letters with "your humble and obedient consort who loves you very much," but after several letters and a few days, "humble" changed to "loyal," and her closing from then on remained "your loyal and obedient consort who loves you more than herself."[48] "Loyal" was more appropriate than "humble" for an *infanta* to use toward a husband she outranked, especially when her husband had entrusted her with governing his duchy and expected complete loyalty from her.[49]

Carlo's secretarial letters usually ended exactly like Catalina's, with "I kiss your hand" and then his signature. He signed his autograph letters, on the other hand, as "Your slave and most faithful consort" (*vuestro esclavo y fidelissimo consorte*).[50] When writing by a secretary, Catalina and Carlo adopted a standard closing formula for addressing a person of higher rank. While they likely gave very little thought to their closing (the valediction), especially as they always used the same expressions, the differing closings between secretarial and autograph letters show Catalina and Carlo reserving more affective language for autograph letters, as they assumed that their autograph letters were solely for the eyes of each other.

The secretarial letters differ even more substantially from the autograph ones in terms of content. Primarily discussing political or military matters—provisions, diplomatic missions undertaken, the outcome of a military venture—the secretarial letters often accompanied a letter or report that Carlo or Catalina had received. They were sometimes brief letters of recommendation for a specific person, who often was the person carrying the letter. Catalina relied on her secretary to convey news that she thought less significant.[51] Rarely do the secretarial letters include any personal or intimate information, and hardly ever did Catalina and Carlo express strong emotions or opinions in letters dictated to a secretary.

They occasionally added autograph postscripts to secretarial letters, and, in many of hers, Catalina refrained from referring to Carlo in the second-person familiar (*tú*), preferring instead to call him Your Highness (*vuestra alteza*).[52] This would suggest that she expected that a secretary would read the letter to Carlo and that she generally reserved familiar, affectionate language for autograph letters. Catalina and Carlo always signed the secretarial letters, and sometimes Catalina dated them as well. Even in her letters to Carlo written by a secretary, she signed toward the bottom right corner, leaving the customary space between the end of the letter and her signature. On a few occasions when she forgot and signed the letter immediately under the last line of text, leaving no space between the body of the letter and her signature (as she did for letters to governors and others who were beneath her in status), she apologized to Carlo, explaining that she had been tired and distracted. In one case she crossed out her name and then signed again in the appropriate place.[53]

Scholars analyzing Isabella d'Este's letters have argued that even though a secretary wrote most of her letters, she still felt free to express her uncensored opinions, as her secretaries were "trusted confidantes."[54] This was not the case with Catalina and Carlo, who chose to withhold information and feelings from their secretary. Catalina trusted their secretary, Agostino Ripa, up to a point, and occasionally told Carlo that Ripa was the only one to know about a particular matter. Once, for example, she informed the duke that she had learned how to intercept and read the letters of René de Val de Stors, French ambassador in Turin, and that Ripa was the only other person who knew her method.[55] On another occasion, she wanted Ripa to befriend someone else's secretary so that he might discover the content of letters.[56] At other times, however, she was more cautious about disclosures to Ripa. Once she told the duke in an autograph letter that she was very reserved in what she said through secretarial letters because, "Up until now Ripa knows nothing of the Geneva venture (*empresa*) nor have I wanted to tell him."[57] On another occasion, she specifically told the duke that Ripa was unable to write about certain matters that had been discussed in a council meeting because she had not wanted him to attend.[58] Seemingly, some political matters were so sensitive that even her secretary was not privy to them.

Carlo, too, recognized that autograph letters allowed more candor than secretarial, specifically telling Catalina that she could share secretarial letters with councilors because he would be careful not to include confidential material: "[Councilors] can see those written by a secretary because I write them in a way that there will be no danger," to which Catalina responded, "you can be sure that I do not say a word to anyone and I never say anything except what you order me to or what you write by secretary, since you have written to me that they can see all these [secretarial letters]."[59] In this exchange with Carlo about the doubtful confidentiality of secretarial letters, Catalina noted that she had showed the marquis d'Este a letter she had written through a secretary.[60] Catalina and Carlo clearly censored what they dictated to secretaries and saw secretarial letters as more public than private, fully expecting that others might read them, or that the secretary himself might indiscreetly reveal confidential matters. If busy or tired, Carlo might have had Catalina's secretarial letters read to him, knowing they were not confidential or intimate. In turn, she might have had Carlo's secretarial letters read to her, especially as they were in Italian.

Unlike secretarial letters, Catalina's and Carlo's autograph ones were not to be shared with anyone. An incident involving a letter from Catalina to Carlo illustrates this point well. In October 1594, Catalina wrote to Carlo but at the same time sent him a letter she had written for Don Jusepe, both Spanish ambassador in Turin and her *mayordomo mayor* from 1588 to 1596, who was with Carlo at the time. In her letter to Carlo she had been somewhat critical of Don Jusepe, doubting something he had told her about mail from Spain.[61] After reading Catalina's letter, Carlo placed it inside the one meant for Don Jusepe, put them both in a pouch, thought no more about it, and went off on his horse to inspect the camp. When an official went looking for him on behalf of Don Jusepe, Carlo gave him Catalina's letter to Don Jusepe without remembering that he had stuck her letter to himself inside it. The next day a very angry Don Jusepe returned the letter Catalina had written to Carlo claiming to be insulted that Carlo had thought to give it to him, but plainly having nonetheless read it.

Carlo confessed his careless misstep to Catalina and admitted that, fearing her reaction, he had waited an entire day to write to her. Apologizing profusely, he begged her forgiveness, adding that "such rudeness (*groseria*) [on Don Jusepe's part] has never been seen and I am desperate."[62] When she heard the news, Catalina became livid, not at

Carlo but at Don Jusepe for reading a letter not addressed to him. What she worried about was "not so much for what [I told you] he had said about [the letters] from Spain but that he should see the foolish things (*nezedades*) that I wrote you." She agreed with Carlo that Don Jusepe's presumption in reading her letter to Carlo was a *groseria*, and added, "I beg you to burn my letters after you have seen them so that they do not suffer the same misfortune."[63] This misadventure of a misdelivered private letter, provoking Catalina's wrath, reveals very clearly her assumption that her autograph correspondence with Carlo was absolutely confidential, allowing unrestrained candor. Carlo's hesitation in admitting a breach of this confidentiality suggests as well, perhaps, that he was uneasily familiar with her ire when provoked.

However, Carlo had breached this confidentiality at least twice before. In August 1589, he read Don Jusepe a section of a letter from the *infanta* in which she told him about a conversation with the papal nuncio.[64] And when in Spain in May 1591, he had allowed Philip II to read the *infanta*'s letter because of something she had written about Venice. In this case, Catalina was not fully surprised, because she had half expected that her father would persuade Carlo to let him read her letters (or would have asked so many questions that it would have been as good as reading her letter), and she admitted that she had refrained from saying a few things precisely for that reason. Claiming not to be mad at Carlo, she noted that she had to "bear it patiently" but wished he had not done it because her father would have read the "hundred foolish remarks" she had made to Carlo.[65] These incidents suggest that Carlo was not as careful as Catalina in keeping their autograph letters private, but apart from Carlo's three forgivable lapses, Catalina and Carlo did not share their autograph letters with anyone.

SENDING LETTERS

For these letters to have political, personal, and emotional effect, they had to reach Carlo and Catalina securely and in a timely fashion. There were at least three different ways by which letters might be conveyed between them. The first and most common was by trusted couriers, sometimes personal servants of the ducal couple. Various men traveled between the court of Turin and the duke's camp, and Catalina's letters are full of references to these ad hoc couriers. Among them were Dominico Belli, who later served as Turinese ambassador at Philip II's court; Acacio de Loaisa, a servant of the *infanta's camarera mayor*, Doña Sancha de Guzmán; Carlo Pallavicino, who was Catalina's *mayordomo mayor* from 1587 until his death in 1588; and Francisco de la Torre, a *repostero de camas*.[66] Catalina or Carlo would sometimes send these men specifically to carry letters, but occasionally when traveling on other business they would also ferry letters between the two.

Another avenue for mail was by ordinary post, a mail system with established routes, stops (*poste*), professional post riders, and usually a postal master at each of the posts. Established in Italy in the late fourteenth century (as similar systems developed elsewhere in Europe) and expanded in subsequent centuries, this system had "fixed departure times and charges that were known to all and accessible to anyone who could afford it, regardless of social class."[67] Typically, private individuals or families bought the right to transport mail along a specific route. For example, the Taxis family (from Bergamo) controlled the early modern imperial Habsburg postal service beginning in the early sixteenth century and was responsible for moving mail from one end of the empire to the other.[68] Within the Italian states, mail went from Rome toward Flanders, branching out to Milan and Venice, as well as to secondary cities such as Turin and Genoa. In Carlo and Catalina's time, Turin was a stopping point for mail bound to France and Flanders, and it also lay on a heavily traveled road to and from Genoa, from which mail was sent directly to Spain. Milan was a major node in the mail network in the Italian lands, with efficient mail service to all the major European centers, and since a Spanish appointed governor was in charge of Milan, Catalina and Carlo would have benefited from this system. Because of greater volume of mail, certain routes were better organized, more reliable, and faster, so occasionally mail took an apparently circuitous route that was in practice speedier.[69]

A third, faster way was by *estafeta*. *Estafeta* derived its name from a horse's stirrup, because this type of mail went by rider on horseback. In its earliest days, ordinary mail had gone by foot, but by the late sixteenth century it too went by horseback, making the distinction between it and *estafeta* less clear.[70] *Estafeta* was usually used for long-distance express mail, the rider going from one post to another and usually relieved by a fresh rider who might ride through the night to ensure that mail was delivered as quickly as possible. Mail that traveled by *estafeta* went in a closed pouch and was therefore more secure than ordinary mail. Both diplomatic and personal mail traveled by *estafeta*, and as with ordinary mail, private individuals could also take advantage of this equestrian relay system. For example, Don Jusepe, Spanish ambassador at the court in Turin, sent an *estafeta* when he wanted a quick response from the duke. *Estafetas* passed by Turin or they were sent by others, and Catalina could take advantage of their passing to send a letter. Catalina used an *estafeta* when she wanted to get a message to the duke quickly. In a letter of 10 April 1589, she noted that she had already sent the duke a letter with his servant, El Forno, but knowing that El Forno was first going home, she feared that he would get a late start. For this reason, she was sending an *estafeta* to convey what she thought was important news to the duke. But Catalina also used an *estafeta* to convey completely personal sentiments, as she did on 29 March 1589 in a brief letter telling him that she was waiting to hear that he was safely in Borgo, that she was going to sung mass for the Easter passion, and that she had received many jasmines from their garden in Miraflores.[71] She also noted that the *estafeta* was departing very quickly, and speed was no doubt one of the advantages of the system. Spanish ambassadors would send dispatches by ordinary mail or *estafeta*, and couriers carrying these dispatches would often stop in Turin on their way to Flanders or Spain, picking up the letters of the Spanish ambassador in Turin. Catalina often sent messages to her father and sister with diplomatic correspondence.

Regardless of which means Catalina and Carlo used, sending letters was never completely secure, especially over long distances. Catalina worried that letters might be seized, as they were on several occasions, infuriating her. In December 1592, for example, Carlo told her that the French had stolen her letters, adding that he had heard that they had praised her letter and were incredulous that a woman had written it. The French Huguenot general, the duke of Lesdiguières, now had her letter in his hands, Carlo claimed, and he asked her to tell him what she had written because he feared that the letter might reveal compromising military information. Catalina responded that "I cannot express how angry I am that my letter is in Lesdiguières's hands."[72] To avoid revealing sensitive matters, she used a cipher for parts of her letters to Carlo when he was far away, as when he was in Spain and when engaged in military campaigns in southern France. In a letter of late October 1590, she worried that she had left too much of the letter free of cipher but at the same time asked Carlo if he had understood the sections that were in cipher. She struggled to use cipher, telling Carlo that she knew she did not write it well.[73]

In 1590, when Carlo was in Provence and she had not heard from him in nine days, she feared that letters had been lost and refrained from writing to him for four days, waiting to see if she received some confirmation that he had received her previous letters. She wrote to him that she was testing all possible roads to see which was the most secure for sending mail. "To live with this fear that they [the letters] will be lost is killing me," she told the duke, "and I will write you at length [and dispatch the letter] with a trustworthy person."[74] As the incident with Lesdiguières illustrates, letters were certainly intercepted sometimes. The state archive in Florence has a sixteenth-century copy of a secretarial letter that Carlo sent Catalina, demonstrating that, at least occasionally, letters were stolen, copied, or just lost.[75]

How long did it take to get a message from Catalina to Carlo and vice versa? Much depended on how far the duke was from Turin and on how quickly a courier could travel. Early in their separation, when the duke was in Saluzzo, which was only about 35 miles from Turin, Catalina could expect to receive a reply to her letters either the same or the next day. For example, Catalina wrote to Carlo on 19 October 1588, telling him, among other things, that she had felt the baby inside her moving. The duke received the letter that evening and responded the next day.[76] When in late October 1589 the duke was in Gex, today in eastern France about 174 miles from Turin, a letter took at most four days to reach Catalina.[77] In Pinerolo (about 31 miles southwest of Turin) in 1593, the duke wrote to Catalina on 11 July, and she responded the next day, and other letters indicate that the duke received her letters the day after she wrote them.[78] When in 1594 Carlo was in Bricherasio, about 25 miles from Turin, he wrote Catalina on 12 October and she responded the next day.[79]

However, when the duke went to Spain in 1591, his letters took over a month to reach Catalina. For example, he wrote to her on 19 May 1591 and she did not receive the letter until 22 or 23 June.[80] Spain was the exception, however, and for most of the other times that they were apart, Catalina could expect that the duke would receive her letters within a day and in turn could respond within a day or two. Of course, much to her dismay, Carlo did not always respond so quickly, mostly because he was busy with military affairs or traveling from one place to another. Nevertheless, for the most part they remained in close touch with a frequent and prompt exchange of letters, consulting with each other about military affairs and state business, telling each other about their lives, and assuring each other of their affection.

THE DAILY ROUTINE OF WRITING

Catalina's letters to Carlo tell us about the place of writing in her daily life. Even if she occasionally suggested that she had a set time for writing, she wrote on and off all day. In different letters, she commented that she was writing in the early morning while still in bed, or before getting dressed, or right after getting dressed.[81] As she indicated in a letter of 2 October 1588 (very early in their correspondence), she made it a practice to write to the duke every morning on waking up: "I do not want to lose the good habit of writing you upon awakening and dressing."[82] In other letters, though, she mentions that she was writing to him before the afternoon meal or in the evening, and very often right before going to bed.[83] As the years went on and Catalina assumed more political responsibilities, she wrote at all times of the day, sometimes waiting to write until she had received his letters or an update about an important matter. Specifying when she was writing seems to have been standard for Catalina, perhaps as a way to help the duke visualize what she was doing and to foster an emotional bond across physical distance. The quantity and length of Catalina's letters suggests that she spent hours of every day writing to Carlo and that writing these letters was the most important part of her day.

Catalina lived for the duke's letters. She left instructions for her attendants to deliver his letters to her whenever they might arrive, and in her own letters she often noted when she had received the duke's— while still in bed, upon waking, as she was getting dressed, when she was washing her hair, as she was going to mass, during mass, after mass, when she was listening to a sermon, when she was at complines, in the evening, at 1 a.m., when she was already in bed.[84] Perhaps she told him when his letters arrived so that he would know how long they had taken to reach her, and her instructions to deliver them to her no matter the time of day or night indicate the importance she attached to them. When she had not heard from him in several days and knew he had been in battle, she began to grow frantic; receipt of his letters then assured her that he was alive and well. Catalina sometimes remarked that she would gladly carry the mail herself in order to see the duke, though she once prefaced her comment by saying that her belly (*barriga*) was so low that she could hardly walk (she would give birth a little over a month later).[85]

Catalina's letters have an immediacy that allows us to reconstruct not only when but also where she wrote. She usually wrote in her bedroom (*aposento*), dressed, but on a few occasions she commented that she still had not yet dressed because the mail carrier was leaving early and she did not want to delay him.[86] Perhaps surprising to a modern reader, she noted on November 1588 that she was writing while sitting on the commode (*la sillica*).[87] Her portable writing desk could have been fitted to the commode, allowing her to write while otherwise engaged.

The duke would have known exactly where she was when she was writing in Turin, but when writing in a less familiar place, she carefully specified the setting to help him visualize it. In late October 1588 when in Savigliano, a town about 30 miles south of Turin, she explained to him that she was writing from the room of her chief lady-in-waiting, Doña Sancha, which looked out in the direction of the battleground where the duke and his men were fighting. In other letters from Savigliano, she noted that she was in her corridor or passageway (*corredor*), evidently a corridor outside her rooms. In 1592, while in Nice, she wrote that she was on his terrace (suggesting that it was a terrace connected to his private apartments), looking out onto the sea while writing.

She did not necessarily write her letters in a single sitting, and brief comments indicate that she would often begin to write a letter and then add material throughout the day. For example, in a letter of 17 March 1589, she told the duke, "after writing this, I heard a sermon with the prayer of the holy Shroud," indicating clearly that she had stopped writing, gone off to hear the sermon, and then returned to resume the letter.[88] She also reported what was happening around her. So, for example, she would often note when her children arrived as she was writing: "I have just heard vespers and the three children are now entering the room and are well."[89] On another day she told him that the children were with her and she had just heard complines. Because this comment came in the middle of the letter, she had clearly stopped writing to go to complines and then resumed the letter.[90]

Catalina's letters suggest that she sometimes continued writing even as she was distracted or interrupted by others. On 16 March 1589, she noted that the children had just arrived and were playing in the room, though their arrival did not stop her from continuing to write. A paragraph later, she reported that Don Jusepe had just spoken to her and shown her a letter, which she then proceeded to summarize.[91] In yet another letter, Catalina wrote that it was too early for the children to be awake, but toward the end of the letter, she reported that the prince (their eldest son) was in the room.[92] Catalina's letters provide a running report on what was going on around her. One can imagine her sitting at her desk, writing intently to the duke, but also taking breaks to greet her children, sew with her ladies, discuss matters with ambassadors, give instructions to her secretary, or attend religious services. Letter-writing was an all-day activity for Catalina, fully integrated into her life at court.

CONVERSING WITH CARLO

Why did Catalina write so often, and why such long, detailed letters? As Carlo's lieutenant in his absence, she needed to keep him informed of political and financial matters, and she commented on issues that he had raised, often expressing her views in animated fashion. Carlo evidently valued her opinion, and though she often apologized for speaking openly, he expected her to give him advice. She also wrote of the arrangements she was making to send him supplies, arms, and money, always reassuring him that she was doing all in her power to keep him well provisioned. The letters, then, served as the means by which they communicated about important matters of state and war and coordinated their actions. Through his correspondence with Catalina, Carlo governed his territories and managed his affairs from afar. The letters certainly document their political partnership, and the bulk of Catalina's letters treat political, military, and administrative issues.

But they also served other purposes. While she usually first commented in a detailed and often lengthy fashion on business matters, later in the letter she moved on to personal or family news. She almost always reported on her health and that of her children—a personal concern for Carlo but also one with political ramifications. After all, if unwell, Catalina could not govern effectively, and his children were his heirs and political capital. Carlo regularly asked her to reassure him that she and the children were well, and she complied, noting their children's health in almost all the letters, sometimes in detail and at other times with only a brief line saying that "our children are well."[93] Catalina also provided news (*nuebas*) of her life, of their children, and of the court, communicating concerns and anecdotes as well as gossip. *Nuebas* could also include her critique of Carlo's ministers, as in a letter of September 1590 remarking that in matters of war, she had more courage (*animo*) than the count of Luzerne, and describing her comments as *nuebas*.[94] Immediately after, she noted that she usually did not begin with *nuebas*, indicating not only that she considered criticism of courtiers as news, but also that she had an organized structure in mind when composing her letters.

Catalina also wrote to distract and entertain Carlo. In one letter, telling him about their dog (and new puppies), she jokingly commented that he could not say that she failed to give him important news (*nuebas de arta importancia*).[95] She told him that she wrote long letters because "you like to know everything."[96] News of their children, their dogs, their gardens, and their household were designed to distract Carlo from stressful affairs, just as, years earlier, news of Aranjuez had distracted Philip II when he was in Portugal. She constantly wrote that she wished she could be with Carlo to treat him regally (*regalarte*), but unable to do so, she entertained him with her letters.

Letters also served as a means to relieve pressure on both Catalina and Carlo. In the middle of a long letter expressing his frustration with his lack of funds and asking for Catalina's assistance in procuring more, the duke begged her to forgive him, but said, "I do not know to whom else to go and let off steam (*esfogarme*), if not to you."[97] Catalina responded using the same verb—*esfogar*—and saying that she, too, needed to vent in her letters to Carlo, and that he should continue to do so.[98] In an earlier letter in which she touched on various subjects in an almost stream-of-consciousness fashion, she told Carlo: "I cannot ever vent except when I write you and so do not be alarmed if I tell you a thousand things."[99] On 2 July 1595, for example, Catalina responded to a letter in which Carlo had complained angrily about Don Jusepe, writing to him, "You have done me a great favor with your letters and in letting off steam with me. I am very sorry that you have been so furious because I know how [anger] hurts you, and [your rage] is justified."[100] There was a limit to how much Catalina and Carlo could express in writing, however, especially if pressed for time, and he commented that if they were together, he would unburden himself (again he used the verb *esfogar*) more fully.[101] Letter-writing provided a means for them to communicate strong emotions, in these cases frustration, when they were not together.

Letter-writing served a further emotional need for Catalina by allowing her to be with her husband vicariously. She told Carlo that she wrote to "endure the solitude" she felt when he was gone.[102] Writing helped her to withstand the "long absence which I feel more with every hour."[103] As she said to Carlo, when she wrote to him she seemed to converse with him; letters were written conversation.[104] "I have no greater pleasure than this"—that is, writing to him—she told Carlo in 1588, "and for that reason I have waited only to get dressed to do so."[105] Seven years later, in January 1595, she was still telling him that she had no greater pleasure than writing to him, and that though she had already written to him once that day, she was writing again because she could not be by his side.[106] She expressed some frustration that Carlo did not write as often as she would have liked. For example, in June 1589, she complained that four days had passed since she had heard from him and she feared that "you now take it as a rule to write only every five days, which seem a million years for someone who would like them [letters] every minute."[107] Nevertheless, she understood that he was busy and that writing tired him, so occasionally she told him not to weary himself by writing and that his secretary should just write a few lines informing her that Carlo was well.[108]

Although military and political matters figure prominently in their correspondence, Catalina and Carlo commented on many other subjects as well: their mutual affection, their children, pets, court gossip, devotional practices, and medicinal recipes, and with their letters they often exchanged gifts such as food, religious objects, family portraits, and flowers. In a typical letter, Catalina fluctuated between political discussions and more mundane subjects; she would voice her complaints about ministers, mention her affection for Carlo, move on to domestic news and gossip, advise Carlo to take good care of himself, and add in a postscript that she was sending Carlo something he liked, such as asparagus.[109] Once she apologized for going on so long by saying that she wrote "as she remembered" things, suggesting that at times there was little structure to her writing.[110] Her letters were indeed like a free-flowing conversation, though she had mastered the courtly art of conversation and no doubt knew when to drop or change the subject. Providing one of the most detailed records of a sixteenth-century aris-tocratic marriage, Catalina and Carlo's correspondence offers us a welcome insight into how an early modern couple, in charge of governing an important duchy, conversed in writing and dealt with the emotional and practical problems of separation.

CHAPTER 5

THE DUKE'S LIEUTENANT
Governing Savoy

You could govern not just that state [the duchy of Savoy] but the world.
Carlo to Catalina, 30 December 1589

CATALINA'S LIFE CHANGED DRAMATICALLY when on 28 September 1588 Carlo attacked and seized Carmagnola, the principal town of the marquisate of Saluzzo. With this assault, the duke embarked on a series of military campaigns that kept him away from Turin for months at a time, during which absences he left Catalina in charge of governing the duchy. Beginning in the fall of 1588, this young woman—she turned twenty-one in October 1588—not only managed the duchy's political and financial matters but also served as Carlo's closest adviser, his eyes and ears in Turin while he was absent. Although young, however, Catalina was not new to political affairs. She had grown up at the court of Philip II, where politics was the family business.

AT THE SPANISH COURT

During her youth, Catalina had many opportunities to observe political negotiations and hear about political matters. Such discussions and decisions were not confined to the rooms where councils met or the monarch's private chambers, and on many occasions Philip II conducted political business in the presence of family. His court chronicler, Luis Cabrera de Córdoba, recounted an occasion on which Philip signed papers; his fourth wife, Anna of Austria, blotted them; and the young *infantas*, Isabel Clara Eugenia and Catalina Micaela, handed them to a trusted attendant, who prepared them to send to the secretaries. When Cabrera de Córdoba recorded this scene in 1573, Catalina was only six years old. Philip also took his paperwork with him when he traveled with his children for pleasure. Making a river excursion from Aranjuez to the Escorial with his daughters and son sometime in 1583 or 1584, he took a portable desk and, as they went down the river, read and signed papers. Although we do not know if Philip II discussed political matters on this outing, he did at other times make political decisions in their presence. The French representative in Madrid, the lord of Longlée, noted that Philip took pleasure in having his daughters present when he discussed affairs of state, because he wanted them to understand and learn from his decisions.[1] No doubt Catalina would have come to know his attitudes and opinions well.

Catalina certainly knew how the Spanish court functioned—who the influential ministers were and how diplomats and others could gain access to her father—and, as evident from her later comments in Turin, she had formed opinions about these ministers. For example, when Philip II dismissed his long-time private secretary Mateo Vázquez in 1591, Catalina told Carlo that she was not upset by his dismissal because "he has always wearied me." When Vázquez died a month later, she noted (without regret) that she was not surprised, attributing his death to his humiliating fall from grace: "He sees himself taken down from his high throne." As her characteristically pungent comment indicates, Catalina had plainly conceived a hearty dislike of Vázquez when she saw him often during her youth in Madrid. On the other hand, she was sorry that her former *mayordomo*, the count of Barajas, had been dismissed from court, commenting that though he must have done something to merit dismissal, he was a good man and his enemies were powerful.[2]

She and her sister grew up surrounded by attendants from some of the most important aristocratic families in Spain, and from these attendants Catalina and Isabel must have heard a great deal of court gossip and grown well aware of political intrigue. In Turin she would put all this background to good use when advising Carlo or sending instructions to his ambassadors in Madrid, and her strong opinions about people and practices at the Spanish court emerge in her advice. When Carlo's ambassador Domenico Belli was in Madrid in August 1589, she commented that although his reports were "not bad," he had been denied permission to go to the Escorial with her father, indicating that he had not fully penetrated important court circles. She recommended sending him more money to help him navigate the Spanish court better, adding that Carlo needed someone in Madrid who was bold enough to speak bluntly, and that Belli did not yet seem able to do that.[3]

Catalina grew up at a court in which women were political actors. Her "second mother," Anna of Austria, met regularly with ambassadors from the imperial court in Central Europe who expected her assistance in negotiating with Philip II. In turn, Philip occasionally asked Anna to serve as his intermediary with ambassadors. In 1574, when two imperial ambassadors had sought to meet with Philip II to discuss the Spanish seizure of the imperial fief of Finale, Philip gave them audiences, but when he returned documents they had given him with his own comments and amendments, he chose to have Anna deliver them, anticipating the ambassadors' displeasure.[4] In subsequent years, Anna continued to meet with Hans Khevenhüller, resident ambassador of Rudolf II in Spain. The *infantas* formed part of the queen's household, and as Anna met with ambassadors in her private apartments, Catalina would have known of and maybe even attended these meetings.

In her last three years in Spain, Catalina had often visited her aunt, Empress María, famously free with her opinions. The empress regularly discussed and negotiated issues with Philip II, ambassadors, and others, providing yet another model for Catalina of a woman active in governance. Empress María would undoubtedly have discussed political matters in Catalina's presence, and Catalina would have seen and interacted with Hans Khevenhüller, who regularly attended the empress in her room at the Descalzas. By the time she went to Turin, Catalina was well familiar with Philip II's concerns and strategies, and aware that women had ways of influencing political decisions.

Catalina also knew that her own marriage had been negotiated for political reasons and that Philip II anticipated that as duchess of Savoy she would strive to protect Spanish interests. In the six months between her formal engagement and wedding, Philip must have instructed her on what he expected of her, and his letters to her when she was in Turin demonstrate that he expected her to rein in the young and ambitious Carlo and prevent him from embarking on aggressive ventures contrary to Philip's wishes. From long before she boarded the ship in Barcelona taking her away forever from Spain, Catalina knew that her father wanted her to press Carlo to follow Philip's will.

Even if she recognized her important political role at the court of Turin, Catalina probably did not expect the duke to leave her in charge of his duchy and tax her with all the responsibilities of governing. In her lifetime, Philip II had neither left a wife in charge of his territories nor himself led an army into battle.[5] Before Carlo left Turin in September 1588, he and Catalina must have discussed her responsibilities during his approaching absence. As he had considered seizing Saluzzo for several years, his decision to invade cannot have come as a surprise to her.[6] All accounts indicate that they spent a great deal of time together, and she would have been well informed of his thinking.

Nevertheless, when Carlo thrust an inexperienced, very young Catalina into the management of the duchy, she was at first disinclined to assume political responsibilities and occasionally tentative in her decisions. Her letters demonstrate that, whether by nature or upbringing, she was forceful and decisive, however, and quickly gaining confidence and growing comfortable with her new duties, she would (as observers soon noted) govern vigorously and effectively.

SALUZZO

Catalina's duties as the duke's lieutenant began with his departure for Saluzzo in the fall of 1588, the first of many extended military campaigns that over the next decade took him from Turin for months at a time. Informally tutored in governance by Philip II since childhood and by Carlo, more intensely, since their marriage three and a half years earlier, she adapted to her new role quickly. What soon became routine for her, however, was at first a test of unproven abilities. Because her experience in 1588–1589 constituted her on-the-job training in governance, established her competence, and set the pattern for her political duties during the rest of her life—the duke was absent campaigning even when she died—a close look at those critical early months is especially valuable.

The duke—and his father before him—had long had their eyes on Saluzzo, a French enclave located about 35 miles south of Turin. Saluzzo had been an imperial fief and self-governing territory until 1548, when Henri II (r. 1547–1559), king of France, seized it, just as he had earlier taken territories of the duchy of Savoy. Because of the territorial aggression of France and the Swiss cantons, for much of the sixteenth century the dukes of Savoy had been forced to live outside the Piedmont, and Carlo's father, Emanuele Filiberto, had dreamed of regaining his ancestral territories. After the Treaty of Cateau-Cambrésis in 1559, Henri II was forced to return the county of Savoy and principality of Piedmont to him. To seal the treaty, Emanuele Filiberto married Henri II's sister and in 1563 moved the capital of his duchy to Turin, beginning the expansion of that city. Saluzzo remained in French hands, however, and from there the French could potentially mount an attack on Savoyard territory.[7]

From the early sixteenth century, Saluzzo had become a center for Waldensians and subsequently for Calvinists. While the majority of the population remained Catholic, Protestantism was "ubiquitous."[8] As Saluzzo was surrounded on all sides by territories under the authority of the duke of Savoy, Emanuele Filiberto argued that he needed to take Saluzzo not only to protect the territorial integrity of his own state but also to prevent Protestantism from spreading to his territories. Saluzzo was the "door," Emanuele Filiberto asserted, through which heresy would spread to his lands. In Saluzzo, therefore, dynastic ambition and religious faith were closely intertwined.[9]

Emanuele Filiberto instilled in Carlo a desire to regain all the territories that had been lost to the French and Swiss and to incorporate Saluzzo into the duchy. In seizing Carmagnola and afterward all of Saluzzo, Carlo was realizing his father's ambitions and following what he thought to be his destiny. Carlo echoed his father's argument, claiming that in seizing Saluzzo he was performing a service to the Catholic faith and even to the French king. He emphasized that this was a defensive, not aggressive, move (Catalina would use similar language when requesting assistance for his campaigns). After taking possession of Saluzzo, he vowed to appoint administrators favorable to France and continued to let Henri III (r. 1574–1589) know that he would gladly hold Saluzzo as a French vassal.[10]

When he went off to seize Carmagnola in late September 1588, Carlo named Catalina his lieutenant, with authority over "everything that occurred" in his territories, including issues of justice, finances, offices, and favors.[11] He did not appoint Catalina regent, an office usually reserved for someone governing for a minor, but in leaving her in charge Carlo was relying on her not only to govern in his place (as the term lieutenant implies), but also to keep him well-informed on all notable matters pertaining to governance of the duchy. Her duties included corresponding with the governors of the forty-six towns, cities, counties, citadels, and fortresses in Carlo's domain, relaying their messages to Carlo, and addressing their concerns.[12] In delegating such large authority to Catalina, Carlo demonstrated his confidence that she could rule effectively in his absence.

By then, Catalina and Carlo had been married and living together for over three years. He had had time to talk at length with Catalina and instruct her on his expectations. (And, given everything we know about Carlo—his effusiveness, his bravado, his self-assurance—it seems certain that he would have lectured her tirelessly about his rights to Saluzzo and other territories.[13]) He had also had opportunity to observe and perhaps even test her ability to make political decisions and mediate informally for him with Philip II and Philip's ministers. He would also have seen that, armed with a forceful character and a strong sense of self, Catalina was comfortable giving orders to their numerous attendants and servants. Nevertheless, by entrusting his ducal authority to his twenty-one-year-old wife, he was calculating that she could negotiate with ambassadors, governors of Savoyard territories, and Carlo's own councilors. It was something of a gamble, and he may have been a little anxious when, leaving her to govern the duchy, he departed from Turin to make war in Saluzzo.

SEIZURE OF SALUZZO

In seizing the stronghold of Carmagnola, Carlo took the most important fortress in the marquisate of Saluzzo, and in the following weeks he would occupy the entire territory.[14] He had already warned Philip that he was considering taking action in Saluzzo, but he moved against Carmagnola without consulting Philip II, who feared that Henri III would think Carlo had acted on Spanish orders.[15] Moreover, Philip worried that Carlo would attempt to seize additional territory and that his aggression would destabilize a region crucial for the movement of troops and supplies to the Netherlands.[16] This tense international situation marked Catalina's formal introduction to governing.

Don Jusepe de Acuña, Spanish ambassador to Turin, described some of the drama of the occasion. On 4 October, after securing Carmagnola, a confident Carlo returned to Turin overnight and met with several ambassadors to inform them of his actions and announce his success. Don Jusepe de Acuña later boasted of the duke's favor to him, proudly reporting that the duke had told him about his seizure of the stronghold before disclosing it to any other ambassador. Catalina, at Carlo's request, had summoned Don Jusepe, that the duke might tell him privately about the seizure. Afterward, Don Jusepe and Carlo joined the ambassador of Venice, the papal nuncio, and René de Val de Stors, French ambassador to Turin, in the walkway of the palace gardens, and Carlo informed all four of his successful action in Carmagnola, presenting it as a victory for the Catholic faith because heretics in Saluzzo had been plotting with heretics in Savoy.[17]

As soon as the duke finished his remarks, René de Val de Stors contradicted him, saying that there were at most 300 heretics in the whole of Saluzzo, and that rather than doing a service to the French king, Carlo was instead inciting "perpetual war" in Italy. Moreover, Stors asserted that it was well known that the duke had dealings with these heretics. Carlo responded by questioning the French ambassador's Catholic faith, saying that the nuncio had told him that in Stors's house, "one lived more liberally than was advisable." The nuncio and Don Jusepe, perhaps to cool the duke's temper, praised him for his "good intention and religious zeal," but the Venetian ambassador said only that he would inform the government of Venice of Carlo's assault on Saluzzo. The heated meeting ended only when the duke left to attend mass, with Don Jusepe reporting that afterward Carlo left Turin in a carriage with his *mayordomo mayor*, his *caballerizo mayor* (chief groom of the stable), and his military commander, all four dressed for battle, preparing to finish subduing the marquisate of Saluzzo.[18]

Catalina is notably absent from Don Jusepe's discussion of the duke's return to Turin from Carmagnola on 4 October, except for a brief mention that Carlo used her as a pretext for talking with him privately. Catalina's correspondence tells a different story. In a letter to Carlo on the following day, she told him that she wished she could have gone with him, if only as his lackey, and hoped he would keep his promise that she could join him soon. Since his departure she had been praying and doing needlework and had also been to vespers, but she added that she would not "forget everything you ordered and this afternoon I will begin to arrange several things."[19]

For Catalina, Carlo's return to Turin had been a chance to see her husband again (and spend a night with him), and her letter indicates her sorrow at being left behind, but her comments also suggest that Carlo had left her with instructions for what she needed to do to help advance his military campaign. Having been given orders which he expected her to follow, she reassured him that she was prepared to get to work fulfilling them. Might he have returned to Turin not only to encourage her but also to ensure that she was handling things well?

In fact, Catalina had begun to take charge as soon as Carlo first left Turin, and her letters document that she immediately began to procure supplies of all kinds for the duke's campaign. As early as 29 September 1588—the day after he seized Carmagnola—she wrote to him four times in one day, telling him that she and her *mayordomo mayor*, Carlo Pallavicino, were sending him oxen, carts, ammunition, and artillery, and in subsequent days she updated him on the progress of these efforts.[20] She informed him that she could not fulfill his order to transfer soldiers from Rivoli to the citadel in Turin because so many had already left Rivoli that none was available to send to Turin. Instead, she told him, twenty men had been found to man the citadel that night, and more would come from other places the next day. She reported meeting with different councilors, commented on their reactions to the duke's news, and noted which would be traveling to see the duke soon. On 29 September, in response to Carlo's news of his victory the previous day, she told him, "I think I need to become a soldier," adding that she would give everything to be with him, to have seen his entrance into Carmagnola, and to ride on a horse "as good as yours."[21]

In the duke's absence, she busily took care of matters to support him from a distance. He needed several tents and had plainly left instructions for her to procure them. Initially, she was going to have two made, but hearing that the marquis d'Este had a very good one, equipped even with a kitchen, she and her *mayordomo mayor* Pallavicino set out to acquire it. Lying to d'Este's *mayordomo*, they told him that the duke had ordered them to send him that specific tent, and a day later she wrote to Carlo that she had the tent in her possession. It was in need of some cords and wooden boards, but she was seeing to that and would dispatch it to him as soon as possible. With Pallavicino's assistance, Catalina procured a second tent in Milan.[22] She had become virtually the duke's quartermaster, even resorting to deceit to acquire what he needed.

She also negotiated for money to send to the duke and in her letters detailed the complicated and difficult means necessary to obtain funds. She noted possible sources, commenting on the likelihood of getting funds from each. Although taking charge, she recognized that certain orders could come only from the duke, and observing that Carlo had not left orders to request money from two of the sources she recommended, she urged him to give her that order without letting the two targets know that she had recommended them. She apologized for going on at length about these logistical matters, qualifying her apology by explaining, "I think you would like for me to write to you about them."[23] In subsequent days she again wrote to the duke about efforts to obtain funds, including loans from the Jewish community of Turin. She explained on 12 October 1588 that the Jewish moneylenders could not come to the court that day because it was their Sabbath, but that five or six of them had promised to come in a day or two to settle on a specific amount they would lend.[24] Three days later she wrote to him that Jewish lenders were coming the following day.[25] She would continue to negotiate with them and others for additional loans.

Even as she sent provisions and materials to the duke and negotiated for loans, she was at first unsure how to see to all her new responsibilities and worried that she was not doing everything the duke expected, or that she would make a mistake. When at the duke's request to send artillery she struggled to send it quickly, she told him she was afraid of seeming negligent in something so important. She reassured him that she was not wasting time in following his instructions but still worried that she and Pallavicino would seem to be remiss in executing his orders. She asked him what funds should be used to pay for the provision of grain for the troops.[26] She informed him that she had been told that the counts of Polonghera had been under house arrest for a small matter and that they now wanted to be freed to serve the duke. Pressed to make a decision, she had allowed this, but she begged the duke to tell her if she had erred in this or anything else.[27] Her uncertainty extended even to issues within her own household, as she told him, for example, which ladies had slept in her room the night before and urged him to tell her if he was displeased with the arrangement. She also asked the duke for instructions on dispatching mail to Spain, Rome, and France.[28]

Assuming a host of new responsibilities, she sought reassurance, asking Carlo to forgive her if she had not negotiated well because "as a novice at this job I cannot get everything right."[29] The duke assured her that he approved of her decisions, even saying on one occasion that Pallavicino, Catalina's *mayordomo mayor* and Carlo's close adviser, could not have done better, and that a letter she had written to the Spanish governor of Milan, the duke of Terranova, was "extremely good."[30]

Even as she threw herself energetically into administrative and financial responsibilities, her letters for the weeks after 5 October 1588 indicate some frustration with having to assume the tasks of governance and a keen desire for the duke's return. In a letter to Carlo of 6 October, she complained that she had spent hours signing official documents (*siñatura*), calling it one of the greatest favors she did for him, and begged him to free her of this burden (*penitenzia*—or penance—was the word she used).[31] For the first time in her life, perhaps, Catalina needed to participate in conciliar meetings and confer with the duke's male councilors, all of whom had strong personalities. As a barely twenty-one-year-old woman, was she reluctant to confer with these councilors, much older and more experienced than she? As an additional challenge, the duke, probably foreseeing logistical difficulties arising from his absence from Turin, had reorganized his council. By late October, faced with in-fighting and constant wrangling for precedence in the newly reconstituted council, Catalina implored the duke, "I beg you to relieve me of this work because without you here nothing is done correctly; at least when I am with you I don't have to see to anything."[32]

In late September and early October 1588, Catalina might have expressed frustration with her political responsibilities, but her letters from this period show that she did not hesitate to express her views, and her readiness with her opinions suggests that she was used to talking about political matters with him and knew he valued her advice. In October 1588, as the duke was preparing to assault the stronghold of Revello, she told him he should not make the attempt until marshalling more troops and installing a new commander to besiege the fortress of Casteldelfino. Annoyed with Andrea Provana di Leynì, the duke's trusted military commander who had not only failed to take Casteldelfino but had even retreated, she counseled Carlo to keep Leynì close by and send another of his commanders to assault the fortress.

She framed her words carefully, apologizing for going on at length and expressing her opinions. After detailing her vexation with Leynì and other military matters, she told Carlo that her opinion differed from that of his commanders at the front, and she urged him not to abandon Casteldelfino but to continue on the offensive. Unlike his commanders, motivated by their private interests, she assured him that she had only the service of God and the duke in mind. Careful not to seem too critical, she modestly professed that her advice was worth little, but then proceeded to tell him exactly what she thought of military developments, adding that Leynì lacked courage and that she, though a woman, would have had greater boldness in the failed assault on Casteldelfino. Further, she told Carlo that, unlike the men with him, she was meticulously seeing to everything and wished only that those around him showed similar diligence. Nine days later she wrote that she wished she could rouse the phlegmatic Leynì and his men—*quitar tanta flema*—and wished she were their commander, to spur them to action.[33] Her comments indicate an unusual self-confidence for a young woman assuming political power for the first time.

Far from being annoyed, Carlo seems to have been pleased with his wife's strong opinions and reactions, and he joked with her about her new-found political vocation. Having at length secured Saluzzo and preparing to return to Turin, he sent Catalina a gift of writing tablets (*tabletas*) from Germany, noting that now that she governed the world, she could use them to write her memoirs.[34]

HER FATHER'S MINISTERS

Catalina served as the duke's adviser on many state affairs, but especially in dealing with Spain and Spanish Milan. In her letters to Carlo, she frequently complained about the duke of Terranova, Spanish governor of Milan, whom she and Carlo clearly disliked. Her actions vis-à-vis Terranova demonstrate that by 1588 her loyalty had shifted from her father and Spain to Carlo and his Savoyard ambitions. Her willingness to use any means, even somewhat devious, to assist her husband in dealing with Terranova also exhibits her self-confidence and resourcefulness.

Carlo d'Aragona e Tagliavia, duke of Terranova, governed Milan from 1582 until 1592. By the time he became governor, he had served as viceroy of Sicily and Philip II's lieutenant in Barcelona. His appointment in Milan was part of a long record of service to the Spanish Habsburgs, and his allegiance was wholly to Philip II. In 1585, Philip rewarded him for his years of loyal service with membership in the Order of the Golden Fleece, the highest military order in the Habsburg lands.[35] After his tenure in Milan, he would return to Spain, where he would join the Council of State, serving there until his death in 1599. In complaining about Terranova, Catalina was criticizing a career bureaucrat whom her father had often promoted.

In 1588, however, Terranova was sixty-eight, and to twenty-one-year-old Catalina, he seemed ancient. In letters to Carlo she regularly referred to him as "*el viejo*" (the old man), indicating her disdain. For his part, Terranova distrusted Carlo's military ventures and thought the duke's determination to enlarge his territories showed little regard to the unrest he was causing in the region. No doubt he had little patience for the youthful ducal couple in Turin, constantly pressing him for support without waiting for Philip's approval and by their aggressiveness, he thought, threatening to destabilize northern Italy and worsen Spanish–French relations.

As Spanish governor of Milan, Terranova was the Spanish minister closest to Turin and Catalina's and Carlo's most accessible source for troops and money. Almost as soon as Carlo left Turin to seize Saluzzo, Catalina, following his instructions, attempted to gain support from Terranova. Without written orders from Spain, Terranova refused.[36] Explaining to Philip II, "I have always refused to give him [Carlo] a [single] man, excusing myself by [saying] that I could not do it without Your Majesty's will and order, because I have it [authority] to see to the security and defense of his lands only when necessary."[37] When Leyni's retreat from Revello placed Carlo in a precarious military situation, both he and Catalina begged Terranova for assistance, soliciting help from the Spanish ambassador in Turin, Don Jusepe de Acuña, in persuading Terranova. But as Catalina explained to Carlo on 15 October, Terranova informed Don Jusepe that he had no intention of sending troops to Carlo without Philip II's approval, or, as Catalina put it disparagingly, "for love of the orders that he was given."[38] In her opinion, Terranova was absurdly wed to his written instructions, unwilling to budge unless Philip issued new orders in writing.

Fortunately for Catalina and Carlo, Don Jusepe located a letter Philip II had written three years earlier, when he had heard, no doubt from Carlo, that there was a plan afoot for the magistrates in Carmagnola to hand the town and citadel over to Carlo.[39] In that ciphered letter, Philip instructed Terranova that if Carlo seized Carmagnola and needed assistance, Terranova should send him 2,000 soldiers.[40] Philip had not sent the letter to Terranova, giving it instead to Don Jusepe's predecessor in Turin, Paolo Sfondrato, to retain in case he needed to use it. Don Jusepe's secretary found it among the late Sfondrato's papers.[41]

Now, eager to please Catalina and Carlo, Don Jusepe wasted no time in sending the three-year-old letter to Terranova. He also wrote to Philip II, informing him of the situation; after all, the letter was more than three years old and had never been delivered to Terranova, and in the interim Philip might well have changed his mind. Catalina reported these developments to Carlo, noting that his councilors (with one exception) knew nothing about them, and begging him to say nothing to them about the letter, though he should write immediately to Philip II "informing him of everything," meaning their negotiations with Terranova and the discovery of the letter. She also told Carlo how pleased Don Jusepe was to have found the letter and urged Carlo to thank the ambassador for his intervention. After these communications, Catalina commented, Terranova "will now have no excuse not to give us the troops."[42] Her use of the first-person plural—to give *us* the troops—reveals how thoroughly she identified herself with Carlo's cause. Even as a novice to governing, Catalina deftly conspired with the Spanish ambassador to put pressure on Terranova to do as she and Carlo desired, trusting that their efforts would secure the troops Carlo needed. She also advised Carlo on diplomatic gestures he should take to ensure his continuance in the good graces of Philip II and Don Jusepe.

Carlo's response indicates not only his joy at Don Jusepe's discovery, but also how much he depended on his wife to take care of his financial and military needs. Calling the letter Don Jusepe had found "a treasure," Carlo wrote that he was so happy about the troops that Terranova would send that he could hardly express his joy. He went on to comment on Catalina's efforts and added further steps he wished her to take:

> The mail that was sent to Milan was very well done because they will be better disposed to provide the troops and . . . as to the letter that he [Don Jusepe] wishes to send to Spain, it seems very good to me but I ask you to have him wait until tomorrow night because I will write tomorrow and my letter will arrive [in Turin] by night-time. I promise you that today I have written two letters by hand and I cannot write more. As to the money for the provisions for the soldiers' munitions, I beg you to have it provided as stipulated by the treasurers, and as I have written more specifically to Pallavicino. I am sending you the letters from France . . .[43]

Though a few days earlier he had referred to Don Jusepe as "a beast," Carlo recognized how important it was to keep themselves in his good graces, and he begged Catalina not to forget to send a gift to Don Jusepe's wife because "the bed can do a lot" (*la cama puede mucho*).[44]

Don Jusepe's and Catalina's plot succeeded. The day after Catalina had informed Carlo of Philip's 1585 letter, Terranova wrote to Philip II and Philip's closest councilor, Juan de Idiáquez, reporting that he had finally (though reluctantly) consented to send troops to the duke. Explaining that he had received letters from the duke, Catalina, and Don Jusepe, as well as a copy of the letter that Philip had written in 1585, he sent copies of all of them to Philip, no doubt to cover his back. Leynì's retreat, Terranova wrote, had been of particular concern to him because it left the duke exposed in Saluzzo with only inexperienced troops to assist and protect him. He did not want to underestimate the danger in which the duke found himself, he explained, and "I did not think it was appropriate to sit with my hands folded" while forces were being raised close by against "the duke, Your Majesty's son."[45]

Yet even as he justified his decision to Philip II and Idiáquez by invoking the familial relation between Carlo and Philip, Terranova pointed out that Carlo was aggressively seizing territory to augment his power, which amounted to starting a war in the region. He explained to Idiáquez that he was reluctant to help the duke because he was afraid other princes might assume that the duke acted on Philip II's orders, but that Leynì's retreat had made him change his mind because "the *infanta* and the duke, finding themselves in Saluzzo, I thought it was necessary not to allow them to lose."[46] Though prevailed on to assist the duke, Terranova was not pleased, stressing that he was making an exception in this one case only.

The episode also allows us to examine Catalina's method of operating and the language she used in trying to win favor. Knowing that an autograph letter from a social superior was a sign of respect and attention, she wrote to Terranova in her own hand, and he noted this when he sent Philip a copy of Catalina's letter labeled "copy of the *infanta*'s autograph letter." In her letter Catalina exploited arguments designed to appeal to Terranova and tried to anticipate his likely objections. Knowing that Terranova saw the seizure of Saluzzo as an aggressive move to extend Carlo's territories, she told him that assistance to the duke would be of service to her father and to Christianity and that he would be aiding Carlo not to gain territory, but rather to conserve what he already possessed.[47] She also suggested that Terranova's loyalty to her father should extend to her as well. In assisting the duke, Terranova would be gratifying her: "For me it would be the greatest pleasure that you could give, since I would not ask it of you if I did not think you could do it without going against the orders that you have . . . and the duke and I would receive so much pleasure if you were to give us [assistance] in this." She concluded by saying she was certain Terranova would "do what I ask of you since you see what I so reasonably desire."[48] Implicit in her rhetoric was the assumption that a Spanish minister should want to please the daughter and son-in-law of his sovereign.

Catalina had also asked Don Jusepe to write to Terranova to pressure him to help, and the Spanish ambassador accordingly wrote to Terranova: "The *señora infanta* asks for [assistance] most tenderly and has called on me and told me that if the duke loses, it will be because her father's ministers did not come to his aid because she knows that His Majesty desires it and she has ordered me to urge you [to aid Carlo]."[49] Terranova in his letters to Philip echoed Catalina and Don Jusepe's language, noting that he had acted to help Catalina and alleviate her anxiety over the duke's fate because she was so "anxious about the person of her husband," adding that "the *infanta*'s anguish and solicitude obligated me to [act] to safeguard his person."[50] He claimed, in other words, to have helped Carlo primarily for Catalina's sake.

In a subsequent letter thanking Terranova for the troops he had sent, Catalina once again used the language of gratitude and patronage.

> The pleasure you have given me in sending the Spaniards and the company [of soldiers] has been so great that I did not want to fail to give you many thanks for it and for the good will that you have demonstrated and I am very happy that it is even more for my father's service than for ours. You will know my [gratitude] on all the occasions that present themselves and in which I know that I can please you. The duke and I wish nothing more than that you know the good will that we have [toward you].[51]

Continuing to emphasize that Carlo had acted as much for Philip as for himself and that she and Carlo might in some way repay Terranova for his assistance, was she suggesting that she would put in a good word for him with her father? After all, many others asked her to write to the Spanish monarch on their behalf. Court etiquette demanded that she thank Terranova, while political necessity required her to win his good will, as this would probably not be the last time she and Carlo needed his assistance. Writing letters to and negotiating with her father's ministers was one of the principal ways she served Carlo, and she told him that she hoped he would repay her by coming to visit her: "I wish . . . you would [come] soon to give me the payment that you promised me for the letter to the duke of Terranova. I would like to write many [more] so that you would repay me in that fashion, although I think it will take you longer to come than I would wish."[52]

Catalina might use ingratiating language in thanking Terranova, but in her letters to Carlo, she struck a very different tone, indicating that she and Carlo both distrusted him. In late October 1588, she noted with pleasure that "the duke of Terranova has started to get on board (*enpezado a enbarcar*) in sending people, because in this way we will get everything we need."[53] (By choosing the verb *embarcar*, which meant to become deeply involved in a difficult and dangerous matter, did Catalina mean to suggest that Terranova would be unable to extricate himself now that he had begun to assist them?[54]) Her focus was hardly on any favor Terranova might have shown them or gratitude for his cooperation, but rather on the benefit they would derive from his acquiescence in their plan. In subsequent months and years, her relationship with Terranova remained shaky, and she regularly referred to him dismissively as "the old man." In May 1589, for example, she told Carlo that:

> Here there is so much [fickleness] on the part of the duke of Terranova that I do not know what to say. You will see all by the [letters] that Don Jusepe writes and it is certain that they do not understand things well. For this reason I think you should write to my father soon and carefully about everything because I am afraid that this old man [Terranova], if he does not have orders, will do us some foolishness. I will do what I can here so that he does not do any [nonsense].[55]

Her animosity toward Terranova was again apparent in early June 1589 in a letter in which she articulated her frustration at his refusal to help Carlo. Negotiating with Don Jusepe and trying her best to secure aid for Carlo, she told the latter:

Believe me when I say that I am doing everything to procure what I think would be of service to you and I am very sorry to see that you have so many burdens without any reason and I beg of you to see how you govern yourself in this because I think this old man from Milan is on his way out (*caduca*—that is, expiring) and he will not fail to do as he says, more for reputation than for anything else.[56]

Catalina's reference to Terranova being "on his way out" is unclear, though she might have heard that Philip was considering replacing him as governor of Milan (which he did in late 1592), but her disdain for Terranova is evident, as is her belief that he cared mostly about his reputation.

Several weeks later, she made even more deprecating comments about Terranova, telling Carlo that "this old man from Milan has so little desire to do anything that it is necessary to wear spurs always to prod him."[57] Her disdain appeared again in early September 1589, when she told Carlo that "from the letters from Milan you will see how this old man deceives me and he does not do anything [to help]." She explained that Don Jusepe had merely asked Terranova to give Carlo the money left over after payments had been made to secure troops, but that Terranova had refused. Catalina added that she did not understand why Terranova looked for excuses, when "he would do better just saying that he does not want to [help.]" She then advised Carlo that "in the end, it is better not to rely on them nor to lose our fortune for their respect," with "them" and "their" apparently referring to Philip II's ministers, especially Terranova and the Spanish ambassador in Rome, Enrique de Guzmán, count of Olivares, whom she disliked so much that she wished her father would send him to the Indies.[58] A week later, still badgering Terranova for assistance, she commented to Carlo that "may it please God that the old man does what we want."[59]

In August 1589, Carlo was in Provence, trying to take advantage of the death of the French king, Henri III. Catalina told him that she was expecting no help from Milan, even though Don Jusepe had written to Terranova. "I fear that the old man does not want us to gain any [territory] but I hope we will do so despite him and even better than he thinks," she wrote to Carlo, making clear that unlike the "old man," she fully endorsed the duke's territorial aggrandizement.[60]

Two years later, she was still enraged about "this old man" who "no longer wants to see to what is necessary for the security of your [Carlo's] person."[61] Nevertheless, when Philip recalled Terranova to Spain in November 1592, Catalina urged Carlo to write him a few kind words because they might need his support in Madrid and because his opinion about matters in northern Italy might influence Philip's ministers.[62] She noted that Terranova's successor might be even worse, moreover, indicating that, in the end, and despite all her complaints, she believed that they had been able to work with Terranova.[63]

Hell-bent on advancing and justifying the duke's expansionist ventures, Catalina had pleaded with, badgered, flattered, deceived, and (to Carlo) regularly mocked Terranova. Cautious from age and experience, Terranova had frustrated her by his reluctance to help Carlo and insistence on getting approval from her father, far away and slow to act. Youthfully and dismissively arrogant, Catalina was used to having her way, without delay.

CHANGING LOYALTIES

As governor of Milan, Terranova was only her father's minister, and Catalina knew to go to the source—her father himself—when she and Carlo needed assistance. She corresponded regularly with her father, partly from affection but almost always, too, with a plea for military or financial assistance.[64] The correspondence between Catalina and Philip from fall 1588 to December 1589—the crucial period during which Carlo seized Saluzzo and subsequently led his army into southern France—reveals that by the beginning of his campaigns Catalina had firmly shifted her loyalties from father to husband. Her letters to Philip are best understood in conjunction with her letters to Carlo, to whom she wrote much more candidly, telling him of the difficulties she faced with her father and his ministers. Her letters to Carlo therefore reveal a new "Savoyard" Catalina, based on her emotional bond with her husband, and her growing distance from her father.

The duke's seizure of Saluzzo was a thorny international issue, and Catalina wrote to her father often as events unfolded. She wrote to him on 30 September—two days after the duke moved into Saluzzo—and again on 7, 8, and 20 October and on 3 November, but Philip, though writing to Carlo three times in November, failed to respond to Catalina until 5 December.[65] (We no longer have her letters to Philip and know of them only because Philip mentioned them in his letter to her of early December.) Catalina's letters, probably detailing and justifying the duke's aggression, provoked Philip to write harshly in return.

Excusing his delay in responding, he explained that he wanted to send his letter with Francisco de Vera, recently appointed Spanish ambassador to Venice, whom he had instructed to stop in Savoy en route to Venice to meet with Catalina and Carlo and persuade Carlo to return Saluzzo to the French king.[66] Two of Philip's three November letters to Carlo had notified him that Vera would communicate Philip's reaction to the duke's invasion and that in the meantime Carlo should take no further action. A third, sterner letter, sent in cipher, had warned him not to encroach on the territory of any other Italian ruler, specifically that of the duke of Mantua.[67] To Catalina now, in December, Philip expressed more bluntly his frustration with Carlo's assault on Saluzzo: "What you first and foremost discuss in them [her letters] is the Saluzzo issue and I never thought that the duke would take such a huge decision without telling me first . . . the troops which the duke of Terranova sent you were for your personal protection and that of the duke and do not let them be used in any other way."

Philip had a further grievance. Catalina had detained mail from Terranova to Spain, probably fearing that his letters criticized the duke's aggression and wanting to allow time for the duke himself to justify to Philip his seizure of Saluzzo.[68] Informed of Catalina's sequestering of Terranova's letters, Philip chastised, "your detaining the mail from Milan can be overlooked this time, but it would be good if you ordered that in the future, this not be done because it could be very damaging."[69] Much unlike his earlier familiar letters to Catalina discussing his health or the weather or responding to her mentions of everyday matters, Philip's December letter was stern and severe.

The letter reveals that, by abetting the duke in a conquest her father strongly disapproved of, Catalina was interfering with Philip's diplomatic policies and interests.[70] Her detention of Terranova's letters to Spain had further ramifications. Writing to the duke, she reported that her *mayordomo mayor* Pallavicino had informed Don Jusepe, the Spanish ambassador, that Terranova's mail could not pass through Savoy without Carlo's approval, indicating that Catalina and Pallavicino were conspiring together to delay Terranova's letters. Furious, Don Jusepe barged into her chambers while she was dining, making such a commotion that Pallavicino and a lady-in-waiting struggled to calm him. Accusing her of neglecting her father's interests, Don Jusepe threatened to complain to both the duke and Philip. "He uttered so many impertinences," Catalina subsequently wrote to the duke, "that I will not bore you with them . . . and I responded that he should do what seemed best to him and I would also write."[71] Despite Philip's anger and Don Jusepe's explosive words, Carlo appreciated Catalina's efforts on his behalf, sympathizing with her indignation at the unmannerly interruption of her meal and characterizing Don Jusepe as a "beast."[72] Following Catalina's advice, he wrote to Philip immediately.

She, too, continued to write to her father, although he refrained from writing to her for two and a half months, from 5 December 1588 to 22 February 1589. He did, however, write to Carlo in late December, expressing his dismay at the seizure of Saluzzo without his approval, and again in late January, both times urging him to refrain from further aggression.[73] On the other hand, René de Lucinge, Savoyard ambassador in Paris, wrote Carlo in late 1588 that the French monarchy was on the verge of collapse and urged him not to stop at Saluzzo but to seize whatever territory he could. By early 1589, relations between Carlo and Henri III of France had deteriorated to the point that Lucinge was compelled to leave the French court, and Carlo was considering deploying troops in Savoyard territories bordering France, fearing an assault.[74] In February Philip was so concerned about the duke's military preparations that he wrote to Catalina twice within two weeks—unusually close together for his correspondence with her.[75] In the first of these, a letter of late February, he noted that she had written to him and Isabel Clara Eugenia "so many letters" that they could not complain and that they had enjoyed hearing from her. He then turned to Carlo's plans to move troops close to France, though leaving the specifics vague, probably for fear that his letter would be intercepted. "You have told me in several of your letters, that the duke wants me to respond to him [about his military plans]. I have answered him and you will learn of it [from Carlo] and from Don Jusepe . . . because it involves you so directly, that it would be good if on your part you help to calm down the duke."[76] In his next letter of two weeks later, he used almost the same words, again telling her that she needed to pacify the duke, because for Carlo "to try anything else right now would be very damaging."[77] The admonition suggests that, wanting Carlo to refrain from aggression against France, Philip expected Catalina to rein in her rash and bellicose husband.

Far from reining in the duke, however, Catalina defended him. On 2 March 1589, Carlo left Turin for the county of Savoy (although Turin was the capital of the duchy of Savoy, it was actually in Piedmont, not Savoy) to protect his Savoyard frontier from French aggression, as Catalina knew when responding to her father's letters (see map, p. xiv). Although her letter to Philip of March 1589 has been lost, she summarized its contents to the duke, explaining to him that she had told her father only that she was missing the duke and "that although it was very necessary for you to go to Savoy, I have felt it very much and that I wish you could have waited for replies [from Philip] to the letters you have written . . . that is all the substance [of her letter to Philip]." Explaining to Carlo that because Don Jusepe had been desperate to dispatch the mail to Spain, she had given him her letter, she added, "Forgive me for not sending you the letter [first]."[78] She reassured the duke that she had divulged no particulars of his military plans to her father. Her summary of her letter to Philip suggests that even as she had used language designed to appease him, she had also defended Carlo's advance into Savoy.

In April 1589, in retaliation for Carlo's seizure of Saluzzo, a French–Swiss coalition invaded Savoy, and Carlo would remain to defend Savoy for the next eight months. Learning of his advance into Savoy, Philip sent separate letters to Carlo and Catalina in early May. To Carlo he expressed surprise and frustration, telling him bluntly that he was mistaken if he thought Philip would assist him, because Spanish resources were stretched too thin, adding "nor is it just for me to do so when you have hurled yourself into such matters without even asking me and so do not think that by committing yourself, you will force me into something that is not advisable."[79] (Philip's finances must indeed have been tight because less than a year had passed since the loss of the Armada and he was contemplating another strike against England.[80]) To Catalina he complained that Carlo had only stirred up trouble (*remover humores*) and that he (Philip) had never thought it a good idea for Carlo to move against French troops. Philip also noted, as he had told Carlo, that, having launched into a war without Philip's approval, the duke should not think that Philip would now feel obligated to assist him. The state of his finances did not allow him to assist the duke, Philip claimed, exhorting Catalina to make sure Carlo understood this, and adding that she should urge the duke to comply with Philip's injunctions against going to war.[81] To convey his message as forcefully as possible, Philip had plainly synchronized his letters to Carlo and Catalina.

Responding to Philip's letter, Carlo claimed to regret Philip's displeasure but justified his campaign in Savoy and southeastern France by arguing that if he had taken no action, he would have lost his lands. "I am in great distress because I see that Your Majesty does not appreciate that [necessity] . . . and I beg you to see that service to you has been my only motivation." Once the French situation was resolved, Carlo continued, he would with Philip's permission go to serve him "with a pike in hand . . . to pay with my blood the many debts that I owe Your Majesty."[82] With no *mea culpa* for his defense of Savoy, Carlo closed his letter by telling Philip that the *infanta* and their children were well.

Philip's admonitory May 1589 letter took two months to reach Catalina, but as soon as she received it she responded strongly, again defending the duke. She reassured Philip that Carlo thought only about following Philip's will, and that although Carlo's campaign would benefit Carlo and Catalina, they would abandon it immediately if it ran contrary to Philip's wishes. Referring to "*our* matters" and "*our* interests" (my italics), Catalina included herself as fully complicit in Carlo's ventures. She also added that, as Philip had requested, she would remind Carlo to follow the king's wishes, adding, though, that it was hardly necessary. Nonetheless, she asserted, Carlo had been forced to act by "such compelling reasons that he cannot do otherwise," and she suggested that Philip's ministers were conveying falsehoods to him.[83] Perhaps to temper her vigorous wifely defense, Catalina then passed seamlessly from political wrangles to her newborn daughter and her three sons.

Her letters to Carlo shed light on her response to Philip. Writing two days before drafting her letter to Philip, Catalina told Carlo that she had received her father's letter and had also talked with Don Jusepe, who had gone on at length about Philip's love for them and "one hundred thousand other things." Her satiric comments on Don Jusepe's effusive chatter about Philip's deep affection, along with the "hundred thousand" other things, suggest that Catalina dismissed the Spanish ambassador's rhetoric as mostly empty blather. Don Jusepe had further assured her, Catalina reported to Carlo, that Philip had no interest in acquiring territories for himself, "because he already has so many kingdoms."[84]

Did she believe this disclaimer? Probably not. A week earlier the duke had written to her that Philip wanted parts of France for himself, particularly a few ports, and that if he succeeded, "afterward there will be nothing left for us," suggesting that Carlo, at least, did not fully credit Don Jusepe's assertion of Philip's indifference to territorial aggrandizement.[85] Responding to Don Jusepe's remarks during their conversation, Catalina had assured him (she told Carlo) that, as she had also written to Philip, she and Carlo desired to obey Philip, and that far from acting impulsively or rashly, Carlo was proceeding with extreme caution. She further told Carlo that Don Jusepe seemed well informed about the situation in Savoy and Provence, and she urged Carlo to impress on Don Jusepe how much he needed Spanish assistance. A good word from Don Jusepe, she reminded Carlo, might make all the difference, and "perhaps with this my father will resolve [to give us] something." Catalina's letter to the duke makes clear that she had come to regard the duke's cause as her own, and that they effectively acted as co-conspirators as they pressed Philip for assistance. Catalina sent Carlo a copy of her letter to Philip, and Carlo complimented her: "I like the letter that you have written to the king, which is very good."[86]

In August 1589, Henri III of France was assassinated, prompting Carlo (and others) to try to exploit the resulting political turmoil to seize French territory. Catalina was fully on board with Carlo's hoped-for land grab. Writing on 25 August, she urged him to write to Emperor

Rudolf II to gain his support, and in subsequent letters she advised Carlo not to wait for assistance from Spain because Philip and his ministers were notoriously slow to respond.[87]

To her father, Catalina wrote that Henri III's death was an opportunity she and Carlo had been waiting for and that Philip should now fulfill his promises to them. While leaving the specifics of these promises unstated, she evidently believed that Philip had pledged to help them secure territories in France, and she reminded him that the territory the duke wanted to seize was "better not to be in someone else's hands as much for Your Majesty's service as for the proximity of these territories [to the duke's lands]." The people of Provence favored the duke, she claimed, and wanted to be under his protection. She apologized to Philip for badgering him for assistance but reminded him that she and the duke had great needs and, most importantly, that they had four children. "I am most certain that Your Majesty, as one who sees how many children we have, and can grant us at once this favor in such a way that we will not cause further [burdens], will not fail to grant it to us."[88] Was she suggesting that one of her children might eventually inherit the disputed territory in Provence, but that for the time being Philip should help Carlo seize it?

Writing to the duke a day later, though, Catalina told him that he should not wait for help from nor rely too much on Spain. (In a letter of the following week she again told Carlo that he was right not to trust Spain or anyone else, because each had its own agenda.) She also noted the "coldness my father's ministers show toward helping us, especially in Provence."[89] Stopping short of blaming Philip himself, she shifted blame to his ministers.

Her letter of 30 August suggests that she found it tricky to write to her father (and his ministers) asking for favors, because after having written to Philip, she told Carlo that she had not known quite what to write because the duke had not returned Philip's letters to her and so "in business matters I have written [only] what I know." Then she added: "I have completely lost the shame in asking," and explained that she could find her way to asking for help only because "it is not for me alone but rather for so many of us." She noted how important it was for him to write to Philip and his ministers often, keeping them updated on his military operations, but in "such a way that they cannot hinder our business (*negozios*)."[90] Her letter to Carlo again highlights that she saw his campaigns as both her own and her children's as well, and also reveals her growing estrangement from Philip and hostility toward his ministers.

In subsequent months, she continued to complain to Philip about his ministers. In November 1589, frustrated that Spanish troops sent to help the duke had been recalled, she told her father that if the troops had remained, the duke would not have found himself in such difficult straits as he now was. It was a situation, she added, for "Your Majesty's ministers to stretch their arms out further" to help remedy.[91] In a letter to the duke, she added, bitterly, that while he and she were struggling and begging for Spanish assistance, Philip II and her sister and brother "are having themselves a good time in Aranjuez; only we are having a tough time."[92]

In October of that year the duke had made peace with the Swiss canton of Bern, which he had been assaulting, a peace allowing some religious freedom for Protestants but allowing Carlo in turn to concentrate on seizing Provence.[93] Although Philip began a letter of 26 November to Catalina by noting that he was pleased that Carlo had recovered territories he had previously lost, he went on to criticize the peace with Bern that Carlo had just concluded, telling Catalina that, as a Spanish *infanta*, she should have known better than to allow the duke to make religious concessions.[94] In response to this reprimand, she offered no apology, but chastised in turn, asserting that if Philip's ministers had helped Carlo, he would not have had to make concessions to the Bern Protestants.

Even as she defended Carlo, however, Catalina privately took up the issue of religion with him. She noted that she had told him that she, like her father, was against any religious concessions—that they were unallowable and resulted in a less honorable peace than she would have wanted. Over the course of several letters, she urged Carlo to repudiate the peace and defended herself when he accused her of being a warmonger. After explaining why the Bern peace was inadvisable, she added that she had given advice in something she did not understand, but that because "you think that I am in favor of war," she could well "give my vote in matters concerning it [war]." She desired peace but a peace to his advantage and which did not damage his reputation. "I am very glad that you think I am so brave and certainly I would be even more so if you had let me go to war. Someday I hope to go with you and you will know it [her bravery] and my not wanting a truce or a suspension of arms is because it seems to me that it cannot be done with your reputation [upheld]." A day later she wrote to him that, "even though you say that I want war up to the eyes (*quiero la guerra asta los ojos*), it [war] seems preferable to a peace that gives them that [religious concessions]."[95] In matters of religion, at least, she did not hesitate to tell Carlo, forcefully, when she disagreed with him.

She stopped short of blaming Carlo himself, however, instead suggesting that Don Jusepe was at fault for encouraging him to seek peace, and conceding that Carlo had been forced to make peace for lack of Spanish financial assistance. "Someday," she remarked, "Spaniards will repent of their lethargy and irresolution." She was losing patience with Spanish ministers, she continued a few days later, and could not understand why Philip and his advisers failed to assist them: "I would rather not have such a bad opinion of them to believe fully that they do not want us to increase [our territorial holdings], although they betray that so often through their deeds . . . I do not know why they should prefer to help others . . . [rather] than their children [Catalina and Carlo].[96] Catalina, belligerent and unused to defeat, found a scapegoat for her frustration in her father's ill-willed ministers.

CONSPIRACY IN CORRESPONDENCE

As one reads the correspondence between Philip and Catalina, it becomes clear that she and Carlo coordinated their letters to her father. She almost always sent the duke drafts (*minutas*) or copies of her letters to Philip, so that Carlo could shape his own letters to conform to what she had written. (The surviving drafts or copies of her letters to Philip are in Catalina's hand.[97]) In most cases, though, she sent her letters to Philip without waiting for the duke's approval, apologizing for doing so and summarizing the content of her letter.[98] On 3 November 1588, for example, she told the duke that she had written Philip a very short letter but had not been able to send the letter first to Carlo or inform him that she was writing to Philip, explaining that a courier carrying mail from Rome to Spain had been passing through Turin and that, as he could not be detained, she had written quickly to her father and sister. Summarizing the letter's contents, she told Carlo that she had written to Philip only that they were well, that the duke was "there" (in Saluzzo), and that fighting had commenced and was going so well that they expected it would soon be over.[99] As she was writing to Philip when Carlo was still consolidating his power over the marquisate and the duke was unable to vet her letter, she reassured him that nothing in it would in any way prejudice his campaign.

Nevertheless, writing to her father at other times about matters of critical importance, Catalina refrained from sending letters without clearing them first with the duke. In November 1590, concerned about the selection of a new pope, she sent Carlo a sealed letter she had written to her father, with an unsealed copy of the same letter for Carlo himself.[100] If he approved of the letter, she instructed him promptly to send the sealed original on to Philip, and if not, he could tear it up. She had sealed it, she explained, because he did not have her seal.[101] Often Catalina relied on Carlo to tell her how he would like her to respond to her father about political matters.[102] Preparing to write to Philip in April 1589, she asked the duke to return the letters Philip and Isabel had sent her, so she would know not only what to respond, but also to "tell me what I have to write so that it will correspond" to what the duke was writing.[103] On one occasion, she hastily sent Carlo copies of letters she had written to Philip and the Count de la Motta, Savoyard ambassador at the Spanish court, before the duke posted his own letters to Spain. "I have wanted to rush to send the copies . . . to see if there is something to add and so that we do not contradict each other."[104] She often reassured Carlo that "when I respond to my father, it will be as you have ordered me," or "today I have written to Spain conforming to what you ordered me."[105]

While Catalina's use of *mandar* (to command) suggests that Carlo was controlling her correspondence with Philip, other aspects of her letters indicate that the two were working in tandem. Her letter to Carlo of 9 April 1589, for example, contains a detailed report on her negotiations with Don Jusepe, who was agreeable to helping them and had told her that all Carlo needed were 2,000 Spanish soldiers. Capitalizing on Don Jusepe's good will, she had immediately urged him to write to Milan asking for the troops, explaining to Carlo: "I think that they [Don Jusepe and Terranova] will agree to give the aid that my father has promised out of fear that if they do not give this [assistance], you will do something [aggressive] elsewhere." She then encouraged Carlo to request this assistance (presumably by writing to Philip, as he did a week later, "very humbly" asking Philip "to order the governor of Milan to come to the rescue of my states") and only later in her letter did she mention that she was writing to Philip, as Carlo had ordered her.[106] Advising Carlo on how to negotiate with Spanish ministers, Catalina saw herself and the duke cooperating in their lobbying campaign, partly teamwork and partly conspiracy.

The duke occasionally sent Catalina draft letters to Philip for her approval. In late October 1588, while besieging Saluzzo, he wrote to Philip, but before dispatching the letter to Spain he sent it to Catalina for her comments. She responded that "the letter to my father is very good . . . there is no need for you to write another one."[107] Several months later, she told the duke that "when the occasion arises [for you] to write my father, I would not hesitate to tell him very clearly that [because of the urgency] this is not a time for talking," and two days later she told him he should write clearly (*claramente*) to her father.[108] In response, the duke told her he would soon write to her father and speak clearly, but in turn he advised her, "when you write to the king, I would complain a little more dispassionately (*con gran flema*), telling him that French matters are not as they think over there [in Spain]."[109] Two months later he sent her the letters to Philip that he had drafted, so that "you will write according to what you see in them."[110] Later the same month she again advised him on what he should write to her father: "I think it would be good for you to insist strongly with my father so that he will want to increase his aid and I will do the same by the post that is going by sea."[111]

Catalina and Carlo's correspondence over the years shows how they continued to coordinate their letters to Philip II so that he would receive essentially the same message from each. In April 1595, over six years after the Saluzzo campaign, she told Carlo that she was writing to her father according to what he had dictated, but two days earlier she had in turn advised him on how to alter a letter he was writing to Philip. Having read Carlo's drafts, she returned them to him with suggestions for two changes he should make.[112]

Such exchanges, just a few examples from their nine years of correspondence, illustrate Catalina and Carlo's cooperative system of negotiating with Philip and his ministers. She advised him regularly, he trusted her opinions, and they had similar goals. As her correspondence with Philip shows, her relationship with her father grew strained because of Carlo's aggressive and expansive ambitions. Philip had hopefully expected Catalina to restrain her eager husband, but rather than restraining him, she encouraged and abetted him, her letters to Philip detailing and justifying Carlo's ventures and laying blame on Philip's ministers for failing to support Carlo fully, if at all. She was not just mechanically following Carlo's instructions and writing to her father as the duke had dictated; she openly shared his ambitions and belligerence. By 1588, she and Carlo had forged a close bond, placing their interests and those of their children above those of Spain and her father.

GAINING CONFIDENCE

When Carlo departed Turin on 2 March 1589 to defend his territories in Savoy, he left Catalina, then seventh months pregnant, in charge. As with his departure for Saluzzo the year before, he left her with specific instructions, and writing to him the day after he left, Catalina told him that she would get started that day on everything he had ordered. She also told the duke that Don Jusepe had been to see her the previous evening, complaining that he had not been notified of the duke's departure, and that to appease him she had assured Don Jusepe that the duke had no intention of seizing territory without Philip II's approval. She also had talked with Domenico Belli, the duke's minister soon to depart for Spain, and with a councilor, Monseñor de la Cruz, and as she detailed the points of their discussion, she begged the duke to forgive her if she had erred, for the previous day was a "day to drive me crazy."

He reassured her of his support, writing, "My life. Do not worry about anything because all will go well despite the harpies of the council in Spain and I know well that it is not your fault."[113] Catalina had attacked political business on the very day of the duke's departure.

Her letters to the duke in March 1589, while he was campaigning in Savoy, reveal a growing self-confidence and comfort with her political responsibilities. She did not beg him to come home to relieve her of her duties, as she had the year before, and seems to have embraced her role as the duke's surrogate with much more assurance than during the previous autumn. In her letters she detailed her negotiations with councilors, relaying their opinions to the duke, and also described her meetings with Don Jusepe, the papal nuncio, and others. When one of the duke's new subjects in recently occupied Carmagnola spread the rumor that the people of Geneva had entered the duke's territories and "a thousand other lies," Catalina ordered him seized.[114]

Whereas in October she had asked the duke what to do with dispatching mail to Spain, Rome, and France, now, five months later, she wrote that she had opened the mail from Rome and read a letter from the duke's ambassador at the papal court. In subsequent days, she opened mail from Spain, read what was not in cypher, sent some to be deciphered so as to spare the duke this task, and then commented on what she had learned from the letters.[115] She also plotted to intercept letters that the French ambassador in Savoy was sending to France, informing the duke that she had set a spy to watch the ambassador's associates, and that the same spy had instructions to intercept the ambassador's outgoing mail and bring it to her.[116] (In July 1589, she in fact intercepted mail coming from Venice for the French ambassador in Turin and sent the letters to Carlo.[117]) She solicited funds from the communities of Mondovì and Val-d'Isère to support the duke's campaigns.[118] No longer a political novice reluctant to take control, Catalina had become a self-confident lieutenant efficiently and even aggressively fostering her husband's agenda.

Their correspondence shows how closely they worked together and re-enforced each other's decisions. Telling the duke that she had shown a deciphered letter to Don Jusepe, she asked Carlo to tell her which letters she could show to whom. Quickly responding, Carlo told her she had done well to share the letter with Don Jusepe and could also show it to a few specified councilors. He apologized for leaving her with so much work but then noted, in a pointed metaphor: "Whoever eats the sweet treats, such as those that you like, must also eat the bitter ones."[119] To what sweets in particular was Carlo referring? The bitter ones were no doubt the responsibilities he had delegated to her. Everything could be more easily borne, he added, if only they were together.

In a letter of 20 March 1589, Catalina informed the duke that letters from Spain had confirmed that, for now, Philip II declined to assist the duke in his quest to annex Provence. She criticized Philip's view of Carlo's plans and his failure to support them, stating that it pained her that "they act so coldly toward us" (*baya[n] tan secos con nosotros*). Her use of the first-person plural "us," especially vs. the third-person "they," closely identifying herself with the duke's goals, once again reveals her shift of loyalties. Nevertheless, she tried to explain to Carlo her father's view of Savoyard affairs, reminding him that Philip felt his resources overtaxed and feared that the duke's aggression in Provence would compromise Spain both financially and militarily. She reported on her negotiations with Don Jusepe, to whom, when he told her that Spain thought the duke over-trusted the pope, she responded that the duke would not let himself be fooled by the pope. Finally, she asked the duke's forgiveness for writing such an unpleasant letter and urged him to write to Philip. Had she said too much to Don Jusepe, she asked Carlo, and what should she write to her father if there were occasion to send mail? Several days later—still upset with her father—she told Carlo she was afraid Philip would not provide substantive assistance, which pained her because, she complained, "what good does it serve us to be his children?"[120]

With Carlo often absent from Turin after 1588, Catalina assumed some of his ceremonial functions for the first time. In March 1589, delegated to perform the investiture ceremony for two of the duke's councilors, she was worried, as she had never done an investiture and wondered if it were even appropriate for a woman to do so; she was particularly worried that the ceremony would require her to wield a sword. Looking for precedent so as not to violate local tradition, she did not ask the duke whether she should wield the ceremonial sword but rather made her own decision. She had the duke's advisers check whether earlier Savoyard duchesses had performed investitures and reported to Carlo that, having learned that not only his paternal grand-mother, the duchess Beatriz (who, like Catalina, had governed in her husband's absence), but many other duchesses as well had used a sword to invest men in office, she would do likewise.[121] After her first investi-ture, she joked with the duke that he would have laughed to see her wielding a sword, but a week later she joked with him that she was so comfortable "with the sword in my hand" that she had invested two other men with their office.[122]

Once again, Catalina had to learn what was expected of her, but she quickly accepted and even embraced her new responsibilities. Among the chief of these was consulting with the duke's councilors, securing their support, summarizing and sending each one's opinion (*parezer*) to him, and procuring supplies for the duke's military campaigns.[123] At one point she bragged to Carlo that one of his councilors had claimed that it was harder to do business with her than with the duke because she drove a harder bargain.[124]

Nevertheless, at times it was difficult to manage Carlo's councilors, and she knew they criticized her, as is evident in a letter from a year and a half after the investitures—August 1590—when his advisers were divided on whether Carlo should continue his assault on Provence. On that occasion, as she gathered all the councilors' opinions to send to Carlo and then had to express her own, she told him that she was reluc-tant to serve as the "judge" who would decide the issue. Mimicking what councilors might say and referring to herself in the third person, she wrote to Carlo that "the *infanta* will be blamed regardless" and that she did not want others to think that it was her emotions (*pasion*) that caused her to side with Carlo and support his assault on Provence. Rather, Carlo should continue, she advised, because his reputation was at stake.[125] Though she ended by apologizing if she had not expressed herself well, confessing that she was no rhetorician, her letter again demonstrates her decisiveness, her concern with Carlo's reputation, and her desire to use reason and not emotion to help guide him. Her letter also shows that Carlo's advisers knew (as did she) that he respected

Catalina's opinion and was likely to follow her advice, making her the "judge" in a particularly contentious matter.

ASSESSING CATALINA'S INFLUENCE

Within a year of being appointed lieutenant, Catalina had grown comfortable governing the duchy and elicited tributes of praise. Francisco de Vera, Philip II's ambassador to Venice, had stopped in Turin on his way to his post and commented on the *infanta*'s abilities.

> Her ability to negotiate is so gratifying that the most important ministers [in Turin], among them the Marquis Pallavicino, have assured me that never has the like been seen in these states, and they wish that her husband would imitate and retain this manner of negotiating. Because the lord duke had no specific day or hour for this, previously there was some disorder by making the busiest ministers wait two or three hours, at times notifying them that he could not attend to business that day, which resulted in much time wasted. Her Highness has reformed this, designating Mondays and Thursdays for signing (*la signatura*). She orders [those days] to begin promptly at 15 o'clock, that is three p.m. in Spain, and there she assigns and distributes [tasks] to the ministers according to the matters, petitions, and memorials given to her, assisted by the Grand Chancellor and the most principal ministers of state, justice, and government. They all say that Her Highness does everything with such good judgment and propriety, that she impresses them, as she resolves in such a prudent manner everything reserved for Her Highness. Those from Carmagnola were so satisfied with the response given them by Her Highness about a certain matter brought before her today, that [though] being so Francophile . . . they have said that they will be [her] perpetual slaves.[126]

Implicit in Vera's description was that Catalina had inherited Philip II's systematic character and profited from his methods, but he also was noting a sharp difference between Carlo's personality and Catalina's. To Vera and apparently to others, Catalina was a woman of business with a more decisive character and a more organized, predictable manner than the impetuous duke.

In March 1589, Don Jusepe reported to Francisco de Idiáquez, secretary for the Council of Italy, Philip's advisory council for matters in Italy, that Catalina governed to everyone's "great satisfaction," adding that because of the speed, wisdom, and "prudence" with which she saw to matters, both the populace and the duke's ministers preferred her to the duke. In short, Don Jusepe commented, she acted as would be expected of the "daughter of such a father" (who after his death would become known as "the prudent king"). Writing on the same day to Don Juan de Idiáquez, one of Philip II's closest ministers and Francisco's cousin, Don Jusepe reported that Catalina was a "great governor, giving rare satisfaction to everyone because she negotiates with steadiness and prudence."[127] Though not an impartial observer and seeking to present Catalina in a good light at the Spanish court, especially by comparing her to her father, he was not alone in his admiration.

Writing to the Venetian senate in September 1589, Francesco Vendramin, Venetian ambassador to Turin, noted the duke's great love for and reliance on Catalina. Because of the duke's military ventures, he had left Catalina in charge, and Vendramin observed that Catalina saw to all matters of state with prudence and wisdom, and that when the duke was in Turin and alone with her, moreover, he communicated all important matters of state to Catalina—as he did when apart via letters—and kept nothing secret from her. The duke wanted her to be in all conciliar meetings, and, according to Vendramin, it was widely known that when asked to express her opinion at these meetings, she did so prudently and excellently, demonstrating, Vendramin added, that she had greater knowledge of political matters than all the duke's councilors put together. He was not surprised because, after all, he noted, she had been raised in "the great school of her father," and the duke deferred to her in everything.[128] In September 1589, Catalina was a month shy of her twenty-second birthday, and yet she had come a long way from the young woman who in the fall of 1588 had seemed uncertain of assuming political authority.

At the end of December 1589, Carlo wrote to Catalina to report on a visit Don Jusepe had paid to him in his encampment in Savoy, noting gleefully that Don Jusepe had told him "the best things in the world about you and that you could govern not just that state [the duchy of Savoy] but the world." Carlo added that he knew Catalina's abilities "a hundred thousand times better" than Don Jusepe, and he went on to say that he wished only that Philip II would allow himself to be governed as well as Catalina governed, a comment that was probably a criticism of Philip's ministers more than of the Spanish king.[129] He concluded by saying that he was sending her beautiful tapestries that, like her, were one of the world's marvels.[130] Although Catalina thought that in saying she was a marvel he was teasing her, Carlo like Don Jusepe and Vendramin appreciated and admired Catalina's ability to govern effectively in his absence.[131] Even Philip II recognized Catalina's strengths. In December 1590, Mario Umolio, Savoyard ambassador to the court in Madrid, told Catalina that when Philip had read a letter from her, he was very pleased, proclaiming that it might have been written by a general.[132] Despite her unwillingness or inability to persuade Carlo to conform to Spanish designs, Philip recognized that his daughter, intelligent and shrewd, could manage the duke's territories in his absence.

These assessments of Catalina's abilities were obviously exaggerated, though Vera's description of the orderly routine she established was probably accurate: only by keeping to a strict schedule could she have devoted so much time to writing letters, attending religious services, and managing the care of the children, in addition to the political, governance, and quartermastering responsibilities that she assumed. She was conscious of her limitations. To the duke's words of praise, she responded that he deceived himself in thinking that she was "a woman of great governance, because I am not at all." People told the duke only what they thought he wanted to hear, she added, and lied about her abilities. In fact, she wanted Carlo never again to leave her governing anything.[133] As she had told him earlier, he was better with the reins of power than she.[134] Regardless of these self-deprecating comments, which suggest that Catalina did not enjoy governing, she proved herself an effective and decisive lieutenant in Carlo's absences—and in the nine years between his seizure of Saluzzo and her death, he was absent from Turin far more than he was present.

CHAPTER 6

FLOWERS, PORTRAITS, AND BANNERS
Conveying Affection and Missing Intimacy

*I do nothing but cry all night finding myself without you and tonight I
have slept embracing your letter.*

Catalina to Carlo, 22 October 1588

WHEN CATALINA MARRIED CARLO in April 1585, she had met him only
the day before. She must have wondered whether, at best, she would
even like the total stranger she was marrying, perhaps never expecting
to develop a truly amorous bond with him. Yet Catalina and Carlo
would grow to love each other, and by the time Carlo left on military
campaign in 1588, they were enjoying an intimate and even passionate
marriage.

How can one evaluate intimacy in an early modern marriage? Our
expectations of marriage have changed so completely from the early
modern period that it is difficult to understand how couples back then
approached marriage and how they articulated affection and desire.
The letters of Catalina and Carlo give us a means to evaluate how
one sixteenth-century couple expressed affection, passion, and sexual
longing. While they might well have been employing conventional
rhetoric of expressing emotions, the frequency with which they articulated their longing for each other, as well as specific details they provided
about their married life, argue strongly that they enjoyed their intimate
and loving bond, both emotionally and physically. Their actions as well
as their letters attest to their desire to be together. She, in particular,

seems to have loved Carlo passionately and missed his company, even counting the days she was apart from him, but Carlo, too, despite his frequent preoccupation with his military campaigning, seems to have cared deeply for Catalina. Missing their sexual intimacy, he made efforts to return to her as often as possible.

In Catalina and Carlo's case, perhaps one could say that having ten children in thirteen years of marriage would offer patent evidence of eager intimacy, but their numerous offspring might also indicate simply abundant fertility and Catalina's not breastfeeding her newborns. Moreover, in an age when many children failed to survive to adulthood, aristocratic couples strove to produce numerous children in order to have an heir and backups. Some women, such as Catalina's paternal aunt, Empress María, gave birth to even more children than did Catalina—sixteen, in nineteen years of marriage. Empress María's cousin, Joanna of Austria (1547–1578), wife of Francesco I de' Medici, Grand Duke of Tuscany, gave birth to eight children in eleven years, even though her husband preferred the company of his mistress, by whom he fathered a son.[1] Joanna herself was the youngest of fifteen. While Catalina and Carlo were at least as fertile as most of their contemporaries, their many children do not alone indicate marital happiness.

But we can begin to document Catalina and Carlo's affectionate relationship by examining what others around them reported, and such observers unanimously claimed that they enjoyed a loving marriage. In 1589, Francesco Vendramin, Venetian ambassador to Turin, reported that the duke "loves her [Catalina] infinitely . . . and she reciprocates with most tender demonstrations of affection toward the duke, who has never up until now abandoned her either with his person or his eyes until the present war; and until the time of the duke's departure for Savoy, they have continuously demonstrated this reciprocal love so warmly, that those who observed these signs judged them to be [signs of] passionate love rather than merely dutiful signs of matrimonial affection." Another Venetian ambassador, Fantino Corraro, writing in 1598, after Catalina's death, remarked that he did not think that "any wife had found a husband who pleased her more nor would it be possible to find a married couple more united and more in accord."[2] These two Venetian ambassadors had frequented the court in Turin, regularly meeting with Catalina and Carlo, and would have been in a good position to observe their interaction. They would also have been privy to court gossip and would not have hesitated to report any rumors of marital discord.

Spanish officials in Turin also noticed that Catalina and Carlo were very happy together. Don Jusepe de Acuña gave Philip II and his ministers regular updates on Catalina, Carlo, and their children. Detailing the first time that Catalina had gone out in public after the birth of her third son, Don Jusepe wrote that she was an "extremely beautiful, plump, and noble woman, who does not seem just to have gone through such labor [childbirth]. She appeared in a very dignified purple and white dress . . . and the duke in the same fashion; their marriage is such that they can be an example for others." As Catalina's *mayordomo mayor*, Don Jusepe accompanied her to Nice in 1592 and remarked how happy Catalina and Carlo were to be together again after not having seen each other for seventeen months. He noted that he did not have much to report about them because for five days after the duke's arrival, they had secluded themselves, "delighting in being able to converse alone."[3] (Nine months later, to the day, she gave birth to her son, Mauricio.) Several months later he reported that they continued greatly to enjoy themselves and described a boat outing Carlo had organized for Catalina and her ladies. When the now-pregnant Catalina grew seasick from the rough water, Don Jusepe added, Carlo gallantly held a basin for her. Back on land she recovered, and after a full day of visits and festivities, Catalina and Carlo returned to their lodgings "happy and tired, and they went to bed at 10 p.m.," which was evidently unusually early for them.[4]

Another Spanish official, the count of Fuentes, who en route to Flanders stopped in Nice to convey a message from Philip II to Carlo, also reported that it was good to see how happy and compatible Catalina and Carlo were. When she suffered from a fever in Nice for twenty-four hours, Don Jusepe commented that, from previous experience, he thought it was due to her pregnancy, but also added, "it is caused by the life they lead of so much love," apparently alluding to the couple's frequent and eager lovemaking. He made this comment in a letter to Juan de Idiáquez, one of Philip II's closest advisers, but to Philip himself

Don Jusepe ascribed Catalina's fever more vaguely to "the changes which she usually experiences when in the duke's company."[5]

Fortunately, we do not have to rely only on second-hand accounts of Catalina and Carlo's relationship because we have their extensive correspondence, which gives us the best evidence for believing that their marriage was not only harmonious but amorous. Catalina and Carlo frequently articulated their longing for each other, documenting their feelings and affection. When analyzing the emotions which the ducal couple expressed in their letters, we need to keep in mind rhetorical and epistolary conventions. We should be careful, for example, not to take at face value hyperbolic expressions of affection in their salutations, because they were sometimes or often conforming to standard epistolary models. Catalina and Carlo also employed conventional expressions of affection in the text of their letters.

Carlo even addressed the issue of rhetorical convention in a letter of December 1595, when he told Catalina that "without you there is no joy or good" and quickly added that "this is not rhetoric but rather pure truth that comes from the interior of the heart."[6] While Carlo's comments do not prove that his proclamations of affection for Catalina were genuine, they nonetheless indicate that he recognized that Catalina might suspect him of insincerity and wanted to reassure her that he meant what he wrote. In this case, after spending five months in Turin with Catalina, he had just left to visit sanctuaries and hermitages in the mountains around the city, while she, feeling unwell, remained behind. In her own letter, written the same day and before she received Carlo's, she lamented that "you have left me, my soul, very alone," and told him to hurry back because nights without him were very lonely.[7]

Catalina, too, addressed the issue of epistolary sincerity, telling Carlo that she believed his expressions of love were true and that she in turn would not embellish her love for him with florid rhetoric. In a letter of 1595, she told Carlo that "I can see well that [the words in your letter] are not words of flattery since I know how much you love me, and I am in such a state that I do not know how to say even rhetorical [words], but I believe you know my will and spirit and you are not gaining on me in feeling lonely and I am eagerly awaiting news of being able to see you."[8] Such affirmations indicate that both Catalina and Carlo, aware of the limitations and unreliability of "written" love, tried to break through those barriers to maintain their loving bond, in turn allowing us years later to understand how they cultivated affection and intimacy at a distance.

GIFTS AND TOKENS

Catalina and Carlo's correspondence documents their affectionate relationship in several concrete ways and provides evidence that their marriage went far beyond mere political convenience. I begin not with their written expressions of affection but rather with the gifts and tokens of affection mentioned in and sent with their letters. The references to gifts are almost too numerous to cover, but certain categories in particular suggest their mutual regard and demonstrate how Catalina and Carlo showed their affection for each other from afar.

"I have had these preserves made from the citrons from Nice and because you like their taste, I am sending them to you."[9] Preserves were only one of the many edibles which Catalina and Carlo sent each other. Among the foods she sent him were pheasants, marzipan, crawfish (*langostinos*), blood sausage, wild boar, and melons, the latter because she knew Carlo loved them.[10] She sent him artichokes and oranges that had come from Nice.[11] When sending him pheasants (*faysanotes*—she used a Portuguese word) in July 1596, she cut short her letter that accompanied them so that they would arrive in time for his evening meal.[12] Carlo in turn sent her *gámbaros azules* (a type of small crawfish), trout, citrons, and game that he had hunted, such as wild boar.[13] Once she thanked him for pork empanadas (*enpanadas del puerco*—most likely from a boar he had hunted) and another time she sent him a sweet milk bread (*pan de leche*) and a ring-shaped roll (*rosca*).[14] Occasionally, Catalina took what Carlo had sent her—such as the citrons mentioned earlier—and had them cooked into preserves, pastries, or a pie and then sent Carlo the finished product. In this way, she reciprocated Carlo's gifts.[15] Like other gifts, food was intended to remind the receiver of the giver, and in Catalina and Carlo's case, food was one of the ways they showed their affection. When she sent him preserves, citrons, and quince in December 1592, she noted that she did so because Carlo ate them regularly and she knew he would enjoy them.[16] Sending food they knew the other liked demonstrated that they were thoughtfully catering to the other's needs and tastes.

Sending him food that she thought beneficial for his health, Catalina solicitously nursed him from afar. Specific foods were thought to be good for particular problems, so when Carlo complained of a stomach upset in June 1589, Catalina sent him preserves made from the flower of a lemon or orange tree in their garden because she had heard that it was good for digestive ailments.[17] Learning that he was suffering from thirst and lack of appetite, she sent him a *búcaro* (a clay pitcher) to hold water. (Thought to have medicinal purposes, the clay perfumed the water, and court women acquired the habit of eating the actual *búcaro*.) She also sent him pomegranates and lemons for his health.[18] When she sent him sweet bread (*pan dulce*) in April 1596, Carlo replied that he thought it would be good for his digestion.[19] She worried that on his campaigns he did not take care of himself and did not eat well or regularly. Believing that food was the culprit for some of Carlo's occasional maladies, Catalina told him, "I am very sorry not to be at your dinners to serve as doctor because I believe that if I were there, you would have no [illness]."[20]

Food could even serve as a stand-in for the other when they were apart, and when Catalina celebrated Epiphany without Carlo in January 1593, she insisted on sending him a few chicks (*pollas*) because "I do not like anything which I cannot share with you."[21] On another occasion, she shared Bergamot pears that she had been given and enjoyed.[22] One time she sent him a dessert (*espejuelos*) made from citrons from Nice, timing its arrival for his evening meal. She commented that she wanted to share the dessert with him not only because it was delicious but also because it would taste good only if she could enjoy it with him.[23] (And in this case, she and Carlo were geographically close enough that she could share prepared food with him.[24])

Catalina also sent him produce from their gardens in and around Turin, as in May 1593, when she sent him asparagus from Valentino, their rural estate, even though she was unsure they would arrive fresh.[25]

As she explained in a letter of April 1596: "I am sending you these slices [of sweet bread] which tasted good to you the other day, and you can repay me with sweets from there [Mondovì, where the duke was visiting the shrine]. I am also sending you these asparagus, which though few, you will [still] receive the goodwill with which they are sent."[26] Other gifts included fish pies made of fish from the Po, which ran through Turin, and apples from their garden. "So that you can see how pretty the garden is," she explained, "I am sending you these apples that come from our tree in front of the windows. They were very ripe so I had them cooked because so many were falling but there were still many that were good so I am sending these for you to try."[27] The thought behind the gift of food was as important as the food itself, as Catalina mentioned, but such gifts must have taken on extra meaning when they evoked memories of their shared life—Valentino, their gardens, the Po.

Sending these items to the duke, Catalina did not refer to them as gifts, even if we would understand them as such today. She would have said she was regaling him, or treating him regally. From the adjective *regalado* or the verb *regalar* comes *regalo*, modern Spanish for "gift." In early modern Spain, *regalar* (to regale) was used to denote caring for someone's corporal needs. The sixteenth-century Spanish lexicographer Sebastián de Covarrubias (1539–1613) defined a person who is *regalada* as one who is "given the delicacies which kings can have and is treated with particular care, diligence, and pleasure, especially in food."[28] In the late sixteenth century, therefore, *regalar* had a direct connection to caring for the material well-being of another, and when Catalina and Carlo sent each other food, they were treating each other regally. She used variations of the word *regalar* often in her letters to him. When apart, she frequently bemoaned her inability to pamper him, writing in October 1592: "God knows how I wish I were there to care for you (*regalarte*)." A week later she noted how sorry she was not to be with the duke and serving him, "because I know that no one there is concerned with your care (*regalo*)."[29] Gifts of toothsome or healthful foods were a gustatory language of affection, more tangible than words.

Catalina and Carlo exchanged more than edible gifts. Many of their gifts to each other were devotional in nature—rosaries, medals, relics, images, ribbons that had touched the Shroud, and other articles that had touched other relics.[30] She sent him a ring that had been rubbed against the skull and finger bone of St. John, for example, and a ribbon that had touched the statue of Our Lady of Savigliano, reportedly endowed with miraculous powers.[31] During Holy Week in 1592, Catalina sent Carlo crosses she had made from palm branches.[32]

They exchanged animals. Sharing her love of exotic species, the duke sent her a dark parrot (which, Catalina reported, would not stop talking) and a monkey that he had acquired in southern France.[33] Catalina, for her part, sent him a pony that had been given to her; she had been told that it ran like a Spanish horse and did not fear harquebuses, she explained, hoping he would like it.[34] Gift exchange was typical of early modern aristocratic culture, and Habsburg women excelled at the practice. For Catalina and Carlo, though, a regular exchange of thoughtfully chosen articles went beyond mere convention.

Catalina and Carlo also sent each other many different varieties of flowers, and while we should not necessarily assume that all the flowers had romantic significance in a few specific cases they clearly did. They had several gardens—one adjacent to their palace in Turin, another in Miraflores, and another in Valentino—and had these carefully cultivated and maintained. (Catalina occasionally used the term *jardin*, which is an ornamental garden, but more often *guerta* [i.e., *huerta*], which would translate more generally as "grounds" or "park.") Their love of their gardens resembled that of Philip II for his gardens in Aranjuez and Aceca, and Carlo, with a keen interest in botany, collected varied, striking, and rare specimens.[35] He made an effort to cultivate a mix of flower varieties in his gardens for both ornamental and botanical interest.[36] His library included an album of detailed drawings of flowers, including several varieties of lilies and orchids.[37] When away from Turin, Carlo reminded Catalina to check on their gardens and also urged her to take exercise by walking to the gardens next to the palace, and she responded by keeping him up to date on the state of their estates. In March 1589, for example, she wrote to him: "I do not want to fail to give you updates on our household tasks (*menajes de casa*) so you will not think me careless. I sent Bernardin to Miraflor to see what is needed . . . and he says it is full of daisies and all the flowers of Constantinople are beginning to come out."[38]

Catalina, too, loved gardens and flowers. She had grown up visiting her father's estates at Aranjuez and Aceca, known for their carefully designed and tended gardens, Aranjuez in particular, and when Carlo visited Spain in 1592, she urged him to visit these places. She incorporated floral designs into her attire. A portrait of her as a young girl, painted by Sofonisba Anguissola, shows her holding a marmoset and wearing a flower in her hair (see plate 4), and Catalina favored hair adornments in the shape of flowers. The inventory of her possessions drawn up shortly after her death contains a separate category listing twenty-four floral hair decorations. These items, richly made of gold and incorporating diamonds, pearls, rubies, and emeralds, included two entries for flowers "of perfect love"—most likely tulips, which symbolized deep and perfect love.[39] In a portrait of Catalina by the court painter El Flamenco, she wears a diadem decorated with "flowers" made of jewels (see plate 7).

Catalina sent Carlo flowers occasionally to satisfy his interest in his gardens and their rare specimens. In September 1590 she sent him a blossom (*azahar*) from a *naranjilla* because "it is surprising that there are any now" (and the flower is still preserved today with the letter). In July 1595, she sent him a rose from their garden because it was unusual; it had emerged from another rose whose petals were already withering, and Catalina described the new flower as "*estrabagante*," or rare.[40] She also sent flowers as proof that she had actually been to the garden (and taken exercise in doing so), as she explained in April 1589: "To obey you, my heart, I have gone this afternoon to the garden and as tokens (*señas*), I am sending you these narcissi of the Constantinople type. All the flowers are coming out, [though] some do not seem to have the stem that they are supposed to have."[41]

In at least one instance, Carlo sent flowers with their bulbs to Catalina to have planted in their garden. In May 1593, as he prepared to fight the French close to Exilles, he wrote to Catalina telling her of the beautiful meadows that he had crossed, filled with narcissi and lilacs. The flowers seemed so beautiful to him that he could not resist gathering and sending some, still in dirt, to Catalina, especially because "they are of the color you like and I like too." She had them planted immediately, and responded, "I have never seen anything so pretty . . .

those meadows must be very pretty with so many narcissi."[42] Flowers from bulbs, such as wild narcissi, were highly appreciated by collectors, and the album of flowers in Carlo's library included drawings of narcissi.[43] The flowers he sent for their gardens illustrate the idea that these were *their* gardens—a locus of shared interest and memories.

Whereas Carlo gathered flowers from places he visited, Catalina sent them from their own garden, and they must have reminded Carlo of home and of her. In March 1589, for example, she sent him hyacinths "from the ones which we planted here in our garden and also in Miraflor," adding, "I am very sorry that you cannot have the pleasure of gathering them as you have these other years." In March 1595, she wrote to him telling him that the hyacinths in their garden were beginning to bloom, and she sent him the first of these highly fragrant flowers.[44] (Covarrubias reports that apothecaries made a confection with hyacinths that was supposed to comfort and cheer the heart. Did hyacinths have this connotation for Catalina and Carlo?) Flowers from their gardens were tangible signs of their life together in Turin and often accompanied other demonstrations of affection. So, for example, in November 1588, she wrote to Carlo: "My life, don't forget me because I am all yours and I will not sleep tonight because I cannot sleep without my life as I had expected, but the thought that I will tomorrow sustains me. I send you this violet which is the first that I have seen this year, though it will fade before you see it as you open the letter."[45] A violet in November, enclosed in a letter with expressions of sorrow at not sleeping with him, and calculated to greet him when he opened the letter, was far removed from being merely a botanical specimen. Perhaps violets had a deeper meaning for Catalina and Carlo, a meaning now lost to us, but she must also have sent it for its simple beauty and its associations with the garden and life she shared with Carlo in Turin.

In early March 1589, Catalina and Carlo sent each other flowers, but in this case, they were part of an exchange of letters suggesting that the flowers might have romantic significance. Catalina and Carlo had been together for the better part of January and February 1589, and shortly after he departed again in early March she tried to express how much she missed him. "Your letter was received with as many tears as go with this one," she told him, and "I hardly sleep and am always either crying or dreaming of you."[46] She also sent him oysters and cauliflower, knowing they would be unavailable in the mountains he was crossing, and he thanked her, saying they were "great."[47] She also responded to a verse (*copla*) he had written, joking about its authorship, and apologizing for her own response. Carlo's verse read as follows:

Memoria sirba a mi bida,
estas memorias qu[e] enbio,
pues la memoria es mi bida,
y es la memoria el mal mio.

Memory serves my life
These memories which I send,
Since the memory is my life
And memory is what ails me.

Catalina responded with her own verse:

No son menester memorias,
por tenerla de mi bida,
pues lagrimas son las memorias,
que me dejo con su ida.

Memories are not necessary
To remember my life
Since tears are the memories
Which he left me when he departed.[48]

A day after sending him the *copla*, she told him she was glad to hear that he had crossed the mountains and enjoyed such good weather, which "we also have here," but added that she was upset he had not taken her with him. Several days later she again complained that she could do nothing but think of Carlo and could hardly hide her sorrow. In addition to the letters, *coplas*, and edibles, she sent flowers.[49]

Responding to Catalina's letters, Carlo tried to express his own yearnings, telling her that "I do not know how I live without my life," and "at least absence does not cause one to forget . . . and I firmly believe that it will not until death separates our lives and even afterward I am certain it will not be able to because our souls are such friends that neither absence nor oblivion can find room there." He thanked Catalina for all she had sent, including the flowers, and in turn sent her flowers he had gathered from the fields, "so that you see that the weather here is better than there." Carlo might have claimed that the flowers were his way of showing that he, too, was enjoying good weather, but more than a meteorological report, the flowers were also a token of his affection for Catalina and an attempt to assuage her sorrow at his parting. In turn, she let him know that she valued the flowers precisely because he had personally gathered them for her and had touched them. Receiving them, she fixed them in her hair because "they came from your hand."[50]

As her comment shows, items the other had touched took on additional meaning for the recipient. In March 1591, the duke sent her a rosary from Marseilles, "which looked pretty to me . . . I beg you to remember me when you pray it." She responded that she would continue to wear it on her arm, though she needed nothing to remind her of him because she thought of him constantly.[51] At the end of September 1594, for an unexplained reason, the duke sent Catalina his rosary. Had he broken it and sent it for repair? Did he want the papal legate, visiting Turin at the time, to bless it? Or did he want Catalina to touch it to the Shroud when she arranged for the legate to see the holy cloth, as he did the day of his visit? Regardless, Catalina returned the rosary the next day, telling him that she had spent the night with it.[52]

These tokens, none of which seems to have been costly in price, gained value by having been touched or worn by the other, and they were meant to remind each of the other. On a rosary she was returning to him, she attached a small cross she had brought with her from Spain, telling him that though the cross was old, she wanted him to have something of hers to prompt him to think of her when he prayed. Likewise, when given a ring by a Franciscan friar peddling handmade religious images, she delayed in sending it to Carlo for a few days, explaining that she had worn it for those days but was now sending it to him "so that you will remember me when you wear it because I always want you to have me in mind as I do [you]." On another occasion, she sent the duke a cross which a Capuchin father had given her, asking him to put it on his rosary and think of her. In January 1590, the duke sent her a ring he had bought because he found it pretty, explaining that "I send it to you as a token (*prenda*) of my coming arrival."[53]

Catalina also sent Carlo objects she had made herself, including sashes (*bandas*), a sheath for a dagger (*bandilla*), and a cord (*cordon*) for the insignia he wore as a member of the Order of the Golden Fleece.[54] In the latter case, she admitted that because it had been made by her, it was not very good. She also made Carlo pouches (*bolsas*; *bolsillos*), one to hold a cross of St. Mauricio, another to hold his winnings from gambling. She sewed crosses of St. Mauricio on tunics which she sent to Carlo to wear in battle. She sent him a small sash "which I have made from the remnants of a veil that I made for Our Lady of Loreto, all by hand, so that you will not think I am lazy."[55] Because handmade gifts, like handwritten letters, took dedicated time and effort, they were tangible tokens of esteem and affection. Sending a handsome gift to Carlo, she almost always noted that she hoped it would remind him of her. Of a sash she made him in 1590, she wrote, "remember me when you wear it." Sending him a needlework sash to wear with the Golden Fleece *insignia*, she explained, "so that you will remember me." The duke in return told her that he kissed her hand "a hundred thousand times" for the band she had made him to wear on his hat (*banda del sombrero*).[56]

Like a chivalrous knight courting his lady, Carlo sent Catalina banners or standards (*banderas*) from his military victories as well as detailed reports about the battles. The captured banners were tokens of his victories and by extension his military prowess (with perhaps a suggestion too of sexual prowess). When he seized Carmagnola in late September 1588, he sent a captured banner, and she reported, "I have the banner here in my room." A month later he sent her another standard "which we have taken." In April 1589, he sent her a banner with a fleur-de-lis, which she thought a good omen for victory against French troops in Savoy and Provence. In October 1589, along with thanks for sending a messenger to give her a full account of a victory in Provence (which Carlo had modestly described as "unbelievable and unimaginable"), she thanked him for the banners taken in the battle.[57]

In July 1593, Carlo sent her "the banner that we have taken," and she thanked him, adding that it now hung in his rooms with all the rest.[58]

Catalina, in turn, made banners for him to carry into battle, designed according to his instructions, and in at least one case he told her he wanted her colors (white, yellow, and purple) on them.[59] Wearing his lady's colors into battle, Carlo again followed a chivalric tradition, and Catalina employed her sewing skills to help him do so. By making the banners and sending them to Carlo, she took part vicariously in his victory, and she was overjoyed to hear that "our standards" were flying from the tower of the fortress in Revello.[60]

Gifts often elicited emotional responses. When Catalina sent Carlo a series of gifts in February 1591—a sheath for his sword which had been touched to relics, a piece of a bell (*pedaso de la campanilla*), a silk ribbon (*listón*), images, medals, a tunic, and a sash that she had sewn—the duke responded "I have received everything as if from the hand of her who sends it and not without many tears." On another occasion, receiving a sash she had made, he told her that he kissed her hand a hundred thousand times, adding "if it was made drenched in tears, it will be worn with perpetual weeping because I am without my life and every time that I look at it, my [tears] will wash it." Carlo liked to be dramatic, and his hyperbole can certainly not be taken literally, but Catalina's gifts, especially those touched or made by her, plainly had sentimental value for the duke. When in January 1591 she failed to send him a bracelet made from her own hair as she had promised, he urged her to send it because "you promised it to me so long ago and it seems to me that if I had it, I would be protected from all disasters."[61] Personalized gifts provoked strong emotions. In embodying the giver's affection, a gift could occasionally even be regarded as a talisman, as Carlo's comment about Catalina's hair bracelet suggests.

Letters themselves were gifts, prompting tears of joy. Catalina and Carlo thanked each other profusely for writing and both reported themselves weeping when they received the other's letters. As gift-giving among equals usually was reciprocal, so letters were also by nature reciprocal, requiring a reply.[62] Catalina reported several times that she had slept all night embracing his letter, suggesting that occasionally letters could also take on erotic suggestions.[63]

PORTRAITS

Portraits figured prominently among the gifts Catalina and Carlo exchanged. Like modern photographs, portraits provided an image of an absent person and helped keep that person visually present to the viewer. While portraits do not themselves indicate affection, they were a means to promote tenderness and love. Carlo, like other aristocratic men, relied on portraits to evaluate the physical appearance of a prospective bride, and as a married couple, he and Catalina used them to bridge the miles sometimes separating them.[64] Early modern portraits undoubtedly followed numerous iconographic conventions and had layers of symbolic meaning, but for Catalina and Carlo, portraits were the closest they could come to being physically present to each other when they were far apart, so that ideally a portrait should recognizably capture each other's likeness and bearing. Receiving a portrait of Catalina in October 1588, the duke told her that he had tearfully received "the prettiest portrait that one could see," but added that she looked thinner and less pretty than she was.[65] (Carlo had been gone so long he had forgotten her expression, Catalina responded, though it had been only fifteen days since they had last seen each other.) A week earlier she had written that she was pleased to see Carlo's expression in a portrait of him that she carried with her and was glad that it looked somewhat like him.[66] When Carlo traveled to Spain in 1591, Catalina instructed him to return with portraits of her family, and his court painter El Flamenco followed the duke to the Spanish court to execute the portraits. When she received that of her sister, whom she had not seen in six years, Catalina remarked that she had changed a great deal. She saw the painting as an almost photographic image of her sister—an accurate means of evaluating her appearance. These family portraits were not necessarily valued for mastery of technique, but rather for the artist's ability to capture the likeness and character of his or her subject. Portraits were sometimes updated to show how a person's appearance had changed over time.

Catalina's and Carlo's comments about these portraits suggest how early modern Europeans used them to foster and maintain affection. She sent him portraits not just of herself but also of their children, even her newborns. In fact, she delayed sending El Flamenco to Spain in 1591 until after she had given birth to her daughter Isabel so that he could paint the infant's portrait. Catalina talked of the portraits as if they were portable manifestations of herself and her children. Telling the duke that El Flamenco was now on his way with the portraits to Spain, she wrote, "we are all going and very true-to-life (*naturales*) and I have detained him until now so that the newborn could go."[67] She also playfully referred to her own image in the third person, as if it were another person. Sending him her portrait in late November 1589, she commented that "I am sending you the portrait . . . of a lady of whom I am very jealous because I know you want to see her as much as [you want to see] me, and she is very altered since you last saw her. I do not say who it is so you can guess." Carlo commented on this portrait in a similar fashion, saying, "the woman whom you have sent me is here with me smiling and certainly I have great desire to see her."[68] On other occasions Catalina commented that the portraits were going to "pay a visit" to the duke, as in October 1588: "I have wanted to send you this visit," meaning that she and the children in the form of portraits were visiting the duke. The portraits took her place (or that of the children), and on more than one occasion she said she longed in turn to take the place of the portrait. In March 1589, when preparing to send several portraits to Carlo, she commented, "I do not want you to be satisfied with the portraits without their owners [i.e., Catalina and her children] going with them. I envy them [the portraits] greatly."[69] She also claimed to worry that the duke would find so much comfort in portraits that he would see no need to return to Turin: "I do not like to send so many portraits because I fear you will postpone seeing me and I wish I were the one going."[70] Carlo, however, insisted that portraits had the opposite effect, making him realize how much he missed her, and "every time I see it, I remember to return [to see you]." Catalina responded that she hoped that "my portrait [will] serve as the means of you remembering me."[71]

The placement of portraits also indicates how they were used to keep the memory of an absent person alive, and both Catalina and Carlo claimed that portraits of each other sustained them. Upset at "not being with my life in bed" and spending so many hours of the night thinking about Carlo, Catalina told him that she took comfort in "a large portrait of you that I have here in my bedroom (*aposento*) because I cannot be without seeing my life." (Carlo responded that she did the large portrait a great honor and he was jealous, apparently because the portrait was with Catalina in her bedroom.[72]) This portrait of Carlo seems to have been the same one she would describe as hanging above the writing desks in front of her bed, allowing her to see the duke not only when she awakened, but also when writing to him. In addition to the portrait above the desks, Catalina carried two smaller portraits of the duke with her.[73] One of these might have been "a very pretty portrait of you that El Flamenco has done on the reverse of the Christ made of lapis which you gave me."[74] Similarly, Carlo had portraits of Catalina in different sizes where he could readily see them. The ones she sent him of her and the children might have been large enough to hang on a wall but must also have been small enough to move from one military encampment to another. Others were even smaller, such as, for example, the portrait of herself that Catalina sent Carlo inside a *libro de memoria*, a blank memoranda book, which must have been small and easily carried.[75] Portraits such as this, or that of Carlo on the reverse of the lapis cross, allowed them to keep an image of the other physically close, even allowing them to touch the portrait. The lapis cross with Carlo's portrait on the reverse combined religious and marital devotion, making Carlo's image a sort of icon.

We think of portraits as objects of art to be looked at and admired, but early modern people interacted with artwork in sometimes unexpected ways. A beloved statue might be painted or dressed, and like many early modern Catholic women, Catalina sewed veils and clothing for Marian statutes.[76] As portraits took the place of people, it is not surprising that both Carlo and Catalina admitted to talking with the portraits.[77] Recovering from being bled because of an illness in July 1589, she told him that she thought his absence was the cause of her malady, and she said, "I am here looking at your portrait that I have in front of me and I speak often with it and this is how I pass the time." Carlo in turn talked to her portrait: "My life, do not forget me because I love you so much that I do not know how to express it. I am all yours and if I did not have your portrait, I do not know how I would do it [survive] because even if it does not respond to what I tell it, it still alleviates the sorrow, because I think that the one whom I love most in the world is here." Catalina responded that she also talked to his portrait as much as the duke talked to hers, and she said, "you do me a great favor to write me these things and they are not follies but rather consolation because I do likewise."[78]

Carlo might even have used Catalina's portrait to keep himself chaste. In the same letter in which he told her that he talked to her portrait, he also told her that he was desperate to conclude his military campaign (in Provence) in order to see her, strongly hinting that he desired her sexually: "I can no longer be without you and at night I wake up a hundred thousand times and I do not find you there . . . and I need to tell you that after these difficulties with the enemy's armies, I have not corrupted myself and I look at you and this is the way it is and you can see that my head is full of troubles."[79] Evidently feeling sexually frustrated, Carlo suggested that looking at Catalina's portrait gave him the ability to resist temptation. Having her image in view allowed him to talk with it until he could feel himself actually with his wife. In responding, Catalina noted that "I die for you" and that only by looking at his portraits did she get some relief. A few days later she told him, "I wake up every hour of the night and time passes as I look at your portrait because now I have your bed with valances and I can see it [your portrait] and this is my consolation."[80] Catalina, who repeatedly told Carlo that nights were endless and lonely without him, was sleeping in his bed (probably because of the summer heat) and able to see Carlo's image while lying down.[81] His portrait helped her cope with his absence, as hers helped him handle sexual abstinence. By providing tangible likenesses of a loved one, portraits could even provide sexual comfort for spouses who were far apart.

FAMILIARITY

While Catalina's and Carlo's letters document the material ways that she and Carlo demonstrated and maintained their affection, they also allow us to glimpse their emotional affinity, as observed by the Venetian ambassador and the count of Fuentes. By 1588, after three years of marriage, they knew each other well and were very comfortable with each other. Much as she knew what food he enjoyed and he knew what gifts she would like, they knew each other's opinions about a range of topics and they shared private jokes. They seem to have kidded, for example, that Catalina was not an early riser, which she cheerfully acknowledged: "And so that you see that I get up early, I am telling you that today after the sermon and before eating, I went to San Lorenzo and the *beluarte* (bulwark), and with all of that it struck noon at the end of the meal, and so you will not always blame me [for getting up late]." When their daughter Margarita was born in April 1589, the duke joked that if she looked like him, she would be ugly; in response, sending him a portrait of the girl, she noted: "You will see if she is ugly and I am very annoyed that you say that if she looks like you, she will be [ugly] . . . you deserve a slap because you have no reason to say so."[82]

Perhaps Catalina was making fun of Carlo's love of pets or his scientific interest in birds when she sent him pheasants on condition that he eat them and not keep them as "guests." She noted that she knew he would laugh at this comment.[83] When she told him that their dog Orianica had given birth to five pups, she added facetiously, "you won't say that I do not give you important news."[84] When in July 1591 she told him about a baptism that had taken place at the cathedral in which their eldest son had served as the godfather, she also told him that one of the court ladies, Doña Leonor, could hardly stomach the ceremony and that she, Catalina, could only laugh to see her. She added that the duke would understand what she meant. (Unfortunately, we don't.) When the duke sent her cider from Nice, he commented that she would laugh because it was the kind of cider that her *camarera mayor*, Doña Sancha, liked.[85] (Did Doña Sancha like cider a little too much?) Their private jokes are mostly lost to us, because we know neither the people nor the circumstances, but the very nature of such jokes is that they depend on a closed circle of sympathy and understanding.

One regular source of frustration but also humor for Catalina and Carlo was Don Jusepe, the Spanish ambassador to Turin and Catalina's *mayordomo mayor*. In their letters, Catalina and Carlo shared stories of his "humors," quick temper, and long monologues. Catalina once reported, for example, that Don Jusepe had been to see her and "he has delivered a long discourse and so extensive that it was almost nighttime when I left to take care of business (*negoziar*) and I could not remain standing any longer" (referring to her practice, adopted from her father, of standing during audiences.) On another occasion, when Don Jusepe had gone to see Carlo, Catalina wrote to Carlo that "Don Jusepe must be giving long discourses . . . and I think will hardly let you speak."[86] Carlo noted on yet another occasion that Catalina was correct that "it is necessary to entertain his humors and listen to his discourses."[87] (Perhaps it was a case of the pot calling the kettle black, because within weeks of his arrival at the court in Turin, Don Jusepe had written to Philip II telling him that Carlo frequently delivered "a thousand discourses" about possibilities for territorial aggrandizement in southern France.[88]) In March 1589, when Don Jusepe tried to enter the citadel in Turin without permission and grew angry when turned away, Catalina reported to Carlo that "you already know his humors and he must think that he can order everyone." She and the duke also agreed that Don Jusepe could not be entrusted with a secret.[89] That they saw Don Jusepe in a similarly ironical light suggests that their close marital bond had superseded Catalina's loyalties to her father and his ministers.

Catalina and Carlo confided in each other in small ways. They had code names for people at both their own court in Turin and the Spanish court. Catalina referred to someone at the court in Turin as the migraine, another as the knife, and to three others as Sagittarius, the mountain, and the boulder respectively. When Carlo went to Spain, he and Catalina used code names to discuss a few people, referring to someone as the parrot (*papagayo*) and to another as the eagle (*aguila*), and Catalina commented that the "fight between the parrot and the eagle amazes me."[90] They shared their opinion on why Catalina's sister, Isabel Clara Eugenia, was not married and pitied her. Catalina even went so far as to allude cryptically to problems she and Isabel had had (and Isabel continued to have) with their younger brother, Prince Philip, who was sickly, childish, withdrawn, and uninterested in governing. As she wrote to the duke: "You are correct to say that God has punished him [Philip II] in his sons because my brother has gotten to such extremes and anyone who has not seen the trouble we had on those occasions cannot but feel pity for my sister, which I feel, [because] she suffers so."[91] She and Carlo also sometimes noted that they were saving a story either too complicated or too sensitive to commit to writing, to share instead when they got together, looking forward to the privacy they might then enjoy.[92] As Carlo observed when he urged her to meet him in Savigliano in November 1588, "I beg you to come to Savigliano because at least we can relax . . . and can discuss everything without a thousand spies." Catalina, too, saw time together as an opportunity to "talk freely about many things."[93] Their bantering and chaffing with each other, their private jokes and mockery, their satiric code names, and their longing to be and talk and sleep together all suggest, in contemporary idiom, a married couple very much on the same page.

LONGING

Catalina and Carlo's marriage went far beyond companionship. They frequently mentioned in their letters how much they missed each other, how lonely they were without the other, and how desperate they were to "end this absence." Their rhetoric of longing, while hyperbolic, was not insincere; they used the language and images they had learned from their culture to articulate their sentiments. Their comments also indicate that when together they comforted each other both emotionally and physically. In expressing their sorrow at being apart, Catalina and Carlo employed language suggesting a much more erotic relationship than that between most early modern aristocratic spouses.

The day they parted from each other when Carlo left for Saluzzo in early October 1588, Catalina expressed her grief, and her letters from the first days of separation often return to her sadness and despair. She wrote to him as soon as he departed to say that from her window she had watched him enter his carriage and wondered whether he had seen her looking out. She explained that she had been so upset at his departure "that I did not know how to say goodbye to you and since then I am regretting that I did not embrace you even though everyone was there." When the duke again left Turin in August 1590, after spending much of that year with her, Catalina was disconsolate, telling him that "I am such that I do not know how I can pick up the pen to write you," though this was her second letter of the day. "I would rather die than pass through this torment, I beg you not to forget me and if you want me to live, we should see each other soon and not part again because I tell you, I will not survive any other way. I love you such that I do not know how to express it because no endearment is sufficient."[94] She did not visit her sick children that day because she did not want others to see her in such a desperate state.

Carlo expressed similar grief, though usually not at Catalina's frequency or high emotional pitch. From Saluzzo in October 1588, when he had been gone from Turin for only about a week, he wrote to her "that it is harder for me [than for you] to be here and it is certain that I can no longer stand it. My life, I love you so, so, so much that I do not know how to say it and I wish I were already there and if you dream of me, I do as much and not finding you, I awake crying." Two weeks later, when Catalina had told him she had cried when he left her, he wrote to her: "I promise you that if you cried when I left you, I was not far from doing so and I am not well unless I am with you. Do not forget me my life because I am all, all yours."[95] Responding to a letter in which Catalina told him she cried when she received his latest letter and that she cried every night, Carlo responded "let's not speak about tears because they are my dinner every night." In 1589 he confessed to her that he could be without the children but not without her and insisted that he could not lie about his passion for her and because of this passion, "I lose my judgment, patience, and composure."[96]

Catalina's sorrow was not confined to the early days of Carlo's departures, and she often struggled to master her grief to conceal it from those around her. Realizing that the duke would be absent when she gave birth in April 1589, she wrote to him:

My life I no longer know what to say of not having hope of seeing you as I had thought because I well see that it is impossible now for you to come. You do not have any advantage in feeling it [sorrow] because I am in such a state that I would not know how to write it. I would like to put myself somewhere where no one could see me, so as to be able to cry without making it seem as if it were caused by what these others [Genevans, who had attacked Carlo's forces and assaulted three different locations] have done, which makes me even sadder. It is necessary for me to make an effort, which is no small feat, and I am already wishing for nighttime when I can let all my groans out (*desgritarme*) in my bed.[97]

Close to two months later and still desperate to see him, she feared she would not any time soon, and said, "without you I cannot live and [I] have to hide what I feel."[98] When she had not had letters from him in a month, she had to hide her despair, as she told him in January 1591: "It was necessary to dissimulate because they [probably councilors and ambassadors] would not get it out of their heads that I was hiding letters." When she finally received letters from the duke, she wrote to him: "If you want to keep me alive, let me hear more often from you."[99] Her comments not only indicate how much she missed the duke but also suggest that it was considered unseemly to demonstrate warm feelings publicly, or at least that Catalina considered such demonstrations inappropriate.

Besides noting their grief, Catalina and Carlo often mentioned their desire to relax together, using the word "*descansar*," a term that the lexicographer Covarrubias defined as "to take a break and recover from work done."[100] Catalina worried, in particular, that Carlo worked too hard and had no one with whom he could be completely at ease. As she wrote in March 1589, she felt sorry for him because "you do not have anyone with whom to take a break (*descansar*) and neither do I." Her answer was for them to find every opportunity to be together, as she said in May 1589: "I would like to see myself there because I believe you miss me and perhaps I could give you a break from certain things. At least I would try because I have no greater contentment than pleasing you." Writing to him in July 1593, she told him, "I firmly believe that you would relax better if we were together and I would desire it more than anything so that I could regale and serve you." Relaxing with her would even cure his melancholy, as she explained in October 1592: "I am giving up on the possibility of being with you to help you relax a bit and to make your melancholy go away."[101] If they were able to relax together, Catalina noted, they could "talk about a hundred million things and resolve them, which is very necessary, because they cannot be put in writing and [we cannot] wait a thousand years for the replies."[102]

Time and again she begged him to let her visit him on his campaigns, saying "you could rest a while, which you need." As if to emphasize that she would not intrude upon his busy schedule, she told him: "I would like to be with you if only when you are on the commode (*sillica*) to give you a short break and certainly I think that both of us need it very much. My life, I am yours and remember me." She often expressed the desire to be with him in this strange way; two months earlier she had also said she would like to be with him, "if only when you are on the commode."[103] Another time she asked him to remember her, "if only when you are on the commode and there is no other place [for you to do so]." On yet another occasion, she said she was frustrated not to be able to serve him if only by bringing him the commode. She explained in another letter that she thought the only time Carlo was free was when he was on the commode, evidently explaining this insistent reference to it.[104]

Carlo also used the term *descansar* to describe how he would like to spend time with Catalina. In early November 1589, frustrated by his ministers and claiming he could rely on no one around him, he wrote to her, "I promise you that I am sometimes in such a purgatory that crying, I ask when was the time when I was relaxing (*descansando*) with my life, happy and serving her." A week and a half later he was still lamenting his inability to "*descansar*" with Catalina after not seeing her for nine months, an absence filling him with rage (*rabia*).[105] "Relax" might even have been a euphemism or a code word for sexual intimacy.

Unable to relax together, they pined for the other. Responding to a letter in which Catalina complained of her loneliness, Carlo told her, "I am much lonelier than you and I do not cry any less in the night." She reassured him of her love and constancy. "Do not forget me because I think of nothing but you," she told him in October 1590, and three months later, "my love do not forget me because I am all, all yours and believe that I do not think of anything but you at all the moments of the world."[106] Writing to Carlo after ten months' separation, she told him, "Margarita is almost eight months and you have not seen her and so one can see how long this absence has been. I do not know how I can live except always with the hope of seeing you and the knowledge that you are well."[107]

Their problem, they claimed, was loving each other too much. Struggling with her first separation from Carlo in October 1588, Catalina wrote to him constantly, though knowing she might be taxing him with a barrage of letters of several folios each. "I do not know if I tire you with such long letters when you have so much to do. They do not seem [long] to me because I have no other rest than this and in loving you so much which makes me say so many foolish things (*disparates*). For the love of God forgive me and do not get annoyed because I want only to please you." Carlo thanked her for remembering him, adding (a little dramatically) that if she failed to remember him, he did not know how he could live. He ended by telling her, "I do not know how to stop [writing]; my life I love you so, so much that I do not know how to say it and this [letter] does not end without tears." In turn, receiving this letter, Catalina claimed she could not stop crying as she read it and responded. She reassured him that she would sooner die than forget him, and she felt better knowing that they shared similar thoughts and worries. She concluded: "All this comes from loving each other so much."[108]

SEXUAL INTIMACY

Far from fulfilling their conjugal obligation merely to produce heirs, Catalina and Carlo relished intimate time together. Although both had their own apartments, they clearly spent nights together, and when Carlo was not in Turin and they had to rely on letters to keep in touch, they regularly mentioned missing each other in bed. Carlo told Catalina in August 1589, for example, that he was off to sleep, "very annoyed not to find you in bed." In October 1589, he wrote to her that he was going to bed soon but did not know how he was going to sleep without her.[109] In a similar fashion, Catalina wrote to him, "it is now midnight and so I am going to bed very lonely without you."[110] On another occasion she told him, "I do not know how I can bring myself to lie in bed without you. I promise you that I am in such a state that I think I will be unable to sleep."[111] She claimed that writing alleviated her loneliness and she was postponing lying down in an empty bed by writing him a long letter: "I do not know how to stop, especially because I am going to bed so alone without you."[112] After spending a few days with Carlo in November 1588, and writing from bed after her first night without him, she told him, "So as not to detain Loaisa [the bearer of the letter], I have not wished to get dressed before writing you and I write now to remind you of the promise to see me tomorrow and afterward to take me [with you] because if that does not happen, I will die from the loneliness with which I remained yesterday and which I have had this past night not having my life in bed. That has caused me many tears."[113] These are not isolated examples but rather appear frequently in Catalina's and Carlo's letters, a repeated lament that goes well beyond mere epistolary convention and indicates the great comfort they took in sharing a bed.

In their letters, Catalina and Carlo also mentioned wanting to spend time together in their bedroom. In December 1589, when they had been apart for more than nine months, Catalina informed him about renovations made in the palace, adding that "I do not see the hour in which I can see myself in the private room (*cabinete*) with you. It has turned out larger than I thought and I know you will like it, because it is very good." By *cabinete*, Catalina was probably referring to the bedroom where they made love, as is suggested by Carlo's response: "If you desire that I were imprisoned there so that we could be close together in the *gabinete*, I do not desire it any less . . . and I am dying at not being able to serve you." Likewise, when he was in Arles in September 1591, he told Catalina that "I am in the usual apartment and in the bedroom (*camara*), which has made me sigh greatly at not finding you there." Catalina responded a few days later that she wanted to know if he was already in Nice and where he was staying, and she noted that "you will be very lonely when you do not find me in your room and I promise you that I have such [loneliness] at not being there that I cry very much every day."[114] In preparation for the duke's return to Turin after a ten-month absence, Catalina sent him the key to her bedroom, always locked at night.[115] Without explicitly saying that they desired to make love, Catalina and Carlo still managed to express their longing for physical intimacy, making it clear in their letters that they enjoyed sleeping together and chafed at the enforced abstinence during his absences on his military campaigns.

Catalina planned for and dreamed of Carlo visiting her at night, as he did occasionally in his first month of absence in fall 1588 or at other absences when he was within a day of Turin. Two days after Carlo left Turin in early October 1588, Catalina wrote, "all night I do nothing but dream that I am with you." When the two days had stretched out to two weeks, Catalina told him that "I am losing hope of having any visit [from you] on any of these nights." Missing him, she wrote that she had dreamed that he had returned to Turin. "I can no longer be so long without my life and all night I dreamed that you had returned and I have been left very sad seeing that it is not the case." A week later she wrote, "I was dreaming that you had arrived and I seemed to hear the door open and I was very upset that it was only a dream."[116]

The door was no doubt the one to her bedroom, and, less than two weeks earlier, anticipating the duke's nocturnal arrival, Catalina had detailed which ladies were sleeping in her bedroom: "Chicha [probably Luisa Mexía] has also slept in my room and therefore the beds are [arranged] as I have told you and hers is at the foot of my bed and Doña Beatriz's bed is by the door (*puerta del retrete*) and that of Doña Mariana is by the two windows. I want to tell you everything because of what you ordered me to do but also in case you come to take me by surprise, you will know how everything is."[117] Her choice of words—"if you come to take me by surprise" (*si benis a tomarme de sobresalto*)—is charged with erotic meaning: she clearly expected Carlo to take her sexually. A day later she updated him on personnel changes in her bedroom, telling him that, because Chicha was sick, Mariana de Tarsis was now sleeping in the bedroom.[118] Expecting Carlo to make love with her, Catalina wanted to inform him of whom he would find in the cots around her.

Her letters from subsequent months (and years) continue to refer frequently to her longing for Carlo's nighttime visits. "I promise that I sleep few hours and [I am] always crying and dreaming of you," she wrote in March 1589. Several weeks later again she wrote to him, "all night all I do is dream I am with you." In December 1589, she told him that "I dreamed this night that you were coming [home] and it cost me many tears when I awoke to see that it was a lie."[119] Dreaming all night of Carlo on yet another occasion and waking to realize he was absent, she wept between dreams.[120] Her description of the circumstances in which she was writing often suggest sexual longing. Lonely, in bed, and still undressed, she wrote to Carlo that she had dreamed they were at their country estate of Miraflores, where they occasionally escaped to relax without most of their attendants: "I write from bed before dressing and certainly very lonely, and what I dreamed this night was that we were together in Miraflor . . . I hope that we will soon be together."[121] Over and over again in her letters, she told him she dreamed about him. In September 1591, after telling him she was desperate to receive letters from him, she added, "I am going to bed now and tonight I will be all alone as on every [night] because I am without you; there is no minute in which I am not dreaming [of] you." In December of the same year, she wrote, "I promise that if you dreamed of me those nights, there is none in which I do not dream of you nor a moment in which I do not think of you."[122]

The duke similarly told Catalina that he dreamed of her and had a hard time sleeping without her. Less than two weeks after first leaving her in Turin in 1588, he wrote: "I love you so, so much that I do not know how to express it and I wish I were already there, and if you dream of me, I do so [dream] of you even more and not finding you, I awake crying." After receiving a letter from her late one night in September 1591, when he was "so sleepy that I could hardly open my eyes," he went back to sleep but not before putting the letter by the head of his bed, and "all night I dreamed of you."[123] In another letter he told her, "I have been with you all night," suggesting that he had been dreaming of her.[124] Responding to a letter from Catalina in which she complained that she could not sleep without him, he wrote: "If you are unable to sleep the night, neither can I. I wake up one hundred thousand times, always thinking I will find you and certainly I grow desperate."[125] Reassuring her that they would see each other soon, Carlo wrote to her: "My life, I am all yours and all I do is dream of you every night."[126] When Catalina told him that she missed him during the day, he responded that he missed her day and night "and it always seems to me that you are talking to me and are with me," adding, "life cannot go on in this way because it is death and we will get together and afterward never be apart."[127]

His letters also make clear that Catalina and Carlo did not merely enjoy sex and then retire to separate bedrooms, but rather spent the entire night together. When he complained of not finding her in bed, Carlo sometimes added that he was freezing in bed without her. Thanking her for treats she had sent to celebrate St. Nicholas's feast day, he wrote: "Last night when I was going to bed, your mail arrived with the shoe for St. Nicholas that you sent me. Seeing it caused me great tears and reminded me that on the eve of this feast day, I am not used to sleeping so alone as I have slept this past night and I was freezing from the cold." In late December 1589, when they had been apart for nine months and when Carlo was looking ahead to the new year, he wrote: "May it please God that we will be together more often than we have been because certainly when I think of this, I go crazy and a tremendous anger (*rabia*) seizes me, and certainly last night on going to bed I cried a lot and at not finding you in bed, my tears doubled, and I tell you for sure that I cannot live in this way and I freeze in bed."[128] Noting how much he missed Catalina, he added the practical consideration that they also kept each other warm on cold nights.

Catalina and Carlo occasionally allude openly to sexual intercourse in their letters. For example, in October 1588, when he was besieging the marquisate of Saluzzo, he responded to a letter in which she said she had felt the baby in her womb move. In his response, he also told her that he was missing sex: "I am glad that the baby can be felt and I am certain that you do not fool yourself because you are very adept at that thing. Life, I give up on Carmagnola and Saluzzo because when I am there, I cannot do *that thing* with my life. I hope in the lord of Leynì [Andrea Provana di Leynì, his military commander] [and] that I will be able to do it soon because the [construction of the] fort is progressing. For the love of God, do not forget me because I would die if that were the case." Catalina responded, "I promise you that I shed many tears and you can be sure that I would sooner die than forget you and . . . I pray very often so that the lord of Leynì finishes his fort . . . I am consoled and hopeful that you remember me and to see that you already miss me *for that business*—you understand me well—and I am not surprised because it has been many days since we saw each other and I beg you not to let more [time] pass."[129]

Was the duke also alluding to sexual intercourse in September 1590 when he responded to Catalina's comment that the baby in her womb was lazy and she had not felt fetal movement yet? He told her: "I know well the recipe for making it move. I wish you were here—I mean now—tonight—because if you count the days, I do too, and if they seem long to you, to me they are even more so."[130] The urgency of seeing Catalina that very same night would suggest that he believed intercourse would prompt the baby to move. And had Catalina been referring to sexual intercourse a month earlier when, upset at being left behind in Turin and almost frantic that she would not see the duke for months, she wrote to Carlo that she would like to see him "if only to rid you of part of that bad humor that you tell me that you have"?[131] Sexual intercourse could be one way to purge the bad and restore the balance of humors in Carlo's body.[132]

These expressions of desire, a regular refrain in their letters, might well have been designed to ignite sexual fires and keep them burning. The timing of at least two of Catalina's pregnancies after 1588, when the duke first left on military campaigns, indicates that they wasted no time when together again. When they met in Nice in early April 1592 after a separation of approximately seventeen months, Catalina got pregnant almost immediately. She gave birth to that child in January 1593. When after another absence he returned to Turin for a short stay four months later, in May, she once again quickly became pregnant. Absence might well have increased the duke's sexual drive, and it is clear that after being separated from Catalina, Carlo returned eagerly to her and to her bed.

MARRIAGE

Catalina and Carlo formed an emotional bond unusual in early modern arranged marriages. She recognized her good fortune in finding emotional intimacy and sexual warmth in her marriage, as is evident in comments she made to Carlo about other, less amorous marriages. When Spanish ambassador Don Jusepe's wife, Juana de Acuña, arrived in Turin in September 1590, Catalina reported that Juana had immediately complained of a terrible headache, and that she and Don Jusepe were already angry with each other. In fact, Don Jusepe was so ill that some thought he was dying, and it was rumored that his malady stemmed from his marital problems, which Catalina found plausible.[133] She was struck with how different she was from Juana de Acuña, telling the duke, "I promise you that if I were to go where you are, I would not have a migraine nor a headache," and lamenting that, unlike Juana de Acuña, she was not so fortunate as to be with her husband. "I love you in a very different way than Doña Juana de Acuña [loves Don Jusepe], because I am and will always be yours."[134] Since Juana's arrival, Don Jusepe was "very thin," "because they love each other so little." Comparing herself and the duke with Doña Juana and Don Jusepe, Catalina added that she did not understand them because "I love you in such a way that I die to see myself without you and I know that you pay me back, no more no less, which is what keeps me alive." Carlo agreed that their marriage was very different from that of Don Jusepe and Juana de Acuña: "The news you write me of Doña Juana de Acuña conforms to what I expected and I had to laugh reading the letters you wrote me about the good marriage. You are correct that we are not like that and I would not want it for the world because it would be dying, not living."[135] Perhaps Catalina relayed the stories concerning Don Jusepe and his wife to amuse Carlo with court gossip, but the other couple's strained relations prompted Catalina to reflect on her own marriage, especially her longing to be with her husband and her certainty of their mutual affection.[136]

She also commented on one other marriage, that of one of her former maids-in-waiting, Juana Manrique, who, after serving in Turin and attracting several admirers for her great beauty, had returned to Spain to marry a wealthy, much older man.[137] Catalina told Carlo that she had received a letter from Juana, who seemed very happy to be marrying. Catalina doubted the happiness would last, though, adding that though Juana was now happy with the union, she would need patience to put up with her husband. Although Catalina was circumspect about detailing her specific doubts about the prospective groom, Carlo was not, noting in his letter that people feared that "he will die in the act of consummation."[138] Although, because Juana Manrique had left Turin without their full consent, Catalina and Carlo might have been moved to make fun of her, Catalina's comments suggest that, sensitive to the disparity of January–May arranged marriages, she rejoiced that she and Carlo were of comparable ages, and that they had been in the full vigor of their youth when they had married.

Unlike other aristocratic wives who might have welcomed separation from their husbands, Catalina wanted to be always with Carlo and envied other wives who had the good fortune always to have their husbands with them. When the count of Frossasco (Andrea Provana di Leynì's son and heir) arrived in Turin in July 1589 to deliver a message from the duke, off on campaign, she was reluctant to send the count back quickly, because his wife, in Turin, was pregnant. She told Carlo that "as someone who feels your absences so much, I think that other women must feel the same, although not as much as I do, and so I am a little gentle in making them [the husbands] leave."[139] On another occasion, she told the duke that she was reluctant to send another of his officials back to Carlo's military encampment quickly, so that his wife could enjoy her good fortune in having her husband at home. "I alone am not allowed this [good fortune]," she complained to the duke.[140] She was filled with anger, she told him, to see other husbands visit their wives while her own husband could not be with her and refused to let her go to him. "God knows the rage that I have that all come to see their wives and home whereas you alone do not allow me to go . . . I promise you that I wake up a hundred times these nights because I am not with you and I go through [the nights] very alone."[141]

Carlo must have told her that a combat front was too dangerous for her, because she often asserted that she had no fear of being close to the fighting. In May 1589, only a week after giving birth, she claimed hyperbolically that she was ready to put on a corslet and join him on the front, telling him that women could fight as well as priests. Yet she was not totally joking. A few weeks later she argued that "I will not be the only woman who has gone to war because there have been many and even if there weren't, it would be enough for me to go with you even if I were the first to have done this. My life, please do me this favor and I will not ask for any other . . . and if you do not, I will tire you every day asking for the same." With her mind bent on joining the duke at the front, she wrote to him a few weeks later: "I am so in shape and without a stomach that a corslet would fit me very well and I have such great desire to go as a soldier that if I could escape [Turin], I would certainly do it."[142]

These were sentiments that she continued to articulate over the years, and in 1594 she even provided Carlo with examples of other women who had gone to war. Commenting that Don Jusepe was feigning illness to avoid joining the duke on the front, she emphasized that, unlike him, she would gladly go:

> Don Jusepe says he is sick in the chest, as if his asthma were begin-ning, I think he does it . . . as an excuse not to go there . . . I do not know how they [Don Jusepe and other ministers] have the spirit to stay here. I am certain that if you gave me permission, I would go to serve you with [more spirit] than he [Don Jusepe] and you can believe me even though I am a woman, because the Catholic queen [Isabel of Castile] and María [unidentified] went to war. I do not know why you do not give me license [to go] and someday I might just take it and I know that afterward you would not mind.[143]

She also noted that German wives went alone to the front to be with their husbands, though without specifying which German wives she had in mind. "They are much luckier because they do what they want while we are unable to do it."[144] Far from imagining herself another Joan of Arc, Catalina longed to go to war simply to be with her husband.

NICE

At the same time that Catalina was commenting on other marriages and complaining of the duke's refusal to let her join him on his campaigns, she was going through her most prolonged separation from him and was struggling with his absence. Her exchange of letters with Carlo during this time demonstrates her compelling need, or at least desire, to be near him. In 1590, with Carlo campaigning in Provence, she was ready to leave everything in Turin behind, including her children, to travel to Nice, where she expected that he would come to see her.

In October that year, Carlo and his troops had entered Provence, and for the next seventeen months Catalina did not see him. She was particularly frustrated because, when leaving Turin in August, Carlo had promised her she could go with him, or at least part way, but their children's illness prevented her. Left behind in Turin in August 1590 with sick children, with the onerous responsibilities of governing, and missing the duke, Catalina in her letters repeatedly detailed her grief. The source of her sorrow was her distance from the duke: "I do not usually tire you out every day by telling you the life that I live without you, my life, because it is death and I cannot say it without crying, especially today when I have not had any news of you because it seems a thousand years to me that I have not had them . . . all my anger is at not being there with you." In another letter, after a sleepless night, she told him that every time she thought she would never see him again, even for a single day, "I would like to kill myself and I think that if I were not pregnant I would have committed some foolishness." Frustrated with adverse events in Provence, and also missing her, Carlo wrote to her that he was so annoyed that he could launch into a knife fight with anyone; that he was in such a "bad mood that anything annoys me . . . I wish you were here . . . I am all yours and you will be mine and nothing can make us stop loving each other."[145]

In late September, a month after departing for Provence, Carlo managed to return to Turin for about a week, satisfying Catalina momentarily, as she wrote soon after he left: "I could have an unhappy life but seeing you, I am always well, as I am now." In turn, the duke reported that he had arrived at his camp wet, exhausted, and coughing, all of which "I feel even more having left you. This pierces the soul and certainly I came [looking] such that anyone could read in my face the pain [I felt] in my heart, and I am sure you experienced the same. Leave everything to me because if you do not, I will certainly die. I will be very pleased for you to come to Nice when the snow falls."[146] Little did Carlo suspect that she would take this casual remark as his permission for her to travel to Nice when winter set in.

In the months following, Catalina continued to remind Carlo that he had promised they would meet in Nice. She could not leave Turin without his permission, at least in part because he had left her governing the duchy, and she grew increasingly angry. In late October 1590, annoyed at the duke's reluctance to let her leave Turin, she wrote: "You know well that you gave me license to go to Nice once the snow arrived and you would send someone else to be here . . . and you told me it was not necessary to ask for further permission to do so . . . and I have been punished enough, but I never thought you would forget [your promise] so quickly." She seems to have anticipated Carlo's objections when she added that, yes, she had agreed that he needed to go to Provence, but she had never thought he would leave her behind indefinitely. Her frustration was palpable: "I did not marry Piedmont and Savoy, but you."[147]

Although frankly telling Carlo that for her, being with him outweighed her political duties, she knew he expected her to oversee the duchy, and she pledged not to abandon her responsibilities. "I would not be so beastly as to go away and leave everything in disorder or mismanaged," she assured him, and, as if to emphasize how desperate she was, she complained: "I promise you that I have to make a considerable effort so that they [the people at court] cannot see it [my frustration]. Write to tell me if you are more annoyed [with me] and if you have not remembered your promise." Worried that she might have gone too far in complaining, she told him in closing that she found it impossible to sleep because "I am afraid that you are unhappy with me." Two days later she remained anxious that he might be angry with her, and urged: "Do not be annoyed with me because if I did not let off steam, I would burst."[148] A week later, however, still waiting for his response, she did not back down from criticism and continued to implore him to let her join him:

> I am eagerly awaiting your response to my letter, because if I had to say the truth, I do not believe your plans . . . that we will be together soon, because you know you propose it many times and afterward nothing happens . . . My soul . . . let me go now that it is winter, [because] in summer and spring there will always be more obstacles and if I stay here, it is certain that I will die. I plead with you again not to deny me what you have so many times promised me because I love you so much . . . and if you would like to be with me, I would [like to be] even more with you and do not be annoyed that I tell you this.[149]

Catalina's forceful personality is evident in these letters, and although she worried that Carlo would be annoyed, she felt free to vent her frustration, trusting that his love for her would persuade him to heed her (sometimes hectoring) entreaties.

He defended himself against Catalina's accusations, at least in part, by reminding her not so much of her political responsibilities as of her maternal duties: "Believe me that I would like to be with you and I will find a way for us to be together ... I know you are not married to Piedmont nor to Savoy but in the end you are the mother of our children and I am trying for us to see each other."[150] Struggling to take possession of Provence, Carlo also had to struggle to appease a strong-willed and unhappy wife averse to governing his duchy and desperate to be with him. The exchange well illustrates that Catalina, more than four months pregnant and charged with governing Savoy in the duke's absence, wanted only to be close to him. While insisting in her letters that she would appoint a surrogate to assume her political responsibilities in Turin, she made no mention of her four children, though she might well have planned to take them with her, as she considered doing when she finally did travel to Nice in 1592.

During the months that she was frustrated in her desperate desire to rendezvous with the duke in Nice, she continued fulfilling all her official duties, such as entertaining the duchess of Brunswick (Christina of Denmark) and hosting the Spanish governor of Milan, the duke of Terranova. She sent Carlo a red band she had made for him and begged him to remember her while wearing it.[151] She also sent him a small portrait of herself, to remind him to think of her. The duke claimed that the portrait made him cry. Though moved to tears, he nonetheless complained that his court painter El Flamenco had not painted her true to life, to which she responded that the portrait was "better than I." By 16 December 1590, however, she was again planning to travel to Nice, happy with the news that the duke was said to be sending someone to replace her in Turin.[152] Thanking him, she professed to be crying as she wrote.

Five days later, though, she was reminding him again of his promise to send someone to replace her in Turin, allowing her to travel to Nice. She did not bother to hide her displeasure when commenting to Carlo that he had failed so often to keep his promise that she entertained little hope, and said: "It is certain that I will not be able to live in this torment and believe me that I say the truth that so much time has passed since I have written you about this that I could not help but let off a bit of steam." Not only would Carlo not summon her to Nice, she realized, but he would not be with her when she went into labor three months hence. Dejected, she told him she did not know what she would do if he were not with her at childbirth, "because if I cannot be with you, I have no interest in life."[153] In January 1591 she reminded him that she was approaching the eighth month of her pregnancy and would soon be unable to travel. She was losing her patience, she continued, "and my wishes are never fulfilled."[154] Now she begged him to let her go after giving birth, urging him to disregard those dissuading him from permitting her to travel. Even as she chided him for blocking her from traveling to Nice, she affirmed her love, telling him that "it is certain that we repay each other well by how much we love each other."[155]

In early March 1591, Catalina gave birth to a daughter—without the duke by her side, as she had dreaded. He was instead on his way to Spain to request military assistance in Provence. She now hoped to make her way to Nice to meet him there on his return from Spain, telling him that she would keep reminding him of his promise and threatening, hyperbolically, that if he did not allow her to go, she would die. Returning to Provence from Spain in June 1591, the duke because of military exigencies again failed to send for Catalina. Again she grew angry. In a letter of late June, going on for nineteen pages, Catalina responded to all the issues that Carlo had mentioned in his letter—his congenial relations with Philip II's ministers; a proposed marriage for Catalina's sister Isabel; the possibility of sending their sons to the Spanish court—but by the end of the letter, she seems to have lost her calm. "I do not know how I have been able to write up until now because all the happiness that I have received from knowing that you are well and had been well treated [in Spain] has been ruined by you not writing even a word about seeing me nor giving me license to go . . . as you had promised me in your letters and which I believed." What she must reluctantly cultivate, she complained, was "Patience, of which in truth I have more than I ever thought. I feel it [displeasure] so much that I have to work to hide [my disappointment] because if I appeared melancholy, people would think it was because you return [from Spain] unhappy. Because you do not live up to what you have promised me so many times, I will not believe you again."[156] She immediately apologized for this rebuke, however, telling him she knew he would understand her frustration and she could let off steam (*esfogarme*) only with him.

As the summer continued and Catalina still had not traveled to Nice to see the duke, she became increasingly feisty. Told by someone who had seen Carlo that he hoped to see her soon, she responded that she would believe it when she saw it, and as she told Carlo, "the great love that I have for you allows me to live but the same [love] does not blind me from seeing clearly whether my departure from here could cause any harm, and in my opinion, it would not, because it [Nice] is not very far and leaving someone here and Savoy well provisioned, as we would do, I will make sure that nothing will happen and from Nice I would work hard and even more to take care of everything as I would staying here . . . I see that if I do not go to Nice, I will not see you."[157] She reassured him that she knew she could not leave without putting political matters in good order: "I am not such a brute (*bestia*) as not to understand that well."[158] In early November, still waiting for his permission, she told him: "Do not make me hopeful; just let me go to Nice because matters here are not dangerous and all would be left well."[159]

She continued to remind the duke of his promise, urging him to give her fair warning to allow her to prepare, and when he finally summoned her to Nice in December 1591, she was overjoyed. "I promise you that I have not slept any of these nights out of happiness and the hours seem a thousand years."[160] She asked Carlo if their three sons could accompany her, but in the end, not hearing from him on this question, she left them behind. Once arrived in Nice, she waited almost two months for the duke to join her there, but then spent six months with him while their children remained in Turin. She became pregnant within days of her reunion with Carlo.

Catalina's determination to get to Nice to meet, talk, and sleep with the duke suggests in capsule form the affection and intimacy of their marriage, as she longed to be in touch, very literally, with her husband.

Was she also afraid, though, that Carlo would not be faithful to her during these long absences? Was she almost frantic to join him in Nice because she feared that in her absence he would find comfort elsewhere? Had she gotten some inkling or heard gossip that Carlo had taken another woman? Nothing in the correspondence suggests this, but Catalina had reason to worry. As a young, virile, privileged man living in an aristocratic culture in which mistresses were common and condoned and men were tacitly expected to indulge their sexual desires, Carlo might well have thought himself justified in seeking pleasure elsewhere for the seventeen months he and Catalina were apart. (After her death he would father eleven illegitimate children.[161]) While she no doubt enjoyed sexual intimacy with her husband, she also knew that, while it meant frequent pregnancies for her, satisfying him sexually had helped rivet his affections. Her determination to go to Nice might reflect a natural fear of his affections wandering during their protracted separation. A strong-willed and possessive woman, she was not ready to allow another woman to take her place in his bed.

CHAPTER 7

CATALINA AS DYNASTIC PROGENITRIX
Eighty-Seven Months of Pregnancy, Ten Childbirths

The one in the belly is well and do not let any of this worry you because there is no reason to do so.

Catalina to Carlo, 4 September 1590

CATALINA AND CARLO'S WARM sexual intimacy and their desire to have heirs led naturally to frequent pregnancy and childbirth. Her reluctance to have Carlo expend his virile energy on a mistress may have been another motive for Catalina to make herself available for sex whenever they were together. Pregnant for 87 of the 152 months that she was married to him, she was more often pregnant than not. She gave birth to their first child, a son, thirteen months after her marriage in Zaragoza, and bore two other sons and a daughter in quick succession, giving birth to four children in four years. She went on to bear six more children in a span of six and a half years in the 1590s. Nine of their ten children survived into adulthood, though their eldest son died at nineteen. Her only child to die in infancy was her last, a girl born prematurely, who was almost certainly stillborn.

Because pregnancy and childbirth were constants in Catalina's married life, she had to factor them into her planning and find ways to continue with her other activities and duties during them, and sometimes despite them. This was particularly true when she took on political responsibilities in Carlo's absence. Comments in her letters suggest that pregnancy did not deter her from most activities and that, despite the strain on her body, she remained healthy and retained her energy. Her greatest frustration was that Carlo was not present for three of the births, and that pregnancy and childbirth kept her in Turin when he was off on his campaigns.

DETECTING PREGNANCY, DATING CONCEPTION, PREDICTING DELIVERY

Providing heirs was an essential part of Catalina's duties and had a direct impact on her status at court and her relationship with Carlo. If she could give Carlo healthy heirs, she would be performing her duty well, securing respect and status at court. At the Spanish court, her female attendants, many of whom had borne children, would probably have taught her to monitor her body and perhaps even to chart her menstrual cycles. Regular periods indicated a healthy, sound body that could conceive and give birth, and because of their significance Philip II kept himself informed about his daughters' periods.[1] Female attendants would have kept Philip abreast of his daughters' periods (or lack thereof), just as Catherine de' Medici's ladies had kept her informed about the menstrual cycles and pregnancies of her daughter, Catalina's mother, Elisabeth of Valois.[2] Catalina's attendants also would have told her that by keeping track of her cycle she would be better prepared to begin married life and sooner able to detect a pregnancy.

Catalina married the duke in March 1585 and by July wrote to her father that she was expecting a child. At the time, she was barely one month pregnant, yet she evidently had some definite way to detect that she had conceived. In July 1585, the Venetian ambassador reported that Catalina's stomach was upset, lending credence to the hopeful rumor that she was pregnant.[3] An account describing Catalina and Carlo's first entrance into Turin as a married couple, in August 1585, recorded that she was vomiting and had "other well-known signs" of pregnancy, so her indisposition might have been an early indication.[4] However, for her pregnancies of 1588 and later, well documented in her correspondence with Carlo, she never referred explicitly to nausea, vomiting, or cravings, although she associated sickliness (*achaques*) with early pregnancy. She also reported headaches, sometimes thought to be a sign of pregnancy.[5]

Like most people of her day, Catalina had a humoral understanding of human physiology, believing that fluids passed naturally through the body and that their flow needed to be managed, balanced, and controlled. She was a firm believer in purges and bleeding.[6] Pregnancy was thought to redirect a woman's fluids to the womb, and it is not surprising that Catalina associated pregnancy with less nasal drainage, telling Carlo that she thought she was pregnant because "I have less catarrh than I usually have."[7]

Indisposition, so frequent in the lives of early modern people, had to be accompanied by other signs to be read as an indicator of pregnancy, and Catalina looked for several. In 1595, for example, about seven weeks pregnant with her eighth child, she wrote to Carlo that her belly (*barriga*) was getting so big that she did not fit into her clothes, and "I am thinking that I am pregnant because I am [otherwise] well." The duke responded by saying that he was like St. Thomas—the doubting Thomas of John 20—because he needed to touch and see before believing. He therefore asked whether she had felt the baby move, because that was a "major sign" of pregnancy.[8] Catalina replied that, although thinking she had perhaps felt the baby move, she was uncertain and would have to wait a little longer before she could assure him, because though her middle was definitely swelling, she was still not feeling the hardness in her belly that she usually felt when pregnant. She was impatient for a month to pass, she added, to remove any doubt. Nine days later she reported that she was certain she had felt the baby move.[9] She was clearly attentive to the quickening, but she was also waiting for a specific length of time—approximately three months—which would suggest that she was calculating either from a specific date when she had had intercourse with the duke or from a missed menstrual period.

As the early weeks of a pregnancy passed and she grew more certain she was pregnant, Catalina occasionally wrote to the duke about changes to her body, including the growing "*criatura*" (creature), as she called it. In October 1588, almost three months pregnant with her fourth child, she wrote that she thought she had felt the baby move, and also, "I have grown wider and my belly has grown such that I have had to remove the *tablilla* [a hard corset used by Spanish women to flatten the abdomen] and if I do not fool myself, it seems to me that I have felt the *criatura*, although it was so slight that I am not certain." Responding, the duke said that he felt sure she was correct about the baby moving, because she was an expert at detecting pregnancy.[10]

Her letters, therefore, reveal that she was monitoring her body closely for early signs of pregnancy and that, before believing, she and Carlo wanted tangible evidence, such as her abdomen growing and hardening and the baby moving. There is no indication from her letters that she relied on a midwife or a doctor to determine pregnancy (her midwives, Cecilia Castellona and Catalina Canola, lived in Milan and were summoned only at the beginning of the ninth month), and Catalina seems to have shared her suspicions with the duke even before she consulted a doctor or midwife, perhaps because she preferred to avoid prompting rumors of pregnancy until she had firm proof.[11]

Yet even before she felt the baby moving or a hardness in her belly, Catalina was attentive to another important sign of pregnancy: cessation of menstruation. Her letters to Carlo make clear that she kept close track of her periods and would have known when one was late. On 1 July 1589, for example, she wrote to the duke to tell him that her menstrual period had ended. She explained that she had not bled much and that the bleeding had not lasted the usual eight days. She added that she would wait until the fifteenth of the month, when her period was due again, to see if she bled more.[12] Catalina therefore kept a record (mental or written) of her periods, and her menstrual cycle was regular. In this specific case, she was writing on 1 July and was noting that she had stopped menstruating and that the bleeding had not lasted eight days. Thus, at least a week would have passed since the bleeding had begun, and at least several days since it had ended, and she was expecting it again in fifteen days. Her comments suggest, therefore, that she expected her period every three to four weeks, and that the bleeding usually lasted about eight days. She kept careful track of how many days her menstrual bleeding ordinarily lasted, as she explained to the duke on Monday, 24 October 1594: "I have already had [my period] for six days and according to what it usually lasts, I will have it only until

Wednesday."[13] Menstruation could be so irregular for many women that its cessation was not always a reliable sign, and thus they looked for a variety of other factors to determine pregnancy.[14] Moreover, some women bled even when pregnant, making it difficult to know when menstruation had stopped, but someone who kept such an exact record of menstrual cycles as Catalina did and whose cycles were predictably regular would have known precisely when she had first missed a period. A letter from Don Jusepe, Spanish ambassador in Turin, to Philip II confirms that Catalina had regular cycles; in September 1588, the ambassador reported that Luisa Mexía, one of Catalina's ladies-in-waiting, had told him that Catalina was pregnant because her period was twelve days late when it was never late by more than a day.[15]

For all her pregnancies which are documented in letters, Catalina calculated when she was entering a new month. In her letters to the duke, she regularly noted how far along she thought her pregnancy was, giving her calculation of the month and sometimes even the exact day since conception. For example, on 17 March 1589 she told the duke that in eight days she would be entering the eighth month of her pregnancy, and a week later, on 24 March, she noted that she had entered that month. A year and a half later, on 18 October 1590—pregnant once again—she informed the duke that "today I have entered the fifth month . . . and I have a considerable belly. I think we will have a girl." (She was right.) She ended a letter to Carlo in July 1593 by noting that she was entering the third month of pregnancy.[16]

How did Catalina know when a new month was beginning and how long did a month last?[17] There were numerous ways to measure time and calculate months in the late sixteenth century, but she seems to have followed a calendar month, beginning with her estimate of when she became pregnant.[18] On 16 December 1590, for instance, she noted that in two days her seventh month would begin, which was exactly two months after she had reported that she had entered her fifth month (on 18 October 1590).[19] Thus, the monthly count in that pregnancy began on the eighteenth day. The meticulous nature of her calculations, with precise noting of when each successive month of a pregnancy began, suggests that she kept a log of her periods and perhaps even a written record of when the duke visited and slept with her. She must have employed some customary method to calculate when she had become pregnant, though the method of determining the date of conception may not always have been accurate, and some births might have been premature.[20]

Cessation of menstruation was key to that calculation. On 17 July 1597, Catalina wrote to Carlo that her period was more than fifteen days late and she feared that she was pregnant with her tenth child. Four days later she told Carlo that "My failure (*falta*) [to get my period] continues and I fear that I will not get my period; soon we will know."[21] For another of her pregnancies, Catalina told the duke that she was in her third month of pregnancy because she had missed her period three times: "I am already in my third month, having passed the three missed menstrual periods (*las tres faltas*)." Catalina's use of this specific phrase— *las tres faltas*—suggests that missing a period for the third time in a row was an important and recognized benchmark for confirming a pregnancy.[22] At the Austrian Habsburg court, the end of the third month of pregnancy was celebrated publicly, indicating that there might have been a wider observance of the *tres faltas*.[23] Even if there is no evidence of a similar celebration at the court in Turin, Catalina's observations verify not only that she knew precisely when she was due to menstruate, but also that she used cessation of menstruation as an indicator of pregnancy.

As a girl, Catalina would have observed that Philip II's fourth wife, Anna of Austria, counted the months of pregnancy. How else would Anna have known when to celebrate a novena in honor of the nine feasts of the Virgin Mary, a ritual performed at the beginning of the ninth month of pregnancy, which she introduced at the Spanish court?[24] In Spain Catalina also learned another Marian ritual, that of feeding nine poor women (for the nine Marian feasts), observed on 25 March, the feast of the Annunciation.[25] Francisco de Vera, Philip II's ambassador to Venice, visited the court in Turin in 1589 and reported that, to mark her upcoming entrance into the ninth month of her pregnancy, Catalina had fed nine poor women, even waiting on them at table. At the end of the meal, Catalina gave the women cloth with which to make themselves dresses, as well as a small bag containing an escudo (gold coin). Vera did not know the origin of this ritual—whether it was a private devotion of Catalina's or a court celebration of the beginning of the ninth month of pregnancy—but he noted that it was connected to the Annunciation.[26] Vera was not completely correct. In 1589, the Annunciation, typically celebrated by Spanish queens with this feeding of poor women, coincided with what Catalina calculated to be the beginning of her eighth and not her ninth month of pregnancy.[27] Nevertheless, Vera seems to have known that the beginning of the ninth month of pregnancy was often accompanied by a religious ceremony and conflated the Annunciation ritual with that for the ninth month. While not requiring exact timing, public rituals of pregnancies in ruling families still mandated that a woman keep close track of when each month of a pregnancy began.

Catalina was not alone in dating her pregnancy to the exact day. In 1617, Curzio di Lorenzo da Picchena, secretary at the Medici court in Florence, reported that the Grand Duchess of Tuscany, Maria Magdalena d'Austria, was entering her ninth month of pregnancy, while in 1621 and again in 1623, the Tuscan ambassador to Spain wrote that Queen Elisabeth of Bourbon, wife of Philip IV, was about to enter the ninth month of her pregnancy.[28] Although these examples are from the early seventeenth century, taken in conjunction with Catalina's and Anna of Austria's practices, they indicate not only that Habsburg women (or women at Habsburg courts) formally observed the beginning of their ninth month of pregnancy, but also that they and other aristocratic women had well-defined ways of calculating conception and establishing when they had begun a specific month of pregnancy. Cessation of menstruation seems to have been the point of departure for these calculations.

No doubt royal women had reasons to chart their menstrual cycles carefully. Medical practitioners encouraged their female patients to keep close track of their menstrual periods, and a woman whose periods were regular could use that information to make practical preparations for menstrual bleeding, to know when intercourse was morally permissible, and to calculate when she might have become pregnant.[29] She might also calculate when she was most likely to conceive, since it was generally accepted that a woman was most fertile immediately after menstruating.[30] On one occasion, Catalina wrote to the duke (because he had asked) that she was no longer menstruating and that she did not bleed at night, encouraging him to come to spend the night with her or to let her go to be with him.[31] He sometimes asked her for clarification—whether she had bled the usual amount, for example, or whether she had finished menstruating.[32] While he no doubt was concerned about her health, he might also have been planning his returns to Turin based in part on the possibility of intercourse with her.

Aristocratic women, especially those such as Catalina whose husbands were away for long periods, had many reasons for dating conception and monitoring the progress of a pregnancy. Careful notes about menstruation, conception, and pregnancy could reassure an absent husband about his wife's fidelity, and public announcements or celebrations at key moments—such as the end of the third month or the beginning of the ninth month—silenced gossip and invoked divine aid for a safe delivery. In Catalina's case, precise calculations also helped with practical concerns such as the timing of the midwife's arrival, the handing over of certain political duties, or the summoning of her husband for the delivery.[33] For personal and political reasons, Catalina kept close track of her reproductive cycle and shared key aspects of this information with Carlo, who wanted to remain informed.[34]

RUMORS AND REPORTS OF PREGNANCY

As the wife of a ruling duke, Catalina's pregnancies were public events—matters of state generating wide interest and discussion. When Catalina first entered Turin, she was barely one month pregnant and yet the rumor already circulated that she was pregnant. Observers commented that she was sick to her stomach, and certain accommodations were made—such as having her ride a tame horse—that in turn would have confirmed the rumors.[35] A pregnancy could become public knowledge very early, and courtiers clearly gossiped about the private life of the ruler's wife. Yet as a young, new bride, Catalina was uncomfortable with an open discussion of pregnancy. In July 1585, less than a month pregnant with her first child, she wrote to Philip II that she thought she was pregnant but complained that she and her pregnancy were the subjects of rumors. Philip responded, "you have no reason to get upset at what is written from there [Turin] about you, because the same has happened to many honorable women . . . and you can no longer deny that you have done what they have and this can be said by letter without you blushing."[36] The experienced Spanish king, who had married four times and sired at least eleven children, counseled his daughter not to be embarrassed by gossip because "many honorable women" had also had sexual relations with their husbands and she had no reason to be ashamed. For Philip II, such speculation was natural, especially because Catalina's duty was to produce heirs. By October he noted that Catalina was freely acknowledging that she was pregnant.[37]

Rumors of pregnancies most likely emanated from Catalina's household, where her ladies-in-waiting and male attendants could detect changes in her health or activities; or they could have come from Carlo, who would have been proud that his new wife was pregnant. In November 1586, for example, when she was pregnant with her second child, he wrote to Philip that both he and Catalina often forgot that she was pregnant because she was feeling so well. Only the growth of her belly reminded them of the pregnancy, and Carlo told Philip that Catalina was already three months along.[38]

Catalina's pregnancies demonstrated her ability to provide heirs, a subject important to Philip II, who no doubt welcomed news that his daughter was to bear a child. There are two extant letters from her *mayordomos* reporting to the Spanish court on her pregnancies. On 14 August 1585, Cristóbal de Briceño wrote to Mateo Vázquez, Philip's influential private secretary, when Catalina was in the second month of her first pregnancy, saying that it was progressing and she was doing well.[39] As her *mayordomo*, Briceño would have had regular access to her apartments and daily contact with her ladies-in-waiting, who would have kept him updated on Catalina's health. Reporting the news to Vázquez, Briceño knew that it would in turn be communicated to Philip.

Likewise, in November 1586, when Catalina was about three months pregnant with her second child, her *mayordomo mayor*, Paolo de Sfrondato, wrote to Juan de Idiáquez, chief minister of Philip II, telling him that the *infanta* was not experiencing any problems with her pregnancy.[40] Though reporting whether she was well or indisposed, neither Briceño nor Sfondrato provided more detailed information about the progress of her pregnancy, probably because Catalina did not discuss her pregnancies with either of them. Their reports are neither extraordinary nor surprising but form part of the regular news Spanish ministers communicated to Philip II in response to his requests for information about the health of his daughter and her family.

Philip recognized that an aristocratic woman's value rested on her ability to bear children and noted with pride that Catalina performed this duty well. On 12 March 1588, as he awaited news that Catalina had given birth to her third child, he wrote telling her that the day before had marked the third anniversary of her marriage, noting that the previous evening had thus been the third anniversary of her initiation into sexual intimacy, "when you began that duty, which you must have learned so well, as can be seen" (by her having three children in three years).[41] Philip's candid comments indicate that he was at ease discussing sexual topics with his married daughter, especially because they had dynastic and political significance.

Philip even felt free to give his daughter obstetrical advice.[42] On the day Catalina gave birth to her third child, Carlo wrote to Philip describing in detail her difficult delivery, explaining that she had expected it to be quick, but that, as she sat in the birthing chair, labor did not progress as expected and, uncomfortable with continuous hip pain, she lay down on a cot. When that did not help, the doctors and midwife suggested she lie down in her usual bed and try to sleep, which she did until waking up with intense labor pains and giving birth at 2:30 am.[43] Carlo's letter was meant to reassure Philip that Catalina had survived the delivery and was well, but Philip reacted strongly to some of the details Carlo had provided and wrote to Catalina instructing her emphatically never to use a birthing chair, but rather to deliver on a bed. As he explained:

> I am as pleased as you might imagine and even more . . . knowing how well you are after labor, and with reason, since it was long and, I am told, difficult, although you do not tell me this, and it would be [difficult] every time that you give birth in a chair and not a bed, because it is very dangerous to get on the chair early, and certainly this was the cause of death of the princess, my first wife. And you

can see how well it went for your two mothers, who gave birth always in bed, which is definitely the best and most secure [method], and the way you have begun, it is to be believed that you will give birth many times, and in every case it should always be in a bed and not a chair. Tell this to the duke for me [so] that he will not allow it any other way, and the chair no doubt was the cause of you taking so long to give birth and the duke quite understandably was very annoyed about it. Never rush [labor], but let it come when it does, and I can give you this good advice because of the many times, as you know, that I have seen it [childbirth].[44]

While scholars familiar with Philip II's obsessive nature would not be surprised at his insistent interest in how Catalina gave birth, his concern also demonstrates his affection for her and his familiarity with the risks of childbirth.[45] As he noted, his first wife had died of complications from childbirth.[46] When Catalina gave birth to her first son in April 1586, Philip wrote to her that he was thrilled with the good news, "which has been the greatest joy imaginable," and that he was very happy she had given him his first grandson but "in exchange for you being very well, I would patiently accept that it were a granddaughter."[47] Far away, worried that his daughter would die in childbirth and unable to control the recommendations of her doctors or the decisions of the duke, Philip II was relieved to hear that his daughter had survived childbirth. Though he claimed that his primary concern was her health and safety, what plainly pleased him as much or more was that she had borne a son.

Catalina herself often told her father which month she was entering, as she did in 1594: "In fifteen days I will be in the ninth month and thus childbirth cannot be too far away." If she wrote Philip more detailed comments, they have been lost, but her letters to Carlo contain many particulars about her pregnancies. She often informed the duke about the health and activities of all their children and when pregnant would add brief updates on the baby she was carrying. For example, she joked with the duke that to forestall any complaints that she did not keep him well informed about the baby in her womb, she was reporting that the baby was well. Missing the duke, she told him that the children were all well and that "the one of the belly" (*el de la barriga*) was very alone without him.[48] On another occasion, she chided the duke for having been gone so long that he no longer remembered what was in her belly. Nevertheless, she added, the baby there greeted him (and Catalina used the typical courtly phrase for showing respect, saying the baby kissed the duke's hands) and was at that moment moving around.[49] At other times, Catalina merely told the duke that her belly was well, making no specific mention of the baby, but rather conflating the belly with the baby.

Most often, Catalina reported the size of her abdomen and whether the child moved—the perceptible signs of the progress of a pregnancy. In September 1590, about two months pregnant with her fifth child, Catalina told Carlo that she was very tired and did not have anything to say about the baby in her womb because he was lazy and hardly moved, and "I think he will take after me in this respect." In October 1590, she wrote, "Today I have entered the fifth month and since three days ago [the baby] has been moving much more and I have a very large belly." Two weeks later, Catalina reported that the doctors had made her stay in bed because of a cough, which concerned them primarily because she was pregnant. She had benefited from the rest and had been able to return to work. "The one in the belly is well and do not let any of this worry you because there is no reason to do so."[50] These regular reports about the status of the child in her womb are not surprising, given the frequency of Catalina's pregnancies and the aristocratic interest in continuing their family line, as well as Carlo's desire to be reassured that all was well.

Catalina's humorous comments indicate that she approached her pregnancies in a good-natured, sometimes playful fashion and was not consumed with worry for nine months. In turn, the duke often responded lightheartedly, calling the baby in her womb the "gentleman of the belly" (*el caballero de la barriga*).[51] Pregnancy was such a normal part of their lives that they could joke and banter about it.

CHILDBIRTH

Childbirth was a different matter, and Catalina did not approach it with the same degree of nonchalance. Not surprisingly, as the ninth month approached she prepared for childbirth and all its accompanying logistical complications, and when the duke was absent she arranged for management of political responsibilities during the post-partum period. Carlo, for his part, seems to have had confidence that she would survive childbirth and be able to resume seeing to his political and military needs immediately after giving birth.

Catalina confronted the possibility that she would die in childbirth and prepared herself by going to confession and receiving communion. As she told the duke in February 1591: "We are all well and I could go into labor at any hour. Yesterday I entered the ninth month and I received communion . . . I trust in God to let me deliver well." In January 1593, in the ninth month of her next pregnancy and knowing she could deliver any day, she went to confession and received communion so that the baby "can come when it wants and God's will be done."[52] But though Catalina clearly considered the possibility of not surviving childbirth, her letters do not indicate that she was overly worried.

Preparing herself for childbirth, Catalina might have found comfort in symbols and talismans of fertility, pregnancy, and safe delivery. The post-mortem inventory of her goods lists a "rose for childbirth," perhaps referring to the rose of Jericho, which was supposed to prevent the risk of hemorrhage in childbirth. The inventory does not clarify, however, whether the rose was decorative or an actual plant.[53] Among the many items which Catalina inherited from her mother was a marten's head made of "gold with forty-one diamonds of different sizes and two small rubies in the eyes, with four small feet made of gold, each one with three diamonds."[54] European ladies attached the jewel-encrusted head to a marten fur and then to a chain belt worn around their waist (see plate 12). From a tale in Book 9 of Ovid's *Metamorphoses*, in which a servant woman who has facilitated her mistress's difficult childbirth is transformed into a marten by an aggrieved divinity, martens had come to be associated with fortunate childbirth, and talismanic virtue was attributed to the jewel-headed marten pelt.[55] As auguring fertility, pregnancy, and safe childbirth, marten furs might be carried or touched by women hoping to conceive or already pregnant.

A portrait of Catalina Micaela (plate 11) shows her touching a jeweled marten's head, and the post-mortem inventory of her possessions lists two martens with gold heads and gold feet. One was undoubtedly the marten she inherited from her mother, which Catalina brought with her to Turin, but the other must have been acquired during her years at the court of Turin. Perhaps her overjoyed husband gave her the second as one of the many presents he showered upon her when she became pregnant for the first time.[56] But though depicted as touching the marten's head in the portrait, Catalina made no reference to the talisman in her letters, and it may have been more a novelty prop for the stiffly posed court portraits than an item for personal use.

Because she feared facing the pain and the danger of childbirth without him, Catalina wished more than anything for the duke's presence when she gave birth. Whenever possible, he did in fact return for the delivery, though sometimes not until the last possible moment. In a letter of 6 January 1593, Catalina urged him to come quickly so that "we do not have to make you rush back for my childbirth," and by the time she gave birth four days later, Carlo had arrived. (In two letters of that same month, he had urged her to tell him how her *barriga* was, so he could time his arrival.[57]) For other pregnancies, too, she wrote asking him to return, telling him that her labor pains would be worse without him. She seems occasionally to have been almost frantic that the duke might fail to appear. In April 1589, as her fourth pregnancy approached term and it became clear to her that he would not appear in time for the delivery, she resigned herself with disappointment. "My life," she wrote to the duke:

> I do not know what to say about losing all hope of seeing you as I had thought, because I now see well that it is impossible for you to come. You do not feel it any worse than I do. I am in such a state that I would not know how to write it and I would like to be somewhere that no one could see me so that I could cry . . . it is necessary for me to restrain myself [from crying] and I wish the night were here so that I could wail my heart out in bed.

In March 1591, facing another childbirth without the duke, she insisted that after recovering she should be allowed to travel to him, "to be with you and not here, banished."[58]

Catalina did not believe she needed to stay in Turin to give birth. Her priority was to be close to Carlo and have him present at the birth, and she urged him to let her go to him and give birth wherever he happened to be. This was particularly true when in 1591, not having seen Carlo in months, she wanted to travel to Nice to give birth and was frustrated when she was not allowed to do so. Writing to Carlo in January that year, she told him that her stomach was very large and that in eight days she would be entering the eighth month. She was losing patience, thinking that Carlo would not be with her when she gave birth and complaining that "my wishes are never met, if only to go to Nice to give birth." The end of the eighth month seemed to have been the cut-off point for her hopes, because once she entered the ninth month, she noted, there was no hope of traveling. She begged Carlo at any rate to let her travel to Nice after giving birth, "if I survive."[59] Carlo, though, wished to keep her far from the fighting and did not want to expose her to the rigors of travel or illness. In February, when she was begging him to allow her to go to Nice, he told her that it was too dangerous and that she was too far along in the pregnancy to travel safely.[60] He reassured her that he would see her when he returned from Spain, where he was journeying to secure Philip's assistance against the French. He never once gave her permission to leave Turin as childbirth approached.

Catalina's comments about needing the duke with her when she gave birth also indicate that she saw childbirth as a conjugal rather than a strictly feminine event; she wanted more than anything to have her husband with her, even perhaps in the birthing room itself. In fact, describing the birth of her daughter Isabel, she wrote to Carlo: "I fear that if you had been here, you would have been no less tired, because all the women have been, their hands swollen from my having pressed them so [hard] . . . I would not have felt [the pain] if I had been with you."[61] Her remarks imply that Carlo would have experienced her delivery as intimately as her ladies-in-waiting, suggesting that in childbirth she was attended not only by women but sometimes by the duke as well; in Turin the birthing room was perhaps not an exclusively female space.[62] When Carlo described to Philip II her difficult delivery in April 1588, he noted that she went from birthing chair to cot to bed, that the doctors and the midwife were advising her, that she sipped soup, ate, and walked around, all suggesting that, while in labor, Catalina was not confined to one place but moved around her apartments, and that male doctors (and Carlo) had access to her rooms. While Carlo might have received this information from Catalina's ladies-in-waiting, he might also have observed Catalina's labor himself, and her later insistence on having him close by would suggest that he had been present at her earlier childbirths, before his military campaigning began.[63]

Similarly, when preparing for her next childbirth, in 1589, Catalina told the duke that without him beside her (*junto a mi*) her labor pains would double. The duke reassured her that he would try his best to be with her, and weeks before the birth of their daughter Margarita in April, he even told Catalina, hyperbolically, that if necessary he would fly through the air to be with her. He also wrote: "If you only knew what I feel not to be with you when you give birth, you would not believe it because I am so, so sorry."[64] Nevertheless, in this case, unable or unwilling to tear himself away from his military campaign, Carlo failed to appear for Margarita's birth.

No doubt Catalina was familiar with the custom of the Spanish court, where the king was often present at royal births.[65] Her father was certainly at the side of her own mother, Elisabeth of Valois, while she was in labor with her first child, administering a special potion sent by her mother, Catherine de' Medici, supposed to lessen labor pains.[66] When he later gave Catalina obstetrical advice, Philip apparently assumed that her husband would be at her side during her labor to ensure that she gave birth on a bed and not a chair. Perhaps from her experience of the Spanish court, Catalina expected the duke to be with her when she went into labor.

She thought that, as a rule, husbands should be present when their wives went into labor. On one occasion, the count of Frossasco, whose wife was soon to give birth, insisted on leaving Turin at once to take a letter from Catalina to the duke. Catalina told Carlo that she had urged the count to wait until his wife delivered, but he had refused. She therefore now requested that Carlo send Frossasco back to Turin within fifteen to twenty days, when his wife expected to give birth, explaining that "because I know how [women] feel to be without their husbands, I have

1. Philip II of Spain, Catalina's father, usually dressed in black, as in this portrait, painted when he was forty-six. When crowned as king of Portugal he had—"much against my will"—worn brocade, as customary for the occasion. For Catalina's wedding he wore black.

2. Catalina's mother, Elisabeth of Valois, eldest daughter of Henri II of France and Catherine de' Medici, died at twenty-three, when Catalina was an infant. Here Elisabeth poses with a jewel-headed marten, likely the same one Catalina poses with in plate 11.

3. The *infantas* Isabel and Catalina at five and four respectively. With garlands of flowers in their hair, dressed in rich fabrics, adorned with costly jewels, and sporting pearl pendant earrings, the two girls also display two of their pets—a green parrot and a small spaniel.

4. A young Catalina with a flower in her hair and holding a marmoset. Inheriting the Habsburg penchant for exotic animals, she and Isabel took them along from one royal residence to another. Catalina would continue to wear flowers and jewels in floral designs as hair adornments.

5. The *infanta* Isabel at twenty or twenty-one, with Magdalena Ruiz, a widowed dwarf Catalina knew well at the Spanish court. In the portrait, painted after Catalina had left Spain, Isabel holds a cameo of Philip II; Magdalena's two monkeys and coral beads were imports from the Americas.

6, facing page top left. In this portrait by his court painter, Jan Kraeck ("El Flamenco"), Carlo Emanuele I poses in armor standing beside a plumed helmet, his hand on a rapier, all probably ceremonial, but apt: military campaigns kept him away from Turin during much of his and Catalina's marriage.

7, facing page top right. This portrait, also by Kraeck, matches that of the duke in armor, both probably from the early 1590s. Catalina, lover and consumer of the latest in feminine fashion, poses in an elaborately ornamented dress and pearl necklace, her hair adorned with a diadem of pearls and jeweled flowers.

8. Catalina and Carlo, the latter in his domestic versus soldierly role, show off their three eldest sons, Filippo, Vittorio (with songbird), and Filiberto, and first daughter, Margarita, wearing a diadem similar to her mother's, but not yet the earrings over which her parents would later spar.

9. Vittorio, Filiberto, and Filippo in fashionable matching outfits chosen by Catalina, with a handsome dog in an elegant collar making a fourth. A parrot in the window and a monkey lurking behind a column suggest the family's heterogeneous menagerie of pets.

10. Maria Apollonia, Catalina and Carlo's seventh child and third daughter, one year old, in a rolling cart similar to those Catalina would have known as a child. A dog and pigeon-like bird flank the girl, adorned with pearls in her hair and pendant pearl earrings—by now, Catalina had prevailed in the tussle over the piercings.

11. Catalina rests her hand on the jewel-encrusted head of a marten pelt (see plate 12), a talisman for fertility and safe childbirth. The portrait's jeweled marten head was probably that inherited from her mother, Elisabeth of Valois, whose portrait also features a marten head (plate 2).

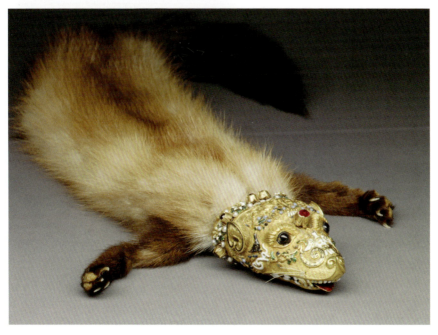

12. This jeweled marten's head from mid-sixteenth-century Venice is probably similar to Catalina's. While the pelt in this museum piece is not original, the artifact gives a good idea of the talisman Catalina inherited.

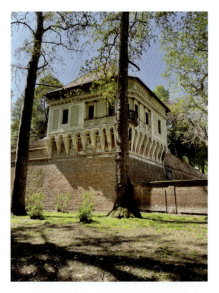

13. A copy of a pencil drawing by Jan Kraeck of Catalina shortly after her 1585 arrival in Turin. Showing her hair in tight ringlets, a high forehead, heart-shaped face, almond eyes, strong nose, and small mouth with full lips, the sketch depicts her youthful countenance in greater detail than formal court portraits, though smallpox scars may have been omitted.

15. Shortly after Catalina's arrival in Turin, this pavilion was built atop a corner bastion on walls bordering the palace grounds and gardens, as a belvedere (now enclosed) from which Catalina could enjoy an open view of the surrounding countryside, just outside the city walls but then home to abundant wildlife.

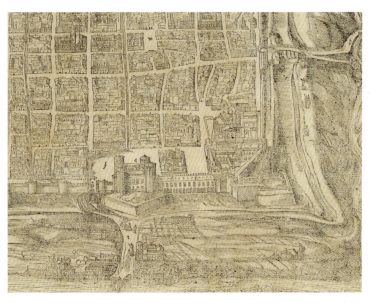

14. This detail of a 1572 plan of Turin shows the castle where Catalina's children lived, connected by the long gallery to the apartments that became the residence of Catalina and Carlo. The Green Bastion pavilion (plate 15), not yet constructed, would be built on the bastion at the lower right.

16. A painting by Kraeck of the Marian statue in Vicoforte, south of Turin, to which healing powers were attributed after it began miraculously to bleed in 1592. Devoted to "Our Lady of Mondovì," Catalina sent the painting to her father, hoping to spread this Marian cult to Spain.

17. The first page of a 1589 letter from Catalina to Carlo, written on a sheet approximately 12.2 × 8.2 inches (31 × 20.5 cm) folded vertically on the left. The salutation ("Lord of my eyes") is centered, with a distinct space between the salutation and the text of the letter. She indented her script on the left to leave a slight margin on this and subsequent pages.

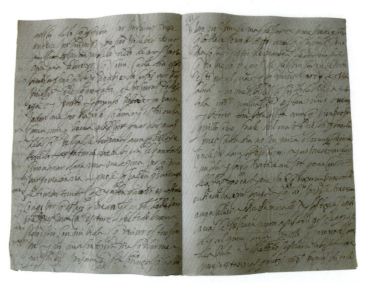

18. The sheet of paper is open, with the fold in the center. The second page of the letter is on the left and the third page is on the right.

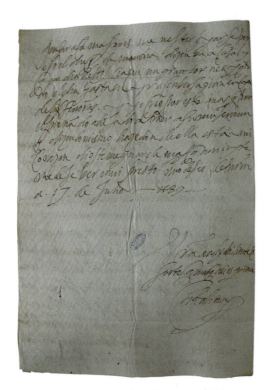

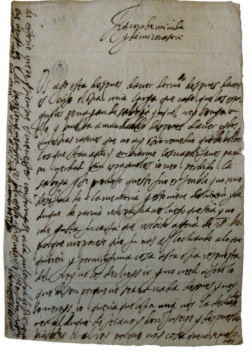

19. In this final page of the letter, the fold is on the right. Catalina's closing and signature are on the bottom right, separated by a wide space after the letter's text. The closing translates, "Your loyal and obedient consort who loves you more than herself."

20. A 1588 letter from Carlo to Catalina whom he addressed as "Lady of my life and my heart." Like Catalina, the duke wrote in Spanish, but his cramped and blotchy script contrasts sharply with Catalina's open, flowing handwriting. To avoid adding another page, he often turned the paper 90 degrees to jam a final sentence or two in the left margin.

sympathy for them [women] and thus I am her advocate." She added that other women were more fortunate than she herself, because their husbands could be with them at childbirth. Clearly she was still smarting from Carlo's failure to be present for her childbirth earlier the same year. She also implied, melodramatically, that if she lived to have another child, she would not put up with Carlo's absence but would rather think of killing herself.[67] Her remarks about Frossasco and his wife indicate that the duke, and probably the count of Frossasco as well, did not always place his wife's labor above political and military priorities.

Carlo, on the other hand, though not necessarily expecting to be at all her deliveries, did expect to receive word as soon as the child was born, and Catalina always wrote immediately after giving birth. These post-delivery letters are only a paragraph long and signed only "Catalina," instead of her usual "your loyal and obedient consort who loves you more than herself, Catalina." She noted that she was not allowed to write more—presumably her doctors forbade her—and would rely on others to give more details. With Catalina's own letter-writing curtailed, the duke asked for a full, detailed report from her *camarera mayor*, Doña Sancha de Guzmán. When the latter showed Catalina the letter she had written to the duke, Catalina joked to the duke that Doña Sancha was very proud of her letter, adding that as a woman (*siendo mujer ella*), Doña Sancha would give all the details.[68] Her meaning seems ambiguous; did she mean that Sancha would have all the details because as a woman she could be with Catalina as she recovered from childbirth, or that women would probably provide more obstetrical details than men? Doña Sancha also wrote to Catalina's father, Philip II, to inform him of the birth, in so doing fulfilling her duties as Catalina's *camarera mayor*.[69] Carlo noted to Catalina: "It is sufficient that Doña Sancha write me everything pertaining to her profession."[70] At the Spanish court, the queen's *camarera mayor* super-vised the baby's delivery.[71] As Catalina's *camarera mayor* at a court which followed Spanish rules of etiquette, Doña Sancha would probably have done this in Turin as well, and in the days right after childbirth, Catalina was attended primarily by women.[72]

While delegating her correspondence to others, especially her *camarera mayor*, in the days immediately after giving birth, Catalina soon returned to her governance responsibilities—among them, securing financial, military, and diplomatic support for the duke's military campaigns and corresponding with several dozen governors and magistrates.[73] Childbirth brought a temporary halt to some of her official responsibilities. After giving birth she could not for a time attend conciliar meetings and had to rely on others to manage financial and military provisions. Carlo, however, expected her to continue with her duties as long as possible before she delivered, and to resume them soon after giving birth.

As her due date approached, Catalina scrambled to settle pressing matters and sometimes warned the duke that she would soon be unable to attend to political duties. In April 1589, for example, only twenty days before giving birth and therefore well into her ninth month, she wrote to the duke: "I want to remind you that . . . if I go into labor there will be no one to take care of all the business." Just nine days before giving birth again, two years later, she reassured Carlo that she was still taking care of all the business of governing, "because for several days, should God give me health after childbirth, I will not be able to deal with business and there will be no trustworthy person [to take care of matters]. I am doing everything that needs to be done."[74] As childbirth approached, Catalina sought to wrap up unfinished business, not only because she knew she might not survive, but also because she could not meet with councilors and ministers while still in bed. However, her phrase "several days" is telling—she expected to resume her political responsibilities within days of delivery.

Prompted by Carlo's expectations, Catalina planned to return to business quickly, and indeed she wasted no time in doing so soon after childbirth. On 30 April 1589, two days after giving birth, she directed her secretary to write to the duke about numerous political matters.[75] By 4 May she was writing in her own hand about business matters, though including particulars about the new baby's baptism and health. A letter of 9 May dealt almost completely with political developments and arrangements for providing the duke with financial support. Two days later, having received several letters from the duke detailing the hardships he and his soldiers were experiencing and his need for money, she expressed her frustration at not being able to confer with councilors and officials as effectively as usual: "Since I have been in bed, nothing has been paid and I wish I were out of bed, better to attend to business and to all you command."[76] Though seeing to business while still recuperating from childbirth, as her letters demonstrate, Catalina nonetheless seems to have worried that the duke would think her negligent in seeing to his funding needs.

Carlo in turn seems to have recognized that she might be frustrated by all his appeals and demands. In a letter of 19 May, otherwise filled with requests and instructions, he wrote that "it hurts me in my soul not to be there to be able to take care of everything" and "forgive me if I give you these afflictions." Three days later he wrote effusively of his love for her and his need to be with her, noting that if they were together, they would not argue or cry.[77]

During these weeks in April and May 1589, Carlo's pressing needs required Catalina to return to political business immediately, and two years later he made similar demands of her after she gave birth to her daughter Isabel, in March 1591.[78] The duke, on his way to Spain to request military assistance from Philip II, was depending on Catalina to manage affairs in Turin. The Spanish ambassador in Turin, Don Jusepe, criticized Carlo for leaving at this critical period, when events in the Piedmont were particularly tense, and he evidently reminded Carlo that Catalina would be unable to see to everything so soon after giving birth, because in a letter to her, Carlo called Don Jusepe a hen (*una gallina*) and said that he had told the ambassador that Catalina was not "a woman like the others."[79] She had given birth seventeen days before Carlo's letter, and he urged her not to write to him because she was still recuperating from childbirth. Nevertheless, the duke felt certain that Catalina could manage things in his absence, and that, if not, she would summon him back from Spain. Catalina in fact did see to political business in the weeks following childbirth. On 18 March 1591, just a week after giving birth, she wrote to Carlo that she was writing from her bed but still doing all she could for him. Thirteen days later, she wrote to assure him that "believe me, I see to everything even though I cannot go out there [outside her private apartments] to see to business, some things are still resolved . . . I think I will go out this next week."[80]

In the days immediately following childbirth, Catalina was by no means freed of her political responsibilities, nor did she enjoy a "privileged position," as scholars have found for other early modern women.[81] Confinement still allowed her to oversee whatever duties she could perform from her apartments, even as she noted that for two weeks she neither got out of bed (except to move to a cot while her bed was made) nor got dressed.[82] In addition to resuming her political duties soon after giving birth, she made preparations for her children's baptisms, usually about two weeks after birth, when Catalina herself was unable to attend.[83] She noted in her letters when she was able to go out in public again, telling Carlo that she had gone out to attend mass (perhaps a mass of purification, as Spanish queens attended after their confinement), usually about three weeks after giving birth.[84] At this point, she was able to resume all political tasks, as she told Carlo on 21 May 1589: "Today I have gone out to mass at San Lorenzo and so I will begin to transact business and I will make sure that everything is done as you order."[85] While she may have been relieved of duties when Carlo returned for her deliveries, this was certainly not the case when he was absent. He expected her to see to political matters even during her confinement, and she complied.

LACTATION AND RETURN TO FERTILITY

Sixteenth-century noble and royal women did not nurse their newborns, in part because menstruation and sexual intercourse were thought to corrupt a woman's milk, and also because to produce more heirs, such women needed a quick return to their menstrual cycle and intercourse. Moreover, because breastfeeding was not socially acceptable for wealthy sixteenth-century women, nursing her children was not an option Catalina even considered, and it is not surprising that after she had given birth, she and Carlo hired a wet nurse, allowing Catalina to return quickly to fertility and sexual intimacy with Carlo.[86]

Thus, after childbirth Catalina immediately attempted to stop the flow of her milk. Lactation seemed almost an illness to her aristocratic contemporaries. In 1566, for example, the French ambassador to the court of Spain had reported to Catherine de' Medici that Catherine's daughter, Elisabeth of Valois, had a fever after childbirth, and that it was due to the milk, which "suffocates her."[87] Catalina also seems to have assumed that lactation, or perhaps lactation without nursing, brought on fever. On 1 May 1589, three days after giving birth, she noted that her milk had started the night before, though without causing a fever. Two days later she begged the duke's forgiveness for having written to him despite his instructions not to do so until she was well, defending herself by saying that writing actually made her feel better and "cures me of milk" (*me sana de la leche*).[88] Several days later she reported that her milk was almost completely gone and caused her no discomfort.

Lactation was in fact one reason Catalina was discouraged from writing after childbirth, and the attempt to stop milk production was probably the cause of her discomfort. Five days after giving birth to Isabel in March 1591, she told the duke that because she was bothered by the milk humor (*umor de la leche*), she was not allowed to move her arms. She also told him that her breasts had become swollen from writing.[89] She needed to recover from lactation just as she recovered from childbirth, and her reward in this case, she hoped, would be to travel to join the duke. Post-partum recovery and lactation confined Catalina to her room and bed, but, feeling well despite still lactating, she chafed at her enforced confinement.

Catalina often informed the duke of the start of her first post-partum period, commenting on whether she had bled her usual eight days. In July 1589, when she had expected the onset of her period but hardly bled, she reported that the doctors had decided to bleed her from a foot—a usual treatment to induce menstrual flow.[90] Telling Carlo that she thought that she would not have had this problem had he been present, she might have been alluding to the belief of physicians that sexual intercourse could cure problems of menstrual flow.[91] On this occasion, after she was bled a second time, Catalina sent Carlo a silk ribbon (*listón*) reddened by her blood during the procedure.[92] Carlo responded, somewhat dramatically, that the bloodied ribbon had made him weep.[93] Her "gift" of the *listón* might also have been her way of providing physical evidence of taking necessary steps to bring on menstruation.

Catalina's terms for describing menstruation suggest that she took a humoral view of menstrual bleeding. In describing her menstrual cycle, she used the very straightforward verb *bajar* (to drop or to lower) for menstruate, a term also used by other aristocratic women trained at the Spanish court.[94] Her use of this verb indicates that she might have regarded menstruation as a form of purging—with the blood dropping from the upper to the lower body—which is how some doctors in late medieval Europe had seen it.[95] Catalina also used the term *con camisa* (with shirt) for menstruation—a Castilian expression that was at least a century old by the time Catalina employed it. As she said in December 1595, about a month and a half after giving birth: "You will find me no longer perspiring as I have written you, but *'con la camisa,'* although it is so little that I wish it were more and so I took the syrup that I normally take for this."[96] Covarrubias explained that this idiomatic expression came from the practice of a menstruating woman not changing her shirt until she stopped bleeding, although there is no indication that Catalina actually followed this practice.[97] She did not employ words such as "the flowers," "courses," or "terms," often used in countries like England and France to describe menstruation.[98]

She reported her menstrual bleeding to her husband not only because it was indicative of her general health, but also because it had implications for resuming sex with him. While it is unclear which days of her cycle Catalina believed to be the most fertile, she might indeed have been letting the duke know that they could soon enjoy sexual intercourse again, and that she was once again fertile.

THE TOLL OF PREGNANCY AND CHILDBIRTH

Catalina lived through the cycle of pregnancy, childbirth, and post-partum recovery nine times and at her death was over halfway through a tenth. Frequent multiple pregnancies can take a cumulative toll on a woman's body, and we can easily speculate that Catalina at thirty was not as vigorous as she had been when she bore her first child at eighteen. Yet, while her letters to Carlo provide detailed information about seven of her ten pregnancies and contain passing references to difficulties and discomforts during them, she never gave the impression that any was serious, and there is no conclusive evidence that her health suffered from having ten children in twelve years.[99] Her only serious illnesses until that leading to her death in 1597 seem to have come in 1588 and

1589. According to a July 1588 report by the Venetian ambassador in Turin, Carlo awakened one morning in Miraflores to find Catalina senseless, her body cold, her mouth foaming. For several days she seemed on the brink of death. The 1589 illness was less serious but still left her exhausted for weeks. Apart from these two grave illnesses and various minor ailments, she evidently enjoyed generally good health during her married years.

In some respects, even pregnancy did not slow Catalina down. She continued to hunt, for example, as in October 1586 when she was three months pregnant with her first child.[100] In July 1596, about four months pregnant with her ninth child, she and her children made an excursion from Turin to Mondovì and hunted along the way.[101] While pregnant she also visited shrines and sanctuaries, traveling in a chair or litter. She assumed as well that she could travel even long distances while pregnant. In 1589, pregnant with her fourth, she told the duke that "being in the seventh month and it not being cold out," she saw no reason why she could not travel with him.[102] Likewise, in October 1597, almost five months pregnant with her tenth (and last) child and eager to be with Carlo, she told him that she could travel safely in a litter or chair to Nice and was not worried about any illnesses she might suffer, though she would prefer that he come to Turin instead.[103] Such examples indicate that Catalina did not languish in pregnancy, nor allow it to cramp her daily life overmuch.

Nevertheless, her letters document that pregnancy could be physically taxing for her and may over time have sapped her strength. Her doctors and Carlo insisted that when pregnant she needed to take particular care of herself. They wanted her to exercise, and she complied, telling Carlo when she was nine months pregnant with their fourth child that most mornings she walked back and forth from the castle where the children resided, a round trip of perhaps a quarter mile.[104] However, pregnancy made it difficult for her to walk. Shortly before the birth of her fourth child, she wrote to Carlo that "my feet and hands are very swollen but I am able to walk better than the usual in other pregnancies."[105] Claiming that she was walking more easily suggests that she had been less mobile during her earlier pregnancies. She had trouble walking not only because of swollen feet but also because, as she told

Carlo when eight months pregnant with her fourth, her belly was so big. A few days later she reported, "I am very burdened with my belly that is very low, more so than [when pregnant] with Vittorio [her second child]."[106] She continued to tell Carlo how uncomfortable she was, adding that he knew well that such discomfort was usual for her in the final months of pregnancy.[107] In September 1590, she wrote to the duke that she was very tired, blaming it on the heat, but she was also three months pregnant with her fifth child.[108] Several months later, she told Carlo that her belly was very large but that the doctors insisted she exercise and that she reluctantly complied by walking on two afternoons to the castle where her children lived. As she noted, "you know well my laziness (*flogedad*) and now it is even worse and I have a very large belly."[109] A few weeks later yet, she reported that "I am so heavy that it is something to see."[110] Although Catalina did not whine, her comments indicate that the burden of carrying an unborn child was difficult for her and that even walking was a chore. Not surprisingly, her autopsy noted that she lived a sedentary life.[111] A large, heavy belly was so low that it prevented her from hunting, she wrote in March 1589.[112] (A month later she gave birth.) Her large belly also hampered her from moving freely in bed, and she wrote to Carlo, then in Spain, that she wished she would give birth, not only so she would be allowed to go where she wanted, but also no doubt so she could move and sleep more easily.[113] Her letters also reveal that she perspired profusely during a few of her pregnancies.[114]

Such difficulties are consistent with what many pregnant women feel and should not surprise us, but unlike most contemporary women in developed countries, who space out their pregnancies, Catalina had hers in quick succession, leaving little time for her body to recover completely. After one of her pregnancies, she was pregnant again within two months, and after another, within three (see the chart at the end of the chapter). Six of her ten pregnancies followed the previous one by no more than six months, and usually less. The two longest gaps (thirteen and fourteen months) came in the years 1589 to 1592, when Carlo was far away—in Savoy, Provence, and Spain. They were again apart in 1593 and 1594, explaining the longer gap between her seventh and eighth pregnancies, but between her final two pregnancies, there was a gap of only six months. No wonder that, after her fourth child in four years and already pregnant with a fifth, Catalina complained to Carlo on just her twenty-third birthday that she was old. Responding to a letter from him thanking her for a rosary, Catalina wrote: "I am glad you liked the rosary and it deserves to be favored because it comes from a holy place and not because it comes from my hands, which are bad and [are those] of an old woman because today I have reached twenty-three years and with four children and another in the belly, they [the years] are many."[115]

Bearing children aged Catalina both mentally and physically, or so she claimed. When their eldest son turned three in April 1589, she told Carlo that "he is already very old . . . and his mother even more so because she is on the verge of having four children." Just four days after Margarita's birth, she described herself as "this very old mother who now is [mother] of four."[116] A month after Margarita's birth in late April, Catalina told Carlo that the baby was getting bigger every day, but that she wished that she were old enough to walk alone, "because I already want to see her grown up." She noted, though, that this would make her—Catalina—old, "although I promise you that I already am, especially in humor . . . and as a mother of four children."[117] Bearing a fourth child seems to have caused Catalina to feel old, though that specific childbirth does not seem to have been particularly difficult for her, and her references to aging are perhaps more lighthearted than serious.

Age was on her mind again in August 1589, perhaps because she was still feeling weary from an illness she had been struggling with since mid-July, for which she had been purged, bled, and medicated, remedies occasionally forcing her to remain in bed all day. In late July, she noted that it had been a bad month and a bad year, and even Philip II commented that he had heard that she had been unwell, bled twice, and purged.[118] In early August she told the duke that she had proof that she was growing old. "You will find me very old if I am lucky enough to live to see you. I promise you that I have gray hair and it is not a joke. Some fell out when I was combing my hair and others are there and still others coming in. You will see [how old] I am, especially having four children who are already so big."[119] As proof that Catalina was speaking the truth (and unbeknownst to Catalina), her *camarera mayor*, Doña

Sancha, took the liberty of sending the duke a few strands of Catalina's gray hair, which the duke gallantly told Catalina he would treasure "as a relic." (She responded that she wished she were holy enough that her gray hair would be relics.[120])

Age was still on her mind three days later when she responded to a letter in which Carlo had commented that he hoped Catalina's sister, Isabel Clara Eugenia, would marry and have as many children "as is necessary and that no more time is wasted because it is a shame that such a pretty thing does not beget other very pretty [things]." Catalina agreed, writing that "my sister wastes too much time, especially because on Saturday she will turn twenty-three," but switching the subject to herself, she added that she, Catalina, was looking much older than twenty-three (she was twenty-two).[121] Her pairing of Isabel's failure to marry and have children with a reference to Isabel's age and her own aging suggests that Catalina worried that bearing four children had made her look old and less attractive. Was she also thinking that with Carlo's compliment to her sister as "such a pretty thing" there might be a suggestion that Isabel had retained her youthful beauty precisely because she had borne no children? Though one would think that, at twenty-two, Catalina could not honestly have felt old and faded, her repeated mentions of aging to Carlo, even if partly playful, suggest an unaffected anxiety.[122] Bearing four children in little over three years had undoubtedly taken a toll on her, and she might have had good reason for feeling much older than her years.

She continued to associate frequent childbearing with rapid aging, and as her children grew older, she felt older yet. In April 1592 she noted, "Today the prince [Filippo Emanuele—their eldest] is six years old, which makes me old." In a letter to Philip II five years later, toward the end of her life, she expressed a similar sentiment: "The newborn baby is eating very well and the rest [of the children] are very big, enough to make me very old."[123] She was twenty-eight. Even as she rejoiced in her active, healthy children, she lamented that in bearing them, she had lost her own youth.

After bearing nine children, Catalina might unwittingly have revealed a reluctance to become pregnant again, thinking that she had by then given birth to enough children. In 1597, suspecting she was pregnant with her tenth, she wrote to Carlo of her suspicions, and three times within a span of a week she used the word "fear" about her state. "I have nothing to say about myself except that I am fearing that I will not get my period," she wrote to Carlo, "because it has not come and I do not feel anything. May it be as God wishes," she added. A few days later, on 17 July 1597, she wrote to him that her period was more than fifteen days late and "it makes me fear that the tenth [child] is in my belly." Four days later she wrote, "My failure (*falta*) [to get my period] continues and I fear that I will not get my period; soon we will know."[124] Although she seems to have accepted her final pregnancy as God's will and did not repine, the drumbeat of "fear" suggests strong reservations about yet another pregnancy. By 1597, the burdens of pregnancy and childbirth had perhaps finally worn her down.

CATALINA'S PREGNANCIES AND GAPS BETWEEN PREGNANCIES

Child #1, Filippo Emanuele, born 2 April 1586
    Pregnant again after 4 months
Child #2, Vittorio Amedeo, born 8 May 1587
    Pregnant again after 2 months
Child #3, Emanuele Filiberto, born 17 April 1588
    Pregnant again after 3 months
Child #4, Margarita, born 28 April 1589 (*Carlo not present at birth*)
    Pregnant again after 14 months
Child #5, Isabel, born 11 March 1591 (*Carlo not present at birth*)
    Pregnant again after 13 months
Child #6, Mauricio, born 10 January 1593
    Pregnant again after 4 months
Child #7, Maria Apollonia, born 8 February 1594
    Pregnant again after 11 months
Child #8, Francesca Caterina, born 6 October 1595
    Pregnant again after 5 months
Child #9, Tommaso Francesco, born 22 December 1596
    Pregnant again after 6 months
Child #10, Giovanna, born prematurely 7 November 1597 (*Carlo not present at birth*)

CHAPTER 8

LOVING HER CHILDREN, LONGING FOR CARLO

I promise you that [I tend to them] more for you than because they are my children. They no longer need me and you could just as well let me go and have a few days of rest with you.

Catalina to Carlo, 5 August, probably 1590

IN THE ELEVEN AND a half years between April 1586 and November 1597, Catalina Micaela bore ten children:

- Filippo Emanuele (1586–1605), named after both grandfathers, and who died at nineteen;
- Vittorio (1587–1637), who would succeed Carlo as duke of Savoy;
- Emanuele Filiberto (1588–1624), who would serve as viceroy of Sicily for the last two years of his life;
- Margarita (1589–1655), who would become duchess of Mantua, rule the duchy, and in later years govern Portugal;
- Isabel (1591–1626), who would marry the heir to the duchy of Modena;
- Mauricio (1593–1657), who would become a cardinal and take religious vows and then renounce them to marry;
- Maria Apollonia (1594–1646), who became a Franciscan nun;
- Francesca Caterina (1595–1640), also a Franciscan nun;
- Tommaso Francesco (1596–1656), prince of Carignano;
- Giovanna (1597), who died at birth.[1]

Catalina knew them only as young children or infants, because she died when her eldest, Filippo (whom she always called "the Prince" in her letters to the duke because as Carlo's heir he held the title of Prince of the Piedmont), was only ten and a half. Though not with her constantly, the children were her frequent companions; she spent time with them almost daily and managed their care. Like other aristocratic women, Catalina handed over the routine care of her children to attendants whom she and the duke had carefully chosen. Left to govern the duchy of Savoy in the duke's absence, she had little choice but to give precedence to her managerial responsibilities, and her letters to Carlo do not indicate that she resented being unable to spend more time with her children. She certainly derived pleasure from them—her letters are filled with affectionate comments about their antics or appearance—but in her priorities, her children came second to her husband, and occasionally she was frustrated by her maternal duties and responsibilities.

"ALL OF OUR CHILDREN ARE HERE"

Catalina's children resided in the medieval castle in Turin now known as Palazzo Madama, a separate building connected to the ducal palace by a long gallery.[2] The two-story gallery, open on the ground level but enclosed on the second, measured approximately 544 × 25 feet (165.81 × 7.58 meters), which did not place the children's residence a great distance from Catalina's apartments, but when pregnant, as she usually was, the walk represented considerable exertion for her, and to the duke she classified it as "getting exercise" and occasionally claimed to be too lazy to go the distance.[3] Attendants brought the children to see her every day, typically in the afternoons, though when the children were ill, Catalina would walk over to see them.[4] On days when she was too busy with political responsibilities, she did not see her children. The weather also occasionally prevented her from seeing the children, as for example one day in October 1588, when it was so windy that neither she nor the children ventured out of their apartments. In January 1590, the cold prevented the children's attendants from taking Catalina's infant daughter, Margarita, outside the castle rooms, prompting Catalina to walk over to see "our Margarita, the prettiest in the world."[5]

Carlo was in the process of converting the extensive gallery linking the castle to the ducal apartments to a grandiose decorated space to display his library, exotica, and other treasures (in 1595 Catalina wrote to him that the newly constructed niches in the gallery were very bare); but it seems also to have served more mundane and family purposes. The children regularly spent part of their days in the gallery, and Catalina noted that she went to see them there, reporting on one occasion that six-year-old Filippo had fallen in the gallery, bruising his forehead.[6] In April 1589, she wrote to Carlo that she had visited the children in the gallery, where they were eating, and that she had stayed there to pray and conduct business.[7]

Catalina was separated from her children for extended periods on only a few occasions. When she went to Savigliano and Revello in 1588 for eighteen days to meet the duke, her three young sons stayed behind in Turin. The longest separation occurred in 1592, when Catalina left Turin in late January and traveled to Nice to be closer to the duke, who was campaigning in Provence. Accompanied by most of her ladies and attendants, she spent most of the year in Nice while the children remained in Turin. She had considered taking her three sons with her (but not her two daughters, the youngest of her then five children), and as late as five days before her departure she was still asking the duke for his approval to bring the boys, writing to him that they "are very well and they could easily go and you would enjoy them very much." Receiving no reply, she left them behind, and only afterward did she receive a letter from the duke telling her that "for now it is not good to bring the boys."[8] This exchange suggests that Catalina was prepared to travel with children, even to a setting as unfamiliar to her as Nice, whereas Carlo, seeing the political and military situation up close and perhaps also fearing for his sons' health, thought it best to leave them in the safety of Turin. The exchange also indicates that when it came to traveling long distances with the children, Catalina was not free to do as she wished without Carlo's permission. While in Nice for more than eight months in 1592, she was separated from her five children (the youngest just days shy of ten months when she left), though through regular correspondence with their attendants she monitored and managed their care from afar.

In most of her letters, Catalina told the duke about their children (whom she sometimes referred to affectionately as "our people"—*nuestra gente*), inserting comments toward the end of letters otherwise detailing political matters, in what had become a pattern of saving domestic news for the closing parts of her letters.[9] Her reports about the children were almost uniformly brief, never approaching the level of detail she provided about political and military matters. She clearly recognized that Carlo needed and wanted to hear more about political topics than news of home, and she gave precedence to those topics. Nevertheless, she regularly updated Carlo on the children, and for a woman who had numerous attendants, children were less a burden than a source of diversion and pleasure. Their antics entertained her, and she shared her amusement with the duke. Their two-year-old, Filiberto, "has been with me here" and although "no one understands what he says," his babbling "is very cute." (Carlo commented that Filiberto must be very cute with his manner of talking, in which he took after his father. Was Carlo suggesting that, like Filiberto, he chattered?[10]) On another occasion, she recounted that Filiberto had been singing all afternoon.[11] Margarita, their one-month-old daughter, nursed so well that Catalina said that if the little girl kept it up, she would eat them out of house and home when she was older.[12] At six months, Margarita was so happy that "all she does is smile."[13] On the day Carlo left after spending five months in Turin, Catalina wrote to him that Maria, their twenty-two-month-old, "has been looking for you all afternoon."[14] Vittorio, two and a half, spent all his time playing with a small tame goat (*cabriol*) someone had given him. Catalina thought Carlo would like the goat and added that none of the dogs seemed to mind it.[15]

In late September 1597, she told the duke that their sons had started to ride and that she had just come away from the window where she had been watching them. Several days later, she wrote to him that Mauricio, their four-year-old, was upset that he was not allowed to ride a horse like his older brothers. She wished the duke had been there to see Mauricio begging to be allowed to ride at least a mule, and Catalina reported that they had finally brought him one and he had ridden the mule so carefully (*mesurado*) and happily that he had declared that he no longer wanted a horse.[16] In one letter relating their children's activities, Catalina closed by saying that she knew this news was really not appropriate to send someone as busy as the duke, but she still wanted to tell him, "and you can't say that I don't tell you enough of the cute things they have done."[17] In fact, these anecdotes were probably meant to entertain the duke—maybe prompt a smile—and distract him for a little while from his military affairs. She wished he could see them play, she wrote, and that she could magically place the boys beside him to free him from business (*desnegoziaros*).[18] "I would pay a lot to have you see him [their eldest son] because I know you would derive great pleasure from that and from seeing all three [sons] . . . and I think your bad humor would go away if you were with them." In the same letter she continued with further anecdotes about their children, telling him that their sons wanted to go to Genoa to practice shooting with their harquebuses, and chiding him that military and political matters had made him forget their children. Carlo replied that he missed his children, recalling that he had cried when he had had to say goodbye to them and noting that he was happy they were well.[19] Catalina's family tales were a wife's prompting to her husband to remember his children and encourage him to return home. Fittingly, among the first gifts she sent Carlo when he left Turin to besiege Saluzzo was a box carved with the names of their three children.[20]

Catalina and Carlo's children were active and rambunctious, and they no doubt tried the patience of those around them.[21] In July 1589, she told Carlo that their three boys were with her and "the noise they make is something to hear."[22] When encouraging the duke to let the older children accompany her to Nice, she warned him that if they stayed behind they would be terribly spoiled by their attendants, who would let them get away with everything, leaving them subsequently hard to control.[23] (Was she suggesting that she herself maintained better discipline and kept them in check?) While in Nice, Catalina received a report that the children were well but more mischievous than usual, driving their attendants crazy pretending to be *matachines* (colorfully dressed dancers who boisterously jumped around, played with swords, and often appeared during the Carnival season).[24] Her children could give Catalina a headache. After Carlo had spent a few days with her and the children in late April 1593 in one of their residences outside Turin, she reported that on their return to the city the children had been distractingly noisy: "I was where you left me until six because it was very hot and afterward the children and I came back [to Turin]. The boys, Margarita, and I were in the carriage, and I don't know how I can even think straight for all they have talked and laughed."[25]

Catalina and Carlo also noted family resemblances in their children. She sometimes commented that a particular child reminded her of one of her siblings, as in May 1589, when she told Carlo that their third son, Filiberto, every day looked more like her sister Isabel.[26] She compared Filiberto to her half-brothers, as well, because like them he was late in learning to talk.[27] She also reported that their sons looked like their grandfathers, and Carlo responded that if that were so, the ladies would be fond of them. In turn, Catalina replied that in truth it would not be long before they were "friends of young girls," and that meanwhile they were quite well and very cute, and Carlo would like them very much.[28] She and the duke were already looking far into their children's future, because when exchanging these comments about their sons' appearance, the oldest was not yet four. (In the sixteenth century, aristocratic betrothals were often arranged when children were still infants.) Playful comments about their children reflected Catalina and Carlo's shared pleasure and pride at having healthy sons and daughters and were also a way for her to keep him up to date on family matters in Turin when he was off on military campaigns. In the same letter reporting their sons' good looks, she added that, to finish with her news of home, she wanted to let him know that their dog, Orianica, had given birth to four white puppies with spots similar to Orianica's own, and Catalina hoped that one of them would be as good a dog as Tojo, who had died a few months earlier and whom Catalina greatly missed.[29] Attractive children and spotted puppies—domestic images Catalina thought would comfort Carlo during his absence from Turin, and keep his family in his thoughts.

Not all her reports of their children were lighthearted or humorous. Catalina managed their children's care and kept Carlo informed about more practical matters of childrearing that she knew would concern him. She always told him when she had changed an infant's wet nurse (usually because either the baby or the nurse was ill) or when she had weaned a child (after about two years).[30] (Weaning was a major step in a child's development and Catalina shared this information with Philip II as well.) When traveling to Nice, she requested Carlo's permission to take the children with her; when changing wet nurses or weaning a child, she made her own decisions and only notified Carlo. He told her that he trusted her to make decisions on these matters because she knew best, although she usually relegated the choice of a new wet nurse to the court doctor, Antonio Lobeto.[31]

She also occasionally recorded having to discipline her children, as in October 1588, when she reported that she had just spanked Filippo, their eldest son (two-and-a-half at the time), because he had soiled himself as soon as he got up from the commode. She prefaced her comment by saying that this had been a "sacrifice" for her and that she had spanked him only once, and she asked Carlo not to get annoyed with her for doing so because their son had to be trained to be clean. Later that day she reported that Filippo had already forgotten about the spanking. Carlo seems not to have been angered, saying that if he had been there, their son would not have gotten off so easily. "You'll say that the war has made me tough (*bravo*)," he wrote, implying that earlier he had been a more lenient father.[32] Another time, Catalina wrote of threatening their son Vittorio with a spanking, but punitive discipline does not seem to have figured largely in her childrearing, though perhaps that was left to attendants and not recorded in the letters.[33]

Catalina and Carlo occasionally quibbled about small issues—such as the piercing of Margarita's ears in January 1590, when she was about eight months. Catalina had given Margarita pendant earrings (*arracadas*) as a New Year's gift, even though the baby still did not have pierced ears (and in fact, the earrings were not even finished by New Year's because, Catalina lamented, "they never finish anything on time for me"). Carlo responded sharply that he wanted no piercing: "I could not suffer Margaritica's [having] golden ears . . . and in truth I would be greatly annoyed if it were done."[34] Though he thought Margarita too young to have her ears pierced, Catalina argued in response that her sister Isabel's had been pierced at three months, and that he could be sure that if there were any danger in piercing Margarita's ears, she would not have it done. Only the cold weather prevented her from having the baby's ears pierced right away. "You do not have to get mad at me about this and it's only because she has such ugly (*bellacas*) ears—I don't know from whom she gets them."[35] This epistolary exchange was probably lighthearted banter, though Carlo perhaps worried that piercing a baby's ears carried some risk of infection. In the end, Catalina delayed having Margarita's ears pierced for another year, timing the piercing with another of Carlo's absences from Turin. Learning of it, he noted that he was upset that she had ordered them to be pierced but happy that Margarita was well.[36]

As her daughter's ears were being pierced, Catalina was entering the final month of her fifth pregnancy. Having a baby girl's ears pierced was plainly a cultural tradition dear to Catalina, and the timing of Margarita's piercing suggests that, regardless of the duke's opposition, Catalina was determined to have her first daughter's ears pierced before she herself faced the risk of childbirth again.[37] A portrait of her younger daughter— Maria Apollonia (plate 10)—would show her wearing earrings as a one-year-old, and the question of piercing her ears does not appear in the correspondence, suggesting that what had been a disputed issue between her and Carlo for their first daughter might have been less of an issue for later ones. At least in some matters, the strong-willed Catalina overbore Carlo.

The anecdotes about their children that Catalina related indicate that even while busy with negotiations, governing the duchy, and keeping Carlo's troops well provisioned, she was also much involved in the daily lives of her children, enjoying their company and delighting in their capers. They often spent a good part of the day in her rooms, as she explained to Carlo in 1596, noting that their sons had come in just as she was sitting down to eat, and their sisters had joined them afterward, and all had stayed with her into the evening. Catalina wrote about this incident on the day the duke had departed from her and the children, and although remarking that she was lonely without him, she was still upbeat—commenting, for example, on some religious objects she was sending him for a shrine he was visiting—because she and the children planned to join the duke in less than a week.[38]

However, in times of stress the children virtually disappear from the letters. In January and early February 1595, as Carlo was defending his territories against the French general Lesdiguières, Catalina was worried about the military uncertainties and anxious for Carlo himself. (In January 1595, when one of Carlo's generals surrendered, she urged Carlo in Draconian fashion to have him punished on the spot.[39]) Her letters of these perilous weeks mention the children only twice, and then only briefly: to tell Carlo that six of their children had been with her to celebrate Mauricio's second birthday, and that they were all going to participate in the procession in honor of St. Mauricio, patron saint of the House of Savoy, to whom she regularly prayed to intercede to protect Carlo and grant him victory.[40] Evidently, Catalina had to be enjoying a lighthearted mood to write with detailed news of the children, and Carlo needed sufficient peace of mind to appreciate hearing about them. In tense times, she did not even attempt to distract him.

TRAINING THE CHILDREN

In her daily and mundane interactions with her children, Catalina informally (sometimes even unconsciously) trained them in court rituals and practices and inculcated values central to aristocratic culture. Religious devotion was one integral part of her children's upbringing. From an early age they joined her for mass and accompanied her to vespers and complines. Her eldest son, Filippo, went to complines with her when only two and a half.[41] On the day of his third birthday, a mass of thanksgiving was offered in Catalina's private oratory, and Catalina remarked that Carlo would have been pleased to see with what gravity their son had behaved. This practice was continued for each of Filippo's birthdays.[42] When he turned nine, the mass was offered at the Cathedral of San Giovanni—a more public place—and by that time Filippo, having no doubt learned the devotional practices expected of him, would have been comfortable as the focus of attention at a public mass in thanksgiving for his birthday.[43] Catalina's children also followed the tradition of making a charitable donation on their birthday, giving escudos equal to the number of years they had turned. This was a ritual of offering—Catalina's treasurer gave the children the escudos from Catalina's funds; she had learned the practice at the Spanish court and taught it to her children.[44]

Likewise, Catalina needed to train her children in seasonal devotional practices and in veneration of the Holy Shroud, the most treasured relic of the Savoyard dynasty. When in 1594 the papal legate asked permission to see the Shroud, Catalina entrusted the keys to her eldest son (as she had done once before), and he and his brothers accompanied the legate. Perhaps her children had seen either her or their father show the Shroud to other guests, but by 1594 her sons were old enough to lead the visit and hold the keys, though undoubtedly they would have been accompanied by adult attendants, if not Catalina herself. With her children, Catalina watched the Holy Week processions, and in 1595 she commented that five-year-old Margarita was afraid of the "*deziplinantes*," the processions' traditional flagellants. The princes also attended plays with religious themes, such as one put on in the ducal apartments by the students of the Jesuits for the feast of St. Mauricio in January 1592. Catalina watched the performance from a doorway while the princes observed the play in the actual room of the performance, and she reported that they had been most attentive, even though the dialogue of the play had been in Latin.[45] In such ways as these, Catalina incorporated her children from an early age into the festive and religious life of the court, introducing them to ceremonies and rituals they would be expected to participate in as they grew older.

She also included the children in an event of religious and political importance for the ruling family of Savoy: the transfer of the bones of St. Mauricio, patron saint of the House of Savoy, from Switzerland to Turin in January 1591. Using language associated with theater, she told the duke that their eldest son Filippo, three months shy of his fifth birthday, had "played his part well" and had held one of the poles of the baldachin, visibly happy and unwilling to accept assistance.[46] Her second son had also participated. This transfer was celebrated every January thereafter, and her children always participated in the annual processions, linking the ducal family with devotion to St. Mauricio, a saint associated with the extirpation of heresy. It was a devotion very dear to Carlo, but it was Catalina who taught her children how to perform their roles in the ceremony.[47]

The children—sometimes all together but occasionally individually or in pairs—ate the late afternoon or evening meal with her (or shared a *merienda*, a light meal), and Catalina often reported that they were her guests (*conbidados*), which suggests that it was a mark of favor for them to share her table.[48] Sometimes meals with her children were unplanned, as in March 1596, when her sons arrived just as she was about to sit down to her midday meal and, impromptu, she invited them to share it with her. By dining with their mother, the children learned the elaborate court etiquette that governed meals. In 1589, she reported that three-year-old Filippo had been frightened to sit at the dinner table and eat off porcelain dishes; in response, she instructed that he be served a capon, presumably served on less fragile dishes.[49] While attending mass and sharing Catalina's dinner table were ordinary daily activities, they were also informal ways she educated her children.

Occasionally, they performed ritual roles they might have learned from the duke rather than from Catalina, who wrote to him about the ceremony even if she did not join in it. In 1589, she informed Carlo that their eldest, Filippo, had participated in the celebrations for the feast of St. John (24 June), traditionally observed with bonfires on the vigil night and with processions and banquets on the feast day itself. Catalina reported that three-year-old Filippo had lit the bonfire (she used the Italian word *falo*) and, she had been told, had done it very well and was reluctant to leave until he saw the fire blaze up. Catalina explained that, because she was going to matins the next day and presumably did not want to stay up late, she had not seen the prince light the bonfire. The prince had also hosted "his dinner" for the harquebusiers while Catalina observed from a gallery, inattentively, she admitted, because she was at the same time reading letters from the Savoyard ambassador to Spain.[50] She also remarked that there had been much commotion (*arrebatyña*), making it difficult for her to observe the dinner. She added, though, that Filippo had worn his wide breeches (*zaraguelles*) and walked so much better in them than in his long tunic that she thought he should continue to wear them. No doubt these rituals were more closely connected with the duke's traditions than with Catalina's own, signaling the introduction of their son into masculine court rituals. Her reference to "his" dinner suggests that this was an annual event typically celebrated by the heir to the duchy or that he was acting in the place of the absent duke. Catalina seems to have been more interested in what Filippo wore than in his table manners.

Dressing in costly garments in the latest fashion was also an important part of noble culture, and Catalina made sure her children's attire reflected their status and upbringing—not surprising in a woman who spent extravagantly on clothes for herself and insisted on dressing in style. As one scholar has shown, Catalina liked to live as a queen and dressed the part.[51] (In 1594, for example, she paid her tailor, Pedro de la Mata, 4,300 florins for clothing for herself and her three daughters, one of whom was still an infant, whereas the next year she gave her almoner only 2,684 florins to spend on alms and food for poor children for six months.[52]) Catalina occasionally remarked on the children's appearance in letters to her husband. In 1588, she reported that two-year-old Filippo was dressed in scarlet, adding humorously that he was wider than he was long. In January 1589, she told Carlo their sons had worn their new outfits (*bestidos*)—"the prettiest in the world." In December 1589, she reported that their two sons were dressed in the same fabric used for the tunic that she had just sent Carlo. As New Year's gifts in 1590, she gave her two eldest sons "gray tunics with cured leather vests with gold buttons." Carlo thanked her for the affection (*voluntad*) that she showed in everything that had to do with their children, and noted that he worked only for them.[53]

Her letters also record styles of dress for children. She noted the change from "long" to "short" gowns, typically occurring when a baby began to crawl or walk. (Long gowns went far beyond the feet, whereas a short one stopped at the ankle; see plate 8).[54] In 1589, she told the duke that the short robe suited their one-year-old son Filiberto. In a letter of 1593 she remarked that all the children were very well dressed (*galanos*) in honor of her sister's birthday and that their youngest, Mauricio, had worn a short tunic and looked very cute (*graziosisimo*).[55] In 1595, Catalina reported that Maria (twenty-two months) looked charming in her *balandran* (long, wide coat), and when eight-month-old Tommaso was going to wear a short gown, she noted that he was "the prettiest in the world."[56] Her comments about clothing also give insight into such cultural practices as the wearing of Franciscan habit on the feast of St. Francis of Assisi (4 October), a custom that her boys and girls both followed.[57] Recorded, too, is an interest in Turkish clothing, which had been in fashion for much of the sixteenth century;

at Margarita's baptism in 1589, Catalina told Carlo that Filippo had worn "his wide pants and Turkish attire" (*sus zaraguelles y ropa turca*).[58]

Catalina's comments about her children's clothing reflect her interest in fashion and her love of costly attire, but they would also help the duke visualize his children, as did the portraits of the children that she regularly sent him. (And these portraits, done by El Flamenco [see plate 9], show the children wearing some of the clothes that Catalina mentioned.[59]) She derived pleasure from her children's appearance, and in almost all of these cases, she remarked that she wished the duke could see the children because, being so attractive, they would distract him from his anxieties and hard work.

Hunting was an aristocratic pursuit Catalina cherished. She and Carlo hunted often, and their children learned the sport early. Carlo encouraged Catalina to enjoy herself by hunting even when he was absent, and although telling him she could enjoy nothing without him, she nonetheless took him at his word and hunted without him.[60] Her children often accompanied her and increasingly participated. In June 1589, two months after giving birth to their first daughter, she told Carlo that she had been to the *guerta* (probably referring to their palace at Valentino, which had woods along with cultivated land), where she had gone to hunt five fox cubs and their mother, but that they had eluded her and she planned to return the next day to try again.[61] Two months later, she reported killing three foxes and many birds from the "*beluarte*" (bulwark) (see plate 15).[62] These birds had first been caught in a wide net that the groundskeeper had set up, and afterward Catalina would shoot them; the children as they grew older also hunted birds.[63] When the ducal family made excursions outside Turin, they often hunted en route. In July 1593, returning from Rivoli to Turin, Catalina and the children shot five hares and a partridge, with Catalina expressing disappointment at not finding even more game. Three years later, after returning from Moncalieri and Rivoli, she told Carlo that their two eldest sons (ten and nine) had spent the afternoon hunting birds with a weasel (*mostela*).[64] From Rivoli she noted with shock that she and the princes had been able to kill only two hares.[65] On this same trip, Catalina reported picnicking on cultivated fields with her sons, listening to music, and traveling partly by boat, on which she was writing the letter, enjoying "a great breeze and we have eaten in [the boat]."[66] In September 1597, telling the duke about their sons' activities, she noted that they went outside in the mornings but hunted later in the day, suggesting that hunting had become a daily activity for the older boys.[67]

Catalina spent a great deal more time writing than hunting, however, and the children grew up knowing that one of their mother's principal duties was to write letters, especially to their father, and from an early age they witnessed and participated in this important aspect of court life. In numerous letters to Carlo, Catalina noted that the children had just arrived or had been there and were playing in the room as she wrote, and she clearly continued to write in the children's presence. A secretarial letter from Catalina to Carlo confirms that the children were close by as she dictated letters. A postscript, also in secretarial hand, added that two-year-old Isabel was seated on Catalina's lap, and the child herself then wrote a few words (*padre mio* [*illegible*]), and one of her brothers then explained in non-cursive script that "sister Isabel has written this."[68]

Occasionally, their games mimicked Catalina's letter-writing; in early October 1588, she reported that their two sons (two and a half and one and a half) were in the room, acting as if they were carrying letters to their father. Aware of their mother's eagerness for letters from their father, the children also played at receiving letters. In September 1588, Catalina told the duke that their sixteen-month-old son Vittorio had prophetic abilities, because the night before he continued to say "in his poor speech" that Carlo would be sending a letter, and that afternoon Vittorio kept calling her to the window, saying that the mail was coming, and in fact, Catalina added, the mail had eventually arrived with a letter from Carlo.[69] (In subsequent months, Catalina continued to refer to Vittorio as "our prophet," especially when she was hoping to hear from the duke, writing on one occasion, for example, "our prophet over here has not said anything for many days . . . I beg you, my soul, to send me news every day and if you are unable to write, order others to do so."[70]) The following month she told the duke that as she wrote, their sons were in the room playing and talking, and that Filiberto, their third, kept looking at a portrait of the duke hanging in Catalina's apartments and talking to it, another habit he must have learned from Catalina.[71]

In early September 1589, Catalina told the duke that, as she wrote, "our children—all four of them—are here talking more than parrots" and added that even their daughter, only five months old, was babbling (*dice sus razones*). Her children's presence in the room did not seem to distract Catalina from her writing, though in one letter she did excuse her sloppy handwriting (only by her high standard), saying that she had been watching her one-month-old daughter smile. Writing in her room shortly after returning from Nice in October 1592, Catalina told the duke that the five children were all in her bedroom, with the youngest sleeping in her bed. In July 1596, happy to receive Carlo's response to her letter telling him she was going to take the children (a few of whom were sick) to Rivoli, she told him that his letter had arrived at a perfect time, and that "if you could see how [excited] the children have been to know what you wrote about them, you would laugh." As late as July 1597, she reported that her children—all nine—were with her and making lots of noise (and that Mauricio, four and a half, was the naughtiest).[72]

Catalina's children began to write letters when very young. In March 1589, she told Carlo that she was sending him a letter which their eldest son, Filippo, three years old, had written to him and that Filippo had gone to the door to try to give the letter to Carlo, as if he were present. Two years later she mentioned that she was sending the duke a letter from Filippo, by then five years old. (When she sent him a letter from the boy five months later, Catalina insisted that he had written it all by himself, though she might well have been exaggerating or joking.[73]) The children also wrote to Catalina when she went to Nice and they stayed in Turin in 1592.[74] Filippo, now six, wrote asking her to send for him (*mandeme pillar*) because "I am big" (*soy grande*). Writing a year later to Carlo, Filippo noted that Catalina had been purged; that Mauricio had a new wet nurse; and that he and his brothers would love to go to serve Carlo.[75] He even reported the marriage of two of Catalina's ladies.[76] He may well have overheard his mother talking about these subjects or knew that Catalina regularly wrote to the duke about them, thereby assuming them appropriate topics for sharing with his father.[77]

On at least one occasion when the children were in her rooms, Catalina was discussing political matters. In November 1589, she told Carlo that the children were "so cute that no one can conduct business because of all the laughter when they [the children] are there. They are with me all day and . . . eat with me and they stay until late." On another occasion, Catalina told Carlo that their eldest son "paid greater attention to political matters (*negozios*)" than she did and that because she had rescheduled an audience for the following day, Filippo, familiar with her routine and not knowing of the change, was confused and kept asking her why she was not giving her usual audience.[78] A mother whose children often spent hours of the day with her while she was governing a duchy undoubtedly discussed and negotiated political matters in their presence.

Because the duke was with her, we do not have letters from Catalina immediately following her other deliveries, but by the evidence of her letters after the births of Margarita and Isabel, her children sometimes visited and spent time with her when she was recovering from childbirth. Convalescing after the birth of her first daughter, Margarita, born eleven days earlier, Catalina wrote to Carlo that all the children were in her bedroom and on the bed, explaining that "our three boys are here every afternoon and are now seated on my bed, committing a hundred thousand follies, the prince [her eldest, Filippo] more than anyone, and I play with them." She added that if the duke's absence lasted any longer, she might not survive. A few days later—the first day she had been able to get up after childbirth—she reported that the children had just left but that they visited her every afternoon and played so much that it was something to see. Nine days later she casually mentioned that all three children were in her room playing. In March 1591, ten days after giving birth to Isabel, Catalina noted that two-year-old Margarita came to see her every afternoon.[79] The children continued to keep her company as Catalina resumed her regular activities after childbirth. A month after Margarita's birth, Catalina reported that she had gone to the garden (*jardin*) two afternoons with the children because the doctors had ordered her to exercise, and she and the children had gathered orange blossoms to make preserves, which she sent him a few days later. A few weeks after this garden visit, she remarked that the children were with her, making a great deal of noise.[80]

Curiously, some aspects of her children's lives Catalina scarcely mentioned. She never refers to her children's tutors (her almoner, Pedro de León, served as their principal tutor), and mentions their lessons only once.[81] On that occasion, Carlo had just left them in Turin, and in the first letter she wrote him after his departure, she reported that she was very alone but that her sons (*los principes*) had entered her room just when she was sitting down to eat, "and so I invited them and they ate with me and afterward their three sisters came and they have been playing and studying all afternoon and early evening."[82] She did not specify which were studying or the subject of their study, but the children—boys and girls—were together in Catalina's room with her and her attendants. Most likely she meant that the three older boys were studying, but she might also have been including Margarita, then nearly seven. For the most part, though, Catalina was little interested in telling Carlo about the children's studies, perhaps because she did not oversee their instruction and their tutors communicated with him directly. Catalina (and her ladies) did, however, teach Margarita (and probably Isabel) to sew, as she noted in August 1597 when she wrote to Carlo that eight-year-old Margarita was with her "working here on my *bastidor* [frame for holding a cloth to sew or embroider]."[83]

SECURING THE CHILDREN'S FUTURE

Catalina kept Carlo up to date on all their children, but her letters indicate that Carlo was particularly pleased with the birth of his first daughter, Margarita, and Catalina chaffed him that he loved Margarita best.[84] When notifying him of her safe delivery in April 1589, Catalina told him, "our girl is all you and I am very happy about that." Carlo's response demonstrates his joy: "Mother of my daughter—the prettiest in the world as long as she does not look like her father because then she would be ugly. I hope she looks like you because then she will be lovely." Joking with Catalina, he called her "Mother of my heart [and] of a daughter all mine and not yours," and told her that he and his men were going through the streets rejoicing, crazy with sheer joy. Almost a month after Margarita's birth, Catalina wrote to Carlo about their three sons but added, "I don't say anything about Margarita because you do not need any [updates] to love her, which makes me jealous on behalf of her brothers."[85]

In subsequent months, Catalina continued to send the duke reports about Margarita. In late May she told him that Margarita got prettier every day (though her comments from May to July suggest that she did not think that her daughter was initially that pretty), but that she hoped that his love for his daughter would not cause him to overlook the other children, who did not deserve to be forgotten. Two months later, however, she joked that he had forgotten his beloved daughter. The following month, August, she reported that Margarita was "so fat that her breasts are larger than mine" and that she wished she could put the baby in Carlo's arms. Carlo did not see or hold Margarita until he returned to Turin in late January 1590, however, when she was almost nine months old. Two years later, when their second daughter Isabel was born, Catalina bantered with Carlo that now she had replaced Margarita as his favorite.[86]

By 1589, when Margarita was born, Carlo and Catalina already had three healthy sons and could afford to rejoice in the birth of a girl. In fact, both had been hoping for a girl. Shortly before the birth, Carlo told Catalina that he was waiting only for her "to console me completely" by telling him that she had borne a daughter. Two days before going into labor, Catalina told Carlo that "everyone says [the baby] will be a girl; you desire it and so do I."[87] Upon learning that the baby was a girl, Carlo told Catalina, "It is certain that I'm going crazy. I have been saying all day that I was wishing for a girl and that has come to pass and you have also done it. I am the happiest man in the world and also I had already told you that [the birth of a daughter] would be the height of joy for me."[88] But while he and Catalina might have been thrilled to have a girl as a change after three boys, girls offered certain political advantages as well.

Carlo's further comments in his letter of rejoicing after Margarita's birth indicate a pragmatic reason for his elation. He suggested that he and Catalina write to Philip II asking his opinion on her name and on her baptism—the latter no doubt meaning the choice of godparents—because "if she is [one day] to be queen of Spain," Philip should be pleased with her name and her godparents. In a later letter, Carlo recommended pursuing imperial connections for the baby girl, proposing Empress María (Catalina's aunt) and Emperor Rudolf II for the newborn's godparents.[89] For the time being, though, Carlo urged Catalina not to let anyone speak to her about such a marriage, "for the reasons that we have discussed many times." His comments indicate that they had previously and repeatedly considered marriage options for a daughter, if they were to have one, and particularly hoped that a daughter might become queen of Spain. This must have been well known at the court, for three years before, when Catalina was about to bear her first child, the Venetian ambassador reported that Catalina and Carlo hoped that, if a daughter, she would one day become queen of Spain.[90] At Margarita's birth, Carlo left it up to Catalina to select her name, because he was "unsure about the name . . . Victoria comes into mind because of the good omen [i.e., a recent military victory] we have had and will have. Isabel pleases me and Margarita does not displease me. Do what seems right to you." Apparently disregarding Carlo's suggestion that they first seek Philip II's approval, Catalina chose to honor Carlo's mother, telling him that she had decided on the name and now it "cannot be taken from her."[91] In a later letter to Philip II, Carlo noted that the *infanta* had insisted on the name Margarita even though he—perhaps thinking of Isabel Clara Eugenia or Catalina's mother, Elisabeth of Valois—would have preferred Isabel.[92]

Carlo's pleasure in the birth of a daughter and his plans for her future marriage tally with his ambitions for his children's political prospects. When Henri III of France died in August 1589 and the throne passed to the Huguenot prince of Navarre, Henri IV, whose right to succeed was widely contested, Carlo immediately sought to press his own family's right to French territories in the south, urging Catalina to write to Philip II reminding him that she and Carlo had several sons whose future the duke needed to secure. Catalina complied, and months later she again wrote to remind Philip II of her many children and connecting their future with Carlo's territorial expansion.[93] (Ironically, however, Philip would seek the French throne for his own daughter, Catalina's sister, Isabel Clara Eugenia.[94])

Like many aristocratic women who tried to place their children in the households of other (preferably influential) aristocrats or royalty, Catalina sought to send her children to the Spanish court, and after her death three of her sons would travel to Madrid, where the two younger would remain for three years and where the eldest son would die. The plan to send the princes to the Spanish court had originated during Catalina's lifetime and is recorded most explicitly in the letters of the count of Lodosa, who in April 1596 replaced Don Jusepe de Acuña as Spanish ambassador in Turin. In a letter of June that year to Philip II, Lodosa praised all the children highly, describing them as courteous and attractive and noting that their tutors and governesses had educated them well. If the ailing Philip could only see them, Lodosa added, they would lengthen his life. Two months later, Lodosa wrote to Philip that the only way to ensure the loyalty of Carlo and Catalina's children to Spain was to summon the children to the Spanish court. He suggested that, in addition to their sons, Philip should also consider sending for their eldest daughter, Margarita, because Catalina and Carlo were considering marrying her to the prince of Condé (1588–1646) in order that she might have a chance to become queen of France.[95] To prevent the dangerous Savoyard alliance with France that such a marriage would create, Carlo and Catalina's children needed to be brought up at the Spanish court in order to fall under Philip's sway and to nurture their loyalty to Spain (suggesting that Carlo was thought to be far too independent). Repeating what he had told Philip in his earlier letter, Lodosa said that the children would add years to Philip's life.

While Lodosa proposed sending the children to Spain to bend them to the Spanish will, he also attributed the idea to Catalina and Carlo themselves, and Catalina's letters to her father corroborate Lodosa's assertion. Writing to Philip about her children, she often noted that she wished they were old enough to serve him. As early as July 1589, when her oldest was only three years old, she told Philip that her sons were doing well, that the third was "more agile than his brothers," and that she wished she could send them as soldiers to serve Philip II. Carlo, for his part, claimed that he wanted to escort his boys to the Spanish court, but that Catalina insisted she be the one to do so. In December 1589, she told Philip that she wished she could be with him in Aranjuez and also that her sons were old enough that she could take them to the Spanish court "to fulfill so many obligations" to Philip.[96] In yet another letter, she told Philip that she wished her sons were old enough to go to serve Philip II and Isabel Clara Eugenia, adding that the boys were "so mischievous that I think they would entertain you." (Philip responded that he was sure that they would please him greatly with their antics.) Later, in 1596, writing to tell her father she had delivered a healthy boy that very day, she expressed the hope that the child would one day be able to go with his brothers to serve Philip.[97] While these comments were routine courtesies from daughter to father, beyond being mere pleasantries they expressed Catalina's genuine hope that one day her father would welcome her children at his court.

She was familiar with the example of her cousins, the Austrian Habsburg archdukes (Rudolf, Ernst, Albert, and Wenceslaus), who had lived for several years at the Spanish court, and she probably had that model in mind, hoping Philip would not only welcome her sons but also award them pensions or important positions. As early as 1591, when Carlo met with Philip II in Spain, they discussed this possibility, and Philip agreed to appoint one of his grandsons Prior of Castile and León, an honorary title in the military order of the Knights Hospitaller (the Order of Malta), which carried a sizeable pension as well as prestige equivalent to that of a Spanish grandee.[98] Philip also agreed to pursue a cardinalate for another of Catalina and Carlo's sons and urged Carlo to send their sons to the Spanish court. When Carlo wrote of this to Catalina, she responded that "it would be very good to send them there because they can only profit." She was particularly pleased by these developments because, as she told Carlo, she had always been of the opinion that their eldest son should inherit all of Carlo's lands and that no territorial concessions should be made to the younger sons.[99]

The boys' appointments were not officially confirmed until a few years later, and Philip allowed Catalina and Carlo to select which sons received the two honors. Catalina suggested her third son, Filiberto (eight years old in 1596), for the priorship and her fourth son, Mauricio (three years old), for the cardinalate.[100] (Presumably she did not choose her second son because he was to inherit if the eldest son were to die, as he did in 1605.) Unwilling to see the Savoyard duchy split up on Carlo's death, Catalina was looking to provide for her younger sons' future by using her connections both to place them at the Spanish court and to secure them lucrative positions and pensions. Although Lodosa wanted to send Margarita as well, Catalina and Carlo never pushed that idea.

Not until 1603, six years after Catalina's death, did the three eldest sons travel to Spain to take up residence at the court. Accompanying them as far as Nice, Carlo left fourteen-year-old Margarita as—at least nominally—supreme governor of the duchy in his absence from Turin.[101]

HEALTH

Most letters were written to share news with others, and recipients expected to hear about a letter-writer's health.[102] In Catalina's case, the duke wanted to hear about not only her health but also that of their children, and it is therefore not surprising that she almost always commented, however briefly, on whether their children were healthy and, if not, on what minor or major ailments they had. Usually, she merely said "the children are all well," but when a child was ill, the reports were much longer. For example, with several sick children in September 1590, she gave the duke details:

> To give you a better report about the children, I have gone this after-noon to see them and I tell you that Vittorio is much better than yesterday. They have given him medicine which has made him have a bowel movement naturally (*echo una camara natural*), which they [the doctors] think is very good. He is quite thin and his coloring is bad, but calmer and not unhappy. He has slept for four straight hours this afternoon and I hope he will get better little by little. The prince [Filippo] is very grouchy and quarrelsome and cries at everything and today it has been so bad that this afternoon he was a little hot but it is only from crying and at bad times the fever sometimes returns but his color is good. Margarita has had so little fever today that I hope that in two or three days she will be completely well. Filiberto is [well] and that is the truth of how they are and *el Proto* [the *protomédico*, the doctor] will give you more particulars, but I have wanted to write you tonight even though I already did this morning.[103]

In such detailed fashion, Catalina updated the duke on the health of all their children, especially if ill, always insisting that she was giving him a complete and honest account.

The children's most common ailments were simple fever (*calentura*) or tertian fever (*tercianas*). *Calentura* was much less serious than tertian fever, which, while common, was more severe and reoccurring, but her letters also make clear that, regardless of terminology, there was no clear way to distinguish between fevers and the treatment was much the same. Catalina also reported her children's colds, coughing bouts, inflamed or infected eyes, and digestive problems, and often tried to explain the illness. When the children had intestinal issues in August 1597, Catalina noted that the fresh fruit must have been the cause.[104] When her children were very young, she often blamed their ailments on teething and downplayed their severity. When Vittorio, her second son, had a fever in October 1588, for example, she reported that the doctors claimed that it was connected to teething, and she herself reached similar conclusions when others of her children had fever.[105] Even diarrhea was thought to be occasionally caused by dental problems, and Catalina reported that Vittorio had had *camaras de dientes* in October 1589.[106] In the case of Vittorio's fever in 1588, Catalina concluded that teeth alone were not the only cause, but that the wet nurse was also implicated, and so, after consulting with the doctors, she had the wet nurse discharged.

Other more serious health issues sometimes appear in her letters. Vittorio began to experience problems urinating in late spring 1589, and they continued through the summer.[107] Her eldest son, Filippo, had a fever in March 1589 that left him with a persistent weakness in his legs until at least mid-June.[108] She updated the duke on Filippo's condition and his doctors' opinions almost daily, but their recommended remedy was so extreme that she preferred to apply her own medication (the duke called it an *emplasto*, a poultice) to Filippo's hips, "without the doctors knowing anything," and she claimed this treatment had done him a world of good.[109] She begged the duke to keep her intervention a secret, which he promised to do, and in turn the duke asked her to have a silver ex-voto (votive offering) shaped like legs made and placed on the altar in the chapel of the Shroud, and also to have several masses said for Filippo's recovery, asking Catalina to do these things quietly, no doubt to avoid drawing attention to their son's ill health.[110] In late March Catalina reported that, thanks to the ex-voto and their devotion to the

Shroud, the prince was much better. Nevertheless, in early June Catalina told the duke that the prince was limping again; she now attributed it to high humidity and felt confident that "one day of sun will take it away."[111]

Filippo seems eventually to have made a full recovery, but his illness discloses how Catalina and Carlo discussed their children's health and coordinated any treatments. Filippo's mobility problem also shows that Catalina was confident enough to follow her own judgment regardless of professional opinion, though in this case, distrusting her reports to Carlo, the doctors themselves reported to him directly. On another occasion when Filippo was ill, she told the duke that she had played the role of doctor and given him three grams of the powder of bezoar stones (stones formed from undigested material in the stomach of animals and thought to have medicinal properties), which brought him relief, though she noted that Filippo would nonetheless need to be purged a second time.[112] In this case, however, as powder of bezoar was a well-respected remedy, she did not think it necessary to conceal her doctoring from the doctors.

The doctors' report about Filippo's health prompted Carlo to urge Catalina to give him the full truth, suggesting that he was concerned that she was not completely forthcoming in informing him of their children's illnesses.[113] In reporting their health, she often added that she was telling him the full truth. For example, after telling him of Vittorio's illness in October 1588, she added that it "is not worse than I have written you because I always tell you the truth. He has had rose honey this morning and is a little grouchy but without fever and you can believe me because I would not tell this to you if it were otherwise." In April 1595, reporting on both their eldest son's and her own improved health, she told Carlo to believe her because "I tell you the truth in everything."[114] Such exchanges involved a delicate balancing: Carlo had to trust that Catalina would be truthful with him, yet while wishing to be honest, she wanted to avoid alarming him unnecessarily.

The poultice that Catalina placed on Filippo's hips is only one example of a remedy recorded in her letters, and perhaps the most usual medicine mentioned was rose honey, used as a gentle laxative when someone had a fever or cold.[115] She reported, for example, that their eldest son had had "his rose honey and I think it will do him much good."[116] She believed strongly in the efficacy of rose honey; when in May 1589 she told the duke that their son Filiberto no longer had fever, she added that he had been given *miel rosada*. On another occasion, she mentioned that the next day their son would be purged, but only with rose honey. Although this remedy was reputed to be mild, this was not always the case, and Catalina reported that when she herself took rose honey in June 1589, it was worse than a medicinal purge.[117]

For more serious illness (or even for routine digestive cleansing), the doctors administered stronger purgatives, and Catalina was a firm believer in the practice. She often urged Carlo to purge himself and also had their children purged. In October 1589, she told Carlo that the prince had been purged "to finish taking away his catarrh."[118] Nevertheless, occasionally she worried about the effect of strong purges on small children, reporting once, for instance, that "today Vittorio has had his tertian fever that comes as strong as on the first day. They [the doctors] wanted to purge him more but I did not [consent] until I could see that he had recovered from the first [purge] or until he is stronger because he is thin and the previous purge left him as you saw. I will let you know what they [the doctors] determine."[119] The duke responded that Vittorio should not be purged again.[120] On another occasion, she noted that Vittorio's tertian fever was lower than the previous day, but as he had not been fever-free for two days he would have to be purged. Expecting that he would protest, she said she might trick him by cloaking the purge in rose sugar.[121] Still another time she reported that only the threat of a strong spanking had persuaded Vittorio to accept purging.[122] Her letters suggest that purging might have been a regular practice used not only to treat illness but also to maintain health. In April 1589, for example, she reported that Filippo "has been purged as usual," when (though he was still recovering from weakness in his legs) her letter gave no indication that he had been sick.[123]

Conforming to early modern notions that excess blood sometimes needed to be expelled in order to balance the humors, Catalina was a strong advocate of bleeding. She herself was bled whenever she was ill, and she had her children bled when they were sick.[124] Twice when their third son, Filiberto, had a bloody nose—in July 1593 and again in December

1595—she told the duke she thought the bleeding was good for him.[125] Catalina and the court doctors did not confine purging and bleeding to people. In June 1589 when Bagot, one of their dogs, became ill, he was purged and bled, Catalina reporting to the duke that Bagot's malady was confined to his rear quarters and came from "the heat and from being with female dogs."[126] Visiting him, she could report that he was now well.

Apart from concern for the children, Catalina was frustrated that their illnesses kept her tied down in Turin and prevented her from following the duke. In this respect, her more frequent comments about the children's health than about their activities betray her occasional restlessness with her maternal duties. One particular exchange of letters in August 1590 reveals her vexation. Carlo had spent much of that summer with her, and when he left in early August, she was disconsolate, writing to him twice in one day, telling him that she would rather die than continue to be separated from him. Though her children had been ill the night before—Filippo had vomited, Vittorio had a tertian fever—she had not gone to see them because "I have not been up to it nor [did I want] to be seen by so many people."[127] In his own letter, written at midnight of the same day as Catalina's and before he received hers, Carlo also claimed that he desired "death more than life," and that he was in extreme torment at having left her so upset.[128] Nevertheless, because she was needed to tend to the children's health, he could not allow her to leave them. As she updated him on the children, she expressed her discontent:

> The prince has been purged and has purged well and he is well [after] he bled from the nose. Vittorio got his tertian [fever] and still has fever and Margarita also got hers [tertian fever] and sweats profusely. I hope she will not be sick long. You can well thank me for all I do for them [their children], as I promise you that [I tend to them] more for you than because they are my children. They no longer need me and you could just as well let me go and have a few days of rest with you.

The duke defended his insistence on her remaining in Turin, though his letter, telling of his comfortable accommodations, might well have annoyed Catalina even further: "Were it not for the illness which has returned to the prince [Filippo] and Vittorio," he wrote, "I would have sent for you to come here and the house is very good and would be comfortable but I would be greatly hurt if you were to leave these children there as they now are."[129] He also assured her that, knowing she was with them, he was not worried about the children's illnesses.[130] Unappeased, Catalina in a rant later that month again complained of her unnecessary detention in Turin:

> The prince . . . has had nothing today and Margarita is also very well and you would enjoy seeing her play. This afternoon Vittorio has had his tertian [fever], though less [than before]. Filiberto is very well and I am enraged that you have wanted to have me here these days because of these children when I could have been with you. I lose my patience every time I think of it and so I do not want to discuss it further because there's nothing to be done and I obey you in everything even though it is very much at my own expense.[131]

Catalina needed the duke's permission to leave Turin, and her letters repeatedly communicate her frustration that their children's illnesses made it impossible for her to join him. A year later—October 1591—she was still pleading to be allowed to travel to meet him, but on that occasion Carlo was concerned not so much for the children's health as for their safety and that of his territories. As he explained to her: "If you leave Turin now it will be placing those states in open ruin, which leads me to beg you that if you desire the good of our children, you will not leave that place until we have some idea of what Lesdiguières will do and what I will do here in Provence."[132] These exchanges from 1590 and 1591–1592 when she was desperate to join him in Nice, even though it would mean leaving their children behind for eight months, demonstrate her priorities. Two days after she finally made it to Nice and was waiting for Carlo, she feared that a recent enemy assault would cause Carlo to take the advice of his general, Andrea Provana di Leynì, and send her back to Turin. (Leynì had suggested that her stay in Nice should be very short.[133]) She told Carlo, however, that she had no intention of leaving Nice: "Let there be no discussion of [my] returning to see the princes because when I am with you I do not remember them so much as to want to leave you in order to see them, so do not think to use this attack to send me back [to Turin], as M[onseñor] de Leynì designs."[134]

Her letters reveal that her affection was to the duke first and only secondarily to their children, whom she would have willingly left behind—even if sick—in order to spend time with Carlo.[135] Moreover, she candidly told him that she was attentive to the children to satisfy him, not because she was their mother. In one emotional letter, she lamented that the children could not console her for missing him: "I promise you that when I am not with you, my solitude is such that they cannot make it go away."[136] Her many children were her dynastic duty to the duke, and often a source of pleasure as well, but when they stood between her and time with Carlo, a source of outspoken discontent.

CHAPTER 9

RELIGIOUS IMAGES, MARIAN DEVOTIONS, CONFESSION, AND COMMUNION
The Catholic Catalina

I never forget to commend you to her [the Virgin] every day in the world.

Catalina to Carlo, 19 September, probably 1597

CATHOLICISM WAS CENTRAL TO Catalina's life, and her letters to Carlo document her devotional practices and strong Catholic faith. In Turin she followed a religious life similar to that she had learned and followed at the Spanish court, where she and her siblings heard sermons, attended sung mass, took part in religious processions, and visited their father's extensive relic collection, comprising nearly 7,500 items by the time of his death. By thirteen, if not earlier, Catalina was attending daily mass and hearing sermons, for in 1581 when Philip II was in Portugal and she and her sister were living at the royal convent of the Descalzas in Madrid, they complained to their father that they were unable "to hear sung mass and sermons." Within two months Philip had had a door cut from their rooms to the church.[1] Her faith had been formed at the court of Philip II and shaped primarily by the religious practices of her father, his fourth wife Anna of Austria, and Catalina's female relatives in the Descalzas convent. Her religious practices were also molded by the Catholic Reformation, and she participated fully in many of the devotional activities encouraged by Tridentine Catholicism.

In Turin, however, she was exposed to other devotions vital to the House of Savoy and to the territories they controlled, and she adopted and helped promote many of these practices as well. She followed a relatively eclectic approach in her devotional life, participating in activities sponsored by different religious orders and not confining herself to furthering the mission of any one order exclusively. Hers was a lived faith—hours of every day were spent in devotion and she was emotionally invested in her faith, deriving comfort and satisfaction from religious observances and rites.

DEVOTIONAL SPACES

Catalina went to daily mass (which would have been a simple or "low" mass), sung masses, and solemn masses, and, typical of the sixteenth century, she confessed and received communion primarily at holy days such as Easter, the Annunciation (25 March), the feast of the Holy Shroud (4 May), the Assumption (15 August), the feast of St. Francis of Assisi (4 October), and All Saints' Day (1 November), or as her delivery dates approached. She attended religious offices such as vespers and complines daily and also listened to sermons, particularly during seasons such as Lent (when there might be two sermons a day), Easter, or Advent, or on particular religious celebrations, as when the relics of St. Mauricio were transferred to Turin in January 1591.[2] (Unlike our modern understanding of sermons as taking place exclusively during a mass or church service, sermons in the sixteenth century were often stand-alone events, though after the Council of Trent, 1545–1563, they were also incorporated into the mass.[3]) She also participated in the different devotions connected to Holy Week, watching processions and venerating the cross on Good Friday.[4] In her letters she rarely mentioned exactly where she attended services—probably because Carlo would have known without being told—but she had a private oratory in her palace apartments, and brief comments in her letters suggest that she engaged in most of these rituals within the ducal palace in Turin or in a church contiguous to the palace in Turin, such as the Cathedral of San Giovanni or the chapel of San Lorenzo.[5]

San Giovanni was the church most directly attached to the court and Don Jusepe described it as "joined to his [the duke's] house" (*pegada a su casa*).[6] Catalina and Carlo could easily go directly from the palace, previously the episcopal residence, to the cathedral by a covered walkway.[7] Moreover, in preparation for the baptism of their eldest son in 1587, an elaborate occasion that Catalina and Carlo choreographed, the choir of the cathedral was altered to add two balconies (*tribunas*), with one, that on the upper right side of the sanctuary, reserved for Catalina and her ladies to hear mass, seated behind an iron grill which allowed them to see into the church while mostly concealed from the mass-goers below.[8] This architectural arrangement furthered the rigid court etiquette governing Catalina's female attendants, whose contact with the outside world was limited in order to maintain their honor and prestige.

But limited visibility or concealment could also magnify a person's or an object's importance, and as Catalina and her ladies sat above the congregation, their detachment and elevation suggested their lofty status.[9] Carlo, not subject to the same rigid court etiquette and able to mix more freely with the public without tarnishing his reputation, sat below with councilors and ambassadors. Access to the balcony seems to have been through the palace, suggesting that a door (either new or longstanding) existed between the palace and the upper level of the cathedral.[10] This physical connection between palace and church was similar to what Catalina had known in Madrid, and at the Escorial Philip II's bedroom had a window overlooking the church's main altar.

In 1587, Catalina and Carlo's eldest son, the heir to the dukedom, was baptized, and for the occasion the Shroud was moved from a private chapel within the palace to a redesigned space within the cathedral, located "over the main altar at the opening to the choir" with marble steps leading up from the altar area. The choir had previously been closed off from view by a wall, which had been torn down and replaced with iron grills and a balustrade. The grills made the Shroud inaccessible and not visible to the public, though it was occasionally hung over the balustrade for public display. Access to this area was restricted and controlled by Carlo and Catalina.[11] Although the Savoyard dynasty rather than the archdiocese held possession of the Holy Shroud and the duke of Savoy could move it at will, San Giovanni remained the Shroud's repository.[12] For the rest of Catalina's life, she and Carlo viewed and venerated the Shroud in this chapel overlooking the main altar of the cathedral.

At San Giovanni, they attended mass, listened to sermons, participated in Holy Week devotions, and attended vespers and complines, often accompanied in these services by ambassadors and members of the court. The cathedral was also at the heart of the ceremonial life in Turin. Their formal entrance into Turin in August 1585 ended at San Giovanni, and the following morning they attended mass there.[13] The baptisms of all the ducal children took place in the cathedral, and although Catalina did not attend their baptisms because she was recovering from childbirth, she planned the ceremony.[14] Her children were typically baptized at two weeks, and Catalina noted, "I do not like days to go by without having them baptized."[15]

She also mentioned attending services at San Lorenzo, in her lifetime a small chapel built into or on top of a defensive wall bordering the palace gardens. The chapel door faced the palace gardens and a covered corridor connected the chapel to the palace and cathedral, incorporating it into the palace complex.[16] Dedicated to the saint on whose feast day Carlo's father had won the battle of St. Quentin, restoring the Piedmont to the dukes of Savoy, the chapel of San Lorenzo was in essence a "ducal chapel," accessible only to members of the court, and Catalina frequented it regularly.[17]

She went to San Lorenzo often, no doubt because of its proximity to the palace, but also because she shared her father's devotion to the saint. As a girl she had often visited the Escorial, then still unfinished, which Philip II had built in honor of and thanksgiving to St. Lorenzo for that same victory so crucial to the House of Savoy. Catalina had seen the Escorial's collection of relics (which included the arm of St. Lorenzo, sent to Philip in 1568 by Carlo's father) and knew well her father's affinity for the saint.[18] Catalina mentioned not only attending mass at San Lorenzo but also keeping vigil at the adoration of the host, hearing the daily offices, listening to a sermon, attending vespers, and participating in a procession on the saint's feast day.[19] The swaddling ceremony for her second daughter, Isabel, was also held in San Lorenzo, as was the mass in thanksgiving for her eldest son's tenth birthday.[20] She helped prepare the altar (*monumento*) of San Lorenzo for the exposition of the Blessed Sacrament during Holy Week, even taking it upon herself to design the decoration and then arguing with the priest over that decoration (she seems to have wanted to place jewels on the altar).[21] When in May 1589 she had recovered from childbirth and went out for the first time to hear mass in public, she went to San Lorenzo.[22] Her visits, activities, and possessions suggest a direct involvement in the chapel's maintenance and a particular devotion to its patron saint.[23] The post-mortem inventory of her possessions lists two images of the saint—an ebony figurine and one embroidered on taffeta.[24]

San Lorenzo's location adjoining the palace gardens also made the chapel appealing to Catalina, allowing her to combine attendance at religious observances at the chapel with visits to the gardens. For example, in March 1595 she told Carlo she had gone to San Lorenzo and "afterward I entered the garden to see the flowers."[25] Her children often accompanied her on these outings. Devotion to St. Lorenzo— shared by the Spanish king and the dukes of Savoy—had special meaning for the young Spanish *infanta*; as the historian Paolo Cozzo has argued in *La geografia celeste*, the cult of St. Lorenzo symbolized the melding of two traditions, two cultures, and two political fates—as was true also of Catalina and Carlo's marriage.[26]

The third—and her only private—devotional space was her personal oratory, located within the palace and probably adjacent to her own bedroom. In the sixteenth century, aristocrats increasingly constructed these devotional spaces within their homes, and because Spanish queens and kings had private oratories—Philip II had one in the Escorial, for example—Catalina was certainly familiar with them.[27] The post-mortem inventory of her oratory gives us some idea of how she chose to decorate the space and what religious objects and devotions were most important to her. For the oratory, Catalina would have chosen images that she thought most conducive to her private prayer and meditation. (The inventory, in Italian, classifies any representation of Christ, Mary, or the saints, whether statues or paintings, as an *imagine*, so it is often difficult to know the form or medium.) She filled her oratory with Marian images: a Madonna with children; Mary nursing the Christ child; an Annunciation with angels; another of the "Conception" (probably referring to the Immaculate Conception, still not Catholic dogma but a devotion promoted by the Habsburgs[28]); a Madonna with St. Anne, St. John the Baptist, and St. Joseph; another of the Madonna with the Christ child in her arms and with St. John the Baptist and St. Anne; the Virgin of Loreto; a Deposition of Christ, which would have featured Mary holding the body of Christ; and four other images of Mary which the inventory fails to detail except to note that one side of one image was scorched and another had an embroidered section. In addition to these Marian images, Catalina's oratory contained images of St. Francis (two), St. Luke, St. Mary Magdalene (two), St. Catherine (three), St. Benedict, and St. Jerome. Some of these images—such as those of the Virgin, St. Anne, John the Baptist and the Christ child; that of St. Francis; that of St. Benedict; and one of the Magdalene—were described as "large," which might suggest that they were more prominently visible than the others, though the inventory does not specify whether they were paintings or statues, or how they were displayed.[29]

Catalina's oratory also had numerous Agnus Dei, waxen images of the Lamb of God, blessed by the pope and often worn on a pendant. Some Agnus Dei were elaborately decorated, with a waxen core adorned with silver or gold. A few of Catalina's incorporated embroidery decorated with ebony, silver, and gold.[30] She kept some of these Agnus Dei in small, ornate boxes—one made of mother of pearl, another decorated with a Christ carved from coral (characteristic of exotica the Habsburgs collected).[31] Following her father's example, Catalina also possessed countless relics—small ones placed in a box, in a reliquary in the form of Christ's head, and in a reliquary cross—and, like the boxes for the Agnus Dei, these reliquaries were variously covered in pearls, coral, lapis lazuli, and gold.

Several of the images in Catalina's oratory featured embroidery, and since we know she did excellent embroidery work, she may well have done the needlework herself or, alternatively, her ladies might have embroidered them.[32] Moreover, her accounts show many purchases for her oratory. From her arrival in Turin, she furnished it with all the items necessary both for her own private devotion and for the celebration of mass. She purchased a chalice, a chasuble (*casulla*) with the arms of Castile and Savoy (thereby incorporating political or dynastic elements in her religious devotion), a missal, and many other items for the mass "which is said regularly" (*de ordinario*) for Catalina.[33] She also acquired fabric for making albs and altar cloths, which she and her ladies sewed, and the post-mortem inventory of her bedroom lists many pieces of finished and unfinished embroidery that might have been destined for the oratory.

The attention she devoted to the furnishing of this oratory reveals that it was central to her devotional life and that she found images and objects conducive to her religion. Through prayer in her oratory, Catalina sought to reach God, with images serving as "visual aids to prayer."[34] These images were also supposed to evoke an emotional response, and for Catalina, mother eventually of ten children, a representation of the Annunciation or of Mary nursing the Christ child (both in the oratory inventory) might well have moved her to prayer.[35] Saints were clearly mediators for her, and she surrounded herself with statues, cloth images, and paintings of those to whom she was particularly devoted. Perhaps she touched or kissed these images, placed candles or jewels by them, or embroidered coverings for them, all typical of devotional practices among sixteenth-century Catholics.[36] The inventory of her oratory lists twenty-nine images, and they would have filled what could not have been a large space.

Through the appointments of their oratories, aristocratic women controlled the images their children would see and also inculcated veneration of such images, a religious practice attacked by Protestant reformers.[37] Catalina's children would have been familiar with her own oratory, but as they grew older and acquired their own oratory, not surprisingly Catalina had a say in how that space, too, was furnished. In their oratory she placed a painting of the Virgin and Child with John the Baptist, inherited from her mother.[38] Her children thus saw a maternal, Marian image that had come from their mother, who in turn had received it from her own mother, their grandmother. In this way, Catalina conveyed a powerful message to her children—the importance of venerating images, of the cult of Mary, and of a mother's role in inculcating religious devotion in her children.

RELIGIOUS ORDERS

On a daily basis, Catalina interacted with members of different religious orders. Her three confessors in Turin, Fr. Mateo de Sarabia, Fr.

Francisco del Villar, and Fr. Andrés Hernández, were Franciscans.[39] Spanish queens traditionally had Franciscan confessors, and as a young girl at the Spanish court, Catalina too had Franciscan confessors (one also serving as confessor to the nuns of the Descalzas Reales and another to Queen Anna of Austria).[40] She would therefore have been influenced by Franciscan models of spirituality, which emphasized absolute poverty and mental prayer. She had two images of St. Francis in her oratory, went to confession and received communion on his feast day, and dressed her children in Franciscan robes in honor of his feast day, all of which indicate a particular devotion to that saint.

In Turin she came in contact with members of other religious orders that probably also influenced her spiritual practices. The Jesuits had established a college in Turin in 1567, and Catalina occasionally heard their sermons, as she did when during Lent in 1595 she told Carlo that he had missed good sermons delivered by the Jesuit provincial.[41] The Jesuit college also staged theatrical representations at different times of the year and invited Catalina to attend.[42] The Jesuits appealed primarily to an aristocratic audience and certainly had enough leverage in Turin to request that Catalina and her children attend their sermons and plays, but although in the following century they would serve as confessors to members of the court, they did not do so in Catalina's lifetime. In her letters she made no mention of seeking spiritual counsel from Jesuits.

In his letters Carlo often mentioned the Capuchins, who were in charge of several hermitages which Carlo visited, and who had a presence in Turin.[43] An offshoot of the Franciscans, the Capuchins were a new religious order founded in Italy in the sixteenth century, largely in response to the Protestant Reformation. Prior to her arrival in Turin, Catalina was probably unfamiliar with the Capuchins, as the order had not yet spread as far as Castile and would not reach Madrid until after her death.[44] Carlo had special devotion to the Capuchins, however, admired their preaching, and encouraged Catalina to visit Capuchin churches.[45] In March 1589 she dutifully reported that, following his wishes, she had gone (while eight months pregnant) to the church of St. Dalmazzo, accompanied by her ladies, and heard a sermon by a Capuchin, whom she described as a saint.[46] In 1589, she issued an order to have a new road constructed from the Po river to the church of the Capuchins, "for public devotion and greater ease for the reverend Capuchin fathers," along which would be many chapels honoring the "holy mysteries of the life of Our Lady."[47] Although this road was not built during Catalina's lifetime, it shows her recognition of the Capuchin priests as well as her desire to promote Marian devotions. In her letters she sometimes mentioned meeting and talking with Capuchin priests and sewing items (such as an altar cloth) for them, and her accounts document donations to Capuchin friars living in Turin.[48] On one occasion, she reported that the papal nuncio had come to see her, bringing with him the Capuchin friars who were now staffing the church of the Consolata in Turin. "They seem to be good people," she wrote to Carlo.[49] As further evidence that she did not patronize any one order exclusively, her accounts also record donations to Augustinian, Franciscan, and Benedictine friars.[50]

Among the practices encouraged by Capuchins, Jesuits, and secular priests such as Carlo Borromeo, Archbishop of Milan, was Forty Hours. During this devotion, the consecrated host was exposed and venerated for forty hours in one church, immediately after which the vigil began in another church, making for continuous exposition of the Blessed Sacrament.[51] Developed in response to the Protestant denial of the Real Presence of Christ in the consecrated host, this Eucharistic devotion was typically enacted during Lent or for a special intention, though Ignatius of Loyola advocated Forty Hours during Carnival as well, to atone for moral laxity during that time of year.[52] When Catalina was gravely ill in July and August 1588, Carlo called for a Forty Hours devotion to pray for her recovery.[53]

Encouraged by Carlo to attend the Forty Hours devotion the Capuchins held during Lent in 1589, Catalina complied, and she did so again two years later. She may have observed this devotion regularly in Lent, without noting it in her letters. In November 1592, Pope Clement VIII officially recognized the devotion and issued a general call to dedicate the Forty Hours to prayer for peace, particularly in France, and Catalina told Carlo that all the churches in Turin had complied; she and Carlo, though, had already been following the devotion, adopting a practice that publicly proclaimed a Catholic dogma denied by Protestants.[54]

While Carlo was off fighting heresy in Saluzzo, Provence, and Geneva—a crusade conveniently meshing with aggrandizement of his duchy's territories—Catalina in Turin was combating heresy by working with the clergy who in the face of Protestant opposition were reaffirming Catholic doctrine and fostering Tridentine culture.

VENERATION OF SAINTS

As Protestants attacked the cult of saints and the veneration of relics, Catalina promoted saints as intercessors and participated in the circulation of relics, much as her Habsburg relatives did elsewhere. For example, she reported the celebration in Turin following the July 1588 canonization of the Spaniard St. Diego of Alcalá, declared a saint through the efforts of Philip II, and the first person canonized after the moratorium the Council of Trent had placed on canonizations. In fact, one of the miracles with which St. Diego of Alcalá was credited with was healing Philip II's son (Catalina's half-brother), Don Carlos, from a life-threatening infection.[55] In November 1588, only four months after St. Diego was canonized, Catalina oversaw a celebration of his feast day (13 November) in Turin, and in April the following year, Philip and Isabel Clara Eugenia sent her a relic—a bone—of the new saint, no doubt expecting her to continue to promote the cult in the Savoyard lands.[56] Catalina in turn sent the relic to the duke, off on campaign. The following year, when she was bled because of illness, she received an image of St. Diego as a gift, and she in turn sent the image as well to the duke.[57] Perhaps this was the image of St. Diego that appears in her post-mortem inventory.[58]

Similarly, in 1588 Catalina had sent the duke a relic of St. Victor, one of the saints of the Theban legion, converts to Christianity traditionally thought to have been martyred in the late third or early fourth century.[59] These ancient stories of martyrdom had gained new life and meaning in the sixteenth century, as Protestant reformers questioned their historical accuracy and claimed that venerating relics was idolatry.[60] When Catalina's "second mother," Anna of Austria, had gone to Spain to marry Philip II in 1570, her mother, Empress María, had sent bones of St. Victor with her, priceless relics, and a reminder that Spain needed to help the Austrian Habsburgs combat Protantism in

Central Europe.[61] The saint's remains, housed within Anna of Austria's fabulously ornate and costly nuptial chest, were placed in the royal convent of the Descalzas Reales in Madrid.[62] Catalina would have been familiar with her family's devotion to St. Victor, seen the reliquary, connected it with the convent where she had lived in 1581 when her father was in Portugal, and associated it with Anna of Austria and Empress María. In 1588, eight years after Anna's death, a nun of the Descalzas sent a relic of St. Victor to Doña Sancha de Guzmán, Catalina's *camarera mayor* in Turin, who in turn gave it to Catalina, who must have treasured this gift but chose to send it to Carlo, explaining that St. Victor was a "great saint."[63] A relic of a saint whose bones had travelled from Central Europe to Madrid now travelled to Turin, passing from Catalina's *camarera mayor* to Catalina and on to Carlo. Carlo and Catalina had named their second son, born in 1587, Vittorio.[64]

Catalina also played a role in furthering devotion to St. Mauricio, patron saint of the House of Savoy, even if she did so primarily in accordance with Carlo's instructions. Like St. Victor, St. Mauricio was one of the Theban legion who had been martyred for refusing to sacrifice to the Roman gods, and legend had it that Mauricio had captained the legion.[65] When Empress María had sent the bones of St. Victor to the Descalzas, she also sent those of St. Mauricio to the Escorial.[66] In her letters Catalina mentioned this saint often, and in particular noted that, following the duke's wishes, she was having the cross of St. Mauricio sewn on the banners and garments that he and his soldiers wore into battle.[67]

In 1591 when some of the bones of St. Mauricio were transferred from Switzerland to Turin, Catalina coordinated the reception and display of the relics. Explaining to Carlo that she had argued with the papal nuncio in Turin, who opposed the transfer, she said she had made sure the relics came because "they are ours and we can take them wherever we want."[68] Nevertheless, she recognized that it was difficult to part with relics and sympathized with the monks of the abbey, "those good people who have felt their loss so much." (Carlo had acquired the relics from the monastery of St. Mauricio in Agaunum, Switzerland.[69]) Among the relics was St. Mauricio's sword, with which Catalina noted she was "infinitely pleased."[70] She reported that the keys to the reliquary were in a "small box made of walnut" and that she had had that box put inside one lined in crimson (*carmesi*) velvet, which she then had had placed by the Shroud.[71]

For the formal ceremony conveying St. Mauricio's relics from the palace in Turin to the adjacent San Giovanni, Catalina, seven months pregnant and describing herself as "very heavy," received them at the foot of the cathedral stairs, "bowing deeply to the saint" and having her children kiss the cover of the relics, before she did the same, publicly displaying the family's reverence for the saint. She and her children participated in all the ceremonies dedicated to this solemn event, and she reported that "I went with authority wearing a ceremonial tunic (*cota*) and my white veil (*toca*) and pearls."[72] Eight months later, she had a silver chest (*arquilla*) made for his remains, directing that the relics thereafter be displayed for public veneration on his feast day.[73] She would claim, later, that her son Vittorio had been miraculously cured of an illness because of his presence at this ceremonial transfer, and two years later she and Carlo would name their fourth son Mauricio.[74]

Are we to understand from these facts that Catalina was particularly devoted to St. Mauricio?[75] When writing in 1589 on the feast of that saint, she noted that, praying for victory for the duke, she was confident that Mauricio would bring him success, but at other times she also said this about other saints (St. Michael, for example, who would have had special significance to her because of her own name.[76]) Moreover, the cult of St. Mauricio was already well developed at the Spanish court and in Habsburg circles, and she would have seen the altar housing his relics at the Escorial. Though she might well have adopted devotion to St. Mauricio readily because of its familiarity to her in Spain and not strictly because of its connection to the House of Savoy, when still in Spain she and her sister had in 1582 mistaken the feast of St. Mauricio for that of St. Victor—perhaps understandably, as they were both of the Theban legion—but suggesting nonetheless that three years before she married the duke of Savoy, Catalina was not fully immersed in the cult of St. Mauricio.[77]

Emphasizing its political significance, at the public ceremony for the arrival of St. Mauricio's bones in Turin the duke's almoner—but not Catalina's—had a principal role. Moreover, the House of Savoy presided

over the military order of St. Mauricio, dedicated not only to the preservation of the House but also to the extirpation of heresy. In the duke's
absence, Catalina oversaw all devotions to St. Mauricio and to events
pertaining to the order. While the letters document her participation in
the cult of St. Mauricio, this does not necessarily indicate keen personal
fervor, and there is no reference to a St. Mauricio in the many images
she possessed.[78] The evidence suggests that her own devotion to
St. Mauricio was perhaps largely a loyal nod to Carlo's.

PERSONAL DEVOTION

Catalina's letters, financial records, and post-mortem inventory shed
valuable light on what we might call her personal or lived faith.

Like many other aristocratic women, she distributed alms and
patronized numerous monasteries and churches, but her letters mention
few of these charitable institutions and make only passing reference to
visits to their sites. Her financial accounts show that in 1585, the year
she arrived in Italy, she gave alms to several convents in Mondovì and
Cuneo, probably when she visited them as she made her way toward
Turin.[79] Her accounts also show that, from 1585 until her death in
1597, Catalina gave alms to monasteries in Turin; that in 1589 she
helped establish a convent for women at risk of falling into prostitution
and afterward regularly gave alms to Angela Ferrara, the mother superior of the convent; that she made regular donations to feed and care for
poor children, and that in 1595 she founded a home for orphans.[80]
Founding and patronizing such institutions were no doubt part of a
larger strategy to place her mark on Turin, as well as to imitate the
charitable patronage characteristic of kings and queens, or, in Catalina's
case, of her Habsburg relatives.[81] Patronage could also bring economic
benefits to Catalina and Carlo; her support for the Albergo di Virtù, a
home she and Carlo founded in Turin in 1587 to train poor children in
manufacturing skills, was a charitable initiative, but one yielding
economic benefits as well. By helping to create skills that could produce
in-demand luxury goods, she helped lessen the court's reliance on Milan
for these goods.[82] Patronage of religious and charitable institutions was
a part of the public performance of piety but was not necessarily vital to

Catalina's own spiritual life, or even central to her shared life with the duke. Judging from the infrequent mention in her letters to the duke, she does not seem to have visited convents as frequently as other Habsburg women, in part because she was too busy with childbearing and matters of state, but perhaps also because such visits were not crucial to her private devotional practices.

Catalina's Franciscan confessors might well have played an important role in shaping her devotional practices, but in fact she rarely mentioned them in her letters to Carlo. On a few occasions she noted items of news that Andrés Hernández, the confessor who served her the longest, had given her about another person or event, but never about spiritual counsel she received from him.[83] Once she told Carlo that she had shown Hernández a document Carlo's confessor had written and in turn was sending Hernández's opinion on the matter to Carlo, describing Hernández as a "good theologian."[84] She no doubt sought his opinion occasionally, but her letters suggest that she did not have an "intensive spiritual relationship" with him as many other early modern women did with their confessors; or at the very least that she would not discuss her confessor's spiritual advice with Carlo.[85]

From March to September 1589, after the death of her previous confessor, Francisco del Villar, she and Carlo seem to have shared a confessor. In March she told Carlo that "his" confessor had been lenient with her, and while writing of this same confessor a week later, Carlo called him "my confessor or to be more precise, our [confessor]."[86] In August, she told Carlo that she was considering asking him to send his confessor to her again because she had no one to hear her confession. The duke must subsequently have sent his confessor to Turin, because several weeks later, he told Catalina that it was fine for her to retain him at the court.[87] Her comments also reveal that when not in Turin Carlo did not keep a confessor with him at all times and sometimes confessed with priests of hermitages, churches, or monasteries where he stopped during his campaigns.[88] Were Carlo and Catalina familiar with the recommendation of such reformers as Carlo Borromeo, who urged families to share a single confessor?[89] Borromeo did not necessarily mean for the highest ruling families to follow his advice, but Catalina and Carlo's correspondence reveals that one ducal couple at least sometimes shared a confessor, and that even though she had an official confessor, at times she confessed to another priest.

An aspect of her personal devotion is evident in her discussion of confession. Both Catalina and Carlo mention going to confession, and their comments provide insight into how one prepared for confession in the late sixteenth century, and also suggest that they differed somewhat in their attitude toward the sacrament. On an evening in October 1588, Catalina concluded a letter to Carlo by saying that "I am in my confession, even though you tell me that I gain nothing by thinking about my sins. I plan to receive communion in the morning. I have heard complines, and after supper I plan to go to bed very lonely because there is no other moment in the day when I am more alone; I think more about you than about confession."[90] Catalina's phrase "in my confession" (*en mi confysion*) appears many times in the correspondence, suggesting that she prepared for receiving the sacrament by reflecting on her transgressions.

This examination of conscience may well have been recommended by her confessors. Confessional manuals stressed that in preparation for confession, penitents should spend some time reflecting on their sins, and Catalina's letters indicate that she did in fact engage in self-examination, though for how long and how earnestly is unclear.[91] Did she perhaps use the "book of seven psalms" (probably the Seven Penitential Psalms), which was among her devotional items when she died?[92]

When preparing to confess, each asked the other's forgiveness for having offended against the other. For example, on Good Friday 1589, mentioning that he planned to confess the next day, the duke asked Catalina's forgiveness in advance. Responding a few days later, she wrote: "If I have [annoyed you] in any way, I ask your pardon and also because I forgot to do so in my other letter where I told you that I had confessed, and you do not need to ask for my forgiveness."[93] These exchanges occur in the correspondence frequently enough that they probably reflect a wider devotional practice among Catholic husbands and wives.

These personal exchanges about confession, rare in the existing literature, give insight into how penitents thought about confession in the late sixteenth century. Drawing their conclusions from confessors' manuals, historians have focused on penance as a one-on-one negotiation between the confessor and the penitent, as no doubt it was.[94] But Catalina and Carlo's practice of asking for each other's forgiveness suggests that confession also had a communal aspect—not just in seeking forgiveness from God through the mediation of a priest but also in seeking forgiveness from intimates whom you might have offended, and in particular one's spouse. Penance had long had a public aspect, but by the late sixteenth century confession was slowly becoming more private (with the gradual use of the confessional, for example) and less communal.[95] Nevertheless, Catalina and Carlo's correspondence shows the persistence of the older tradition, as they clearly believed that asking forgiveness from the other was very much a part of preparation for the sacrament. In addition to these regular confessions, prior to which she had time for a period of reflection and preparation, she is also known to have confessed and afterward received communion on at least one urgent occasion. In 1588, recovering from the grave illness she suffered that July, she immediately asked to confess and afterward received communion.[96]

The correspondence also indicates that Catalina was selective about her private devotional practices and could sometimes be critical of preachy moralizing. She certainly had pronounced opinions about the many sermons she heard, commenting on their merits or lack thereof. In March 1589 she wrote to Carlo that the rector (probably of Turin's San Giovanni) had given a very good (and short) sermon, and a month later she told him that the rector's sermon had been most inspiring.[97] She also heard sermons delivered by Francesco Panigarola, a Franciscan priest who served as bishop of Asti and was considered the "greatest" preacher of the day.[98] His advent sermon of 1590 was very lovely (*lindisimo*), she told Carlo. She was intrigued by Panigarola, who had spent years in France preaching to combat the spread of Calvinism, and she must have heard stories about the hardship and deprivation he had endured, because she commented—skeptically—that "he looks so fat that he does not seem to have eaten rats."[99] A month later, when the bones of St. Mauricio were brought to Turin, Panigarola preached, and she reported that his sermon had been very good (*bonisimo*).[100] He was known to give fiery sermons strongly defending orthodox Catholicism, suggesting that Catalina was drawn to such oratory and themes.

On another occasion, she told Carlo that a Theatine priest had given the sermon, and "he did not talk too long and he preached well and with less scolding than usual."[101] On yet another occasion, she told the duke that she had heard a sermon she had plainly disliked, citing the preacher's criticism of women: "Today's sermon has treated us women very poorly, claiming that we do not know how to keep quiet. I will not say more."[102] Responding to a sermon about women's volubility with an emphatic "no comment," Catalina might have been sharing a private joke with the duke. Nevertheless, her sometimes negative assessments of sermons reveals that she could be critical of homiletic rhetoric.

The correspondence also indicates that Catalina and Carlo sometimes disagreed on her devotional practices. On at least one occasion, having just received a report about her daily routine, he advised her not to spend all her time in "sermons and prayers," but to "go outside a bit" for physical exercise.[103] This would suggest that her religious exercises seemed a little exaggerated to him, and that perhaps such practices at the Savoyard court were less rigorous than those in Madrid. The duke's comments also need to be put in the context of other remarks of his. He plainly advocated exercise for her, urging that she get outside and stay active, even and especially when pregnant, and she more than once told him that she had listened to his (and the doctors') advice and gone out for a stroll.[104]

Catalina also sometimes laughed at her own time-consuming attention to religious devotions, suggesting that, with the duke gone, she had little option but to devote her time to prayer and services of the canonical hours. Her letters document daily attendance at sung mass, complines, and vespers, and she noted that she prayed when she woke up, after the midday meal, and before she went to sleep.[105] On one occasion, writing at eleven in the morning, she remarked that she had been praying up until then.[106] As she wrote in October 1588, in the duke's absence she was spending all her time going to mass, hearing the daily offices, and listening to sermons, to the point that she was, she joked, in danger of becoming a saint.[107] So occupied was she with religious observances during Holy Week in 1591 that she told Carlo, "This Easter has flown by in sermons and vespers."[108] Participation in religious observances was fundamental to Catalina's faith, and while political responsibilities might have taken her away from a few of them, she always found time for daily mass, the hours, and private prayer. However, as she told Carlo, and as Carlo undoubtedly knew, "I am far from a saint," and as proof she noted that God had not listened to her prayers to have Carlo return home.[109] Alternately, she told Carlo that she wished she were a saint so that God would listen to her prayers.[110] In March 1592, she wrote to Carlo saying that she thought only of him and that if she were to think as often of God as she did of the duke, she would be a saint.[111] She seems to have had no illusions about her own sanctity.

Often Catalina remarked that she had received letters from the duke during mass—quite literally, that they had been given to her as she attended mass. These masses may well have been in her private oratory, celebrated by her own confessor, so that delivery of a letter might not have been distracting to others or disruptive. No doubt she was praying for the duke at the moment she received his letter, as she often told him. His letters, too, became objects of devotion, and she occasionally took the duke's letters to bed with her. The line between the religious and the worldly was not always clearly drawn in her personal religious sensibility, and Catalina's attachment to Carlo intertwined with her religious observances.

RELICS AND ROSARIES

As duchess of Savoy, Catalina quickly embraced veneration of the House of Savoy's most sacred relic: the Holy Shroud. Her devotion to the Shroud did not develop until she arrived in Turin, although she might well have seen a copy of it in Spain (Philip II owned a copy that had been touched to the original).[112] It was not exposed for veneration as part of the celebration of Catalina's entrance into Turin in August 1585, but she saw it shortly thereafter. Responding to a letter she had written a few months after her arrival in Turin, Philip II complimented her for visiting the Shroud, claiming that her prayers on that visit had improved his health, and asking her to pray for her brother's health when she next viewed it. Philip's comments suggest that Catalina visited the Shroud regularly, though it was stored under lock and key, and her letters to Carlo confirm her veneration.[113] She noted reciting a prayer to the Shroud, which was probably the same as that on the prayer card she sent Carlo in July 1595, explaining that it had been newly printed.[114] The prayer might well have been connected to a novena, because in its printed version, it could be reproduced for wide circulation. Catalina may also have sent the prayer card to her Habsburg relatives.

Her financial accounts show that she bought silk ribbons to keep on hand for occasions when the Shroud was exposed, to have them touched to the sacred cloth and sent as gifts to the duke, to her father and sister in Spain, and to others. In September 1588, she sent the duke one such ribbon, instructed him to use it to hang a reliquary cross that she had also given him, and gave him detailed instructions about how to wear it.[115] As noted earlier, when Catalina and Carlo's eldest son suffered a weakness in his legs and had trouble walking, the duke instructed Catalina to place an ex-voto of legs at the Holy Shroud to ask for God's help in healing the boy.[116] She also donated a piece of damask and embroidered another cloth to adorn the reliquary in which the Shroud was kept.[117] In venerating the Shroud privately through the ex-voto or touching a ribbon to it, or publicly by participating in processions or celebrating the feast of the Holy Shroud on 4 May, Catalina was adopting a devotion in most respects new to her but closely connected to the House of Savoy.

At times Catalina acted almost as a custodian for the Shroud and manifested proprietary interest in it. In 1589 she told Carlo that when she had allowed the Spanish ambassador to Venice, Francisco de Vera, to view the Shroud, she had tried to do so in secret, but that there were so many people in the cathedral that she had permitted them also to view it, especially since their prayers were needed.[118] After the Shroud had been exposed for Vera and others, she saw to it that it was folded properly, directing several of her attendants (her *mayordomo* Carlo Pallavicino; her *camarera mayor* Sancha de Guzmán; and her almoner Pedro de León) and a few cathedral sacristans to refold the Shroud "correctly," because she had been displeased with how it had been folded previously.[119]

With the sacred cloth kept under lock and key, Catalina believed Carlo should take care to retain the right to display it. In October 1588, she told him that the priest entrusted with the keys to the chapel holding the Shroud had given them to a young assistant, and Catalina complained that she did not think it appropriate that the young man opened the grill to whoever asked. Several months later, when the priest left Turin to see Carlo and left the keys with Catalina's almoner, she commented that they were now in better hands than those of the overly obliging young assistant. A few months later yet, sending the keys to Carlo, she noted that the cord on which they hung was so dirty that she had replaced it and that she had also made a bag for the keys for safe-keeping.[120] Although she had access to the keys, she always asked the duke's permission before allowing anyone to view the Shroud.

As duchess of Savoy, Catalina helped to spread the cult of the Shroud, sending copies in linen to Habsburg relatives throughout Europe.[121] In preparation for the visit of her cousin Archduke Albert in 1595, she had silver candelabra made for the chapel of the Shroud and went with him to the cathedral for the public exposition of the holy cloth.[122] Her devotion to the Shroud was heartfelt, and in giving thanks for her recovery from an illness in July 1588, she cited her faith in the Shroud and had a silver statue placed by the holy cloth.[123]

Complementing her devotion to the Shroud was her devotion to another relic, the veil of Veronica, referred to occasionally as the shroud of Veronica, or simply a Veronica. She possessed a copy of the veil and her post-mortem inventory lists a "shroud, that is, a Veronica." The original cloth, housed in St. Peter's in Rome, was reputed to have been used to wipe Christ's face as he bore the cross to Golgotha, upon which the likeness of his face was imprinted on it. A cult surrounding this relic developed during the medieval centuries. Catalina would have been familiar with this devotion from her years in Spain; El Greco, for example, active there during Catalina's youth, painted several represen-tations of Veronica's veil. She also owned an ebony image and a jewelry piece with an image of St. Veronica, further suggesting her devotion.[124]

As the ribbons touched to the Shroud suggest, Catalina's private or personal piety was centered on the material and the tactile. When, for example, she and her children welcomed the arrival of the bones of St. Mauricio in Turin, they touched their rosaries and crowns (*corone*) to the bones, and even kissed the relics.[125] She often received religious objects from travelling friars—images, medals, rosaries—and sent them to the duke, often after the objects were blessed or touched to the Holy Shroud. In turn, the duke acquired rosaries and Agnus Dei in the hermitages and churches that he visited and sent them to Catalina and the children. Catalina and Carlo both noted that they carried an Agnus Dei or a rosary not only as a religious talisman but also as a sign of the other's affection. In March 1589, the duke thanked Catalina for a rosary she had sent him, telling her that he always wore it on his arm. On one occasion, the duke sent Catalina a rosary which she then carried with her before returning it to him, writing to him that she had slept with it.[126] This rosary could certainly be used for prayer, but it acquired, when she slept with it, a suggestion of a further emotional and even sensual meaning.

MARIAN DEVOTIONS

Catalina showed particular fervor for Marian devotions, and in examining this aspect of her religious life, we approach even closer to what might be considered her inner piety, or more heartfelt feelings of religious devotion. Although occasionally her promotion of Marian cults had political implications, she plainly derived personal satisfaction from honoring the mother of Christ. From Spain, Catalina brought Marian devotions and feasts, such as the ritual of feeding nine poor women on the feast of the Annunciation, as she did when heavily pregnant in 1589, and her financial records indicate that she observed the same ritual in 1597, suggesting that this was an annual practice.[127] The feast of the Annunciation was important in the Marian calendar but also for the House of Savoy, whose military order was called the Annunziata. Perhaps for that reason, in a letter to Carlo Catalina referred to the feast of the Annunciation as "our feast."[128] She also observed the other Marian feasts, going to confession and receiving communion on the octave of the Assumption, for example.[129]

Catalina herself was instrumental in promoting and spreading the devotion to Our Lady of Mondovì.[130] According to legend, in the late fifteenth century a woman in the town of Vico (in the province of Mondovì) had a painting of Mary hung on a pillar, and a small local following developed in the early sixteenth century, gaining ground in the 1560s when two young Jesuits began to encourage penitents to visit what came to be called Our Lady of Mondovì. In 1592, a young hunter unintentionally shot an arrow into the pillar, piercing the painting, and the Virgin of the image began to bleed.[131] Reports of people being healed through visits to the image of the Virgin caused a local deacon to begin to raise funds to have a church built; until then the pillar had probably been in a small chapel.[132]

When news of the miraculous bleeding of the image of the Virgin of Mondovì began to spread, Catalina demonstrated great interest, wanting to make a pilgrimage to visit the site and immediately requesting paintings and copies of the image of Mary.[133] Making sure to claim for herself the first copy of Mondovì's painting of the Virgin, she displayed two representations of it in her bedroom.[134] She also wrote to her Habsburg relatives about the miraculous image, and thanks to her report, Archduke Albert, her cousin, stopped first at Mondovì on his way to visit her and Carlo in Turin in November 1595.[135]

While plans had been made to construct a modest church at Mondovì, Carlo and Catalina favored a more grandiose edifice which would accommodate pilgrims from throughout Europe and which was intended to serve eventually as their own mausoleum. In April 1596, Carlo accompanied by Don Jusepe visited Vico, but road conditions prevented a pregnant Catalina from accompanying them, as she explained to her father: "I greatly wish that the roads had been such that I could have gone as well but I hope to do so after Easter."[136] In later letters to Philip and Carlo, she wrote that she was "excited" to visit the Virgin soon.[137] Carlo also wrote to Philip II, telling him that he had just returned from visiting "that holy image of which one cannot begin to tell the great devotion there is and the miracles she has worked," adding that he would be sending him certifications from prelates and inquisitors confirming the miracles. When Catalina sent images of the Virgin to Carlo in April 1596 and asked him to touch them to the painting of Our Lady of Mondovì, she anticipated sending several of them to Spain. Carlo did in fact send Philip images of the Virgin that had been touched to the original painting, as well as the plans for the church and a monastery they hoped to build there.[138] Both he and Catalina were eager to share the news of this Marian devotion with Philip, probably also hoping for a contribution toward the building of the new shrine. In 1597, Catalina sent Philip a painting of the Mondovì Madonna, done by El Flamenco and now in the Escorial (see plate 16).[139]

When Carlo visited Mondovì in April 1596, he took with him a gold and enameled necklace with rubies that Catalina had sent with him to be offered to the Madonna.[140] Catalina also sent a veil she had made, along with a silver rod (*barilla*) and some cords, though it is unclear what purpose the rod and cords served. A *frontal* (a cloth covering the front of an altar) was not completely finished, but she promised to send it soon. She expressed frustration that more images had not been completed but asked Carlo to have those that she sent to him be touched to the painting of the Virgin, and also asked him to measure the painting, perhaps to have it reproduced accurately.[141]

Although she would have wanted construction of the church to begin in April 1596 when Carlo and Don Jusepe visited, she was happy that "they will wait for me to lay the first stone." In July of that year, she and Carlo with their five eldest children traveled with the entire court to Mondovì for the groundbreaking ceremony, and she and Carlo laid the cornerstone. For that ceremony, she contributed many costly gifts for the sanctuary, including a gold baldachin; a chalice; a veil she had had made of gold, silver, and silk; and two crowns made of pearls, emeralds, and rubies.[142] When her son Tommaso was baptized later that year, Catalina sent another gold crown for the Virgin in thanksgiving.[143] Catalina's female attendants followed her example, offering expensive gifts to the Virgin. Devotion to Our Lady of Mondovì spread quickly, and nobles from Spain, Central Europe, and other parts of Italy also sent gifts.[144]

As these examples show, Catalina fervently embraced this new Marian cult in lands belonging to the House of Savoy. While recognizing that she "intimately lived" her Marian devotion, one scholar has also argued that by promoting the cult of the Virgin of Mondovì, the *infanta* along with the duke also sought to establish Turin and other lands of the House of Savoy as a center of Marian devotion.[145] Endorsement of this cult had political ramifications, as it fostered the idea of a ruling family blessed by the hand of God. No doubt Catalina and Carlo recognized that they stood to gain from having it widely known that the Virgin had graced their territory. Even as her interest in the Virgin of Mondovì and in the construction of an impressive shrine to her may have had political implications, Marian devotion was a prominent aspect of Catalina's religious feeling long before 1592, and the two paintings of Our Lady of Mondovì in Catalina's bedroom suggest that, rather than promoting the cult primarily for political reasons, she felt a personal devotion to the Virgin.[146]

In addition to sending gifts to the Virgin of Mondovì and promoting her cult, Catalina sewed objects for other Marian images, such as a veil for a "very old and miraculous" image of the Virgin in a church in Cuneo and another for one in Savigliano; a painting of this Madonna of Savigliano hung in her bedroom.[147] Her private oratory contained a painting or statue of the Virgin of Loreto, to whom she prayed when ill in 1588.[148] (Carlo vowed they would make a pilgrimage to Loreto if she recovered, but never making it to Loreto, they instead visited the sanctuary of Varallo, much closer to Turin, to offer their thanksgiving.) She had several other figurines of the Virgin of Loreto among her possessions, one made of ebony, another of glass.[149] All three of these Madonnas (Cuneo, Savigliano, and Loreto) were in Italian lands, and as those of Cuneo and Savigliano enjoyed only a local following, Catalina's devotion to them probably began only after her arrival in Turin. Her accounts also show that she bought fabric to make a cloak for "Our Lady of the Cathedral," apparently a statue of the Virgin in the Cathedral of San Giovanni.[150] The images in her oratory were overwhelming Marian, and of fifteen paintings in her room at her death, six portrayed Mary.[151] Moreover, a long list of Agnus Dei and medals among her personal belongings at her death includes numerous images of Mary, many richly carved in lapis lazuli and jasper and adorned with diamonds, pearls, emeralds, and rubies. The post-mortem inventory of all her possessions lists more than 100 Marian images of various kinds.

To be sure, Catalina possessed paintings and statuary of other saints and of Christ, and of secular subjects as well, but she surrounded herself with representations of the Virgin Mary, praying to her frequently. After complines and vespers, which she attended daily, she prayed the *Salve*, a Marian prayer dating back to the medieval period and by

Catalina's day regularly prayed at complines, the last of the canonical hours, from Pentecost to Advent. (After 1568, the *Salve* was also prayed at the end of vespers during the same weeks.[152]) The prayer was important enough to Catalina that she specifically told Carlo that she had gone to "complines and the *salbe*."[153] She clearly took great comfort from devotion to the Virgin. In a Christmas Eve letter of 1590 to Carlo, she remarked that though she had just come from vespers, they had not prayed the *Ave Maria* (Hail Mary), the omission of which had left her feeling very lonely.[154]

Along with her letter-writing, political responsibilities, attention to children, and visits to Miraflores and Valentino, religious devotions gave rhythm to Catalina's days. She found comfort in praying the rosary, attending mass and the canonical hours, venerating images of saints, confessing, and receiving communion, perhaps especially when Carlo was absent. Missing him and often worried about his safety and health, she often prayed for him, invoking the intercession of her favorite saints, especially the Virgin Mary, as in July 1596 when on her way to visit the Madonna at Cuneo, she told Carlo that she would entrust him to the Virgin's care.[155] And she was certainly not exaggerating when in September 1597, with the duke defending Savoy against the French, she assured him that "I never forget to commend you to her [the Virgin] every day in the world."[156]

Among her last acts, two months later, she requested that the Shroud be brought to her deathbed, after which she received the Church's last rites.[157]

CHAPTER 10

THE WORLD LOSES "THAT
INCOMPARABLE WOMAN"

*My soul, look after yourself and don't work so hard because you are not
made of stone.*
Catalina to Carlo, 22 September, most likely 1597

IN SPRING 1597, THE French Huguenot general François de Bonne,
duke of Lesdiguières, invaded Savoy, attacking the Maurienne and
Tarentaise valleys and breaking the truce that Carlo had made two years
earlier with Henri IV of France.[1] Carlo departed from Turin in late June
to defend his territories, leaving Catalina behind with their nine children. Again she took over governance of the duchy, as well as coordi-
nating efforts to keep Carlo and his troops supplied. Within weeks of
his departure, moreover, she discovered she was pregnant. For the next
four months she worked unceasingly to support Carlo's campaign, until
on 7 November she died a day and a half after miscarrying.

The autograph correspondence between Catalina and Carlo for
these final months is spotty, with both relying more than usual on
secretaries. When he added brief postscripts to secretarial letters, Carlo
wrote in his native Italian, probably because he was pressed for time
and expected that a secretary in Turin might read the letter to Catalina.
Though she, too, often relied on a secretary, she nonetheless wrote in
her own hand every second or third day. It is hard to know if the extant
letters represent all that Catalina and Carlo exchanged during these
final months, but several times she specifically explained a lapse in her

own letters, explaining that she had delayed writing for a few days in order that she might update him on military or financial affairs. In September Carlo reported that recent letters had gone missing, apparently intercepted by the French but, while these and others may have been lost, there is no firm evidence that either Catalina or Carlo wrote a great many more autograph letters than those that have survived.[2] Nevertheless, they were plainly aware that communication between them was insecure, and that awareness might well have restrained the candor of the content and lessened the frequency of their letters.

Catalina's letters during these months are often shorter than those of earlier years, probably because of the press of business, but at least occasionally she seems purposely to have kept her letters brief. As she said at the end of a long letter of August of that year, "you are so busy that I am afraid I tire you with such a long letter."[3] Only once during these months did she tell him that she felt as if she were talking with him while writing, and even then she also apologized for writing such a long letter. Though welcoming his autograph letters, she worried that Carlo was staying up too late in order to write to her: "My life, you have done me a great favor in writing me everything but I do not want that to be the cause of you going to bed at four."[4] All she needed was to know that he was alive and well, she assured him, and a letter he dictated to a secretary would suffice.[5]

Catalina's letters show her continued wholehearted support for Carlo, not only in defense of his own territories but also in an attempt to seize French Huguenot territories. She urged him to press on in his campaigns, telling him that his decision to move into the French Dauphiné was "very good" and that he should not lose what she saw as a "good opportunity" to seize new territory to augment their duchy.[6] If he could make some type of assault into Grenoble (which Lesdiguières had taken for the Huguenots in 1590), "I would do it."[7] While consistently expressing her desire to hear from Carlo, her anxiety for his safety, her impatience at not receiving his letters and joy when she finally did, her letters despite these fluctuating emotions document her complete commitment to his military ventures. From early July until the end of October 1597, Catalina worked tirelessly to secure supplies, troops, and money for Carlo, including even personal apparel; on one occasion, she sent him fourteen pairs of shoes and ten pairs of socks and told him shirts would follow shortly.[8] She was constantly negotiating on his behalf with councilors, governors of towns, the Spanish governor of Milan, and the Spanish ambassador in Turin.

Going even further, though, she urged, planned, and coordinated assaults she thought necessary to their cause. While Carlo was besieging towns around Grenoble, for example, she recommended an assault on Pragelato, a town in the Chisone valley some 37 miles west of Turin. In early August 1597, she told Carlo that she and others were making preparations for an attack on Pragelato and that all that was needed was his approval. Frustrated when he failed to address this issue in his letters, she wrote to him a week later remarking that his silence "shocked" her. A week later yet, still waiting to hear from him, she reminded Carlo that this assault was "extremely important" in order to keep Lesdiguières away from Susa (a principal town north of Pragelato), exhorting him that it was crucial "not to lose time."[9] In subsequent days, she continued to press for his approval, and Carlo at length evidently acceding, the assault on Pragelato was launched in late August, Catalina reporting that though not all of the venture had gone well, at least they had gained a "foothold in Pragela[to], though not very far in."[10]

Several days later, she told Carlo she wished that she herself could fortify the mountain passes and that all of his ministers in Turin were helping her. If only the men around Carlo would help him similarly, she exclaimed. As on previous occasions when Carlo was away at the front, Catalina commented that she longed to be a soldier serving him, because she had more spirit (*animo*) than those with him.[11] Hearing rumors that the French would soon renew the truce to end the fighting, she interpreted it as a sign of French weakness and prompted Carlo to remain on the offensive, even urging, "we should hurry."[12]

Catalina also consistently offered Carlo her opinion on military decisions, noting that he had requested it, as in a letter of July 1597 telling her that they should keep each other informed and that he was looking forward to having her opinion. In early August, when rumor had it that Lesdiguières intended to attack the Piedmont, she wrote to Carlo, "you command me to tell you my opinion, and it is that if the enemy comes here without artillery and if you could manage the enterprise of

Grenoble, I think it would be good to try it." In the same letter she again suggested mounting an assault against Pragelato, or if that were too ambitious, at least to take Moriana. Acknowledging that she was removed from the actual tactical difficulties he was confronting, she added, "remember that this is said by one who does not know anything about war matters and so forgive me if it is not on the mark but you are to blame because you asked for my opinion."[13] In the months before her death, her letters reveal that Carlo's campaigns were uppermost in her mind. But though soliciting her advice, which she eagerly offered—and which usually favored aggressive action—Carlo certainly knew, as she acknowledged, that what might be called her armchair generalship did not always accord with battlefield realities.

For the most part, however, Carlo and Catalina's military endeavors failed, for Lesdiguières occupied the Maurienne and Tarentaise valleys until a peace was concluded the following year, and Catalina struggled to understand their failure.[14] "I am furious that everything seems to turn out wrong," she wrote to Carlo.[15] She criticized their commanders, including Carlo's half-brother, Amedeo, and also blamed her father's ministers (Juan Fernández de Velasco, governor of Spanish Milan, and Godofredo de Mendoza, count of Lodosa, Spanish ambassador in Turin) for not providing troops in a timely fashion.[16] In letters to her father, she begged him to ensure that his ministers send provisions and troops more quickly to Carlo, making sure to note that Carlo's military campaigns were securing Spanish supply lines to Flanders.[17] If Carlo failed—as he would if Philip's ministers continued to drag their feet—the Spanish Road to Flanders would be severed, she warned her father.[18] While she was careful not to criticize Philip, her letters convey frustration at not receiving any response from him. As she wrote to him in late September, "a thousand days have passed since we have received any news from you," and to her sister she wrote, "I no longer know how to explain going so long not only without letters from you but also without any news from there [Spain], which has me very worried."[19] No letters of 1597 from Philip II or Isabel to Catalina survive.

But Catalina also questioned why God did not give Carlo and her victories. When the attack on Pragelato did not succeed, she told Carlo that God must have allowed failure so that "we would not have vainglory," and although she claimed not to have boasted of certain victory, she admitted that she had been happy at the thought.[20] She and Carlo saw God's hand in their campaigns. When the duke considered undertaking an assault in a new location, he looked for a sign from God and asked Catalina to pray to the Virgin Mary for guidance (and keep the intention secret from his councilors). Facing difficulties in getting Spanish reinforcements to Carlo's current location, Catalina suggested that it must be a sign that God wanted him to move on to the next place.[21] In late October, however, confronting stalled, aborted, and failed military ventures, a discouraged Catalina commented that God had to give them a victory somewhere, because they had had so many losses everywhere.[22]

Working long hours daily and writing to Carlo regularly about her efforts to help him—all while in the early months of her tenth pregnancy—Catalina pushed herself to exhaustion, and her letters convey both non-stop activity and frustration. In a very long letter of 28 October, she told Carlo that, among other things, she had written to the Spanish governor in Milan and met with the Spanish ambassador in Turin. She praised Carlo's design for a fort he was building and commented at length about whether his troops should attack Moriana, concluding that it was unwise to postpone an attack any longer. Detailing her efforts to procure funds for him, she reassured him that she was doing all in her power, adding, "you must believe that I am doing everything humanly possible."[23] Consumed by Carlo's military needs, she worried that her efforts might be insufficient, or that Carlo would find them so. The doctors who would soon conduct her autopsy prefaced their report by saying that in the weeks before her death, Catalina had been working tirelessly and "excessive labors of mind and body, both night and day, overcame her: giving audiences, both in public and in private, from the midday meal on and writing before dinner; providing for all things in this time of war."[24]

Carlo no doubt recognized how hard she was working, because when she became ill in late September—we have no letters from her to Carlo for five days—he became concerned and told her to take better care of herself.[25] He must have suggested that she scale back her governance duties and get fresh air and physical exercise, for she responded that, pregnant as she was, she did not want to go out in a carriage and did not like to be carried in a chair. He would have to be satisfied with her walking out to the palace grounds, she told him, though it had been so windy lately that she could not do even that. It was impossible, she added, to work (*negoziar*) less, and this work brought "a hundred annoyances, that I do not deny are very exhausting," but "I will look out more for myself because you command it." She went on to note that troops would be sent to Susa, that she expected to procure money for him, that Amedeo's mistress had given birth to a daughter, and that she was sending amber and other items that their court doctor, Lobeto (now with Carlo), had requested. In short, even recovering from illness, Catalina did not rest.[26]

Throughout these months she was, conversely, anxious about the duke's health. When in August he told her that plague was spreading in the areas where he and his men were encamped, she urged Carlo to take care of himself. She sent him bezoar stones, telling him to use them to protect himself from illness and to take them seriously.[27] She also had Lobeto concoct an ointment from amber and "unicorn" that was to provide protection from plague and told him of another remedy she had heard of: to soak rue in rose vinegar and dab it behind the ears, under the arms, and on the inside of the thighs.[28] She sent Carlo a prayer he should recite every day to ward off plague and urged him not to accept any letters that were not perfumed.[29] Thanking her for the vinegar recipe, he reassured her that he was wearing a bracelet with the bezoar stones and was following all her instructions.[30]

When Carlo occasionally reported that he did in fact have medical issues—a cold, a sore throat, a cough, an upset stomach—Catalina insisted that he was not taking care of himself. He needed to sleep more, if not at night then during the day, and she was upset that he always slept with his clothes on, probably because it suggested to her that, always on the alert, he seldom slept soundly. Wanting him to eat well, she sent him melons because she knew how much he liked them.[31] Concerns about Carlo's health increased her anxiety about his safety, especially when several days passed with no letters from him, as in mid-October when after eight days without hearing from him she was "very worried."[32]

Even as their correspondence from July to November 1597 shows that Catalina and Carlo were both working continuously, their letters sometimes return to the spirit of less stressful times in the past. In the midst of planning military campaigns, Carlo thought to send Catalina a painting and earrings, the latter from Montmélian, and she told him she had worn them.[33] She sewed a band for him on which to display the emblem of the Order of the Golden Fleece or to put on his hat. Carlo sent her two heads—apparently relics of saints—which he had won and wanted to add to their treasury. He also noted that the landscape around him was the prettiest he had ever seen (typical of his superlatives) and asked her to send El Flamenco to paint it.[34] In Turin, Catalina had been supervising construction of Carlo's oratory in the palace and reported that it was finished and beautiful.[35] She sent him fish pies (*enpanadas*) made from sturgeon caught in the Po, along with asparagus from their garden.[36]

Her brother's and sister's marriages were also on Catalina's mind: Philip II had finally chosen spouses for Prince Philip and the *infanta* Isabel. For his son, the king had earlier decided to choose among three daughters of his cousin, Archduke Charles of Styria, and requested portraits of all three.[37] Before Philip even saw the portraits, however, the decision was made for him when, first, the oldest archduchess died in June 1595, and then, in September 1597, the next eldest also died, prompting Catalina to comment on her brother's marriage prospects and sexual inexperience. To Carlo, Catalina reported that she had heard that her brother (nineteen at the time) had yet to have sex with a woman (*aun no a conozido ninguna mujer*) or fall in love, and to her sister, Catalina admitted that it was high time for their brother to marry.[38] She was gloomily struck by the death of the two archduchesses, however. As she explained, rather darkly, to Carlo, "the one who was supposed to marry my brother has died; another sister who is a year younger is still available, but already two [archduchesses] have died, and it seems to me that he [Prince Philip] will kill as many [wives] as my father," even if he still had yet to marry any of them.[39] To Isabel, she added that, since the remaining archduchess was only a year younger than the one who had just died, she assumed the marriage would be arranged quickly and she was sorry only for the mother, who had lost two daughters already and was losing a third to marriage.[40]

Catalina was also interested in Isabel's marriage—a matter that had long concerned her and Carlo and which had finally been settled. In August 1597 Isabel's betrothal to her cousin, Archduke Albert, was confirmed but was still not public knowledge, nor were the exact terms of the agreement yet known, though Catalina had some knowledge of the negotiations.[41] She worried that among the letters of hers which had fallen into French hands was one in which she discussed the marriage, and she feared that her sister might be hurt by the news spreading prematurely. In the same letter to her sister in which she had discussed their brother's betrothal, she referred to Isabel's marriage obliquely, telling her that she awaited the mail to see if it brought news of yet "other marriages," adding that it would please her to be congratulating her soon ("kissing your hands," she wrote). To Carlo, Catalina commented that rumor had it that both Prince Philip's and Isabel's marriages had been decided and that she had heard that when told of the nuptial agreement, Isabel had responded that she would follow her father's will. Nevertheless, the terms had not been settled, and it was still unclear if Isabel and Albert would be given "that country," referring to the Low Countries.[42] Carlo, who had hoped Philip would give Catalina territory as part of her dowry, was no doubt annoyed at the prospect of Isabel inheriting the Netherlands, and the Venetian ambassador to Turin reported that Carlo could not refrain from saying that, compared to her sister, Catalina had been treated like a bastard child.[43]

In the weeks prior to her death, then, Catalina was thinking about these marriages in addition to worrying about Carlo's health, military matters, and her failure to receive letters from her father and sister. Nothing in Catalina and Carlo's correspondence from early July until late October 1597 was much out of the ordinary, except that there are almost no references to missing each other in bed or to any of the sexual longing found in earlier letters, suggesting that both were too preoccupied with Carlo's military campaigns to have leisure for amatory yearnings.[44] Despite setbacks and fear of enemy attack, Catalina was still hoping to spend the winter with Carlo, even if she had to travel. She told him, though, that she would prefer to have him come to Turin, that they might then go off by themselves to relax. Carlo in turn reassured her that he would be home for the winter, but that it was too dangerous for her to meet him where he then was, and that they would not, in any case, be able to relax there.[45] With Carlo's promise, Catalina anticipated returning to their more domestic life soon.

In late October, Catalina developed a cold, though she told Carlo not to worry, that she and the children were otherwise well and that she had gone with them to the grounds beyond the palace, where her sons had shot three foxes.[46] Her letters from the last few days of October hardly mention her health and are filled rather with detailed reports about business matters and political developments. On 28 October, she told Carlo that she had just entered the fifth month of her pregnancy, though remarking that, from the size of her belly and fetal movement, she seemed further along.[47]

In early November, Catalina was thinking more of Carlo's health than of her own. Between her letter of 28 October and that of 3 November, she heard that he was ill with a high fever. On 30 October, he had written to reassure her that he was better after being bled, but in a brief letter of 3 November, she explained that her anxiety would not lessen until she heard from him again, and that she wished she were going to see him. She hoped that if his illness continued, he would allow her to go to him, "because in a chair or litter, I would not feel the cold or anything else and perhaps I would be more successful in serving you than those who are there, because being like this, I do not know how I live."[48] She was sending him a clay pitcher (*búcaro*), pomegranates, and lemons because Carlo had reported being very thirsty and with little appetite. Her servant Acacio de Loaisa was carrying these gifts to Carlo, which pleased her because Loaisa could then give her a full report on Carlo's health and could also tell her about the rooms where Carlo was staying, because "if you remain there this winter, even if you are well, I cannot refrain from going to be with you."[49]

The following day, however, Catalina woke up with chills and a fever, and that evening her doctors decided to bleed her. She was well enough by the following afternoon, 5 November, to write to Carlo, telling him, matter-of-factly:

> I am concerned at not having any news from you. I will give you mine. Yesterday I awoke with chills and fever and they bled me.

Today they have purged me and afterward I miscarried a very big daughter who has been baptized, which makes it [the girl's death] bearable, and I hope with this I will be better soon and do not be upset, and because the doctors will send you a long report, I will not and I beg you to let me know how you are.[50]

In keeping with her steady stream of letters over nine years, Catalina wrote to Carlo to the very end of her life, asking, as usual, that he let her know how he was, but her letter of 5 November 1597 would be her last. Less than forty-eight hours later, she died.

The marquis of Lodosa, Spanish ambassador at the court in Turin, wrote to Philip II soon after her death, giving him particulars. When Catalina had learned that Carlo was sick with a high fever, she herself also developed a fever. Later that day she began to suffer from a pain in her side, and her doctors, choosing her life over that of the child in her womb, decided to bleed her, improving her condition somewhat. Noting this improvement, the doctors decided to go further and purge her, but when that purge took effect, she experienced abdominal pains and shortly thereafter miscarried. Although she initially seemed better after the miscarriage, she soon relapsed, and by the early hours of 7 November no medicine or treatment could help her.[51] Asking for the Shroud to be brought to her, she received the last rites from the archbishop of Turin before dying at 5:30 in the morning.[52]

Lodosa attributed the onset of Catalina's fever to news of Carlo's illness.[53] As Lodosa wrote, "at three [o'clock] today the most exalted *infanta* received news that the lord duke was indisposed with double tertian [fevers] that oppressed him, from which resulted that same day at night that Her Highness developed a very high fever."[54] Likewise, Fantino Corraro, Venetian ambassador in Turin, claimed that news of Carlo's illness had caused her fever to rise, which in turn disordered her pregnancy. Lodosa's and Corraro's analysis of Catalina's illness was informed by humoral theory, holding that changes in one's physical or mental environment could upset the balance of humors. Imbalance caused illness, and a doctor's task was to maintain or reestablish humoral equilibrium.[55] In keeping with this theory, Lodosa and Corraro alleged that the emotional stress of learning of Carlo's illness had caused a humoral imbalance in Catalina, leading directly to her death. Bloodletting and purging were key components of restoring humoral balance, and as a firm believer in both these practices, Catalina would have accepted her doctors' decision to bleed and purge her even though five months pregnant.

Others, such as a monk in the Escorial, Jerónimo de Sepúlveda, would later report that Catalina had gone into shock after receiving a letter reporting (wrongly) that Carlo had died, the shock causing her to miscarry and die.[56] Fantino Corraro, too, claimed that the immediate cause of her death was thinking that Carlo had died; according to Corraro, as death approached, the *infanta* was heard to say, "the duke my lord is dead." Corraro noted additional complicating factors, however: she was pregnant (in her fifth month; he mistakenly thought it the seventh), she suffered from a severe cold, and she was "full of bad disposition."[57] Exactly what he meant by "bad disposition" is unclear. Was he suggesting that Catalina was inflexible and prone to lose her temper, qualities that would have disordered her bodily humors?[58] Was he implying that she was emotionally distraught? Recognizing that Catalina's health was already compromised when she heard of Carlo's illness, Corraro added, tellingly, that many thought that in their desire to help her, the doctors had proceeded too forcefully and too quickly, applying "violent remedies."[59] Perhaps because of these reports, Philip II insisted that Catalina's final illness had been mismanaged and accused the doctors of incompetency.[60]

Had the doctors intentionally induced an abortion in order to save Catalina's life? Corraro wrote that the doctors were eager to help her *"disperdere,"* which means to eliminate a fetus through natural or induced methods, but if they helped her to miscarry, the miscarriage was not entirely natural. As Corraro and Lodoso recognized, her doctors clearly knew that bleeding might cause her to miscarry.

The report of the doctors who performed the autopsy on Catalina gives an even more detailed picture of the *infanta's* last few days. The doctors conjectured that overwork alone was not responsible for Catalina's anxiety, citing also the "heretical Waldensians" (Protestants who lived in areas where Carlo was fighting) and news that her father was mortally ill.[61] Feeling a sharp pain in her chest, the autopsy report continued, she retired to the chapel to "grieve and mourn, to let out deep sighs, and finally to break out in sobbing, tears, and lamentation, and indeed, even in secret wailings." Eventually recognizing that she was ill but preferring to hide it from her doctors, she told her ladies-in-waiting that "I am fevered, but you must not tell the doctors, because I am weighed down with a multitude of grave matters, which compel me to write" (by which she meant conduct business).[62] When she finally went to bed, chills and body aches prevented her from sleeping, and against her will the doctors were called. By then the fever was acute and she was suffering from pain on her right side. The following day—4 November—the fever persisted and she had "a very serious cough." Fearing that the baby in her womb was further sapping her strength, the doctors gave her a concoction of cooked plums, bread, broth, and seed pulp. After they bled her of 10 ounces of blood at midnight, she seemed to improve and was able to sleep.

The following day, because she could not endure further fasting, the doctors gave her broth of capon with two pieces of meat and her pain seemed to diminish, but presently she began to experience violent contractions. The midwife delivered the baby, whose head, middle, and one leg were bruised in the process, and who had probably died *in utero*. Based on the state of the infant's body, the doctors claimed— perhaps to defend their actions—that, contrary to what everyone had thought, the pregnancy had been progressing badly. That evening and into the night, they monitored her progress, let her drink, and gave her medicines, but by the afternoon of 6 November, Catalina's condition grew worse. She died the following morning, the autopsy noting that with her death the world had lost "that incomparable woman, to be lamented through the ages . . . the most prudent woman of her age, the most steadfast, of strongest character, second to none in justice."[63]

The autopsy itself was performed in her bedroom (*dormitorio*) forty hours after her death, with Catalina's *camarera mayor*, Sancha de Guzmán, and a few other female attendants serving as witnesses.[64] The autopsy described the state of her stomach, intestines, lungs, heart, liver, and uterus, noting, for example, that the lungs were bruised, with one exhibiting a dark spot. The report also noted that during the autopsy, Sancha de Guzmán and the other attending women had noticed that

Catalina's rectum had been "turned inside out" (perhaps a rectal prolapse) because of the "violent strain in childbirth," but the men present could not confirm this because "it was illicit for the men to see." This detail from the autopsy indicates that the women were not just passive witnesses but could register their opinions. The autopsy suggests that Catalina was suffering from a respiratory infection with a high fever, possibly pneumonia, and developed sepsis that likely involved the uterine cavity, leading to fetal death and then her own death.[65]

But the autopsy also suggests that Catalina's health toward the end of her life was poor. The doctors reported that she had suffered from irregular breathing, shortness of breath, and catarrh of the eyes, nostrils, throat, and chest, and they made a connection between these ailments and an enlarged thyroid. They also noted that she was corpulent, led a sedentary life, ate and drank often and immoderately, and had to pause while eating for fear of suffocation. Her coughing caused her to have convulsions, and the doctors added frequent childbirths to her list of medical conditions, implying that ten pregnancies in twelve years had weakened her.

After an autopsy, the organs were typically removed and the body embalmed, dressed, and displayed in the church for public viewing, after which a requiem mass would have been said before the body was placed in a coffin at night.[66] It is unclear whether Catalina's body was publicly displayed, because Carlo was not in Turin and her funeral was postponed until he could return. Catalina's coffin was placed in the Cathedral of San Giovanni, with the expectation that it would be moved to the sanctuary of Mondovì once its chapel, under construction, was finished. The whereabouts of her remains today are unknown.[67]

Carlo did not hear about Catalina's death until about twenty-four hours later. Ironically, in a letter dated 8 November—the day after her death—he wrote to her (in Italian, by his secretary) that he was unwell and that the only consolation he received during his illness was seeing her image, particularly her eyes. The large portrait he had of her was lost, though, and he added in Spanish and in his own hand that someone had taken all the paintings he had left in the fortress where he was staying and he begged her to send him a large and a small portrait of herself.[68] At the time, Carlo was in Montmélian, a Savoyard Alpine town 120 miles northwest of Turin. Difficult terrain and distance would have made it hard for news to reach him quickly, and he had been traveling in the days prior to her death, so a courier might have set out from Turin without knowing his exact location.

Catalina's death did not bring Carlo rushing back to Turin to comfort his children or seek solace in their presence, however. The military situation remained precarious, and he had not secured his Savoyard territories from French invasion.[69] Continuing to suffer from tertian fevers, moreover, he was unfit to travel, but rather than returning to Turin when he finally recovered, he retreated briefly to the Cistercian monastery of Hautecombe overlooking Lake Bourget, about 150 miles northwest of Turin. Founded by his ancestors, many of whom were buried there, Hautecombe lay in a remote mountain spot—a "desolate place," Carlo called it—and he sought comfort in the solitude and rugged terrain where he might contemplate his "wretched condition."[70]

Was it at Hautecombe that he composed poems about Catalina, entitled "Verses at the Death of a Wife"? In these laments, written in Italian, Carlo bemoaned his loss, remembering places and sights they had enjoyed together, "the fountains, the shadows, the grass, and the flowers," and noting that without her, he hated his life. "Everywhere I seek my hope," but having lost his beloved, he wished to be dead.[71]

Not until two and a half months after Catalina died did Carlo write an autograph letter to Philip II. Carlo's nephew, the marquis d'Este, personally delivered the letter and expressed the duke's condolences, while also asking Philip to continue to provide military support. Considering that Carlo usually wrote to Philip regularly to request assistance and inform him of military developments, it seems curious that he waited two and a half months before writing to him about Catalina's death. He justified the delay in his letter, dated 22 January 1598, claiming not only illness but also that he had felt lost without Catalina. As he explained: "For the past three months, after having lost all the good that I had, I have been unable to hold a pen nor has it been possible for me to remember what I needed to do."[72] He was sure that Philip would pardon the delay because he shared the "very sad and incurable pain" and felt just as sharply the "blow that kills us." Carlo told Philip that his illness had been so bad that he had no relief night or day and "the doctors feared what I desired," but that he had asked to be taken to Hautecombe and had found some peace there.

Not for long, though, and Carlo explained that the generals in charge of Spanish troops and the governors of Savoyard towns had complained so much to him about disorder among the troops that he had been forced to leave the monastery and go to Chambéry, where he had been able to restore some order. He was sending the marquis d'Este, Carlo wrote, to beg Philip not to forget the "deplorable state of this House [of Savoy]" and to continue to assist him. D'Este was further to inform Philip of Catalina's illness and death and also to tell him of the mausoleum where she would be buried, which, Carlo explained, had already been designed and would be next to that "miraculous and holy image of Our Lady of Mondovì." In death they would enjoy what they were unable to enjoy in life, Carlo wrote dramatically, probably alluding to his plan to have both himself and Catalina buried at Mondovì. (He had in fact sketched out a joint funerary monument for them and asked Ascanio Vitozzi, his chief engineer, to take on the project.[73])

Mindful that funerals were occasions to display dynastic glory, Carlo soon after Catalina's death (and long before he wrote to Philip II) began to plan her funeral, asking his councilors to research other funerals, specifically those of his mother, Holy Roman Emperor Charles V, and Francis of France (perhaps Francis I) and other French kings.[74] He possessed printed descriptions of these funerals and told his councilors where to look for them.[75] He also asked his court painter, El Flamenco, to design a "*capilla ardente*"—a "fiery chapel," which typically consisted of "a wooden baldachin on columns" decorated with hundreds of candles and placed in front of the main altar during a funeral.[76] Writing ten days after Catalina's death, Carlo said the funeral should take place when he returned to Turin. Although the date of Catalina's funeral is unrecorded, it most likely occurred in late January 1598 when Carlo finally returned.[77]

While we have no description of the funeral, a proposal drafted by Antonio Cornuato, Carlo's almoner, for her funeral survives, and expense records from March 1598 suggest that Carlo followed Cornuato's plan.[78] Cornuato had proposed a carefully designed ceremony to begin in the palace, followed by a procession throughout the city and ending with a mass in the cathedral.[79] A heavy casket was to be displayed in the palace, perhaps with the *infanta's* corpse, but a lighter wooden casket would be carried in the procession. In front of the cathedral's high altar a *capilla ardente* was to be constructed, topped by a pyramid in the form of a cross, which was typical of funerary structures for dukes.[80] Noteworthy was Cornuato's proposal to display Catalina's wedding dress on a table by the head of the casket in the palace and then have it carried in procession through the city and finally placed beside the casket at the cathedral.[81] The wedding dress was to be covered by a black veil and, when conveyed from the palace to the cathedral, to be carried on a gold cloth. Whereas a king might have his throne or scepter displayed, or in Carlo's father's case, his nuptial bed along with his sword, scepter and crown, a wedding dress would be more emblematic of Catalina, signifying the importance of her marriage.[82] By marrying her, Carlo had allied himself with the most powerful monarch in Europe, and the marriage had resulted in nine healthy children, including five male heirs. Through the marriage, moreover, Carlo had gained a spouse with whom he shared an intimate, affectionate bond, and he would have found it fitting to symbolize that bond with Catalina's wedding dress.

He was not alone in mourning her. The death of a daughter "whom he so dearly loved" and who was known for her "great courage and manly spirit and great authority" caused Philip such anxiety and despair that he locked himself in his apartments for three hours with the *infanta* Isabel and prince Philip. His servants and ministers reported that they had never seen him grieve so deeply before—not for the death of any of his other children or any of his wives or the loss of the Armada.[83] Khevenhüller claimed that the confirmation of Catalina's death provoked fever and gout in the king.[84] The distraught Philip declared a period of mourning during which all theaters in Madrid were closed. He himself would die just ten months later, and Jerónimo de Sepúlveda, a chronicler in the Escorial, claimed that the news of Catalina's death had shortened his life.[85]

In late December 1597, on a snowy day a little over a month after Catalina's death, a memorial service was held for her at the royal chapel in Madrid. A crown was placed on a pillow next to the catafalque, and the chapel was draped with velvet and damask cloths in black and gold, decorated with the arms of Savoy and Castile.[86] Francisco Aguilar de Terrones delivered the eulogy, designed primarily to console Philip and commenting very little on Catalina herself. (In a printed version of twenty-one folios, Catalina is discussed only in the last folio.) Aguilar de Terrones remarked that Catalina had been a good Christian and was ready to meet her God. He praised her "heroic virtues" and her "valor, spirit, and her most prudent counsel about war and on matters of state." He noted that Carlo communicated all matters of state to her, and that her responses were so wise that they could have been given by Tacitus or Cato. The eulogist also claimed that every Saturday Catalina gave audiences for the poor, listening to their pleas and providing for them (though Catalina never mentioned these in her letters).[87] Philip should not bemoan that God had given his "saintly and valorous" daughter the crown she so richly deserved.

While Aguilar de Terrones addressed his sermon to Philip II and probably did not know Catalina personally, three additional funeral sermons (delivered in Milan, Chambéry, and Turin) might have been of greater importance to the ducal family, as the state archive in Turin has preserved copies of them. All three are conventional, emphasizing Catalina's lineage and connections to important men and noting her charity, piety, and devotion to her husband. They compare her to Biblical figures, such as Deborah, or to saints, such as Elizabeth of Hungary, and cite classical authors as authorities on virtues and on dealing with sorrow and loss. But the sermons also note certain key features of her life: her close and affectionate marriage with Carlo; her giving birth to many children; her governance of the duchy; and her role as councilor to Carlo. Eulogists also compared her to other Habsburg women who ruled (such as Maria of Austria, sister of Charles V, and Margaret of Austria, natural daughter of Charles V) and to Isabel of Castile.[88] They presented her as a good mother, whose children would sorely miss her. Francesco Caccia, whose sermon was printed in Milan, noted that her young sons and daughters were looking everywhere for her, crying out, "Where are you mother?" According to Caccia, the entire court was filled with sorrow and melancholy at Catalina's death.[89]

Of the three sermons, the Chambéry sermon, by Guillaume de Oncieu, is of particular note because in all likelihood he delivered the sermon at a memorial that Carlo attended and must have tailored his remarks to what he thought would appeal to Carlo.[90] He praised Catalina's prudence, justice, temperance, grandeur, and piety, and singled out her devotion to Our Lady of Mondovì, noting that even when still uncomfortable while recovering from the birth of her son Tommaso, she had journeyed to Mondovì because of her great affection for the Virgin. Oncieu claimed that, giving up all festivities and outings when the duke was gone, she attended strictly to business, and praised her ability to govern, give audiences, and deal justly with everyone. Even learned people and grand orators were impressed by her prudence. Though mostly conventional, his comments nonetheless suggest some familiarity with Catalina's life and concerns, and he did not shy away from noting her political role, asserting that, recognizing Catalina's abilities early in their marriage, Carlo asked her to help him govern, and that she provided him with wise, judicious advice.[91]

But the most noteworthy part of Oncieu's sermon is the significance he gave to Catalina's relationship with Carlo. If in considering a woman's virtues one gave pre-eminence to friendship (*l'amitié*) with one's husband, Oncieu argued, Catalina would surpass all others. He noted that Catalina greatly loved Carlo and that she was a model wife. Her only wish was to please her husband, and they were "two souls with the same will and two bodies in one." Oncieu singled out her affection for Carlo as one of her highest virtues. Calling her a "phoenix of conjugal friendship," Oncieu argued that Catalina's magnanimity, prudence, valor, elegance, and sweetness contributed to and resulted from her friendship with him.[92] His sermon suggests that he knew (or had heard) of the close bond between the duke and the *infanta* and thought that Carlo would welcome hearing that side of his marriage extolled.

In the end, though, the sermons give us only brief glimpses into Catalina's life. Eulogistic by nature, written by men who did not interact with her often, if at all, and designed to console those left behind or provide a conjugal model for others, they offer little insight into the strong, feisty woman who emerges in the letters to Carlo. Far more cogent than the pieties of funeral panegyrics as a testament to Catalina's character, and as her lasting legacy, is her correspondence with Carlo, bringing her alive to us centuries later, and showing that she died as she had lived—writing, praying, working, thinking of Carlo and her father, giving birth, touching a relic, and living fully until the very end. The value of the letters is not simply their quantity or even their candor and record of conjugal intimacy, but the strength, capacity, and emotional intensity of the woman who wrote them. Long overlooked by scholars, the *infanta* Catalina deserves to be numbered among the most able and interesting of early modern women.

ENDNOTES

ARCHIVAL SOURCES (WITH ABBREVIATIONS)

ACA	Archivo de la Fundación Casa de Alba, Madrid
AGP	Archivo General de Palacio, Madrid
SAG	Sección Administración General
SH	Sección Histórica
AGS	Archivo General de Simancas, Simancas
E	Estado
PTR	Patronato Real
ASC	Archivio Storico Civico, Milan
Bel.	Fondo Belgioioso
ASdT	Archivio Storico, Turin
ASF	Archivio di Stato, Florence
MP	Mediceo del Principato
ASRT	Archivio di Stato (Sezione Riunite), Turin
AST	Archivio di Stato (Sezione Corte), Turin
LDRC	Lettere Diverse Real Casa
LDS	Lettere di Duchi e Sovrani
LM(S)	Lettere Ministri, Spagna
LPF(S)	Lettere di Principi Forestieri, Spagna
LPDS	Lettere di Principi Diversi di Savoia
ASV	Archivio di Stato, Venice
SDS	Senato: Dispacci Spagna
SDSa	Senato: Dispacci Savoia
AZ	Archivo Zabálburu, Madrid
BAV	Biblioteca Apostolica Vaticana, Vatican City
BL	British Library, London
Add. MSS	Additional Manuscripts
BN	Biblioteca Nacional, Madrid
BNU	Bilbioteca Nazionale Universitaria, Turin
BPG	Bibliothèque Publique et Universitaire, Geneva
CEF	Collection Edouard Favre

BPR	Biblioteca del Palacio Real, Madrid
BR	Biblioteca Reale, Turin
HHStA	Haus-, Hof-, und Staatsarchiv, Vienna
DK	Diplomatische Korrespondenz
SV	Spanien Varia
IVDJ	Instituto Valencia de Don Juan, Madrid
MAP	Medici Archive Project
RAH	Real Academia de la Historia, Madrid

ABBREVIATIONS USED IN THE ENDNOTES

C	*Caja*
Cart.	*Cartone*
ENV	*Envío*
exped.	*expediente*
fasc. / fasz.	fascicolo / faszikel
K	Karton
L	*Legajo*
M	*Mazzo*
MS	Manuscript
MSS	Manuscripts
no.	number (of a document)
r	recto
T	*Tomo*
v	verso

INTRODUCTION

1. Carlo to Catalina, 26 April 1591, AST, M16, fasc. 8, fol. 1009r. The duke was referring to the house of the archbishop of Zaragoza where the royal family stayed for the wedding.
2. Catalina to Carlo, 20 May 1591, AST, M38, fasc. 5, fol. 776av; Altadonna, II:187.
3. Anonymous report, 1585 Bia, Doc. ID no. 22824 (ASF, MP 5037, fol. 525), MAP. The golden key was the key that gave access to the private apartments of a king, and having the key was a mark of status among court attendants. In this case, the golden key was the key that gave access to the private room where Catalina awaited Carlo on their marriage night. For definition, see *Diccionario de la lengua española*, Real Academia Española (RAE), https://dle.rae.es/.
4. "Nuptials at the Court of Philip II," 12 March 1585, in Matthews, *News and Rumor*, 103. Rumors that Carlo was hunchback persist to this day but are discounted in Gal, *Charles-Emmanuel de Savoie*, 17–19, 40.
5. Catalina to Carlo, 20 May 1591, AST, M38, fasc. 5, fol. 776bv; Altadonna, II:187.
6. Sánchez Hernández, *Mujeres en la corte*, 7.
7. Zane, "Relazione di Spagna," 365–6.
8. Juan Ruiz de Velasco to Mateo Vázquez, quoted in Gonzalo Sánchez-Molero, "L'educazione devozionale," 59. Geoffrey Parker identifies him as a valet. See *Imprudent King*, 81.

9. Duchess of Alba to Catherine de' Medici, 7 January 1570, in Morel-Fatio, "La duchesse d'Albe," 381.
10. Gabriel de Zayas to Don Francés de Alava, Madrid, 16 May 1569, in Alava y Beaumonte, *Correspondencia inédita de Felipe II*, 335.
11. Throughout, I have used Georg Graf Khevenhüller-Metsch's typescript of Hans Khevenhüller's dispatches. Khevenhüller to Rudolf II, 11 April 1583, HHStA, DK, K10, 254v; 4 July 1583, HHStA, DK, K10, 269; 22 September 1584, HHStA, DK, K11, 46v.
12. Klingenstein, *The Great Infanta*; Llanos y Torriglia, *La novia de Europa*; Rodríguez Villa, *Correspondencia*.
13. Betegón Díez, *Isabel Clara Eugenia*; Wyhe, *Isabel Clara Eugenia*. A volume of essays on Isabel and her husband was also published. See Thomas and Duerloo, *Albert and Isabella*.
14. Fórmica, *La infanta Catalina Micaela*; Mansau, *La femme aux lynx*.
15. Raviola and Varallo, *L'Infanta*.
16. Klingenstein, *The Great Infanta*, 13, 26.
17. Zane, "Relazione di Spagna," 366.
18. Villermont, *L'Infante Isabelle*, 24, 30.
19. As Susan Broomhall writes, Alba knew that Catherine wanted "lavish praise of her talented granddaughters." "Ordering Distant Affections," 71.
20. Wyhe, *Isabel Clara Eugenia*, 19n3.
21. Quoted in Villermont, *L'Infante Isabelle*, 47.
22. Matthew Vester points out in his introduction to *Sabaudian Studies* that the Savoyard dynasty "ruled over a set of contiguous lands that, taken together, formed one of the more sizeable territorial states in early modern Europe (after the kingdoms of France, England, Spain, Portugal, and Naples)" (3).
23. Gonzalo Sánchez-Molero, "L'educazione devozionale," 83–4; Villermont, *L'Infante Isabelle*, 35. Martínez Hernández, "Enlightened Queen," 38–42; García Prieto, *Una corte*, 171–2.

CHAPTER 1

1. "Relacion de la orden que la magestad del rey nuestro señor tubo en las prebenciones de la entrada y desposorio y casamiento de sus altezas de la infanta doña Catalina y duque de Saboya su marido. Para el illᵐᵒ señor mi señor el baron Adam de Dietrichstein," 1585, HHStA, SV 3, fasz. 3, fol. 69v. I refer to this as the Dietrichstein wedding account. Corazzino, *Sposalizio*, 24, 26 (Italian), 58, 60 (Spanish); Cock, *Relación del viaje hecho*, 72–3, 76, 79–80.
2. Parker, *Imprudent King*, 163; Rodríguez Salgado, "'Una perfecta princesa.' . . . Segunda parte," 92–3.
3. Duchess of Alba to Catherine de' Medici, 12 November 1567 and 1 December 1567, in Morel-Fatio, "La duchesse d'Albe," 371.
4. Letter of December 1567, in Amezúa y Mayo, *Isabel de Valois*, 3:52. Translation by Cathy Yandell. I would like to thank Florence Jurney and Cathy Yandell for their assistance in translating this passage.
5. Ana of Dietrichstein to Margarita of Cardona, 22 May 1576, in Dietrichstein, *Cartas*, 86.
6. Rodríguez Salgado, "'Una perfecta princesa.' . . . Segunda parte," esp. 97–8. See also Rodríguez Salgado, "'Una perfecta princesa.' . . . Primera parte," 79.

7. Kamen, *Philip of Spain*, 204; Philip II to the marquis of Ladrada, 25 October 1570, BL, Add. MSS 28354, fol. 51v.

8. When Philip II charged Ladrada with codifying the rules, Ladrada talked with people who had served in the queen's household and who were able to tell him what the rules were. For the oral transmission of the *etiquetas*, see Gómez-Centurión Jiménez, "La herencia de Borgoña," 11–31.

9. Rodríguez Salgado, "'Una perfecta princesa.' . . . Primera parte," 79; Río Barredo, "De Madrid a Turín," 103.

10. AGP, SH, C 49, exped. 3, fol. 122v–123r.

11. Marquis of Ladrada to Philip II, 24 November 1571, BL, Add. MSS 28354, fol. 289r; Gamberini, "Sofonisba Anguissola, a Painter and a Lady-in-Waiting," 105–6; Gonzalo Sánchez-Molero, "L'educazione devozionale," 43–4.

12. For examples, see Ana of Dietrichstein to Margarita of Cardona, 12 June 1575 and 20 December 1575, in Dietrichstein, *Cartas*, 68, 83; López-Cordón Cortezo, "Entre damas," 130; Sánchez, "Privacy, Family, and Devotion," 369.

13. See Ana of Dietrichstein to Margarita of Cardona, Good Friday, 1580, 4 June 1580, 3 October 1580, in Dietrichstein, *Cartas*, 126, 132, 136, 137.

14. Ana of Dietrichstein to Margarita of Cardona, 6 March 1581, in Dietrichstein, *Cartas*, 155. Pressuring her to play with them: 6 February 1581, 150. Hipólita playing with them: Second day of Easter, 1581, 146, and 9 January 1581, 149.

15. Río Barredo, "De Madrid a Turín," 104–12.

16. On Juana of Austria, see the essays in García Pérez, *The Making of Juana of Austria* and Cruz, "Juana of Austria," 103–22.

17. Parker, *Imprudent King*, 166; Philip II to Catherine de' Medici, 4 July 1569, in Alava y Beaumonte, *Correspondencia inédita de Felipe II*, 186.

18. Kamen, *Philip of Spain*, 206.

19. Badoero, "Relazione di Spagna," 276.

20. Parker, *Imprudent King*, 165. For examples of references to letter exchanges between Anna and Philip, see marquis of Ladrada to Philip II, BL, Add. MSS 28354, 21 February 1571, fol. 158r; 23 February 1571, fol. 160r; 5 April 1571, fol. 176r; 11 April 1571, fol. 186r.

21. Parker says that she gave birth to seven children (*Imprudent King*, 165), but his chart (157) shows only five children. She miscarried at least one child. See Ana of Dietrichstein to Margarita of Cardona, 22 May 1576, in Dietrichstein, *Cartas*, 86.

22. Kamen, *Philip of Spain*, 206.

23. Philip II to Catalina, 14 June 1588, in Bouza, *Cartas*, 156.

24. Ana of Dietrichstein to Margarita of Cardona, 25 November 1578, in Dietrichstein, *Cartas*, 113.

25. Parker, *Imprudent King*, 164.

26. Fourquevaux to Catherine de' Medici, 16 December 1571, in Douais, *Dépêches de M. de Fourquevaux*, II:411.

27. "*Juramento del Prince D. Felipe*, 1584," in Simón Díaz, *Relaciones de actos*, 20, 21, 24. See also Sepúlveda, "Historia de varios sucesos," I:4r–v.

28. García Prieto, "Isabel Clara Eugenia of Austria," 131–53.

29. Empress María to Philip II, 29 November 1590, in Galende Díaz and Salamanca López, *Epistolario*, 200–1; Fourquevaux to Catherine de' Medici, 29 October 1568, in Douais, *Dépêches de M. de Fourquevaux*, II:11.

30. Ana of Dietrichstein to Margarita of Cardona, 19 July 1576, 30 January 1580, 10 December 1582, in Dietrichstein, *Cartas*, 88, 118, 212.

31. Ana of Dietrichstein to Margarita of Cardona, 1 November 1580, in Dietrichstein, *Cartas*, 142.
32. See Philip II to the *infantas*, 2 October 1581 (helping Diego learn to write, 58); 23 October 1581 (teaching Diego to read and write, 60), 20 November 1581 (sends *perdones, cuentas*, and rosaries to give siblings, 64); 1 October 1582 (teaching Diego Portuguese and how to write, 93–4), in Bouza, *Cartas*.
33. Duerloo, *Dynasty and Piety*, 21.
34. González Cuerva, *Maria of Austria*, 84–7, 116–22, 179–80; Fichtner, *Emperor Maximilian II*, 42–9, 51–2, 107–8, 114–16.
35. See Kamen, *Philip of Spain*, 98, 207. On Albert at the Spanish court, see Martínez Millán, "El archiduque Alberto," 27–37.
36. On their daily schedule, see Duerloo, *Dynasty and Piety*, 21–2.
37. Sigüenza, *Fundación*, 97.
38. Amezúa y Mayo, *Isabel de Valois*, 412; Gonzalo Sánchez-Molero, "L'educazione devozionale," 42–3.
39. On the Descalzas, see the essays in García Pérez, *The Making of Juana of Austria*, esp. García Sanz, "A Personal Project," 195–219 and Toajas Roger, "The *Cuarto Real*," 220–51. See also Sánchez, "Where Palace and Convent Meet," 53–82.
40. Marquis of Ladrada to Philip II, 21 February 1571, BL, Add. MSS 28354, fol. 158r.
41. Parker, *Imprudent King*, 85, 167, 169–70.
42. Khevenhüller, *Diario*, 286.
43. Philip II to the *infantas*, 16 April 1582, in Bouza, *Cartas*, 79.
44. Philip II to the *infantas*, 8 November 1582, in Bouza, *Cartas*, 99.
45. Philip II to the *infantas*, 3 January and 17 January 1583, in Bouza, *Cartas*, 100, 101.
46. Carvajal, *Autobiography*, in Carvajal, *Life and Writings*, 121, 118; Redworth, *The She-Apostle*, 14.
47. Albaladejo Martínez, "Las infantas," 116.
48. For Charles V's instructions to Philip, see Ball and Parker, *Cómo ser rey*. For Philip's education, see Gonzalo Sánchez-Molero, *Felipe II*.
49. Gonzalo Sánchez-Molero, "L'educazione devozionale," 45, 86, 73, 74–5, 183. Zúñiga also became the queen's royal almoner, following a tradition that the royal children's tutor would hold that position. Martha K. Hoffman says that it was typical for royal children to begin their formal education at the age of seven, but she notes that some of Philip III's children began even earlier. See Hoffman, *Raised to Rule*, 57–8. Philip II began his formal education at age seven.
50. Gonzalo Sánchez-Molero, "L'educazione devozionale," 82; Duerloo, *Dynasty and Piety*, 21–2.
51. Translation by Geoffrey Parker. Philip II to the marquis of Ladrada, 17 May 1572, BL, Add. MSS 28354, fol. 394v.
52. See, for example, the marquis of Ladrada to Philip II, 6 March 1571, BL, Add. MSS 28354, fol. 166r, reporting that the queen and *infantas* had gone with Juana of Austria to the Descalzas to see one of their ladies-in-waiting take vows.
53. Gonzalo Sánchez-Molero, "L'educazione devozionale," 75, 82.
54. Cruz Medina, "Y porque sale la reyna," 437; Gonzalo Sánchez-Molero, "L'educazione devozionale," 88–9.
55. Fray Buenaventura de Santibáñez to Philip II, with Philip's response, 27 May 1581, BL, Add. MSS 28342, fol. 322; Philip II to the *infantas*, 10 July 1581, in Bouza, *Cartas*, 49.

56. The original source for this claim seems to be Llanos y Torriglia, *La novia de Europa*, 35–6, who based this on Luis Gálvez de Montalvo's *El pastor de Fílida*. In that work, Gálvez de Montalvo listed the girls from aristocratic families who were in the *infantas'* entourage and put on plays with them; see 353–88. Other scholars have repeated Llanos y Torriglia's claim. See Albaladejo Martínez, "*Las infantas*," 118; Martínez Hernández, "'Enlightened Queen'," 30; Zuese, "Ana Caro and the Literary Academies," 196.

57. Philip III and his children, though, do not seem to have been educated with other aristocrats. See Hoffman, *Raised to Rule*, 56.

58. Duerloo, *Dynasty and Piety*, 22.

59. Gonzalo Sánchez-Molero, "L'educazione devozionale," 85–6.

60. Blanco Mourelle, "Reinventing the Wheel," 293–311; Gonzalo Sánchez-Molero, "L'educazione devozionale," 89–93.

61. King, "Book-lined Cells," 436.

62. Corazzino, *Sposalizio*, 13 (Italian), 47 (Spanish); Kamen, *Philip of Spain*, 257.

63. Catalina to Carlo, 11 June 1589, AST, M35, fasc. 9, fol. 225av; Altadonna, I:203.

64. Catalina to Carlo, 15 January 1592, AST, M40, fasc. 1, fol. 1054v; Altadonna, III:9.

65. Santiago Martínez Hernández mentions Johanna de Jacincourt as a possible teacher of French. See "Enlightened Queen," 28.

66. Philip II to the *infantas*, 1 October 1582, 17 September 1582, in Bouza, *Cartas*, 93, 91.

67. Vanessa de Cruz Medina discusses the evolution of the script of one of the *infantas'* attendants, Ana of Dietrichstein. See Cruz Medina, "Manos que escriben cartas," 173–6.

68. Martínez Hernández, "'Enlightened Queen," 30; Philip II to the *infantas*, 3 April 1581, in Bouza, *Cartas*, 34–5.

69. For Isabel's letters to Lerma, see Rodríguez Villa, *Correspondencia*.

70. Robledo Estaire, "La música," 200.

71. "Scriptura firmada de las señoras Infantas Doña Isabel y doña Catalina, que se otorgó en Barcelona a 11 de junio 1585," IVDJ, ENV 35, C 48, no. 28; Cristóbal de Briceño to Mateo Vázquez, 11 September 1585, IVDJ, ENV 5, T III, fol. 257v.

72. Marquis of Ladrada to Philip II, 25 October 1570, BL, Add. MSS 28354, fol. 51v.

73. Amezúa y Mayo, *Isabel de Valois*, III:515–20; Rodríguez Salgado, "'Una perfecta princesa.' . . . Primera parte," 67, 73; Cuentas de casa de la Reina, AGP, SAG, C 10276.

74. Marquis of Ladrada to Philip II, 21 February 1571, BL, Add. MSS 28354, fol. 158r. For Juana of Austria's sponsorship of theater, see Cruz, "Juana of Austria," 113–15; Jordan, "Las dos águilas," 433–43.

75. San Gerónimo, "Memorias," 227–8.

76. García Prieto, *Una corte*, 182.

77. Ana of Dietrichstein to Margarita of Cardona, 30 June 1575, in Dietrichstein, *Cartas*, 67; Gálvez de Montalvo, *El pastor de Fílida*, 353–88. For reference to Vázquez's house, see Gonzalo Sánchez-Molero, "L'educazione devozionale," 59.

78. Ana of Dietrichstein to Margarita of Cardona, 5 February 1574, in Dietrichstein, *Cartas*, 43.

79. Cole, *Sofonisba's Lesson*, 271n2; Gonzalo Sánchez-Molero, "L'educazione devozionale," 50–1.

80. Ana of Dietrichstein to Margarita of Cardona, 1 August 1576, in Dietrichstein, *Cartas*, 92–3.
81. Llanos y Torriglia, *La novia de Europa*, 35–6.
82. Martín de Gaztelu to the marquis of Ladrada, 1 April 1570, BL, Add. MSS 28343, fol. 25r.
83. San Gerónimo, "Memorias," 168.
84. Sepúlveda, "Historia de varios sucesos," I:fol. 16v.
85. Philip II to the *infantas*, 16 April 1582, in Bouza, *Cartas*, 78.
86. Pérez de Tudela, "Regalos y retratos," 103–4; Carlo Pallavicino to Juan de Idiáquez, 26 February 1588, AGS, Estado, L1264, no. 120.
87. García García, *El ocio*, 29.
88. Cuentas de casa de la Reina, AGP, SAG, C 10276; Rodríguez Salgado, "'Una perfecta princesa.' . . . Primera parte," 71.
89. Parker, *Imprudent King*, 168.
90. Fourquevaux to Catherine de' Medici, 21 December 1570, in Douais, *Dépêches de M. de Fourquevaux*, II:310.
91. Catalina to Carlo, 20 May 1591, AST, M38, fasc. 5, fol. 776br; Altadonna, II:187. See also her letter to Carlo from 26 December 1589, in which she suggested that Isabel was more patient than she. AST, M36, fol. 474ar; Altadonna, I:394.
92. Pérez de Tudela, "Regalos y retratos," 103n54.
93. Jordan and Pérez de Tudela, "Renaissance Menageries," 439, 439n77.
94. Jordan and Pérez de Tudela, "Renaissance Menageries," 435; Philip II to the *infantas*, 30 July 1582, in Bouza, *Cartas*, 88–9.
95. San Gerónimo, "Memorias," 368–9; Kamen, *Philip of Spain*, 249; Jordan and Pérez de Tudela, "Renaissance Menageries," 443. Khevenhüller reported that when he returned to Madrid from Portugal, Philip II lodged the rhinoceros in the general hospital of Madrid and the elephant in that of Antón Martín. See Khevenhüller to Rudolf II, 13 March 1583, HHStA, DK, K10, 251v; 18 July 1583, HHStA, DK, K10, 271r.
96. Some authors have suggested that all they did was engage in religious activities and that the court was like a convent. See Villermont, *L'Infante Isabelle*, 32, though Villermont was primarily commenting on the period when Philip was in Portugal.
97. San Gerónimo, "Memorias," 130; Camelot, "Confirmation," 149.
98. Marquis of Ladrada to Philip II, 1 February 1571, BL, Add. MSS 28354, fol. 164v.
99. Philip II to the *infantas*, 10 July and 20 November 1581, in Bouza, *Cartas*, 48, 63.
100. San Gerónimo, "Memorias," 285.
101. San Gerónimo, "Memorias," 168.
102. San Gerónimo, "Memorias," 127, 352.
103. San Gerónimo, "Memorias," 166, 267.
104. San Gerónimo, "Memorias," 132, 385. Philip II established a seminary at the Escorial, which drew boys as young as twelve. See Kamen, *The Escorial*, 201.
105. San Gerónimo, "Memorias," 171. Philip II disliked and avoided bullfights. See Alves, *The Animals of Spain*, 91; Kamen, *Philip of Spain*, 226.
106. Quoted in García Prieto, *Una corte*, 89. In 1581, the *infantas* met with the imperial ambassador. See Ana of Dietrichstein to Margarita of Cardona, Second day of Easter 1581 and 3 January 1581, in Dietrichstein, *Cartas*, 146. In a letter of

14 August 1581, Philip wrote that he thought that four Venetian ambassadors would be in Madrid, suggesting that the girls would meet with them. Bouza, *Cartas*, 53

107. Philip II to the *infantas*, 19 February 1582, in Bouza, *Cartas*, 71. Don Antonio de Castro was a Portuguese nobleman whom Philip sent to Barcelona to greet the empress on her arrival in the Spanish kingdoms. See Bouza, *Cartas*, 62n100.

108. For another discussion of these letters, see Parker, *Felipe II*, 462–7.

109. Parker, *Imprudent King*, 169; Philip II to the *infantas*, 29 January 1582, in Bouza, *Cartas*, 67.

110. Philip II to the *infantas*, 30 July 1582, 16 April 1582, 1 May 1581, in Bouza, *Cartas*, 88, 79, 39.

111. Parker, *Imprudent King*, 115; Bouza, *Cartas*, 39–40n22. On these *gente de placer*, see Moreno Villa, *Locos, enanos, negros y niños*; Bouza, *Locos, enanos y hombres*; and Bouza, "La estafeta del bufón," 95–124.

112. Bouza, *Cartas*, 40n24.

113. Philip II to the *infantas*, 23 October 1581, 1 May 1581, in Bouza, *Cartas*, 61, 39. For references to them writing to the girls, see Bouza, *Cartas*, 46, 61, 66, 87.

114. Philip II to the *infantas*, 3 April 1581, in Bouza, *Cartas*, 35.

115. Philip II to the *infantas*, 15 January 1582, 20 November 1581, in Bouza, *Cartas*, 66–7, 63–4. *Perdones* were probably *cuentas de perdón*, which were a type of rosary that when prayed conferred an indulgence. See *Diccionario de autoridades*, vol. 2 (1729), https://apps.rae.es/DA_DATOS/TOMO_II_HTML/CUENTA_008416.html.

116. Philip II to the *infantas*, 2 October 1581, 3 September 1582, 17 September 1582, in Bouza, *Cartas*, 60, 90, 91.

117. Philip II to the *infantas*, 2 October 1581, 26 June 1581, 21 August 1581, in Bouza, *Cartas*, 60, 47, 56. Catalina continued to have swollen cheeks, connected to molar pain, when in Turin. See, for example, Catalina to Carlo, 11 November [1588], AST, M35, fasc. 2, fol. 62v; Altadonna, I:71.

118. Philip II to the *infantas*, 7 May 1582, in Bouza, *Cartas*, 82–3.

119. Philip II to the *infantas*, 14 August 1581, 4 June 1582, in Bouza, *Cartas*, 53, 85.

120. The French representative reported that the *infantas* saw the empress every fifteen days. See Monsieur de Longlée to Catherine de' Medici, 31 December 1583, in Mousset, *Dépêches Diplomatiques*, 7.

121. Khevenhüller to Rudolf II, 29 November 1583, HHStA, DK, K10, 288r.

122. Khevenhüller to Rudolf II, 28 July 1584, HHStA, DK, K11, 38v.

123. Catalina to Carlo, 20 May 1591, AST, M38, fasc. 5, fol. 776bv; Altadonna, II:187. For Carlo's letter, see 26 April 1591, AST, M16, fol. 1009–1009bv.

CHAPTER 2

1. The marriage to Marguerite had sealed the Treaty of Cateau-Cambrésis that returned the duchy of Savoy to the House of Savoy. See Moriondo, *Testa di ferro*, 82–4; Merlin, "Il cinquecento," 71–3. See BL, Add. MSS 28418, fol. 74v–76r for the Spanish ambassador's discussion of several of Carlo's ministers and their leanings.

2. Cabrera de Córdoba, *Historia de Felipe II*, III:1054. When Emanuele's wife died in 1574, Philip also proposed that Emanuele marry Philip's niece, Archduchess Elisabeth of Habsburg, although the marriage did not take place. Friedrich

Edelmayer adds two other factors to explain Philip's desire to ally with Emanuele Filiberto: Philip wanted to show his appreciation to Emanuele Filiberto for not pressing his own right to the Portuguese throne and also to strengthen his own family's ties with the House of Valois. Both Catalina and Carlo had claims to the French throne, so by joining them, their collective claim would be stronger. See Edelmayer, *Philipp II*, 162–3.

3. Pérez de Tudela, "Regalos y retratos," 106. For Carlo's options, see Sfondrato's reports to Philip II in "Relacion de una carta del Varon Sfondrato para su Md de Verceli," 13 June 1581, BL, Add. MSS 28418, fol. 17r–17v. See also Merlin, *Tra guerre e tornei*, 4. On Borromeo's canonization, see Weber, "The Promises and Pitfalls."

4. "Relacion de una carta del Varon Sfondrato para su Md de Verceli," 13 June 1581, BL, Add. MSS 28418, fol. 16v; Guillén de San Clemente to Philip II, 18 June 1581, BL, Add. MSS 28392, fol. 17r. See also Mongiano, "Quale dote," 148. San Clemente reported that the duke spoke openly to Sfondrato, so much so that several of Carlo's ministers disapproved of him. See report of Guillén de San Clemente to Philip II, 17 June 1581, BL, Add. MSS 28392, fol. 9v. San Clemente claimed that Carlo's Francophile advisers urged him to demand territory because they knew that Philip would not give any and that that would incline Carlo to marry a French princess. See Guillén de San Clemente to Philip II, 18 June 1581, BL, Add. MSS 28392, fol. 17v.

5. Paolo Sfondrato to Philip II, 13 June 1581, BL, Add. MSS 28418, fol. 23r, 12r. Sfondrato reported that Carlo wanted to be inducted into the Order of the Golden Fleece before any other Italian prince. See "Relacion de una carta del Varon Sfondrato para su Md de Verceli," 13 June 1581, BL, Add. MSS fol. 17v.

6. For Carlo's sense of his own grandeur, see Gal, *Charles-Emmanuel de Savoie*, *passim*. See also Merlin, *Tra guerre e tornei*, 4.

7. Pérez de Tudela, "Regalos y retratos," 109. My discussion of these early negotiations for the marriage between Catalina and Carlo is indebted to Pérez de Tudela's essay, 105–12.

8. Guillén de San Clemente was appointed ambassador to the court of Savoy in 1581, but almost immediately afterward, Philip named him his ambassador to the imperial court in Prague. Paolo Sfondrato replaced him as ambassador in Turin. On San Clemente, see Arienza Arienza, "La historia de Guillén de San Clemente," 73–98; Jurado Riba, "Clientelismo, servicio militar," 325–52. For San Clemente's report, see Guillén de San Clemente to Philip II, 18 June 1581, BL, Add. MSS 28392, fol. 14r–18r.

9. Pérez de Tudela, "Regalos y retratos," 107n77.

10. Pérez de Tudela, "Regalos y retratos," 110, 105n66, 108; Philip II to the *infantas*, 2 January 1583, in Bouza, *Cartas*, 100; Pallavicino to Carlo, 13 December 1582, AST, LM(S), M3, n.p. For exchange of portraits, see Warnke, *The Court Artist*, 218–24; for English examples, see Sowerby, "'A Memorial and a Pledge of Faith'," 303–9.

11. Pérez de Tudela, "Regalos y retratos," 109–10. See also Carlo Pallavicino to Carlo Emanuele, 1 May 1584, AST, LM(S), M3, n.p.; Khevenhüller to Rudolf II, 10 January 1583, HHStA, DK, K10, 239v.

12. Carlo Pallavicino to Carlo Emanuele, 1 May 1584, AST, LM(S), M3, n.p.

13. Paolo Sfondrato to Juan de Idiáquez, 23 August 1584, AGS, PTR, L46, 9, fol. 41r; Pérez de Tudela, "Regalos y retratos," 111–12. Philip wrote to Catalina that

he hoped she was not badly scarred. Philip II to the *infantas*, 17 January 1583, in Bouza, *Cartas*, 101.

14. Carlo Pallavicino to Carlo Emanuele, 11 September 1584, AST, LM(S), M3, n.p. Pallavicino sent Carlo portraits of the two *infantas*, both identified on the back.

15. Khevenhüller to Rudolf II, 4 July 1583, HHStA, DK, K10, 269r; 15 August 1583, HHStA, DK, K10, 274r–274v; 12 September 1583, HHStA, DK, K10, 276v; 30 June 1584, HHStA, DK, K11, 34v; 22 September 1584, DK, K10, 46v–47r.

16. Longlée to Henri III, 29 February 1584, in Mousset, *Dépêches Diplomatiques*, 31; Longlée to Henri III, 30 June 1584, in Mousset, *Dépêches Diplomatiques*, 89.

17. He was "permanent resident" and not ambassador. Ribera, *Diplomatie et Espionnage*, 548–9.

18. Pallavicino to Carlo, 1 March 1584, AST, LM(S), M3, n.p.

19. Khevenhüller to Rudolf II, 15 August 1584, HHStA, DK, K11, 44r.

20. Carlo and Elisabeth of Valois, Catalina's mother, were first cousins. For Gregory XIII's dispensation, see AGS, PTR, L46, no. 7. AST, Matrimonio, M20, no. 11, fol. 3r–3v, 20 October 1584. Mongiono remarks on the difficulty of comparing the size of Catalina's dowry to that of others but stresses that it was certainly large. See "Quale dote," 148.

21. AST, Matrimonio, M20, no. 11, fol. 4r, 20 October 1584. See also Mongiano, "Quale dote," 150. After Catalina's death, the dowry would remain a bone of contention between Spain and Savoy for many years. In particular, Carlo and his successors demanded that Spain pay the annual allowance of 40,000 ducats. See Antolín Rejón, "Pricing an Ally."

22. AST, Matrimonio, M20, no. 11, fols. 4r–4v, 5r, 20 October 1584. Briceño claimed that the duke had promised to provide 20,000 ducats a year to sustain Catalina's household. See Cristóbal de Briceño to Juan de Zúñiga, 13 December 1585, BPG, CEF, MS 23, fol. 402r. I am grateful to Rocío Martínez López for clarifying this aspect of the contract and for discussing at length Catalina's marriage contract with me.

23. AST, Matrimonio, M20, no. 11, fol. 5r, 20 October 1584; Martínez López, "El Imperio y Baviera," 34.

24. The Venetian ambassador noted that, with the consent of Philip II, Catalina's title would be *Infanta* of Spain and duchess of Savoy; *Infanta* would come before duchess. Giovanni Mocenigo to Nicolò da Ponte, 5 July 1585, ASV, SDSa, filza 8, no. 20.

25. AST, Matrimonio, M20, no. 11, fol. 3v, 20 October 1584. See also "Rinunzia dell' Infanta di Spagna Cattarina d'Austria Duchessa di Savoia a favore del Re Filippo II," AST, Matrimonio, M20, no. 14, 13 June 1585.

26. The account was written by someone who addressed Adam von Dietrichstein, former imperial ambassador to Spain, as "my lord." The author wrote from the Spanish court and was probably someone in the household of Hans Khevenhüller. I would like to thank Suzanne Belz for photographing the account for me. "Relacion de algunas menudencias desta corte hasta los 23 de septiembre de 1584," HHStA, SV 3, fasz. 3, fol. 12r–16. Adam of Dietrichstein had many informants at the Spanish court. See Edelmayer, "Honor y dinero," 112–13, and 113n122 for a discussion of the provenance of these accounts. For Pallavicino's report on this occasion to Carlo, see 22 September 1584, AST, LM(S), M3, n.p.

27. "Relacion de algunas menudencias desta corte hasta los 23 de septiembre de 1584," HHStA, SV 3, fasz. 3, fol. 12v. Khevenhüller reported that he had been told that in early August 1584, before Carlo signed the contract in Chambéry, Philip had informed the emperor, the pope, and the French king that he had agreed to marry Catalina to the duke of Savoy. If so, all of these men found out before Catalina that she was betrothed. See Khevenhüller to Rudolf II, 22 September 1584, HHStA, DK, K11, 51r.

28. "Relacion de algunas menudencias desta corte hasta los 23 de septiembre de 1584," HHStA, SV 3, fasz. 3, fol. 13r. Henry Kamen discusses Catalina's reaction to the letter, but his translation is slightly different from mine. While noting that Catalina blushed when she saw the signature and refused to read the letter, he does not note that observers claimed she had tears in her eyes. He also says that Philip spent the rest of the afternoon with the "delighted princesses," when Catalina's reaction suggests that she was far from delighted. Kamen gives the date as September 1583, when it was 1584. See Kamen, *Philip of Spain*, 249.

29. Pallavicino to Carlo, 22 September 1584, AST, LM(S), M2, n.p.

30. Pallavicino to Carlo, 22 September 1584, AST, LM(S), M3, n.p. Khevenhüller reported that Philip had reprimanded Pallavicino for his attire, refusing to show him the courtesies usually given to ambassadors on celebratory occasions, and Pallavicino had returned very upset to Madrid. Although Khevenhüller commiserated with him, he thought Pallavicino had shown ill judgment. See Khevenhüller to Rudolf II, 22 September 1584, HHStA, DK, K11, 52v; Khevenhüller, *Diario*, 289.

31. Martínez López, "Los derechos sucesorios femeninos," 76. For the empress's disapproval, see González Cuerva, *Maria of Austria*, 181.

32. Khevenhüller, *Diario*, 288.

33. Khevenhüller, *El khurzer Extrakt*, 437. Khevenhüller gave the wrong date. Pallavicino presented the duke's letter to Philip on 16 September 1584. For his complaints, see Khevenhüller to Rudolf II, 22 September 1584, HHStA, DK, K11, 50v–52r.

34. Khevenhüller, *Diario*, 288.

35. See, for example, Longlée to Henri III, in Mousset, *Dépêches Diplomatiques*, 97; Pallavicino to Carlo, 8 November 1583 and 11 September 1584, AST, LM(S), M3, n.p.

36. Fra Bongianni di Piero Gianfigliazzi to Francesco de' Medici, 9 March 1585, ASF, MP, filza 4916, fol. 446v; Khevenhüller to Rudolf II, 27 September 1584, HHStA, DK, K11, 54v; 9 February 1585, HHStA, DK, K11, 93v; 11 March 1585, HHStA, DK, K11, 97r.

37. "Relacion de algunas menudencias desta corte hasta los 17 de noviembre de 84," HHStA, SV 3, fasz. 3, 41r–41v.

38. Khevenhüller, *Diario*, 289. On the use of "Your Excellency," see Medina Morales, "Las formas nominales," 1338. The Venetian ambassador to Turin also reported that Philip had allowed Amedeo to keep his head covered at all times. Giovanni Mocenigo, report of 4 November 1584 in *Due anni,* 35.

39. Fra Bongianni di Piero Gianfigliazzi to Francesco I de' Medici, 20 October 1584, ASF, MP, filza 4916, fol. 312v; Khevenhüller, *El khurzer Extrakt*, 438.

40. "Llegada de Don Amadeo Hermano del duque de Saboya al Pardo," ACA, Carpeta 143-101, fol. 57r. The Alba document is not dated, but in his diary Khevenhüller says that Amedeo went to El Pardo on 8 October. The previous day, the *infantas* had begun to wear *chapines*. See Khevenhüller, *Geheimes Tagebuch*, 139. See also Giovanni Mocenigo, report of 4 November 1584, in *Due anni*, 35.

41. "Llegada de Don Amadeo . . . al Pardo," ACA, Carpeta 143-101, fol. 57r.

42. "Llegada de Don Amadeo . . . al Pardo," ACA, Carpeta 143-101, fol. 57r–57v. As a ten-year-old *infanta*, Empress María had also refused to take the hand of a French envoy. See González Cuerva, *Maria of Austria*, 15.

43. Fra Bongianni di Piero Gianfigliazzi to Francesco I de' Medici, 12 October 1584, ASF, MP, filza 4916, fol. 304r.

44. Bouza, *Cartas*, 74n140.

45. Pallavicino to Carlo Emanuele, 20 October 1584, AST, LM(S), M3, n.p.

46. "Relacion de algunas menudencias desta corte hasta los 17 de noviembre de 84," HHStA, SV 3, fasz. 3, fol. 37v. It is unclear whether Amedeo was present, and Pallavicino affirmed that no male courtiers were allowed to attend. See his letter to Carlo Emanuele, 20 October 1584, AST, LM(S), M3, n.p.

47. Pallavicino to Carlo Emanuele, 20 October 1584, AST, LM(S), M3, n.p.; "Relacion de algunas menudencias desta corte hasta los 17 de noviembre de 84," HHStA, SV 3, fasz. 3, fol. 37v–38r.

48. Pallavicino to Carlo Emanuele, 11 September 1584, AST, LM(S), M3, n.p.; Mulcahy, "Sánchez Coello at the Prado," 664.

49. Pallavicino to Carlo, 24 November 1584, AST, LM(S), M3, n.p. Pallavicino relayed the *infanta*'s message in Spanish, suggesting that he might have been quoting her exact words.

50. For partition of goods, see "Scriptura firmada de las señoras Infantas Doña Isabel y doña Catalina, que se otorgó en Barcelona a 11 de junio 1585," IVDJ, ENV 35, C 48, no. 28.

51. On the marten as a fertility symbol, see Carlos Varona, *Nacer en palacio*, 51–5; Carlos Varona, "Representar el nacimiento," 232–3. See also the English version of this article: "Giving Birth at the Habsburg Court," 153–6.

52. Roses made of gold were blessed by the pope on the fourth Sunday of Lent and then given as gifts to prominent persons. See Rock, "Golden Rose."

53. Amezúa y Mayo, *Isabel de Valois*, Appendix VII, 539.

54. Sbaraglia, "Las joyas de Catalina Micaela," 42–3; Ruffino, "Vestire l'infanta," 355. The jewels that Catalina left her children were valued at 281,400 ducats. On Catalina's jewels, see also Rodríguez López-Abadía, "Las joyas de la infanta Catalina Micaela," 105–14.

55. Cock, *Relación del viaje hecho*, 145.

56. Consultas, 1 October 1584, 20 March 1585, and 8 June 1585, AZ, Altamira, Carpeta 85, nos. 69, 29, 38; Río Barredo, "De Madrid a Turín," 104–5.

57. After Diego de Alcalá's canonization, Philip II had his legs severed from his uncorrupted body so that he and his family could keep the relics. See Eire, *From Madrid to Purgatory*, 452. For the discussion of the visit to Alcalá, see Corazzino, *Sposalizio*, 13 (Italian), 47 (Spanish).

58. Cock, *Relación del viaje hecho*, 22, 10–11, 13–14, 16, 21, 22.

59. Cock, *Relación del viaje hecho*, 24, 29.

60. Ruiz, "Philip II's Entry into Zaragoza," 274, 277.

61. Ruiz, *A King Travels*, 276.

62. "Relacion de la orden," HHStA, SV 3, fasz. 3, fol. 73r.

63. "Relacion de la orden," HHStA, SV 3, fasz. 3, fol. 73r. On the tapestries, see Cock, *Relación del viaje hecho*, 52; and Fundación Carlos de Amberes, http://tapestries. flandesenhispania.org/index.php/The_Conquest_of_Tunis_series. Replicas of the tapestries were ordered immediately after the originals were completed, and

Mary of Hungary had one such set that was smaller than the original. Juana of Austria inherited this smaller series, which passed to Philip at her death. These must have been the ones that he took with him, displaying them first at the wedding and later at the *Cortes* in Monzón.

64. Cock, *Relación del viaje hecho*, 41; Merlin, *Tra guerre e tornei*, 5.

65. Philip II to Paolo Sfondrato, 13 January 1585, AGS, Estado, L1260, no. 200.

66. Khevenhüller, *Diario*, 312.

67. Corazzino, *Sposalizio*, 20 (Italian), 55 (Spanish).

68. Cock, *Relación del viaje hecho*, 48.

69. Giovanni Mocenigo to Nicolò da Ponte, 29 March 1585, ASV, SDSa, filza 8, no. 5; Giovanni Mocenigo, report of 29 March 1585, in *Due anni*, 47. The author of the Dietrichstein account commented that once the duke arrived in the palace, the *infantas* did not greet him because they were with other ladies. "Relacion de la orden," HHStA, SV 3, fasz. 3, fol. 67v.

70. See Schroeder, *The Decrees of the Council of Trent*, 184. For marriage in Spain, see Usunáriz, "Marriage and Love," 201–24.

71. Kamen, *The Phoenix and the Flame*, 282–3.

72. Catalina to Carlo, 11 March 1592, AST, M40, fasc. 3, fol. 1091v; Altadonna, III:40.

73. Cock, *Relación del viaje hecho*, 52; Corazzino, *Sposalizio*, 22 (Italian), 58 (Spanish); "Relatione delli nozze del Duca di Savoia," BAV, fol. 494r; Gómez River, "Antonio Perrenot de Granvela."

74. "Relatione delli nozze del Duca di Savoia," BAV, fol. 491v; Cock, *Relación del viaje hecho*, 52; "Relacion de la orden," HHStA, SV 3, fasz. 3, fol. 69r; Letter (unknown writer and recipient) from Zaragoza, 11 March 1585, ACA, Carpeta 143-110, no. 5.

75. Corazzino, *Sposalizio*, 24 (Italian), 58 (Spanish); "Relacion de la orden," HHStA, SV 3, fasz. 3, fol. 69v.

76. Carlo to the marquis d'Este from Zaragoza, 14 March 1585, quoted in Varallo, *Da Nizza a Torino*, 16n14.

77. See Cock, *Relación del viaje hecho*, 57.

78. Schroeder, *The Decrees of the Council of Trent*, 184; Donahue, "The Legal Background," 36.

79. "Relacion de la orden," HHStA, SV 3, fasz. 3, fol. 70v; "Relatione delli nozze del Duca di Savoia," BAV, fol. 494v.

80. Giovanni Mocenigo to Nicolò da Ponte, 29 March 1585, ASV, SDSa, filza 8, no. 5; Giovanni Mocenigo, report of 29 March 1585 in *Due anni*, 49; Usunáriz, "Marriage and Love," 201.

81. "Relacion de la orden," HHStA, SV 3, fasz. 3, fol. 71r–71v.

82. "Relatione delli nozze del Duca di Savoia," BAV, fol. 495v–496r.

83. Giovanni Mocenigo to Nicolò da Ponte, 29 March 1585, ASV, SDSa, filza 8, no. 5; Giovanni Mocenigo, report of 29 March 1585 in *Due anni*, 49, 50.

84. Catalina's *mayordomo*, Cristóbal Briceño, noted that Carlo had a child by a woman at court. See Cristóbal Briceño to Mateo Vázquez, 15 September 1585, IVDJ, ENV 5, T III, fol. 257r–v.

85. Corazzino, *Sposalizio*, 26 (Italian), 60 (Spanish).

86. Cock, *Relación del viaje hecho*, 60.

87. Giovanni Mocenigo to Nicolò da Ponte, 29 March 1585, ASV, SDSa, filza 8, no. 5; Giovanni Mocenigo, report of 29 March 1585 in *Due anni*, 50.

88. Giovanni Mocenigo to Nicolò da Ponte, 26 March 1585, ASV, SDSa, filza 8, no. 4; Giovanni Mocenigo, report of 26 March 1585 in *Due anni*, 41.

89. "Relacion de la orden," HHStA, SV 3, fasz. 3, fol. 75r.

90. "Relacion de la orden," HHStA, SV 3, fasz. 3, fols. 74v, 75r.

91. Giovanni Mocenigo to Nicolò da Ponte, 29 March 1585, ASV, SDSa, filza 8, no. 5; Giovanni Mocenigo, report of 29 March 1585 in *Due anni*, 50.

92. "Relatione delli nozze del Duca di Savoia," BAV, fol. 496r–v.

93. Giovanni Mocenigo to Nicolò da Ponte, 29 March 1585, ASV, SDSa, filza 8, no. 5; Giovanni Mocenigo, report of 29 March 1585 in *Due anni*, 50–1.

94. Giovanni Mocenigo to Nicolò da Ponte, 26 April 1585, ASV, SDSa, filza 8, no. 11; Giovanni Mocenigo, report of 26 April in *Due anni*, 51.

95. Carlo to Philip II, 5 October 1586, AGS, Estado, L1261, no. 13. Catalina remembered the difficulty of having to climb to the hermitages. See Catalina to Carlo, 20 May 1591, AST, M38, fasc. 5, fol. 776av; Altadonna, II:187.

96. Cock, *Relación del viaje hecho*, 141.

97. Giovanni Mocenigo to Nicolò da Ponte, 24 May 1585, ASV, SDSa, filza 8, no. 13; Giovanni Mocenigo, report of 24 May 1585 in *Due anni*, 51–2.

98. Corazzino, *Sposalizio*, 33, 35 (Italian), 70–1 (Spanish). Carlo also gave costly gifts to Philip II, the *infanta* Isabel, and Prince Philip. "Relatione delli nozze del Duca di Savoia," BAV, fol. 504v.

99. "Relacion de carta de Zaragoza," RAH, L38, Carpeta 1, no. 5, fol. 274r.

100. Storrs, *War, Diplomacy and the Rise of Savoy*, 193–4; Wyllie, *Orders, Decorations, and Insignia*, 153; Pera Museum Blog, http://blog.peramuzesi.org.tr/en/haftanin-eseri/savoyali-filippo-emanuele/.

101. Cock, *Relación del viaje hecho*, 76–8.

102. Gamberini, *Sofonisba*, 100.

103. See "Embarcacion y despedida de la infanta D. Catalina y del duque de Saboya," ACA, Carpeta 143-121, no. 12; "Relacion de carta de Zaragoza," RAH, L38, Carpeta 1, no. 5, fol. 274v; Parker, *Imprudent King*, 168.

104. Quoted in Kamen, *Philip of Spain*, 259.

105. "Embarcacion y despedida de la infanta D. Catalina y del duque de Saboya," ACA, Carpeta 143-121, no. 12.

106. Cock, *Relación del viaje hecho*, 145. An anonymous report also notes the tears and sadness. See "Relacion de la embarcacion de la S. Ynfanta Doña Catalina y duque de Saboya pa yr a su estado y de el recebimynto que en el se les hizo," RAH, Salazar y Castro, fol. 78r.

107. "Embarcacion y despedida de la infanta D. Catalina y del duque de Saboya," ACA, Carpeta 143-121, no. 12.

108. Fra Bongianni di Piero Gianfigliazzi to Francesco I de' Medici, 9 March 1585, ASF, MP, filza 4916, fol. 446v.

109. Sepúlveda, "Historia de varios sucesos," I:fol. 23v.

110. Parker, *Imprudent King*, 385. For a reordering of Sepúlveda's account, see Zarco-Bacas y Cuevas, *Documentos para la historia del monasterio*. However, Zarco-Bacas y Cuevas does not include the incident with the pearls.

111. Philip II, for example, had felt compelled to remove many of Elisabeth of Valois's French attendants because they clashed regularly with her Spanish attendants. Rodríguez Salgado, " 'Una perfecta princesa.' . . . Primera parte," 51.

112. Vincenzo Gradenigo to Nicolò da Ponte, 6 April 1585, ASV, SDS, filza 18, no. 8.

CHAPTER 3

1. Toward the end of their stay in Spain, the duke and several of his men fell seriously ill, and two of his courtiers died. Carlo might have been suffering from this illness and not from seasickness. See Giovanni Mocenigo to Nicolò da Ponte, 3, 15, and 24 June 1585, ASV, SDSa, filza 8, nos. 15, 16, 19. For published accounts, see Giovanni Mocenigo, 24 May 1585, 15 and 24 June 1585 in *Due anni*, 52–3. For Sfondrato's letter, see Paolo Sfondrato to Juan de Idiáquez, 14 June 1585, AGS, Estado, L1261, no. 10. See also Andrea Provana di Leynì to the marquis d'Este, 5 June 1585, Barcelona, ASC, Bel., cart. 41. Leynì said that the duke had been so sick that no one wanted him to board the ship.
2. Paolo Sfondrato to Juan de Idiáquez, 14 June 1585, AGS, Estado, L1261, no. 10.
3. Andrea Provana di Leynì to the marquis d'Este, 5 June 1585, ASC, Bel., cart. 41.
4. For the entrance into Nice, see "Relatione degli apparati," 96–104. From Nice they proceeded to Ceva, Savona, Mondovì, Cuneo, Fossano, Savigliano, Racconigi, Carignano, Viconovo, and Moncalieri. See "Relatione degli apparati," 105, and Álvarez González, "Pageantry," 33. Stéphan Gal says Carlo wanted to seduce Catalina with the grandeur of his lands. See *Charles-Emmanuel de Savoie*, 91. For entrance into Turin, see "De la llegada del duque de Saboya a Turín," 10 August 1585, AGS, Estado, L1260, no. 194. Before they reached Turin, the *infanta*'s pregnancy was confirmed and led to her reception in Turin being altered slightly. Catalina was supposed to step from her litter to a triumphal carriage pulled by six horses, but instead she mounted a "very calm palfrey," richly adorned and better suited to someone who was pregnant. See "Relatione degli apparati," 113.
5. Councilors debated whom they would choose to represent Turin when the *infanta* entered. Forty men were to greet Catalina outside the city, and six needed to be chosen to carry the staffs of the baldachin that would be placed over the ducal couple. See Álvarez González, "Pageantry," 36n21; Varallo, *Da Nizza a Torino*, 32n67.
6. For a detailed discussion of these preparations, the duke's role in the preparations, and how specific communities greeted Carlo and Catalina, see Varallo, *Da Nizza a Torino*, 38–78. See 38n80 about Pinerolo's refusal to contribute. For specific structures, see Paolo Antonio Pallavicino to the marquis d'Este, 20 June 1585, ASC, Bel., cart. 41, fasc. 2, fol. 52.
7. Governor of Savigliano to the marquis d'Este, 15 July 1585, ASC, Bel., cart. 41, fasc. 3, fol. 248r; Governor of Cuneo to the marquis d'Este, 15 July 1585, ASC, Bel., cart. 41, fasc. 3, fol. 244; Governor of Carignano to the marquis d'Este, 19 July 1585, ASC, Bel., cart. 41, fasc. 3, fol. 256.
8. ASRT, Camera dei Conti, Art. 224, Cuentas 1585–87, limosnas de 1585, n.p.
9. "Relatione degli apparati," 105; Varallo, *Da Nizza a Torino*, 79–80.
10. Varallo, *Da Nizza a Torino*, 85; "Relatione degli apparati," 112; Cristóbal de Briceño to Mateo Vázquez, 14 August 1585, IVDJ, ENV 5, T III, fol. 256r.
11. "De la llegada del duque de Saboya a Turin," 10 August 1585, AGS, Estado, L1260, no. 194. The document does not state author, day, or month but seems to have been written by someone close to Catalina, possibly Paolo Sfondrato.
12. "Entrata della Ser[enissi]ma Infanti di Spagna Catharina d'Austria Duchessa di Savoya e Principessa di Piamonte," ASdT, Ordinati, vol. 135, fol. 61r–v; "Relatione degli apparati," 113, 116–18.

13. "Relatione degli apparati," 121; "De la llegada del duque de Saboya a Turin," 10 August 1585, AGS, Estado, L1260, no. 194; Cristóbal de Briceño to Mateo Vázquez, 14 August 1585, IVDJ, ENV 5, T III, fol. 256r.

14. "De la llegada del duque de Saboya a Turin," 10 August 1585, AGS, Estado, L1260, no. 194. The Venetian ambassador, who had been reporting rumors that Catalina was pregnant, noted on 5 August 1585 that she was in fact pregnant and for this reason they were cutting the trip short to reach Turin as quickly as possible. See Giovanni Mocenigo to Nicolò da Ponte, ASV, SDSa, filza 8, no. 25.

15. Pollak, *Turin*, 13–15; Cardoza and Symcox, *A History of Turin*, 114–19; Merlin, *Manuel Filiberto*, 145–6, 148–9. Pollak argues that Emanuele Filiberto chose the episcopal palace in order to disassociate himself from the French and emphasize his family's divinely sanctioned right to rule but Merlin says that the French governors had lived in the episcopal residence.

16. Merlin, *Manuel Filiberto*, 150n13; Cuneo, "Gli anni spagnoli," 148; Varallo, *Da Nizza a Torino*, 22.

17. The duke also instructed D'Este to have a covered *loggetta* constructed where a table for twelve to fourteen people could be placed, connected to a room where the *infanta* could retire. Varallo, *Da Nizza a Torino*, 22–3, 23n33.

18. Cuneo, "Gli anni spagnoli," 146. For the Racconigi house, see Varallo, *Da Nizza a Torino*, 19–20, esp. 19n28; Cuneo, "Le residenze," 237–8.

19. Giovanni Mocenigo to Nicolò da Ponte, 29 March 1585, ASV, SDSa, filza 8, no. 5.

20. Cristóbal de Briceño to Juan de Zúñiga, 7 January 1586 and 6 March 1586, BPG, CEF, MS 23, fols. 404v, 415v.

21. It is difficult to get a sense of the architectural layout of the extended palace complex because none of it remains. At some point Catalina and her ladies probably moved into rooms in the new palace, but the timing is unclear and the date uncertain.

22. "La orden que es nuestra voluntad que guarden los criados y criadas de la Serenísima Infanta Doña Catalina mi muy cara y muy amada hija, en lo que toca a su servicio, uso y ejercicio de sus oficios," BPR, II/3127, fol. 59–155; Río Barredo, "De Madrid a Turín," 106–14.

23. Consulta del Comendador Mayor de Castilla sobre cosas del cargo del Baron Sfondrato, 25 May 1585, AGS, Estado, L1260, no. 184.

24. Merlin, *Tra guerre e tornei*, 8.

25. Sfondrato was the brother of Niccolò Sfrondato, who became Pope Gregory XIV in 1590. See Giuliani, "Il barone Paolo Sfondrati," 169–87; Giannini, "Sfondrati, Paolo."

26. Consulta of Juan de Zúñiga to Philip II, 25 May 1585, AGS, Estado, L1260, no. 184; Río Barredo, "De Madrid a Turín," 112.

27. Cristóbal de Briceño to Juan de Zúñiga, 13 December 1585, BPG, CEF, MS 23, fol. 402v.

28. "De la llegada del duque de Saboya a Turin," 10 August 1585, AGS, Estado, L1260, no. 194.

29. Cristóbal de Briceño to Juan de Zúñiga, 13 December 1585, BPG, CEF, MS 23, fol. 402v.

30. The salaries of the women of the *cámara*, except for that of Luisa Mexía, were significantly lower than those given to the ladies and to *mayordomos* such as Briceño. See ASRT, Camera dei Conti, Art. 224, Cuentas 1585–87, n.p. Luisa

Mexía seems to have been the attendant Catalina called "Chicha," who had probably served Catalina at the Spanish court. In Catalina's household there were two attendants named Luisa Mexía. The second Luisa Mexía might have been the elder Luisa's niece. I am indebted to María José del Río Barredo for helping me identify Luisa Mexía as Chicha.

31. Cristóbal de Briceño to Juan de Zúñiga, 11 June 1586, BPG, CEF, MS 23, fol. 438v. For a discussion of the carriage as a social privilege reserved for those designated by the king, see López Álvarez, *Poder, lujo y conflicto*, 156–67.

32. Cristóbal de Briceño to Juan de Zúñiga, 11 June 1586, BPG, CEF, MS 23, fol. 438v–439r. See also Fórmica, *La infanta Catalina Micaela*, 16.

33. Cristóbal de Briceño to Juan de Zúñiga, 11 June 1586, BPG, CEF, MS 23, fol. 438v. Pallavicino noted that Luisa Mexía had arranged for a friend to come from Spain to serve as governess of one of Catalina's children. He explained that the woman would bring four daughters with her, which would greatly add to the court's expense. Although Pallavicino did not specifically say that Mexía was taking advantage of her influence with Catalina, he implied it. See Carlo Pallavicino to Juan de Idiáquez, 26 February 1588, AGS, Estado, L1264, no. 120; Cristóbal de Briceño to Juan de Zúñiga, 7 January 1586, BPG, CEF, MS 23, fol. 404v.

34. In this same letter, Briceño complained that men kept their hats on in Catalina's presence and, whereas at the beginning only Amedeo and an occasional ambassador had done so, now at least four others covered their heads and Briceño worried that others would follow their example. Cristóbal de Briceño to Juan de Zúñiga, 7 January 1586, BPG, CEF, MS 23, fol. 405r–v.

35. Cristóbal de Briceño to Mateo Vázquez, 20 October 1586, IVDJ, ENV 5, T III, no. 258; Cristóbal de Briceño to Juan de Zúñiga, 7 January 1586, BPG, CEF, MS 23, fol. 406r.

36. Cristóbal de Briceño to Juan de Zúñiga, 6 June 1586, BPG, CEF, MS 23, fol. 434v; Cristóbal de Briceño to Mateo Vázquez, 20 October 1586, IVDJ, ENV 5, T III, no. 258.

37. Cristóbal de Briceño to Juan de Zúñiga, 5 February 1586, BPG, CEF, MS 23, fol. 408r–409r; Fórmica, *La infanta Catalina Micaela*, 23–4.

38. Cristóbal de Briceño to Juan de Zúñiga, 6 June 1586, BPG, CEF, MS 23, fol. 436r; Fórmica, *La infanta Catalina Micaela*, 19–20.

39. Cristóbal de Briceño to Juan de Zúñiga, 6 June 1586, BPG, CEF, MS 23, fol. 434r–436v. Briceño says that Miraflores was 2 leagues outside Turin (a Spanish league was about 3 miles) but the Venetian ambassador says 2 miles. It was approximately 5 miles from the palace. See Francesco Vendramin to Pasquale Ciconi, 20 June 1586, ASV, SDSa, filza 8, no. 78.

40. Cristóbal de Briceño to Mateo Vázquez, 15 September 1585, IVDJ, ENV 5, T III, fol. 257r–v.

41. Cristóbal de Briceño to Juan de Zúñiga, 6 June 1586, BPG, CEF, MS 23, fol. 434r–v.

42. Cristóbal de Briceño to Juan de Zúñiga, 11 June 1586, BPG, CEF, MS 23, fol. 438r.

43. Philip II to Catalina, 28 July 1586, in Bouza, *Cartas*, 143.

44. Cristóbal de Briceño to Mateo Vázquez, 20 October 1586, IVDJ, ENV 5, T III, no. 258. Briceño might also have been in poor health, because he died in March 1587. See Paolo Sfondrato to Philip II, 17 March 1587, AGS, Estado, L1262, no. 128. See also Bouza, *Cartas*, 150n347.

45. I will refer to Kraeck as "El Flamenco," since that is how Carlo and Catalina referred to him. On Kraeck, see Astrua, Bava, and Spantigati, "*Il nostro pittore fiamengo.*"

46. Among the verses is one to Lavinia Guasco, who entered Catalina's household only in late 1585 or early 1586 but was definitely at the court by March 1586. The verses must therefore have been composed after Lavinia's arrival at court. For these verses, see AST, Storie della Real Casa, M15-2; for his poetry, see Doglio, "Il 'teatro poetico' del principe," 165–89.

47. Roggero and Scotti, *Il castello del Valentino*, 9.

48. Roggero and Scotti, *Il castello del Valentino*, 9–10; Roggero Bardelli, Vinardi, and Defabiani, *Villa sabaude*, 158. The residence was called Miraflores even before Catalina's arrival and she often referred to Miraflores in the singular, as Miraflor.

49. On 6 November 1586, Catalina and Carlo went to Miraflores after their midday meal and returned in the evening. See Paolo Sfondrato to Juan de Idiaquez, AGS, Estado, L1261, no. 31; Cuneo, "Le residenze," 243; Francesco Vendramin to Pasquale Ciconi, 20 June 1586, ASV, SDSa. Savoia, filza 8, no. 78.

50. Philip II to Catalina, 2 January 1586 and 10 April 1586, in Bouza, *Cartas*, 132, 138.

51. One author argues that Carlo probably planned to invest Catalina's dowry in Valentino. See Roggero and Scotti, *Il castello del Valentino*, 9–10. He gave d'Este the palace of Lucento in exchange for Valentino. See Roggero Bardelli, Vinardi, and Defabiani, *Villa sabaude,* 143.

52. Cuneo, "La fabbrica del Valentino," 266.

53. For these accounts, see ASRT, Camerale Piemonte, Art. 252, 12, 1, fol. 2–26v (accounts from 1589 to 1594); 12, 2, fol. 5–14 (accounts for repairs done in 1590); and 12, 3, fol. 1–6v (accounts from M. Alessandro Mangarda from 1595). The accounts record that Catalina employed a gardener, day laborers, and women to work in the gardens. See Catalina's letter of 28 September 1595 in ASRT, Camerale Piemonte, Art. 252, 12, 1, fol. 4v.

54. Catalina to Carlo, 20 June, AST, M45, fasc. 3, fol. 2089r, no year given but from internal evidence I would date it to 1590. See also Catalina to Carlo, 2 May [1593], AST, M41, fasc. 3, fol. 1303r–v; Altadonna, III:91.

55. Cuneo, "La fabbrica del Valentino," 267.

56. ASRT, Camera dei conti, Real Casa, Art. 224, Cartas de Pago, July 1589, entry 440, n.p.

57. Cristóbal de Briceño to Juan de Zúñiga, 6 June 1586, BPG, CEF, MS 23, fol. 436r.

58. See the many entries in ASRT, Real Casa, Camerale, Art. 384, Cuentas de Sayas y Vestidos, 15 October 1585, 25 October 1585, n.p. and ASRT, Camera dei conti, Real Casa, Art. 224, n.p. On Catalina's attire, see Varallo, "Catalina Micaela en la corte de Saboya," 63–85. In the sixteenth century, a bed was essentially textiles on or over a frame, and "*cama*" could refer to all the textiles used to cover a bed frame. These might include curtains and pillows. See Ágreda Pino, "Vestir el lecho," 20–1.

59. ASRT, Real Casa, Camerale, Art. 384, 31 December 1585, 8 March 1586, 10 April 1586, 15 April 1586, n.p. Catalina and Carlo served as godparents of Mariana's child.

60. ASRT, Real Casa, Camerale, Art. 384, 12 February 1586, 15 April 1586, 29 October 1586, 12 December 1590, 15 November 1586, n.p.

61. ASRT, Real Casa, Camerale, Art. 384, 24 May 1586, n.p.
62. ASRT, Real Casa, Camerale, Art. 384, Cuentas de Sayas y Vestidos, 26 August 1585, n.p.
63. ASRT, Camera dei conti, Real Casa, Art. 224, Cartas de Pago, entry 170, n.p. The accounts do not specifically say that the small gifts were for Catalina's birthday, but the entry is sandwiched between purchases made to celebrate her birthday.
64. On Catalina's embroidery, see Binaghi Olivari, "I ricami dell'infanta," 359–69.
65. ASRT, Camera dei Conti, Real Casa, Art. 224, 3 May 1586, n.p.
66. Catalina to Carlo, 9 October [1588], AST, M35, fasc. 1, fol. 25v; Altadonna, I:30.
67. Cristóbal de Briceño to Juan de Zúñiga, 5 February 1586, BPG, CEF, MS 23, fol. 408r–408v.
68. Philip II to Catalina, 16 February 1586, in Bouza, *Cartas*, 136.
69. For evidence of Catalina hunting while pregnant, see Philip II to Catalina, 14 March 1587, in Bouza, *Cartas*, 148. In March 1587, Catalina was in her seventh month of pregnancy. Carlo Pallavicino to Juan de Idiáquez, 26 February 1588, AGS, Estado, L1264, no. 120.
70. Cristóbal de Briceño to Juan de Zúñiga, 5 February 1586, BPG, CEF, MS 23, fol. 408v–409r; ASRT, Camera dei Conti, Real Casa, Art. 224, Cuentas 1585–87, 22 February 1586, n.p.
71. Tylus, "Women at the Windows," 329; McKendrick, *Theatre in Spain*, 186.
72. *Gregüesco* referred to the style of pants supposedly worn by Greeks, and Lope de Vega used the adjective as a synonym for Greek. See Lope Félix de Vega Carpio, *La Dorotea*, 354n214. ASRT, Camera dei Conti, Real Casa, Art. 224, entry 168, n.p.
73. ASRT, Real Casa, Camerale, Art. 384, 14 January 1586; 25 February 1586, n.p. For examples of other payments for materials related to *comedias*, see ASRT, Camera dei conti, Real Casa, Art. 224, Cartas de Pago, 20 October 1585.
74. Philip II to Catalina, 16 February 1586, in Bouza, *Cartas*, 136.
75. Cristóbal de Briceño to Juan de Zúñiga, 5 February 1586, BPG, CEF, MS 23, 409r; Smith, *The Commedia dell'Arte*, 7.
76. On Martinelli and the creation of Arlecchino, see Ferrone, *Arlecchino*; Henke, *Performance and Literature*, 158; Ferrone, "Journeys," 71; Schrickx, "Italian Actors in Antwerp in 1576," 804.
77. Shergold, "Ganassa and the 'Commedia dell'arte'," 60–1. On the commedia dell'arte in Spain, see Sanz Ayán and García García, "El 'oficio de representar'," 475–500.
78. ASRT, Camera dei Conti, Real Casa, Art. 224, Cuentas 1585–87, 10 March 1586, n.p.
79. Smith, *The Commedia dell'Arte*, 6–7; Fernández Valbuena, "Influencing Gender Roles," 117.
80. Catalina to Carlo, 18 April 1591, AST, M37, fasc. 5, fol. 542; Altadonna, II:170.
81. Catalina to Carlo, 20 May 1591, AST, M38, fasc. 5, fol. 776br; Altadonna, II:187.
82. Pellicer, *Tratado histórico*, 64; Sanz Ayán, "Felipe II," 53n13.
83. Cristóbal de Briceño to Juan de Zúñiga, 7 January 1586 and 17 February 1586, BPG, CEF, MS 23, fols. 406r, 412r.

84. Years later, Isabel Clara Eugenia would shoot the popinjay at the festival in Brussels. Thomas, "Isabel Clara Eugenia and the Pacification," 187–90. Fraser describes similar midsummer festivities in Aix involving archery, popinjays, and bonfires. See *The Golden Bough*, 630.

85. ASRT, Camerale, Art. 384, 29 October 1586, n.p.

86. Carlo to Philip II, 5 October 1586, AGS, Estado, L1261, no. 13.

87. Cristóbal de Briceño to Mateo Vázquez, 20 October 1586, IVDJ, ENV 5, T III, no. 258; Carlo to Philip II, 5 October 1586, AGS, Estado, L1261, no. 13. Carlo's report to Philip corroborates Briceño's account. On Catalina's illness in July 1588, see Francesco Vendramin, 30 July 1588, ASV, SDSa, filze 9, no. 87; Carlo to Philip II, 30 July 1588, AGS, Estado, L1263, no. 158; Doctor Madera to Jusepe de Acuña, 4 August 1588, AGS, Estado, L1263, no. 107.

88. Giovanni Mocenigo to Pasquale Ciconi, 10 April 1586, ASV, SDSa, filza 8, no. 68.

89. Giovanni Mocenigo to Pasquale Ciconi, 10 and 25 April 1586, ASV, SDSa, filza 8, nos. 68, 70.

90. Bucci, *Il solenne battesimo*, *passim*, but for specific references, see fols. 16v, 28v, 33v, 36v–37r.

91. Carlo Pallavicino to Don Juan Idiáquez, 26 February 1588, AGS, Estado, L1264, no. 120.

92. Giovanni Mocenigo to Pasquale Ciconi, 18 December 1585, ASV, SDSa, filza 8, no. 54.

93. Giovanni Mocenigo to Pasquale Ciconi, 25 April 1586, ASV, SDSa, filza 8, no. 70; Francesco Vendramin to Pasquale Ciconi, 13 July 1586, ASV, SDSa, filza 8, no. 81.

94. In his letter of 10 April 1586, Philip II noted that Catalina had made several requests. See also Philip's letter of 27 April 1586 in which he told Catalina that he would talk with the duke's ambassador to the Spanish court about a matter that she had specifically requested. Philip's decision to communicate through Carlo's ambassador and not by letter to Catalina suggests that the matter was political and perhaps sensitive. See Bouza, *Cartas*, 138–9.

95. Vendramin, "Relazione di Savoia," 173.

96. Vendramin, "Relazione di Savoia," 178. Pierpaolo Merlin cites Vendramin's report to argue that from the beginning of her stay in Turin, Catalina kept to herself and did not mix with courtiers. In fact, Vendramin specifically notes that Catalina had retired to her room in 1588 precisely to display her sorrow at the duke's absence. The evidence suggests that, up until that point, Catalina went out often and interacted frequently with courtiers. See Merlin, *Tra guerre e tornei*, 160.

CHAPTER 4

1. By August of that year, Empress María would begin her journey to Spain. See Ceña Llorente, "El viaje," 55.

2. Philip II to the *infantas*, 3 April 1581, in Bouza, *Cartas*, 34–5.

3. Bouza, *Cartas*, 35n6; Parker, *Imprudent King*, 271.

4. Ana of Dietrichstein to Margarita de Cardona, 19 July 1576, quoted in Cruz Medina, "Manos que escriben cartas,"179; Cruz Medina, "Y porque sale la reyna," 437.

5. Philip II to Catalina, 5 June 1581, in Bouza, *Cartas*, 42.

6. Cruz Medina, "Cartas, mujeres y corte," 38.
7. Gonzalo Sánchez-Molero, "L'educazione devozionale," 76.
8. Parker calls Don Carlos's script when he was twenty-two "virtually illegible." He notes, though, that Carlos was left-handed but forced to write with his right hand. The contrast between his handwriting and that of Catalina and Isabel when they were roughly his age is striking. See an example of Carlos's script in Parker, *Imprudent King*, plate 35. See also Gonzalo Sánchez-Molero, "L'educazione devozionale," 51.
9. Philip II to the *infantas*, 16 April 1582, in Bouza, *Cartas*, 78–9.
10. Philip II to the *infantas*, 1 October 1582 and 23 October 1581, in Bouza, *Cartas*, 93–4, 60.
11. García García, "Los regalos," 22; García García, "Bruselas y Madrid," 73.
12. Philip II to the *infantas*, 14 February 1583 and 30 July 1582, in Bouza, *Cartas*, 103, 88.
13. With one exception, Isabel Clara Eugenia's letters to Catalina are missing, and we have only two of Catalina's letters to Isabel. We know that the two sisters corresponded, but as of now, the letters have not surfaced. For the one surviving letter from Isabel, see Isabel to Catalina, 16 September 1594, in Bouza, *Cartas*, 195n411. For Catalina's letters to her sister, see Catalina to Isabel, 25 September 1597 and 12 October 1597, BL, Add. MSS 28419, fols. 298r–9r, 304r–5r. On the destruction of early modern letters, see Hunt, " 'Burn this Letter'," 189–209.
14. Paolo de Sfondrato to Juan de Idiáquez, 14 June 1585, AGS, Estado, L1261, no. 10; Philip II to Catalina, 18 June 1585, in Bouza, *Cartas*, 116.
15. James Daybell distinguishes between holograph and autograph letters, explaining that holograph means written completely in one hand. Thus, a letter written completely and signed (in another's name) by a secretary would be a holograph letter. An autograph letter, on the other hand, is written completely by the person who also signs the letter. Most of Catalina's and Carlo's letters fall into this latter category, and I am therefore referring to them as autograph, not holograph. See Daybell, *The Material Letter*, 23; Daybell, *Women Letter-Writers*, 64n10.
16. Cockram, *Isabella d'Este*, 29. For Isabella's correspondence, see Shemek, *Isabella d'Este*.
17. Cockram, *Isabella d'Este*, 31; James, "Marriage by Correspondence," 326–7, 342, 348; Shemek, *Isabella d'Este*, 11–12.
18. Another collection of letters between spouses is that of Magdalena Behaim and Balthasar Paumgartner, a merchant couple from Nuremberg, contemporaries of Catalina and Carlo. See Ozment, *An Intimate Portrait*.
19. Anna of Saxony wrote or received around 25,000 letters, and most of the ones she wrote were written by scribes. See Keller, *Kurfürsin Anna von Sachsen*, 72–3. Another comparison would be Elizabeth Stuart, whose voluminous correspondence has been edited and published by Nadine Akkerman. Unfortunately, the letters from Elizabeth to her husband Frederick have not survived. See Akkerman, *The Correspondence of Elizabeth Stuart*; Akkerman, *Elizabeth Stuart: Queen of Hearts*.
20. Daybell, *Women Letter-Writers*, 1. Wiggins says 242 letters both from and to Hardwick survive, and they span six decades. They are distinctive as well for being from a woman born into the lesser gentry. See *Bess of Hardwick's Letters*, 22.
21. Catalina to Carlo, 28 July 1597, AST, 44, fasc. 7, fol. 1939dv; Altadonna, III:313. This letter is five folios back and front, so it is longer than others. It has a few blots

only on the last folio. She must have been referring to its composition. She uses a similar expression—about talking with him through letters—in AST, M35, 2 April 1589, fasc. 7, fol. 128d; Altadonna, I:131.

22. Gibson, "Significant Space," 2–4; Braunmuller, "Accounting for Absence," 53–6; Daybell, *Women Letter-Writers*, 47–60; Steen, "Reading Beyond the Words," 61–3.

23. For writing on the side of the paper, see Catalina to Carlo, 13 January [1595], AST, M43, fasc. 1, fol. 1664a. For two examples of postscripts in her letters to Carlo, see letter of 19 January 1590, AST, M37, fasc. 3, fol. 535v; Altadonna, II:25; letter of 20 May 1591, AST, M38, fasc. 5, fol. 776dv; Altadonna, II:188–9.

24. James Daybell explains that cream-colored paper was the most desirable and the most expensive. See *Women Letter-Writers*, 52.

25. Catalina to Carlo, 16 August, AST, M45, fasc. 4, fol. 2068r–2068a, no year given but from internal evidence I would date it to 1593.

26. Carlo to Catalina, 13 December 1589, AST, M14, fasc. 4, fol. 558.

27. Catalina to Carlo, 30 September [1592], Nice, AST, M40, fasc. 9, fol. 1135r; Altadonna, III:55. For the duke's letter, see 29 September 1592, AST, M18, fasc. 7, fol. 1291.

28. Carlo to Catalina, 30 October 1592, AST, M18, fasc. 8, fol. 1303.

29. Catalina to Carlo, 28 July 1597, AST, M44, fasc. 7, fols 1939r–1939dv; Altadonna, III:312–15. Another letter that she described as long was three and a half folios, front and back. See Catalina to Carlo, 9 March 1589, AST, M35, fasc. 6, fol. 96r–96cr; Altadonna, I:97–100.

30. Catalina to Carlo, 1 October 1588, AST, M35, fasc. 1, fol. 5; Altadonna, I:14. See, for example, her references to her poor script in the following letters to Carlo: Letter of 29 September [1588], AST, M35, fasc. 1, fol. 2v; Altadonna, I:5. Letter of 5 October 1588, AST, M35, fasc. 1 fol. 17b; Altadonna, I:11. Letter of 15 October 1588, AST, M35, fasc. 1, fol. 33c; Altadonna, I:41. Letter of 9 March 1589, AST, M35, fasc. 6, fol. 96bv; Altadonna, I:99. Letter of 28 May 1589, AST, M35, fasc. 8, fol. 208bv; Altadonna I:189. Letter of 23 January [1595], AST, M43, fasc. 1, fol. 1086a; Altadonna, III:218. Letter of 17 September 1597, AST, M44, fasc. 9, fol. 1980av–1980br; Altadonna, III:339. This last letter has about four blots on it, and when she wrote the letter—September 1597—Catalina was feeling overwhelmed by political and military developments. She may have been rushing when writing to Carlo.

31. Catalina to Carlo, AST, M36, 9 September [1589], fasc. 3, fol. 336v–336ar; Altadonna, I:287.

32. For example, Catalina to Carlo, 13 September [1597], AST, M45, fasc. 4, fol. 2088br. Here she misspells *balia* (wet nurse) as "*bayla*." In a letter of 20 September [1594], she spells it "*baila*," as also in a letter of 10 September 1597. (AST, M42, fasc. 2, fol. 1476a; AST, M41, fasc. 7, fol. 1445cv; Altadonna, III:142, 337.) The latter mentions their daughter Catalina, born in October 1595, and as Catalina and Carlo were together during all of September 1596, September 1597 is the only possibility.

33. Catalina to Carlo, 21 March 1591, AST, M38, fasc. 3, fol. 734v; Altadonna, II:160. Giovanna Altadonna notes yet other examples of "italianisms." See Altadonna, I:xx.

34. See Catalina's letters to Carlo: 20 March 1589, AST, M35, fasc. 6, fol. 109r; Altadonna, I:115. 21 March [1589], AST, M35, fasc. 6, fol. 112r; Altadonna, I:118. 9 September [1589], AST, M36, fasc. 3, fol. 336v–336a; Altadonna, I:287. 18 December 1589, AST, M36, fasc. 6, fol. 463c; Altadonna, I:385.

35. Catalina to Carlo, 18 September, no year, AST, M42, fol. 1469v.

36. Catalina to Carlo, 22 March 1589, AST, M35, fasc. 6, fol. 116a; Altadonna, I:122. For the postscript in Italian, see Carlo to Catalina, 7 October 1589, AST, M14, fasc. 2, fol. 497v.

37. Catalina to Carlo, 23 October [1589], AST, M36, fasc. 4, fol. 401av; Altadonna, I:327. Ripa was the ducal secretary, serving both Catalina and Carlo. He subsequently became a councilor of state, of finance, and of the order of the Annunziata. In 1594, he was made count of Giaglione, and he died in 1613. Merlin says that Ripa was very pro-Spanish and communicated information to Spain. See Merlin, "Il governo dell'Infanta," 164n21. On Ripa, see Cibrario, *Storia di Torino*, 242; Claretta, "I marmi scritti di Torino," 369. Catalina does not specify which marquis, but from other letters I have deduced that he was probably the marquis d'Este, who had arrived at the court in Turin in late September 1589.

38. Juan de Zúñiga to Philip II, 26 May 1585, AGS, Estado, L1260, no. 185.

39. Sfondrato was no doubt aware of Philip II's effort to formalize modes of address, which in 1586 resulted in the Spanish court issuing the *Pragmática en que se da la orden y forma que se had de tener y guarder en los tratamientos y cortesías*. This decree, though published in 1586, was well underway when Catalina was still at the Spanish court.

40. For discussion of Sfondrato's questions about the secretary, see Juan de Zúñiga to Philip II, 26 May 1585, AGS, Estado, L1260, no. 185, and for the response, see "Los puntos que cita la instruccion que se ha dado al Baron Sfondrato para el cargo de mayordomo mayor de la Señora Infanta Doña Catalina," AGS, Estado, L1260, no. 187. Philip's advisers, Juan de Zúñiga and Juan de Idiáquez, seem to have advised the king about this matter, but the final instructions most likely came from Philip himself.

41. "Los puntos que cita la instruccion que se ha dado al Baron Sfondrato para el cargo de mayordomo mayor de la Señora Infanta Doña Catalina," AGS, Estado, L1260, no. 187.

42. Usunáriz, "Sentimientos e historia," 251–73, esp. 268.

43. Catalina to Carlo, 23 November, no year, AST, M45, fasc. 7, fol. 2184r.

44. Catalina to Carlo, 28 April [1589], AST, M35, fasc. 7, fol. 162; Altadonna, I:160. Catalina to Carlo, AST, M45, fasc. 4, fol. 2103. This letter is undated but has to have been written between May 1587 and December 1591.

45. Carlo to Catalina, 17 March 1591, AST, M16, fasc. 7, fol. 990.

46. The early modern Spanish lexicographer, Sebastían de Covarrubias, explained that *serenissimo* was higher even than *excelentissimo* (most excellent) and was a title befitting princes. Covarrubias, *Tesoro de la lengua*, 935. Juan de Icíar, who wrote a letter-writing manual in 1552, informed his reader that *serenissimo* was the title used for a king's heir, and Antonio de Torquemada said that queens and princesses should be referred to as *serenissimas*. Quoted in Cruz Medina, "Cartas, mujeres y corte," 86 and 89. For manuals, see Tejeda, *Cosa nueva*; Torquemada, *Manual de escribientes*; Manzanares, *Estilo y formulario de cartas familiares*.

47. The *pragmática* issued in 1586 specifically decreed that in letters, the king should be addressed only as *señor*. See *Pragmática en que se da la orden*, fol. 2v.

48. "*Vuestra humilde y obediente consorte que mucho os quiere,*" changed to "*vuestra leal y obediente consorte q mas que a si os quire.*" The timeframe was from 29 September to 2 October 1588. The undated letter which Catalina wrote from Miraflores ends with "*vuestra consorte humilde*" and in this way deviates sharply from the norm. However, her use of the term "*humilde*" suggests that she wrote this letter very early in her epistolary exchange with Carlo, before she switched to "loyal." See Catalina to Carlo, AST, M45, fasc. 4, fol. 2103.

49. Letter-writing manuals such as that of Gaspar de Tejeda recommended that in writing to his lord, a vassal or servant should refer to himself as obedient and humble. The lexicographer, Sebastián de Covarrubias, noted that the term "loyal" could be used not only by an inferior to a superior but also between equals. Tejeda, *Cosa nueva*, n.p.; Covarrubias, *Tesoro de la lengua*, 705, 755.

50. Usunáriz cites one example of an early modern Spanish love letter where the sender closes by calling himself a slave of the recipient's tyranny. See Usunáriz, "Sentimientos e historia," 269–70. Nuns also sometimes called themselves slaves. See Beatriz of Dietrichstein to her brother in Cruz Medina, "Cartas, mujeres y corte," 193. Catalina also called herself Carlo's slave in a letter of 8 March 1589, AST, M35, fasc. 6, fol. 93av; Altadonna, I:97.

51. Catalina to Carlo, 9 October [1588], AST, M35, fasc. 1, fol. 25a; Altadonna, I:30.

52. See, for example, Catalina to Carlo, 15 October 1594, AST, M42, fasc. 3, fol. 1557r–v; Catalina to Carlo, 18 October 1594, AST, M42, fasc. 3, fol. 1564. Both of these letters were written by a secretary, but Catalina added an autograph postscript.

53. Catalina to Carlo, 3 July 1595, AST, M43, fasc. 7, fol. 1828av; Catalina to Carlo, 9 July 1589, AST, M36, fasc. 1, fol. 258a; Catalina to Carlo, 2 October 1597, AST, M44, fasc. 10, fol. 1993a.

54. James, "Marriage by Correspondence," 326; Shemek, Introduction to *Isabella d'Este*, 11–12. For a brief discussion of authorship in Isabella d'Este's letters, see Cockram, *Isabella d'Este*, 31–2. For more on Isabella's secretary acting as an intermediary between Isabella and Francesco, see Cockram, 71–73.

55. Catalina to Carlo, 5 July 1589, AST, M36, fasc. 1, fol. 250av; Altadonna, I:226.

56. Catalina to Carlo, 20 December 1589, AST, M36, fasc. 6, 468v; Altadonna, I:390.

57. Catalina to Carlo, 16 April [1589], AST, M35, fasc. 7, fol. 147b; Altadonna, I:146.

58. Catalina to Carlo, 1 July [1589], AST, M36, fasc. 1, fol. 246d; Altadonna, I:222. She previously had mentioned an issue with Ripa's brother-in-law, so perhaps she did not want the secretary in the council because they were going to discuss issues concerning a family member.

59. Carlo to Catalina, 11 March 1589, AST, M13, fasc. 2, fol. 282cr–v. Carlo was responding to Catalina's letter from 9 March 1589 in which she asked him to tell her if she could share news that he wrote with Don Jusepe and with councilors. See Catalina to Carlo, 9 March 1589, M35, fasc. 6, fol. 96av; Altadonna, I:98. For Catalina's subsequent letter to Carlo, see AST, M35, 2 April 1589, fasc. 7, fol. 128cr; Altadonna, I:130.

60. See Catalina to Carlo, 21 March [1589], AST, M35, fasc. 6, fol. 112r; Altadonna, 1:118.

61. The letter in question seems to have been her letter to Carlo of 10 October [1594]. See AST, M42, fol. 1542r–1542av; Altadonna, III:177–8.

62. Carlo to Catalina, 10 October 1594, AST, M20, fol. 1715.

63. Catalina to Carlo, 12 October 1594, AST, M42, fasc. 3, fol. 1549v; Altadonna, III:180–1.
64. Don Jusepe to Philip II, 12 August 1589, AGS, Estado, L1266, no. 78.
65. Catalina to Carlo, 30 May 1591, AST, M40, fasc. 5, fol. 1117bv; Altadonna, II:193.
66. For examples of people who carried letters for or to Catalina, see Catalina to Carlo, AST, M35, fascs. 1 and 2, letters of 7, 9, 12, 13 October 1588; 20 October 1589 (2 letters); 22 October 1589, 2, 13, 20 November 1589. Catalina to Carlo, AST, M36, fasc. 6, letters of 9, 16, 18 March 1589; Altadonna, I:26, 30, 34, 36, 37, 46, 47, 49, 64, 74, 83, 97, 109, 112.
67. Schobesberger et al., "European Postal Networks," 27; Alonso García, *El Correo en el Renacimiento Europeo*, 39.
68. The Dutch Revolt hurt them significantly, but Rudolf II gave them a monopoly over the mail in the empire and they then became financially stable again. See Schobesberger et al., "European Postal Networks," 21.
69. Schobesberger et al., "European Postal Networks," 28, 29 for map, and 31.
70. Covarrubias, *Tesoro de la lengua*, 562. For the difference between *correo ordinario* and *estafeta*, see González Corchado, "Nuevas aportaciones," n.p., http://archivos.afinet.org/estudios/Nuevas_aportaciones_corresp_certif_Espana_siglos_XVI_XVII.pdf.
71. Catalina to Carlo, 16 November [1588], AST, M35, fasc. 2, fol. 71r; 31 October [1588], AST, M35, fasc. 1, fol. 54r; 10 April [1589], AST, M35, fasc. 7, fol. 137r; 29 March [1589], AST, M35, fasc. 6, fol. 123; Altadonna, I:80, 61, 137, 127.
72. See Catalina to Carlo, 17 December 1592, AST, M40, fasc. 12, fol. 1228r; Altadonna, III:85. She mentions other letters lost in a letter of 15 December, AST, M45, fasc. 4, fol. 2075r, no year; letter of 19 September, AST, M45, fasc. 5, fol. 2110b, no year given but probably 1597; AST, M45, fol. 2121v–2121ar, 10 September, no year; 23 November 1590, AST, M38, fasc. 5, fol. 931v–931ar; Altadonna, II:106. For Carlo's letter, see AST, M18, fasc. 10, fol. 1390.
73. Catalina to Carlo, 28 October 1590, AST, M37, fasc. 9, fol. 641; Altadonna, II:84. Catalina to Carlo, 29 November 1590, AST, M37, fol. 671r; Altadonna, II:109.
74. Catalina to Carlo, 27 November 1590, AST, M37, fol. 669r; Altadonna, II:107.
75. Avisos de Torino, ASF, MP, filza 2962, fol. 397r–398v.
76. Catalina to Carlo, 19 October 1588, AST, M35, fasc. 1, fol. 37–37bv; Altadonna, I:43. Carlo to Catalina, 20 October 1588, AST, M12, fasc. 20, fol. 240.
77. See Carlo to Catalina, 26 October 1589, AST, M14, fasc. 2, fol. 514, and Catalina responded on 1 November 1589. For Catalina's response, see 1 November 1589, AST, M35, fasc. 5, fol. 412r–412c; Altadonna, I:335–7. Catalina received the letter no later than 31 October and possibly even earlier.
78. See Catalina to Carlo, 12 July 1593, AST, M41, fol. 1390–1390av; Altadonna, III:117–18. See Carlo to Catalina, 11 July 1593, AST, M19, fasc. 9, fol. 1611. Carlo said he received Catalina's letter of 7 July on 8 July.
79. The duke closed his letters from these days by saying he was at the military camp but did not state his specific location. He was besieging Bricherasio in fall 1594, so his camp must have been very close to there. See Gómez Canseco, *Epopeyas*, 15–16.
80. Carlo to Catalina, 19 May 1591, AST, M16, fasc. 2, fol. 1032r–1032bv. Catalina received it a month later, on 23 June 1591. See Catalina to Carlo, 24 June 1591, AST, M38, fasc. 5, fol. 784r–784i; Altadonna, II:204–10.
81. Catalina to Carlo, 14 March 1589, AST, M35, fasc. 6, fol. 102r–v; Altadonna, I:105, 106.

82. Catalina to Carlo, 2 October 1588, AST, M35, fasc. 1, fol. 8r; Altadonna, I:15.
83. See the following letters from Catalina to Carlo: (Before getting dressed): 23 December, no year given, AST, M45, fasc. 4, fol. 2195r; 20 November [1588], AST, M35, fasc. 2, fol. 64; Altadonna, I:82. (Right after getting dressed): 20 December 1595, AST, M43, fasc. 8, fol. 1842r; Altadonna, III:277; and 5 July 1593, AST, M41, fasc. 5, fol. 1371v; Altadonna, III:111–12. (Right before going to bed): 27 February 1592, AST, M40, fasc. 2, fol. 1081; Altadonna, III:33. (Received letter at 7 a.m.): 21 November 1592, AST, M40, fasc. 11, fol. 1183r; Altadonna, III:74. (Writing at 8 p.m.—just got home and is writing before she goes to bed): 1 May 1593, AST, M41, fasc. 3, fol. 1299r; Altadonna, III:90. (Has written to him before eating): 28 October 1588, AST, M35, fasc. 1, fol. 49; Altadonna, I:58.
84. See Catalina's letters to Carlo: (While hearing sermon): 17 March 1589, AST, M35, fasc. 6, fol. 107r; Altadonna, I:110. (At complines): 9 October [1588], AST, M35, fasc. 1, fol. 25r; Altadonna, I:29. (Going to church): 11 March 1592, AST, M40, fasc. 3, fol. 1091r; Altadonna, III:40. (Receives letter during mass): 22 September [1594], AST, M42, fasc. 2, fol. 1482r; Altadonna, III:144; 18 January 1595, AST, M43, fasc. 1, fol. 1678r; Altadonna, III:214. (Went to confession, received communion, and then they gave her his letter): 3 May 1593, AST, M41, fasc. 3, fol. 1305r; Altadonna, III:91–2. (Received his letter after eating): 2 May [1593], AST, M41, fasc. 3, fol. 1304r; Altadonna, III:91. (Commode): 15 November 1588, AST, M35, fasc. 2, fol. 70r; Altadonna, I:77. (Gave her his letter just as she was about to go to bed): 22 May 1593, AST, M41, fasc. 3, fol. 1347r; Altadonna III:106–7. (Received his letter at midnight): 15 August [1593], AST, M41, fasc. 6, fol. 1426r; Altadonna, III:133. (Writing close to midnight): 30 June [1595], AST, M43, fasc. 6, fol. 1820b; Altadonna, III:269. (Washing her hair): 29 August, no year given but probably 1591, AST, M45, fol. 2019a.
85. Catalina to Carlo, 9 March 1589, AST, M35, fasc. 6, fol. 96bv; Altadonna, I:99. See also Catalina to Carlo, 22 July, AST, M45, fasc. fol. 2079a, no year given but from internal evidence, I have dated it 1589.
86. Catalina to Carlo, 20 November [1588], AST, M35, fasc. 2, fol. 64; Altadonna, I:82.
87. Catalina to Carlo, Feast of San Martin (11 November) [1588], AST, M35, fasc. 6, fol. 83r; Altadonna, I:70. 20 March 1589, AST, M35, fasc. 6, fol. 108r; Altadonna, I:114. In Italian, the word for commode was *seggetta* (little chair), and *sillica* is the diminutive of *silla* and also would mean little chair. From this evidence and from evidence internal to Catalina's letters, it seems clear that she was referring to a commode. For example, she said that she had spanked her son because he had gotten himself dirty (*enzuziado*) after getting up from the *sillica*. See Catalina to Carlo, 9 October [1588], AST, M35, fasc. 1, fol. 25a; Altadonna, I:30. For *seggetta*, see Cavallo and Storey, *Healthy Living*, 263.
88. Catalina to Carlo, 17 March 1589, AST, M35, fasc. 6, fol. 107br; Altadonna, I:111. This letter provides other examples that she was writing it at different sittings. For another example, see Catalina to Carlo, 9 March 1589, AST, M35, fasc. 6, fol. 96c; Altadonna, I:99.
89. Catalina to Carlo, 30 October [1588], AST, M35, fasc. 1, fol. 53a; Altadonna, I:61; Catalina to Carlo, 3 October [1588], AST, M35, fasc. 1, fol. 12; Altadonna, I:18; 3 October [1588], AST, M35, fasc. 1, fol. 13av; Altadonna, I:21; Catalina to Carlo, 6 October [1588], AST, M35, fasc. 1, fol. 21v; Altadonna, I:26. For comments that suggest she was writing in installments: Catalina to Carlo, 15 October 1588, AST, M35, fasc. 1, fol. 33r–33c; Altadonna, I:39.

90. Catalina to Carlo, 26 October [1588], AST, M35, fasc. 1, fol. 47v; Altadonna I:54.

91. Catalina to Carlo, 16 March [1589], AST, M35, fasc. 6, fol. 105bv–105c; Altadonna, I:109.

92. Catalina to Carlo, 3 October [1588], AST, M35, fasc. 1, fol. 12; Altadonna, I:18.

93. See, for example, Catalina to Carlo, 3 July 1589, AST, M36, fasc. 1, fol. 249a; Altadonna, I:225.

94. Catalina to Carlo, 28 September, AST, M45, fasc. 4, fol. 2089v, no year written but from internal evidence and comparison to other letters, I have concluded that this letter is from 1590.

95. Catalina to Carlo, 23 September, AST, M45, fasc. 4, fol. 2094a, no year written but from internal evidence, it has to be from after 1593.

96. Catalina to Carlo, 10 October [1588], AST, M35, fasc. 1, fol. 26v; Altadonna, I:32.

97. Carlo to Catalina, 3 June 1589, AST, M13, fasc. 5, fol. 364v.

98. Catalina to Carlo, 7 June 1589, AST, M35, fasc. 9, fol. 119av; Altadonna, I:198.

99. Catalina to Carlo, 16 March [1589], AST, M35, fasc. 6, fol. 105r; Altadonna, I:107.

100. Catalina to Carlo, 2 July 1595, AST, M43, fasc. 7, fol. 1825r; Altadonna, III:270.

101. Carlo to Catalina, 11 March 1589, AST, M13, fasc. 2, fol. 282a.

102. Catalina to Carlo, 7 August 1592, AST M40, fasc. 8, fol. 1126r; Altadonna III:54.

103. Catalina to Carlo, 2 October 1588, AST, M35, fasc. 1, fol. 8r; Altadonna, I:15.

104. Catalina to Carlo, 28 July 1597, AST, M44, fasc. 7, fol. 1939dv; Altadonna, III:313.

105. Catalina to Carlo, 1 October [1588], AST, M35, fasc. 1, fol. 4r; Altadonna I:12.

106. Catalina to Carlo, 13 January [1595], AST, M43, fasc. 1, fol. 1664r; Altadonna, III:209.

107. Catalina to Carlo, 27 June [1589], AST, M38, fasc. 9, fol. 242r; Altadonna, I:217.

108. Catalina to Carlo, 10 October [1588], AST, M35, fasc. 1, fol. 26v; Altadonna, I:32.

109. See, for example, Catalina to Carlo, 26 September, AST, M45, fasc. 4, fol. 2089r, no year but probably from 1590.

110. Catalina to Carlo, 23 September [1594], AST, M42, fasc. 2, fol. 1487v–1487ar; Altadonna, III:147.

CHAPTER 5

1. Cabrera de Córdoba, *Historia de Felipe II*, II:655; "De la embarcacion de S.M. con el principe y las serenissimas Infantas sus hijos en Vacia al Madrid para Aranjuez y Aceca," BN, MS 5938; Longlée to Henri III, 1 May 1584, in Mousset, *Dépêches Diplomatiques*, 64.

2. Catalina to Carlo, 25 April 1591 and 20 May 1591, AST, M38, fasc. 4 and 5, fols. 761c, 776c; Altadonna, II:175, 188.

3. Catalina to Carlo, 8 and 17 August [1589], AST, M36, fasc. 2, fols. 299av, 311v; Altadonna, I:261, 268.

4. Khevenhüller, *Diario*, 100; Sánchez, "Privacy, Family, and Devotion," 368.

5. About the most Philip did was let his third wife, Elisabeth of Valois, represent him in the meeting with her mother, Catherine de' Medici, in Bayonne to encourage Catherine to be firm against the Huguenots. See Kamen, *Philip of Spain*, 101–3.

6. Philip II to the duke of Terranova, 17 July 1585, AGS, Estado, L1264, no. 91. This is a copy of the original letter.

7. On Saluzzo in the sixteenth century up to the Treaty of Lyon (1601), see Merlin, "Saluzzo, il Piemonte, l'Europa," 15–57, and Battistoni, "Reshaping Local Public Space," 242–3. See also Gal, *Charles-Emmanuel de Savoie*, 134–9.

8. Battistoni, "Reshaping Local Public Space," 243. Gal adds that the Protestant threat was not imaginary. See Gal, *Charles-Emmanuel de Savoie*, 143–4. Carlo claimed that Huguenots from the Dauphiné had designs on Saluzzo and in turn were threatening his lands. See Carlo to Philip II, 2 August 1588, AGS, Estado, L1263, no. 160.

9. Merlin, "Saluzzo, il Piemonte, l'Europa," 17; Gal, *Charles-Emmanuel de Savoie*, 135. Merlin maintains (18) that interest in acquiring Saluzzo was part of Emanuele Filiberto's plan to expand toward the sea.

10. Merlin, "Saluzzo, il Piemonte, l'Europa," 21, 29; Gal, *Charles-Emmanuel de Savoie*, 143. E. Armstrong noted that Carlo went in "taking possession in the name of Henry III and posing in French dress as governor for France." In September 1589, when after Henri III's assassination a Protestant prince succeeded as French king, Carlo had Saluzzo swear allegiance to him (Carlo). French kings, however, especially Henri IV (r. 1589–1610), refused to heed Carlo's arguments or accept his seizure, and Savoy's annexation of the marquisate remained a thorny issue until 1601, when, in the Treaty of Lyon, France formally recognized Carlo's possession in exchange for Savoy's territories west of the river Rhone. See Gal, *Charles-Emmanuel de Savoie*, 143–5; Armstrong, "Tuscany and Savoy," 414; Parker, *The Army of Flanders*, 68–9; Pitts, *Henri IV of France*, 227.

11. Merlin, "Etichetta e politica," 311–12. For the decree of 30 September 1588, see AST, Tutele, Reggenze e Luogotenenze, M2, no. 4.

12. Raviola, "La imagen de la infanta," 1733–47; Merlin, "Caterina d'Asburgo," 220–2.

13. Stéphane Gal paints a vivid portrait of Carlo and his effusive personality. See *Charles-Emmanuel de Savoie, passim*.

14. The duke and his troops attacked and seized the strongholds of Centallo, Saluzzo, and Revello, though these proved more difficult to take than Carmagnola. By late November 1588, Carlo was in possession of the marquisate. Cano de Gardoqui argued that the seizure of Carmagnola came only after Carlo had secretly negotiated with and bribed the governor and the lieutenant. See Cano de Gardoqui, *La cuestión de Saluzzo*, 12; Merlin, "Saluzzo, il Piemonte, l'Europa," 15–30.

15. In his letter of 23 December 1588 to Carlo, Philip noted that Carlo had acted completely on his own accord but Carlo had certainly warned Philip of his plans. In July 1588, Carlo had written to him that authorities in Saluzzo were prepared to hand the marquisate to Huguenots, which would threaten Carlo's states and Milan. He added that he was informing Philip so that "come what will, I cannot be blamed." See Philip II to Carlo, AST, LPF(S), M97, fasc. 4, fol. 87r–v; Altadonna, "Cartas de Felipe II," 170. Philip's letter is not autograph. For Carlo's letter, see AGS, Estado, L1263, 11 July 1588, no. 157.

16. Gal, *Charles-Emmanuel de Savoie*, 142.

17. Jusepe de Acuña to Philip II, 5 October 1588, AGS, Estado, L1264, no. 160.

18. Jusepe de Acuña to Philip II, 5 October 1588, AGS, Estado, L1264, no. 160.

19. Catalina to Carlo, 5 October [1588], AST, M35, fasc. 1, fol. 15v; Altadonna, I:23.

20. Catalina to Carlo, 29 September [1588], AST, M35, fasc. 1, fol. 2v bis; Altadonna, I:7. For other references to *sending artillery*, see Catalina to Carlo, 29 September

[1588], AST, M35, fasc. 1, fol. 2v; 29 September [1588], fol. 82r; 30 September 1588, fol. 18r–v; 1 October [1588], fol. 6v–6ar; 12 October [1588], fol. 29av; Altadonna, I:5, 6, 10, 13, 35.

21. Catalina to Carlo, 29 September [1588], AST, M35, fasc. 2, fol. 82r–v; Altadonna, I:6; Catalina to Carlo, 29 September [1588], AST, M35, fasc. 1, fol. 2bis–a; Altadonna, I:8.

22. Catalina to Carlo, 30 September 1588, 1 and 3 October [1588], AST, M35, fasc. 1, fols. 17v, 4v, 12; Altadonna, I:11, 12, 18.

23. Catalina to Carlo, 8 October 1588, AST, M35, fasc. 1, fol. 23a–av; Altadonna, I:28–9.

24. Catalina to Carlo, 12 October [1588], AST, M35, fasc. 1, fol. 29v; Altadonna, I:35. For other examples from Catalina's letters to Carlo, see letters of 23 and 28 May 1589, AST, M35, fasc. 8, fols. 203r, 207b; Altadonna, I:182, 188. Letter of 2 June 1589, AST, M35, fasc. 9, fol. 210a; Altadonna, I:192. Letter of 11 September [1589], AST, M36, fasc. 3, fol. 341v; Altadonna, I:290.

25. Catalina to Carlo, 15 October 1588, AST, M35, fasc. 1, fol. 33a; Altadonna, I:40. Her accounts also list a payment to a "judio Ysaje Bilione," for two pieces of cloth (*holanda*) that "sua Alteza hizo tomar para su servicio al duque." ASRT, Camera dei Conti, Real Casa, Art. 224, 1585–7, n.p.

26. Catalina to Carlo, 29 September [1588], 11, 12, 14 October 1588, AST, M35, fasc. 1, fols. 2v bis, 24a, 29v, 29a, 31r; Altadonna, I:8, 33, 35, 38.

27. Catalina to Carlo, 29 September [1588], AST, M35, fasc. 2, fol. 82av; Altadonna, I:7.

28. Catalina to Carlo, 30 September 1588, 29 September [1588], AST, M35, fasc. 1, fols. 18r, 2v; Altadonna, I:10, 5.

29. Catalina to Carlo, 13 November [1588], AST, M35, fasc. 2, fol. 67a; Altadonna, I:75.

30. Carlo to Catalina, 14 November 1588, AST, M12, fasc. 20, fol. 253r. In a letter from 28 March 1589, the duke told Catalina that she should not ask his pardon for how she had negotiated a particular issue because he himself could not have negotiated as well. See Carlo to Catalina, 28 March 1589, AST, M12, fasc. 20, fol. 234bv. Note that the archive has dated this letter March 1588 but Carlo mentions Don Jusepe, who did not arrive until May 1588, so this letter has to be from March 1589 (and corresponds to the contents of other letters from March 1589).

31. Catalina to Carlo, 6 October [1588], AST, M35, fasc. 1, fol. 21v; Altadonna, I:25.

32. Catalina to Carlo, 28 October [1588], AST, M35, fasc. 1, fol. 51ar; Altadonna, I:57–8.

33. Catalina to Carlo, 3, 13, 17, 22 October 1588, AST, M35, fasc. 1, fols. 13v, 13a, 30a, 35r, 41v; Altadonna, I:20–1, 37, 41–2, 51.

34. Carlo to Catalina, 20 November 1588, AST, M12, fasc. 16bis, fol. 164c. The tablets were probably the erasable writing tablets popular in Renaissance Europe. See Stallybrass et al., "Hamlet's Tables," 385–403.

35. On Terranova's connections to Philip II's court before he was sent to Milan, see Scalisi, "El Duque de Terranova," 358–70; Bazzano, "Carlo d'Aragón."

36. Catalina to Carlo, 3 October [1588], AST, M35, fasc. 1, fol. 13r; Altadonna, I:20. On 13 October 1588, she again noted that she would write to Terranova "as you command me to do." Catalina to Carlo, AST, M35, fasc. 1, fol. 30av; Altadonna, I:38.

37. Duke of Terranova to Philip II, 16 October 1588, AGS, Estado, L1264, no. 86.

38. Catalina to Carlo, 15 October 1588, AST, M35, fasc. 1, fol. 33r; Altadonna, I:39.

39. Philip wrote the letter on 17 July 1585, a little over a month after saying goodbye to Catalina and Carlo. The timing of the letter suggests that Carlo must have discussed his plans with Philip and demonstrates that Carlo was planning to seize territory in the area of Saluzzo long before 1588. For a copy of the letter, see Philip II to Terranova, 17 July 1585, Monzón, AGS, Estado, L1264, no. 91. For a discussion of Carlo's early efforts to gain Philip's support for his seizure of Carmagnola, see Barquero Cerdán, "Dinastía y oeconómica," 19–21.

40. Catalina to Carlo, 15 October 1588, AST, M35, fol. 33v; Altadonna, I:39–40.

41. Catalina to Carlo, 15 October 1588, AST, M35, fasc. 1, fol. 33r–33c; Altadonna, I:39–40.

42. Catalina to Carlo, 15 October 1588, AST, M35, fasc. 1, fol. 33ar–v; Altadonna, I:39–40.

43. Carlo to Catalina, 16 October 1588, AST, M12, fasc. 20, fol. 238v.

44. Carlo to Catalina, 7 October 1588, AST, M12, fasc. 20, fol. 239; Carlo to Catalina, 16 October 1588, AST, M12, fasc. 20, fol. 238v.

45. Duke of Terranova to Philip II, 16 October 1588, AGS, Estado, L1264, no. 86.

46. Duke of Terranova to Juan de Idiáquez, 16 October 1588, AGS, Estado, L1264, no. 867.

47. In an undated autograph draft of a letter to Terranova, Catalina emphasized that Carlo's actions were not aggressive. She wrote that, because Don Jusepe had told her "the difficulties you [Terranova] raise in allowing my father's people to assist the duke in the forts, I have not wanted to leave off doing this [writing Terranova] because I think you must not have understood that they are for the defense of the duke's territories . . . We ask for nothing except that which is necessary for the defense and conservation of the duke's territories and the recovery of what was lost." She added that she was very sure that Terranova would not fail to give her "this great pleasure." See Catalina to the duke of Terranova, AST, M45, fol. 2028r–v. Catalina does not specify that she was writing to Terranova, but internal and contextual evidence makes it clear that Terranova was the recipient. This letter seems to be a draft, because she crossed out many words and added a few words in the margins.

48. Catalina to the duke of Terranova, 13 October 1588, AGS, Estado, L1264, no. 90. This is a copy of Catalina's autograph letter.

49. Jusepe de Acuña to the duke of Terranova, 12 October 1588, AGS, Estado, L1264, no. 175. This is a copy of Don Jusepe's letter.

50. Duke of Terranova to Philip II, 16 October 1588, AGS, Estado, L1264, no. 86 Also duke of Terranova to Philip II, 19 November 1588, AGS, Estado, L1264, no. 95.

51. Catalina to the duke of Terranova, 19 October 1588, AST, M35, fasc. 1, fol. 36. This is a draft of the letter, which Catalina probably sent to Carlo.

52. Catalina to Carlo, 15 October 1588, AST, M35, fasc. 1, fol. 33b; Altadonna, I:41.

53. Catalina to Carlo, 26 October [1588], AST, M35, fasc. 1, fol. 46r; Altadonna, I:53.

54. Covarrubias defines "embarcar" as "entrar en la barca" and "embarcarse en un negocio es averse como engolfado en el, descubriendo muchas dificultades y peligros." See Covarrubias, Tesoro de la lengua, 504.

55. Catalina to Carlo, 10 May 1589, AST, M35, fasc. 8, fol. 181r; Altadonna, I:169.

56. Catalina to Carlo, 2 June 1589, AST, 35, fasc. 9, fol. 210br–bv; Altadonna, I:193.

57. Catalina to Carlo, 20 June 1589, AST, M35, fasc. 9, fol. 233a; Altadonna, I:210.

58. Catalina to Carlo, 4 September [1589], AST, M36, fasc. 3, fol. 332av; Altadonna, I:284. See also Catalina to Carlo, 25 April 1591, AST, M38, fasc. 1, fol. 761c; Altadonna, II:175.

59. Catalina to Carlo, 12 September 1589, AST, M36, fasc. 3, fol. 346v; Altadonna, I:291.

60. Catalina to Carlo, 25 August 1589, AST, M36, fasc. 2, fol. 320ar; Altadonna, I:276.

61. Catalina to Carlo, 10 September 1591, AST, M39, fasc. 3, fol. 853gr; Altadonna, II:252–3.

62. Catalina to Carlo, 10 November 1592, AST, M40, fasc. 11, fol. 1163v; Altadonna, III:68–9.

63. The duke of Frías succeeded Terranova as Spanish governor of Milan, and Catalina also complained about him. See Río Barredo and Sánchez, "Le lettere familiari," 207.

64. For a discussion of the correspondence between Catalina and Philip, see Río Barredo and Sánchez, "Le lettere familiari," 189–212.

65. Philip II to Catalina, 5 December 1588, in Bouza, *Cartas*, 160.

66. Bouza, *Cartas*, 160n362; López Álvarez, "Francisco de Vera y Aragón."

67. Philip II to Carlo, 1, 8, 9 November 1588, AST, LPF(S), M97, fasc. 4, fols. 82.1, 83, 85; Altadonna, "Cartas de Felipe II," 169–70.

68. The mail was actually going to Lyon but Catalina explained to Carlo that she had no doubt that the mail would continue on to Spain. See Catalina to Carlo, 6 October 1588, AST, M35, fasc. 1, fol. 20; Altadonna, I:24.

69. Philip II to Catalina, 5 December 1588, in Bouza, *Cartas*, 160–1.

70. Catalina to Carlo, 6 October 1588, AST, M35, fasc. 1, fol. 20r–v; Altadonna, I:24.

71. Catalina to Carlo, 6 October 1588, AST, M35, fasc. 1, fol. 20r; Altadonna, I:24.

72. Carlo to Catalina, 7 October 1588, AST, M12, fasc. 20, fol. 239.

73. Philip II to Carlo, 23 December 1588 and 20 January 1589, AST, LPF(S), M97, fasc. 4, fols. 87.1, 91.1; Altadonna, "Cartas de Felipe II," 170–1.

74. Gal, *Charles-Emmanuel de Savoie*, 146, 148. Lucinge was a humanist and political theorist who, among other works, published his memoirs of his years at the French court. He also greatly influenced the works of Giovanni Botero. See *Lettres de 1588*; *Lettres sur les débuts de la Ligue (1585)*; Bireley, *Botero*, xvii.

75. He also wrote to Carlo three times in February, twice on one day because he received Carlo's letter after writing and so wrote a second time. Philip II to Carlo, 19 and 20 February 1589, AST, LPF(S), M97, fasc. 4, fol. 96–8; Altadonna, "Cartas de Felipe II," 171–72.

76. Philip II to Catalina, 22 February 1589, in Bouza, *Cartas*, 162.

77. Philip II to Catalina, 9 March 1589, in Bouza, *Cartas*, 163.

78. Catalina to Carlo, 5 March 1589, AST, M35, fasc. 6, fol. 119av; Altadonna, I:95. She had written to her sister and Empress María as well.

79. Philip II to Carlo, 7 May 1589, AST, LPF(S), M97, fasc. 4, fol. 102r–v; Altadonna, "Cartas de Felipe II," 173. In April 1589, Carlo wrote to Philip consistently informing him of his actions and asking him to have the duke of Terranova give him military support for the "conservation" of his lands. See Carlo to Philip II, 12, 15, 21, 23 April 1589, AGS, Estado, L1263, nos. 171, 172, 173, 175.

80. See Parker, *Imprudent King*, 330–1.

81. Philip II to Catalina, 7 May 1589, in Bouza, *Cartas*, 163–4.

82. Carlo to Philip II, 3 July 1589, AGS, Estado, L1263, no. 184.

83. Catalina to Philip II, 8 July 1589, AST, M36, fasc. 1, fol. 259v. This is a draft or copy of her letter.

84. Catalina to Carlo, 6 July 1589, AST, M36, fasc. 1, fol. 255r; Altadonna, I:227.

85. Carlo to Catalina, AST, M13, fol. 379v, not dated, but the duke was responding to a letter from Catalina of 24 June 1589, so probably late June or early July. Six months later, Catalina would tell Carlo that having heard that Philip II had already seized four territories in France, she thought she and the duke should be allowed to do likewise. See Catalina to Carlo, 13 December 1589, AST, M36, fasc. 6, fol. 459f; Altadonna, I:380–1.

86. Catalina to Carlo, 6 July 1589, AST, M36, fasc. 1, fol. 255v; Altadonna, I:227; Carlo to Catalina, 14 July 1589, AST, M13, fasc. 6, fol. 394av.

87. Catalina to Carlo, 25 and 27 August 1589, AST, M36, fasc. 2, fols. 320av, 324r–v; Altadonna, I:276–7.

88. Catalina to Philip II, 29 August 1589, in Bouza, *Cartas*, 168n376 and also Catalina to Philip II, 29 August 1589, AST, M36, fasc. 6, fol. 480r–480a. The letter in Turin seems to be the copy because it has no date on it, although the archive has (wrongly) dated it to December. The letter in Bouza is the original and is dated.

89. Catalina to Carlo, 30 August 1589, AST, M36, fasc. 2, fols. 325b–325bv, 325av; Catalina to Carlo, 9 September [1589], AST, M35, fasc. 3, fol. 336av; Altadonna, I:280, 287, 279.

90. Catalina to Carlo, 30 August 1589, AST, M36, fasc. 2, fol. 325b; Altadonna, I:280.

91. Catalina to Philip II, 26 November 1589, AST, M36, fasc, 5, fol. 443.

92. Catalina to Carlo, 26 November [1589], AST, M36, fasc. 5, fol. 442v; Altadonna, I:359.

93. The peace allowed for Protestant worship in seven villages. See Bouza, *Cartas*, 170n381.

94. Philip II to Catalina, 26 November 1589, in Bouza, *Cartas*, 170.

95. Catalina to Carlo, 18 and 19 December 1589, AST, M36, fasc. 6, fols. 463b–bv, 464v–464a; Altadonna, I:385, 384, 388.

96. Catalina to Carlo, 19 and 26 December 1589, AST, M36, fasc. 6, fols. 464v, 464a, 474a–av; Altadonna, I:388, 394.

97. In letters to Carlo, Catalina noted when she was sending him copies or briefs (*minutas*) of the letters she had written to her father. See, for example, such letters as that from Catalina to Carlo of 20 June, AST, M45, fol. 2054v, no year given; that of 9 October, AST, M45, fol. 2061r, no year given but probably 1589; that of 3 June, AST, M45, fol. 2096r, no year given but probably 1589; an undated letter, AST, M45, fol. 2118av, also probably 1589; a letter of 13 March [1589], AST, M35, fasc. 6, fol. 99v; Altadonna, I:103. A draft might differ from the final letter but a copy would not, and in every case Catalina had already dispatched the letter to Spain before sending Carlo the draft or copy.

98. Catalina to Carlo, 13 March [1589], AST, M35, fasc. 6, fol. 99v; Altadonna, I:103. She also sent him the *minuta* of what she wrote to her father on 22 April 1589 and apologized if it was not to his liking. See Catalina to Carlo, AST, M35, fasc. 7, fol. 155a; Altadonna, I:156.

99. Catalina to Carlo, 3 November 1588, AST, M35, fasc. 2, fol. 57v; Altadonna, I:67. In March 1589, she again summarized what she had written to her father. See Catalina to Carlo, 5 March 1589, AST, M35, fasc. 6, fol. 119av; Altadonna, I:95.

100. From 27 September until 5 December 1590, there was no pope (*sede vacante*). Catalina and Carlo tried to influence the selection of a new pope and did not necessarily agree with Philip's choice. On the vacant see, see Hunt, *The Vacant See in Early Modern Rome*.

101. Catalina to Carlo, 23 November 1590, AST, M37, fasc. 10, fol. 670; Altadonna, II:106.

102. See, for example, Catalina to Carlo, 20 March 1589, AST, M35, fasc. 6, fol. 109cv; Altadonna, I:117.

103. Catalina to Carlo, 16 April [1589], AST, M35, fasc. 7, fol. 147bv; Altadonna, I:145. Catalina regularly sent Carlo the letters she received from her father and her sister, urging him to return them to her as soon as possible.

104. Catalina to Carlo, 8 May 1595, AST, M43, fasc. 5, fol. 1803; Altadonna, III:259.

105. Catalina to Carlo, 9 April [1589], AST, M35, fasc. 7, fol. 134c; Altadonna, I:135. Catalina to Carlo, 1 April 1595, AST, M43, fasc. 4, fol. 1742v; Altadonna, III:240. In both cases, she used the verb *mandar*, which has several meanings. See Covarrubias, *Tesoro de la lengua*, 784.

106. Catalina to Carlo, 9 April [1589], AST, M35, fasc. 7, fol. 134b; Altadonna, I:135; Carlo to Philip II, 15 April 1589, AGS, Estado, L1263, no. 171, deciphered.

107. Catalina to Carlo, 20 October [1588], AST, M35, fasc. 1, fol. 39av; Altadonna, I:46. Although outside the chronological scope of this chapter, a letter from the duke to Catalina in January 1595 also shows that the duke sought his wife's input on what he wrote to Philip. Carlo sent Catalina a letter written by his secretary but added a personal note telling her that he was enclosing a letter he had written to Philip and that she should tell him if she thought it was good. See Carlo to Catalina, 25 January 1595, AST, M21, fasc. 1, fol. 1911. His letter to Philip seems to have been a draft, because he said that if she approved, he would write it again.

108. Catalina to Carlo, 20 March 1589, AST, M35, fasc. 6, fol. 109cr; Altadonna, I:117. Catalina to Carlo, 22 March 1589, AST, M35, fasc. 6, fol. 114a; Altadonna, I:120.

109. Carlo to Catalina, 28 March 1589, AST, M12, fasc. 20, fol. 234bv–c.

110. Carlo to Catalina, (8?) May 1589, AST, M13, fasc. 4, fol. 333.

111. Catalina to Carlo, 18 May [1589], AST, M35, fasc. 8, fol. 196r; Altadonna, I:178.

112. Catalina to Carlo, 29 March 1595, AST, M43, fasc. 3, fol. 1740v; Altadonna, III:239.

113. Catalina to Carlo, 3 March 1589, AST, M35, fasc. 6, fol. 90v–90av; Altadonna, I:91. Carlo to Catalina, 4 March 1589, AST, M13, fasc. 2, fol. 277b.

114. Catalina to Carlo, 5 March 1589, AST, M35, fasc. 6, fol. 119a; Altadonna, I:95.

115. Catalina to Carlo, 14 and 20 March 1589, AST, M35, fasc. 6, fol. 102r, 109bv; Altadonna, I:105, 117.

116. Catalina to Carlo, 5 April 1589, AST, M35, fasc. 7, fol. 131v–131a; Altadonna, I:132.

117. Catalina to Carlo, 11 July 1589, AST, M36, fasc. 1, fol. 261ar; Altadonna, I:233. She identifies her source/spy as "*un secretario de la posta clerigo.*"

118. Catalina to Carlo, 9 March 1589, AST, M35, fasc. 6, 94r–v.

119. Catalina to Carlo, 9 March 1589, AST, M35, fasc. 6, 96v–96av; Altadonna, I:98. Carlo to Catalina, 11 March 1589, AST, M13, fasc. 2, fol. 282ar. Catalina responded in her letter of 13 March [1589], AST, M35, fasc. 6, fol. 99r; Altadonna, I:103.

120. Catalina to Carlo, 20 and 22 March 1589, AST, M35, fasc. 6, fol. 109bv–cv, 114a; Altadonna, I:117, 120.

121. See Merlin, *Manuel Filiberto*, 24–5. On Beatriz of Portugal, duchess of Savoy (1503–1538), see Buescu, "L'infanta Beatrice di Portogallo," 43–77. See also Merlin, "Beatrice di Portogallo," 79–102; Marini, "Beatrice di Portogallo, duchessa di Savoia."

122. For first investiture, see Catalina to Carlo, 9 March 1589, AST, M35, fasc. 6, fols. 94a, 96c; Altadonna, I:99. For second, see Catalina to Carlo, 13 March [1589], AST, M35, fasc. 6, fol. 99b; Altadonna, I:104. Catalina did not explain the context for these investitures.

123. See Catalina to Carlo, 14 October 1588, AST, M35, fasc. 1, fol. 31r–v; Altadonna I:38. See also Catalina to Carlo, 2 November 1588, AST, M35, fasc. 1, fol. 56v; Altadonna, I:64–5.

124. Catalina to Carlo, 20 March 1589, AST, M35, fasc. 6, fol. 109dr; Altadonna, I:118.

125. Catalina to Carlo, 23 August, AST, M45, fasc. 5, fol. 2139r–v, no year given but from internal evidence I would date to 1590.

126. Francisco de Vera to Philip II, 28 March 1589, AGS, Estado, L1266, no. 147.

127. "Copia de capitulos de carta de Don Jusepe de Acuña a Francisco de Idiáquez," 14 March 1589, AGS, Estado, L1266, no. 30, 1; Jusepe de Acuña to Francisco de Idiáquez, 14 March 1589, AGS, Estado, L1266, no. 41; Parker, *Imprudent King*, xviii.

128. Vendramin, "Relazione di Savoia," 178–9.

129. Carlo to Catalina, 30 December 1589, AST, M14, fasc. 4, fol. 589. He specifically criticized the way that Cristóbal de Moura and Juan de Idiáquez were exercising power.

130. The post-mortem inventory of her possession lists a tapestry with the wonders of the world, which is probably the same tapestry that Carlo sent her. ASRT, Gioie e Mobili, M1, no. 6, fol. 37v.

131. Carlo to Catalina, 30 December 1589, AST, M14, fasc. 4, fol. 539; Catalina to Carlo, 1 January 1590, AST, M37, fasc. 3, fol. 520; Altadonna, II:6.

132. Mario Umolio to Catalina, 8 December 1590, AST, LM(S), M5, n.p.

133. Catalina to Carlo, 1 January 1590, AST, M37, fasc. 3, fol. 520v; Altadonna, II:5.

134. Catalina to Carlo, 4 June 1589, AST, M35, fasc. 9, fol. 240v; Altadonna, I:194.

CHAPTER 6

1. On Joanna of Austria, see Ferrari, "Kinship and the Marginalized Consort," 45–68; Bercusson, "Johanna of Austria," 128–53.

2. Vendramin, "Relazione di Savoia," 178; Corraro, "Relazione dello stato di Savoia," 379–80.

3. Jusepe de Acuña to Philip II, 24 May 1588, AGS, Estado, L1264, no. 136; Jusepe de Acuña to Philip II, 10 April 1592, AGS, Estado, L1271, no. 105.

4. Jusepe de Acuña to Philip II, 15 August 1592, AGS, Estado, L1271, no. 16.

5. Conde de Fuentes to Philip II, 30 August 1592, AGS, Estado, L1271, no. 20; Jusepe de Acuña to Juan de Idiáquez, 7 May 1592, AGS, Estado, L1271, no. 38; Jusepe de Acuña to Philip II, 6 May 1592, AGS, Estado, L1271, no. 33.

6. Carlo to Catalina, 13 December 1595, AST, M21, fasc. 5, fol. 2035.

7. Catalina to Carlo, 13 December 1595, AST, M43, fasc. 8, fol. 1833v; Altadonna, III:274–5.

8. Catalina to Carlo, 26 June 1595, AST, M43, fasc. 6, fol. 1806r; Altadonna, III:262.

9. Catalina to Carlo, 11 October 1588, AST, M35, fasc, 1, fol. 24a; Altadonna, I:32–3.

10. See the following letters from Catalina to Carlo: wild boar (*javalí*): AST, M40, fasc. 11, fol. 1166a, 12 November 1592. Melon: AST, M41, fasc. 5, fol. 1400r, 21 July 1593; Blood sausage: AST, M41, fasc. 8, fol. 1447v, 28 November 1593; Altadonna, III:70, 122–3, 137.

11. Catalina to Carlo, 10 October [1588], AST, M35, fasc. 1, fol. 26a; Altadonna, I:31–2.

12. Catalina to Carlo, 18 July 1596, AST, M44, fasc. 3, fol. 1889v; Altadonna, III:291–92.

13. Catalina to Carlo, 9 October [1588], AST, M35, fasc. 1, fol. 25v; Altadonna, I:30.

14. See the following letters from Catalina to Carlo: *empanadas*: AST, M35, fasc. 6, fol. 112a, 21 March [1589]; Altadonna, I:119. She also told him on another occasion that she would send him pork *empanadas* from a boar that had been caught and, if possible, its head. AST, M45, fasc. 5, fol. 2134b, 20 September, no year given. *Rosca* and *pan de leche*: AST, M45, fasc. 6, fol. 2186b, 25 August, no year given but I would date it to 1589 or 1590.

15. Aristocrats in early modern Europe often gave food items to show deference toward or win favor with a social superior. Social equals might exchange food items as signs of friendship, and sending rare or expensive articles might flaunt the giver's wealth. See Heal, "Food Gifts," 55.

16. Catalina to Carlo, 3 December 1592, AST, M40, fasc. 12, fol. 1806v; Altadonna, III:79.

17. Catalina to Carlo, 14 June 1589, AST, M35, fasc. 9, fol. 229c; Altadonna, I:207. The preserves were made from the *azahar*, which was the white flower of an orange or lemon tree, though Catalina did not specify which it was. She also said that she dared to do so because it came from their garden, so she was suggesting that she thought it could be trusted.

18. Catalina to Carlo, 3 November [1597], AST, M44, fasc. 11, fol. 2019; Altadonna, III:363. On court women and *búcaros*, see Oliván Santaliestra, "The Countess of Harrach," 213. Covarrubias was critical of the use of *búcaros*. See *Tesoro de la lengua*, 239. See also "Covered jar," https://www.metmuseum.org/art/collection/search/662161.

19. Carlo to Catalina, 2 April 1596, AST, M22, fasc. 7, fol. 2190.

20. Catalina to Carlo, 3 October, AST, M45, fasc. 4, fol. 2128r, no year given but I have dated it to 1590 from internal evidence.

21. Catalina to Carlo, 6 January 1593, AST, M41, fasc. 1, fol. 1297av; Altadonna, III:89–90.

22. Catalina to Carlo, 9 April [1595], AST, M43, fasc. 4, fol. 1763v; Altadonna, III:250.

23. Catalina to Carlo, 11 November [1588], AST, M35, fasc. 2, fol. 62v–a; Altadonna, I:71.

24. The letter is from Savigliano and Carlo was in Revello, about 15 miles away.

25. Catalina to Carlo, 2 May [1593], AST, M41, fasc. 3, fol. 1303v; Altadonna, III:90–1.

26. Catalina to Carlo, 1 April 1596, AST, M44, fasc. 2, 1871v; Altadonna, III:281. In his letter of 2 April 1596, Carlo thanked Catalina for the asparagus and the *pan dulce* which she had sent him, and therefore I think the reference to slices is to the sweet bread. For Carlo's letter, see 2 April 1596, AST, M22, fasc. 7, fol. 2190. He told her a day later that he had two beautiful gifts for her but she would never guess what they were. See Carlo to Catalina, 3 April 1596, AST, M22, fasc. 7, fol. 2191.

27. Catalina to Carlo, 19 October [1588], AST, M35, fasc. 1, fol. 37b–bv; Altadonna, I:45.

28. Covarrubias, *Tesoro de la lengua*, 900.

29. Catalina to Carlo, 31 October 1592 and 4 November 1592, AST, M40, fasc. 10, fol. 1145r, and fasc. 11, fol. 1152v; Altadonna, III:61, 64.

30. For rosary, see Catalina to Carlo, 20 March 1589, AST, M35, fasc. 6, fol. 109c; Altadonna, I:118, and on 24 March 1589, the duke wrote that he was wearing it on his arm. See Carlo to Catalina, AST, M13, fasc. 2, fol. 293v.

31. Catalina to Carlo, 20 May 1591, AST, M38, fasc. 5, fol. 776d; Altadonna, II:188. Catalina to Carlo, 21 September [1591], AST, M39, fasc. 3, fol. 865c; Altadonna, II:262.

32. Catalina to Carlo, 23 March [1592], AST, M38, fasc. 3, fol. 742; Altadonna, III:49.

33. Catalina to Carlo, 3 April [1592], AST, M38, fasc. 4, fol. 750v; Altadonna, III:51–2. Carlo collected different types of parrots. See Mamino, "Reimagining the Grande Galleria," 80–81n30.

34. Catalina to Carlo, 24 December [1590], AST, M39, fasc. 6, fol. 954e; Altadonna, II:128. The archive has listed this letter as 1591, but Altadonna has dated it, I think correctly, to 1590.

35. Escudero, *Felipe II*, 124. See also Amezúa, *Felipe II y las flores*.

36. Cultivating flowers in gardens arranged for aesthetic purposes was part of the court culture that emerged in the sixteenth century. Carlo was interested in all types of plant and animal life. He even drew up a study of natural history where he discussed numerous flowers and plants. See Mamino, "Reimagining the Grande Galleria," 80–8.

37. Siniscalco, Caramiello, and Guglielmone, "Disegnatori piemontesi," 136, 150.

38. Catalina to Carlo, 24 March 1589, AST, M35, fasc. 6, fol. 117a; Altadonna, I:123.

39. ASRT, Gioie e Mobili, M1, no. 6, fol. 10v–11v.

40. Catalina to Carlo, 4 September 1590, AST, M37, fasc. 8, fol. 570; Altadonna, II:43; Catalina to Carlo, 4 July 1595, AST, M43, fasc. 7, fol. 1829a; Altadonna, III:273.

41. Catalina to Carlo, 10 April [1589], AST, M35, fasc. 7, fol. 137b; Altadonna, I:139.

42. Carlo to Catalina, 11 May 1592, AST, M19, fasc. 7, fol. 1534; Catalina to Carlo, 12 May 1593, AST, M41, fasc. 3, fol. 1324r; Altadonna, III:97.

43. Siniscalco, Caramiello, and Guglielmone, "Disegnatori piemontesi," 136 (no. 50).

44. Catalina to Carlo, 29 March [1589], AST, M35, fasc. 6, fol. 123; Altadonna, I:127; Catalina to Carlo, 19 March [1595], AST, M43, fasc. 3, fols. 1713r, 1757; Altadonna, III:227; and Catalina to Carlo, 5 April 1595, AST, M43, fasc. 4, fol. 1752br; Altadonna, III:246.

45. Catalina to Carlo, 21 November 1588, AST, M35, fasc. 2, fol. 75v; Altadonna I:86.

46. Catalina to Carlo, 3 and 4 March 1589, AST, M35, fasc. 6, fols. 90r, 91r; Altadonna, I:90, 92.

47. Catalina to Carlo, 3 March 1589, AST, M35, fasc. 6, fol. 90br; Altadonna, I:92. Catalina to Carlo, 14 January, AST, M45, fasc. 3, fol. 2024a, no year but probably from 1592. Cauliflower had been introduced to Italy only in the sixteenth century. In seventeenth-century England, oysters were considered aphrodisiacs, as were crawfish, lobster, and game, and were also thought to promote sexual health. This might also have been true in sixteenth-century Italy and Spain. See Evans, *Aphrodisiacs*, 101.

48. For the verses, see AST, M35, fasc. 5, fol. 88b. The *coplas* are not dated, but Catalina mentions them in her letter of 3 March 1589, AST, M35, fasc. 6, fol. 90br; Altadonna, I:92n3. She says that a capuchin sent the *coplas*, but Carlo seems to have been the poet, and Catalina wrote the response. She says "forgive me that the response is not very good because it was done in haste and the poet is not very good, because [the poet] does not know how to say how she feels being without her love."

49. Catalina to Carlo, 3 March 1589, 4 March [1589], 6 March 1589, AST, M35, fasc. 6, fols. 90br, 91r, 92r; Altadonna, I:92, 96. She does not say she is sending him flowers, but he thanks her for flowers in his letter, so she must have sent them.

50. Carlo to Catalina, AST, M13, fasc. 2, fol. 280r, undated; Catalina to Carlo, 8 March 1589, AST, M35, fasc. 6, fol. 93r; Altadonna, I:96.

51. Carlo to Catalina, 14 March 1591, AST, M16, fasc. 6, fol. 988av; Catalina to Carlo, 31 March [1591], AST, M38, fasc. 3, fol. 745v; Altadonna, II:167.

52. Catalina to Carlo, 1 and 2 October 1594, AST, M42, fasc. 3, fol. 1513r–v, 1517av; Altadonna, III:162–3. The legate saw the Shroud on 2 October 1594. See Catalina to Carlo, 2 October 1594, AST, M42, fasc. 3, fol. 1517v; Altadonna, III:162.

53. Catalina to Carlo, 23 November, AST, M45, fasc. 7, fol. 2184r, no year given; Catalina to Carlo, 8 October 1588, 12 October [1588], AST, M35, fasc. 1, fols. 26a, 29; Altadonna, I:36, 29; Catalina to Carlo, 18 November 1591, AST, M39, fasc. 5, fol. 930ev; Altadonna, II:305; Carlo to Catalina, 5 January 1590, AST, M15, fasc. 1, fol. 675v.

54. Catalina to Carlo, 20 June 1589, AST, M35, fasc. 9, fol. 233ev; Altadonna, I:213; Catalina to Carlo, 10 November [1588], AST, M35, fasc. 2, fol. 61r; Altadonna, I:69.

55. Catalina to Carlo, 1 and 9 October [1588], AST, M35, fasc. 1, fol. 6av, 25a; Altadonna, I:14, 30; Catalina to Carlo, 16 February, AST, M45, fasc. 3, fol. 2052v, no year given but must be 1591; Catalina to Carlo, 10 September 1591, AST, M39, fasc. 3, fol. 853hv; Altadonna, II:253.

56. Catalina to Carlo, 14 November [1590], AST, M37, fasc. 10, fol. 657; Altadonna, II:100; Catalina to Carlo, 12 July [1597], AST, M44, fasc. 3, fol. 1916bv; Altadonna, III:302; Carlo to Catalina, 11 September 1590 (?), AST, M15, fasc. 5, fol. 788. When she sent Carlo a *banda* and *sombrero* on 20 January 1591, she also said that she hoped they would remind him of her. See Catalina to Carlo, 20 January [1591], AST, M35, fasc. 1, fol. 87; Altadonna, II:137.

57. Catalina to Carlo, 29 September [1588], AST, M35, fasc. 1, 2bisb; Altadonna, I:6; Carlo to Catalina, November 1588, AST, M12, fasc. 20, fol. 257; Catalina to Carlo, 19 April 1589, AST, M35, fasc. 7, fol. 148r; Altadonna, I:147; Carlo to Catalina, 27 September 1589, AST, M14, fasc. 1, fol. 480; Catalina to Carlo,

6 October, AST, M45, fasc. 5, fol. 2120r, no year given but from internal evidence I would date it to 1589. For other examples, see Catalina to Carlo, 1 August 1592, AST, M40, fasc. 8, fol. 1123r; Altadonna, III:53; Carlo to Catalina, AST, M19, fol. 1625.

58. Carlo to Catalina, 18 July 1593, AST, M19, fasc. 8, fol. 1625. Catalina received them the next day. See Catalina to Carlo, 19 July [1593], AST, M41, fasc. 5, fol. 1396r–v; Altadonna, III:120–1.

59. Carlo to Catalina, 21 October 1588, AST, M12, fasc. 20, fol. 241v. For Catalina's colors, see Pérez de Tudela, "Lujo en el matrimonio," 380. When he arrived in Zaragoza for the wedding, the duke and his entourage dressed in Catalina's colors. See Matthews, *News and Rumor*, 103. Catalina had *banderas* made according to his specifications. See Catalina to Carlo, 20 October [1588], AST, M35, fasc. 1, fol. 38v; Catalina to Carlo, 20 October 1588, AST, M35, fasc. 1, fol. 40v; Altadonna, I:47, 48. For the purchase of crimson damask to make a banner, see ASRT, Real Casa, Camerale, Art. 384, Cuentas de Sayas y Vestidos, 5 November 1597, n.p.

60. Catalina to Carlo, 20 November 1588, AST, M35, fasc. 2, fol. 74r; Altadonna, I:83.

61. Carlo to Catalina, 7 February 1591, AST, M15, fasc. 1, fol. 686br; 22 August 1589, AST, M15, fasc. 3, fol. 692ar; 16 January 1591, AST, M16, fasc. 5, fol. 917v.

62. Daybell, *Women Letter-Writers*, 159–60. For letters provoking tears, see Catalina to Carlo, 7 October [1588], AST, M35, fasc. 1, fols. 22v, 22av; Altadonna, I:26–7; Catalina to Carlo, 22 July [1589], AST, M45, fasc. 4, fol. 2079r; Carlo to Catalina, 22 August 1589, AST, M15, fasc. 3, fol. 692r. On the reciprocal nature of gifts, see Mauss, *The Gift*, esp. 41–2; Davis, *The Gift in Sixteenth-Century France*, 11–14.

63. Catalina to Carlo, 22 October [1588], AST, M35, fasc. 1, fol. 42av; 2 November 1588, AST, M35, fasc. 2, fol. 55v; Altadonna, I:50, 63; Catalina to Carlo, 9 March 1589, AST, M35, fasc. 6, fol. 96br; Altadonna, I:99.

64. On early modern portraits, see Bass, *The Power of the Portrait*; Sowerby, "'A Memorial and a Pledge of Faith'," 296–331; Sommer-Mathis and Standhartinger, "Le suplico me ynbíe un rretrato," 397–429; Bolland, "'Both the Fairest Ladies'," 91–5; Falomir Faus, "De la cámara a la galería," 126–40. Falomir Faus demonstrates persuasively that the same portraits had different meanings for different people.

65. Carlo to Catalina, 18 October 1588, AST, M12, fasc. 20, fol. 239. For Catalina's response, see letter of 19 October [1588], AST, M35, fasc. 1, fol. 37v; Altadonna, I:43.

66. Catalina to Carlo, 11 October 1588, AST, M35, fasc. 1, fol. 27r; Altadonna, I:33.

67. Catalina to Carlo, 18 March 1591, AST, M38, fasc. 3, fol. 731v; Altadonna, II:157.

68. With her portrait, Catalina also sent a portrait of Carlo's mother that he had requested. Catalina to Carlo, 23 November [1589], AST, M36, fasc. 5, 433d; Altadonna, I:353; Carlo to Catalina, 30 November 1589, AST, M14, fasc. 3, fol. 553.

69. Catalina to Carlo, 17 October 1588, AST, M35, fasc. 1, fol. 35av; Altadonna, I:42; Catalina to Carlo, 16 March [1589], AST, M35, fasc. 6, fol. 105bv; Altadonna, I:109.

70. Catalina to Carlo, 24 March 1589, AST, M35, fasc. 6, fol. 117r; Altadonna, I:123.

71. Carlo to Catalina, 18 October 1588, AST, M12, fasc. 20, fol. 239; Catalina to Carlo, 19 October [1588], AST, M35, fasc. 1, fol. 37v; Altadonna, I:43.

72. Catalina to Carlo, 20 March 1589, AST, M35, fasc. 6, fol. 108av; Altadonna, I:114; Carlo to Catalina, 28 March 1589, AST, M12, fasc. 20, fol. 234bv.

73. Catalina to Carlo, 5 July 1589, 1 July [1589], AST, M36, fasc. 1, fols. 250br, 246fr; Altadonna, I:226, 223. Years later at her court in Brussels, Isabel Clara Eugenia also wrote her letters in a gallery surrounded by portraits of her relatives. García García, "Los regalos," 22.

74. Catalina to Carlo, 28 August, AST, M45, fasc. 4, fol, 2074bv, no year given but from internal evidence I would date it to 1590.

75. Catalina to Carlo, 4 December 1590, AST, M37, fasc. 11, fol. 673; Altadonna, II:112. On *libros de memoria*, see Gómez-Bravo, *Textual Agency*, 153.

76. For people's devotional interaction with religious images, see Kasl, "Delightful Adornments," 147–63. Among other examples, Kasl discusses Sor Margarita de la Cruz's interaction with statues of the baby Jesus. For further discussion of Sor Margarita's devotion, see Tiffany, " 'Little Idols'," 35–48; and García Sanz, *El Niño Jesús*.

77. Juana of Austria received a portrait of her soon-to-be husband, Prince Juan of Portugal, and hung it in her bedroom, where she spent the better part of the day admiring and talking to it. See Falomir Faus, "De la cámara a la galería," 126, 129. Isabel Clara Eugenia claimed she hugged the portrait of her niece. See García García, "Los regalos," 72–3.

78. Catalina to Carlo, 16 July 1589, AST, M36, fasc. 1, fol. 268ar; Altadonna, I:240; Carlo to Catalina, 29 June 1589, AST, M13, fasc. 4, fol. 376v; Catalina to Carlo, 1 July [1589], AST, M36, fasc. 1, fol. 246fr; Altadonna, I:223.

79. Carlo to Catalina, 29 June 1589, AST, M13, fasc. 5, fol. 376v.

80. Catalina to Carlo, 1 July [1589] and 5 July 1589, AST, M36, fasc. 1, fols. 246fr, 250br; Altadonna, I:223, 226. Catalina meant that the bed did not have curtains, only valances at the top which allowed her to see out into the room. Perhaps in the summer she did not sleep in a bed encircled with curtains. I thank Bernardo García for clarifying "*de volante*" for me. On early modern beds, see Ágreda Pino, "Vestir el lecho," 20–41.

81. On 20 July 1589, she said she was eating and sleeping in his apartment because of the heat. She may well have slept there all month. See Catalina to Carlo, 20 July [1589], AST, M36, fasc. 1, 276v; Altadonna, I:242.

82. In writing "*beluarte*," Catalina was referring to a bulwark (*baluarte* in Spanish; *balvardo* in Italian). In particular, she was referring to the belvedere that Carlo had built on top of the Green Bastion (Bastion Verde), one of the bastions of the wall that bordered the palace grounds, from which the ducal family could enjoy the fauna and flora of the palace grounds and the countryside beyond the walls. Catalina to Carlo, 5 April 1596, AST, M44, fasc. 2, fol. 1878v–1878ar; Altadonna, III:286; Catalina to Carlo, 3 May [1589], AST, M35, fasc. 8, fol. 169a; Altadonna, I:162.

83. Catalina to Carlo, 17 July 1596, AST, M44, fasc. 3, fol. 1889v; Altadonna, III:290.

84. Catalina to Carlo, 10 November 1592, AST, M40, fasc. 11, fol. 1163v; Altadonna, III:69.

85. Catalina to Carlo, 26 July [1591], AST, M37, fasc. 6, fol. 544; Altadonna, II:227. The archive has this letter dated 1590 but Altadonna has dated it 1591. Carlo to Catalina, 10 October 1590 or 1591, AST, M17, fasc. 3, fol. 1114.

86. Catalina to Carlo, 15 November, AST, M45, fasc. 4, fol. 2072bv, no year given but probably from 1589; Catalina to Carlo, 15 August 1589, AST, M45, fasc. 5, fol. 2114ar, no year given but from internal evidence I have dated it to 1589.

87. Carlo to Catalina, 17 March 1589, AST, M13, fasc. 2, fol. 289av.

88. Jusepe de Acuña to Philip II, 14 June 1588, AGS, Estado, L1263, no. 87.

89. Catalina to Carlo, 17 March 1589, AST, M35, fasc. 6, fol. 107ar–v; Altadonna, I:111; Catalina to Carlo, 5 January 1592, AST, M40, fasc. 1, fol. 1215; Altadonna, III:6.

90. Catalina to Carlo, 10 November 1591, AST, M39, fasc. 5, fol. 995ar; Altadonna, II:302; Catalina to Carlo, 20 May 1591, AST, M38, fasc. 5, fol. 776cr; Altadonna, II:188. The eagle might have been Empress María, because the eagle was the symbol of the Habsburgs.

91. Kamen, *Philip of Spain*, 305. Catalina to Carlo, 9 April [1589], AST, M35, fasc. 7, fol. 134bv–c; Altadonna, I:135.

92. See, for example, Catalina to Carlo, 26 May, AST, M45, fasc. 4, fol. 2102v, no year given. See also Catalina to Carlo, 16 May [1593], AST, M41, fasc. 3, fol. 1332v; Altadonna, III:101.

93. Carlo to Catalina, 3 November 1589, AST, M12, fasc. 20, fol. 248; Catalina to Carlo, 9 March 1589, AST, M35, fasc. 6, fol. 96br; Altadonna, I:99.

94. Catalina to Carlo, 5 October [1588], AST, M35, fasc. 1, fol. 15r; Altadonna, I:23; Catalina to Carlo, 21 August 1590, AST, M37, fasc. 7, fol. 548; Altadonna, II:34.

95. Carlo to Catalina, 15 October 1588, AST, M12, fasc. 20, fol. 238r; Carlo to Catalina, 25 October 1588, AST, M12, fasc. 20, fol. 242v.

96. Carlo to Catalina, 28 March 1589, AST, M12, fasc. 20, fol. 234v; Carlo to Catalina, 22 August 1589, AST, M15, fasc. 3, fol. 692ar.

97. Catalina to Carlo, 16 April [1589], AST, M35, fasc. 7, fol. 147v; Altadonna, I:144–5. For what the Genevans had done, see Carlo to Catalina, 14 April 1589, AST, M13, fasc. 3, fol. 308r.

98. Catalina to Carlo, 7 June 1589, AST, M35, fasc. 9, fol. 219ar; Altadonna, I:198.

99. Catalina to Carlo, 20 January [1591], AST, M35, fasc. 1, fol. 87; Altadonna, II:133.

100. Covarrubias, *Tesoro de la lengua*, 288.

101. Catalina to Carlo, 20 March 1589, AST, M35, fasc. 6, fol. 109d; Altadonna, I:118; Catalina to Carlo, 30 May [1589], AST, M35, fasc. 8, fol. 209r; Altadonna, I:189; Catalina to Carlo, AST, M41, fasc. 5, 19 July [1593], fol. 1396r; Altadonna, III:120; Catalina to Carlo, 6 October 1592, AST, M45, fasc. 3, fol. 2050v, no year given but was written from Nice so has to be from 1592.

102. Catalina to Carlo, 2 March 1592, AST, M40, fasc. 3, fol. 1086; Altadonna, III:34.

103. Catalina to Carlo, 10 April, AST, M45, fasc. 3, fol. 2067–2067v, no year given; Catalina to Carlo, 10 May 1589, AST, M35, fasc. 8, fol. 181v; Altadonna, I:169–70; Catalina to Carlo, 17 March 1589, AST, M35, fasc. 6, fol. 107av; Altadonna, I:111. See also Catalina to Carlo, 18 December 1595, AST, M43, fasc. 8, fol. 1821v; Altadonna, III:276–7.

104. Catalina to Carlo, 13 November [1588], AST, M35, fasc. 2, fol. 67av; Altadonna, I:75; Catalina to Carlo, 21 October, AST, M45, fasc. 3, fol. 2037bv, no year given but I would date it to 1588 or 1589; Catalina to Carlo, 30 July 1589, AST, M36, fasc. 1, fol. 287v; Altadonna, I:251.

105. Carlo to Catalina, 10 and 21 November 1589, AST, M14, fasc. 3, fol. 524, 540.
106. Carlo to Catalina, 12 November 1588, AST, M12, fasc. 20, fol. 252; Catalina to Carlo, 30 October 1590, AST, M37, fasc. 9, fol. 645v; Altadonna, II:86; and Catalina to Carlo, 11 January 1591, AST, M38, fasc. 1, fol. 698c; Altadonna, II:132.
107. Catalina to Carlo, 13 December [1589], AST, M36, fasc. 6, fol. 459g; Altadonna, I:381.
108. Catalina to Carlo, 2 October 1588, AST, M35, fasc. 1, fol. 9a; Altadonna, I:17; Carlo to Catalina, 10 October 1588, AST, M12, fasc. 20, fol. 236b; Catalina to Carlo, 12 October [1588], AST, M35, fasc. 1, fol. 29r; Altadonna, I:34.
109. Carlo to Catalina, 15 August 1589, AST, M13, fasc. 7, fol. 445bis/ar–v, 422; Carlo to Catalina, 3 October 1589, AST, M14, fasc. 1, fol. 492.
110. Catalina to Carlo, 23 September [1594], AST, M42, fasc. 2, 1487a; Altadonna, III:148.
111. Catalina to Carlo, 20 September 1590, AST, M37, fasc. 8, fol. 589r; Altadonna, II:49.
112. Catalina to Carlo, 13 April, AST, M45, fasc. 5, fol. 2132av, no year given.
113. Catalina to Carlo, 20 November [1588], AST, M35, fasc. 2, fol. 64; Altadonna, I:82.
114. Catalina to Carlo, 15 December 1589, AST, M36, fasc. 11, fol. 460c; Altadonna, I:383; Carlo to Catalina, 22 December 1589, AST, M14, fasc. 3, fol. 581; Carlo to Catalina, 24 September 1591, AST, M17, fasc. 2, fol. 1091; Catalina to Carlo, 27 September, AST, M45, fasc. 6, fol. 2197av, no year given.
115. Catalina to Carlo, 19 January 1590, AST, M37, fasc. 1, fol. 535; Altadonna, II:25.
116. Catalina to Carlo, 7, 20, 26 October [1588], AST, M35, fasc. 1, fols. 22v, 39ar, 46v; Altadonna, I:26, 46, 53; Catalina to Carlo, 2 November 1588, AST, M35, fasc. 2, fol. 55ar; Altadonna, I:63–4.
117. Catalina to Carlo, 25 October 1588, AST, M35, fol. 44v; Altadonna, I:52. She used a similar expression (*nos tomareys de sobresalto*) on 19 January 1590 when she sent him the key to her room. See Catalina to Carlo, 19 January 1590, AST, M37, fasc. 1, fol. 535; Altadonna, II:25.
118. Catalina to Carlo, 26 October [1588], AST, M35, fasc. 1, fol. 47ar; Altadonna, I:54.
119. Catalina to Carlo, 4 and 28 March [1589], AST, M35, fasc. 6, fols. 91r, 122av; Altadonna, I:92, 126; Catalina to Carlo, 19 December 1589, AST, M36, fasc. 6, fol. 464av–b; Altadonna, I:389.
120. Catalina to Carlo, 1 September, AST, M45, fasc. 6, fol. 2151v, no year given.
121. Catalina to Carlo, 18 May 1591, AST, M38, fasc. 3, fol. 732ar; Altadonna, II:184.
122. Catalina to Carlo, 23 September [1591], AST, M39, fasc. 3, fol. 866v; Altadonna, II:265; Catalina to Carlo, 2 December 1591, AST, M39, fasc. 6, fol. 938a–av; Altadonna, II:309.
123. Carlo to Catalina, 16 October 1588, AST, M12, fasc. 10, fol. 238v; Carlo to Catalina, 23 September 1591, AST, M17, fasc. 2, fol. 1089r.
124. Carlo to Catalina, 11 September, no year, AST, M15, fasc. 5, fol. 788.
125. Carlo to Catalina, 24 August, year illegible, AST, M15, fasc. 3, fol. 695av.
126. Carlo to Catalina, 22 November 1592, AST, M18, fasc. 9, fol. 1341.
127. Carlo to Catalina, 2 February 1590, AST, M15, fasc. 1, fol. 686ar.

128. Carlo to Catalina, 6 and 30 December 1589, AST, M14, fasc. 4, fols. 560, 589. A St. Nicholas tradition was to fill a shoe with treats, and Carlo was referring to that.

129. Author italics for both. Carlo to Catalina, 20 October 1588, AST, M12, fol. 240; Catalina to Carlo, 21 October 1588, AST, M35, fol. 40r; Altadonna, I:48.

130. Carlo to Catalina, 5 September 1589, AST, M15, fasc. 3, 716av. Note that this letter appears to say 1589 but has to be from 1590 because it goes along with Catalina's letter to Carlo from 4 September 1590. See AST, M37, fasc. 8, fol. 570; Altadonna, II:43. She also was not pregnant in September 1589. On the moral and social norms of sexual intercourse during pregnancy, see Kremmel, "Sexual Intercourse during Pregnancy," 79–81.

131. Catalina to Carlo, 30 August, AST, M45, fasc. 4, fol. 2090r, no year given but from internal evidence I have dated it to 1590.

132. There was some debate as to whether sexual intercourse was helpful or damaging to men's health. Catalina believed in purging, and intercourse was seen as one way of purging excess semen, so she may well have thought it important for Carlo to return to Turin to have sex with her to rid himself of bad humor. See Cavallo and Storey, *Healthy Living*, 268. Male humoral balance was considered important for procreation. See McClive, *Menstruation*, 84.

133. Catalina to Carlo, 25 September, AST, M45, fasc. 4, fol. 2080ar, no year given but probably from 1590.

134. Catalina to Carlo, 14 October, AST, M39, fasc. 9, fol. 896[d]; Altadonna, II:70–1. The archive has this as 1591 but Altadonna has dated it to 1590, which would make logical sense since they were discussing Don Juana de Acuña in other letters in October 1590.

135. Catalina to Carlo, 15 October [1590], AST, M37, fasc. 9, fol. 627; Altadonna, II:72; Carlo to Catalina, 22 October 1590, AST, M17, fasc. 2, fol. 1127fr.

136. Catalina to Carlo, 25 September, AST, M45, fasc. 4, fol. 2080ar, no year given but probably from 1590.

137. On Juana's great beauty, see, Cristóbal de Briceño to Juan de Zúñiga, 6 June 1586, BPG, CEF, MS 23, fol. 434r–436v. See also García Prieto, *Una corte*, 203–4.

138. Carlo to Catalina, 26 April 1591, AST, M16, fasc. 8, fol. 1009av.

139. Catalina to Carlo, 22 July, AST, M45, fasc. 4, fol. 2079cv, no year given but from internal evidence I have dated it to 1589.

140. Catalina to Carlo, 15 November, AST, M45, fasc. 3, fol. 2039a–av, no year given but probably from 1590.

141. Catalina to Carlo, 4 July 1595, AST, M43, fasc. 7, fol. 1829r–v; Altadonna, III:273.

142. Catalina to Carlo, 5 May [1589], 28 May 1589, AST, M35, fasc. 8, fol. 173r, 208v; Altadonna, I:164, 188; Catalina to Carlo, 7 June 1589, AST, M35, fasc. 9, fol. 219dr; Altadonna, I:200.

143. Catalina to Carlo, 19 October 1594, AST, M42, fasc. 3, fol. 1569v; Altadonna, III:192–3.

144. Catalina to Carlo, 4 June 1589, AST, M35, fasc. 9, fol. 240av; Altadonna, I:195; Catalina to Carlo, 5 August [1589], AST, M36, fasc. 2, fol. 294r–v; Altadonna, I:255.

145. Catalina to Carlo, 26 August 1590, AST, M37, fasc. 7, fol. 553; Altadonna, II:36; Catalina to Carlo, 30 August, AST, M45, fasc. 4, fol. 2090r, no year given but from internal evidence I have dated it to 1590; Carlo to Catalina, 29 August 1590, AST, M15, fasc. 3, fol. 704.

146. Catalina to Carlo, 26 September 1590, AST, M45, fasc. 4, fol. 2089b, no year given but I have dated it to 1590; Carlo to Catalina, 22 September 1590, AST, M15, fasc. 4, fol. 738r–v.

147. Catalina to Carlo, 28 October 1590, AST, M37, fasc. 9, fol. 641v; Altadonna, II:81.

148. Catalina to Carlo, 28 and 30 October 1590, AST, M37, fasc. 9, fols. 641, 645; Altadonna, II:81, 86.

149. Catalina to Carlo, 5 November 1590, AST, M37, fasc. 10, fol. 649v; Altadonna, II:88–9.

150. Carlo to Catalina, 2 February 1591, AST, M16, fasc. 6, fol. 928b. The archival record makes it a little difficult to fully understand Carlo's response. His letter addressing the issues that Catalina raised in her letter of October 1590 is dated February 1591. Did Carlo misdate his letter or did he wait that long to respond to her letter? In his letter dated February 1591, he expressed his concern that she had a cough, which she had mentioned in her October letter, but made no mention of in any later letters. Would he have waited four months to respond to her report of a cough, knowing she was no longer ill? More likely, he misdated his letter, which was probably written in late October or in November 1590.

151. See Catalina to Carlo, 23 November 1590, AST, M39, fasc. 5, fol. 931dv; Altadonna, II:106; Catalina to Carlo, 23 November 1590, AST, M37, fasc. 5, fol. 670v; Altadonna, II:107. For Terranova, see Catalina to Carlo, 29 November 1590, AST, M37, fasc. 10, fol. 671v; Altadonna, II:109.

152. Catalina to Carlo, 4 and 16 December 1590, AST, M37, fasc. 11, fols. 673, 678; Altadonna, II:112, 121.

153. Catalina said that Carlo had promised to send "Monseñor il Gran," who was Silla Roero, count of Revigliasco and *Gran Scudiere* of Savoy, to replace her in Turin. Catalina to Carlo, 21 December 1590, AST, M37, fasc. 11, fol. 680; Altadonna, II:123, 125.

154. Catalina to Carlo, 9 January 1591, AST, M38, fasc. 1, fol. 693. This letter is not in Altadonna.

155. Catalina to Carlo, 20 January [1591], AST, M35, fasc. 1, fol. 87; Altadonna, II:134.

156. Catalina to Carlo, 24 June 1591, AST, M38, fasc. 6, fol. 784hv–i; Altadonna, II:209–10.

157. Catalina to Carlo, 18 August 1591, AST, M39, fasc. 2, fol. 832cr; Altadonna, II:239.

158. Catalina to Carlo, 18 August 1591, AST, M39, fasc. 2, fol. 832cv; Altadonna, II:239.

159. Catalina to Carlo, 8 November 1591, AST, M39, fasc. 5, fol. 924; Altadonna, II:301.

160. Catalina to Carlo, 23 December 1591, AST, M39, fasc. 6, fol. 951r–951v; Altadonna, II:313.

161. Of those eleven illegitimate children, four of them were by Marguerite de Rossillon, an aristocratic woman whom he eventually married. For the number and fate of his illegitimate children, see Osborne, *Dynasty and Diplomacy*, 44–6, and Oresko, "Bastards as Clients," 45.

CHAPTER 7

1. McClive, *Menstruation*, 116–17.

2. Catherine de' Medici sought to monitor her daughter's reproductive health from a distance, insisting on receiving reports from Elisabeth's female attendants as well

as from French ambassadors in Spain. Years later, Empress Maria Theresa would expect monthly reports from her daughter, Marie Antoinette, about her menstrual cycles. See Broomhall, "Women's Little Secret," 4; Wolff, "Habsburg Letters," 70–86; McClive, *Menstruation*, 118–19, 139–40.

3. Philip II to Catalina, 23 August 1585, in Bouza, *Cartas*, 125; Giovanni Mocenigo, 14 July 1585, report from Mondovì, ASV, SDSa, filze 8, no. 22.

4. "De la llegada del duque de Saboya a Turin," 10 August 1585, AGS, Estado, L1260, no. 194.

5. Catalina to Carlo, 17 July 1597, AST, M44, fasc. 7, fol. 1924r; Altadonna, III:306. For a list of symptoms, see Carbón, *Libro del arte*, 41–4.

6. For reports of purging, see Catalina to Carlo, 9 October, AST, M45, fasc. 2, fol. 2061v, no year given but I have dated it to 1589; Catalina to Carlo, 9 June 1589, AST, M35, fasc. 9, fol. 223ar; Altadonna, I:202; Catalina to Carlo, 13 May 1593, AST, M41, fasc. 3, fol. 1326r; Altadonna, III:99.

7. Catalina to Carlo, 9 August 1597, AST, M44, fasc. 8, fol. 1949c; Altadonna, III:321.

8. Catalina to Carlo, 25 March [1595], AST, M43, fasc. 3, fol. 1732b; Altadonna, III:236; Carlo to Catalina, 26 March 1595, AST, M21, fasc. 2, fol. 1949.

9. Catalina to Carlo, 27 March 1595, AST, M43, fasc. 3, fol. 1736v; Altadonna, III:237; Catalina to Carlo, 5 April 1595, AST, M43, fasc. 4, fol. 1753v, Altadonna, III:246.

10. Catalina to Carlo, 19 October [1588], AST, M35, fasc. 1, fol. 37v; Altadonna, I:43–4; Bernís, *El traje*, 214; Carlo to Catalina, 20 October 1588, AST, M12, fol. 240.

11. For the name of her midwives, see ASRT, Camera dei Conti, Real Casa, Art. 224, 1585-87, n.p. and Conto del Sig. Isidoro de Robles, ASRT, Camera dei Conti, Real Casa, Art 224, 1594–96, entry no. 106. Typically, one of Catalina's attendants traveled to Milan to bring the midwife to Turin. See ASRT, Camera dei Conti, Real Casa, Art. 224, 1585–87, n.p.

12. Catalina to Carlo, 1 July [1589], AST, M36, fasc. 1, fol. 246d; Altadonna, I:222.

13. Catalina to Carlo, 24 October, AST, M45, fasc. 5, fol. 2142–2142v, no year given but internal evidence indicates 1594.

14. McClive, *Menstruation*, 10–11, 139–52, 161–2.

15. Jusepe de Acuña to Philip II, 3 September 1588, AGS, Estado, L1263, no. 120.

16. Catalina to Carlo, 17 and 24 March 1589, AST, M35, fasc. 6, fol. 107av, 117av; 18 October 1590, AST, M37, fasc. 9, fol. 630; Altadonna, I:111, 122 and II:74; Catalina to Carlo, 17 July, AST, M45, fol. 2064a, no year but internal evidence indicates 1593.

17. Perhaps she relied on a lunar calendar, but her calculations do not correspond to a lunar month. In March 1589, the lunar month would have begun on 16 March with the new moon, but Catalina calculated that the new month began on 24 March, when the moon entered its first quarter. In 1590, she said that she was beginning a new month on 18 October, when astronomers have calculated that the moon was in its last quarter. For the lunar months, see http://astropixels.com/ephemeris/phasescat/phases1501.html.

18. For different calculation of months, see McClive, *Menstruation*, 106–8; D'Amelia, "Becoming a Mother," 230.

19. Catalina to Carlo, 18 October and 16 December, AST, M37, fasc. 9, fol. 630 and fasc. 11, fol. 678; Altadonna, II:74, 121.

20. She does not always seem to have determined the date of conception correctly. On 24 March 1589, she said she entered the eighth month, which would mean that on 24 April she entered the ninth. The baby was born on 28 April—only four days into the ninth month. On 30 January 1594, Catalina wrote to Philip that in fifteen days she would enter the ninth month of her pregnancy. She gave birth on 8 February, sooner than she expected even to enter the final month. In 1591, on the other hand, her calculations were much more accurate. On 19 February, she told Carlo that the day before she had entered her ninth month. She gave birth on 11 March. It could also be that she did not miscalculate but rather that several of her children were born prematurely.

21. Catalina to Carlo, 14, 17, 21 July 1597, AST, M44, fasc. 7, fols. 1317c, 1924r, 1931b; Altadonna, III:304, 306, 309–10.

22. Catalina to Carlo, 2 September, AST, M45, fasc. 6, fol. 2156c–2156cv, no year.

23. Vocelka and Heller, *Die private Welt*, 27. Vocelka and Heller say that Habsburg empresses were bled three times when pregnant, and these bleedings were accompanied by elaborate court festivities. There seems no evidence of this practice at the court in Turin. Unfortunately, Vocelka and Heller do not cite any of their sources and often generalize over the centuries, making it difficult to determine the origins of specific rituals.

24. Carlos Varona, "Entre el riesgo," 282. In 1576, when Anna of Austria was queen of Spain, the royal tailor bought cloth to dress nine women on the feast of the Annunciation, so the ritual was observed at least when she was queen. See García Prieto, "La infanta Isabel Clara Eugenia," 141n285.

25. Margarita de Austria, wife of Philip III of Spain, celebrated this ritual in 1609 and also trained her daughter Ana to perform it, but the practice was already established at the court in Madrid. See Carlos Varona, "Entre el riesgo," 284; Hoffman, *Raised to Rule*, 84–5.

26. Francisco de Vera to Philip II, 28 March 1589, AGS, Estado, L1266, no. 147.

27. Catalina to Carlo, 24 March 1589, AST, M35, fasc. 6, fol. 117a; Altadonna, I:124. Catalina dated the beginning of the eighth month of this pregnancy to 24 March 1589 but, in fact, she was probably much closer to the beginning of her ninth month. She gave birth on 28 April.

28. Curzio di Lorenzo da Picchena to Caterina di Ferdinando I di Medici-Gonzaga, 3 October 1617, MAP, document 6710 [MdP vol. 6108, fol. 950r]; Giuliano de' Medici di Castellina to Curzio di Lorenzo da Picchena, 1 August 1621, MAP, document 7959 [MdP vol. 4949, fol. 949r]; Averardo di Raffaello de' Medici di Castellina to Curzio di Lorenzo da Picchena, 16 October 1623, MAP, document 9289 [MdP vol. 4952, n.p.].

29. McClive, *Menstruation*, 103, 116. McClive argues (66–7) that in the sixteenth century, several influential Spanish theological texts downgraded intercourse during menstruation from a mortal to a venial sin.

30. McClive, *Menstruation*, 94. Other scholars have argued that physicians debated whether conception occurred at the beginning or at the end of a menstrual cycle. See King, *Midwifery*, 56; Castiglione, "Peasants at the Palace," 93.

31. Catalina to Carlo, 24 October, AST, M45, fasc. 5, fol. 2142r–v, no year.

32. See, for example, Carlo to Catalina, 18 July 1589, AST, M13, fasc. 6, fol. 401.

33. For the midwife's arrival, see Catalina to Carlo, 13 April 1589, AST, M35, fasc. 7, fol. 144c; Altadonna, I:144.

34. See, for example, Catalina to Carlo, 10 October, AST, M45, fol. 2077a, no year.

35. See "De la llegada del duque de Saboya a Turin," 10 August 1585, AGS, Estado, L1260, no. 194, and "Relatione degli apparati," 113.

36. Philip II to Catalina, 23 August 1585, in Bouza, *Cartas*, 125.

37. Philip II to Carlo, 30 October 1585, AST, LPF(S), M97, fasc. 4, no. 59; Altadonna, "Cartas de Felipe II," 158.

38. Carlo to Philip II, 7 November 1586, AGS, Estado, L1261, no. 35.

39. Cristóbal de Briceño to Mateo Vázquez, 14 August and 15 September 1585, IVDJ, ENV 5, T III, fol. 256r, 257v.

40. Paolo Sfrondato to Juan de Idiáquez, 6 November 1586, AGS, Estado, L1261, no. 31.

41. Philip II to Catalina, 12 March 1588, in Bouza, *Cartas*, 155.

42. Parker, *Felipe II*, 85, 451–2, 456–7.

43. Carlo to Philip II, 17 April 1588, AST, E1263, no. 142.

44. Philip II to Catalina, 14 June 1588, in Bouza, *Cartas*, 156–7.

45. On the birthing chair and its use by Spanish queens, see Carlos Varona, *Nacer en palacio*, 91–5. Catalina probably used a chair when giving birth to her second child, because her accounts list a purchase of red velvet to cover the chair where she had given birth. See ASRT, Camera dei Conti, Real Casa, Art. 224, Cartas de Pago, 1586–1595, fol. 23, entry 344.

46. His first wife, Maria Manuela of Portugal, died four days after giving birth to a son. His third wife, Elisabeth of Valois, died after giving birth, but she had been ill for the entire pregnancy. Parker, *Imprudent King*, 30. Kamen, *Philip of Spain*, 204.

47. Philip II to Catalina, 27 April 1586, in Bouza, *Cartas*, 139.

48. Catalina to Philip II, 30 January 1594, BL, Add. MSS 28419, fol. 79r, Turin; Catalina to Carlo, 3 October, AST, M45, fasc. 5, fol. 2128r, no year given but almost certainly from 1590; Catalina to Carlo, 12 November, AST, M45, fasc. 5, fol. 2112av, no year.

49. Catalina to Carlo, 27 August, AST, M45, fasc. 5, fol. 2138cv, no year but most probably from 1590. For another example of her saying that the baby kissed his hand, see Catalina to Carlo, 15 October [1590], AST, M37, fasc. 9, fol. 627; Altadonna, II:72.

50. Catalina to Carlo, 4 September 1590, AST, M37, fasc. 8, fol. 570; Altadonna, II:43; Catalina to Carlo, 18 and 28 October 1590, AST, M37, fasc. 9, fol. 630, 641; Altadonna, II:74–5, 83.

51. Carlo to Catalina, 6 January 1591, AST, M16, fasc. 5, fol. 909; also Carlo to Catalina, 16 January 1591, AST, M16, fasc. 5, fol. 917v.

52. Catalina to Carlo, 19 February 1591, AST, M35, fasc. 5, fol. 89. The archive dates this letter 1589, but internal evidence indicates 1591; Catalina to Carlo, 6 January 1593, AST, M41, fasc. 1, fol. 297v; Altadonna, III:89.

53. AST, Gioie e Mobili, M1, no. 6, fol. 38v.

54. "Relacion de la forma en que parece se pueden partir las joyas entre sus Altezas por la tasación que está hecha," 11 June 1585, IVDJ, ENV 35, C 48, no. 28. For a discussion of these portraits and the marten in the culture of pregnancy, see Carlos Varona, *Nacer en palacio*, 51–5.

55. Carlos Varona, "Representar el nacimiento," 233; Musacchio, *The Art and Ritual*, 136.

56. An anonymous observer reported to Philip II that the duke went out of his way to please and give presents to Catalina. See "De la llegada del duque de Saboya a Turín," 1585, AGS, Estado, L1260, no. 194.

57. Catalina to Carlo, 6 January 1593, AST, M41, fasc. 1, fol. 297v; Altadonna, III:89; Carlo to Catalina, 5 and 6 January 1593, AST, M19, fasc. 7, fol. 1518, 1519.
58. Catalina to Carlo, 16 April [1589], AST, M35, fasc. 7, fol. 147v–147a; Altadonna, I:144–5; Catalina to Carlo, 7 March 1591, AST, M38, fasc. 3, fol. 723; Altadonna, II:156.
59. Catalina to Carlo, 9 January 1591, AST, M38, fasc. 1, fol. 633.
60. Carlo to Catalina, February 1591, AST, M20, fasc. 1, fol. 1671v.
61. Catalina to Carlo, 16 March 1591, AST, M38, fasc. 3, fol. 728v; Altadonna, II:157.
62. For artistic evidence of men's presence in the birthing room, see Musacchio, *Art and Ritual*, 22–3; Carlos Varona, 'Representar el nacimiento," 232, 240n5 and Carlos Varona, *Nacer en palacio*, 95–8.
63. As María Cruz de Carlos Varona has argued, women cared deeply about who was in the birthing room and also about being attended by the same midwife in all the births. See *Nacer en palacio*, 100.
64. Catalina to Carlo, 24 April [1589], AST, M35, fasc. 7, fol. 158av; Altadonna, I:158; Carlo to Catalina, 31 March 1589, AST, M13, fasc. 2, fol. 298av; Carlo to Catalina, April 1589, AST, M13, fasc. 3, fol. 319.
65. Catalina's half-brother Philip III (r. 1598–1621) was present at the birth of all his children, and Philip II was present at least at some and possibly at all the births of his children. See Carlos Varona, *Nacer en palacio*, 96–7.
66. Parker, *Felipe II*, 451. See the French ambassador's account in Douais, *Dépêches de M. de Fourquevaux*, 111. For Catherine de' Medici's advice to her daughter, see Broomhall, "Women's Little Secret," 6–7, 8–14.
67. Catalina to Carlo, 10 August, AST, M45, fasc. 4, fol. 2076c, no year given but from internal evidence I would date it to 1589.
68. Catalina to Carlo, 3 May [1589], AST, M35, fasc. 8, fol. 169v; Altadonna, I:162.
69. For drafts of Philip II thanking Doña Sancha for her letters, see AGS, Estado, L1261, no. 14 (1586); AGS, Estado, L1262, no. 169 (27 May 1587); AGS, Estado, L1265, no. 182 (23 May 1589) and 186 (6 February 1590); AGS, Estado, L1937, no. 106 (2 August 1592).
70. Carlo to Catalina, probably 1 May 1589, AST, M13, fasc. 4, fol. 325a.
71. Carlos Varona, "Entre el riesgo," 274.
72. As Juan de Idiáquez wrote to Baron Paolo Sfondrato, "During the days after childbirth . . . it is appropriate that women serve Her Highness." See his letter of 8 April 1586, AGS, Estado, L1261, no. 138.
73. On Catalina's correspondence with governors, see Raviola, "La imagen de la infanta," 1733–48.
74. Catalina to Carlo, 9 April [1589], AST, M35, fasc. 7, fol. 134cv; Altadonna, I:136; Catalina to Carlo, 7 March 1591, AST, M38, fasc. 3, fol. 723; Altadonna, II:155.
75. Catalina to Carlo, 30 April 1589, AST, M35, fasc. 7, fol. 166r–av. This letter was written by a secretary.
76. Catalina to Carlo, 4 May [1589], 9 May 1589, 11 May [1589], AST, M35, fasc. 8, fols. 171r–av, 178v, 183bv; Altadonna, I:163–4, 166–8, 172.
77. Carlo to Catalina, 19 and 22 May 1589, AST, M13, fasc. 4, fols. 348r–v, 349a.
78. In April 1589, he was fighting a coalition of forces in Geneva. See Castronovo, "Carlo Emanuele I."

79. Carlo to Catalina, 26 March 1591, AST, M16, fasc. 7, fol. 998r.

80. Catalina to Carlo, 18 March 1591 and 31 March [1591], AST, M38, fasc. 3, fol. 731v, 745v; Altadonna, II:158, 168.

81. Rublack, "Pregnancy," 85. For confinement in early modern Europe, see Harris, *English Aristocratic Women*, 104–7; Davis, *Society and Culture*, 145; Wilson, *The Making of Man-Midwifery*, 26–30; Cressy, *Birth, Marriage, and Death*, 82–7.

82. Catalina to Carlo, 5 May [1589], AST, M35, fasc. 4, fol. 173r; Catalina to Carlo, 10 May 1589, AST, M35, fasc. 4, fol. 181v; Catalina to Carlo, 12 May 1589, AST, M35, fasc. 4, fol. 186v–186ar; Catalina to Carlo, 17 May [1589], AST, M35, fasc. 4, fol. 194r; Altadonna, I:164, 169, 172–3, 177.

83. Catalina to Carlo, 13 May 1589, AST, M35, fasc. 8, fol. 188av; Altadonna, I:174; Catalina to Carlo, 25 March [1591], AST, M38, fasc. 3, fol. 743; Altadonna, II:166.

84. The Venetian ambassador reported that Catalina went out publicly to hear mass at San Giovanni on 1 May 1586; her son had been born on 3 April. See Giovanni Mocenigo to Pasquale Ciconi, 8 May 1586, ASV, SDSa, filza 8, fol. 72. Don Jusepe reported that twenty-two days after giving birth in April 1588, Catalina went out in public for the first time. See Jusepe de Acuña to Philip II, 24 May 1588, AGS, Estado, L1264, no. 136. After giving birth in April 1589, she went to mass publicly on 21 May 1589. See Catalina to Carlo, 21 May [1589], AST, M35, fasc. 8, fol. 200r; Altadonna, I:179. The period of confinement for Spanish queens was usually forty days, but it varied depending on the queen and the time she needed to recuperate. Confinement for Spanish queens ended with a mass of purification. See Carlos Varona, *Nacer en palacio*, 105–6. Catalina's confinements were shorter, probably because she needed to return to her official duties.

85. Catalina to Carlo, 21 May [1589], AST, M35, fasc. 8, fol. 200r; Altadonna, I:179.

86. See Castiglione, "Peasants at the Palace," 81; Fildes, *Breasts*, 98–102.

87. Douais, *Dépêches de M. de Fourquevaux*, 113.

88. Catalina to Carlo, 1 and 3 May [1589], AST, M35, fasc. 8, fol. 167, 169r; Altadonna, I:161, 162.

89. Catalina to Carlo, 16 and 22 March 1591, AST, M38, fasc. 3, fols. 728v, 741v; Altadonna, II:156–7, 160.

90. Catalina to Carlo, 14 July 1589, AST, M36, fasc. 1, fol. 264r; Altadonna, I:237. On ways to induce menstrual bleeding, see Paré, *On the Generation of Man*, 948; Carbón, *Libro del arte*, 93.

91. Crawford, *Blood, Bodies*, 26.

92. Catalina to Carlo, 22 July, AST, M45, fasc. 4, fol. 2079a, no year given but from internal evidence I would date it to 1589. For the second bleeding, see Catalina to Carlo, 16 July 1589, AST, M36, fasc. 1, fol. 268v–268ar; Altadonna, I:239–40.

93. Carlo to Catalina, 18 July 1589, AST, M13, fasc. 6, fol. 401.

94. Ana of Dietrichstein to Margarita de Cardona, 25 March 1575 and 16 September 1575, in Dietrichstein, *Cartas*, 65, 73. The countess of Alba used the term in her letters to Catherine de' Medici about Elisabeth of Valois. See Duchess of Alba to Catherine de' Medici, 26 December, no year given but probably from 1567, in Morel-Fatio, "La duchesse d'Albe," 372.

95. Bynum, *Wonderful Blood*, 18. The association of menstruation with purgation was more general; Sebastián de Covarrubias listed *el menstruo* (menstruation) as one definition of *purgación* (purgation). Covarrubias, *Tesoro de la lengua*, 889.

96. Catalina to Carlo, 20 December 1595, AST, M43, fasc. 8, fol. 1842v–1842a; Altadonna, III:277. For other examples, see Catalina to Carlo, 17 July 1597, AST, M44, fasc. 7, fol. 1924r; Altadonna, III:306. Catalina to Carlo, 21 July 1597, AST, M44, fasc. 7, fol. 1931b; Altadonna, III:309–10.

97. Covarrubias, *Tesoro de la lengua*, 278.

98. For alternate names for menstruation, see Read, *Menstruation and the Female Body*, 24–34.

99. Her correspondence with Carlo gives some information about seven of her ten pregnancies. We have far less information about her first three pregnancies, though she did comment briefly about them in letters to Philip II.

100. Cristóbal de Briceño to Mateo Vázquez on 20 October 1586, ENV 5, T III, no. 258; Catalina to Carlo, 28 October 1597, AST, M44, fasc. 10, fol. 2014cv; Altadonna, III:359.

101. Catalina to Carlo, 17 July [1596], AST, M44, fasc. 3, fol. 1887r; Altadonna, III:290.

102. Catalina to Carlo, 4 March [1589], AST, M35, fasc. 6, fol. 91r; Altadonna, I:92.

103. Catalina to Carlo, 14 October 1597, AST, M44, fasc. 10, fol. 2002v; Altadonna, III:349–50. Catalina was probably referring to a sedan chair, which was integrated into princely culture in the second half of the sixteenth century. See López Alvarez, "Some Reflections," 309–10.

104. Catalina to Carlo, 2 April 1589, AST, M35, fasc. 7, fol. 128a; Altadonna, I:129.

105. Catalina to Carlo, 26 April 1589, AST, M35, fasc. 7, fol. 159r; Altadonna, I:159.

106. Catalina to Carlo, 9 and 22 March 1589, AST, M35, fasc. 6, fol. 96bv, 116r; Altadonna, I:99, 122.

107. Catalina to Carlo, 15 April 1589, AST, M35, fasc. 7, fol. 143c; Altadonna, I:152.

108. Catalina to Carlo, 29 January 1590, AST, M37, fasc. 3, fol. 539v; Altadonna, II:29. The letter is clearly dated 1590, but Catalina was not pregnant in January 1590. I think she misdated the letter and it is actually from January 1591, when she was pregnant.

109. Catalina to Carlo, 20 January [1591], AST, M35, fasc. 5, fol. 87; Altadonna, II:136.

110. Catalina to Carlo, 6 February [1591], AST, M35, fasc. 5, fol. 88; Altadonna, II:141.

111. "Relazione della malattia e morte dell'infanta donna Catalina d'Austria duchessa di Savoia," ASC, Bel., cart. 54, fasc. iv, doc. 281, fol. 281r.

112. Catalina to Carlo, 22 March 1589, AST, M35, fasc. 6, fol. 116r; Altadonna, I:122.

113. Catalina to Carlo, 27 February, AST, M45, fasc. 3, fol. 2051, no year given but must be from 1591.

114. During the same pregnancy, she reported that she was not perspiring as she had in other pregnancies. See Catalina to Carlo, 25 February [1591], AST, M38, fasc. 2, fol. 718; Altadonna, II:151.

115. Catalina to Carlo, 10 October 1590, AST, M45, fasc. 3, fol. 2036v.

116. Catalina to Carlo, 5 April 1589, AST, M35, fasc. 7, fol. 131v; Altadonna, I:133; Catalina to Carlo, 3 May [1589], AST, M35, fasc. 8, fol. 169a; Altadonna, I:162.

117. Catalina to Carlo, 28 May 1589, AST, M35, fasc. 8, fol. 208b; Altadonna, I:188–9.

118. Catalina to Carlo, 26 July 1589, AST, M36, fasc. 1, fol. 280b; Altadonna, I:246. For Philip II's letter, see Philip II to Catalina, 4 September 1589, in Bouza, *Cartas*, 166.

119. Catalina to Carlo, 5 August [1589], AST, M36, fasc. 2, fol. 294bv; Altadonna, I:257.
120. Carlo to Catalina, 5 August 1589, AST, M13, fasc. 7, fol. 427v; Catalina to Carlo, 8 August [1589], AST, M36, fasc. 2, fol. 299v; Altadonna, I:260.
121. Carlo to Catalina, 5 August 1589, AST, M13, fasc. 7, fol. 427a–av; Catalina to Carlo, 8 August [1589], AST, M36, fasc. 2, fol. 299av; Altadonna, I:261.
122. On women's perception of aging, see Beam, "'Should I as Yet Call You Old?'," 95–116.
123. Catalina to Carlo, 3 April [1592], AST, M38, fasc. 4, fol. 750; Altadonna, III:51–2; Catalina to Philip II, 13 March 1596, BL, Add. MSS 28419, fol. 166v.
124. Catalina to Carlo, 14, 17, 21 July 1597, AST, M44, fasc. 7, fol. 1917c, 1924r, 1931b; Altadonna, III:304–5, 306, 309–10.

CHAPTER 8

1. Filippo Emanuele signed his letters Emanuele, suggesting that he was called by his middle rather than his first name. Perhaps for that reason the third son, Emanuele Filiberto, went by his middle name. On these children, see Morales, Santarelli, and Varallo, *Il Cardinale*; Geevers, "Dynasty and State," 267–91; Antolín Rejón, "Diplomacia, familia y lealtades," 5–19 (and *passim*); Raviola, "The Three Lives," 59–76; Raviola, "'En el real serbicio de vuestra majestad'," 242–59; Raviola, "Le infante di Savoia," 471–502; Río Barredo, "El viaje de los príncipes de Saboya," 407–34.
2. The architect Juvarra designed the façade in the seventeenth century, long after Catalina's death. During her lifetime, the building looked like what is now the rear side of Palazzo Madama. On the gallery, see Varallo and Vivarelli, *La Grande Galleria*; Visconti, "La Grande Galleria," 53–63; Tosino, "La Grande Galleria," 65–73.
3. See Catalina to Carlo, 2 April 1589, AST, M35, fasc. 7, fol. 128a; Altadonna, I:129. For too lazy, see Catalina to Carlo, 25 April 1591, AST, M38, fasc. 4, fol. 761d; Altadonna, II:176. For the size of the gallery, see Mamino, "Reimagining the Grande Galleria," 293.
4. On 12 October 1588, she told Carlo that the children had not yet been to see her because it was morning. This would suggest that their visits were usually in the afternoon. Catalina to Carlo, AST, M35, fasc. 1, fol. 28; Altadonna, I:34.
5. Catalina to Carlo, 12 October [1588], AST, M35, fasc. 1, fol. 28; Altadonna, 1:34; Catalina to Carlo, 4 January 1590, AST, M37, fasc. 3, fol. 522; Altadonna, II:10.
6. Catalina to Carlo, 9 March 1589, AST, M35, fasc. 6, fol. 96av; Altadonna, I:98; Catalina to Carlo, 7 November 1592, AST, M40, fasc. 11, fol. 1159a; Altadonna, III:68.
7. Catalina to Carlo, 5 and 13 April 1589, AST, M35, fasc. 7, fols. 131av, 144cv; Altadonna, I:133, 144.
8. Catalina to Carlo, 18 January 1592, AST, M40, fasc. 1, fol. 1055v; Altadonna, III:10. Catalina said "*principes*," but it is unclear if she meant all three sons; Carlo to Catalina, 5 January 1592, AST, M18, fasc. 1, fol. 1208av.
9. For examples of Catalina's use of "*nuestra gente*," see Catalina to Carlo, 13 July 1589, AST, M36, fasc. 1, fol. 262; Altadonna, I:237. Catalina to Carlo, 30 September [1592], AST, M40, fasc. 9, fol. 1135a; Altadonna, III:56. Catalina to Carlo, 2 May [1593], AST, M41, fasc. 3, fol. 1303v; Altadonna, III: 91. Catalina to Carlo, 17 July 1597, AST, M44, fasc. 7, fol. 1924r; Altadonna, III:306.

10. Catalina to Carlo, 28 September 1590, AST, M37, fasc. 8, fol. 601; Altadonna II:53; Carlo to Catalina, 5 September 1590, AST, M15, fasc. 4, fol. 716a.
11. Catalina to Carlo, 24 September, AST, M45, fasc. 3, fol. 2048d, no year given but might be from 1589.
12. Catalina to Carlo, 13 May 1589, AST, M35, fasc. 8, fol. 188av; Altadonna, I:174.
13. Catalina to Carlo, 14 October [1589], AST, M36, fasc. 4, fol. 382a; Altadonna, I:317.
14. Catalina to Carlo, 13 December 1595, AST, M43, fasc. 8, fol. 1833v; Altadonna, III:275.
15. Catalina to Carlo, 28 October 1588, AST, M36, fasc. 4, fol. 50v; Altadonna, 1:59.
16. Catalina to Carlo, 2 October 1597, AST, M44, fasc. 10, fol. 1992av; Altadonna, III:344.
17. Catalina to Carlo, 27 June [1589], AST, M35, fasc. 9, fol. 242bv; Altadonna, I:219.
18. Catalina to Carlo, 17 May [1589], AST, M35, fasc. 8, fol. 194a; Altadonna, I:178.
19. Catalina to Carlo, 27 June [1589], AST, M35, fasc. 9, fol. 242bv; Altadonna, I:218–19; Carlo to Catalina, 3 July 1590, AST, 15, fasc. 3, fol. 690r–v. For another example of Catalina saying the children would amuse Carlo, see Catalina to Carlo, 31 March 1592, AST, M38, fasc. 3, fol. 746v; Altadonna, III:49.
20. Catalina to Carlo, 17 October 1588, AST, M35, fasc. 1, fol. 35a; Altadonna, I:42.
21. Don Jusepe described the eldest son as mischievous but said that everyone enjoyed seeing him. Jusepe de Acuña to Philip II, 24 May 1588, AGS, Estado, L264, no. 136.
22. Catalina to Carlo, 14 July 1589, AST, M36, fasc. 1, fol. 264a; Altadonna, I:238.
23. Catalina to Carlo, 27 September 1591, AST, M39, fasc. 3, fol. 871bv; Altadonna, II:266.
24. Catalina to Carlo, 22 February 1592, AST, M40, fasc. 2, fol. 1078; Altadonna, III:29. During Carnival in 1591, Catalina told Carlo that their eldest son "*haze los matachines.*" See Catalina to Carlo, 23 February, AST, M45, fasc. 3, fol. 2051. For definition of *matachines,* see *Diccionario de la lengua española*, RAE. *Matachines* were also connected to the commedia dell'Arte. Covarrubias, *Tesoro de la lengua*, 793.
25. Catalina to Carlo, 1 May [1593], AST, M41, fasc. 3, fol. 1299r; Altadonna, III:90.
26. Catalina to Carlo, 28 May 1589, AST, M35, fasc. 8, fol. 208b; Altadonna, I:189.
27. Catalina to Carlo, 26 September [1589], AST, M36, fasc. 3, fol. 395b; Altadonna, I:304. In December she noted that she thought Margarita would talk before he did. See Catalina to Carlo, 26 December 1589, AST, M36, fasc. 6, fol. 474e; Altadonna, I:396.
28. Catalina to Carlo, 14 January 1590, AST, M37, fasc. 3, fol. 529; Altadonna, II:18.
29. Catalina to Carlo, 1 January 1590, AST, M37, fasc. 3, fol. 520; Altadonna, II:7. For other reports about their dogs, see Catalina to Carlo: letter of 9 March 1589, AST, M35, fasc. 6, fol. 96bv; Altadonna, I:99; letter of 30 September 1590, AST, M37, fasc. 8, fol. 603; Altadonna, II:54–5; letter of 26 June 1595, AST, M43, fasc. 6, fol. 1807v; Altadonna, III:261.
30. For comments about weaning the children, see Catalina to Carlo, 20 September [1594], AST, M42, fasc. 2, fol. 1476a; Altadonna, III:142; Catalina to Carlo, 24 March 1595, AST, M43, fasc. 3, fol. 1727v; Altadonna, III:234; Catalina to Carlo, 7 September 1597, AST, M44, fasc. 9, fol. 1975b; Altadonna, III:335; Catalina to Carlo, 22 September, AST, M45, fasc. 5, fol. 2108b, no year given but from internal evidence I have dated it to 1597.

31. In November 1588, Catalina reported that she had written to the doctor, Lobeto, to have Vittorio's wet nurse changed. See Catalina to Carlo, 16 November [1588], AST, M35, fasc. 2, fol. 71a; Altadonna, I:81. In April 1589, Catalina told them that they had weaned Vittorio, and Carlo responded telling her to follow her own judgment because she knew best. See Carlo to Catalina, 14 April 1589, AST, M13, fasc. 3, fol. 308v.

32. Catalina to Carlo, 9 October [1588], AST, M35, fasc. 1, fol. 25a; Altadonna, I:30. For second letter, see 9 October 1588, AST, M35, fasc. 1, fol. 24v; Altadonna, I:31; Carlo to Catalina, 10 October 1588, AST, M12, fasc. 20, fol. 236b.

33. Catalina to Carlo, 29 August, AST, M45, fasc. 4, fol. 2091a, no year given but probably from 1590.

34. Catalina to Carlo, 1 January 1590, AST, M37, fasc. 3, fol. 520; Altadonna, II:6–7; Carlo to Catalina, 12 January 1590, AST, M15, fasc. 1, fol. 679v.

35. Catalina to Carlo, 14 January 1590, AST, M37, fasc. 3, fol. 529; Altadonna, II:18.

36. Catalina told him on 15 February 1591 that she had had Margarita's ears pierced. See Catalina to Carlo, AST, M40, fasc. 2, fol. 1074; Altadonna, II:151; Carlo to Catalina, 9 March 1591, AST, M16, fasc. 7, fol. 986a.

37. Catalina to Carlo, 7 March 1591, AST, M38, fasc. 3, fol. 723; Altadonna II:155.

38. Catalina to Carlo, 30 March 1596, AST, M44, fasc. 1, fol. 1869; Altadonna, III:279. Her first letter of 1596 is from 30 March, and the letters continue only until 5 April and then do not resume until 11 July. Thus, Catalina probably knew that she would be spending several months with Carlo.

39. Catalina to Carlo, 24 January 1595 and 25 January [1595], AST, M43, fasc. 1, fols. 1690, 1692; Altadonna III:219–21.

40. Catalina to Carlo, 10 January, AST, M45, fasc. 5, fol. 2105b, no year given but from internal evidence I would date to 1595. See also Catalina to Carlo, 15 January [1595], AST, M43, fasc. 1, fol. 1669cv; Altadonna, III:212.

41. Catalina to Carlo, 2 October 1588, AST, M35, fasc. 1, fol. 9v; Altadonna, I:16, 17.

42. Catalina to Carlo, 5 April 1589, AST, M35, fasc. 7, fol. 131av; Altadonna, I:133.

43. Catalina to Carlo, 3 April 1595, AST, M43, fasc. 4, fol. 1747v; Catalina to Carlo, 3 April 1596, AST, M44, fasc. 2, fol. 1874b; Altadonna, III:242, 283.

44. AGP, SAG, Cuentas del Tesorero de la Reina de los gastos. Nóminas de criados y criadas, pensiones y limosnas ocurridas en la casa de la Reina, Príncipe e Infanta. Años de 1576 a 1589, accounts from 18 April 1580; 19 October 1582; 11 August 1581; 9 October 1581. These donations were not necessarily made exactly on the birthday. See also, Hoffman, "Childhood and Royalty," 83–4.

45. Catalina to Carlo, 2 October 1594, AST, M42, fasc. 3, fol. 1517v; Altadonna, III:162; Catalina to Carlo, 24 March 1595, AST, M43, fasc. 1, fol. 1727v; Altadonna, III:234; Catalina to Carlo, 15 January 1592, AST, M40, fasc. 1, fol. 1054v; Altadonna, III:9.

46. Catalina to Carlo, 20 January [1591], AST, M35, fasc. 1, fol. 87; Altadonna II:137.

47. Catalina to Carlo, 15 January 1592, AST, M40, fasc. 1, fol. 1054v; Altadonna, III:9.

48. When she says "*comer*," I am assuming this is the afternoon meal. "*Cenar*" is the evening meal. For *merendar*, see Catalina to Carlo, 2 November 1588, AST, M35, fasc. 2, fol. 56a; Altadonna, I:65. For *conbidados*, see Catalina to Carlo, 5 January 1592, AST, M40, fasc. 12, fol. 1215; Altadonna, III:7; 21 May 1593, AST, M41, fasc. 3, fol. 1346a; Altadonna, III:106; Catalina to Carlo, 2 February 1595, AST, M43, fasc. 2, fol. 1697a; Altadonna, III:222–3.

49. Catalina to Carlo, 30 March 1596, AST, M44, fasc. 1, fol. 1869; Altadonna, III:279; Catalina to Carlo, 17 May [1589], AST, M35, fasc. 8, fol. 194a; Altadonna, I:178. Catalina wrote porcelain but she might have meant another kind of ceramic. Covarrubias explains that ceramic from Pozzuoli, Italy was also commonly called porcelain. See Covarrubias, *Tesoro de la lengua*, 877.

50. Catalina to Carlo, 24 June 1589 and 27 June [1589], AST, M35, fasc. 9, fol. 241dv, 242b; Altadonna, I:216, 218–19. The duke responded that he was glad that the prince had lit the bonfire. See Carlo to Catalina, late June 1589, AST, M13, fasc. 5, fol. 379v.

51. Varallo, "Catalina Micaela en la corte en Saboya," 69.

52. Accounts of Isidro de Robles, Treasurer, ASRT, Entries from 1594 to 96, fol. 31r (entry 92) and fol. 31v (entry 96).

53. Catalina to Carlo, 10 October [1588], AST, M35, fasc. 1, fol. 26a; Altadonna, I:32; Catalina to Carlo, 8 January [1589], AST, M35, fasc. 5, fol. 86ar; Altadonna, I:90; Catalina to Carlo, 10 December 1589, AST, M36, fasc. 6, fol. 466g; Altadonna, I:375; Catalina to Carlo, 1 January 1590, AST, M37, fasc. 3, fol. 520; Altadonna II:6; Carlo to Catalina, 7 January 1589, AST, M13, fasc. 1, fol. 276a.

54. Catalina to Carlo, 31 March 1592, AST, M38, fasc. 3, fol. 746v; Altadonna, III:49.

55. Catalina to Carlo, 26 April 1589, AST, M35, fasc. 7, fol. 159b; Altadonna, I:160; Catalina to Carlo, 12 August 1593, AST, M41, fasc. 6, fol. 1432a; Altadonna, III:131. For another example, see Catalina to Carlo, 6 October 1597, AST, M44, fasc. 10, fol. 1996b; Altadonna, III:346.

56. For María: Catalina to Carlo, 13 December 1595, AST, M43, fasc. 8, fol. 1833v; Altadonna, III:275. For Tommaso: Catalina to Carlo, 7 September 1597, AST, M44, fasc. 9, fol. 1975b; Altadonna, III:335.

57. Catalina to Carlo, 4 October, AST, M45, fasc. 6, fol. 2164r, no year given but probably from 1590. For other examples, see Catalina to Carlo, 4 October [1588], AST, M35, fasc. 1, fol. 16r; 4 October [1594], AST, M42, fasc. 3, fol. 1524r; Altadonna, I:22; III:166.

58. Catalina to Carlo, 4 May [1589], AST, M35, fasc. 8, fol. 171av; Altadonna, I:164. The prince wore *zaragüelles* again in July 1589. The *Diccionario de la lengua española*, RAE, defines *zaragüelles* as "*calzónes anchos.*" On European interest in Turkish fashion, see Jirousek and Catterall, *Ottoman Dress and Design*, 97–105.

59. Sending Philip II a *librillo* with small portraits of his four children, Carlo commented that he preferred these portraits to the larger ones because they were more true-to-life—*naturales*. In fact, he had earlier criticized the portraits, saying that Filiberto was prettier than he appeared and that El Flamenco had made Filippo's mouth too harsh. See Carlo to Philip II, 4 June 1589, AGS, Estado, L1263, no. 181. See also Carlo to Catalina, 31 March 1589, AST, M13, fasc. 2, fol. 298r.

60. Catalina to Carlo, 24 June 1589, AST, M35, fasc. 9, fol. 241e; Altadonna, I:217. See also Catalina to Carlo, 23 August 1589, AST, M36, fasc. 2, fol. 381av; Altadonna, I:275.

61. Catalina to Carlo, 24 June 1589, AST, M35, fasc. 9, fol. 241e; Altadonna, I:217.

62. Catalina to Carlo, 23 August 1589, AST, M36, fasc. 2; fol. 318a; Altadonna, I:275. On the occasion that Catalina noted, she and the children must have gone to the bastion and from there hunted on palace grounds, or more probably the surrounding countryside. This belvedere on the bastion, renovated in the seventeenth century, survives today. See Cuneo, "Gli anni spagnoli," 148. See also https://www.museotorino.it/view/s/12b2f409db40425fbe67a310b73418ef.

63. Catalina to Carlo, 6 August 1589, AST, M36, fasc. 2, fol. 295av; Altadonna, I:258.
64. Catalina to Carlo, 16 July, AST, M45, fasc. 5, fol. 2104v, no year given but from internal evidence I have dated it to 1596.
65. Catalina to Carlo, 17 July [1596], AST, M44, fasc. 3, fol. 1887r; Altadonna, III:290.
66. Catalina to Carlo, 15 July [1596], AST, M44, fasc. 7, fol. 1919v; Altadonna, III:287.
67. Catalina to Carlo, 25 September 1597, AST, M44, fasc. 9, fol. 1987r; Altadonna, III:340.
68. Catalina to Carlo, 16 May 1593, AST, M41, fol. 1334c.
69. Catalina to Carlo, 3 October [1588], AST, M35, fasc. 1, fol. 13av; Altadonna, I:21; Catalina to Carlo, 29 September [1588], AST, M35, fasc. 1, fol. 2 bis b; Altadonna, I:9.
70. Catalina to Carlo, 22 April [1589], AST, M35, fasc. 7, fol. 155b; Altadonna I:157. She was also referring to Vittorio when she mentions a *"profeta"* in her letters from March 1589 and May 1589. See Catalina to Carlo, 16 March [1589], AST, M35, fasc. 6, fol. 105a; 21 March [1589], AST, M35, fasc. 6, fol. 112a; 4 May [1589], AST, M35, fasc. 8, fol. 171av; Altadonna, I:108, 119, 164. The duke responded on 28 March 1589. See Carlo to Catalina, AST, M12, fasc. 20, fol. 234ar.
71. Catalina to Carlo, 24 May 1589, AST, M35, fasc. 8, fol. 205v; Altadonna, I:183. See also Carlo to Catalina, 29 (?) June 1589, AST, M13, fasc. 5, fol. 376v.
72. Catalina to Carlo, 1 September [1589], AST, M36, fasc. 3, fol. 328av; Altadonna, I:282; Catalina to Carlo, 28 May 1589, AST, M35, fasc. 8, fol. 208bv; Altadonna, I:189; Catalina to Carlo, 1 November 1592, AST, M40, fasc. 11, fol. 1146v; Altadonna, III:62; Catalina to Carlo, 16 July 1596, AST, M44, fasc. 3, fol. 1885; Altadonna, III:289; Catalina to Carlo, 17 July 1597, AST, M44, fasc. 3, fol. 1924r; Altadonna, III:306.
73. Catalina to Carlo, 16 March [1589], AST, M35, fasc. 6, fol. 105c; Altadonna, I:110; Catalina to Carlo, 18 April 1589, AST, M37, fasc. 5, fol. 542; Altadonna, II:171; Catalina to Carlo, 2 September 1591, AST, M39, fasc. 3, fol. 847c; Altadonna, II:247.
74. Catalina to Carlo, 22 February 1592, AST, M40, fasc. 2, fol. 1078; Altadonna, III:29; Catalina to Carlo, 11 March 1592, AST, M40, fasc. 3, fol. 1091cv; Altadonna, III:43.
75. Filippo Emanuele to Catalina, 1592, AST, LPDS, M1, fol. 33; Filippo Emanuele to Carlo, 1593, AST, LPDS, M1, fol. 37; Filippo Emanuele to Carlo, 1592, AST, LPDS, M1, fol. 36. Of ten extant letters Filippo wrote to Carlo before Catalina's death, one was in Spanish, two in French, and seven in Italian. His letters written after Catalina's death are primarily in Italian, with a few in French.
76. Filippo Emanuele to Carlo, 1593, AST, LPDS, M1, fol. 38.
77. For letters of Catalina and Carlo's other children, almost all written after Catalina's death, see AST, LPDS, M2–M18. For a brief discussion of part of this correspondence, see Antolín Rejón, "Diplomacia, familia y lealtades," 19–21.
78. Catalina to Carlo, 11 November 1589, AST, M36, fasc. 5, fol. 417d; Altadonna, I:342; Catalina to Carlo, 22 November, AST, M45, fasc. 3, fol. 2059a, no year.
79. Catalina to Carlo, 9 May 1589, 12 May 1589, 21 May [1589], AST, M35, fasc. 8, fol. 180–180v, 186a, 201a; Altadonna, I:169, 173, 181; Catalina to Carlo, 21 March 1591, AST, M38, fasc. 3, fol. 734; Altadonna, II:160.

80. Catalina to Carlo, 11 June 1589, AST, M35, fasc. 9, fol. 225av; Altadonna, I:203; Catalina to Carlo, 14 July 1589, AST, M36, fasc. 1, fol. 264a; Altadonna, I:238.

81. Pedro de León became bishop of Fossano in 1602. On Pedro de León, see Río Barredo, "De Madrid a Turín," 15.

82. Catalina to Carlo, 30 March 1596, AST, M44, fasc. 1, fol. 1869; Altadonna, III:279.

83. Catalina to Carlo, 9 August 1597, AST, M44, fasc. 8, fol. 1949bv; Altadonna, III:320. Catalina also made no mention of the children learning to dance, which was an important part of an aristocratic upbringing.

84. We should remember, though, that this was the first time that Catalina gave birth without the duke by her side, so while we have letters to document Catalina's and Carlo's reactions to Margarita's birth, we lack similar documentation for the birth of their first three sons.

85. Catalina to Carlo, 29 April [1589], AST, M35, fasc. 7, fol. 164; Altadonna, I:160; Carlo to Catalina, 1 May 1589, AST, M13, fasc. 4, fol. 325r–325a; Catalina to Carlo, 24 May 1589, AST, M35, fasc. 8, fol. 205v; Altadonna, I:183.

86. Catalina to Carlo, 24 May 1589, AST, M35, fasc. 8, fol. 205v; Altadonna, I:183; Catalina to Carlo, 26 July 1589, AST, M36, fasc. 1, fol. 280b; Altadonna, I:246; Catalina to Carlo, 13 August 1589; AST, M36, fasc. 2, fol. 303d; Altadonna, I:264; Catalina to Carlo, 25 March [1591], AST, M38, fasc. 3, fol. 743; Altadonna, II:166.

87. Carlo to Catalina, 23 April 1589, AST, M13, fasc. 3, fol. 317; Catalina to Carlo, 26 April 1589, AST, M35, fasc. 7, fol. 159r; Altadonna, I:159.

88. Carlo to Catalina, late April/early May 1589, AST, M34, fasc. 23, fol. 4983.

89. Carlo to Catalina, undated letter, AST, M34, fasc. 23, fol. 4983. See Hoffman, Raised to Rule, 7–9 on godparenting at the Spanish court of Philip III.

90. Carlo to Catalina, 1 May 1589, AST, M13, fasc. 4, fol. 325a; Giovanni Mocenigo, report from 15 March 1586, ASV, SDSa, filze 8, no. 64.

91. Carlo to Catalina, AST, M34, fasc. 23, fol. 4983, no date given but must be late April 1589 or early May at the latest; Catalina to Carlo, 1 May [1589], AST, M35, fasc. 8, fol. 167; Altadonna, I:161. See also Catalina to Philip II, 18 May 1589, AST, M35, fasc. 8, fol. 197. This is a copy of the letter she wrote to Philip.

92. Carlo to Philip II, 4 June 1589, AGS, Estado, L1263, no. 181.

93. Carlo to Catalina, 26 August 1589, AST, M13, fasc. 7, fol. 449; Catalina to Philip II, AGS, Estado, L1263, no. 193. The letter is also printed in Bouza, Cartas, 168n376; Catalina to Philip II, 29 December 1589, AST, M36, fasc. 6, fol. 480.

94. García Prieto, "Isabel Clara Eugenia of Austria," 139–45.

95. The count of Lodosa to Philip II, 4 June 1596, AGS, Estado, L1280, no. 157; the count of Lodosa to Philip II, 5 August 1596, AGS, Estado, L1280, no. 159; Río Barredo, "El viaje de los príncipes de Saboya," 7–8.

96. Catalina to Philip II, 8 July 1589, AST, M36, fol. 259av; Carlo to Philip II, 4 June 1589, AGS, Estado, L1263, no. 181; Catalina to Philip II, 26 December 1589, AST, M36, fasc. 6, fol. 475a.

97. Catalina to Philip II, AST, M45, fasc. 3, fol. 2029r, undated but most likely written in 1589; Philip II to Catalina, 6 July 1589, in Bouza, Cartas, 165; Catalina to Philip II, 26 December 1596, BL, Add. MSS 28419, fol. 241r.

98. Carlo to Catalina, no day or month, 1591, AST, M16, fasc. 11, fol. 1046dv.

99. Catalina to Carlo, 24 June 1591, AST, M38, fasc. 6, fol. 784fr–v; Altadonna, II:208.

100. Jusepe de Acuña to Philip II, 9 January 1595, AST, Estado, L1279, no. 6; Philip II to Catalina, 7 September 1596, in Bouza, *Cartas*, 199. For a discussion of the office of Prior of Castile and León, see Antolín Rejón, "Diplomacia, familia y lealtades," 122–42 and Bouza, *Cartas*, notes on 198–9. On Emanuele Filiberto, see Geevers, "Dynasty and State Building," 267–92. Filiberto was appointed prior in 1596 and naturalized as a Spaniard in 1597. See Geevers, "Dynasty and State Building," 277 and Antolín Rejón, "Diplomacia, familia y lealtades," 121–58.

101. Raviola, "The Three Lives," 61–2; Raviola, "Il filo di Anna," 333.

102. Daybell, *Women Letter-Writers*, 266. Letter-writing manuals suggested that letters begin with reports of the writer's health, but Catalina did not do this. On reporting illness in letters, see Thorpe, " 'I Haue Ben Crised and Besy'," 85–108.

103. Catalina to Carlo, 21 September, AST, M45, fasc. 4, fol. 2126v, no year given but I have dated it to 1590.

104. Catalina to Carlo, 27 August 1597, AST, M40, fasc. 8, fol. 1128br; Altadonna, III:331.

105. Catalina to Carlo, 20 October [1588], AST, M35, fasc. 1, fol. 38v; Altadonna, I:46. For other examples in Catalina's letters to Carlo, see 9 April [1589], AST, M35, fasc. 7, fol. 134e; 13 May 1589, AST, M35, fasc. 8, fol. 188av; 25 September 1589, AST, M36, fasc. 3, fol. 355b; Altadonna, I:137, 174, 303.

106. Catalina to Carlo, 19 October [1589], AST, M36, fasc. 4, fol. 393; Altadonna, I:321.

107. Catalina to Carlo, 16 July 1589, AST, M36, fasc. 1, fol. 268b; Altadonna, I:240.

108. Almudena Pérez de Tudela argues that at this time Filippo was learning to walk. However, as early as October 1588, Catalina reported that two-and-a-half-year-old Filippo was walking fine. The weakness in his legs in March 1589 was a change related to illness. The prince had developed a fever from a cold. See also Catalina to Carlo, 3 March 1589, AST, M35, fasc. 6, fol. 90br; Altadonna I:91, where Catalina reports that "*el prinzipe esta algo mejor de sus piernas aunq[ue] a tosido un poco.*" It is unclear whether the fever preceded the weakness or vice versa, but they were related and had little to do with the prince learning to walk. See Pérez de Tudela Gabaldón, "Copies of the Holy Shroud," 324; Catalina to Carlo, 8 October 1588, AST, M35, fasc. 1, fol. 23av; Altadonna, I:29; Catalina to Carlo, 4 March [1589], AST, M35, fasc. 6, fol. 91a–av; Altadonna, I:93.

109. Catalina to Carlo, 13 March [1589], AST, M35, fasc. 6, fol. 99av; Altadonna, I:104.

110. Carlo to Catalina, 17 March 1589, AST, M13, fasc. 2, fol. 289av, where he says that he will keep it a secret; Carlo to Catalina, 11 March 1589, AST, M13, fasc. 2, fol. 282bv.

111. Catalina to Carlo, 2 June 1589, AST, M35, fasc. 9, fol. 210c; Altadonna, I:194.

112. Catalina to Carlo, 27 August, AST, M45, fasc. 5, fol. 2138v, no year.

113. See, for example, this exchange: Catalina to Carlo, 16 March [1589], AST, M35, fasc. 6, fol. 105v; Altadonna, I:108; Carlo to Catalina, 13 March 1589, AST, M13, fasc. 2, fol. 284av. He said: "I beg you always to write me the truth, which I know you do."

114. Catalina to Carlo, 22 October [1588], AST, M35, fasc. 1, fol. 42a; Altadonna, I:50; Catalina to Carlo, 28 April 1595, AST, M43, fasc. 4, fol. 1785r; Altadonna, III:256–7.

115. Catalina might have used rosehips, which are a gentle laxative. Gómez de Ortega, *Continuación de la flora española*, 208–9.

116. Catalina to Carlo, 18 March [1589], AST, M37, fasc. 4, fol. 540; Altadonna, I:113. In October 1589, she said that her children had a cold and were therefore going to be given rose honey. See Catalina to Carlo, 6 October, AST, M45, fasc. 5, fol. 2120b, no year given but I would date it to 1589.

117. Catalina to Carlo, 16 May 1589, AST, M35, fasc. 8, fol. 192v; Altadonna, II:177; Catalina to Carlo, 17 March 1589, AST, M35, fasc. 6, fol. 107c; Altadonna, I:111–12; Catalina to Carlo, 5 June 1589, AST, M35, fasc. 9, fol. 215v; Altadonna, I:196. For other examples of *miel rosada* being used to purge, see Catalina to Carlo, 5 April 1595, AST, M43, fasc. 4, fol. 1753v; Altadonna, III:246–7; Catalina to Carlo, 3 June, AST, M45, fasc. 4, fol. 2096a, no year given but probably 1589. Don Jusepe reported that Catalina had a cold and had been purged with 2 ounces of *miel rosada*. Because she was pregnant, doctors had been careful not to give her too much purgative. Jusepe de Acuña to Philip II, 5 and 7 May 1595, AGS, Estado, L1279, nos. 57 and 55.

118. Catalina to Carlo, 17 October 1589, AST, M36, fasc. 4, fol. 389c; Altadonna, I:321.

119. Catalina to Carlo, 30 September 1590, AST, M37, fasc. 8, fol. 603; Altadonna, II:54.

120. Carlo to Catalina, 3 October 1590, AST, M17, fasc. 3, fol. 1102av.

121. Catalina to Carlo, 27 August, AST, M45, fasc. 5, fol. 2138a, no year given.

122. Catalina to Carlo, 29 August, AST, M45, fasc. 4, fol. 2091a, no year given but probably from 1590.

123. Catalina to Carlo, 11 April [1589], AST, M35, fasc. 7, fol. 142; Altadonna, I:139. She often urged Carlo to let himself be purged, and while sometimes it was because he was not feeling well (on a few occasions because he was sweating excessively), at other times it was merely to remain healthy. See Catalina to Carlo, 10 October, AST, M45, fasc. 3, fol. 2036c, no date given but from internal evidence I would date it to 1590. See also Catalina to Carlo, 25 September, AST, M45, fasc. 4, fol. 2080b, probably from 1590; 30 August 1590, AST, M45, fasc. 4, fol. 2090b.

124. A good example of her purging are in her letters to Carlo, 26–28 September 1594, AST, M42, fasc. 2, fol. 1495–1502a; Altadonna, III:152–6. She noted that the first purging had caused her to evacuate ten times. She also received gifts, probably because of the purges.

125. Catalina to Carlo, 6 July 1593, AST, M41, fasc. 5, fol. 1379v; Catalina to Carlo, 16 December 1595, AST, M43, fasc. 8, fol. 1838r; Altadonna, III:114, 275.

126. Catalina to Carlo, 7 June 1589, AST, M35, fasc. 9, fol. 219d; Altadonna, I:200.

127. She mentions that this was her second letter of the day, but the first letter has not survived. See Catalina to Carlo, 21 August 1590, AST, M37, fasc. 7, fol. 548; Altadonna, II:35.

128. Carlo defended his departure, claiming that it was necessary for his honor, and could not believe that she was more concerned about his life than his honor. Carlo to Catalina, 21 August 15(90?), AST, M15, fasc. 3, fol. 691r.

129. Catalina to Carlo, 5 August, AST, M45, fol. 2113b, no year given but possibly from 1590; Carlo to Catalina, 15 August 1589, AST, M13, fasc. 7, fol. 445bis; emphases added by the author. He might have misdated this letter. He dated it 1589, but the topics he mentioned fit with topics Catalina raised in August 1590.

130. Carlo to Catalina, 24 August 1590, AST, M15, fasc. 3, fol. 635a.

131. Catalina to Carlo, 28 August, AST, M45, fasc. 4, fol. 2074br, no year given but probably from 1590.

132. Carlo to Catalina, 22 October 1590 or 1591, AST, M17, fasc. 3, fol. 1127v.

133. See her letter from February 1592 in which she discussed Leyni's comments with respect to having her sons join her in Nice. Catalina to Carlo, 2 February 1592, AST, M40, fasc. 2, fol. 1064d; Altadonna, III:16.

134. Catalina to Carlo, 2 February 1592, AST, M40, fasc. 2, fol. 1064d; Altadonna, III:16.

135. Perhaps Catalina subscribed to the Habsburg ethos as described by Sheila Ffolliott: "The Habsburgs had a clear sense of family, but keeping parents and children together was not an essential component." "Juana and her Peers," 168.

136. Catalina to Carlo, AST, M45, fasc. 3, fol. 2025, no date given but most probably from July 1590.

CHAPTER 9

1. Philip II to the *infantas*, 21 August 1581 and 2 October 1581, in Bouza, *Cartas*, 53, 56. For his relics, see Lazure, "Possessing the Sacred," 61.

2. For attendance at two Lenten sermons, see Catalina to Carlo, 17 March 1589, AST, M35, fasc. 6, fol. 107b; Altadonna, I:11.

3. Hilary Dansey Smith notes that sermons were usually given only on Sundays, holy days, and feast days, or during Lent, novenas, or retreats, and that Carlo Borromeo argued that sermons did not have to be preached in a church. See Smith, *Preaching in the Spanish Golden Age*, 10, 15.

4. See, for example, Catalina to Carlo, 1 April 1589, AST, M35, fasc. 7, fol. 125v; Altadonna, I:127.

5. For the inventory of her oratory, see AST, Corte, Gioie e Mobili, M1, no. 6, fol. 43r–46r.

6. Jusepe de Acuña to Philip II, 10 July 1588, AGS, Estado, L1263, no. 95.

7. For the *pasadizo* and the *tribuna*, see Roco de Campofrío, *España en Flandes*, 37. Don Jusepe also mentioned the *pasadizo* in his letter to Philip II, 10 July 1588, AGS, Estado, L1263, no. 95.

8. On this baptism, see Bucci, *Il solenne battesimo*, fol. 33v.

9. Elliott, "The Court of the Spanish Habsburgs," 154; Sánchez, "Privacy, Family, and Devotion," 374–5.

10. See Bucci, *Il solenne battesimo*, fol. 33v. Don Jusepe's description of the entrances suggests that Carlo and his servants went directly from the palace to the cathedral without going to the street. Jusepe de Acuña to Philip II, 10 July 1588, AGS, Estado, L1263, no. 95.

11. Bucci, *Il solenne battesimo*, fol. 33v. The Shroud was in the chapel of San Lorenzo when Carlo Borromeo, the famous archbishop of Milan, visited Turin in 1578. Borromeo did not think this tiny chapel appropriate for such an important relic because it could not accommodate even private exposition of the Shroud. On that occasion, the cloth had to be moved to the cathedral for Borromeo and his attendants to venerate it and out to the Piazza Castello for the public to do so as well. Evidence suggests that by the time Borromeo returned to Turin in 1582, the Shroud was kept in a chapel within the palace and that from that chapel it was moved to the cathedral in 1587. See Scott, *Architecture for the Shroud*, 63–75.

12. Cozzo, *La geografia celeste*, 67; Scott, *Architecture for the Shroud*, 66.

13. "Relatione degli apparati," 121–2.
14. She made all the arrangements when two-week-old Margarita was baptized on 14 May 1589, and in 1591 when Isabel was baptized two weeks after she was born. Although she asked the duke for his input about certain aspects of the baptism, she orchestrated the event and then had a report (*relación*) drawn up to send to the duke. See Catalina to Carlo, 4 May [1589], AST, M35, fasc. 8, fol. 171a–av; Altadonna, I:164. Catalina must have misdated this letter, because the baptism took place on 14 May 1589.
15. Catalina to Carlo, 6 February [1591], AST, M35, fasc. 5, fol. 88; Altadonna, II:142 and Catalina to Carlo, 23 February, AST, M45, fasc. 3, fol. 2051, no year given but from internal evidence I would date it to 1591.
16. In 1582, Paolo Sfondrato noted that Carlo had an oratory dedicated to St. Lorenzo in the palace. Sfondrato referred to an "*oratorio de San Lorenzo que está en su propia casa.*" It could be that Sfrondrato was referring to the garden chapel. The covered corridor may have been added after Catalina's time, but the ease of attending services at San Lorenzo suggests that the corridor already existed. Carlo's father, Emanuele Filiberto, had vowed to endow a church in St. Lorenzo's honor but did not have the financial resources to endow a new church so he rededicated the small chapel of Santa Maria del Presepe to the saint, and renamed and reno-vated the chapel. See Paolo Sfrondrato to Philip II, 3 August 1582, BL, Add. MSS 28418, fol. 45v; Scott, *Architecture for the Shroud*, 62–4. In a document in which he divided his household possessions among his children, Carlo mentioned relics housed in "the garden chapel of San Lorenzo." Quoted in Mamino, "Culto delle reliquie," 58. In the seventeenth century, after Carlo's death, a new church of San Lorenzo, designed by the architect Guarino Guarini, would be built on the square outside the palace. See Meek, *Guarino Guarini and his Architecture*; Daradanello, Klaiber, and Millon, *Guarino Guarini*.
17. Scott says that it was "within the complex of ducal palace and administrative buildings" and was open for "courtly devotion." Scott, *Architecture for the Shroud*, 63. On the church of San Lorenzo, see Klaiber, "The First Ducal Chapel," 329–43.
18. Pérez de Tudela Gabaldón, "Copies of the Holy Shroud," 314–15.
19. See the following from Catalina to Carlo: Undated letter, AST, M45, fasc. 4, fol. 2024a; letter of 10 August, AST, M45, fasc. 4, fol. 2076cr, no year given but I have dated it to 1589; letter of 19 March [1595], AST, M43, fasc. 3, fol. 1713r; Altadonna, III:227; letter of 31 March 1596, AST, M44, fasc. 1, fol. 1870v; Altadonna, III:280; letter of 5 April 1596, AST, M44, fasc. 2, fol. 1878v; Altadonna, III:286; letter of 11 August 1597, AST, M44, fasc. 8, fol. 1953bv; Altadonna, III:322.
20. The mass for his ninth birthday was in the cathedral, which would suggest that Catalina divided her devotions between the cathedral and the chapel. Catalina to Carlo, 23 March [1591], AST, M38, fasc. 5, fol. 769; Altadonna, II:164; Catalina to Carlo, 3 April 1596, AST, M44, fasc. 2, fol. 1874br; Altadonna, III:283.
21. Catalina to Carlo, 24 March 1589, AST, M35, fasc. 6, fol. 117av; Altadonna, I:124; 1 April 1589, AST, M35, fasc. 7, fol. 125; Altadonna, I:127.
22. Catalina to Carlo, 21 May [1589], AST, M35, fasc. 8, fol. 200r; Altadonna, I:179.
23. In the sanctuary of la Consolata in Turin, Catalina's portrait hung below a statue of St. Lorenzo, suggesting that her devotion to the saint was well-known. See Franchetti, *Storia della Consolata*, 218, and discussed in Cozzo, "Intus Mirabile Magis," 218–19n27.

24. AST, Corte, Gioie e Mobili, M1, no. 6, fol. 86v.
25. Catalina to Carlo, 19 March [1595], AST, M43, fasc. 3, fol. 1713r; Altadonna, III:227–8.
26. Cozzo, *La geografia celeste*, 55, 58.
27. See Banner, "Private Rooms," 89–93; Malo Barranco, "Los espacios de religiosidad," 175–93. For a detailed discussion of Queen Margarita de Austria's oratory in Madrid, see Carlos Varona, *Nacer en palacio*, 177–223.
28. On Spanish promotion of the Immaculate Conception, see Stratton, *The Immaculate Conception, passim*; Hernández, *Immaculate Conceptions*, 31–40.
29. AST, Corte, Gioie e Mobili, M1, no. 6.
30. Nalle, "Private Devotion," 255–72; Muller, "The Agnus Dei," 2. See AST, Corte, Gioie e Mobili, M1, no. 6, fol. 43v.
31. For Catalina's exotica, see Varallo, "Exotica e oggetti preziosi," 371–88; Albaladejo Martínez, "Lo exótico," 95–110. For the Habsburgs' collections of exotica, see Pérez de Tudela and Jordan, "Luxury Goods," 1–127.
32. Binaghi Olivari, "I ricami dell'infanta," 359–69.
33. ASRT, Real Casa, Camera dei Conti, Art. 224, Cartas de Pago, entries 3–5.
34. Kasl, "Delightful Adornments," 149.
35. Rodríguez G. de Ceballos, "Image and Counter-Reformation," 30.
36. Kasl, "Delightful Adornments," 149.
37. Malo Barranco, "Los espacios de religiosidad," 177–8.
38. "Libro donde se asientan sayas y vestidos y otras cosas de su alteza," ASRT, Camerale, Art. 384, n.p. This might have been the oratory only of her sons. The term used is *hijos*, which can be strictly sons but might also include her daughters.
39. Her first confessor, Fray Mateo de Sarabia, returned to Spain in 1587. Her second, Francisco del Villar, died in Turin in February 1589. Her third, Andrés Hernández, arrived in Turin in 1589 and remained her confessor until her death. Pedro de León became bishop of Fossano in 1602 and served until his death in 1606. See Cozzo, *La geografia celeste*, 222 and "Intus Mirabile Magis," 219n29. See also https://www.catholic-hierarchy.org/bishop/bleop.html.
40. In the 1570s her confessor was Melchor Sánchez de Yebra, who was also confessor in the Descalzas. From 1581 to 1584, her confessor was Buenaventura de Santibáñez and from 1584 to 1585, Andrés de la Iglesia. Martínez Hernández, "Enlightened Queen," 31.
41. Catalina to Carlo, 22 March [1595], AST, M43, fasc. 3, fol. 1724v; Altadonna, III:232.
42. Grendler, *The Universities of the Italian Renaissance*, 98.
43. In 21 March 1595, he told Catalina that he had heard a sermon and then complines given by Capuchins in Pinerolo. See Carlo to Catalina, AST, M21, fasc. 2, fol. 1936.
44. The Capuchins established a base in Barcelona in 1578 and the order spread slowly in the kingdom of Aragon. Resistance to the order persisted outside Aragon, and the Capuchins did not reach Madrid until the early seventeenth century. See Cuthbert, *The Capuchins*, I:212–14.
45. His mother ascribed his birth to the devotion she showed to Franciscans, and Carlo had great fervor for the Franciscans but even more so for the Capuchins. See Cozzo, *Un eremita*, 84–6; Cozzo, "Il clero," 370–1; Cuthbert, *The Capuchins*, II:274–5.
46. Catalina to Carlo, 28 March [1589], AST, M35, fasc. 6, fol. 122a; Altadonna, I:126.

47. Quoted in Mamino, "Culto delle reliquie," 66.

48. On the religious orders in Turin and Carlo's devotion to the mendicant orders, see Cozzo, "Il clero," 370–1. For her interactions with or patronage of Capuchins, see Catalina to Carlo, 13 April 1589, AST, M35, fasc. 7, fol. 144cv; letter of 11 May [1589], AST, M35, fasc. 8, fol. 183bv; Altadonna, I:144, 172. She noted that a Capuchin from Paris had stopped to see her on his way to Rome. Catalina to Carlo, 5 April 1595, AST, M43, fasc. 4, fol. 1752b; Altadonna, III:246. For donation, see ASRT, Real Casa, Camera dei Conti, Art. 224, Cuentas 1585–87, Limosnas del año 1586, n.p.

49. Catalina to Carlo, 10 October, AST, M45, fasc. 4, fol. 2077r–v, no year given.

50. ASRT, Real Casa, Camera dei Conti, Art. 224, Cuentas 1585–87, n.p.

51. On the Forty Hours Devotion, see Villiers, "A History of the 40 Hours Devotion;" Thurston, "Forty Hours Devotion." See also Norman, "Social History of Preaching," 161.

52. Thurston, "Forty Hours Devotion."

53. Cozzo, La geografia celeste, 168.

54. Pope Paul III (d. 1549) had issued an indulgence to those who took part in the practice to pray for peace and safety against the Turks. Pope Clement VIII issued the Constitution "Graves et diuturnae" on 25 November 1592 in response to the situation in France and provided some instructions for how the devotion should be done. https://www.newadvent.org/cathen/06151a.htm. See Carlo to Catalina, 17 March 1589, AST, M13, fasc. 2, fol. 289b.

55. On the canonization of St. Diego and Philip II's role in petitioning for his canonization, see Villalon, "San Diego de Alcalá," 691–715. On Prince Carlos, see Parker, Imprudent King, 179–91.

56. The sanctuary of Our Lady of the Angels in Cuneo has an altar dedicated to St. Diego de Alcalá. Built long after Catalina's death, the altar suggests that devotion to the Spanish saint continued in Savoy.

57. Catalina to Carlo, 9 June 1589, AST, M35, fasc. 9, fol. 223a; Altadonna, I:202.

58. The post-mortem inventory of her possessions lists an image of St. Diego that had a curtain to cover it. See AST, Corte, Gioie e Mobili, M1, no. 6, fol. 87r.

59. On St. Victor and the other Theban saints, see Baldesano, Historia sacra de la ilustrissima legion Tebea; Wattenberg García, "San Mauricio y la legión Tebana," 13–23. See also Mediavilla Martín and Rodríguez Díez, Las reliquías del real monasterio del Escorial, I:155n21. While the legion had 6,661 soldiers, only about 40 were considered saints.

60. Wattenberg García, "San Mauricio y la legión Tebana," 16.

61. Cruz Medina, "The Relicario of the Descalzas Reales," 313–14. See also Pérez de Tudela, "Los relicarios de la reina Ana de Austria."

62. García Sanz and Ruiz, "Linaje regio y monacal," 150; Cruz Medina, "The Relicario of the Descalzas Reales," 314.

63. Catalina to Carlo, 9 October [1588], AST, M35, fasc. 1, fol. 25a; Altadonna, I:30. Perhaps Habsburg women showed favor to their camareras by allowing them to serve as mediators for the transfer of religious objects. Empress María had Anna de Austria's camarera mayor present several relics to the abbess of the Descalzas. Cruz Medina, "The Relicario of the Descalzas Reales," 314.

64. Cozzo, La geografia celeste, 194n150.

65. Wattenberg García, El estandarte de San Mauricio, 13. On St. Mauricio and the Theban saints, see Bosco, "I santi Tebei nella Torino del primo seicento," 101–30.

66. Cruz Medina, "The Relicario of the Descalzas Reales," 313; Mediavilla Martín and Rodríguez Díez, *Las reliquías del real monasterio del Escorial*, I:186.

67. See, for example, the following letters from Catalina to Carlo: 3 October 1588, AST, M35, fasc. 1, fol. 11; Altadonna, I:20; letter of 16 February, AST, M45, fasc. 3, fol. 2052, no year given but probably 1591; letter of 22 July AST, M45, fasc. 4, fol. 2079dv, no year given but probably 1589.

68. Catalina to Carlo, 20 January [1591], AST, M35, fasc. 5, fol. 87; Altadonna, II:137.

69. Catalina to Carlo, 11 January 1591, AST, M38, fol. 698br; Altadonna, II:132; Wattenberg García, *El estandarte de San Mauricio*, 21–2.

70. She also described the reliquary for the sword, noting it had a *boina del santo*. See Catalina to Carlo, 20 January [1591], AST, M35, fasc. 5, fol. 87; Altadonna, II:137.

71. Catalina to Carlo, 20 January [1591], AST, M35, fasc. 5, fol. 87; Altadonna, II:137.

72. See the account in "L'Ordine che si è osservato nella traslatione del glorioso Corpo di Santo Mauritio nella Città di Torino," AST, Corte, Materie Ecclesiastiche, Reliquie, M1, n.p. On 11 January 1591, Catalina reported that she had the relics, so they must have gone from the palace to the cathedral. Catalina to Carlo, 20 January [1591], AST, M35, fasc. 5, fol. 87; Altadonna, II:136–7.

73. Catalina to Carlo, 21 September [1591], AST, M39, fasc. 3, fol. 865bv; Altadonna, II:262.

74. See also Paolo Cozzo's discussion and analysis of these ceremonies in "Intus Mirabile Magis," 223–5; and *La geografia celeste*, 70–4.

75. Cozzo argues that she was devoted to St. Mauricio. He cites her conclusion of a letter to Carlo saying that the next day was the feast of St. Mauricio and that she hoped he and St. Michael would bring Carlo success in his military ventures. It is noteworthy that she did not say only St. Mauricio but also St. Michael, to whom she was certainly devoted. Her prayer to St. Mauricio might have had more to do with Carlo's devotion than hers. See "Intus Mirabile Magis," 223–5.

76. For references to Catalina praying to St. Michael, see, for example, her letters to Carlo, 29 September [1589], AST36, fasc. 3, fol. 364a; Altadonna, I:307; 20 September 1594, AST, M42, fasc. 2, fol. 1475–1475v; Altadonna, III:143; 29 September 1597, AST, M44, fasc. 9, fol. 1989b; Altadonna, III:342.

77. The Escorial housed twenty relics of St. Mauricio. Cozzo, "Idiomi del sacro," 290; Cozzo, "Intus Mirabile Magis," 223n52. See Philip II to the *infantas*, in Bouza, *Cartas*, 94.

78. For St. Catherine, see AST, Corte, Gioie e Mobili, M1, no. 6, item 4 (no folio number), fol. 18r, 38v, 85v, 86v; for St. Michael, fol. 18v; for St. Jerome, fol. 18r; for St. Lorenzo, fol. 39r; St. Magdalene, fol. 45r.

79. Conto del Sig. Gaspare Anastro, 1585–1587, ASRT, Camera dei Conti, Real Casa, Art. 224, n.p.

80. Raviola, "'Una delle prime principesse del mondo'," 491–2. The Confraternity of San Paolo established the home for penitent women with Catalina's support. On this confraternity, see Barberis and Cantaluppi, *La Compagnia*. For donations to poor children, see Conto del Sig. Isidoro de Robles Tesoriere della Ser.ma infant Dona Cattalina d'Austria, 1594 to 1596, ASRT, Camera dei Conti, Real Casa, Art. 224, fol. 11v, entry no. 23; fol. 31v, entry no. 96. See ASRT, Camera dei Conti, Real Casa, Art. 224, 1594–96, entries for "Angela Ferrara, madre de las convertidas," nos. 27, 28, 29. The latter are only a selection.

81. Her father founded the Augustinian monastery at the Escorial; her aunt Juana of Austria founded the convent of the Descalzas Reales in Madrid; another aunt, Empress María, patronized the Jesuit college in Madrid.

82. Members of the Confraternity of San Paolo founded the Albergo in 1580 but it "existed only on paper until Duke Carlo Emanuele I took it over in 1587." Cavallo, *Charity and Power*, 89. On the Albergo, see Cavallo, 89–91; Ruffino, "Vestire l'infanta," 342–3.

83. For example, on 2 July [1597], she wrote to Carlo that her confessor had told her why another priest had been put into custody and that she would send a message to the papal nuncio with her almoner. See Catalina to Carlo, AST, M44, fasc. 7, fol. 1923; Altadonna, III:298.

84. Catalina to Carlo, AST, M45, fasc. 3, fol. 2063, 27, no month and no year given but since it was written from Nice I have dated it to 1592.

85. The phrase comes from Boer, *The Conquest of the Soul*, 177.

86. Catalina to Carlo, 3 March 1589, AST, M35, fasc. 6, fol. 90av–b; Altadonna, I:91. His confessor was Francesco Martinengo, who was also his almoner. He was also a Franciscan. See Cozzo, *La geografia celeste*, 222. Carlo to Catalina, 11 March, AST, M13, fasc. 2, fol. 282bv, no year given but internal evidence suggests 1589.

87. Carlo to Catalina, 18 September 1589, AST, M14, fasc. 1, fol. 472.

88. For example, in 1588, 1594, and 1595, he asked Catalina to send him his confessor. See Carlo to Catalina, 25 October 1588, AST, M12, fasc. 20, fol. 242a; 17 September 1594, AST, M20, fasc. 1, fol. 1676a; 20 March 1595, AST, M21, fasc. 2, fol. 1933. For the duke confessing to priests along the way, see Carlo to Catalina, 17 March 1589, AST, M13, fasc. 2, fol. 298av; 31 March 1589, AST, 13, fasc. 2, fol. 298; 6 December 1589, AST, M14, fasc. 4, fol. 559. Catalina to Carlo, 17 September [1594], AST, M42, fasc. 2, fol. 1468v; Altadonna, III:139.

89. Boer, *The Conquest of the Soul*, 180.

90. Catalina to Carlo, 3 October [1588], AST, M35, fasc. 1, fol. 11; Altadonna, I:19–20.

91. O'Banion, *The Sacrament of Penance*, 48.

92. AST, Corte, Gioie e Mobili, M1, no. 6, fol. 62v.

93. Carlo to Catalina, 31 March 1589, AST, M13, fasc. 2, fol. 298av; Catalina to Carlo, 2 April 1589, AST, M35, fasc. 7, fol. 128a; Altadonna, I:129. For another example of asking him to forgive her, see letter of 22 November, AST, M45, fasc. 3, fol. 2059a, no year. For examples of Carlo asking her pardon when he confessed, see Carlo to Catalina, 31 March 1589, AST, M13, fasc. 2, fol. 298av; Carlo to Catalina, 6 December 1589, AST, M14, fol. 559.

94. See, for example, O'Banion, *The Sacrament of Penance*, 57–68.

95. Bossy, "The Social History of Confession," 27–30; Boer, *The Conquest of the Soul*, 181.

96. Francesco Vendramin, 30 July 1588, ASV, SDSa, filze 9, no. 87.

97. Catalina to Carlo, 4 March [1589], AST, M35, fasc. 6, fol. 91a; Altadonna, I:93 and Catalina to Carlo, 1 April 1589, AST, M35, fasc. 7, fol. 125v; Altadonna, I:127.

98. Norman, "Social History of Preaching,"136. See also Ardissino, "Italian Sermons," 60.

99. Catalina to Carlo, 16 December 1590, AST, M37, fasc. 11, fol. 678bv; Altadonna, II:122.

100. Catalina to Carlo, 20 January [1591], AST, M35, fasc. 1, fol. 87; Altadonna, II:137.

101. Catalina to Carlo, 5 March 1589, AST, M35, fasc. 6, fol. 199b; Altadonna, I:95.

102. Catalina to Carlo, 2 April 1589, AST, M35, fasc. 7, fol. 128av; Altadonna, I:129.

103. Carlo to Catalina, 28 March 1588, AST, M12, fasc. 20, fol. 234v.

104. See, for example, Catalina to Carlo, 19 October 1594, AST, M42, fasc. 3, fol. 1570av; Altadonna, III:194. For an example of the duke urging her to get exercise, see Carlo to Catalina, 2 February 1591, AST, M15, fasc. 1, fol. 686b.

105. The references are almost too numerous to note, but see particularly her letters to Carlo from September 29 until the end of October 1588, in AST, M35, fasc. 1; Altadonna, I:5–62.

106. Catalina to Carlo, AST, M45, fasc. 4, fol. 2043, Saturday, 11 a.m., no other date given.

107. Catalina to Carlo, 1 October [1588], AST, M35, fasc. 1, fol. 4r; Altadonna, I:12. On 22 October 1588, she said that "all I do is hear mass." Catalina to Carlo, AST, M35, fasc. 1, fol. 42v; Altadonna, I:50.

108. Catalina to Carlo, 18 April 1591, AST, M37, fasc. 5, fol. 542; Altadonna, II:171.

109. Catalina to Carlo, 22 October 1588, AST, M35, fasc. 1, fol. 41v; Altadonna, I:51.

110. Catalina to Carlo, 2 November 1588, AST, M35, fasc. 2, fol. 55v; Altadonna, I:63.

111. Catalina to Carlo, 2 March 1592, AST, M40, fasc. 3, fol. 1086; Altadonna, III:34.

112. There were two copies of the Shroud in the province of Jaén, and in 1568 Philip received a copy that had been made the previous year. See Pérez de Tudela Gabaldón, "Copies of the Holy Shroud," 313–14.

113. Philip II to Catalina, 2 January 1586, in Bouza, *Cartas*, 133–4; Catalina to Carlo, 28 October [1588], AST, M35, fasc. 1, fol. 51av; Altadonna, I:58.

114. Catalina to Carlo, 17 March 1589, AST, M35, fasc. 6, fol. 107b; Altadonna, I:111. In March 1589, Catalina said she had been lonely and so she had said the prayer to the Shroud and heard a sermon. Catalina to Carlo, 4 March [1589], AST, M35, fasc. 6, fol. 91a; Altadonna, I:93.

115. ASRT, Camera dei Conti, Real Casa, Art. 224, Cartas de Pago, 1586–1595, no. 482; Catalina to Carlo, 30 September 1588, AST, M35, fasc. 1, fol. 18a; Altadonna, I:10.

116. Carlo to Catalina, 11 March, AST, M13, fasc. 2, fol. 282bv, no year given but from internal evidence can be dated 1589.

117. ASRT, Camera dei Conti, Real Casa, Art. 224, Cartas de Pago, 1586–1595, no. 290; no. 548.

118. Catalina to Carlo, 11 May [1589], AST, M35, fasc. 8, fol. 183av; Altadonna, I:171.

119. Catalina to Carlo, 26 May 1589, AST, M35, fasc. 8, fol. 207cv; Altadonna, I:186.

120. Catalina to Carlo, 4 June 1589, AST, M35, fasc. 9, fol. 240a; Altadonna, I:195.

121. Cozzo, *"Intus Mirabile Magis,"* 220–2. On the spread of the devotion of the Shroud with political ramifications, see Cozzo, "Et per maggior divotione," 397–410. On the circulation of copies of the Shroud, see Cozzo, "Idiomi del sacro," 27–96.

122. "Relazione del ricevimento fatto dal Duca Carlo Emanuele I all'arciduca Cardinale Alberto in occasione del suo passaggio a Nizza ed in Piemonte," AST, Ceremoniale, M1, n.p.; Roco de Campofrío, *España en Flandes*, 36–7.

123. For July 1588, see Cozzo, *La geografia celeste*, 169, esp. note 73. See also Cozzo, "Intus Mirabile Magis," 223.

124. AST, Corte, Gioie e Mobili, M1, no. 6, fols. 87r, 53v.

125. Cozzo, "Intus Mirabile Magis," 224 and 227. For the interaction between the faithful and their devotional objects, see Kasl, "Delightful Adornments," 147–63. For the kissing of the relics, see "L'Ordine che si è osservato nella traslatione del glorioso corpo di Santo Mauritio nella città di Torino," AST, Corte, Materie Ecclesiastiche, Reliquie, M1, n.p.

126. Carlo to Catalina, 24 March 1589, AST, M13, fasc. 2, fol. 293v; Catalina to Carlo, 2 October 1594, AST, M42, fasc. 3, fol. 1517av; Altadonna, III:162.

127. ASRT, Real Casa, Camera dei Conti, Art. 224, Cuentas, 1596–99, no. 73. Because in Turin the ceremony occurred in Catalina's apartments and involved only women, her daughters would probably have observed and taken part. In Spain, the *infanta* Ana observed the ritual when she was nine. Hoffman, *Raised to Rule*, 84.

128. Catalina to Carlo, 31 March [1591], AST, M38, fasc. 3, fol. 745; Altadonna, II:168.

129. Catalina to Carlo, 22 August, AST, M45, fasc. 7, fol. 2190v, no year.

130. Cozzo, "*Regina Montis Regalis*," 130–45.

131. Cozzo, "*Regina Montis Regalis*," 52–72. Roco de Campofrío tells a slightly different story—two hunters, presumably heretics, died after shooting the Virgin. See *España en Flandes*, 29.

132. Cozzo, "*Regina Montis Regalis*," 55, 67–8. Roco de Campofrío describes it as an "*hermita . . . donde en una pared de tapia sobre cal estaba pintada una imagen de Nuestra Señora.*" *España en Flandes*, 29.

133. Cozzo, "*Regina Montis Regalis*," 131.

134. Cozzo, "Intus Mirabile Magis," 226. See the inventory of her possessions in AST, Corte, Gioie e Mobili, M1, no. 6, fol. 96.

135. Roco de Campofrío, *España en Flandes*, 29; Cozzo, "*Regina Montis Regalis*," 131–2.

136. Catalina to Philip II, 1 April 1596, BL, Add. MSS 28419, fol. 174r. Cozzo, "*Regina Montis Regalis*," 131. The Spanish governor of Milan, Juan Fernández de Velasco, also visited Vico with his son.

137. Catalina to Philip II, 10 April 1596, BL, Add. MSS 28419, fol. 178. For her letter to Carlo, see 4 April 1596, AST, M44, fasc. 2, fol.1877; Altadonna, III:285.

138. Carlo to Philip II, BL, Add. MSS 28419, 10 April 1596, fol. 176r; and Cozzo, "Intus Mirabile Magis," 227.

139. Pérez de Tudela, "Entre Madrid y Turín." The painting was done in 1596 and sent in 1597.

140. Cozzo, "*Regina Montis Regalis*," 133.

141. Catalina to Carlo, 30 and 31 March 1596, AST, M44, fasc. 1, fol. 1869, 1870; Altadonna, III:279–80. For ruby necklace, see Cozzo, "*Regina Montis Regalis*," 133.

142. Catalina to Carlo, 3 April 1596, AST, M44, fasc. 2, fol. 1874v; Altadonna, III:283; Cozzo, "*Regina Montis Regalis*," 133–4. For a detailed description of these gifts, see Cozzo, "Intus Mirabile Magis," 226n67.

143. Cozzo, "*Regina Montis Regalis*," 134. For these accounts see ASRT, Real Casa, Camera dei Conti, Art. 224, 1596–99, no. 75, no. 84. The accounts are dated 27 May 1597.

144. For gifts to Our Lady of Mondovì, see Cozzo, "*Regina Montis Regalis*," 134–7. See Catalina's letter to the duke in which she says that the Pernstein family must have been the ones to send gifts to the Virgin of Mondovì and that she was happy that there was devotion to that Virgin in German lands. See letter of 2 April 1596, AST, M44, fasc. 2, fol. 1872v; Altadonna, III:281.

145. Paolo Cozzo says that piety was part of her identity, "intimately lived and publicly advertised." See Cozzo, "Intus Mirabile Magis," 231; Cozzo, *La geografia celeste*, 179.

146. Cozzo, "*Regina Montis Regalis*," 129, and Cozzo, "Intus Mirabile Magis," 228–9.

147. AST, Corte, Gioie e Mobili, M1, no. 6, fol. 96r. For Cuneo, see Catalina to Carlo, 15 July, AST, M45, fasc. 5, fol. 2104r, no year given but from internal evidence I have dated it to 1596.

148. Report of Francesco Vendramin, 30 July 1588, ASV, SDSa, filze 9, no. 87; Cozzo, "*Regina Montis Regalis*," 130. Years later, Catalina's niece, Maria of Austria, would visit the sanctuary to the Virgin of Loreto, and she and her ladies-in-waiting publicly demonstrated their great devotion to that Virgin. For an account of this trip and devotions, see Río Barredo, "De Madrid à Vienne," 218–22.

149. Cozzo, *La geografia celeste*, 170–1, 170n81. Inventory in AST, Gioie e Mobili, M1, fasc. 6, fol. 45r, 85v, 87r; Cozzo, "Intus Mirabile Magis," 228n81.

150. ASRT, Camerale, Art. 384, n.p.

151. AST, Corte, Gioie e Mobili, M1, no. 6, fols. 45r, 96r.

152. Snow, "Salve Regina," 1002.

153. For two examples from her letters to Carlo, see 15 October 1588, AST, M35, fasc. 1, fol. 33bv; Altadonna I:41; and 19 March [1595], AST, M43, fasc. 3, fol. 1713r; Altadonna, III:227.

154. "*Aora acabo de oyr bisperas que no an dicho el ave que me a hecho mucha soledad.*" Catalina to Carlo, 24 December [1590], AST, 37, fasc. 11, fol. 954ev; Altadonna, II:128. After Trent, the Hail Mary had been added along with the Our Father as introductory prayers at vespers. See Schidel, "Vespers," 631.

155. Catalina to Carlo, 12 July, AST, M45, fasc. 4, fol. 2092, no year given but from internal evidence I would date it to 1596.

156. Catalina to Carlo, 19 September, AST, M45, fasc. 4, fol. 2110c, no year given but from internal evidence I would date it to 1597.

157. The count of Lodosa to Philip II, 7 November 1597, AGS, E1284, no. 71.

CHAPTER 10

1. For a discussion of these events, see Gómez Canseco, *Epopeyas*, 10–17. See also Parker, *The Army of Flanders*, 68.

2. Catalina mentions the seizure of letters in a letter to Carlo of 13 September, probably 1597. See AST, M45, fasc. 4, fol. 2088a. (Though she did not give a year, internal evidence makes it almost certain that it was written in 1597.) None of her letters survives from 3–9 July, 23–26 August, or 1–6 September, longer gaps than usual, suggesting that letters might have been lost. In surviving letters immediately following these gaps, Catalina did not mention any failure to write, which would be unusual had she not written. On 15 July, she said the longest she had gone without writing was one day, so the letters from 3–9 July were very likely

lost. Perhaps she was sick and unable to write during these days, but the extant correspondence does not mention any serious illness.

3. Catalina to Carlo, 22 August 1597, AST, M44, fasc. 8, fol. 1964c; Altadonna, III:329.

4. Catalina to Carlo, 28 July 1597, AST, M44, fasc. 7, fol. 1939dr–v; Altadonna, III:314, 315.

5. Catalina to Carlo, 11 August 1597, AST, M44, fasc. 8, fol. 1953b; Altadonna, III:322; Catalina to Carlo, 11 October 1597, AST, M44, fasc. 10, fol. 1999a; Altadonna, III:348.

6. See, for example, her letters of 22 August (the word she uses is *bonisima*) and 26 October 1597: Catalina to Carlo, 22 August 1597, AST, M44, fasc. 8, fol. 1964r; and 26 October 1597, fasc. 10, fol. 2011r; Altadonna, III:327, 356.

7. Catalina to Carlo, 22 August 1597, AST, M44, fasc. 8, fol. 1964r; Altadonna, III:327. The Catholic League had taken Grenoble from the Huguenots but lost it to Lesdiguières in 1590.

8. Catalina to Carlo, 1 August 1597, AST, M44, fasc. 8, fol. 1941r; Altadonna, III:315.

9. Catalina to Carlo, 5, 11, and 17 August 1597, AST, M44, fasc. 8, fols. 1945a–av, 1953ar, 1960av; Altadonna, III:317, 321, 325–6.

10. Catalina to Carlo, 17 September 1597, AST, M44, fasc. 9, fol. 1980av; Altadonna, III:339. For other letters in which she brought up Pragela with Carlo, see 27 August 1597, AST, M40, fasc. 8, fol. 1128ar; 30 August 1597, AST, M44, fasc. 8, fol. 1969–1969bv; 7 September 1597, AST, M44, fasc. 9, fol. 1975r; Altadonna, III:329, 330, 331, 334.

11. Catalina to Carlo, 19 October 1597, AST, M44, fasc. 10, fol. 2007a; Altadonna, III:353. On the eve of her thirtieth birthday, she told him that she was old and that he might as well let her go to war because perhaps she would help him more than those he had with him. See Catalina to Carlo, 9 October 1597, AST, M44, fasc. 10, fol. 1997b; Altadonna, III:347.

12. Catalina to Carlo, 7 August 1597, AST, M44, fasc. 8, fol. 1946v; Altadonna, III:319 and 28 October 1597, AST, M44, fasc. 10, fol. 2014b, Altadonna, III:358.

13. Carlo to Catalina, 12 July 1597, AST, M23, fasc. 4, fol. 2253bis; Catalina to Carlo, 5 August [1597], AST, M44, fasc. 8, fol. 1945v, 1945av; Altadonna, III:316, 317. On 28 October, she also asked him to forgive her for expressing her opinion. Catalina to Carlo, 28 October 1597, AST, M44, fasc. 10, fol. 2014av; Altadonna, III:358.

14. Carlo's struggles with Lesdiguières were part of a larger war between France and Spain. Lesdiguières's advances severed the Spanish Road for transporting troops and supplies to the Netherlands. See Parker, *The Army of Flanders*, 68–9.

15. Catalina to Carlo, 14 September 1597, AST, M44, fasc. 9, fol. 1979v; Altadonna, III:338.

16. In a letter to Prince Philip from 12 October 1597, Catalina said that the provisions from Milan "were so late that they cause much damage to everything." See BL, Add. MSS 28419, fol. 206r.

17. See her letter of 8 July 1597 where she noted that the duke had not been able to proceed as quickly as he would have liked because the Spanish governor of Milan had delayed in sending money and troops. She urged Philip to write to the duke of Frías, Governor of Milan, telling him to supply Carlo, and her frustration with Frías is palpable. Catalina to Philip II, BL, Add. MSS 28419, fol. 292v.

18. She specifically said that if the Tarnataise was lost, the path to Flanders would be lost. Catalina to Philip II, 8 July 1597, BL, Add. MSS 28419, fol. 293r.

19. Catalina to Philip II, 25 September 1597, BL, Add. MSS 28419, fol. 296r and Catalina to the *infanta* Isabel, 25 September 1597, BL, Add. MSS 28419, fol. 298r.

20. Catalina to Carlo, 7 September 1597, AST, M44, fasc. 9, fol. 1975r; Altadonna, III:334.

21. The letters do not clarify the location. See Catalina to Carlo, 16 October [1597] and 19 October 1597, AST, M44, fasc. 10, fols. 2004b, 2007a; Altadonna, III:352–3.

22. Catalina to Carlo, 30 October [1597], AST, M44, fasc. 10, fol. 2015b; Altadonna, III:361.

23. Catalina to Carlo, 28 October 1597, AST, M44, fasc. 10, fol. 2014bv; Altadonna, III:358.

24. "Relazione della malattia e morte dell'infanta donna Catalina d'Austria duchessa di Savoia," ASC, Bel., cart. 54, fasc. iv, doc. 281, fol. 281r. Transcription of autopsy from the Latin by Jaume Marce Sánchez. English translation by Matthew Lubin, edited for clarity.

25. In a letter to her sister Isabel from 29 September 1597, Catalina mentioned that she had been sick but downplayed her illness, saying she had been confined to bed only one day, and more than anything for just a headache. See Catalina to the *infanta* Isabel, BL, Add. MSS 28419, fol. 299r. In a letter to her father, she said she had been sick two days. See Catalina to Philip II, 25 September 1597, BL, Add. MSS 28419, fol. 296v.

26. Catalina to Carlo, 25 September 1597, AST, M44, fasc. 9, fol. 1987r–av; Altadonna, III:339–40.

27. Catalina to Carlo, 7 September 1597, AST, M44, fasc. 9, fol. 1975a; Altadonna, III:334. Catalina to Carlo, 10 September 1597, AST, M41, fasc. 9, fol. 1445v; Altadonna, III:336. She said one was "oriental" and the other from Peru.

28. Catalina to Carlo, 25 September 1597, AST, M44, fasc. 9, fol. 1987a; and 14 October 1597, fasc. 10, fol. 2002b; Altadonna, III:340, 350.

29. Catalina to Carlo, 17 September, AST, M44, fasc. 9, fol. 1980av–b; and 14 October 1597, fasc. 10, fol. 2002b; Altadonna, III:339, 349.

30. Carlo to Catalina, 19 October 1597, AST, M23, fasc. 5, fol. 2344c.

31. Catalina to Carlo, 24 July 1597, AST, M44, fasc. 7, fol. 1933av; 1, 17, 27 August 1597, fasc. 8, fols. 1941r, 1960v; AST, M40, fasc. 8, fol. 1128b; Altadonna, III:311, 315, 325, 331.

32. See Catalina to Carlo, 14 October 1597, AST, M44, fasc. 10, fol. 2002bv; Altadonna, III:348; Catalina to the *infanta* Isabel, 12 October 1597, BL, Add. MSS 28419, fol. 304r.

33. For the painting, see Carlo to Catalina, 26 June 1597, AST, M23, fasc. 4, fol. 2230bis. For the earrings, see Catalina to Carlo, 12 July [1597], AST, M44, fasc. 7, fol. 1916c: Altadonna, III:302.

34. Carlo to Catalina, 12 (?) July 1597, AST, M23, fasc. 4, fol. 2253bis.

35. Catalina to Carlo, 14 October 1597, AST, M44, fasc. 10, fol. 2002b; Altadonna, III:350.

36. Catalina to Carlo, 17 July 1597, AST, M44, fasc. 7, fol. 1924a; Altadonna, III:307.

37. Parker, *Imprudent King*, 350.

38. Catalina to Carlo, 13 September 1597, AST, M45, fasc. 9, fol. 2088av. For Catalina's letter to Isabel, see 12 October 1597, BL, Add. MSS 28419, fol. 304v.

39. Catalina to Carlo, 9 October 1597, AST, M44, fasc. 10, fol. 1997av; Altadonna, III:347.
40. Catalina to the *infanta* Isabel, 12 October 1597, BL, Add. MSS 28419, fol. 304v.
41. The pope gave his approval in April 1597 and in August the ambassador of the duke of Mantua congratulated Albert formally, so it was known by then. See Duerloo, *Dynasty and Piety*, 52; Roco de Campofrío, *España en Flandes*, 157.
42. Catalina to Carlo, 13 September, AST, M45, fasc. 4, fol. 2088ar–av, no date given but from internal evidence I have dated it to 1597.
43. Corraro, "Relazione dello stato di Savoia," 373.
44. An exception is the letter from 13 September 1597, AST, M45, fasc. 4, fol. 2088b, where at the end she says she is going to bed and will miss him.
45. Catalina to Carlo, 14 October 1597, AST, M44, fasc. 10, fol. 2002b; Altadonna, III: 350; Carlo to Catalina, 17 October 1597, AST, M23, fasc. 5, fol. 2344c.
46. Catalina to Carlo, 28 October 1597, AST, M44, fasc. 10, fol. 2014cv; Altadonna, III: 359.
47. Catalina to Carlo, 28 October 1597, AST, M44, fasc. 10, fol. 2014dv; Altadonna, III:360.
48. Catalina to Carlo, 3 November [1597], AST, M44, fasc. 11, fol. 2019; Altadonna, III:363. For Carlo's letter, see 30 October 1597, AST, M23, fasc. 5, fol. 2348r. Note that some scholars have argued that Catalina's death also resulted from anxiety at not hearing from Carlo, but she seems to have received this letter from 30 October, so she had not gone that long since hearing from him. See Varallo, *Il Duca e la corte*, 33.
49. Catalina to Carlo, 3 November [1597], AST, M44, fasc. 11, fol. 2019; Altadonna, III:363.
50. Catalina to Carlo, 5 November, AST, M45, fasc. 3, fol. 2044, no year given but from internal evidence I have dated it to 1597.
51. Lodosa also wrote to the Spanish ambassador in Venice giving a similar report, though he added that at the very end Catalina's womb had risen to her stomach. See the count of Lodosa to Iñigo de Mendoza, 7 November 1597, AGS, Estado, L1284, no. 119.
52. Corraro, "Relazione dello stato di Savoia," 379.
53. Oncieu, *Oraison funèbre*, 45.
54. The count of Lodosa to Philip II, 7 November 1597, AGS, E1284, no. 71.
55. Dols and Immisch, *Majnūn*, 18.
56. Sepúlveda, *Historia de varios sucesos*, II:fol. 34r.
57. Corraro, "Relazione dello stato di Savoia," 379.
58. I would like to thank María José del Río Barredo for their assistance in translating and understanding "*mala abitudine*."
59. Corraro, "Relazione dello stato di Savoia," 379.
60. Cozzo, "Stratégie dynastique," 220; Giachino, "Un panegirico," 482.
61. "Relazione della malattia e morte dell'infanta donna Catalina d'Austria duchessa di Savoia," ASC, Bel., cart. 54, fasc. iv, doc. 281, fol. 281v. Marco Battistoni explains that Waldensians lived in Saluzzo and "the Savoyard Piedmont, the Dauphiné, and upper Provence." See Battistoni, "Reshaping Local Public Space," 243. On the introduction of Protestantism to this area, see Bruening, "The Pays de Vaud," 118–39 and Fiume, "Geneva, the Italian Refuge," 377–9.
62. "Relazione della malattia e morte dell'infanta donna Catalina d'Austria duchessa di Savoia," ASC, Bel., cart. 54, fasc. iv, doc. 281, fol. 281v.

63. "Relazione della malattia e morte dell'infanta donna Catalina d'Austria duchessa di Savoia," ASC, Bel., cart. 54, fasc. iv, doc. 281, fols. 283v, 284r.

64. See "Relazione della malattia e morte dell'infanta donna Catalina d'Austria duchessa di Savoia," ASC, Bel., cart. 54, fasc. iv, doc. 281, fol. 284r. Beginning in the sixteenth century, autopsies were performed at the court of Savoy in order to understand the cause of death and perhaps to rule out poison. See Giachino, "Un panegirico," 482, and Cozzo, "Stratégie dynastique," 219. An autopsy was performed on the corpse of Carlo's father, and Carlo's body was also autopsied when he died in 1630, so it is not surprising that Catalina's body underwent an autopsy.

65. I am grateful to Dr. Pablo J. Sánchez and Dr. Jonathan Baum for reading the autopsy and suggesting this possibility.

66. The length of time that the body was displayed varied. Carlo's father died in August and his body was displayed for only a few hours. Carlo Emanuele II died in June and his body was displayed for three days. See Cozzo, "Stratégie dynastique," 222.

67. Cozzo, "*Regina Montis Regalis*," 161n223. Luisella Giachino says that she was buried in the Sacra di San Michele in Val di Susa, but when I visited, I did not see evidence of her tomb. Mons. Oliviero Iozzi noted that in 1836 many of the remains of Savoyard princes were moved from the cathedral in Turin (especially from the palace chapel) to the Sacra di San Michele, where some were placed in a communal grave. Iozzi does not mention Catalina, but at the time of this removal her body might well have been in the cathedral still, and from there transferred to the Sacra di San Michele and interred in the common grave. See Giachino, "Un panegirico," 483; Iozzi, *Le tombe dei reali*, 17.

68. Carlo to Catalina, 28 October 1597, AST, M23, fasc. 5, fol. 2352. His letter suggests that he kept portraits of Catalina stored in cabinets.

69. Gómez Canseco, *Epopeyas*, 16–17; Merlin, "Saluzzo, il Piemonte, l'Europa," 54–61. In his letter of 22 January 1598 to Philip II, Carlo said that he had been sick for three months. See Carlo to Philip II, BL, Add. MSS 28419, fol. 310r.

70. Carlo to Philip II, 22 January 1598, BL, Add. MSS 28419, fol. 310r. The term he used was "*lugar áspero.*"

71. Vayra, *Il museo storico*, 227.

72. Carlo to Philip II, 22 January 1598, BL, Add. MSS 28419, fol. 310r.

73. Varallo, *Il Duca e la corte*, 34.

74. Carlo to his councilors and governors, 18 November 1597, AST, M23, fasc. 9, fol. 2442. See Brero, "Recollecting Court Festivals," 121.

75. One of these books was probably Guichard, *Funérailles*, which the author dedicated to Carlo and which discussed Charles V's funeral and that of French kings and queens.

76. For a discussion of the *capilla ardente* and comparison to the catafalque, see Schraven, *Festive Funerals*, 10–15. The quoted words are from Schraven. Carlo to his ministers of state, 18 November 1597, AST, M23, fasc. 9, fol. 2442.

77. Varallo, *Il Duca e la corte*, 34–5. Scholars disagree on when Catalina's funeral took place and on whether Carlo was present. Cozzo says that Carlo was unable to be there, but as Cornuato's plan includes the duke, Carlo must have planned to be present. Varallo concludes that the funeral probably took place in late 1597 or early 1598, and Carlo's letter to Philip of 22 January suggests that at that point he had yet to return to Turin, so the funeral was probably in late January or early February.

78. Varallo, *Il Duca e la corte*, 94n9 and 94n11.
79. Franca Varallo says that the funeral was not particularly elaborate or sumptuous because of political and economic exigencies and because of the fear of plague. See Varallo, *Il Duca e la corte*, 36, 93n3.
80. Schraven, *Festive Funerals*, 57.
81. Cornuato, "Dispozione intorno il funerale," 76, 82.
82. Cozzo says that Emanuele Filiberto had used the nuptial bed only on his wedding night, and then it was used again for his funeral. Cozzo, "Stratégie dynastique," 218.
83. Sepúlveda, *Historia de varios sucesos*, II:fol. 34r–v; Cabrera de Córdoba, *Historia de Felipe II*, III:1630.
84. Khevenhüller to Rudolf II, 3 December 1597, HHStA, DK, K12, 343r.
85. Sepúlveda, *Historia de varios sucesos*, II:fol. 34r.
86. Cabrera de Córdoba, *Historia de Felipe II*, III:1630.
87. Terrones Aguilar del Caño, *Sermón que predicó*, fol. 19r.
88. Oncieu, *Oraison funèbre*, 33, 37.
89. Caccia, *Oratione di Francesco Caccia*, fol. 17v.
90. Giachino, "Un panegirico," 487.
91. Oncieu, *Oraison funèbre*, 8, 20–27v, 29–32, 53.
92. Oncieu, *Oraison funèbre*, 41, 42, 46, 50.

BIBLIOGRAPHY

PRINTED PRIMARY SOURCES

Akkerman, Nadine, ed. *The Correspondence of Elizabeth Stuart, Queen of Bohemia.* 2 vols. Oxford: Oxford University Press, 2011 and 2015.

Alava y Beaumonte, Don Francés de. *Correspondencia inédita de Felipe II con su embajador en París (1564–1570).* Ed. Pedro Rodríguez and Justina Rodríguez. San Sebastián: Donostia, 1991.

Altadonna, Giovanna, ed. "Cartas de Felipe II a Carlos Manuel II [*sic*], Duque de Saboya (1583–1596)," *Cuadernos de Investigación Histórica*, 9 (1986): 137–90.

Altadonna, Giovanna, ed. *Catalina Micaela d'Austria: Lettere inedite a Carlo Emanuele I (1588–1597).* 3 vols. Messina: Il Grano, 2012.

Badoero, Alberto. "Relazione di Spagna (1578)," in Eugenio Albèri, ed., *Relazioni degli ambasciatoria veneti al Senato durante il secolo decimosesto*, 273–80. Florence: A spese dell'editore, 1861.

Baldesano, Guillermo. *Historia sacra de la ilustrissima Legion Tebea.* Trans. Fernando de Sotomayor. Madrid: Pedro Madrigal, 1594.

Bollea, L.C., ed. *Un anno di carteggio epistolare fra Carlo Emanuele I di Savoia e l'Infante Caterina d'Austria, sua moglie (1594).* Turin: Carlo Clausen, 1905.

Bouza, Fernando, ed. *Cartas de Felipe II a sus hijas*, 2nd edn. Madrid: Akal, 1998.

Bucci, Domenico Filiberto. *Il solenne battesimo del serenissimo prencipe [sic] di Piemonte, Filippo Emanuelle.* Turin: Bevilacqua, 1588.

Cabrera de Córdoba, Luis. *Historia de Felipe II, Rey de España.* Ed. José Martínez Millán and Carlos Javier de Carlos Morales. 4 vols. Salamanca: Junta de Castilla y León, 1998.

Caccia, Francesco. *Oratione di Francesco Caccia, Dottor di Leggi, oratore, e consigliere di stato del Serenissimo Duca di Savoia, Carl'Emmanuello, fatta nella morte della Serenissima Infante donna Caterina d'Austria, Duchessa di Savoia.* Milan: Pandolfo Malatesta, 1598.

Carbón, Damián. *Libro del arte de las comadres o madrinas* (1541). Ed. Francisco Susarte Molina. Alicante: Universidad de Alicante, 1995.

Carvajal y Mendoza, Luisa. *Epistolario y poesías.* Ed. Camilo María Abad. Madrid: Atlas, 1965.

Carvajal y Mendoza, Luisa. *The Life and Writings of Luisa de Carvajal y Mendoza.* Ed. and trans. Anne J. Cruz. Toronto: Iter Press, 2014.

Cock, Henrique [Henry]. *Relación del viaje hecho por Felipe II en 1585, á Zaragoza, Barcelona y Valencia.* Ed. Alfredo Morel-Fatio and Antonio Rodríguez Villa. Madrid: Aribau, 1876.

Corazzino, Angelo. *Sposalizio di Carlo Emanuele Duca di Savoia con Caterina d'Austria Infanta di Spagna in Zaragoza 10.III.1585.* Ed. Cesare Malfatti. Barcelona: n.p., 1968.

Cornuato, Antonio. "Dispozione intorno il funerale da farsi in Torino alla su serenissima infanta donna Caterina d'Austria duchessa di Savoia," in Franca Varallo, ed., *Il Duca e la corte*, 75–95. Geneva: Slatkine, 1991.

Corraro, Fantino. "Relazione dello stato di Savoia di Fantino Corraro, 1598," in Eugenio Albèri, ed., *Relazioni degli ambasciatori veneti al Senato durante il secolo decimosesto: Appendice*, 353–84. Florence: A spese dell'editore, 1863.

Covarrubias, Sebastián de. *Tesoro de la lengua castellana o española.* Madrid: Turner, 1984.

Dietrichstein, Ana de. *Cartas*, in Vanessa de Cruz Medina, ed., *Una dama en la corte de Felipe II: Cartas de Ana de Dietrichstein a su madre, Margarita de Cardona.* Unpublished manuscript.

Douais, C. *Dépêches de M. de Fourquevaux, ambassadeur du roi Charles IX en Espagne, 1565–1572.* Paris: E. Leroux, 1896.

Due anni alla corte di Carlo Emanuele I, Duca di Savoia: Da dispacci al senato di Giovanni Mocenigo, ambasciatore veneto a Torino, 1583–1585. Venice: Antonelli, 1884.

Galende Díaz, Juan Carlos and Manuel Salamanca López, eds. *Epistolario de la emperatriz María de Austria: Textos inéditos del Archivo de la Casa de Alba.* Madrid: Nuevosescritores, 2004.

Gálvez de Montalvo, Luis. *El pastor de Fílida.* Ed. Julián Arribas Rebollo. Valencia: Albatros-Hispanófila Siglo XXI, 2006.

Guichard, Claude. *Funérailles et divers manières d'ensevelir des Romains, Grecs et autres nations, tant anciennes que moderne.* Lyon, 1581.

Khevenhüller, Hans. *Diario de Hans Khevenhüller, embajador imperial en la corte de Felipe II.* Ed. Félix Labrador Arroyo. Madrid: Sociedad Estatal para la Conmemoración de los Centenarios de Felipe II y Carlos V, 2001.

Khevenhüller, Hans. *El khurzer Extrakt*, in Alfredo Alvar Esquerra, ed., *El Embajador Imperial Hans Khevenhüller en España*, 221–627. Madrid: Ministerio de Asuntos Exteriores y de Cooperación, 2015.

Khevenhüller, Hans. *Geheimes Tagebuch 1548–1605.* Graz: Akademische Druck- u. Verlagsanstalt, 1971.

Lucinge, René de. *Lettres de 1588: Un monde renversé.* Ed. James Supple. Geneva: Droz, 2006.

Lucinge, René de. *Lettres sur les débuts de la Ligue (1585).* Ed. Alain Dafour. Geneva: Droz, 1964.

Manzanares, J. Pablo de. *Estilo y formulario de cartas familiares, según el gobierno de prelados, y señores temporales, donde se ponen otras cartas con sus respuestas, y algunas de oficios de república.* Alcalá de Henares, Spain: Diego Martínez, 1582.

Martinelli, Tristano. *L'epistolario d'Arlecchino (Tristano Martinelli 1556–1631).* Ed. Raccolto da Jarro. Florence: Salvadore Landi, 1895.

Matthews, George T., ed. *News and Rumor in Renaissance Europe (The Fugger Newsletters)*. New York: Capricorn Books, 1959.

Mousset, Albert, ed. *Dépêches Diplomatiques de M. de Longlée, Résident de France en Espagne (1582-1590)*. Paris: Librarie Plon, 1912.

"Naratione delle nozze di sua Altezza il Duca di Savoia con la Serenissima Donna Caterina infante di Spagna. 11 March 1585," in Emanuele Federico Bollati di Saint-Pierre, *Nelle faustissime nozze della nobile damigella Giuseppina Panissera di Veglio col conte Augusto Giriodi di Monastero*. N.p.: Vicenzo Bona, 1882.

Oncieu, Guillaume de. *Oraison funèbre sur le décez de très-haute, très-illustre, & sérénissime Infante Catherine d'Austriche, Duchesse de Savoye*. Chambéry: Claude Pomar, 1598.

Paré, Ambroise. *On the Generation of Man*, in *The Collected Works of Ambroise Paré*. Trans. Thomas Johnson, from the 1st English edn, London 1634. New York: Milford House, 1968.

Pragmática en que se da la orden y forma que se had de tener y guarder en los tratamientos y cortesías de palabra y por escripto. Alcalá, Spain: Juan Iñiguez de Lequerica, 1586.

"Relatione degli apparati e feste fatte nell'arrivo del Serenissimo Signor Duca di Savoia con la Serenissima Infante sua consorte in Nizza, nel passaggio del suo stato, e finalmente nella entrata di Turino," in Franca Varalla, ed., *Da Nizza a Torino: I festeggiamenti per il matrimonio di Carlo Emanuele I e Caterina d'Austria*. Turin: Centro Studi Piemontesi, 1992.

Roco de Campofrío, Juan. *España en Flandes: Trece años de gobierno del Archiduque Alberto (1595–1608)*. Madrid: Gráficas Yagües, 1973.

Rodríguez Villa, Antonio, ed. *Correspondencia de la infanta Isabel Clara Eugenia de Austria con el Duque de Lerma*. Madrid: Fortanet, 1906.

San Gerónimo, Fray Juan de. "Memorias," in *Colección de documentos inéditos para la historia de España*, Vol. 7. Madrid: Viuda de Calero, 1845.

Schroeder, H.J., trans. *The Decrees of the Council of Trent*. St. Louis, MO: B. Herder, 1960.

Sepúlveda, Fray Jerónimo de. "Historia de varios sucesos y de las cosas notables que han sucedido de veinte años a esta parte en toda España y en toda la iglesia católica." 2 vols. *Biblioteca Digital Hispánica*, Biblioteca Nacional, Madrid, http://bdh-rd.bne.es/viewer.vm?id=0000009947&page=1.

Shemek, Deanna, ed. *Isabella d'Este, Selected Letters*. Toronto: Iter Press, 2017.

Sigüenza, Fray José de. *Fundación del monasterio de el Escorial por Felipe II*. Madrid: San Bernardo, 1917.

Simón Díaz, José, ed. *Relaciones de actos públicos celebrados en Madrid*. Madrid: Instituto de Estudios Madrileños, 1982.

Tejeda, Gaspar de. *Cosa nueva: Estilo de escribir cartas mensageras sobre diversas materias como se usa con los títulos y cortesías, compuesta por un cortesano. Segunda Parte*. Valladolid: Sebastián Martínez, 1549.

Terrones Aguilar del Caño, Francisco. *Sermon que predico a la magestad del Rey don Felipe nuestro señor, en su capilla real el Doctor Aguilar de Terrones su predicador, en las honras que se hizieron por la serenissima infanta doña Catalina, Duquesa de Saboya a sabado, veynte de diziembre de 1597*. Madrid: n.p., 1598.

Torquemada, Antonio de. *Manual de escribientes*. Ed. María Josefa Canellada and Alonso Zamora Vicente. Madrid: Anejos del Boletín de la Real Academia de la Historia, 1970.

Vega Carpio, Lope Félix de. *La Dorotea*. Ed. Edwin S. Morby. Berkeley, CA: University of California Press, 1958.

Vendramin, Francesco. "Relazione di Savoia, 1589," in Eugenio Albèri, ed., *Relazioni degli ambasciatori veneti al senato*, 129–96. 1858. Reprint. Vol. 11. New York: Cambridge University Press, 2012.

Zane, Matteo. "Relazione di Spagna, 1584," in Eugenio Albèri, ed., *Relazioni degli ambasciatori Veneti al senato*, 341–86. 1861. Reprint. Vol. 13. New York: Cambridge University Press, 2012.

Zarco-Bacas y Cuevas, Julián, ed. *Documentos para la historia del monasterio de San Lorenzo el Real del Escorial*. Madrid: Helénica, 1916.

SECONDARY SOURCES

Ágreda Pino, Ana María. "Vestir el lecho: Una introducción al ajuar textil de la cama en la España de los siglos XV y XVI," *Res Mobilis: Revista internacional de investigación en mobilario y objectos decorativos*, 6, no. 7 (2017): 20–41.

Akkerman, Nadine. *Elizabeth Stuart: Queen of Hearts*. Oxford: Oxford University Press, 2021.

Albaladejo Martínez, María. "Las infantas Isabel Clara Eugenia y Catalina Micaela: Modelos de la perfecta princesa educada e instruida," *Anales de Historia del Arte*, 24 (December, 2014): 115–27.

Albaladejo Martínez, María. "Lo exótico y lo inusual en los retratos e inventarios de las infantas Isabel Clara Eugenia y Catalina Micaela," *Ars Bilduma*, no. 4 (2014): 95–110.

Albadalejo Martínez, María. "Ritos y Ceremonias en la corte de Felipe II: Lutos en honor a la infanta de España Catalina Micaela," *Potestas*, 7 (2014): 147–57.

Alonso García, Fernando. *El Correo en el Renacimiento Europeo: Estudio postal del Archivo Simón Ruiz, 1553–1630*. Madrid: Fundación Albertino de Figueiredo para la Filatelia, 2004.

Álvarez González, Marta. "Pageantry and the Projection of Status: The Triumphal Entries of Catherine of Austria (1585) and Christine of France (1620) in Turin," *Mélanges de l'École française de Rome: Italie et Méditerranée*, 115, no. 1 (2003): 29–50.

Alves, Abel. *The Animals of Spain: An Introduction to Imperial Perceptions and Human Interaction with other Animals, 1492–1826*. Leiden: Brill, 2011.

Amezúa, Agustín G. de. *Felipe II y las flores*. N.P.: Reino de Cordelia, 2010.

Amezúa y Mayo, Agustín G. *Isabel de Valois, reina de España (1546–1568)*. Madrid: Gráficas Ultra, 1949.

Antolín Rejón, Carlos. "Diplomacia, familia y lealtades: El príncipe Filiberto de Saboya (1588–1624) entre las cortes de Madrid y Turín." PhD diss., Universidad Autónoma, Madrid, 2021.

Antolín Rejón, Carlos. "Pricing an Ally: The House of Savoy and the Dowry of the Spanish Infanta Catherine Michaela," in Rocío Martínez López, ed., *Pricing a Bride: Medieval and Early Modern Dowries and Nuptial Economic Policies*. Forthcoming.

Ardissino, Erminia. "Italian Sermons in Early Modern Europe," *MLN*, 145, no. 1 (January 2020): 55–83.

Arienza Arienza, J. "La historia de Guillén de San Clemente, un embajador hispano en el corazón de Europa entre los años 1581 y 1608," *Ibero-Americana Pragensia*, 45 (2017): 73–98.

Armstrong, E. "Tuscany and Savoy," in Sir A.W. Ward, G.W. Prothero, and Stanley Leathes, eds, *The Cambridge Modern History*, Vol. 3: *The Wars of Religion*, 383–421. Cambridge: Cambridge University Press, 1907.

Astrua, Paola, Anna Maria Bava, and Carla Enrica Spantigati, eds. *"Il nostro pittore fiamengo": Giovanni Caracca alla corte dei Savoia (1568–1607)*. Turin: Umberto Allemandi & C., 2006.

Ball, Rachael and Geoffrey Parker, eds. *Cómo ser rey: Instrucciones del emperador Carlos V a su hijo Felipe. Mayo de 1543*. Madrid: Centro de Estudios Europa Hispánica, 2014.

Banner, Lisa. "Private Rooms in the Monastic Architecture of Habsburg Spain," in Andrew Spicer and Sarah Hamilton, eds, *Defining the Holy: Sacred Space in Medieval and Early Modern Europe*, 81–93. London: Routledge, 2006.

Barberis, Walter and Anna Cantaluppi. *La Compagnia di San Paolo*. 2 vols. Turin: Giulio Einaudi, 2013.

Barquero Cerdán, Iván. "Dinastía y oeconómica: El matrimonio y casa de la infanta Catalina Micaela de Austria, duquesa de Saboya." MA thesis, Universidad Autónoma, Madrid, 2024.

Bass, Laura. *The Power of the Portrait: Theater and Visual Culture in Early Modern Spain*. University Park, PA: Penn State University Press, 2009.

Battistoni, Marco. "Reshaping Local Public Space: Religion and Politics in the Marquisate of Saluzzo between the Reformation and Counter-Reformation," in Matthew Vester, ed., *Sabaudian Studies: Political Culture, Dynasty, and Territory, 1400–1700*, 240–58. Kirksville, MO: Truman State University Press, 2013.

Bava, Anna Maria and Enrica Pagella. *Le meraviglie del mondo: Le collezioni di Carlo Emanuele I di Savoia*. Genoa: Sagep, 2016.

Bazzano, Nicoletta. "Carlo d'Aragón (o Aragona) Tagliavia y Aragona," *Diccionario Biográfico: Real Academia de la Historia*, http://dbe.rah.es/biografias/15810/carlo-d-aragon-o-aragona-tagliavia-y-aragona.

Beam, Aki C.L. "'Should I as Yet Call You Old?': Testing the Boundaries of Female Old Age in Early Modern England," in Erin Campbell, ed., *Growing Old in Early Modern Europe: Cultural Representations*, 95–116. Aldershot: Ashgate, 2006.

Bercusson, Sarah. "Johanna of Austria and the Negotiation of Power and Identity at the Florentince Court," in Giovanna Benadusi and Judith C. Brown, eds, *Medici Women: The Making of a Dynasty in Grand Ducal Tuscany*, 128–53. Toronto: Centre for Reformation and Renaissance Studies, 2015.

Bernís, Carmen. *El traje y los tipos sociales en El Quijote*. Madrid: El Viso, 2001.

Betegón Díez, Ruth. *Isabel Clara Eugenia: Infanta de España y soberana de Flandes*. Barcelona: Plaza Janés, 2004.

Binaghi Olivari, Maria Teresa. "I ricami dell'infanta," in Blythe Alice Raviola and Franca Varallo, eds, *L'Infanta: Caterina d'Austria, duchessa di Savoia (1567–1597)*, 359–69. Rome: Carocci, 2013.

Bireley, Robert, ed. *Botero: The Reason of State*. Cambridge: Cambridge University Press, 2017.

Blanco Mourelle, Noel. "Reinventing the Wheel: Pedro de Guevara's *Nueva y sutil invención* as pedagogical technology," *Journal of Spanish Cultural Studies*, 21, no. 3 (2020): 293–311.

Boer, Wietse de. *The Conquest of the Soul: Confession, Discipline, and Public Order in Counter-Reformation Milan*. Leiden: Brill, 2001.

Bolland, Charlotte. "'Both the Fairest Ladies in their Countries': Elizabeth and Mary's Encounters through Portraiture," in Susan Doran, ed., *Elizabeth and Mary: Royal Cousins, Rival Queens*, 91–5. London: British Library, 2021.

Bosco, Maria Grazia. "I santi Tebei nella Torino del primo seicento," in Maria Grazia Bosco et al., eds, *Torino: I percorsi della religiosità*, 101–30. Turin: Archivo Storico della Città di Torino, 1998.

Bossy, John. "The Social History of Confession in the Age of the Reformation," *Transactions of the Royal Historical Society*, 25 (1975): 21–38.

Bouley, Bradford A. *Pious Post-Mortems: Anatomy, Sanctity, and the Catholic Church in Early Modern Europe*. Philadelphia, PA: University of Pennsylvania Press, 2017.

Bouza, Fernando. "La correspondencia del hombre práctico: Los usos epistolares de la nobleza española del Siglo de Oro a través de seis años de cartas del tercer conde de Fernán Núñez (1679–1684)," *Cuadernos de Historia Moderna, Anejo* [supplement] 4 (2005): 129–54.

Bouza, Fernando. "La estafeta del bufón: Cartas de gente de placer en la España de Velázquez," *Madrid: Revista de arte, geografía e historia*, no. 2 (1999): 95–124.

Bouza, Fernando. *Locos, enanos y hombres de placer en la corte de los Austrias: Oficio de burlas*. Madrid: Temas de Hoy, 1996.

Braunmuller, A.R. "Accounting for Absence: The Transcription of Space," in W. Speed Hill, ed., *New Ways of looking at Old Texts: Papers of the Renaissance English Text Society, 1985–1991*, 47–56. Binghamton, NY: Renaissance English Text Society, 1993.

Brero, Thalia. "Recollecting Court Festivals: Ceremonial Accounts in Sixteenth-Century Savoy," in Matthew Vester, ed., *Sabaudian Studies: Political Culture, Dynasty, and Territory, 1400–1700*, 240–58. Kirksville, MO: Truman State University Press, 2013.

Broomhall, Susan. "Ordering Distant Affections: Fostering Love and Loyalty in the Correspondence of Catherine de Medici to the Spanish Court, 1568–1572," in Susan Broomhall, ed., *Gender and Emotions in Medieval and Early Modern Europe: Destroying Order, Structuring Disorder*, 67–86. London: Routledge, 2016.

Broomhall, Susan. "'Women's Little Secret': Defining the Boundaries of Reproductive Knowledge in Sixteenth-century France," *Social History of Medicine*, 15, no. 1 (2002): 1–15.

Bruening, Michael. "The Pays de Vaud: First Frontier of the Genevan Reformation," in Jon Balserak, ed., *A Companion to the Reformation in Geneva*, 118–39. Leiden: Brill, 2021.

Bryant, Diana Rowlands. "Affection and Loyalty in an Italian Dynastic Marriage." PhD diss., University of Sydney, 2011.

Buescu, Ana Isabel. "L'infanta Beatrice di Portogallo e il suo matrimonio con il duca di Savoia (1504–1521)," in Maria Antónia Lopes and Blythe Alice Raviola, eds, *Portogallo e Piemonte. Nove secoli (XII–XX) di relazioni dinastiche e politiche*, 43–77. Rome: Carocci, 2014.

Bynum, Caroline Walker. *Wonderful Blood: Theology and Practice in Late Medieval Northern Germany and Beyond*. Philadelphia, PA: University of Pennsylvania Press, 2007.

Camelot, P.T. "Confirmation," *New Catholic Encyclopedia*, Vol. 4, 145–50. New York: McGraw-Hill, 1967.

Cano de Gardoqui, José Luis. *La cuestión de Saluzzo en las comunicaciones del imperio español*. Valladolid: Estudios y Documentos Cuadernos de Historia Moderna, 1962.

Cardoza, Anthony L. and Geoffrey W. Symcox. *A History of Turin*. Turin: Giulio Einaudi, 2006.

Carlos Varona, María Cruz de. 'Entre el riesgo y la necesidad: Embarazo, alumbramiento y culto a la Virgen en los espacios femeninos del Alcázar de Madrid (siglo XVII)," *Arenal*, 13, no. 2 (July–December 2006): 263–90.

Carlos Varona, María Cruz de. "Giving Birth at the Habsburg Court: Visual and Material Culture," in Anne J. Cruz and Maria Galli Stampino, eds, *Early Modern Habsburg Women: Transnational Contexts, Cultural Conflicts, Dynastic Continuities*, 151–73. Farnham and Burlington, VT: Ashgate, 2013.

Carlos Varona, María Cruz de. *Nacer en palacio: El ritual del nacimiento en la corte de los Austrias*. Madrid: Centro de Estudios Europa Hispánica, 2018.

Carlos Varona, María Cruz de. "Representar el nacimiento: Imágenes y cultura material de un espacio de sociabilidad femenina en la España altomoderna," *Goya*, 319 (2017): 231–45.

Castiglione, Caroline. "Peasants at the Palace: Wet Nurses and Aristocratic Mothers in Early Modern Rome," in Jutta Gisela Sperling, ed., *Medieval and Renaissance Lactations*, 79–100. Farnham: Ashgate, 2013.

Castronovo, Valerio. "Carlo Emanuele I, duca di Savoia," *Dizionario Biografico degli Italiani*, Vol. 20. Treccani Enciclopedia, 1977, http://www.treccani.it/enciclopedia/carlo-emanuele-i-duca-di-savoia_(Dizionario-Biografico)/.

Cavallo, Sandra. *Charity and Power in Early Modern Italy: Benefactors and their Motives in Turin, 1541–1789*. Cambridge: Cambridge University Press, 1995.

Cavallo, Sandra and Tessa Storey. *Healthy Living in Late Renaissance Italy*. Oxford: Oxford University Press, 2013.

Ceña Llorente, Rafael. "El viaje de la emperatriz María de Austria a España con estancia prolongada en las Descalzas Reales," *Reales Sitios*, 75, 1 (1983): 49–56.

Chartier, Roger, Alain Boureau and Cécile Dauphin. *Correspondence: Models of Letter-writing from the Middle Ages to the Nineteenth Century*. Princeton, NJ: Princeton University Press, 1997.

Cibrario, Luigi. *Storia di Torino*, Vol. 2. Turin: Alessandro Fontana, 1846.

Claretta, G. "I marmi scritti di Torino e suburbio," *Atti della società di archeologia e arti per la provincial di Torino*, Vol. 2, 349–78. Turin: G.B. Paravia e Comp., 1878.

Cockram, Sarah D.P. *Isabella d'Este and Francesco Gonzaga: Power Sharing at the Italian Renaissance Court*. Farnham: Ashgate, 2013.

Cole, Michael W. *Sofonisba's Lesson: A Renaissance Artist and her Work*. Princeton, NJ: Princeton University Press, 2019.

Condulmer, Piera. "Un matrimonio dinastico ispano-piemontese," *Studi Piemontesi*, 6, no. 2 (November 1977): 320–29.

Cozzo, Paolo. "'Et per maggior divotione vorrebbe che fusse della medesima grandezza et che avesse tocato la istessa santa Sindone': Copie di reliquie e politica sabauda in età moderna," *Annali di storia moderna e contemporanea*, 16 (2010): 397–410.

Cozzo, Paolo. "Idiomi del sacro fra Savoia e Impero (secoli XVI–XVII)," in Marco Bellabarba and Andrea Merlotti, eds, *Stato sabaudo e Sacro Romano Impero*, 29–96. Bologna: Il Mulino.

Cozzo, Paolo. "Il clero di corte nel ducato di Savoia fra XVI e XVII secolo," in Paola Bianchi and Luisa G. Gentile, eds, *L'affermarsi della corte sabauda: Dinastie, poteri, élites in Piemonte e Savoia fra tardo medioevo e prima età moderna*, 361–86. Turin: Silvio Zamorani, 2006.

Cozzo, Paolo. "'Intus Mirabile Magis': L'orizzonte devozionale dell'infanta Caterina," in Blythe Alice Raviola and Franca Varallo, eds, *L'Infanta: Caterina d'Austria, duchessa di Savoia (1567–1597)*, 213–31. Rome: Carocci, 2013.

Cozzo, Paolo. *La geografia celeste dei Duchi di Savoia: Religione, devozioni e sacralità in uno Stato di età moderna (secoli XVI–XVII)*. Bologna: Il Mulino, 2006.

Cozzo, Paolo. *"Regina Montis Regalis": Il santaurio di Mondovì da devozione locale a tempio sabaudo*. Rome: Viella, 2002.

Cozzo, Paolo. "Stratégie dynastique chez les Savoie: Une ambition royale, XVIe–XVIIIe siècle," in Juliusz A. Chrościcki, Mark Hengerer and Gérard Sabatier, eds, *Les funérailles princières en Europe, XVIe–XVIIIe Siècle*, Vol. 1: *Le grand théâtre de la mort*, 217–35. Versailles: Centre de recherche du château de Versailles, 2010.

Cozzo, Paolo. *Un eremita alla corte dei Savoia: Alessandro Ceva e le origini della congregazione camaldolese di Piemonte*. Milan: FrancoAngeli, 2018.

Cozzo, Paolo, Andrea Merlotti, and Andrea Nicolotti, eds. *The Shroud at Court: History, Usages, Places and Images of a Dynastic Relic*. Leiden: Brill, 2019.

Crawford, Patricia. *Blood, Bodies and Families in Early Modern England*. London: Pearson/Longman, 2004.

Cressy, David. *Birth, Marriage, and Death: Ritual, Religion, and the Life-Cycle in Tudor and Stuart England*. New York: Oxford University Press, 1997.

Cruz, Anne J. "Female Governance in Early Modern Spanish Courts," in Noelia García Pérez, ed., *The Making of Juana of Austria: Gender, Art, and Patronage in Early Modern Iberia*, 25–43. Baton Rouge, LA: Louisiana State University Press, 2021.

Cruz, Anne J. "Juana of Austria: Patron of the Arts and Regent of Spain, 1554–59," in Anne J. Cruz and Mihoko Suzuki, eds, *The Rule of Women in Early Modern Europe*, 103–22. Urbana, IL: University of Illinois Press, 2009.

Cruz, Anne J. and Maria Galli Stampino, eds. *Early Modern Habsburg Women: Transanational Contexts, Cultural Conflicts, Dynastic Continuities*. Farnham and Burlington, VT: Ashgate, 2013.

Cruz Medina, Vanessa de. "Cartas, mujeres y corte en el siglo de oro." PhD diss., Universidad Complutense, Madrid, 2010.

Cruz Medina, Vanessa de. "Ladies-in-Waiting at the Spanish Habsburg Palaces and Convents, the Alcázar and the Descalzas Reales (1570–1603)," in Jeremy Roe and Jean Andrews, eds, *Representing Women's Political Identity in the Early Iberian World*, 146–68. London: Routledge, 2020.

Cruz Medina, Vanessa de. "Manos que escriben cartas: Ana de Dietrichstein y el género epistolar en el siglo XVI," *Litterae: Cuadernos sobre Cultural Escrita*, 3–4 (2003–2004): 161–85.

Cruz Medina, Vanessa de. "The Relicario of the Descalzas Reales: Juana of Austria's Collection of Relics," in Noelia García Pérez, ed., *The Making of Juana of Austria: Gender, Art, and Patronage in Early Modern Iberia*, 289–320. Baton Rouge, LA: Louisiana State University Press, 2021.

Cruz Medina, Vanessa de. "Y porque sale la reyna a senar acabo, que es mi semana de serbir: La vida en palacio de la Reina Ana, las infantas Isabel Clara Eugenia y Catalina Micaela en las cartas de Ana de Dietrichstein," in M.V. López Cardón and G. Franco Rucio, eds, *La reina Isabel y las reinas de España*, 427–45. Madrid: Fundación Española de Historia Moderna, 2005.

Cuneo, Cristina. "Gli anni spagnoli alla corte sabauda: Le residenze urbane ed extraurbane dell'Infanta Caterina d'Austria e di Carlo Emanuele I di Savoia," in Monique

Chatenet and Krista De Jonge, eds, *Le prince, la princesse et leurs logis: Manieres d'habiter dans l'élite aristocratique européenne (1400–1700)*, 141–58. Paris: Picard, 2014.

Cuneo, Cristina. "La fabbrica del Valentino tra cinquecento e seicento," *Atti e Rassegna Tecnica Società Ingegneri e Architetti in Torino*, 46, nos. 5–7 (May–July 1992): 261–70.

Cuneo, Cristina. "Le residenze dell'Infanta: architettura e *loisir*," in Blythe Alice Raviola and Franca Varallo, eds, *L'Infanta: Caterina d'Austria, duchessa di Savoia (1567–1597)*, 233–46. Rome: Carocci, 2013.

Cuthbert, Fr. *The Capuchins: A Contribution to the History of the Counter-Reformation*. 2 vols. London: Sheed and Ward, 1928.

D'Amelia, Marina. "Becoming a Mother in the Seventeenth Century: The Experience of a Roman Noblewoman," in Anne Jacobson Schutte, Thomas Kuehn, and Silvana Seidel Menchi, eds, *Time, Space, and Women's Lives in Early Modern Europe*, 223–44. Kirksville, MO: Truman State University Press, 2001.

Daradanello, Giuseppe, Susan Klaiber, and Henry A. Millon, eds. *Guarino Guarini*. Turin: Allemandi, 2006.

Davis, Natalie Zemon. *Society and Culture in Early Modern France*. Stanford: Stanford University Press, 1975.

Davis, Natalie Zemon. *The Gift in Sixteenth-Century France*. Madison, WI: University of Wisconsin Press, 2000.

Daybell, James. *The Material Letter in Early Modern England: Manuscript Letters and the Culture and Practices of Letter-Writing, 1512–1635*. Basingstoke, Hampshire: Palgrave Macmillan, 2012.

Daybell, James. *Women Letter-Writers in Tudor England*. London: Oxford University Press, 2006. Reprint, 2012.

Daybell, James. "Women's Epistolary Rhetoric in Sixteenth-Century Letters of Petitions," *Women's Writing*, 13, no. 1 (March 2006): 2–33.

Doglio, Maria Luisa. "Il 'teatro poetico' del principe: Rime inedite di Carlo Emanuele I di Savoia," in Mariarosa Masoero, Sergio Mamino, and Claudio Rosso, eds, *Politica e cultura nell'età di Carlo Emanuele I. Torino, Parigi, Madrid*, 165–89. Florence: Leo S. Olschki, 1999.

Dols, Michael W. and Diana E. Immisch. *Majnūn: The Madman in Medieval Islamic Society*. New York: Oxford University Press, 1992.

Donahue, Charles Jr. "The Legal Background: European Marriage Law from the Sixteenth to the Nineteenth Century," in Silvana Seidel Menchi, ed., *Marriage in Europe, 1400–1800*, 33–60. Toronto: University of Toronto Press, 2016.

Duerloo, Luc. *Dynasty and Piety: Archduke Albert (1598–1621) and Habsburg Political Culture in an Age of Religious Wars*. Farnham and Burlington, VT: Ashgate: 2012.

Earle, Rebecca. "Letters and Love in Colonial Spanish America," *The Americas*, 62, no. 1 (July 2005): 17–46.

Edelmayer, Friedrich. "Honor y dinero: Adán de Dietrichstein al servicio de la casa de Austria," *Studia Historica. Historia Moderna*, 11 (1993): 89–116.

Edelmayer, Friedrich. *Philipp II: Biographie eines Weltherrschers*, 2nd edn. Stuttgart: W. Kohlhammer, 2009.

Eire, Carlos. *From Madrid to Purgatory: The Art and Craft of Dying in Sixteenth-Century Spain*. New York: Cambridge University Press, 1995.

Elliott, J.H. "The Court of the Spanish Habsburgs: A Peculiar Institution?," in *Spain and Its World, 1500–1700*, 142–61. New Haven and London: Yale University Press, 1992.

Escudero, José Antonio. *Felipe II: El rey en el despacho*. Madrid: Editorial Complutense, 2002.

Esteban Estríngana, Alicia and José Antonio López Anguita, eds. *Mujeres en la alta política de la Europa moderna: Visibilidad, ocultación y memoria*. Madrid: Doce Calles, 2024.

Evans, Jennifer. *Aphrodisiacs, Fertility and Medicine*. Woodbridge: The Boydell Press, 2014.

Falomir Faus, Miguel. "De la cámara a la galería: Usos y funciones del retrato en la corte de Felipe II," in *D. Maria de Portugal, Princesa de Parma (1565–1577) e o seu tempo: as relações culturais entre Portugal e Itália na segunda metade de quinhentos*, 126–40. Porto: Instituto de Cultura Portuguesa, 1999.

Fargas Peñarrocha, Mariela. "Explicar el cuerpo y entregar el alma: Los embarazos y partos de Estefanía de Requesens (siglo XVI)," *Avisos de Viena*, no. 4 (August 2022): 137–48.

Fernández Collado, Ángel. "García de Loaysa y Girón," *Diccionario Biográfico: Real Academia de la Historia*, https://dbe.rah.es/biografias/18465/garcia-de-loaysa-y-giron.

Fernández Fernández, José Antonio. "Entre el juego y el coleccionismo: Las muñecas de las reinas e infantas de España (1560–1621)," *Hipogrifo*, 11, no. 1 (2023): 913–48.

Fernández Valbuena, Ana. "Influencing Gender Roles: Commedia dell'Arte in Spain," in Anne J. Cruz and María Cristina Quintero, eds, *Beyond Spain's Borders: Women Players in Early Modern National Theaters*, 113–28. London: Routledge, 2016.

Ferrari, Catherine. "Kinship and the Marginalized Consort," *Early Modern Women*, 11, no. 1 (Fall 2016): 45–68.

Ferrone, Siro. *Arlecchino: Vita e avventure di Tristano Martinelli attore*. Rome: Laterza, 2006.

Ferrone, Siro. "Journeys," in Christopher B. Blame, Piermario Vescovo, and Daniele Vianello, eds, *Commedia dell'Arte in Context*, 67–75. Cambridge: Cambridge University Press, 2018.

Ffolliott, Sheila. "Juana and Her Peers: Queens, Regents, and Patronage in Sixteenth-Century Europe," in Noelia García Pérez, ed., *The Making of Juana of Austria: Gender, Art, and Patronage in Early Modern Iberia*, 167–94. Baton Rouge, LA: Louisiana State University Press, 2021.

Fichtner, Paul Sutter. *Emperor Maximilian II*. New Haven and London: Yale University Press, 2001.

Fildes, Valerie. *Breasts, Bottles, and Babies: A History of Infant Feeding*. Edinburgh: Edinburgh University Press, 1986.

Fiume, Emanuele. "Geneva, the Italian Refuge, and Contact with Italy," in Jon Balserak, ed., *A Companion to the Reformation in Geneva*, 369–87. Leiden: Brill, 2021.

Fórmica, Mercedes. *La infanta Catalina Micaela en la corte alegre de Turín*. Madrid: Fundación Universitaria Española, 1976.

Franchetti, D. *Storia della Consolata, con illustrazioni critiche e documenti inediti*, Vol. 1. Turin: Pietro Celanza, 1904.

Fraser, James. *The Golden Bough: The Roots of Religion and Folklore*. New York: Gramercy, 1993.

Freedberg, David. *The Power of Images: Study on the History and Theory of Response*. Chicago, IL: University of Chicago Press, 1989.

Gal, Stéphane. *Charles-Emmanuel de Savoie: La politique du précipice*. Paris: Payot, 2012.

Gamberini, Cecilia. *Sofonisba Anguissola*. Los Angeles: Getty Publications, 2024.

Gamberini, Cecilia. "Sofonisba Anguissola, a Painter and a Lady-in-Waiting," in Tanja L. Jones, ed., *Women Artists in the Early Modern Courts of Europe, c. 1450–1700*, 91–112. Amsterdam: Amsterdam University Press, 2021.

García García, Bernardo. "Bruselas y Madrid: Isabel Clara Eugenia y el duque de Lerma," in Werner Thomas and Luc Duerloo, eds, *Albert and Isabella, 1598–1621*, 67–77. Leuven: Brepols, 1998.

García García, Bernardo. *El ocio en la España del siglo de oro*. Madrid: Akal, 1999.

García García, Bernardo. "Los regalos de Isabel Clara Eugenia y la corte española: Intimidad, gusto y devoción," *Reales Sitios*, 37, no. 143 (2000): 16–27.

García García, Bernardo and María Luisa Lobato, eds. *Dramaturgia Festiva y Cultura Nobilaria en el Siglo de Oro*. Madrid: Iberoamerica, 2007.

García Pérez, Noelia, ed. *The Making of Juana of Austria: Gender, Art, and Patronage in Early Modern Iberia*. Baton Rouge, LA: Louisiana State University Press, 2021.

García Prieto, Elisa. "Isabel Clara Eugenia of Austria: Marriage Negotiations and Dynastic Plans for a Spanish Infanta," in Cordula van Wyhe, ed., *Isabel Clara Eugenia: Female Sovereignty in the Courts of Madrid and Brussels*, 131–53. London: Centro de Estudios Europa Hispánica and Paul Holberton Publishing, 2011.

García Prieto, Elisa. "La infanta Isabel Clara Eugenia de Austria, la formación de una princesa europea y su entorno cortesano." PhD diss., Universidad Complutense, Madrid, 2012.

García Prieto, Elisa. *Una corte en femenino: Servicio áulico y carrera cortesana en tiempos de Felipe II*. Madrid: Marcial Pons, 2018.

García Sanz, Ana. "A Personal Project: The Founding of Madrid's Descalzas Reales," in Noelia García Pérez, ed., *The Making of Juana of Austria: Gender, Art, and Patronage in Early Modern Iberia*, 195–219. Baton Rouge, LA: Louisiana State University Press, 2021.

García Sanz, Ana. *El Niño Jesús en el monasterio de las Descalzas Reales de Madrid*. Madrid: Patrimonio Nacional, 2010.

García Sanz, Ana and Leticia Ruiz. "Linaje regio y monacal: La galería de retratos de las Descalzas Reales," in *El linaje del Emperador: Iglesia de la preciosa sangre, Centro de exposiciones, San Jorge, Cáceres*, 135–58. Madrid: Sociedad Estatal para la Conmemoración de los Centenarios de Felipe II y Carlos V, 2000.

Geevers, Liesbeth. "Dynasty and State Building in the Spanish Habsburg Monarchy: The Career of Emanuele Filiberto of Savoy (1588–1624)," *Journal of Early Modern History*, 20 (2016): 267–91.

Giachino, Luisella. "Un panegirico per l'Infanta: Le orazioni funebri," in Blythe Alice Raviola and Franca Varallo, eds, *L'Infanta: Caterina d'Austria, duchessa di Savoia (1567–1597)*, 481–98. Rome: Carocci, 2013.

Giannini, Massimo Carlo. "Sfondrati, Paolo," *Dizionario Biografico degli Italiani*, Vol. 92. Trecanni Enciclopedia, 2018, https://www.treccani.it/enciclopedia/paolo-sfondrati_(Dizionario-Biografico)/.

Gibson, Jonathan. "Significant Space in Manuscript Letters," *The Seventeenth Century*, 12, no. 1 (1997): 1–10.

Giuliani, Marzia. "Il barone Paolo Sfondrati tra Milano, Torino e Madrid: Diplomazia e affari di famiglia," in Danilo Zardin, ed., *Lombardia ed Europa: Incroci di Storia e Cultura*, 169–87. Milan: Vita e Pensiero, 2014.

Gleason, Elizabeth G. "The Capuchin Order in the Sixteenth Century," in Richard L. DeMolen, ed., *Religious Orders of the Catholic Reformation*, 31–57. New York: Fordham University Press, 1994.

Gómez-Bravo, Ana M. *Textual Agency: Writing Culture and Social Networks in Fifteenth-Century Spain*. Toronto: University of Toronto Press, 2013.

Gómez Canseco, Luis, ed. *Epopeyas de una guerra olvidada*. Madrid: Iberoamericana-Vervuert, 2002.

Gómez-Centurión Jiménez, Carlos. "La herencia de Borgoña: el ceremonial real y las casas reales en la España de los Austrias (1548–1700)," in Luis Antonio Ribot García, ed., *Las sociedades ibéricas y el mar a finales del siglo XVI*, Vol. 1: *La corte: Centro e imagen del poder*, 11–31. Madrid: Sociedad Estatal Lisboa, 1998.

Gómez de Ortega, Casimiro. *Continuación de la flora española o historia de las plantas que se crian en España que escribía Don Joseph Quer*, Vol. 6. Madrid: Joachin Ibarra, 1784.

Gómez River, Ricardo. "Antonio Perrenot de Granvela," *Diccionario Biográfico: Real Academia de la Historia*, https://dbe.rah.es/biografias/11263/antonio-perrenot-de-granvela.

González Cuerva, Rubén. *Maria of Austria, Holy Roman Empress (1528–1603): Dynastic Networker*. London: Routledge, 2022.

Gonzalo Sánchez-Molero, José Luis. *Felipe II: La educación de un felicísimo príncipe, 1527–1545*. Madrid: Polifemo, 2014.

Gonzalo Sánchez-Molero, José Luis. "L'educazione devozionale delle infante," in Blythe Alice Raviola and Franca Varallo, *L'Infanta: Caterina d'Austria, duchessa di Savoia (1567–1597)*, 25–95. Rome: Carocci, 2013.

Gowing, Laura. "Secret Births and Infanticide in Seventeenth-Century England," *Past and Present*, 156 (August 1997): 87–115.

Grendler, Paul. *The Universities of the Italian Renaissance*. Baltimore, MD: Johns Hopkins Press, 2002.

Hairston, Julia L. "The Economics of Milk and Blood in Alberti's *Libri della famiglia*: Maternal versus Wet-Nursing," in Jutta Gisela Sperling, ed., *Medieval and Renaissance Lactations*, 187–212. Farnham and Burlington, VT: Ashgate, 2013.

Harris, Barbara J. *English Aristocratic Women, 1450–1550: Marriage and Family, Property and Careers*. Oxford: Oxford University Press, 2002.

Harris, Barbara J. "Women and Politics in Early Tudor England," *The Historical Journal*, 33, no. 2 (June 1990): 259–81.

Heal, Felicity. "Food Gifts, the Household and the Politics of Exchange in Early Modern England," *Past and Present*, 199 (May 2008): 41–70.

Henke, Robert. *Performance and Literature in the Commedia dell'Arte*. Oxford: Oxford University Press, 2002.

Hernández, Rosalie. *Immaculate Conceptions: The Power of the Religious Imagination in Early Modern Spain*. Toronto: University of Toronto Press, 2019.

Hoffman, Martha K. "Childhood and Royalty at the Court of Philip III," in Grace E. Coolidge, ed., *The Formation of the Child in Early Modern Spain*, 123–42. Burlington, VT: Ashgate, 2014.

Hoffman, Martha K. *Raised to Rule: Educating Royalty at the Court of the Spanish Habsburgs, 1601–1634*. Baton Rouge, LA: Louisiana State University Press, 2011.

Hunt, Arnold. "'Burn this Letter': Preservation and Destruction in the Early Modern Archive," in James Daybell and Andrew Gordon, eds, *Cultures of Correspondence in Early Modern Britain*, 189–209. Philadelphia: University of Pennsylvania Press, 2016.

Hunt, John M. *The Vacant See in Early Modern Rome: A Social History of the Papal Interregnum*. Leiden: Brill, 2016.

Iozzi, Oliviero. *Le tombe dei reali di Savoia*. Rome: Ermanno Loescher, 1910.

James, Carolyn. "Marriage by Correspondence: Politics and Domesticity in the Letters of Isabella d'Este and Francesco Gonzaga, 1490–1519," *Renaissance Quarterly*, 65, no. 2 (Summer 2012): 321–52.

Jirousek, Charlotte and Sara Catterall. *Ottoman Dress and Design in the West: A Visual History of Cultural Exchange*. Bloomington, IN: Indiana University Press, 2019.

Jordan, Annemarie. "Las dos águilas del emperador Carlos V: Las colecciones y el mecenazgo de Juana y María de Austria en la corte de Felipe II," in Luis Antonio Ribot García, ed., *La monarquía de Felipe II a debate*, 429–72. Madrid: Sociedad Estatal para la Conmemoración de los Centenarios de Felipe II y Carlos V, 2000.

Jordan, Annemarie and Almudena Pérez de Tudela. "Renaissance Menageries, Exotic Animals and Pets at the Habsburg Courts in Iberia and Central Europe," in K.A.E. Enenkel and P.J. Smith, eds, *Early Modern Zoology: The Construction of Animals in Science*, 419–47. Leiden: Brill, 2007.

Jurado Riba, Victor. "Clientelismo, servicio militar y promoción nobilaria: La activi-dad de don Guillén de San Clemente hasta su nombramiento como embajador en el Imperio," *Investigaciones Históricas, época moderna y contemporánea*, 42 (2022): 325–52.

Kamen, Henry. *Philip of Spain*. New Haven and London: Yale University Press, 1997.

Kamen, Henry. *The Escorial: Art and Power in the Renaissance*. New Haven and London: Yale University Press, 2010.

Kamen, Henry. *The Phoenix and the Flame: Catalonia and the Counter Reformation*. New Haven and London: Yale University Press, 1993.

Kasl, Ronda. "Delightful Adornments and Pious Recreation: Living with Images in the Seventeenth Century," in Ronda Kasl, ed., *Sacred Spain: Art and Belief in the Spanish World*, 147–63. New Haven and London: Yale University Press, 2009.

Keller, Katrin. *Kurfürsin Anna von Sachsen, 1532–1585*. Regensburg: Friedrich Pustet, 2010.

King, Helen. *Midwifery, Obstetrics and the Rise of Gynaecology: The Uses of a Sixteenth-Century Compendium*. Aldershot: Ashgate, 2007.

King, Margaret. "Book-lined Cells: Women and Humanism in the Early Italian Renaissance," in Albert Rabil, ed., *Renaissance Humanism*, Vol. 1: *Foundations, Forms, and Legacy*, 434–54. Philadelphia: University of Pennsylvania Press, 1988.

Klaiber, Susan. "The First Ducal Chapel of San Lorenzo," in Mariarosa Masoero, Sergio Mamino, and Claudio Rosso, eds, *Politica e cultura nell'età di Carlo Emanuele I: Torino, Parigi, Madrid*, 329–43. Florence: Leo S. Olschki, 1999.

Klestinec, Cynthia. *Theaters of Anatomy: Students, Teachers, and Traditions of Dissection in Renaissance Venice*. Baltimore, MD: Johns Hopkins University Press, 2011.

Klingenstein, Lucy. *The Great Infanta: Isabel, Sovereign of the Netherlands*. New York: G.P. Putnam's Sons, 1910.

Kremmel, Nina. "Sexual Intercourse during Pregnancy and the Postpartum Period in Early Modern Spain," *Revista Historia Autónoma*, 16 (2020): 71–81.

Labrador Arroyo, Félix. "From Castile to Burgundy: The Evolution of the Queens' Households during the Sixteenth Century," in Anne J. Cruz and Maria Galli Stampino, eds, *Early Modern Habsburg Women: Transnational Contexts, Cultural Conflicts, Dynastic Continuities*, 119–48. Farnham and Burlington, VT: Ashgate, 2013.

Labrado Arroyo, Félix and José Eloy Hortal Muñoz. "Presentación: Las casas de las reinas, de los príncipes, de los infantes y de las infantas, ¿modelo borgoñón o castellano?," in José Eloy Hortal Muñoz and Féliz Labrador Arroyo, eds, *La Casa de Borgoña: Las casas del rey de España*, 461–82. Leuven: Leuven University Press, 2014.

Lazure, Guy. "Possessing the Sacred: Monarchy and Identity in Philip II's Relic Collection at the Escorial." *Renaissance Quarterly*, 60 (2007): 58–93.

Llanos y Torriglia, Félix de. *La novia de Europa: Isabel Clara Eugenia*. Madrid: Ediciones Fax, 1928. Reprint, 1944, 1962.

Lobato, María Luisa y Bernardo J. García García, eds. *La Fiesta Cortesana en la Época de los Austria*. Valladolid: Junta de Castilla y León, 2003.

López Álvarez, Alejandro. "Francisco de Vera y Aragón," *Diccionario Biográfico: Real Academia de la Historia*, https://dbe.rah.es/biografias/30364/francisco-de-vera-y-aragon.

López Álvarez, Alejandro. *Poder, lujo y conflicto en la corte de los Austrias: Coches, carrozas y sillas de mano, 1550–1700*. Madrid: Polifemo, 2007.

López Álvarez, Alejandro. "Some Reflections on the Ceremonial and Image of the Kings and Queens of the House of Habsburg in the Sixteenth and Seventeenth Centuries," in René Vermeir, Dries Raeymaekers, and José Eloy Hortal Muñoz, eds, *Constellation of Courts: The Courts and Households of Habsburg Europe, 1555–1665*, 267–322. Leuven: Leuven University Press, 2014.

López-Cordón Cortezo, M.V. "Entre damas anda el juego: Las camareras mayores de palacio en la edad moderna," *Cuadernos de Historia Moderna, Anejo* [supplement] 2 (2003): 123–52.

López Santamaría, Anna. "Great Faith is Necessary to Drink from the Chalice," in Joan-Lluís Palos and Magdalena S. Sánchez, eds, *Early Modern Dynastic Marriages and Cultural Transfer*, 115–38. Farnham and Burlington, VT: Ashgate, 2016.

McClive, Cathy. *Menstruation and Procreation in Early Modern France*. Farnham: Ashgate, 2015.

McKendrick, Melveena. *Theatre in Spain, 1490–1700*. Cambridge: Cambridge University Press, 1992.

Malo Barranco, Laura. "Los espacios de religiosidad y la devoción femenina en la nobleza moderna: El ejemplo de los linajes Arande e Híjar," *Cuadernos de Historia Moderna*, 42, 1 (2017): 175–93.

Mamino, Sergio. "Culto delle reliquie e architettura sacra negli anni di Carlo Emanuele I," in Maria Grazia Bosco et al., eds, *Torino I percorsi della religiosità*, 53–100. Turin: Archivo Storico della Città di Torino, 1998.

Mamino, Sergio. "Reimagining the Grande Galleria of Carlo Emanuele I of Savoy," *Anthropology and Aesthetics*, 27 (Spring 1995): 70–88.

Mansau, Andrée. *La femme aux lynx*. Moncalieri: Centro interuniversitario di ricerche sul "Viaggio in Italia," 2002.

Marchandisse, Alain. "The Funeral of Charles V," in Monique Chatenet, Murielle Gaude-Ferragu, and Gérard Sabatier, eds, *Princely Funerals in Europe, 1400–1700*, 223–45. Turnhout: Brepols, 2021.

Marini, Lemigio. "Beatrice di Portogallo, duchessa di Saovia," *Dizionario Biografico degli Italiani*, Vol. 7. Treccani Enciclopedia, 1970, https://www.treccani.it/enciclopedia/beatrice-di-portogallo-duchessa-di-savoia_(Dizionario-Biografico)/.

Martínez Hernández, Santiago. "'Enlightened Queen, clear Cynthia, beauteous Moon': The Political and Courtly Apprenticeship of the Infanta Isabel Clara

Eugenia," in Cordula van Wyhe, ed., *Isabel Clara Eugenia: Female Sovereignty in the Courts of Madrid and Brussels*, 21–59. London: Centro de Estudios Europa Hispánica and Paul Holberton Publishing, 2011.

Martínez López, Rocío. "El Imperio y Baviera frente a la sucesión de Carlos II: Relaciones diplomáticas con la monarquía de España (1665–1699)." PhD diss., Universidad Nacional de Educación a Distancia, 2018.

Martínez López, Rocío. "Los derechos sucesorios femeninos en la dinastía Habsburgo: Diferencias y enfrentamientos (1500–1740)," in Gonzalo del Puerto, Mercedes Llorente, Renato Epifânio, Alice Santiago Faria, and Maria Barreto Dávila, eds, *Mulheres da realeza ibérica mediadoras politicas e culturais*, 67–93. Lisbon: MIL, 2019.

Martínez Millán, José. "El archiduque Alberto en la corte de Felipe II (1570–1580)," in Werner Thomas and Luc Duerloo, eds, *Albert and Isabella, 1598–1621*, 27–37. Leuven: Brepols, 1998.

Martínez Millán, José. "La casa y servidores de la infanta Catalina Micaela en Turín," in Blythe Alice Raviola and Franca Varallo, eds, *L'Infanta: Caterina d'Austria, duchessa di Savoia (1567–1597)*, 391–479. Rome: Carocci, 2013.

Martínez Millán, José and Santiago Fernández Conti, *La monarquía de Felipe II: La casa del rey*. 2 vols. Madrid: MAPFRE, 2005.

Masoero, Mariarosa, Sergio Mamino, and Claudio Rosso, eds. *Politica e cultura nell'età di Carlo Emanule I: Torino, Parigi, Madrid*. Florence: Leo S. Olschki, 1999.

Mauss, Marcel. *The Gift: The Form and Reason for Exchange in Archaic Societies*. Trans. W.D. Halls. New York: W.W. Norton, 1990.

Mediavilla Martín, Benito and José Rodríguez Díez. *Las reliquías del Real Monasterio del Escorial, documentación hagiográfica*. San Lorenzo de El Escorial: Ediciones Escurialenses, 2005.

Medina Morales, Francisca. "Las formas nominales de tratamiento en el Siglo de Oro," *AISO, Actas*, VI (2002): 1329–41.

Meek, H.A. *Guarino Guarini and his Architecture*. New Haven and London: Yale University Press, 1988.

Merlin, Pierpaolo. "Beatrice di Portogallo e il governo del ducato sabaudo (1521–1538)," in Maria Antónia Lopes and Blythe Alice Raviola, eds, *Portogallo e Piemonte: Nove secoli (XII–XX) di relazioni dinastiche e politiche*, 79–102. Rome: Carocci, 2014.

Merlin, Pierpaolo. "Caterina d'Asburgo e l'influsso Spagnolo," in Franca Varallo, ed., *In assenza del re: Le reggenti dal XIV al XVII secolo (Piemonte ed Europa)*, 209–34. Florence: Leo S. Olschki, 2008.

Merlin. Pierpaolo. "Etichetta e politica: L'infante Caterina d'Aspurgo tra Spagna e Piemonte," in José Martínez Millán and María P. Marçal Lourenço, eds, *Las relaciones discretas entre la monarquías hispana y portuguesa: Las casas de las reinas (Siglos XV–XIX)*, Vol. 1, 311–38. Madrid: Ediciones Polifemo, 2008.

Merlin, Pierpaolo. "Il cinquecento," in Pierpaolo Merlin, Claudio Rosso, Geoffrey Symcox, and Giuseppe Ricuperati, eds, *Il Piemonte sabaudo: Stato e territori in età moderna*, 3–172. Turin: UTET, 1994.

Merlin, Pierpaolo. "Il governo dell'Infanta: un bilancio tra luci e ombre," in Blythe Alice Raviola and Franca Varallo, eds, *L'Infanta: Caterina d'Austria, duchessa di Savoia (1567–1597)*, 159–74. Rome: Carocci, 2013.

Merlin, Pierpaolo. *Manuel Filiberto: Duque de Saboya y General de España*. Madrid: ACTAS, 2008.

Merlin, Pierpaolo. "Saluzzo, il Piemonte, l'Europa: La politica sabauda dalla conquista del marchesato alla pace di Lione," in Marco Fratini, ed., *L'annessione sabauda del marchesato di Saluzzo: Tra dissidenza religiosa e ortodossia catolica (secc. XVI–XVIII)*, 15–30. Turin: Claudina, 2004.

Merlin, Pierpaolo. *Tra guerre e tornei: La corte sabauda nell'età di Carlo Emanuele I.* Turin: Società Internazionale, 1991.

Mongiano, Elisa. "Quale dote per un'infanta di Spagna?: Il contratto di matrimonio di Caterina d'Austria," in Blythe Alice Raviola and Franca Varallo, eds, *L'Infanta: Caterina d'Austria, duchessa di Savoia (1567–1597)*, 145–57. Rome: Carocci, 2013.

Mora Afán, Juan Carlos. "Francisco de Idiáquez," *Diccionario Biográfico: Real Academia de la Historia*, https://dbe.rah.es/biografias/29421/francisco-de-idiaquez.

Morales, Jorge, Cristina Santarelli, and Franca Varallo, eds. *Il Cardinale: Maurizio di Savoia, mecenate, diplomático e político (1593–1657)*. Rome: Carocci, 2023.

Morel-Fatio, Alfred, ed. "La duchesse d'Albe Dª María Enríquez et Catherine de Médicis," *Bulletin Hispanique*, 7, no. 4 (1905): 360–86.

Moreno Villa, José. *Locos, enanos, negros y niños palaciegos: gente de placer que tuvieron los Austrias en la Corte española desde 1563 a 1700*. Mexico: Presencia, 1930.

Moriondo, Carlo. *Testa di ferro: Vita di Emanuele Fliberto de Savoia*. Turin: UTET, 2007.

Mulcahy, Rosemarie. "Sánchez Coello at the Prado: Madrid," *The Burlington Magazine*, 132, 1050 (September 1990): 663–5.

Muller, Aislinn. "The Agnus Dei, Catholic Devotion, and Confessional Politics in Early Modern England," *British Catholic History*, 34, 1 (May 2018): 1–28.

Musacchio, Jacqueline Marie. *The Art and Ritual of Childbirth in Renaissance Italy*. New Haven and London: Yale University Press, 1999.

Nalle, Sara. "Private Devotion, Personal Space: Religious Images in Domestic Context," in María Cruz de Carlos Varona, ed., *La imagen religiosa en la Monarquía Hispánica: Usos y espacios*, 255–72. Madrid: Casa de Velázquez, 2008.

Norman, Corrie E. "Social History of Preaching: Italy," in Larissa Taylor, ed., *Preachers and People in the Reformations and Early Modern Period*, 125–91. Leiden: Brill, 2001.

O'Banion, Patrick J. *The Sacrament of Penance and Religious Life in Golden Age Spain*. University Park, PA: Pennsylvania State University, 2013.

Oliván Santaliestra, Laura. "The Countess of Harrach and the Cultivation of the Body between Madrid and Vienna," in Joan-Lluís Palos and Magdalena S. Sánchez, eds, *Early Modern Dynastic Marriages and Cultural Transfer*, 213–34. Farnham and Burlington, VT: Ashgate, 2016.

Oresko, Robert. "Bastards as Clients: The House of Savoy and its Illegitimate Children," in Roger Mettam and Charles Giry-Deloison, eds, *Patronages et Clientélismes 1550–1750 (France, Angleterre, Espagne, Italie)*, 39–67. London: L'Institut français du Royaume-Uni, 1995.

Osborne, Toby. *Dynasty and Diplomacy in the Court of Savoy: Political Culture and the Thirty Years' War*. Cambridge: Cambridge University Press, 2007.

Ozment, Steven. *An Intimate Portrait of Life in 16th-Century Europe Revealed in the Letters of a Nuremberg Husband and Wife*. New Haven and London: Yale University Press, 1989.

Parker, Geoffrey. *The Army of Flanders and the Spanish Road, 1567–1659*. London: Cambridge University Press, 1972.

Parker, Geoffrey. *Felipe II: La biografía definitiva*. Barcelona: Planeta, 2010.

Parker, Geoffrey. *Imprudent King: A New Life of Philip II*. New Haven and London: Yale University Press, 2014.

Pellicer, Casiano. *Tratado histórico sobre el origen y progreso de la comedia y del histrionismo en España*. Ed. José María Diez Borque. Barcelona: Labor, 1975.

Pérez de Tudela, Almudena. "Entre Madrid y Turín: La infanta Catalina Micaela," *Agenart: La agencia artística de la mujeres de la Casa de Austria, 1532–1700*, 9 November 2022, https://agenart.org/entre-madrid-y-turin-la-infanta-catalina-micaela/.

Pérez de Tudela, Almudena. "La vida festiva de la infanta Catalina en la corte de Turín en la correspondencia del barón Paolo Sfondrato," *Ars & Renovatio*, 1 (2013): 148–66.

Pérez de Tudela, Almudena. "Los relicarios de la reina Ana de Austria en el real monasterio de El Escorial," *Agenart: La agencia artística de las mujeres de la Casa de Austria, 1532–1700*, 1 March 2022, https://agenart.org/los-relicarios-de-la-reina-ana-de-austria-en-el-real-monasterio-de-el-escorial/.

Pérez de Tudela, Almudena. "Lujo en el matrimonio de la infanta Catalina Micaela con el duque de Saboya en Zaragoza en 1585," *Ars & Renovatio*, 7 (2019): 379–400.

Pérez de Tudela, Almudena. "Regalos y retratos: Los años de la infanta Catalina Micaela en la corte de Madrid (1567–1584), in Blythe Alice Raviola and Franca Varallo, eds, *L'Infanta: Caterina d'Austria, duchessa di Savoia (1567–1597)*, 97–141. Rome: Carocci, 2013.

Pérez de Tudela, Almudena and Annemarie Jordan. "Luxury Goods for Royal Collectors: Exotica, Princely Gifts, and Rare Animals Exchanged between the Iberian Courts and Central Europe in the Renaissance (1560–1612)," *Jahrbuch des Kunsthistorischen Museum Wien*, 3 (2001): 1–127.

Pérez de Tudela Gabaldón, Almudena. "Copies of the Holy Shroud for the Court of King Philip II of Spain (1527–1598)," in Paolo Cozzo, Andrea Merlotti, and Andrea Nicolotti, eds, *The Shroud at Court: History, Usages, Places and Images of a Dynastic Relic*, 313–34. Leiden: Brill, 2019.

Pitts, Vincent J. *Henri IV of France: His Reign and Age*. Baltimore, MD: Johns Hopkins University Press, 2009.

Pollak, Martha D. *Turin, 1564–1680: Urban Design, Military Culture, and the Creation of the Absolutist Capital*. Chicago, IL: University of Chicago Press, 1991.

Pollock, Linda A. "Childbearing and Female Bonding in Early Modern England," *Social History*, 22, no. 3 (October 1997): 286–306.

Pollock, Linda A. "Embarking on a Rough Passage: The Experience of Pregnancy in Early Modern Society," in Valerie Fildes, ed., *Women as Mothers in Preindustrial England*, 39–67. New York: Routledge, 1990.

Raulich, Italo. *Storia di Carlo Emanuele I, duca di Savoia*, Vol. 1. Milan: Ulrico Hoepli, 1896.

Raviola, Blythe Alice. " 'En el real serbicio de vuestra majestad': El cardenal Mauricio de Saboya entre Turín, Roma, Madrid y París," *Libros de la Corte*, Monográfico, 1, no. 6 (2014): 242–59.

Raviola, Blythe Alice. "Il filo de Anna: La marchesa d'Alençon, Margherita Paleologo e Margherita di Savoia-Gonzaga fra stati italiani ed Europa," in Franca Varallo, ed., *In assenza del re: Le reggenti dal XIV al XVII secolo (Piemonte ed Europa)*, 317–41. Florence: Leo S. Olschki, 2008.

Raviola, Blythe Alice. "La imagen de la infanta en la correspondencia de los goberna-dores piamonteses," in José Martínez Millán and M.P. Marçal Lourenço, eds, *Las Relaciones discretas entre las monarquías hispana y portuguesa: Las casas de las reinas (siglos XV–XIX): Arte, música, espiritualidad y literatura*, 3: 1733–48. Madrid: Editorial Polifemo, 2008.

Raviola, Blythe Alice. "Le infante di Savoia: Percorsi dinastici e spirituali delle figlie di Catalina Micaela e Carlo Emanuele I fra Piemonte, stati italiani e Spagna," in José Martínez Millán, Rubén González Cuerva, and Manuel Rivero Rodríguez, eds, *La corte de Felipe IV (1621–1665): Reconfiguración de la monarquía católica*. Vol. 4: *Los reinos y la política internacional*, 471–502. Madrid: Polifemo, 2018.

Raviola, Blythe Alice. "The Three Lives of Margherita of Savoy-Gonzaga, Duchess of Mantua and Vicereine of Portugal," in Anne J. Cruz and Maria Galli Stampino, eds, *Early Modern Habsburg Women: Transnational Contexts, Cultural Conflicts, Dynastic Continuities*, 59–76. Farnham and Burlington, VT: Ashgate, 2013.

Raviola, Blythe Alice. "'Una delle prime principesse del mondo': Catalina Micaela y la Corte de Turín al final del siglo XVI," in José Eloy Hortal Muñoz and Félix Labrador Arroyo, eds, *La casa de Borgoña: La casa del rey de España*, 483–500. Leuven: Leuven University Press, 2014.

Raviola, Blythe Alice and Franca Varallo, eds. *L'Infanta: Caterina d'Austria, duchessa di Savoia (1567–1597)*. Rome: Carocci, 2013.

Read, Sara. *Menstruation and the Female Body in Early Modern England*. Basingstoke: Palgrave Macmillan, 2013.

Redworth, Glyn. *The She-Apostle: The Extraordinary Life and Death of Luisa de Carvajal*. Oxford: Oxford University Press, 2008.

Rhodes, Elizabeth. *The Tight Embrace: Luisa de Carvajal y Mendoza (1566–1614)*. Milwaukee: Marquette University Press, 2000.

Ribera, Jean-Michel. *Diplomatie et Espionnage: Les ambassadeurs du roi de France auprès de Philippe II: Du traité du Cateau-Cambrésis (1559) à la mort de Henri III (1589)*. Paris: Honoré Champion, 2007.

Río Barredo, María José del. "De Madrid a Turín: El ceremonial de las reinas espa-ñolas en la corte ducal de Catalina Micaela de Saboya," *Cuadernos de Historia Moderna*, Anejo [supplement] 2 (2003): 97–122.

Río Barredo, María José del. "De Madrid à Vienne: La dévotion à la Vierge de Marie de Habsbourg, reine de Hongrie et impératrice (1606–1646)," trans. Cécile Vincent-Cassy, in Murielle Gaude-Ferragu and Cécile Vincent-Cassy, eds, *"La dame de cœur": Patronage et mécénat religieux des femmes de pouvoir*, 209–27. Rennes: Presses universitaires de Rennes, 2016.

Río Barredo, María José del. "El viaje de los príncipes de Saboya a la corte de Felipe III (1603–1606)," in Paola Bianchi and Luisa Clotilde Gentile, eds, *L'affermarsi della corte sabauda: Dinastie, poteri, élites in Piemonte e Savoia fra tardo medioevo e prima età moderna*, 406–34. Turin: Silvio Zamorani, 2006.

Río Barredo, María José del and Magdalena S. Sánchez. "Le lettere familiari di Caterina di Savoia," in Blythe Alice Raviola and Franca Varallo, eds, *L'Infanta: Caterina d'Austria, duchessa di Savoia (1567–1597)*, 189–212. Rome: Carocci, 2013.

Robledo Estaire, Luis. "La música en la casa de la reina, príncipe e infantas," in Luis Robledo Estaire, Tess Knighton, Cristina Bordas Ibáñez, and Juan José Carreras, eds, *Aspectos de la Cultura Musical en la Corte de Felipe II*, 195–212. Madrid: Alpuerto, 2000.

Rock, P.M.J. "Golden Rose," in *The Catholic Encyclopedia*. New York: Robert Appleton Company, 1909, https://www.newadvent.org/cathen/06629a.htm.

Rodríguez G. de Ceballos, Alfonso. "Image and Counter-Reformation in Spain and Spanish America," in Ronda Kasl, ed., *Sacred Spain: Art and Belief in the Spanish World*, 15–35. New Haven and London: Yale University Press, 2009.

Rodríguez López-Abadía, Arturo. "Las joyas de la infanta Catalina Micaela, duquesa de Saboya, y la dama del manto de armiño," *Digilec*, 6 (2019): 105–14.

Rodríguez Salgado, M.J. "'Una perfecta princesa': Casa y vida de la reina Isabel de Valois (1559–1568). Primera parte," *Cuadernos de Historia Moderna*, Anejo [supplement] 2 (2003): 39–96.

Rodríguez Salgado, M.J. "'Una perfecta princesa': Casa y vida de la reina Isabel de Valois (1559–1568). Segunda parte," *Cuadernos de Historia Moderna*, 28 (2003): 71–98.

Roggero, Costanza and Aurora Scotti. *Il castello del Valentino*. Turin: Politecnico di Torino, 1994.

Roggero Bardelli, Costanza, Maria Grazia Vinardi, and Vittorio Defabiani. *Villa sabaude: Piemonte 2*. Milan: Rusconi, 1990.

Rublack, Ulinka. "Pregnancy, Childbirth and the Female Body in Early Modern Germany," *Past and Present*, no. 150 (1996): 84–110.

Ruffino, Maria Paola. "Vestire l'infanta: Abiti, stoffe e monili di Caterina d'Austria," in Blythe Alice Raviola and Franca Varallo, eds, *L'Infanta: Caterina d'Austria, duchessa di Savoia (1567–1597)*, 341–57. Rome: Carocci, 2013.

Ruiz, Teofilo F. *A King Travels: Festive Traditions in Late Medieval and Early Modern Spain*. Princeton, NJ: Princeton University Press, 2012.

Ruiz, Teofilo F. "Philip II's Entry into Zaragoza in 1585: A Theater of Power or Contestation?," in Nancy Van Deusen and Leonard Michael Koff, eds, *Mobs: An Interdisciplinary Inquiry*, 269–84. Leiden: Brill, 2011.

Sánchez, Magdalena S. "'I would not feel the pain if I were with you': Catalina Micaela and the Cycle of Pregnancy at the Court of Turin, 1585–1597," *Social History of Medicine*, 28, no. 3 (2017): 445–64.

Sánchez, Magdalena S. "'Lord of my Soul': The Letters of Catalina Micaela, Duchess of Savoy, to her Husband, Carlo Emanuele I," in Anne J. Cruz and Maria Galli Stampino, eds, *Early Modern Habsburg Women: Transnational Contexts, Cultural Conflicts, Dynastic Continuities*, 79–95. Farnham and Burlington, VT: Ashgate, 2013.

Sánchez, Magdalena S. "Privacy, Family, and Devotion at the Court of Philip II," in Marcello Fantoni, George Gorse, and Malcolm Smuts, eds, *The Politics of Space: European Courts ca. 1500–1750*, 361–81. Rome: Bulzoni, 2009.

Sánchez, Magdalena S. "'She Grows Careless': The *Infanta* Catalina and Spanish Etiquette at the Court of Savoy," in Joan-Lluís Palos and Magdalena S. Sánchez, eds, *Early Modern Dynastic Marriages and Cultural Transfer*, 21–44. Farnham and Burlington, VT: Ashgate, 2016.

Sánchez, Magdalena S. "Vísperas, misas cantadas y sermones: Prácticas devocionales de la duquesa de Saboya Catalina Micaela," in Bernardo J. García García, Katrin Keller, and Andrea Sommer-Mathis, eds, *De puño y letra: Cartas personales en las redes dinásticas de la Casa de Austria*, 51–78. Madrid: Iberoamericana, 2019.

Sánchez, Magdalena S. "Where Palace and Convent Meet: The Descalzas Reales in Madrid," *Sixteenth Century Journal*, 46, 1 (2015): 53–82.

Sánchez Hernández, María Leticia, ed. *Mujeres en la corte de los Austrias*. Madrid: Polifemo, 2019.

Sanz Ayán, Carmen. "Felipe II y los orígenes del teatro barroco," *Cuadernos de Historia Moderna*, 47–8, no. 23 (1999): 47–78.

Sanz Ayán, Carmen and Bernardo J. García García. "El 'oficio de representar' en España y la influencia de la comedia dell'arte (1567–1587)," *Cuadernos de Historia Moderna*, 16 (1995): 475–500.

Sbaraglia, Daniela Alejandra. "Las joyas de Catalina Micaela de Austria, duquesa de Saboya: Circulación de orfebrerías entre Madrid y Turín en el tardo Renacimiento (1580–1600)," *Valori Tattili: Ornamenta* (July–December 2011): 41–7.

Scalisi, Lina. "El Duque de Terranova en la corte de Felipe II entre contiendas cortesanas, avisos prudentes y relaciones peligrosas," *Libros de la Corte*, 13, no. 23 (2021): 358–70.

Schidel, G.E. "Vespers," *New Catholic Encyclopedia*, Vol. 14. New York: McGraw-Hill, 1967.

Schobesberger, Nikolaus, Paul Arblaster, Mario Infelise, André Belo, Noah Moxham, Carmen Espejo, and Joad Raymond. "European Postal Networks," in Joad Raymond and Noah Moxham, eds, *News Networks in Early Modern Europe*, 19–63. Leiden: Brill, 2016.

Schraven, Minou. *Festive Funerals in Early Modern Italy: The Art and Culture of Conspicuous Consumption*. Farnham and Burlington, VT: Ashgate, 2014.

Schrickx, Willem. "Italian Actors in Antwerp in 1576: Drusiano Martinelli and Vincenzo Beladno," *Revue belge de philology et d'histoire*, 50, no. 3 (1972): 796–806.

Scott, John Beldon. *Architecture for the Shroud: Relic and Ritual in Turin*. Chicago, IL: University of Chicago Press, 2003.

Shergold, N.D. "Ganassa and the 'Commedia dell'arte' in Sixteenth-Century Spain," *The Modern Language Review*, 51, no. 3 (July 1956): 359–68.

Siniscalco, Consolata, Rosanna Caramiello, and Laura Guglielmone. "Disegnatori piemontesi, album dei fiori," in Anna Maria Bava and Enrica Pagella, eds, *Le meraviglie del mondo: Le collezioni di Carlo Emanuele I di Savoia*. Genoa: Sagep, 2016.

Smith, Hilary Dansey. *Preaching in the Spanish Golden Age: A Study of some Preachers of the Reign of Philip III*. London: Oxford University Press, 1978.

Smith, Winifred. *Italian Actors of the Renaissance*. New York: Benjamin Blom, 1968.

Smith, Winifred. *The Commedia dell'Arte*. New York: Benjamin Blom, 1964.

Snow, R.J. "Salve Regina," *New Catholic Encyclopedia*, Vol. 12. New York: McGraw-Hill, 1967.

Sommer-Mathis, Andrea and Christian Standhartinger. "Le suplico me ynbíe un rretrato chiquito suyo para que le pueda traer conmigo, La emperatriz María Ana de Austria (1606–1646) y el uso de los retratos en la corte imperial de Viena," *Libros de la Corte*, no. 28 (Spring–Summer 2024): 397–429.

Sowerby, Tracy A. "'A Memorial and a Pledge of Faith': Portraiture and Early Modern Diplomatic Culture," *English Historical Review*, 129, no. 537 (2014): 296–331.

Spangler, Jonathan. *Monsieur: Second Sons in the Monarchy of France, 1550–1800*. New York: Routledge, 2022.

Stallybrass, Peter, Roger Chartier, J. Franklin Mowery, and Heather Wolfe. "Hamlet's Tables and the Technologies of Writing in Renaissance England," *Shakespeare Quarterly*, 55, no. 4 (Winter 2004): 379–419.

Steen, Sara Jayne. "Reading Beyond the Words: Material Letters and the Process of Interpretation," *Quidditas*, 22 (2001): 55–69.

Storrs, Christopher. *War, Diplomacy and the Rise of Savoy, 1690–1720*. Cambridge: Cambridge University Press, 1999.

Stratton, Suzanne L. *The Immaculate Conception in Spanish Art*. Cambridge: Cambridge University Press, 1994.

Thomas, Werner. "Andromeda Unbound: The Reign of Albert and Isabella in the Southern Netherlands, 1598–1621," in Werner Thomas and Luc Duerloo, eds, *Albert and Isabella, 1598–1621*, 1–14. Leuven: Brepols, 1998.

Thomas, Werner. "Isabel Clara Eugenia and the Pacification of the Southern Netherlands," in Cordula van Wyhe, ed., *Isabel Clara Eugenia: Female Sovereignty in the Courts of Madrid and Brussels*, 181–201. London: Centro de Estudios Europa Hispánica and Paul Holberton Publishing, 2011.

Thomas, Werner and Luc Duerloo, eds. *Albert and Isabella, 1598–1621*. Leuven: Brepols, 1998.

Thorpe, Deborah. "'I Haue Ben Crised and Besy': Illness and Resilience in the Fifteenth-Century Stoner Letters," *The Mediaeval Journal*, 5, no. 2 (2015): 85–108.

Thurston, Herbert. "Forty Hours Devotion," *The Catholic Encyclopedia*. New York: Robert Appleton Company, 1909, https://www.newadvent.org/cathen/06151a.htm.

Tiffany, Tanya. "'Little Idols': Royal Children and the Infant Jesus in the Devotional Practice of Sor Margarita de la Cruz (1567–1633)," in Matthew Averett, ed., *The Early Modern Child in Art and History*, 35–48. London: Pickering and Chatto, 2015.

Toajas Roger, M. Ángeles. "The *Cuarto Real* of the Descalzas Reales: The Uses and Forms of Architecture," in Noelia García Pérez, ed., *The Making of Juana of Austria: Gender, Art, and Patronage in Early Modern Iberia*, 220–51. Baton Rouge, LA: Louisiana State University Press, 2021.

Tosino, Patrizia. "La Grande Galleria di Federico Zuccari a Torino: Il capolavoro mancato," in Anna Maria Bava and Enrica Pagella, eds, *Le meraviglie del mondo: Le collezioni di Carlo Emanuele I di Savoia*, 65–73. Genoa: Sagep, 2016.

Tylus, Jane. "Women at the Windows: 'Commedia dell'arte' and Theatrical Practice in Early Modern Italy," *Theater Journal*, 49, no. 3 (October 1997): 323–42.

Usunáriz, Jesús M. "Marriage and Love in Sixteenth- and Seventeenth-Century Spain," in Silvana Seidel Menchi, ed., *Marriage in Europe, 1400–1800*, 201–24. Toronto: University of Toronto Press, 2016.

Usunáriz, Jesús M. "Sentimientos e historia: La correspondencia amorosa en los siglos XVI–XVIII," in Antonio Castillo and Verónica Sierra Blas, eds, *Cinco siglos de cartas: Historia y prácticas epistolares en las épocas moderna y contemporánea*, 251–73. Huelva, Spain: Universidad de Huelva, 2014.

Varallo, Franca. "Catalina Micaela en la corte de Saboya," in José Luis Colomer and Amalia Descalzo, eds, *Vestir a la española en las cortes europeas (siglos XVI y XVII)*, Vol. 2, 63–85. Madrid: Centro de Estudios Europa Hispánica, 2014.

Varallo, Franca, ed. *Da Nizza a Torino: I festeggiamenti per il matrimonio di Carlo Emanuele I e Caterina d'Austria: Relatione degli apparati e feste fatte nell'arrivo del serenissimo signor duca di Savoia con la Serenissima Infante sua Consorte in Nizza, nel passaggio del suo Stato, e finalmente nella entrata in Turino 1585*. Turin: Centro Studi Piemontesi, 1992.

Varallo, Franca. "*Exotica* e oggetti preziosi: Note sull'inventario della infanta," in Blythe Alice Raviola and Franca Varallo, eds, *L'Infanta: Caterina d'Austria, duchessa di Savoia (1567–1597)*, 371–88. Rome: Carocci, 2013.

Varallo, Franca. *Il Duca e la corte: Cerimonie al tempo di Carlo Emanuele I de Savoia*. Geneva: Slatkine, 1991.

Varallo, Franca, ed. *In Assenza del Re: Le reggenti dal XIV al XVII secolo (Piemonte ed Europa)*. Florence: Leo S. Olschki, 2008.

Varallo, Franca and Maurizio Vivarelli, eds. *La Grande Galleria: Spazio del sapere e rappresentazione del mondo nell'età di Carlo Emanuele I di Savoia*. Rome: Carocci, 2019.

Vayra, Pietro. *Il museo storico della casa di Savoia nell' archivio di stato in Torino*. Rome: Fratelli Boca Librai di S.M., 1880.

Venturelli, Paola. "La moda española entre las damas de Milán y Mantua," in José Luis Colomer and Amalia Descalzo, eds, *Vestir a la Española en las cortes europeas (siglos XVI y XVII)*, Vol. 2, 87–115. Madrid: Centro de Estudios Europa Hispánica, 2014.

Vester, Matthew, ed. *Sabaudian Studies: Political Culture, Dynasty, and Territory, 1400–1700*. Kirksville, MO: Truman State University Press, 2013.

Vilacoba Ramos, Karen Maria. *El Monasterio de las Descalzas Reales y sus confesores en la edad moderna*. Madrid: Vision Libros, 2013.

Villalon, L.J. Andrew. "San Diego de Alcalá and the Politics of Saint-Making in Counter-Reformation Europe," *The Catholic Historical Review*, 83, no. 4 (October 1997): 691–715.

Villermont, Marie H. de. *L'Infante Isabelle, gouvernante des Pays-Bas*. Paris: Librarie S. François, 1912.

Villiers, Henri de. "A History of the 40 Hours Devotion by Henri de Villiers," trans. Gregory Dipippo, *New Liturgical Movement*, 7 March 2018, https://www.newliturgicalmovement.org/2018/03/a-history-of-40-hours-devotion-by-henri.html.

Visconti, Maria Carla. "La Grande Galleria di Carlo Emanuele I: L'architettura attraverso le immagini dei secoli XVI e XVII," in Anna Maria Bava and Enrica Pagella, eds, *Le meraviglie del mondo: Le collezioni di Carlo Emanuele I di Savoia*, 53–63. Genoa: Sagep, 2016.

Vocelka, Karl and Lynne Heller. *Die private Welt der Habsburger: Leben und Alltag einer Familie*. Vienna: Styria, 1998.

Warnke, Martin. *The Court Artist: On the Ancestry of the Modern Artist*. Trans. David McLintock. Cambridge: Cambridge University Press, 1993.

Wattenberg García, Eloísa. "San Mauricio y la legión Tebana: Difusión y controversia de su leyenda," in *El estandarte de San Mauricio del Museo de Valladolid: Reliquias de Flandes en la Corte de España, 1604*. Valladolid: Museo de Valladolid, 2012.

Weber, Samuel. "The Promises and Pitfalls of a Family Saint: The Borromeos and the Canonization of Carlo (c. 1590–1620)," in Birgit Emich, Daniel Sidler, Samuel Weber, and Christian Windlers, eds, *Making Saints in a "Glocal" Religion: Practices of Holiness in Early Modern Catholicism*, 249–78. Leiden: Böhlau, 2024.

Wiggins, Alison. *Bess of Hardwick's Letters: Language, Materiality, and Early Modern Epistolary Culture*. London: Routledge, 2016.

Wilson, Adrian. *The Making of Man-Midwifery: Childbirth in England, 1660–1770*. Cambridge, MA: Harvard University Press, 1995.

Wolff, Larry. "Habsburg Letters: The Disciplinary Dynamics of Epistolary Narrative in the Correspondence of Maria Theresa and Marie Antoinette," in Anne Fehn, Ingeborg Hoesterey, and Maria Tatar, eds, *Neverending Stories: Toward a Critical Narratology*, 70–86. Princeton, NJ: Princeton University Press, 1992.

Wyhe, Cordula van, ed. *Isabel Clara Eugenia: Female Sovereignty in the Courts of Madrid and Brussels*. London: Centro de Estudios Europa Hispánica and Paul Holberton Publishing, 2011.

BIBLIOGRAPHY

Wyllie, Robert E. *Orders, Decorations, and Insignia Military and Civil with the History and Romance of their Origin and a Full Description of Each*. New York: G.P. Putnam's Sons, 1921.

Zarco-Bacas y Cuevas, Julián. *Documentos para la historia del monasterio de San Lorenzo el Real del Escorial*. Madrid: Helénica, 1916.

Zarri, Gabriella, ed. *Per lettera: La scrittura epistolare femminile tra archivio e tipografia, secli XV–XVII*. Rome: Viella, 1999.

Zuese, Alicia R. "Ana Caro and the Literary Academies of Seventeenth-Century Spain," in Anne J. Cruz and Rosilie Hernández, eds, *Women's Literacy in Early Modern Spain and the New World*, 191–208. Burlington, VT: Ashgate, 2011.

INDEX